Principles of Information Technology

Preparing for IC³ Certification

Texas Edition

Boston • Columbus • Indianapolis • New York • San Francisco
Amsterdam • Cape Town • Dubai • London • Madrid • Milan • Munich • Paris • Montréal • Toronto
Delhi • Mexico City • São Paulo • Sydney • Hong Kong • Seoul • Singapore • Taipei • Tokyo

Cover Art: Courtesy of Brandstock/Shutterstock

330 Hudson Street, New York, NY 10013

Hardcover ISBN 10: 0-13-444654-2
Hardcover ISBN 13: 978-0-13-444654-7

Pearson

6 17

Table of Contents

Table of Contents

Table of Contents

Table of Contents

To the Student

USING YOUR TEXTBOOK

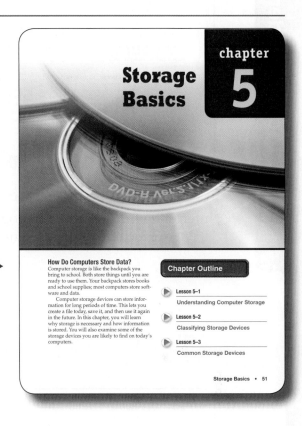

Chapter Overview ▶

Each chapter begins with an introduction to concepts and a chapter outline.

◀ ### Lesson Overview

At the start of each lesson you will find helpful tools that guide you through the learning process.

As You Read Ideas for how you can best organize information for maximum learning.

Objectives Tasks you should be able to complete by the end of the lesson.

Key Terms Key words you should know after you complete the lesson.

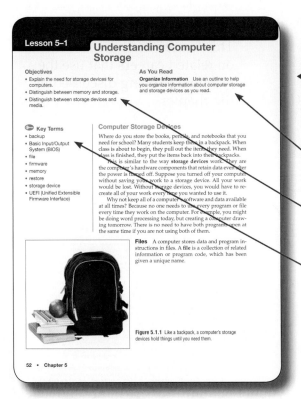

Additional features in each chapter enhance and support the text.

Sequential Versus Random Access When equipped with a tape drive, business computers can store data on a long piece of tape, similar to an old-fashioned cassette tape. A tape drive is an example of a **sequential storage device**, which requires the computer to scan from the beginning of the medium to the end until it finds the data it needs. While cheaper and slower than other types of storage, the highest capacity tape cartridges can hold five terabytes of uncompressed data. Because it can take several minutes to locate a piece of data on a high-capacity tape, tapes are used chiefly by businesses that want to back up their computer systems—often after the business day is over.

A **random access storage device** lets a computer go directly to the needed information. The device does not have to search the entire medium to find data. For this reason, random access storage devices are much faster, and more expensive, than sequential devices. A hard drive is an example of a random access storage device.

Magnetic Versus Optical Storage Magnetic storage devices are specially treated disks or tapes, such as those mentioned above, that record information using magnetically sensitive materials. These devices use electricity to shift magnetic particles so they form a pattern that the computer reads and stores as information. Common magnetic storage devices include hard drives and tape drives

Other storage devices use laser beams to read information that has been stored on the reflective surface of a disc. These are called **optical storage devices**. Popular types of optical storage devices for computers include CD-ROM and DVD-ROM drives.

Technology@School

Some schools have a dedicated computer "lab," but more and more schools have computers in every classroom or tablets for every student. Expensive equipment may be damaged if a student mishandles it, costing the school—or the student—money to replace it.

Think About It!
Rate the computer equipment that you think is most sensitive to mishandling and needs the most care. On a scale of 1 to 5, use 1 for most sensitive and 5 for least.

- CD-ROM/DVD
- Flash drive
- Hard drive
- Power cord
- Laser printer
- Tablet

Technology@Home
Technology@School
Technology@Work

These include relevant information on how you can use the technology that you are learning about. They put the topics being discussed into real-world context.

Did You Know?

Interesting facts about technology are included in this feature.

Did You Know?

Most computers only have enough RAM to store programs and data while a computer is using them. This is because RAM is relatively expensive to make and to buy. As a result, makers of computers limit the amount of RAM in their machines to help lower initial computer costs and to allow users who want more RAM to purchase it separately.

Storage Versus Memory New computer users sometimes get confused about temporary memory (RAM) and permanent storage (disks and disk drives). They will say "memory" when they actually mean to say "storage." Adding confusion, both are measured with the same units: bytes. One byte equals about 8 bits, or a single character. A kilobyte, or 1KB, is 1 thousand bytes. A megabyte, or 1MB, is 1 million bytes. A gigabyte, or 1GB, is 1 billion bytes. A terabyte, or 1TB, is 1 thousand billion bytes. A petabyte, or 1PB, is one million gigabytes. To avoid this problem, remember two key differences between storage and memory:

- The two work differently. Remember that RAM uses chips to temporarily store information. These chips depend on a constant supply of power to keep their contents; when the power is lost, the chips lose their contents. Storage uses different methods to store data permanently, so it isn't lost when the power is turned off.
- A PC has more storage capacity than memory. Even though some PCs have several gigabytes of RAM, their hard drives will be many times larger.

Storage Media and Storage Devices

Storage has two components: storage media and storage devices.

Storage Media In terms of storage, a medium is an object that physically holds data or program instructions. Flash drives, tapes, compact disc... and Blu-ray Disc... age medi...

Magneto-Optical (MO) Drives A popular method of data storage for many businesses, this type of drive combines both magnetic and optical drive technologies. A magneto-optical drive uses a removable disk that is inserted via a slot in the front of the drive. These drives can be internal or external. Their disks can store several gigabytes of information.

Online Storage Many online—or cloud—storage sites such as Google Drive, Dropbox, Microsoft OneDrive, and Apple iCloud, are available where you can store files on a network server at a remote location. You access your data by logging in through the Internet using a secure password. Some programs, including Microsoft Office, come with free online storage space. You can also pay a storage service provider (SSP) for space. Online storage offers these three benefits: 1) it is expandable; 2) it allows you to share files with others; and 3) data stored in a remote location is protected if your computer is stolen or damaged.

Career Corner

Computer Security Specialist
Today, security specialists are in demand to work with various computer storage systems, such as tape warehouses and online storage companies.

Computer security specialists study ways of improving the overall security of their systems. For example, some goals include improving recording or access time or the safety of the protected information in case of a natural disaster.

Career Corner

This feature includes information on related careers that use the technology being discussed in the chapter.

Capacities of Common Storage Devices

Device	Capacity
Internal hard drive	500 GB–1 TB and more
External hard drive (USB or Firewire connection)	500 GB–8 TB and more
	...64 GB a...

Figure 5.3.2 A USB flash drive has a USB connector, a flash memory chip, a mass storage controller, and a crystal oscillator that allow the device to c... the c...

Connections

This cross-curricular feature explains how the technology covered in the chapter is used in other areas, including the arts, science, social studies, language arts, and mathematics.

Connections

Mathematics In math class, you are accustomed to a system that combines ten possible digits, or numbers, in a certain order to represent larger numbers. In binary code, only 0 and 1 are used.

- In math class, you carry a number over to the next column when numbers in a column add to 10 or more. With binary numbers, a number is carried if the items add to 2. In an eight-bit example, the number 35 would be written as 100011.
- While numbers in math class refer to specific quantities, binary code numbers refer to specific actions. A 1 turns a circuit on, while a 0 turns a circuit off.

Solid State Disks Solid state disks or drives, or SSDs, are a mass storage device similar to a hard disk drive. Even though SSDs serve the same purpose as hard drives, their internal parts are much different. SSDs do not have any moving parts, like the hard drive's magnetic platters; they store data using flash memory. SSDs have better read performance because the data does not get fragmented into many locations, and, since they are not magnetic, SSDs do not lose data when next to a strong magnetic field.

SSDs do have disadvantages, though. This newer technology costs about ten times more per gigabyte, so people tend to buy SSDs with smaller capacity than most hard drives. Their limited number of write cycles means their performance declines over time. Yet, with improvements in SSD technology, these devices will advance, and the prices may come down.

Flash Memory Devices Several types of storage devices using flash memory offer the speed of memory with the high capacity of a magnetic storage device. Flash memory drives work faster than magnetic drives, because they have no moving parts, and they do not require battery power to retain their data. Flash drives installed inside computers resemble magnetic hard drives in size and shape.

A **USB flash drive** is a portable, self-contained storage device that uses **flash memory**. In addition to portability, these drives offer the advantages of speed, capacity, and cost. A USB flash drive has a USB connector that plugs into the USB port on... memory chip... ng; a USB m...

Additional Chapter Features

Throughout the text are Spotlight on. . . and Real-World Tech features.

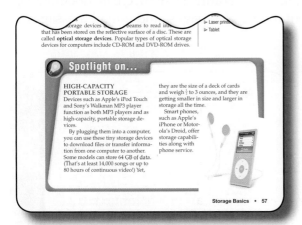

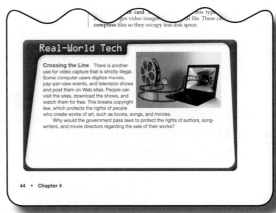

▲ **Spotlight on . . .**

There are so many individuals who have made a difference in the technology that we use today. Spotlight on . . . highlights some of these people.

▲ **Real-World Tech**

This is a technology-awareness feature that introduces a technology concept relating to the current topic.

At the End of Each Chapter

▼ **Use the Vocabulary**

Matching exercises to check your understanding of key terms in the chapter

▼ **Thinking Critically**

Short-answer questions to demonstrate your understanding of concepts

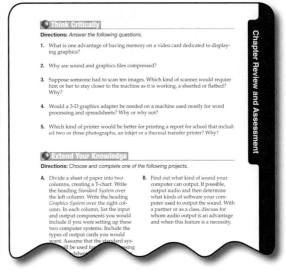

▲ **Check Your Comprehension**

Questions to self-check your reading comprehension

▲ **Extend Your Knowledge**

Projects incorporating all the skills you have learned in a fun and challenging activity

Hands-on Application Activities

In chapters where application skills are discussed, hands-on activities are included. These projects give you the opportunity to use the operating system, create documents, spreadsheets, databases, multimedia presentations, Web pages, and e-mail messages.

Activity Directions

An overview of what skills are to be used in the activity, along with a scenario of what you'll be creating

Activity Steps

Step-by-step directions indicate what needs to be done in order to complete the project

Illustrations

Activity illustrations help you check your work

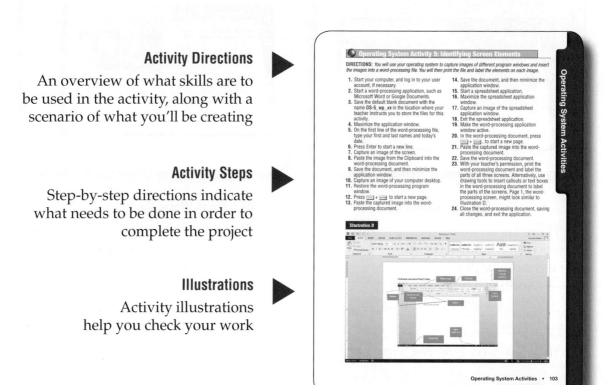

Data Files

There are data files and data record sheets for use with some of the application activities. These files can be accessed from the NavigateIT Web site (www.pearsonhighered.com/navigateit). Select "Student" and browse for "Principles of Information Technology."

Computing Fundamentals

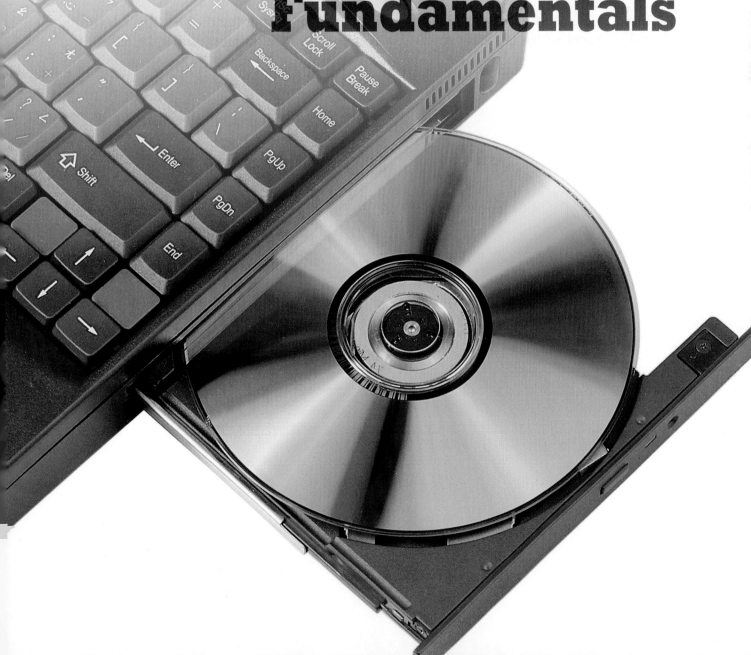

Computer Basics

How Do Computers Work? The answer to this question can be very long and complicated, even though computers work in a fairly simple way. At its core, a computer contains a set of on/off switches; by turning these switches on and off very rapidly, the computer can represent information. Imagine a wall covered with a thousand light bulbs, each with its own on/off switch. By turning switches on and off in a certain way, you could use the lights to spell words or create pictures. Computers work in a similar way.

But a computer cannot use its switches without instructions. That's where software and you, the user, come into play. By giving the computer instructions and data to work with, you and your software programs tell it how to work its switches—turning them on and off millions of times each second.

Chapter Outline

 Lesson 1–1

What Is a Computer?

 Lesson 1–2

What Is Computer Hardware?

 Lesson 1–3

What Is Computer Software?

What Is a Computer?

Objectives

- Describe the four operations of computers.
- Contrast analog and digital computers.
- Explain why data and instructions for computers are coded as 0s and 1s.
- Identify three benefits of computers.
- Explain the hexadecimal system of displaying color.

As You Read

Sequence Information   Use a sequence chart to help you organize the four operations of computers as you read the lesson.

Key Terms

- bit
- byte
- computer
- data
- hexadecimal value
- input
- output
- processing
- program
- storage

Computer Basics

A **computer** is a machine that changes information from one form into another by performing four basic actions. Those actions are input, processing, output, and storage. Together, these actions make up the information processing cycle. By following a set of instructions, called a program, the computer turns raw data into organized information that people can use. Creation of usable information is the primary benefit of computer technology. There are two kinds of computers:

- Analog computers measure data on a scale with many values. Think of the scales on a mercury thermometer or on the gas gauge of a car.
- Digital computers work with data that has a fixed value. They use data in digital, or number, form. The computers that run programs for playing games or searching the Internet are digital computers.

Input

Input is the raw information, or **data**, that is entered into a computer. This data can be as simple as letters and numbers or as complex as color photographs, videos, or songs. You input data by using a device such as a keyboard or digital camera.

Bits of Data   Data is entered into a computer in a coded language. The building blocks of that language are units called **bits**. *Bit* is short for *binary digit*. Each bit is a number, or a digit. A bit can have only two possible values—0 or 1.

Bits into Bytes   Every letter, number, or picture is entered into the computer as a combination of bits, or 0s and 1s. The bits are combined into groups of eight or more. Each group is called a **byte**. Each letter or number has a unique combination of bits. For instance, on most personal computers, the letter *A* is coded as 01000001. The number *1* is 00110001.

Even images are formed by combinations of bytes. Those combinations tell the computer what colors to display and where to put them.

Color can be represented by a three-byte combination where each byte represents the red, green, or blue (RGB) component of the displayed color. The intensity of each component is measured on a scale from 0 to 256 since there are 256 possible combinations of 1 or 0 in each group of eight bits. To represent a color, the three byte RGB codes are simplified into a 6-digit **hexadecimal** value where the first two digits represent the intensity of red, the second two are green, and the last two are blue.

A hexadecimal number has sixteen possible values, so the RGB values are assigned a number from 0 to 15. But since 10 through 15 are two digit numbers they are expressed with the letters A through F, where A equals 10 and F equals 15. In this way, the 256 possible combinations of each byte can be expressed in two digits. For example, the hexadecimal value for pure, intense red is FF0000 since red has highest intensity and both green and blue are at zero. The hexadecimal for white is FFFFFF, or complete intensity of all three colors, and black is 0000000.

Processing

The second step of the information processing cycle is called **processing**. In this step, the computer does something to the data.

Coded Instructions What the computer does depends on the instructions, or **program**, given to the computer. The instructions are also written in binary code, using combinations of 0s and 1s. They might tell the computer to add two numbers, or they might have the computer compare two numbers to see which is larger.

Speed of Processing Computers can process data very rapidly, performing millions of operations every second. The ability to process data with lightning speed is another reason computers are so valuable.

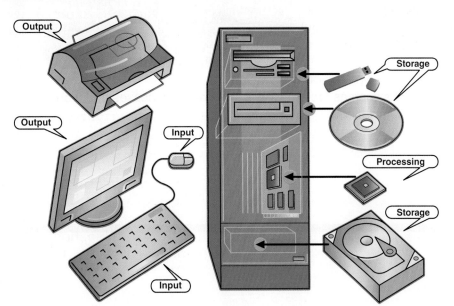

Figure 1.1.1 Each computer component plays a role in one of the system's four primary functions.

Output

The third step shows what happens after the computer processes the data. This is the **output** step. If the program tells the computer to add two numbers, the output stage displays the result. To create output, the computer takes the bytes and turns them back into a form you can understand, such as an image on the screen or a printed document.

Output can take many forms. A program might convert the 0s and 1s into a report. It might become an image you are drawing on the computer. If you are playing a game, the output might be a car zooming along a road and the sound of its engine. A computer provides output through a device such as a monitor, speaker, or printer.

Storage

The fourth operation is **storage**, in which the computer saves the information. Without storage, all the work you do on the computer would be lost. Computers have a temporary memory that is used during the processing stage. When the computer is turned off, however, any data in that temporary memory is lost.

By storing the data in a permanent form, you can access the information over and over. This is another great advantage of computers—what you do one day can be saved and reused on another day.

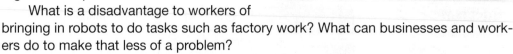

Real-World Tech

Robots at Work Some output is very unusual. Computer-controlled robots work in some auto factories. Their output is cars. The robots are perfect for the tasks that take place on an assembly line. These tasks are done over and over again without change. For instance, robots weld parts together and paint car bodies.

What is a disadvantage to workers of bringing in robots to do tasks such as factory work? What can businesses and workers do to make that less of a problem?

What Is Computer Hardware?

Objectives
- Summarize how a CPU and RAM work together.
- Contrast primary and secondary storage.
- Compare the features of four secondary storage devices.
- Identify three types of connectors and the peripherals that use each.

As You Read
Compare and Contrast   Use a chart to help you compare and contrast computer hardware as you read.

What Is Hardware?

When you think about a computer, you probably picture its **hardware**, the computer's physical parts. You use hardware devices such as a keyboard or mouse to input data. The processor is a hardware **device** that turns the raw data into usable information. Hardware devices such as a monitor or a disk drive show output and store data for later access.

Inside the Case

Much of a computer's hardware is found inside the computer case, hidden from view. Most of this hardware is used for processing and storing data.

Processing Devices   Perhaps the most important piece of hardware in a computer is the **central processing unit**, or **CPU**. This is the device that processes data. The CPU is a small, thin piece of silicon attached to a **circuit board**. The CPU is covered with tiny electrical **circuits**. By moving data along these circuits in specific ways, the CPU can do arithmetic and compare data very quickly.

Primary Storage   Some hardware used to store data is inside the computer case near the CPU. The computer uses **random access memory**, or **RAM**, to store data and instructions while the computer is working. In this way, the CPU can quickly find the data it works with. This type of storage is called primary storage. RAM is volatile memory, which means data in RAM is lost when the computer is turned off.

Secondary Storage Devices   Other pieces of storage hardware are secondary storage. The following devices let you store data permanently—even when the computer is turned off.

Key Terms
- central processing unit (CPU)
- circuit
- circuit board
- cloud storage
- device
- hardware
- peripheral
- random access memory (RAM)
- terabyte
- universal serial bus (USB)

Figure 1.2.1 The CPU fits in a socket on a circuit board.

Service Technician Computer hardware sometimes fails. When that happens, people call service technicians. These people work for computer companies. They might work in the offices of the company that employs them, or they might travel to business sites to fix machines. Technicians need to know about software and hardware because problems are sometimes caused by a computer's programs and not by its equipment.

- Hard drives use a stack of disk platters to store large amounts of information permanently on the computer. External hard drives, which are plugged into the computer, are used to store back-ups of your data. They can be desktop or portable devices. They usually connect to the computer via a **universal serial bus**, or **USB**, port.

- Flash, jump, thumb, or pen drives—all names for the same kind of storage device—connect to the computer through a USB port. They hold anywhere from 4 gigabytes to as many as 32 gigabytes or more.

- Compact Discs (CDs), Digital Video Discs (DVDs), and Blu-ray Discs (BDs) are optical storage devices. You insert the CD or DVD into your computer through the disc drive. A CD can store 650 to 700 megabytes of data. DVDs can store anywhere from 4.7 gigabytes to double that amount if the DVD is double-sided. Blu-ray Discs hold from 25 gigabytes to 128 gigabytes.

- **"Cloud" storage** is online storage offered on various Web sites. Most of them will give you a few gigabytes for free, but then require you to pay for more space.

- Memory cards store data for mobile devices like smart phones and digital cameras. Some memory cards can store 256 gigabytes.

Secondary Storage Capacity Hard disk drives hold the most data. Many computers now have hard drives that can store several hundred gigabytes. A gigabyte is just over a billion bytes. Some external hard drives can store more than 30 **terabytes** (tb). A terabyte is about 1,000 gigabytes. Thumb or flash drives hold the next largest amount of data, sometimes going over 128 gigabytes. CDs and DVDs hold the least amount of data—from around 700 megabytes to almost 10 gigabytes. A megabyte is just over a million bytes, but still several hundred of them on a CD can store entire encyclopedias, including images, maps, and sound.

Figure 1.2.2 Today, nearly all computers feature a built-in hard drive. Some have capacities of 4 terabytes or more. Some external hard drives are able to store 30 terabytes of data.

Peripherals

For most desktop systems, input devices, such as the keyboard and mouse, are separate from the case. So are output devices, such as monitors and printers. Hardware that is separate but can be connected to the case is called a **peripheral**.

Not all computers have all this equipment as peripherals. Apple's iMac® computers include the monitor as a physical part of the main system. Other computers may have built-in storage devices. Portable computers have the keyboard, a type of mouse, and a monitor all attached to the main unit.

Peripherals need to be connected to the computer so that data can be moved back and forth. Some use a wireless connection and some are linked to the computer by a cable. Both wireless connections and cables connect to the computer with a plug. Most plugs join the computer at a connector on the computer case, but some are installed internally. Connectors can be unique for the peripheral. Monitors have specific plugs designed for transferring image data. Speakers and microphones have unique plugs as well. Many devices such as keyboards, printers, and mice use USB ports.

Connectors There are several main types of connectors, or ports:

- Serial ports move data one bit at a time. For example, they connect computers to modems for Internet access.

- Parallel ports move data in groups.

- Multiple device ports, such as Small Computer Systems Interface (SCSI) and Universal Serial Bus (USB) ports, connect several peripherals to a computer at one time. They all move data faster than serial ports can.

One problem with computer hardware is the tangle of cables that can result from lots of peripherals. Bluetooth™ is a wireless way of communicating that uses radio waves to communicate between electronic devices.

Many cell phones and other portable devices use Bluetooth to send signals to each other. For example, many people use Bluetooth to send photos from their cell phones to their computers. These users may also use Bluetooth to send commands from their telephones and computers to DVD players, data video recorders, refrigerators, and other computer- controlled appliances.

Figure 1.2.3 Ports are usually labeled, making it easy to know what plugs in where.

USB ports   Ethernet

What Is Computer Software?

Objectives

- Describe what an operating system does.
- Explain what utility software does.
- Identify four types of application software and ways to obtain them.

As You Read

Classify Information Use a concept web to help you classify different types of computer software as you read.

Key Terms

- application software
- operating system (OS)
- software
- system software
- utility software

What Is Software?

Hardware includes all the physical pieces that make up a computer. Hardware is useless without software, however. **Software** includes all of the programs that tell a computer what to do and how to do it. Think of a computer as a sports team. Hardware is the players, and software is the coach. No matter how talented the players are, the team will only perform properly if the coach gives it the right instructions.

Figure 1.3.1 Operating systems that run on computers, tablets, and smart phones are examples of system software.

Types of Software

Software is divided into two main types: system software and application software. **System software** includes programs that help the computer work properly. You are probably more familiar with **application software**, which are programs designed to help you do tasks such as writing a paper or making a graph. This type of software also includes programs that allow you to use the computer to listen to music or play games.

System Software

There are two types of system software: operating systems and system utilities. Both help computers run smoothly.

Operating Systems   The **operating system (OS)** lets the hardware devices communicate with one another and keeps them running efficiently. It also supports the hardware when applications programs are running. The two most widely used operating systems are the Macintosh® OS and Microsoft® Windows®.

System Utilities   Programs that help the computer work properly are called **utility software**. They usually do maintenance and repair jobs that the operating system cannot do itself. Some utility programs repair damaged data files or save files in certain ways so they take up less space. Others translate files created in one OS so they can be read and worked on in another.

Spotlight on...

BILL GATES

Bill Gates has a simple idea about the future of computing. "The goal," he says, "is information at your fingertips." It will not surprise anyone if Gates and his company, Microsoft, play a major role in making that goal become a reality. Gates started writing software in high school. He and a childhood friend, Paul Allen, wrote a programming language to run on a machine called the Altair, the first personal computer. Allen and Gates then formed Microsoft, which is now one of the leading software companies in the world.

A software program's version is usually indicated by a number, such as "Version 4" or "Version 8.5." Software is upgraded to remove programming errors and to add new features. Some revisions are major, and the version number jumps from, for example, 9.0 to 10. Minor fixes typically change the number after the decimal point, such as 10 to 10.2.

Think About It!

For which items below would it be worthwhile for you to buy the new version of the program?

➤ a program you use all the time that is moving from 4.3 to 5.0

➤ a program you rarely use that is moving from 2.2 to 2.3

➤ a program you often use that is moving from 5.1 to 5.2

➤ a program you often use that is moving from 1.0 to 3.0

Figure 1.3.2 You can buy off-the-shelf software from a bricks-and-mortar store or online from a retail Web site.

Application Software

There are many different applications. They can be grouped into four main categories:

- Productivity software helps people be more productive at work. People use these programs to write reports, prepare financial plans, and organize data.
- Graphics software makes it possible to draw, paint, and touch up photos.
- Communication software allows computers to connect to the Internet and to send e-mail.
- Home, education, and entertainment software helps people manage their money or figure their taxes. Other products can be used to learn new skills or simply to have some fun.

Custom Software   There are two ways to obtain application software. Some organizations need software programs to do very specific jobs. They hire people to write custom software designed to do those jobs. Because these programs are custom written, they are usually quite expensive.

Off-the-Shelf Software   Most people use software to do standard jobs. They might want to write letters or organize an album of photos. They can choose from many ready-made programs to handle these common tasks. These are called "off-the-shelf" programs because stores and companies that sell software online stock them. Most off-the-shelf software purchased online can be downloaded directly onto the buyer's computer. Because software publishers can sell many copies of this software, it is less expensive than custom software.

Use the Vocabulary

Directions: *Match each vocabulary term in the left column with the correct definition in the right column.*

_____ **1.** input
_____ **2.** bit
_____ **3.** byte
_____ **4.** output
_____ **5.** hardware
_____ **6.** central processing unit
_____ **7.** random access memory
_____ **8.** peripheral
_____ **9.** software
_____ **10.** utility software

a. program that tells the computer what to do

b. group of 8 bits

c. area where data and instructions are stored while the computer is working

d. physical parts of a computer

e. raw data entered into a computer

f. program that does maintenance or repair tasks

g. part of a computer that processes data

h. basic unit of data a digital computer can understand

i. hardware separate but connected to the computer

j. the results of the computer's processing

Check Your Comprehension

Directions: *Complete each sentence with information from the chapter.*

1. A(n) _____ is a machine that changes information from one form into another.

2. _____ is a basic operation of computers.

3. Data and instructions in computers are coded with a(n) _____ because computers only understand two values.

4. The CPU uses _____ to hold data it is working on.

5. Data in RAM is _____ when the computer is turned off.

6. A(n) _____ is an example of a connector that works with only one kind of peripheral.

7. SCSI and USB connectors connect _____ peripherals at the same time.

8. Some organizations need _____ software programs to do very specific jobs.

9. _____ software is used to connect to the Internet and send e-mail.

10. Off-the-shelf software is _____ expensive than custom software because publishers sell more units.

 **Think Critically**

Directions: *Answer the following questions.*

1. How do analog and digital computers differ?

2. What is the RGB hexadecimal value for a pure intense green? Explain your answer.

3. What are the differences between primary and secondary storage?

4. What is the difference between system software and application software? Give at least one example of each.

5. What type of application software do you use most? Explain.

Extend Your Knowledge

Directions: *Choose and complete one of the following projects.*

A. Look at a computer. Create a five-column chart. In the first column, list all the hardware that you can identify. In the remaining columns, state whether each item is used for inputting, processing, outputting, or storage. Examine how the different pieces are connected to the computer. What other hardware do you think the computer has that you cannot see? With your teacher's permission, unplug and replug all of the computer components, including external drives, a printer, mouse, keyboard, monitor, projector, and the power supply. Start the system. Record your observations. Discuss your findings with the class.

B. Using the Internet or library resources, research at least three types of processing devices used in laptop computers. Keep track of your sources. Create a chart that compares and contrasts the price, top speed, and number of operations per second each one can perform. Determine which device would be most appropriate for working with text, graphics, and math. Write a brief summary explaining your findings, including a list of sources or bibliography. Read your summary out loud to a partner and listen as your partner reads his or hers out loud to you.

Understanding Computers

Working Together Computers come in many different shapes and sizes. Some are large enough to fill a room. Others can be held in the palm of your hand. Whatever their size and capabilities, all these computers have something in common. They use electronic parts and instructions to perform specific tasks.

The electronic parts or components are called hardware. Hardware includes things like computer chips, circuit boards, hard drives, keyboards, monitors, and speakers. These hardware pieces, however, cannot perform the tasks by themselves. They require power and instructions. Electricity provides the power and software provides the instructions to work. Software programs unlock the potential of the hardware so that you can use the computer to do amazing things.

Chapter Outline

 Lesson 2–1

Exploring Computer Systems

 Lesson 2–2

Basic Programming Concepts

 Lesson 2–3

Group and Individual Computing

Exploring Computer Systems

Objectives

- Explain how input devices are suited to certain kinds of data.
- Distinguish between RAM and ROM.
- Identify an appropriate output device for different types of data.
- Explain Ohm's Law and its effect on electricity in a circuit.
- Summarize the tasks of operating systems.
- Identify two leading operating systems and explain why compatibility is an issue.

As You Read

Identify Information   Use a chart to help you organize details about devices used to perform computing functions as you read the lesson.

🔑 Key Terms

- circuit
- command
- computer system
- current
- flash drives
- handwriting-recognition software
- motherboard
- multicore processor
- Ohm's Law
- read-only memory (ROM)
- resistance
- screen-magnifier software
- speech-recognition software
- stylus
- transformer
- transistors
- voltage

Parts Make a Whole

It takes many different parts working together for a computer to do its job. A **computer system** includes several devices that perform the four basic functions of computing: input, processing, output, and storage.

Input Devices

Input means entering data, such as text, images, or sounds. Computer users can choose from several different input devices.

Text and Commands   Perhaps the most basic input device is the keyboard. You can type on it to input text (letters, numbers, and symbols) and commands. Keyboards may be localized for a specific language, such as Arabic or Chinese. A **command** is an instruction for the computer to perform some action. For example, the Print command tells the computer to send the file you are working on to a printer. With **speech-recognition software**, users can input text by speaking into a microphone, and with **handwriting-recognition software**, users can input text by writing with a **stylus** directly on a device such as a tablet or screen. The software changes the words into digital data the computer can read. This software can be used by people with disabilities that prevent them from typing.

A mouse moves a pointer on the monitor, which allows you to move around a document, or to select commands. Some individuals cannot use a mouse. For them, keyboard equivalents for mouse commands provide access to the data. Adaptive devices can help users type without using their fingers on the keyboard.

A trackball, touchpad, or trackpad function similarly to a mouse. Touch screens let you input some commands by touching the monitor directly. There are also motion-recognition software programs that let you input some commands by moving your hand across the display or by looking at a location on the screen. A joystick, often used in computer games, is yet another input device.

Images   A mouse or stylus can also be used to input images by drawing in a graphics program. You can also input images using a digital camera or scanner, by importing them from a storage device or smart phone, or by downloading them from the Internet.

Sounds   Microphones can be used to input sounds. As with images, sounds stored on a storage device or on the Internet can also be brought into the computer as input.

Processing Devices

Inside the computer, data travels from one device to another through the computer's **motherboard**. This board is covered with electrical circuits and switches, and it connects vital pieces of hardware such as the CPU and memory.

The CPU   The main processing device in a computer is the central processing unit, or CPU. The CPU is a chip that receives data from input devices and changes it into a form that you can use, such as text, pictures, or sounds. The processor also follows your commands to do something to that data, such as change a word or move a picture.

CPUs can carry out fewer than 1,000 instructions. However, they can perform millions of these operations every second. That ability is what makes computers able to work so quickly.

Multicore processors have two or more CPUS so can process data faster. Most personal computers have at least a dual core processor (two CPUs), and some have quad core processors (four CPUs). The more cores on the CPU, the higher the price. But, the improved processing speed is probably worth it.

RAM   The CPU temporarily stores the instructions and data it is using on chips called random access memory, or RAM. Once the computer is turned off, RAM no longer stores any data. Reading information from RAM takes very little time—just billionths of a second. Because programs today are complex, they need a large amount of RAM to run properly.

ROM   A second kind of memory is called **read-only memory**, or **ROM**. These chips contain the instructions that start the computer when you turn it on. The instructions in ROM typically do not change once this memory is placed on the motherboard.

CPU vs. RAM vs. Hard Disk   Factors that impact computer performance include processing speed, memory speed and size, and storage device speed and size. Most important, however, is how well these three components work together. Even if you have the fastest, most-efficient CPU available, it cannot process data quickly if there is not enough RAM available. If there is not enough RAM to hold the data, the CPU is forced to keep accessing the disk. As a result, the computer can only perform as fast as the disk drive.

Technology @ Home

A sudden loss of power that shuts down a computer may result in the loss of unsaved work. Users can prevent that loss by buying a backup device that runs a battery if the power shuts down. The battery can keep the computer running for 20 to 45 minutes, which gives the user enough time to save valuable data.

Think About It!

Think about what would be harmed by a loss of power. Which kinds of data listed below would suffer from a loss of power?

➤ data on a hard drive

➤ data on a DVD

➤ unsaved data in RAM

➤ data in ROM

➤ data on a CD-ROM encyclopedia

Figure 2.1.1 The motherboard houses all the chips and circuits a computer needs in order to function.

Output Devices

Output is the results of the computer's processing. The output that users see or hear can lead them to give the computer new instructions for processing their data.

A computer needs output devices to display the results of its processing. Text and images are displayed on a computer screen. They can also be printed by a printer. Sound data is sent to speakers inside, or connected to, the computer. You can also connect headphones to a computer to listen to sounds. Some output devices and features help make computers more accessible to users with disabilities.

Monitors   Both text and images are displayed on the monitor. **Screen-magnifier software** can make images on the monitor much larger for people who have difficulty seeing. The program enlarges the area where the cursor is. The user can also change the colors on the monitor to make text easier to see.

Printers   Another form of output for text and images is print. A high-quality output at a large font size may help some people with poor vision read printed text more easily. Braille printers can also provide output in a format some people with visual disabilities can read.

Speakers   To hear recorded voices, sounds, and music, you need external speakers or headphones. Software lets you choose which recording to hear and adjust the volume. Windows has a feature called Show Sounds. When activated, this feature shows a visual symbol when it plays a sound and displays spoken words as text. This feature can help people who have hearing difficulties. Many programs can display audio as printed text so people with hearing difficulties can see the spoken words.

Storage Devices

Because memory is temporary, a computer needs a secondary location for storing data permanently. Devices such as hard disk drives, **flash drives**, CDs/ DVDs, and online storage are all popular types of secondary storage.

Figure 2.1.2 Headphones let you hear sounds output from the computer.

Electricity Powers the Computer

All computer components are powered by electricity. When you plug the computer into an outlet, the electricity flows from the outlet to the **circuits** of the computer. A circuit is a network of electronic components. The computer circuits contain switches, or **transistors**, that use the electricity to complete tasks.

But how does the electricity get to your house? Power companies send electricity from a power plant to your house through power lines. Before the electricity goes into your house it travels into a **transformer**, which is a device that transfers electricity from one circuit to another. Wires, called windings, in the transformer lower the **voltage**, or electric pressure, of the electricity before it reaches your house.

The electricity flowing through your computer behaves in a constant fashion and follows scientific rules. **Ohm's Law** is a rule that describes how electricity will behave as it travels through circuits. Ohm's Law says that the **current**, or flow of electricity, through a wire is directly proportional to the voltage pushing electricity through the wire. Think of water moving through pipes. If you increase the pressure in the pipes, the water moves faster. Electricity acts in the same way. If you increase the voltage, the current moves faster.

Electronics in your house do not use a constant flow of electricity, called **direct current (DC)**. Instead, they use an **alternating current (AC)**. With AC current, the electricity briefly travels in one direction and then reverses direction. The back and forth happens very rapidly: over 50 times a second! Computers plug into the same type of AC outlet that other appliances use, but once the current reaches the computer's power supply it is converted to DC. That's because the internal computer components require DC.

Ohm's law also says that if there is more **resistance** in a wire, the current will move more slowly. Resistance is caused by anything that obstructs or inhibits current. Think about when you have a clog in your pipe: the water pressure is still the same but less water can flow through. There are many different types of conductors, or materials that electricity flows through, and each creates a different amount of resistance. Length and width of wires can affect resistance, as well. Resistance can be added to a circuit by using different materials or changing the thickness of the wires. Devices that add resistance to a circuit are called resistors. Computers use the relationship between voltage, resistance, and current in a circuit to control either the voltage or the current through the different components.

Connections

Math   Ohm's Law can be summarized in the math equation:

$$V = IR.$$

This equation states that the voltage (V) equals current (I) multiplied by resistance (R). If you had a constant voltage but increased the resistance, the current would decrease. The equation shows that there is a direct relationship between voltage and current and an inverse relationship between current and resistance. Because this relationship is constant, it is possible to adjust one variable within the circuit by controlling the other two.

Give it a try: if you had a circuit with a voltage of 6 and a resistance of 2 what would the current be? The measurements for voltage is volts, resistance is ohms, and current is amps. Now what would happen if you kept the voltage at 6 volts but then changed the resistance to 3 ohms?

Figure 2.1.3 In transistors, three terminals are connected to an external circuit. Altering the current in one terminal changes the current in the other two. Many transistors together make up the integrated circuits used in modern electronics.

The total resistance of all resistors in a circuit depends on both their individual values and how they are connected. When resistors are in a series, or straight line, the current from the voltage source flows through them sequentially, or one after the other. So, the total resistance in the circuit is equal to the sum of the individual resistances. When resistors are placed parallel, with each resistor connected directly to the voltage source, each resistor gets the full voltage of the source. More current flows from the source, so the total resistance is lower. In fact, the total resistance in the circuit is equal to the sum of the inverse, or opposite, of each individual resistance.

Software Controls the System

Recall that the software that tells a computer how to do its work is the operating system, or OS. The OS does many different jobs:

- Working with peripherals: moving data and commands between the CPU and monitors, printers, and disk drives

- Managing data: finding the needed programs and files

- Using memory: storing data and programs in RAM or on the hard drive

- Coordinating data processing: doing many tasks at once without interfering with one another

- Providing the user interface: organizing and displaying the options you see on your screen when you turn on your computer

Systems Compatibility The two most popular operating systems are Microsoft® Windows® and the Macintosh OS®. Both use text and images to represent data and programs. The Macintosh OS runs on Apple® computers.

For many years the two systems were not compatible, meaning that files saved in one OS had formats that could not be read by the other OS. Today, cross-platform compatibility, or the ability to use a file on any device no matter what operating system is being used, is important. Versions of many programs are written to run on many operating systems. For example, versions of Microsoft Office applications are available for PCs running Windows, Macs running Mac OS, mobile devices running iOS, and mobile devices running Android OS.

In addition, most programs include a Save As command that lets you save files in different formats, and an Open command that lets you open files saved in a different format. There are also utility programs that can translate files that previously may have been unreadable so that can be used on devices running a different OS.

Figure 2.1.4 This is a Windows 8 Start Screen, which is the main starting place for working with Windows and programs.

Windows 8, Microsoft Corporation.

Basic Programming Concepts

Objectives

- Explain the binary system used by computers.
- Describe how software is written and translated.
- Explain why Boolean Algebra is used in computers.
- Explain the function of algorithms and how they are used in programming.
- Identify the three components of structured programming.

As You Read

Outline Information Use an outline as you read to help you organize information about how software makes computers work.

Software Provides Directions

How does a computer know what to do with data in digital form? Software gives it the instructions it needs. Experts called **programmers** write the instructions that become software. Programmers write these instructions, called **source code**, using a programming language.

Procedural or Object-Oriented Programming There are two basic categories of programming, procedural and object-oriented. **Procedural programming** uses step-by-step instructions to tell a computer what to do. Procedural programming languages include C, Fortran, Pascal, and Basic. **Object-oriented programming** provides rules for creating and managing **objects**, which are items that include both data and how to process the data. Object-oriented programming languages include Java, Alice, Python, and VBScript. Some programming combines the two. C++ is an example of a **programming language** that uses both procedural and object-oriented programming.

Compilers and Interpreters Special programs called **compilers** translate the source code into binary form, using only 0s and 1s. The result, called **object code**, can be read and acted on by a computer. Sometimes, programs called **interpreters** are used to translate the source code directly into actions, by-passing the need for a compiler. Interpreters are able to immediately follow the instructions in the binary code while compilers must first wait and translate the binary. Even though the compilers take longer to get started, they are able to complete task much faster than interpreters.

Representing Data Some programming languages require the programmer to assign a data type to variable data. Some common data types include string, which is a sequence of characters that does not contain numbers used for calculations; numeric, which is numbers or amounts that are used in calculations; character, which is text; integers, which represent whole numbers; and date, which is the method of coding dates.

🔑 Key Terms

- algorithm
- ASCII
- Boolean algebra
- character set
- compatibility
- compiler
- IF- statements
- interpreter
- logic gate
- object
- object code
- object-oriented programming
- operator
- procedural programming
- programmer
- programming language
- source code
- subroutine
- Unicode

Technology @ Home

By backing up your data, you make copies of data stored on your computer's hard drive to an external hard drive, USB flash drive, online storage service, or CDs/DVDs. Using an external hard drive with backup software or an online service lets you backup automatically. If you use CDs/DVDs or flash drives, you must back up data on your own.

Think About It!

Before deciding *how* to back up your hard drive, think about *why* it is important to back up. Sequence the importance of backing up each item in the list below using a scale of 1 (lowest) to 5 (highest):

➤ A program you can download from the Internet
➤ A report that you spent four hours on
➤ A file not used for a year
➤ Photos of friends
➤ Stored files of a game

Digital Computing

The computers widely used today are digital machines. Each piece of information used in the computer is identified by a distinct number. As a result, the computer acts on each piece of data by comparing its value to the value of other data or by performing a mathematical operation on it.

The Binary World   Most computers are not just digital but binary, too. That is, they only recognize two possible values. Think of a television's power switch. It, too, is binary: The switch is either on or off. There are no other possibilities.

Computers break data into pieces called bits and give each bit a value of either 0 or 1. A byte is a group of bits—usually 8. Using 8 bits in different combinations, each byte can represent a different value. For example, one byte might be 00000000, another might be 01010101, and another might be 00110011. There are 256 possible combinations!

Data in Bytes   Every piece of data that a computer works on, therefore, must be expressed in 0s and 1s and organized into bytes. These bytes can alone represent characters and numbers or be taken in combination to express more complex instructions like displaying color.

Digitizing Text   Programmers use 0s and 1s arranged in 8-digit bytes to represent the letters of the alphabet and many standard punctuation marks. American Standard Code for Information Interchange (**ASCII**) is a common system, or **character set**, for coding letters that uses 8 bits. **Unicode**, which uses 16 bits, is another.

 Spotlight on...

GRACE MURRAY HOPPER

Grace Hopper was a talented mathematician who joined the Naval Reserve during World War II. She worked on a computer the Navy was building, and she became the computer's first programmer. She also was a key figure in the development of compilers. Hopper's work helped make computers what they are today—tools that process text as easily as numbers.

Programming Creates the Software

The Language of Computers People communicate using words made up of 26 letters. Computers communicate using programs made up of two numbers—1s and 0s. No matter how complex, all computer tasks within a program are based on directions given in 1s and 0s.

To write computer code, programmers use math called **Boolean algebra**. Boolean algebra only has two values: true and false. This form of algebra is perfect for programming because binary also has two values. While using Boolean math in programming, 1 is true and 0 is false.

When you solve a math problem, you use an operation like addition or multiplication to find the relationship between two numbers. Boolean calculations are solved with the Boolean **operators** *AND*, *OR*, and *NOT*. These operators compare one or more Boolean values. When using the *AND* operator, if two values are true, then the solution is true; otherwise it is false. With the *OR* operator, if either of two values is true, then the solution is true. The *OR* operator is only false when both values are false. The *NOT* reverses a value from true to false.

Computers use physical devices consisting of a group of switches called a **logic gate** to preform Boolean equations. Using a combination of logic gates, programs direct the computer to perform more complex functions like computing advanced math or playing a song from an audio file.

Did You Know?

Boolean operators are used outside of algebra as well. When you use a search engine to search for information online you can use Boolean operators to fine-tune your search results.

- If you search for George Washington *AND* the American Revolution, the search engine would display links to Washington's efforts during the revolution.
- If you search for Washington *OR* the Revolution, the list includes links about Washington and links about the Revolution.
- If you search for Washington *AND NOT* the Revolution, the list includes links to Washington's life outside the American Revolution.

Solving Boolean Algebra with Truth Tables

AND				OR		
X	Y	Z		X	Y	Z
0	0	0		0	0	0
0	1	0		0	1	1
1	0	0		1	0	1
1	1	1		1	1	1

Figure 2.2.1 Charts called Truth Tables can be used as a quick reference to find the solutions to Boolean algebra problems. The values in the equation are X and Y. The solution is Z. For example, with the AND truth table, when X and Y equal 0, or false, then Z equals false.

Programs are Directions

Programs are a sequence of instructions that result in the computer performing a specific task. This linear sequence of instructions is called an **algorithm**. In a program, the algorithm is a designated sequence of calculations. The calculations are always done in the same order and steps are never skipped, so the result is always the same. Algorithms do not have to be a sequence of calculations. They can be a sequence of instructions that result in a predictable outcome, or solve a specific problem. When you bake a cake, the recipe is your algorithm. If you follow the recipe steps precisely and in the correct order, the result is a successful cake.

The Structure of a Program

There are three main components in programs: *sequence, decision,* and *loop*. Programs follow the same linear *sequence* of actions every time they run. If a program is solving the equation $2(x+1)$, it always adds 1 then multiplies by 2. If it performs the operations in a different order—say, multiplies by 2 and then adds 1—the answer would not be correct. The computer ends each action with a *decision*. The decision is the choice the program takes at the end of each step. The decisions are determined with **IF- statements**. An IF-statement defines conditions that must be met for the program to move to the next step. For example, *IF* you have finished adding the ingredients to the cake batter, *then* you can put the cake in the oven. Sometimes an action is repeated in a *loop,* or iteration, until a desired result occurs. You can illustrate the structure of an algorithm using a flowchart, using arrows to indicate the linear sequence, and the iterative loops.

Some sequences are described in a single line of code called a **subroutine**. With a subroutine, a programmer can tell the computer to perform an entire sequence without having to type every step.

Figure 2.2.2

Algorithms can be illustrated using a flowchart, which has boxes connected with arrows, showing the order of steps. This flowchart shows the sequence of steps involved in following the steps in a cake recipe.

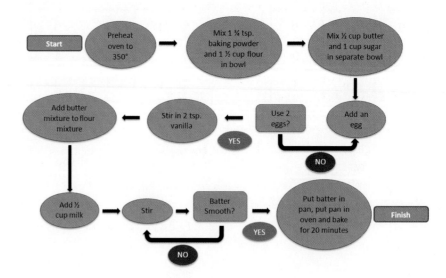

Group and Individual Computing

Objectives

- Compare and contrast different kinds of computers used in organizations.
- Compare and contrast different kinds of computers used by individuals.

As You Read

Compare and Contrast   Use a Venn diagram to help you compare and contrast information about the types of computers as you read the lesson.

A Dizzying Variety

Computers range in size from huge machines as big as a room to devices so small they can fit in your pocket. Each type of computer is suited to handling a particular set of jobs in particular settings. When thinking about this great variety of computers, it is helpful to look at them in two groups: those used by organizations and those used by individuals.

Computers for Organizations

Companies and other organizations use the full range of computers. Large organizations can afford the largest and most expensive machines, and such companies are more likely to need all the processing power that these huge machines have. Many companies also want some of their workers, such as salespeople, to have small **handheld computers**.

Supercomputers   The largest and most powerful computers can process huge amounts of data very quickly. These superfast scientific computers are called **supercomputers**. Where most CPUs can perform millions of calculations a second, supercomputers can perform millions upon millions of calculations a second. The organizations using supercomputers do very complex work, such as forecasting the weather or creating detailed models of nuclear reactions.

Supercomputers are not only the largest and most powerful type of computer, they are also the most expensive. A single supercomputer can cost hundreds of thousands of dollars or tens of millions of dollars. They are also extremely rugged and dependable systems, so users place constant heavy workloads on them.

 **Key Terms**

- desktop computer
- emerging technology
- evolving technology
- handheld computer
- mainframe
- server
- smart phone
- subnotebook computer
- supercomputer
- tablet computer
- wearable computer

Figure 2.3.1 Some organizations use very large computer systems and house them in their own special environments.

When computers are linked in a network, the network is set up to prevent people who have no right to be in the network from having access to the information. Typically, users use a password to gain access.

Think About It!

Think about the kind of information stored on a school network. Which informational items listed below do you think should have blocked access?

➤ class schedules

➤ students' grades

➤ students' health records

➤ sports team results

➤ scheduled school events

Mainframes The **mainframe** is another type of computer used by government agencies and large corporations. Mainframe computers are used in centralized computing systems as the storage location for all or most of the data. Other, less powerful computers connect to the mainframe so users can access the data. For example, airline company employees use mainframes to store and process reservations. In this way, reservations agents and travel agents all around the world can locate and use the same information at the same time. The trend now is to replace mainframes with servers. Even many government agencies have reduced the amount they rely on mainframes.

Servers Most organizations connect their computers together in a network. All the computers that are part of the network are connected to a computer called a **server**. The server holds data and programs that people on the network can use on their personal computers. A computer connected to a network, called the host, uses a special program called the client to contact the server and get data from it. Unlike terminals, computers on a network can have their own disk storage, but the main source of data for the network is still the server. Servers can be host- or client-based. If the server is host-based, the server runs the programs and receives directions from the client computers. In a client-bast server the programs and processing are split between the client and host computers. The networking found in servers can also be found in peer-to-peer networks, where computers in a system share resources and there is no host computer.

Real-World Tech

The Intelligent Room Some businesses are using a powerful new approach to working together called the Intelligent Room. The room looks like a normal conference room, but computer-controlled microphones and cameras placed around the room make sure that the speaker is always in view. This is especially helpful for video conferencing, in which a video of a meeting in one room is  sent to another group of workers in another room. Screens mounted on the wall can be used to display data from computers simply by touching the screen.

Why is the camera's ability to follow the speaker useful for video conferencing?

Computers for Individuals

Most individuals do not need as much computing power as organizations do. They can use smaller—even mobile—devices for their computing needs.

Workstations   The most powerful and expensive personal computers are workstations. Architects, engineers, designers, and others who work with complex data use these machines for their power and speed.

Personal Computers   Most individuals use personal computers to do everyday jobs more quickly and easily. **Desktop computers** are personal computers that are small enough to fit on or under a desk but too large to move around easily. Desktop computers may be connected to a network or they may be stand-alone, which means they are not connected to any network.

Small portable computers such as laptops and notebooks are as powerful as a desktop but can be easily carried around. They usually include an internal hard drive. They can connect to an AC power source or run on battery power. Laptops usually have a monitor, keyboard, and pointing device built-in, as well as ports and Wi-Fi for connecting to peripherals and the Internet. Some, called all-in-ones, have touch screens, as well.

Tablet Computers   Tablet computers are small, portable computers that have a flat panel display. The display is usually a touch screen, which can be used with a finger or a stylus. They may have ports and usually allow wireless connection to peripherals and a network. The primary characteristic of a tablet is its small size. Most are about 6-inches wide by 8-inches tall and weigh less than 1 pound.

Smart Phones   A **smart phone** is a telephone with computing capabilities. Most smart phones are mobile, or cellular. Smart phones provide Internet access using 3G, 4G, or Wi-Fi technology. They run apps, which are small programs designed for one purpose, such as checking the weather, finding a nearby restaurant, or playing a game. Smart phones have built-in devices such as cameras, microphones, and speakers. They have internal storage for saving data such as pictures, music, contact information, and a calendar. Smart phones also have the capability to send and receive e-mails and text messages. Some smart phones have attached keyboards, but most use a pop-up keyboard on the touch screen display.

Career Corner

Computer Engineer   Designing compact, powerful machines like subnotebooks and PDAs is the work of computer engineers. They design and test components and then put them together to make sure they work properly. Engineers need to know software and programming as well as understand the workings of hardware. Demand for computer engineers is expected to be good in the coming years.

Mobile Devices While all portable computers are mobile, including laptops, notebooks, and tablets, the term generally refers specifically to smart phones and handheld or **wearable computers**.

- A **personal digital assistant (PDA)** is a small, highly portable handheld computer that is used for taking notes or keeping track of appointments. Some similar devices include the ability to read barcodes and smart cards.

- Wearable computers are designed to be worn on the body, leaving the hands free for other tasks. They are usually intended for a specific purpose, such as inventory control or for monitoring body systems, such as heartrate. They may be worn on the arm or wrist or around the waist like a belt. Smartwatches are worn on the wrist and tell the time along with having the ability to run apps. Some wearable computers are worn as eyewear and can affect vision or display information.

Evolving and Emerging Technologies Technology is always changing and adapting. As new needs are identified, technology is developed to meet those needs. As a technology becomes widely used, it may be modified to be more efficient or to meet a new or different need. A new, innovative technological development is called an emerging technology. Augmented reality, in which digital information is layered over someone's real-world view, is an **emerging technology**. An existing technology that changes to be more efficient or meet a different need is called an **evolving technology**. For example, using a smart phone to pay for products is one way existing technologies are evolving.

Figure 2.3.2 Smart phones and tablets are small, light, and powerful.

Use the Vocabulary

Directions: *Match each vocabulary term in the left column with the correct definition in the right column.*

_____ 1. command
_____ 2. motherboard
_____ 3. read-only memory
_____ 4. programmer
_____ 5. compiler
_____ 6. supercomputer
_____ 7. algorithm
_____ 8. server
_____ 9. desktop computer
_____ 10. circuit

a. a sequence of instructions

b. instruction for the computer to do something

c. a network of connected electronic components

d. where the CPU is located

e. high-speed computer for complex work

f. another name for personal computer

g. set of chips that starts the computer when it is turned on

h. language that translates source code into binary form

i. writes instructions for a computer to follow

j. computer accessed by users on a network

Check Your Comprehension

Directions: *Determine the correct choice for each of the following.*

1. What would you most likely use a microphone to input?
   a. commands
   b. images
   c. sound
   d. text

2. Data from which part of a computer is lost when it is turned off?
   a. the CD-ROM
   b. the hard drive
   c. RAM
   d. ROM

3. Which is NOT a component in programs?
   a. loop
   b. choice
   c. sequence
   d. decision

4. Which is an example of a binary number?
   a. 10011001
   b. –342
   c. 67439622
   d. .0000002

5. Which of the following is NOT a task performed by operating systems?
   a. controlling a printer
   b. managing memory
   c. coordinating how programs run
   d. compiling a program

6. What kind of machine is more powerful than a server?
   a. desktop computer
   b. portable computer
   c. mainframe
   d. handheld computer

 **Think Critically**

Directions: *Answer the following questions.*

1. What are the functions of compilers and interpreters?

2. Explain the difference between the operation of compilers and interpreters.

3. Identify and explain the concept of an algorithm.

4. Explain how the following data types are used to represent variable data in software development: string, numeric, character, integer, and date.

5. List at least three object-oriented programming languages and three procedural programming languages. Explain how they are used in software development.

Extend Your Knowledge

Directions: *Choose and complete one of the following projects.*

A. Make a flowchart to illustrate a linear sequence of actions you do every day, such as getting ready for school or packing your lunch. Does your flowchart contain the main components of programs: sequence, decision, and loop? Create an IF-statement for one step of your flowchart to illustrate the iterative instructions.

B. Collect three advertisements for home computer systems. List the components that are offered in each ad. Compare the three systems for their appropriateness for inputting and outputting text, images, and sounds. Compare their capacity to store data. Based on the features, write a brief explanation of which machine you think is best and why. Read your explanation out loud to a partner and listen as your partner reads his or hers out loud to you.

C. Work with a partner to practice using a digital multimeter (DIMM). Being sure to follow all safety protocols, use the DIMM to measure AC and DC voltages. Then, measure AC and DC current. Finally, measure the resistance of a circuit consisting of resistors. If possible, construct simple circuits on a breadboard or with a soldering iron.

Input/Output Basics

Input and Output If you think of the computer as a person, its brain would be the central processing unit, or CPU. Like a brain, a CPU receives and organizes data from many different sources into useful information.

Also, like a person, a computer needs more than just a brain to work properly. It needs a way to receive the unorganized data and to show the results of its processing of the data. The brain receives data through the senses: sight, hearing, smell, taste, and touch. It shows the results of its processing of the data through speech, movement, and writing. The CPU receives its data from input devices such as the keyboard and mouse. It shows the results of its processing through output devices such as a monitor, printer, or speakers.

Chapter Outline

 Lesson 3–1

Basic Input Devices

 Lesson 3–2

Basic Output Devices

Basic Input Devices

Objectives

- Distinguish among four types of input.
- Compare and contrast basic input devices.
- Discuss the health risks of using some input devices.

As You Read

Organize Information   Use a concept web to help you organize information about basic input devices as you read.

 Key Terms

- command
- digital camera
- ergonomic
- pointer
- pointing device
- repetitive strain injury (RSI)
- scanner
- webcam

What Is Input?

As you already learned, input is any kind of information, or instructions, that is entered into a computer's memory. There are four basic types of input: data, software instructions, user commands, and responses.

Data   Words, numbers, images, and sounds that you enter into a computer are data. This is the raw material that a computer processes.

Software Instructions   To perform any job, a computer must follow instructions from a software program. Software typically is installed from a CD or downloaded from the Internet onto the hard drive. Launching a program moves it into the computer's RAM. That makes the program available to the CPU—and to you.

User Commands   A **command** is an instruction that tells a software program what action to perform. For example, to open a program, save your work, or close a program, you must issue a command to the computer.

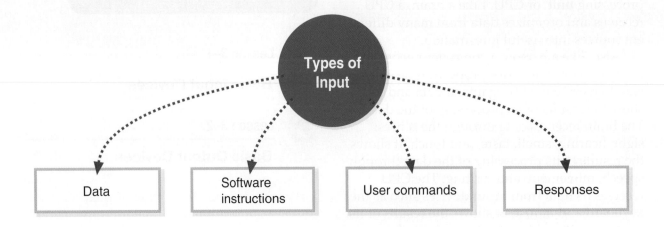

Responses Sometimes a program asks you to enter information or make a choice so that it can carry out a command or process data. For example, if you try to close a program without saving your work, the program will ask if you wish to save it. Before you can continue, you must input a response.

What Is an Input Device?

An input device is any hardware used to input data. Recall that two common input devices are the keyboard and the mouse. A mouse is a type of **pointing device**. Moving the mouse over a surface moves a **pointer** on the screen. Notebook computers often use a touchpad, or trackpad, as the pointing device. It is built into the computer. Moving your finger on the touchpad moves the pointer. Smart phones, some computers, and tablets use touch screens that allow you to move your finger directly on the screen. Some can sense motion and react to a hand moving in front of the screen or even respond to eye movements. There are also specialized input devices, such as digital cameras, for capturing and inputting photos and videos, microphones for inputting sound, and even global positioning systems (GPS) used to input maps and locations.

Game Controllers Game controllers are handheld devices that let you input command and interact with video and computer games. They usually have buttons, directional pads, and even motion sensors. A joystick is a lever that can be moved in all directions to move objects on the screen. It may be used with computer games, flight simulators, or virtual reality programs.

Technology @ Work

Some people have disabilities that prevent them from working a mouse with their fingertips. Two companies make joysticks that can be controlled by mouth. Moving the stick up and down or from side to side moves the cursor on the screen.

Think About It!

Which mouse actions do you think need to be considered in an adaptive input device for people with physical disabilities?

➤ select text

➤ scroll through a document

➤ create art in a drawing program

➤ click the mouse button to select a menu option

➤ cut text

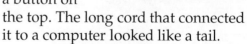
Spotlight on...

DOUG ENGELBART

❝We were looking for the best—the most efficient—device. We . . . said 'let's test them,' and determine the answer once-and-for-all. . . . It quickly became clear that the mouse outperformed all the [other devices].❞

Doug Engelbart

In the 1960s, Doug Engelbart created the mouse—a device that could be used to move a cursor around a computer screen.

The first mouse was a crude wooden box with two round discs on the bottom and a button on the top. The long cord that connected it to a computer looked like a tail.

A visionary, Engelbart also thought computers could be used as writing machines, or word processors.

You might think that repetitive strain injury only affects adults who work all day at a computer. Researchers are trying to find out if children can also be affected by repeated use of the keyboard and mouse. They have learned that children run some risk of injury.

One thing that can reduce this risk is to have the keyboard and mouse positioned lower than the computer. Many students, though, prefer to have these devices on top of a table. They want to be able to see the keys as they type!

Microphone   To input sounds, you can use a microphone or a sound card (inside the computer) to record and play back sounds. Many computers, including smart phones and tablets, use sound input for direction. Voice recognition programs, like Apple's Siri or Google's "OK Google," are used to start searches on smart phones.

Digital Cameras, Webcams, and Scanners   Digital cameras connect to the computer by a cable or a wireless link to input photos. When you video chat with a friend you're using a **webcam**, a small camera that either attaches to the computer monitor, sits on your desk, or—like Apple's iSight—is built into the computer. Webcams usually come with software that enables you to record video or stream the video on the Web. **Scanners** are devices that let you copy printed images into a computer and can be stand-alone or part of your printer. The scanner changes the printed image into a digital form.

Modem and Routers   Modems and routers direct the input of data between multiple computers. A modem converts data from one form to another. Originally modems were used send computer data over telephone lines so computers could access the Internet through dial-up. Modern modems can send information through cable, satellite, or DSL. Routers forward data from one source to another, such as between two computers or between a computer and the Internet. For Internet access, a router is connected to a modem. The modem connects to an Internet provider and the router directs the flow of data between the Internet and computers.

Health Risks of Some Input Devices

When you use a keyboard or mouse a lot, you make the same hand movements over and over again. This can cause damage to nerves in the hand. The problem is called **repetitive strain injury**, or **RSI**. **Ergonomic** keyboards have been designed to reduce RSI. Some people who suffer from this problem use a mouse controlled by foot pedals or some other kind of pointing device. Proper posture and lighting and limiting the amount of time you spend looking at a screen can help prevent health problems.

Figure 3.1.1 Specially designed keyboards, like this one, can reduce the risk of repetitive strain injuries.

Basic Output Devices

Objectives

- Distinguish among the four types of output.
- Compare and contrast basic output devices.
- Explain how visual display systems work.
- Summarize printing technology.

As You Read

Outline Information Use an outline format to help you organize information about output as you read.

What Is Output?

After a computer has processed data, it provides the results in the form of output. There are four types of output: text, graphics, video, and audio.

Text Characters such as letters, symbols, and numbers are called text. To be considered text, the characters must be organized in a coherent way. For example, random letters on a page are not considered text, but paragraphs in a book report are text.

Graphics Drawings, photographs, and other visual images are called graphics.

Video Moving images are known as video. Images captured by a digital video camera, and which can be played on a computer, are one example of video. The use of animation is another example.

Audio Sound output is called audio. This includes music or speech that the computer plays through its speakers or headphones.

 **Key Terms**

- All-in-One printer
- cathode ray tube (CRT)
- impact printer
- liquid crystal display (LCD)
- nonimpact printer
- output device

Figure 3.2.1 This is an LCD monitor—an output device for displaying text and graphics.

What Is an Output Device?

An **output device** is any piece of hardware that displays or plays back the result of computer processing in one of the four forms of output. For example, monitors and printers create a visual record of the processing completed by the computer.

Monitors

The computer displays information on a monitor, a hardware device that receives and shows images on a screen. The images the monitor displays change as the computer processes data.

LCDs Modern monitors use the **liquid crystal display**, or **LCD**. In an LCD, two transparent surfaces are placed on either side of a layer of cells containing tiny crystals. Electrical signals sent to the crystals cause them to form images on the surface.

LCDs are very light and have a flat screen. They use little power and can even be operated using just batteries. Also, there are now two different techniques for producing color: thin film transistor (TFT) and passive matrix technology. TFT produces sharper color and images, so it is becoming the standard.

CRTs An older type of monitor is the **cathode ray tube**, or CRT. In a CRT, the monitor receives electrical signals from the computer. The signals cause "guns" in the CRT to shoot a stream of electrons at the back of the screen. The electrons strike materials called phosphors, which begin to glow. The glowing phosphors appear as points of light on the screen.

Touch Screen Monitors Touch screen monitors, used on smart phones, tablets, and some computers, are designed to respond to input from a finger or stylus touching the screen. There are pros and cons of using a touch screen with the most important being personal preference. The trend is moving toward touch screens, as many people find swiping with a finger easier, faster, and more intuitive than using a keyboard, mouse, or touch pad.

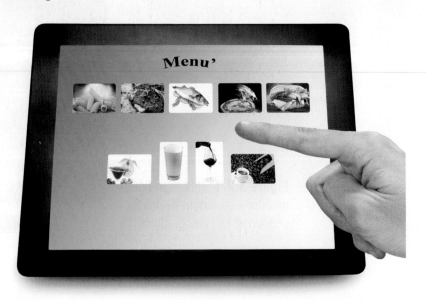

Figure 3.2.2 Touch screens are used for tablets, smart phones, and some notebook PCs.

Currently, there are two main types of touch screens:

- Analog resistive touch screens are made of two layers: usually one is glass and the other is plastic film. They are each covered with a grid of electrical conductors. When you touch the screen, there is contact between the grid on the glass and the grid on the film, creating a circuit. The monitor detects and responds to the change in electric current resistance at the spot of the touch.
- Projected capacitance (pro-cap) touch screens also use two layers of conductors, but they rely on electrical capacitance, which is the build-up of electrons in an object. When you touch the top layer of the screen, the screen takes some electrons—or charge—from the other layer. The monitor responds to the change in the charge.

Color monitors have three electron guns, each one shooting a beam of a different color: red, blue, or green. CRTs today are now capable of producing thousands of colors. Some of the first monitors and televisions were CRTs. However, these monitors are not only heavy and take up a lot of desk space, but they also heat up easily. CRTs use more electricity than LCDs. As LCDs became more affordable, companies stopped producing and selling CRTs in the United States.

Printers

A printer makes a paper copy of the display shown on a monitor. The most common types of printers are nonimpact printers, which have made impact printers almost obsolete.

Real-World Tech

e-cycling You've probably noticed that your printer ink cartridges can be recycled at your local office supply stores. However, did you realize that you can recycle your old computer or other electronic equipment that still works? The best way to do this is to donate them to schools, other nonprofits, or low-income families in need. To help you do this—and keep our country greener—the Environmental Protection Agency has a Web site that lets you find local programs, manufacturer-retailer programs, and government supported donation and recycling programs:

http://www.epa.gov/osw/conserve/materials/ecycling/donate.htm

Nonimpact Printers   Most computer users today use these inkjet and laser printers to produce paper copies. Inkjet printers make images by spraying a fine stream of ink onto the paper. Laser printers use a powder called toner and operate like a copier machine. Heat fuses the toner to the paper to create the image. Laser printers create more crisp images than inkjet. Both inkjet and laser printers are available in **All-in-One** versions that add fax, copier, and scanner capabilities at a very low cost.

Impact Printers   Dot matrix printers are a kind of impact printer that uses hammers or pins to press an ink-covered ribbon. They are noisy and the image quality is poor, but some are still used in businesses to provide copies of multi-part forms, like invoices.

Real-World Tech

Three-Dimensional Printers

Three-dimensional objects can be modeled in software and then created by computers using a three-dimensional (3D) printer. 3D printers build objects by slicing the digital model into thin layers and then printing the layers as sheets. These sheets are then joined together to produce the three-dimensional object. Many 3D printers build objects with plastic or metal. 3D printers are used for product design in many industries ranging from footwear to medical devices.

If you had a 3D printer, what would you print?

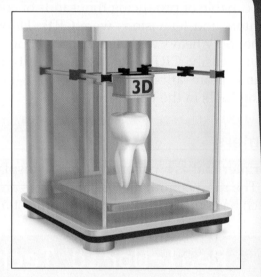

Use the Vocabulary

Directions: *Match each vocabulary term in the left column with the correct definition in the right column.*

_____ **1.** command
_____ **2.** pointer
_____ **3.** output device
_____ **4.** digital camera
_____ **5.** scanner
_____ **6.** repetitive strain injury
_____ **7.** All-in-One printer
_____ **8.** liquid crystal display
_____ **9.** impact printer
_____ **10.** nonimpact printer

a. produces images by sending electrical signals to crystals

b. any piece of hardware that displays or plays back the result of computer processing

c. device with hammers or pins that strike a ribbon to leave ink on paper

d. lets you input printed images into a computer

e. a printer that contains fax, copier, and scanner capabilities

f. follows a mouse's movements

g. device such as an inkjet or laser printer

h. takes photographs that a computer can read

i. condition caused by making the same movements again and again

j. instruction to a software program to take an action

Check Your Comprehension

Directions: *Determine the correct choice for each of the following.*

1. Which type of input provides answers to questions issued by programs?
  a. commands
  b. data
  c. responses
  d. software

2. Which device can be used to connect a computer to the Internet?
  a. keyboard
  b. modem
  c. pointing device
  d. scanner

3. Which of the following devices can be designed to reduce the problem of RSIs?
  a. scanner
  b. digital camera
  c. monitor
  d. keyboard

4. What do output devices provide?
  a. data to be processed
  b. software code
  c. text and images only
  d. results of processing

5. Which of the following is NOT descriptive of a CRT?
  a. heavy
  b. uses little power
  c. heats up easily
  d. affordable

6. What kind of output device would NOT be used to output images?
  a. CRT
  b. LCD
  c. printer
  d. speaker

Chapter Review and Assessment

Directions: *Answer the following questions.*

1. Why are microphones or digital cameras unlikely to cause the damage that is found in repetitive strain injury?

2. Identify the type and purpose of at least three specialized input devices.

3. What type(s) of monitor(s) do you use at school? What are the advantages and disadvantages of the different types of monitors?

4. How is video similar to ordinary graphics? How is it different?

5. Why have nonimpact printers all but replaced impact printers?

Extend Your Knowledge

Directions: *Choose and complete one of the following projects.*

A. Open a word-processing program. Use the keyboard to input the definition of the word "Text" on page 33. Input the paragraph a total of five times. Each time you do so, time yourself. Print the five paragraphs. Compare the five times. Determine whether you were able to type faster and more accurately with practice.

B. With your teacher's permission, practice disconnecting and connecting your computer system's input and output devices. For example, disconnect and connect the mouse, keyboard, and printer. Then, verify that the devices are working correctly by opening a word-processing document and typing a paragraph about the different input and output devices you are working with. Move around in the document using the keyboard and the mouse, and edit the paragraph to include an explanation of which device you think is easier to work with and why. With your teacher's permission, print the document. Read your paragraph to a partner or to the class and answer any questions.

Understanding Specialized Input/Output

From Text to Moving Pictures Modern personal computers work in basically the same way that early personal computers did. Both perform the same four operations: input, processing, storage, and output. Both turn different sources of data into useful information. There is a major difference between what earlier and more recent computers can do, however.

Early personal computers could work with text and numbers. Today's computers can also handle different types of data, such as still images, sound, and video. Hardware makers have designed new devices to allow users to input data and output information in new ways. These devices have taken computers from the still and silent world of text and numbers into a dazzling multimedia world of sound, images, and motion.

Chapter Outline

 Lesson 4–1

Specialized Input Devices

 Lesson 4–2

Specialized Output Devices

Lesson 4–1

Specialized Input Devices

Objectives

- Explain how sound cards process sound.
- Compare and contrast traditional and digital cameras.
- Compare digital cameras, scanners, and digital video cameras.

As You Read

Organize Information   Use a concept web to help you organize information about devices used to input sound, still images, and video as you read.

 Key Terms

- compress
- digital video camera
- fax machine
- optical character recognition (OCR)
- video capture card

Inputting Sound

The microphone is the most basic device for inputting sound into a computer. You use it for all types of sound, including music, narration, and speech for voice recognition software. Microphones capture sounds in analog form—as a series of rapidly changing waves or vibrations. To be usable by a computer, sounds must be in digital form, that is, the waves must be converted to binary code (1s and 0s) that the computer can recognize. The sound card does this work.

A sound card is a circuit board that processes sounds in multiple ways. First, it digitizes sounds by changing them from analog to digital form. Then, it processes the digital sounds by following a set of built-in instructions. For example, it can prepare the digital sound files for use with voice recognition software. Sometimes the sound card reduces the size of sound files by compressing the data. That way, the files take up less space in memory. Finally, the sound card reverses the digitizing process so you can play analog sounds through the computer's speakers.

Figure 4.1.1 A sound card handles the audio-processing tasks in a computer.

Inputting Still Images

There are several different ways to input still images into a computer. They include facsimile (fax) machines, digital cameras, and scanners.

Facsimile Machines A **fax machine**, or facsimile machine, scans printed documents and sends them over phone lines to another fax machine. Though fax machines are still used by some companies, many documents that were once sent as a fax are now sent online as image files.

Digital Cameras A digital camera, like a traditional camera, takes pictures. In a traditional camera, light enters the lens and strikes a piece of film coated with chemicals that are sensitive to light. The chemicals produce an image on the film. In a digital camera, a computer chip takes the information from the lens and records it as pixels, or small dots, that form the image. A digital camera has memory to store the pictures you take.

Some digital cameras store images on a memory card that can be removed. If a computer has the correct device, it can read the images from the memory card. Many digital cameras, including smart phones, can connect to a computer via a cable or wireless link. When the camera is connected, the computer treats it like a disk drive and the pictures can be copied to the computer.

Connections

The Arts A digital camera can take pictures that use from 4 to 20 million dots (pixels) to make the picture. The more dots it uses, the sharper the image is. But more dots also take up more space on the memory card where the pictures are stored in the camera.

Photographers can choose to take photos of lesser quality to save space. They can also delete photos from the camera's memory to make space for new ones.

Figure 4.1.2 Digital cameras capture and store images electronically.

Scanners Any printed document can be digitized by using a scanner. Scanners shine a light onto the material to be copied and change the image into pixels. This creates a digital image that can be input.

Most scanners have **optical character recognition**, or **OCR**, software. When you scan printed text using this software, the text is turned into a digital file. In this way, you can input printed text, including handwriting, without having to type it.

There are different types of scanners:

- With a sheetfed scanner, you insert the pages you want copied and the scanner pulls them through one at a time.

- Flatbed scanners work more like copy machines. You lay material on a flat glass panel to make the copy. All-in-one printers have flatbed scanner capability.

- Handheld scanners are portable models that you hold in your hand. They are useful for copying small originals.

Inputting Video

You can input and display full-motion video and animation on a computer. Like all other forms of input, the videos must be in digital form. **Digital video cameras** record moving images in digital form. Most smart phones can record video, too.

To convert analog videos to digital format, a computer needs a **video capture card**. Like a sound card, this type of circuit board changes video images into a digital file. These cards also **compress** files so they occupy less disk space.

Real-World Tech

Crossing the Line   There is another use for video capture that is strictly illegal. Some computer users digitize movies, pay-per-view events, and television shows and post them on Web sites. People can visit the sites, download the shows, and watch them for free. This breaks copyright law, which protects the rights of people who create works of art, such as books, songs, and movies.

Why would the government pass laws to protect the rights of authors, songwriters, and movie directors regarding the sale of their works?

Specialized Output Devices

Lesson 4–2

Objectives

- Distinguish among different video adapters.
- Compare and contrast different printers.
- Compare and contrast other output devices.
- Identify kinds of audio output.

As You Read

Gather Information   Use a chart to help you gather information about output and output devices used for still images, video, and sound as you read.

Video Adapters

The images you see on your monitor are created by a **video adapter**. The adapter is a circuit board that receives data from an operating system or software application. It changes that data into electrical currents and sends them to the monitor. In a color monitor, the amount of current sent by the video adapter determines the color the monitor will produce. Like a sound card, a video adapter processes data so that the computer's CPU can take care of other jobs. It also has its own memory, called **video memory**, or **VRAM**, to free up space in the computer's memory.

Special Video Adapters   Some video adapters send images to the monitor very quickly. They are called video accelerators.

Key Terms

- data projector
- high-definition television (HDTV)
- Musical Instrument Digital Interface (MIDI)
- OLED
- speech synthesis software
- thermal transfer printer
- video adapter
- video memory (VRAM)

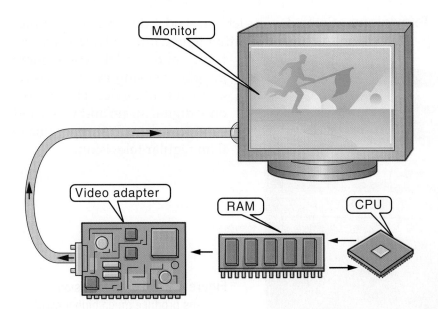

Figure 4.2.1 The video adapter processes video data for display on the monitor, allowing the CPU and RAM to handle other tasks.

Another new technology might help users of small video screens to see better in sunlight. **OLED**, or Organic Light Emitting Diode, technology consumes less power and produces better displays than current LCD screens. OLED screens also have very good video quality—the manufacturers call it "full motion" video.

Think About It!

Think of the small display screens that you have seen in use. Think also of the lighting conditions in which they are used. Which of the following products do you think could best use OLED display?

➤ Cell phone

➤ PDA

➤ Netbook computer

➤ MP3 player, like the iPod

Most computers today have highly specialized video adapters, called 3-D video adapters. Images on a monitor have only two dimensions—height and width. 3-D video adapters add a third dimension to an image—depth.

Outputting Images with Printers

Recall that image quality varies based on which type of printer is used to output an image. Both impact and nonimpact printers create images by printing tiny dots on the paper. Inkjet and laser printers have much higher print quality. Therefore, they are more often used for printing graphic images.

The best printer for printing color images is a **thermal transfer printer**. These printers use heat to transfer color dyes or inks onto paper. Thermal transfer printers do not make pictures out of tiny dots. Instead, the colors actually blend together on the paper. These printers only work with glossy paper.

Outputting Video

You can use three types of devices to output video.

Data Projectors You may be familiar with **data projectors**, which show a computer's video output on a projection screen so many people can view it at once. These projectors are often used to display presentations for educational or business meetings.

Digital light processing, or DLP, projectors use millions of tiny mirrors to create a very sharp image. That image is then projected through a lens and onto a screen. Because the image they produce is so sharp, DLP projectors can be used with large audiences. They can even be used in brightly lit rooms.

Televisions Some devices let you send video from a computer to a television. As **high-definition television**, or **HDTV**, has become more widely used, more people are using their television as an output device. HDTV uses only digital audio and video and produces a much sharper image than regular television.

Figure 4.2.2 Digital television systems produce much higher quality output than standard televisions.

Headsets A headset, which has two LCD panels, is worn over the head. The computer sends video images to each panel. To the person wearing the headset, it seems as if he or she is walking in a three-dimensional space.

A similar but larger device is the Cave Automated Virtual Environment, or CAVE. This is a room in which three-dimensional images are shown on the floor, walls, and ceiling. A person in the room wears 3-D glasses. The glasses and images create the illusion of interacting in three-dimensions.

Outputting Sound

To output sound to headphones or speakers, your computer must have a sound card and speakers. The sound card changes digital sound files stored in the computer's memory into an electrical current. It sends that current to the speakers to produce audio output.

The sound a computer can produce depends on the computer's software. Two kinds of software allow audio output:

- **Speech synthesis software** allows the computer to read text files aloud.

- **Musical Instrument Digital Interface (MIDI)** software allows the computer to create music. With this software, you can send instructions to a digital musical instrument called a synthesizer. This device then sounds the notes it has been instructed to play.

 Spotlight on...

RAYMOND KURZWEIL

Raymond Kurzweil's reading machine turned printed text into spoken language, opening a world of information to people with visual impairments.

Kurzweil also devised the first electronic musical instrument. After Kurzweil spoke with singer and songwriter Stevie Wonder, he had the idea of making a better music synthesizer. Kurzweil's synthesizer could make the music of an entire orchestra.

Use the Vocabulary

Directions: *Match each vocabulary term in the left column with the correct definition in the right column.*

_____ **1.** compress
_____ **2.** fax machine
_____ **3.** optical character recognition
_____ **4.** digital video camera
_____ **5.** video capture card
_____ **6.** video adapter
_____ **7.** VRAM
_____ **8.** thermal transfer printer
_____ **9.** speech synthesis software
_____ **10.** MIDI

a. turns text into audio

b. prints high-quality output suitable for photos

c. software that lets the computer play like an electronic instrument

d. software that scans text and turns it into a digital file

e. memory on a video adapter

f. to make files smaller

g. captures still images, which are then shown rapidly

h. controls video output to the monitor

i. converts analog video into digital

j. scans documents and sends them over phone lines

Check Your Comprehension

Directions: *Complete each sentence with information from the chapter.*

1. To play sound that has been stored in a computer, it must be converted to _____ format.

2. Digital photos can be input from a camera by transporting them on a disk or sending them to the computer using a(n) _____.

3. _____ software allows people to scan text instead of rekeying it.

4. Photos that haven't been taken with a digital camera can still be input into a computer using either a fax machine or a(n) _____.

5. The amount of current that a video adapter sends to the monitor determines the _____ display on the monitor.

6. Three-dimensional graphics include height, width, and _____.

7. DLP projectors are better than LCD projectors for giving a presentation to many people because the _____ appear sharper.

8. Standard printers create output by printing tiny _____ on paper.

9. Headsets and the room-sized _____ create virtual three-dimensional environments.

10. Audio can be output to headphones or _____.

Think Critically

Directions: *Answer the following questions.*

1. What is one advantage of having memory on a video card dedicated to displaying graphics?

2. Why are sound and graphics files compressed?

3. Suppose someone had to scan ten images. Which kind of scanner would require him or her to stay closer to the machine as it is working, a sheetfed or flatbed? Why?

4. Would a 3-D graphics adapter be needed on a machine used mostly for word processing and spreadsheets? Why or why not?

5. Which kind of printer would be better for printing a report for school that included two or three photographs, an inkjet or a thermal transfer printer? Why?

Extend Your Knowledge

Directions: *Choose and complete one of the following projects.*

A. Divide a sheet of paper into two columns, creating a T-chart. Write the heading *Standard System* over the left column. Write the heading *Graphics System* over the right column. In each column, list the input and output components you would include if you were setting up these two computer systems. Include the types of output cards you would want. Assume that the standard system will be used for word processing and spreadsheet work. Assume that the graphics system will be used for high-quality photographs.

B. Find out what kind of sound your computer can output. If possible, output audio and then determine what kinds of software your computer used to output the sound. With a partner or as a class, discuss for whom audio output is an advantage and when this feature is a necessity.

Storage Basics

chapter 5

How Do Computers Store Data?

Computer storage is like the backpack you bring to school. Both store things until you are ready to use them. Your backpack stores books and school supplies; most computers store software and data.

Computer storage devices can store information for long periods of time. This lets you create a file today, save it, and then use it again in the future. In this chapter, you will learn why storage is necessary and how information is stored. You will also examine some of the storage devices you are likely to find on today's computers.

Chapter Outline

 Lesson 5–1

Understanding Computer Storage

 Lesson 5–2

Classifying Storage Devices

 Lesson 5–3

Common Storage Devices

Understanding Computer Storage

Objectives

- Explain the need for storage devices for computers.
- Distinguish between memory and storage.
- Distinguish between storage devices and media.

As You Read

Organize Information   Use an outline to help you organize information about computer storage and storage devices as you read.

🔑 Key Terms

- backup
- Basic Input/Output System (BIOS)
- file
- firmware
- memory
- restore
- storage device
- UEFI (Unified Extensible Firmware Interface)

Computer Storage Devices

Where do you store the books, pencils, and notebooks that you need for school? Many students keep them in a backpack. When class is about to begin, they pull out the items they need. When class is finished, they put the items back into their backpacks.

This is similar to the way **storage devices** work. They are the computer's hardware components that retain data even after the power is turned off. Suppose you turned off your computer without saving your work to a storage device. All your work would be lost. Without storage devices, you would have to re-create all of your work every time you wanted to use it.

Why not keep all of a computer's software and data available at all times? Because no one needs to use every program or file every time they work on the computer. For example, you might be doing word processing today, but creating a computer drawing tomorrow. There is no need to have both programs open at the same time if you are not using both of them.

Files   A computer stores data and program instructions in files. A **file** is a collection of related information or program code, which has been given a unique name.

Figure 5.1.1 Like a backpack, a computer's storage devices hold things until you need them.

The type of file people most often use is called a document. A document can be any kind of file that a user can create, save, and edit. For example, you can use a word-processing program to create a letter, which is one type of document. A digital photo is another type of document.

System Startup Computer storage devices are a key part of a computer's startup process. Without a storage device to hold startup information permanently, a computer would not know what to do when you turned it on.

When you start a computer, it looks for information that tells it what to do. The **Basic Input/Output System**, or **BIOS**, is a set of programs, called **firmware**, that tells the computer equipment how to start up. When a computer is built, the BIOS is set up with this basic information. The BIOS is permanently stored in special memory chips called read-only memory, or ROM. Usually, the BIOS instructs the computer to look for the operating system. The operating system contains all the commands required to run the computer. It provides the tools to operate the system and to run programs. Most Apple Macintosh computers and personal computers built to run Windows 8 and later use **UEFI (Unified Extensible Firmware Interface)** instead of BIOS. UEFI allows for faster startup, supports large capacity storage drives, and is more secure than BIOS.

Memory and Storage

When people talk about computer **memory**, they usually mean a set of chips that acts as a temporary workspace in the computer. This memory, called random access memory, or RAM, stores data and program instructions needed by the CPU.

RAM and ROM are different in two important ways, as the following chart shows. First, ROM is nonvolatile, which means it stores its contents permanently, even when the computer is turned off. RAM, on the other hand, is volatile and only stores its contents temporarily; if the computer loses power, RAM's contents are lost.

Second, because ROM stores instructions that are needed only by the computer, you seldom need to think about ROM or the information it holds. But RAM holds data and programs while they are being used. As you use the computer, you constantly work with the contents of RAM.

Connections

Science   Nanotechnology is a field of science and technology that studies how to make things by arranging individual atoms and molecules. Nanotechnology has contributed to advances in computer technology.

For example, nanotechnology has made it possible for computer hard drives to hold ever larger amounts of data. They can do so because the parts that retrieve and record data—called the read/write heads—are made from an extremely thin layer of magnetic material. The material is less than one billionth of a meter thick, or close to 7,000 times thinner than a strand of a spider web.

ROM and RAM		
	Storage	**Holds**
ROM	Permanent	Startup instructions and configuration information for the computer
RAM	Temporary	Program instructions and data that are being used by the CPU

Storage Versus Memory New computer users sometimes get confused about temporary memory (RAM) and permanent storage (disks and disk drives). They will say "memory" when they actually mean to say "storage." Adding confusion, both are measured with the same units: bytes. One byte equals about 8 bits, or a single character. A kilobyte, or 1KB, is 1 thousand bytes. A megabyte, or 1MB, is 1 million bytes. A gigabyte, or 1GB, is 1 billion bytes. A terabyte, or 1TB, is 1 thousand billion bytes. A petabyte, or 1PB, is one million gigabytes. To avoid this problem, remember two key differences between storage and memory:

- The two work differently. Remember that RAM uses chips to temporarily store information. These chips depend on a constant supply of power to keep their contents; when the power is lost, the chips lose their contents. Storage uses different methods to store data permanently, so it isn't lost when the power is turned off.

- A PC has more storage capacity than memory. Even though some PCs have several gigabytes of RAM, their hard drives will be many times larger.

Storage Media and Storage Devices

Storage has two components: storage media and storage devices.

Storage Media In terms of storage, a medium is an object that physically holds data or program instructions. Flash drives, magnetic tapes, compact discs, DVDs, and Blu-ray Discs are examples of storage media. (The word *media* is the plural of *medium*.) One important use of storage media is for making a **backup** of computer data. When you back up data you copy the data to a different location for safekeeping. If the original data is lost or damaged you can **restore** the data from the backup files.

Figure 5.1.2 Nearly all PCs use the storage devices and media shown here.

Storage Devices A storage device is a piece of hardware that holds the storage medium, sends data to the medium, and retrieves data from the medium. Hard drives, flash drives, and CD and DVD drives are all examples of storage devices.

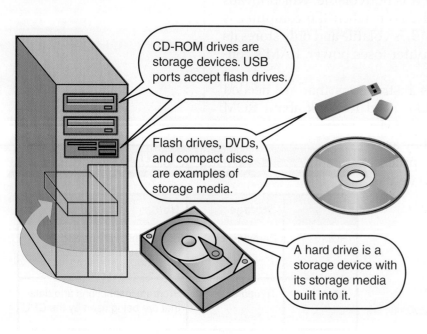

CD-ROM drives are storage devices. USB ports accept flash drives.

Flash drives, DVDs, and compact discs are examples of storage media.

A hard drive is a storage device with its storage media built into it.

Classifying Storage Devices

Objectives

- Explain how computer storage devices are classified.
- Compare and contrast primary, secondary, and archival storage devices.
- Describe the categories of storage devices.

As You Read

Classify Information   Use a spider map to help you classify storage devices as you read.

Hierarchy of Storage Devices

Computer storage devices are sometimes classified in a hierarchical structure—that is, primary or secondary.

Primary Storage Devices   The term **primary storage** is sometimes used to describe the main memory, or RAM, in a computer. This is because when the CPU needs data or instructions, it looks in memory before looking anywhere else.

Most knowledgeable computer users, however, avoid using the term *storage* when talking about RAM. This is because RAM works very differently from storage devices such as disks or flash drives. RAM also loses any data it contains when the computer is turned off, while disks and flash drives can hold data permanently.

Secondary Storage Devices   The term **secondary storage** is sometimes used to describe devices that can store data permanently, such as a hard drive, flash drive, compact disc, DVD, or external hard drive. This is because the computer will look for data on one of these devices if the data is not in RAM.

Many kinds of secondary storage devices can hold much more data than a computer's RAM can. For example, while most of today's PCs have from 4 to 16 gigabytes of RAM, they have hard drives that can store up to a terabyte.

Because they can store data permanently (or until you erase it), secondary storage devices are sometimes called **archival storage devices**. This refers to the fact that you can store data on a drive or disk and then put it away for a long time, only using it again when you need it.

Key Terms

- archival storage device
- optical storage device
- primary storage
- random access storage device
- read/write device
- read-only device
- secondary storage
- sequential storage device

Figure 5.2.1 Compact discs and digital video discs are popular storage media.

Technology @ Home

You probably use a variety of storage devices in your home. Some of these may be computerized, while others are not.

Think About It!

Some of the devices listed below are based on read-only technology, while others are based on read/write technology. Which storage devices in the list do you think are based on read-only technology?

➤ Smart phone

➤ CD-ROM drive

➤ CD burner

➤ DVD-ROM drive

Categories of Storage Devices

Storage devices (but not RAM) are divided into three categories. Each category has two options based on the device.

Read-Only Versus Read/Write A **read-only device** can only read data from the storage medium. You cannot change the data on the medium or save new data onto it. A CD-ROM drive is an example of a read-only device, because it does not have the capability to write data onto a disc.

The media used with read-only devices come with data already saved on them. Music CDs or software programs on CDs are CD-Rs. Your CD-ROM drive will be able to play the music or read the program instructions from the disc, but you can't change the disc's contents. Standard DVD players are another example of a read-only device.

A **read/write device** not only can read data from the storage medium, but can write data onto the medium, as well. These devices let you read data from a disk or tape, make changes to the data, and save new data onto the medium. Hard drives, USB flash drives, CD-Rewritable drives (CD-RW), and DVD-RAM drives are commonly used examples of read/write devices.

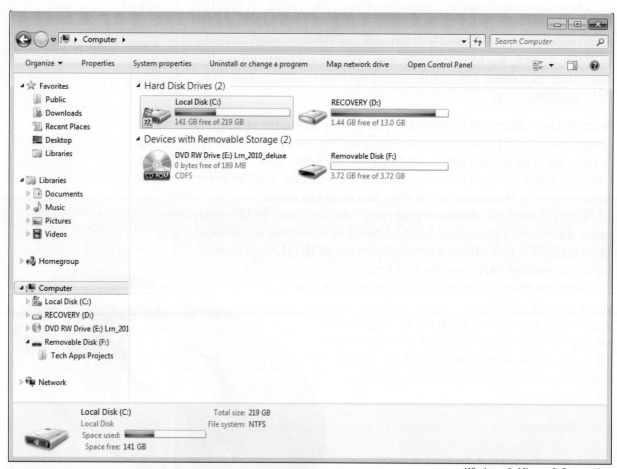

Windows 8, Microsoft Corporation.

Figure 5.2.2 Use an operating system such as Windows to view a list of storage devices connected to your computer.

Sequential Versus Random Access When equipped with a tape drive, business computers can store data on a long piece of tape, similar to an old-fashioned cassette tape. A tape drive is an example of a **sequential storage device**, which requires the computer to scan from the beginning of the medium to the end until it finds the data it needs. While cheaper and slower than other types of storage, the highest capacity tape cartridges can hold five terabytes of uncompressed data. Because it can take several minutes to locate a piece of data on a high-capacity tape, tapes are used chiefly by businesses that want to back up their computer systems—often after the business day is over.

A **random access storage device** lets a computer go directly to the needed information. The device does not have to search the entire medium to find data. For this reason, random access storage devices are much faster, and more expensive, than sequential devices. A hard drive is an example of a random access storage device.

Magnetic Versus Optical Storage Magnetic storage devices are specially treated disks or tapes, such as those mentioned above, that record information using magnetically sensitive materials. These devices use electricity to shift magnetic particles so they form a pattern that the computer reads and stores as information. Common magnetic storage devices include hard drives and tape drives

Other storage devices use laser beams to read information that has been stored on the reflective surface of a disc. These are called **optical storage devices**. Popular types of optical storage devices for computers include CD-ROM and DVD-ROM drives.

Technology @ School

Some schools have a dedicated computer "lab," but more and more schools have computers in every classroom or tablets for every student. Expensive equipment may be damaged if a student mishandles it, costing the school—or the student—money to replace it.

Think About It!

Rate the computer equipment that you think is most sensitive to mishandling and needs the most care. On a scale of 1 to 5, use 1 for most sensitive and 5 for least.

➤ CD-ROM/DVD

➤ Flash drive

➤ Hard drive

➤ Power cord

➤ Laser printer

➤ Tablet

 Spotlight on...

HIGH-CAPACITY PORTABLE STORAGE

Devices such as Apple's iPod Touch and Sony's Walkman MP3 player function as both MP3 players and as high-capacity, portable storage devices.

By plugging them into a computer, you can use these tiny storage devices to download files or transfer information from one computer to another. Some models can store 64 GB of data. (That's at least 14,000 songs or up to 80 hours of continuous video!) Yet,

they are the size of a deck of cards and weigh $\frac{1}{2}$ to 3 ounces, and they are getting smaller in size and larger in storage all the time.

Smart phones, such as Apple's iPhone or Motorola's Droid, offer storage capabilities along with phone service.

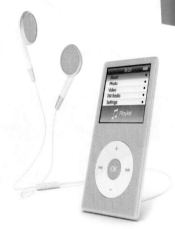

Common Storage Devices

Objectives

- Differentiate between internal and external storage devices.
- List commonly used magnetic storage devices.
- Summarize optical storage options.

As You Read

Classify Information   Use a T-chart to help you classify information about magnetic and optical storage devices as you read.

Key Terms

- CD-ROM drive
- hard drive

Internal and External Storage Devices

Storage devices can be installed in your computer or connected to it. A storage device installed inside your computer is called an internal storage device. One that is positioned outside your computer is referred to as an external storage device.

Magnetic Storage Devices

The most common magnetic storage device installed in computers is a **hard drive**. You cannot see the hard drive because it is installed inside your computer. Often, a small flashing light on the front of a computer shows when the hard drive is in use. Hard drives hold a great deal of data, but they are not portable.

External Magnetic Devices   Other forms of magnetic storage devices include a variety of USB- or firewire-connected external hard drives. These can hold up to as much as 8 terabytes of data, and they are portable. External drives communicate with the computer via a high-speed interface cable. By using the external hard drive with an automatic backup program, like the Mac's TimeMachine, computer users have peace of mind. They know their data is always recoverable if their computer crashes or is hit by a virus.

Figure 5.3.1 If you removed a PC's internal hard drive, it would look something like this.

Magneto-Optical (MO) Drives A popular method of data storage for many businesses, this type of drive combines both magnetic and optical drive technologies. A magneto-optical drive uses a removable disk that is inserted via a slot in the front of the drive. These drives can be internal or external. Their disks can store several gigabytes of information.

Online Storage Many online—or cloud—storage sites such as Google Drive, Dropbox, Microsoft OneDrive, and Apple iCloud, are available where you can store files on a network server at a remote location. You access your data by logging in through the Internet using a secure password. Some programs, including Microsoft Office, come with free online storage space. You can also pay a storage service provider (SSP) for space. Online storage offers these three benefits: 1) it is expandable; 2) it allows you to share files with others; and 3) data stored in a remote location is protected if your computer is stolen or damaged.

Capacities of Common Storage Devices

Device	Capacity
Internal hard drive	500 GB–1 TB and more
External hard drive (USB or Firewire connection)	500 GB–8 TB and more
MP3 player	16 GB–64 GB and more
Smart phones	128 GB flash storage
Magneto-Optical (MO) drives	100 MB–several GB
Flash memory cards and drives	4 GB–256 GB and more
CD-ROM	650 MB–700 MB
DVD	9.5 GB
Blu-ray disc	25 GB

Career Corner

Computer Security Specialist
Today, security specialists are in demand to work with various computer storage systems, such as tape warehouses and online storage companies.

Computer security specialists study ways of improving the overall security of their systems. For example, some goals include improving recording or access time or the safety of the protected information in case of a natural disaster.

Figure 5.3.2 A USB flash drive has a USB connector, a flash memory chip, a mass storage controller, and a crystal oscillator that allow the device to communicate with the computer.

Flash Memory Storage Devices

Flash media use a non-magnetic storage medium called flash memory. Flash memory is a special kind of storage used in ROM chips within your computer itself to store basic information about the computer's configuration. It is also used in memory cards and memory sticks for digital cameras that require removable, reusable storage and in USB flash drives (also called jump, pen, and key drives). Flash drives connect to the computer through a USB (universal serial bus) port.

Most removable flash memory devices include a chip that stores data and a microcontroller that permits the operating system to communicate with the chip. As the technology of flash memory improves, the capacity of flash devices increases significantly. Early flash devices only held 32–256 MB, but capacities of up to 512 GB are now available but very expensive. The small size, increasing capacity, and ease of connection of these removable devices make them widely used.

Optical Storage Devices

Optical storage devices store data by etching tiny pits onto a disc. A laser then scans the disc and changes the data into a form the computer can work with. CDs, DVDs, and Blu-ray Discs are the most common types of optical storage media. On a PC, a button on the front of the drive opens a tray on which you insert a CD. You push the button to close the tray so you can read the disc's contents. On Macs the **CD-ROM drive** is simply a slot into which you insert a disc, and you can eject it electronically by moving the disc icon into the "trash."

Standard CD-ROM and DVD drives can only read data stored on an optical disc. Only optical drives labeled CD-R, CD-RW, or DVD/CD-RW can be used to record data onto blank discs.

A standard CD can store 650 megabytes of data, or around 74 minutes of audio. Newer CDs can store 700 megabytes of data, or about 80 minutes of audio. Digital video discs can store about 4.7 gigabytes of data on each side. These discs are used for storing programs, games, data, and movies.

Figure 5.3.3 CDs and DVDs are popular components in both computers and home entertainment centers.

Use the Vocabulary

Directions: *Match each vocabulary term in the left column with the correct definition in the right column.*

_____ **1.** storage device
_____ **2.** memory
_____ **3.** primary storage
_____ **4.** secondary storage
_____ **5.** read/write device
_____ **6.** random-access storage device
_____ **7.** optical storage device
_____ **8.** hard drive
_____ **9.** read-only device
_____ **10.** CD-ROM drive

a. temporary workspace on a computer

b. sometimes used when referring to a computer's RAM

c. uses laser to read information

d. users access from and save information to this type of device

e. common secondary storage device

f. computer component that retains data even after power is shut off

g. storage device that lets computer go directly to the needed information

h. read-only optical device

i. can only read data from the storage medium

j. any type of storage device that holds data permanently; not RAM

Check Your Comprehension

Directions: *Complete each sentence with information from the chapter.*

1. Storage devices _____ information even when a computer is turned off.

2. Information saved as a(n) _____ is identified by a unique name.

3. The _____ is a set of programs that directs a computer to start up.

4. RAM stores its contents _____ and is cleared when the computer is shut down.

5. A computer's BIOS is usually stored in a special memory chip, called _____.

6. Apple's iPod is an example of _____ that stores data in the popular _____ format.

7. The most common secondary storage device is a(n) _____.

8. _____ storage allows users to access rarely used computer files.

9. A magnetic tape is an example of a(n) _____ storage device.

10. _____ lets you store data on a remote computer.

 **Think Critically**

Directions: *Answer the following questions.*

1. Which type of secondary storage device do you use most at school? Do you think this will change in the near future? If so, why?

2. What can you do with a CD-RW that you cannot do with a CD-R?

3. Why do you think computer hard drives locate information directly, rather than sequentially?

4. What are the ways in which computer users would use a CD-ROM drive at home? At work? At school?

5. Where do you think users of computer games sold on CDs and DVDs store their information? Why?

Extend Your Knowledge

Directions: *Choose and complete one of the following projects.*

A. Look at your computer at school and find out how much memory it currently has. Next, use online documentation or other resources, such as the manufacturer's Web site, to compare your computer memory to the maximum amount of memory your computer can hold. Identify advantages to having more random access memory and compare this to the cost. As a class, conclude whether or not your school computers have sufficient memory to meet students' needs.

B. Go online and do research on storage service providers. Take notes and keep track of your sources as you work. Be sure to evaluate the information and only use it if it is accurate, relevant, and valid. What services and features do they offer? How do they protect the data they store? How easy is it for customers to access their data once they have given it to the service? Can customers share the stored data with other people? What fees do these services charge? Do you think such services can be useful to individuals as well as to companies? Discuss your findings with a partner, or as a class.

Understanding How Data Storage Works

Why Is Computer Storage Important?

Once you understand the basics of computer storage, you can begin to understand why storage is so important. In fact, the true power of a computer is its ability to store data for future use. Without storage, a computer would be similar to a calculator; useful for a one-time task, but not much more than that.

In this chapter, you will examine how different types of storage devices work. You will learn more about the advantages and drawbacks of storage devices, and the steps you can take to protect your data.

Chapter Outline

 Lesson 6–1

Understanding Hard Drives and Flash Drives

 Lesson 6–2

Optical Storage Devices

 Lesson 6–3

Storage Trends

Understanding Hard Drives and Flash Drives

Objectives

- Identify the parts of a hard drive.
- Explain the role platters play in storing information.
- Compare and contrast the access time of different storage devices.

As You Read

Organize Information Use a concept web to help you organize key concepts related to hard-drive storage as you read.

🔑 Key Terms

- access time
- cylinder
- data loss
- flash memory
- platter
- property
- read/write head
- sector
- solid state disk (SSD)
- storage media
- track
- USB flash drive
- write
- write-protect switch

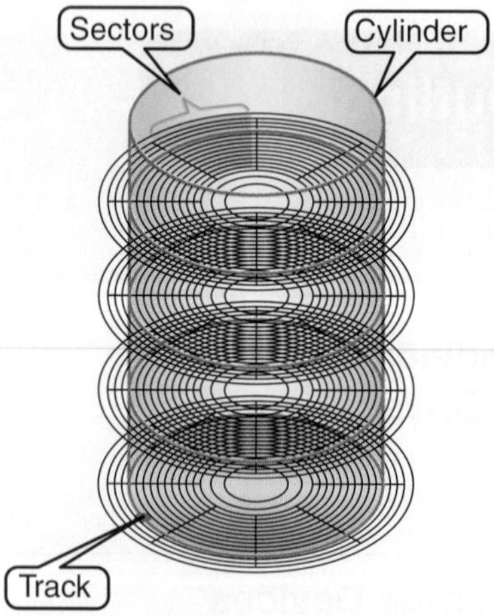

Figure 6.1.1 In a stack of platters, the same track creates a cylinder.

Parts of a Hard Drive

Recall that a hard drive is a storage device that is usually installed inside a computer, although some hard drives are external. Its main function is storing information. Several rigid disks, coated with a magnetically sensitive material, are enclosed with recording heads in a hard metal container that is sealed to protect it from dirt and other damaging items.

Platters Inside the sealed container is a stack of metal disks, known as **platters**, that store information. The platters rotate around a spindle inside the sealed container. These platters are so close together that only a thin layer of air separates them. The platters are **storage media**, coated with a special material that allows information to be saved on them.

Each platter is divided into **tracks**, or a set of circles on the surface of the platter, on which the data is recorded. A **cylinder** is the same track location on all the stacked platters. Each track is divided into segments, called **sectors**.

The process of storing information on storage media is called **writing**. Information can also be deleted from the platters. This is done when you no longer need a file or want to make room for another one.

Read/Write Heads A hard drive has a motor that spins the platters at a high speed. Usually, these platters spin continuously when your computer is on. A small, needle-like component, called the **read/write head**, travels back and forth across the surface of each platter, retrieving and storing data. Most hard drives have at least one head on the top and one on the bottom of each platter for storage on each side of the platter.

Storing Data on a Hard Drive

When a file is saved to the hard drive, the read/write head locates a spot on a platter. It then generates a magnetic field on the surface of the platter. The magnetic field records a string of 1s and 0s, or binary code, to generate the information a computer can read.

If the hard drive is damaged or if the read/write head changes the field in order to modify or delete the file, the magnetic field will not remain intact. A head crash, or the collision of a read/write head with the surface of the disk, could occur. If this were to happen, data could no longer be stored on the damaged sector of the drive.

Limitations of Hard Drives

The amount of information a hard drive can hold depends on several factors. One factor is the number of platters contained in the hard drive. The greater the number of platters, the more information a drive can store.

Another factor is the number of read/write heads. Generally, there is a read/write head for each side of each platter. However, sometimes one side of one platter will not have its own read/write head. That means information cannot be stored on that side.

Effects of Performance   The performance of your hard drive directly affects how fast your computer works. The faster the hard drive, the faster your computer will read and write data. Because the platters in a hard drive are rigid, they can spin at very high speeds. The platters in most hard drives can spin at a rate of 7,500 rpm (revolutions per minute), but some can spin at rates as high as 15,000 rpm.

Hard Drive Speed   A storage device's most important performance characteristic is the speed at which it locates the desired data. This is measured by its **access time**, the amount of time it takes for the device to begin reading the data. For hard drives, the access time includes the time it takes the read/write head to locate the data before reading begins.

The speed of storage devices varies considerably, but all storage devices are significantly slower than RAM. RAM speed is measured in nanoseconds, or billionths of a second. A storage device's speed is measured in milliseconds, or thousandths of a second.

Hard Drive Capacity   The first PC hard drives held only about 10 MB of data and program instructions. Recent personal computers feature hard drives with capacities of 500 GB and higher—you can even buy hard drives with capacities of 1 to 3 terabytes!

Alternative Storage Options

Manufacturers of computer chips are working to provide faster alternatives to magnetic storage.

Solid State Disks **Solid state disks** or drives, or **SSDs**, are a mass storage device similar to a hard disk drive. Even though SSDs serve the same purpose as hard drives, their internal parts are much different. SSDs do not have any moving parts, like the hard drive's magnetic platters; they store data using flash memory. SSDs have better read performance because the data does not get fragmented into many locations, and, since they are not magnetic, SSDs do not lose data when next to a strong magnetic field.

SSDs do have disadvantages, though. This newer technology costs about ten times more per gigabyte, so people tend to buy SSDs with smaller capacity than most hard drives. Their limited number of write cycles means their performance declines over time. Yet, with improvements in SSD technology, these devices will advance, and the prices may come down.

Flash Memory Devices Several types of storage devices using flash memory offer the speed of memory with the high capacity of a magnetic storage device. Flash memory drives work faster than magnetic drives, because they have no moving parts, and they do not require battery power to retain their data. Flash drives installed inside computers resemble magnetic hard drives in size and shape.

A **USB flash drive** is a portable, self-contained storage device that uses **flash memory**. In addition to portability, these drives offer the advantages of speed, capacity, and cost. A USB flash drive has a USB connector that plugs into the USB port on a computer; a flash memory chip that stores data; a USB mass storage controller that allows the computer to read, write, and erase data on the drive; and a crystal oscillator that controls the speed with which the drive works.

The electronic parts of the flash drive are protected by a hard plastic or metal case. The USB connector usually has a cover to protect it as well. Most USB flash drives have a light that comes on when the drive is plugged in. The drive may have a **write-protect switch**. When the switch is in the on position, the computer can read from the drive but cannot write to it or delete data from it.

Protecting Your Information

The information saved on computer storage media is important to the individuals, schools, businesses, and government agencies that wanted to keep it. Computers store information about virtually every aspect of life. We use them to store school grades, lists of business contacts, names of registered voters, bank account balances, and many other kinds of crucial data. Since this information can be so important, computer users should be aware of data loss and protection.

Data Loss When a storage device experiences **data loss**, the data is damaged or made unusable. Storage devices and computers can also be lost, stolen, or destroyed, resulting in data loss. The data may be gone forever. It may be time-consuming or impossible to reconstruct the information that had been stored.

Data Protection One way to reduce the impact of data loss is to back up your data. Storing information on removable storage media, which may be locked in high-security areas or stored at a different location, makes it difficult for people to steal the information, or to lose it due to a disaster such as fire, flood, or system failure. Many businesses use magnetic tape to back up large amounts of data, because it is relatively inexpensive and reliable. Some organizations hire storage service providers, or SSPs, to store data on offsite computers, and online storage is becoming increasingly popular.

Information can also be accidentally deleted, overwritten, or stolen by unauthorized users. One way to protect data is to apply password protection to a file or drive so only authorized users can access it, or to set a read-only property so the data may be read but cannot be changed. A **property** is a piece of data, sometimes called metadata, attached to or associated with a file, program, or device. Typical properties include name, type, storage location, and size. You can view and customize properties in the Properties dialog box.

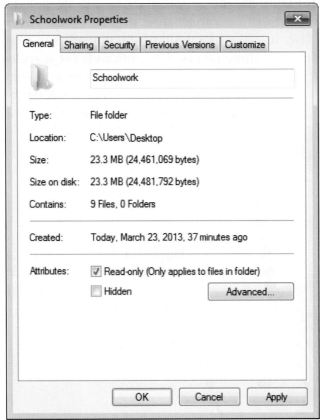

Windows 8, Microsoft Corporation.

Figure 6.1.2 To keep a file from being changed or overwritten, you can set its properties to Read-only.

Optical Storage Devices

Objectives

- Compare and contrast CD-ROM and DVD-ROM drives.
- Summarize how compact discs and digital video discs store data.

As You Read

Organize Information Use a spider map to help you organize information about optical storage devices and how they work as you read.

 Key Terms

- data transfer rate
- land
- laser sensor
- pit

CD-ROM and DVD-ROM Drives

The most recent advancements in storing data are in optical storage. These include CD-ROM (compact disc read-only memory), DVD-ROM (digital video disc read-only memory), laserdiscs, PhotoCDs, and similar storage devices. Optical storage media—the discs themselves—are easy to transport and can store large amounts of information. Many computers have built-in DVD or Blu-ray drives, or ports for connecting external drives. In part to distinguish optical media from magnetic media, some people prefer changing the spelling of disc (optical) to disk (magnetic).

Compact Disc Media Optical drives are storage devices into which you insert a compact disc, or CD. When you look at an optical disc, it looks like a shiny, circular mirror. Optical discs are made up of three layers. The bottom layer is a clear plastic. The middle layer is a thin sheet of aluminum. The top layer is a lacquer coating that protects the disc from scratches and dust.

Figure 6.2.1 You can use a computer's built-in DVD or Blu-ray drive to install programs, watch movies, back up files, or play audio.

Reading Optical Information

All storage devices read information at a speed measured by the unit's **data transfer rate**, or the number of bits of data the device can transfer to memory or to another device in a single second. In CD-ROM drives, the speed is measured in a multiple of 150,000 bits—the speed per second of the first CD-ROM drives. A 2X drive transfers data at double speed, or 300,000 bits per second. Some drives transfer data at 7.8 million bits per second, about as fast as slower hard drives.

Laser Sensors   A **laser sensor**, a laser-operated tool that reads information, is housed inside the optical drive. Optical drives read information by shining a laser on the disc in the drive. A laser sensor starts to read from the center of the disc's spirals and moves outward. The sensor notices changes in the physical properties of the disc and reads these changes as binary code: 0s and 1s.

Lands and Pits   The surface of an optical disc stores data as a series of lands and pits. A **land** is a flat, reflective area on the surface of a disc. Lands reflect light from a laser's sensor and are recorded as a 1 by a computer. A **pit** is an indented area on the surface of a disc that scatters the light from a laser's sensor. Since no light is reflected by a pit, it is recorded as a 0. The binary code represents the information encoded on the surface of the disc.

Technology @ Work

Because information storage is important to many businesses, a growing number of companies are using DVDs to store large amounts of information.

Think About It!

Which of the following businesses might need the storage capacity of DVDs to record their business transactions?

➤ graphic-arts firm

➤ dry cleaner

➤ grocery store

➤ insurance company

➤ auto repair shop

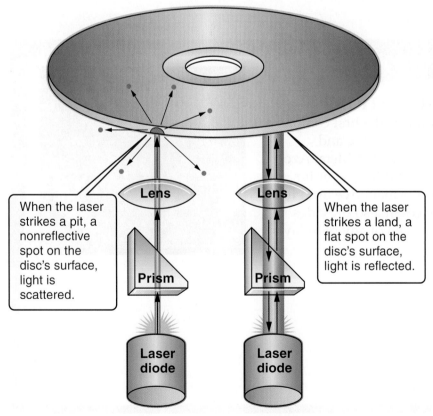

Figure 6.2.2 How an optical drive reads data on an optical disc.

Storing Optical Information

CD-ROM, laserdisc, and DVD-ROM drives are read-only devices. CD-R, CD-RW, and DVD-RAM drives read *and* write information.

CD-R Drives   These drives let you insert a blank recordable CD and then save data to it. After the information is stored, the disc's surface is changed so that the recorded information cannot be changed or erased.

CD-RW, DVD-RAM, DVD-R/RW, and PhotoCDs   Optical devices that let you record, change, or overwrite data multiple times are called read/write storage devices. CD-RW, DVD-RAM, and DVD-R/RW drives provide read/write capabilities using erasable discs. The information on that disc can be deleted after it is written, and additional information can be added. PhotoCDs can save photographs from the Internet and from digital cameras.

Spotlight on...

VERBATIM CORPORATION
Verbatim Corporation was the first company to offer DVDs in both write-once and read/write formats. A patented Metal Azo dye that serves as the recording layer for the discs has become the main dye used for write-once DVD devices. It also provides the fastest recording speed of any of today's DVD formats.

Storage Trends

Objectives

- List limitations of current storage technologies.
- Compare solid-state storage devices to magnetic and optical storage devices.

As You Read

Identify Key Concepts Use a spider web to help you identify key concepts about future storage devices as you read.

Limitations of Storage Devices

All technologies change over time. Existing technologies evolve to become more efficient and meet changing needs, and new technologies emerge to solve problems and meet new needs. Technological breakthroughs have helped correct these common storage-device problems:

- slow retrieval
- data decay
- friction

Slow Retrieval Tape devices are limited by slow retrieval speeds. Because devices must search from the beginning to the end of the tape to find the data, and magnetic tape cannot spin as fast as hard drives, it can take several minutes or even hours to locate information. Also, because tapes are usually stored in a remote location, you must first retrieve them.

Data Decay One limitation of current storage devices is the possibility of **data decay**, or the loss of information resulting from the gradual wearing down of a storage medium. Information stored on magnetic tapes and disks will, over time, become unusable. Air, heat, and humidity can break down the surface of magnetic storage media. As this breakdown occurs, the information stored may be lost.

People once thought optical storage devices did not decay. However, studies have shown that user-recorded discs can lose information in as few as five to ten years. Factory-recorded, or pressed, compact discs may decay in 10 to 25 years. In addition to being vulnerable to gradual decay, magnetic storage devices can lose data in an instant if exposed to a strong magnetic field.

Friction As a magnetic tape travels through the tape heads, friction is created. This causes heat, which can stretch and burn a tape. Companies are trying to develop read/write heads that decrease this friction and preserve magnetic media.

Key Terms

- cloud computing
- data decay
- data integrity
- enterprise storage system
- holographic data storage system (HDSS)
- storage area network (SAN)
- virtualization

Figure 6.3.1 Time and environmental conditions can take their toll on any storage medium.

Data Integrity

When information is stored, it must be maintained correctly. **Data integrity** means that stored information is usable and available in the location in which you expect to find it. Data integrity can be maintained using RAID, Redundant Array of Inexpensive Disks.

RAID is a term used to describe a collection of drives or disks that run together to store data. For example, a computer using RAID may have two or more hard drives installed. The hard drives work together as one to read data from and write to the drive at the same time. This backup process ensures that copies of files can be retrieved in case one drive fails.

Enterprise Storage

Computers linked together by a cable or wireless medium are called networked computers. In a network environment, computers can share data using an **enterprise storage system**. This technology allows networked computers to access storage devices linked to the network, such as servers, RAID systems, tapes, and optical disc systems.

New and Future Technologies

As computer use increases, the need also grows for faster, more reliable, and higher capacity storage.

Cloud Computing and Virtualization Both cloud computing and virtualization make computers more efficient by using centralized storage, memory, and processing. **Cloud computing** uses the Internet and central remote servers to host data and applications.

Figure 6.3.2 Solid-state devices store large amounts of data, despite being very small.

Virtualization is when physical storage is pooled from multiple network storage devices into what seems to be one single storage device managed from a central console. Storage virtualization is usually used in a **storage area network (SAN)**, a network of storage devices that can be accessed by multiple computers. Many businesses use virtualization to consolidate many different servers onto one piece of physical hardware that then provides a simulated set of hardware to two or more operating systems. While cloud computing and virtualization are two distinct storage options, many cloud computing providers use virtualization in their data centers.

New Magnetic Media   In the future, by manipulating molecules and atoms, magnetic hard drives will store as much as 1 terabyte (TB) per square inch of disk space. That's an increase of 100 times the 10 gigabytes per square inch of current hard drives.

New Optical Media   DMDs, or digital multilayer discs, contain multiple layers of a fluorescent material that stores information on each layer. A disc can hold 1 terabyte of data.

Holographic Media   A **holographic data storage system**, or **HDSS**, stores data in images called holograms on optical cubes the size of a sugar cube. These devices will hold more than 1 terabyte of storage and will be ten times faster than today's hard drives.

Technology @ Work

As more businesses use computers at work, the need for faster, more reliable, higher capacity storage devices is also on the rise.

Think About It!

Some businesses are storage-intensive while others require only basic components. The businesses listed below might benefit from a variety of storage technologies. Which would benefit more from new magnetic media? Which from DMD? Which from HDSS?

> graphic-design company

> school district

> online catalog

> hospital

> airline

 Spotlight on...

MARVIN THEIMER

After a major earthquake hit California in 1989, many file storage systems were not working, and even backup data had been destroyed. It was then that Marvin Theimer started thinking about creating a disaster-tolerant storage system.

As a result, Theimer has been developing Farsite, a system which will let people back up their data on a system of networked computers. The exciting news about Farsite is that it uses the additional hard drive space that machines aren't using. That way,

even if 99 out of 100 machines in the network are destroyed, people will still be able to retrieve their information from the machine that is still working.

Use the Vocabulary

Directions: *Match each vocabulary term in the left column with the correct definition in the right column.*

_____ 1. storage media
_____ 2. platter
_____ 3. write
_____ 4. read/write head
_____ 5. access time
_____ 6. USB flash drive
_____ 7. SSD
_____ 8. data transfer rate
_____ 9. laser sensor
_____ 10. pit

a. amount of time it takes storage device to begin reading data
b. one of the disks in a hard drive
c. removable, portable storage device inserted into a USB slot
d. save information on a storage medium
e. indentation on optical disc that does not reflect light
f. a mass storage device, similar to a hard disk drive that uses flash memory
g. needle-like device that retrieves and stores data on a magnetic disk
h. tool in optical drive that reads information
i. number of bits per second at which data is moved from a storage device to RAM
j. material that retains stored information saved by a computer storage device

Check Your Comprehension

Directions: *Determine the correct choice for each of the following.*

1. What type of media are used in a computer hard drive?
   a. magnetic
   b. optical
   c. solid state
   d. photo

2. What does the performance of a hard drive affect?
   a. if a read/write head can store data
   b. where a read/write head stores data
   c. how fast a computer reads and writes data
   d. the computer's memory

3. Which medium stores the least amount of information?
   a. DVD
   b. CD
   c. hard drive
   d. USB flash drive

4. Optical drives read information by using a _____.
   a. memory chip
   b. magnetic sensor
   c. laser sensor
   d. binary code

5. How many layers of material make up an optical disc?
   a. one
   b. two
   c. three
   d. four

6. Which of the following storage devices allow you to write data to a medium multiple times?
   a. CD-Rs
   b. read/write storage devices
   c. DVD-ROMs
   d. laserdiscs

Directions: *Answer the following questions.*

1. Why are disks (and discs) considered secondary—and not primary—storage devices?

2. Why is it important to be sure data is protected and secure? Give an example of how you can keep your data safe.

3. What can happen if a read/write head is disturbed?

4. How are magnetic storage devices organized?

5. If USB flash drives and CD-Rs cost about the same per megabyte of storage, which do you think is more advantageous? Why?

Extend Your Knowledge

Directions: *Choose and complete one of the following projects.*

A. Find out the age and the storage capacity of the hard drive on the computer you use at school. By using computer ads or visiting a local retailer, find out what improvements have been made to hard drives currently on sale. What conclusions can you draw about today's computers?

B. Research evolving and emerging storage technologies. Take notes and keep track of your sources. What kinds of storage devices do you think computers will have in five to ten years? What trends, if any, do you predict? Present an oral report on the topic to your class.

System Software Basics

What Is an Operating System? Have you ever wondered what happens when you turn on your computer? For many users, just seeing that the computer starts and that they can begin working is enough to meet their needs. But to become a more knowledgeable user, you should know how your computer works. One of the main behind-the-scenes contributors is the operating system.

The operating system is like the control center of your computer: it controls everything that happens with your computer. The operating system makes sure that files are stored properly on storage devices, software programs run properly, and instructions to peripherals are sent, among other jobs. Without an operating system, your computer would not be able to perform even basic tasks.

Chapter Outline

 Lesson 7–1

Introducing the Operating System

 Lesson 7–2

Operating Systems and Utilities

Introducing the Operating System

Objectives

- Explain what an operating system is and what it does.
- Identify types of operating systems.
- Describe a graphical user interface.

As You Read

Organize Information   Use a concept web to help you collect information about operating systems as you read.

Key Terms

- crash
- desktop
- graphical user interface (GUI)
- icon
- interface
- update
- upgrade

What Operating Systems Do

An operating system (OS) is a set of instructions designed to work with a specific type of computer, such as a Dell® PC or a Macintosh® computer. The OS controls all the computer's functions. It also provides an **interface**, the on-screen tools you use to interact with the computer and your programs. The operating system performs several tasks:

- manages the central processing unit (CPU) so that processing tasks are done properly
- manages computer memory
- manages files stored on the computer's disks
- manages input and output devices
- loads application programs into memory

Avoiding Conflicts   In most computers, especially personal computers, the operating system is stored on the hard drive. Before you can use the computer, a portion of the operating system must be loaded into memory. This is true of all programs; they may permanently reside on a disk but must be copied into RAM before you can use them.

Some operating systems enable a computer run more than one program at a time. To do this, the operating system has to assign each program some space in RAM, and then protect that space. Otherwise, conflicts can occur when two programs try to occupy the same space in RAM. When this happens, one or both of the programs may **crash**, or stop working, until the conflict is resolved.

Updates and Upgrades   When companies that develop operating system software make improvements, they release new versions. A minor **update** fixes problems such as bugs, security issues, and the ability to work with new hardware and is usually delivered for free automatically over the Internet. A major **upgrade** introduces new features. Users wishing to upgrade purchase the software.

Types of Operating Systems

All computers require an operating system. There are four kinds of operating systems.

Real-Time Systems   Real-time operating systems are used to control large equipment, such as heavy machinery and scientific instruments, and to regulate factory operations. In order for these systems to run, they require very little user interaction.

Single-User/Single-Task Systems   This kind of system lets one person do one task at a time. An example is the operating system that controls a handheld computer.

Single-User/Multitasking Systems   A multitasking system allows the computer to perform several jobs, either one after the other or at the same time. For example, you could use your computer to write a letter as it downloads a page from the Internet and prints another letter. Most desktop and laptop computers today use this kind of system. Windows and the Macintosh OS are examples of this type of operating system.

Multi-User Systems   These systems allow many individuals to use one large computer. The OS balances all the tasks that the various users ask the computer to do. UNIX® is an example of this type of operating system.

Real-World Tech

An Operating System—in Your Dog?   Robots are devices that can move and react to input from sight, hearing, touch, and balance. How are those "senses" and those reactions controlled? Through an operating system, of course! Robots are used to explore outer space and to do factory jobs. Now, however, they're also available as pets. Some robotic "dogs" can learn their own name and your name. They can show joy, anger, and surprise through lights, sounds, and gestures.

For what purposes do you think robots would be useful or fun?

Technology @ School

Fingerprint identification programs allow scanned fingerprints to be matched to electronic fingerprints stored in the computer.

Think About It!
For which activities below do you believe such a fingerprint identification system would be an advantage at school?

▷ paying for a school lunch

▷ checking out a library book

▷ taking attendance

▷ turning in homework

▷ accessing computer files

Operating Systems for Mobile Devices

Mobile devices such as smart phones and tablets are computers and therefore need an operating system to run properly. However, they cannot just use a PC's operating system, like Windows or Linux. Mobile operating systems have been designed to maximize the efficiency of a smaller touch screen, limited memory, and limited storage capacity. They are optimized to use wireless networks and to provide access to the specific apps most people expect from their mobile devices. Smart phones actually contain two operating systems: one that supports the user's software and one that operates the phone's hardware. Three common mobile device operating systems are Apple's iOS, Microsoft's Windows Phone, and Google's Android.

The User Interface

The operating system's user interface lets you start programs, manage disks and files, and shut down the computer safely. To start the OS, you turn the computer on. During the startup procedure, the OS places part of itself into the computer's memory.

Desktop   Nowadays, computer operating systems are based on visual displays. The **graphical user interface**, or **GUI** (*GOO-ee*), lets you use a pointing device to interact with the workspace on the computer screen, called a **desktop**.

Icons   On the screen, pictures called icons or tiles represent resources on the computer such as a program, a document, a hardware device, or a Web site. You click or double-click an icon or tile to perform an action, such as starting a program or opening a file.

Options   You can use the operating system to customize some features of the desktop, such as the look of the background or the placement of the icons. You can also change how other components work, such as keyboard functions and the speed at which the cursor blinks on the screen. Use the documentation that came with your system or the Help program to explore these options.

Figure 7.1.1 Options for personalizing the Windows 8 Start Screen.

Windows 8, Microsoft Corporation.

Operating Systems and Utilities

Objectives

- Examine different operating systems.
- Discuss the function of the file manager in an operating system.
- Describe how system utilities help operating systems function.

As You Read

Outline Information Use an outline to help you note details about operating systems and system utilities as you read.

Popular Operating Systems

The first widely-used operating system for personal computers was called MS-DOS. It was developed in the early 1980s by Microsoft for IBM-compatible PCs. Now, three operating systems dominate the computer world—Microsoft Windows®, the Macintosh OS, and UNIX. The computer you use at school or at home probably has a version of Windows or the Macintosh OS installed. UNIX, and adaptations of it, is most often found running on large business or scientific networks.

Mac OS X® In 1984, Apple® became the first computer maker to sell consumers a personal computer equipped with a graphical user interface (GUI). *Macintosh* names both the computer and its operating system. Easy for beginners to use, some version of the Mac OS runs all Macintosh computers.

Microsoft Windows Although Microsoft Windows was not the first OS to have a GUI, the Windows OS is currently the market leader, installed on more than 90 percent of personal computers. Early versions of Windows were based on MS-DOS. In fact, Windows 98 was the last version of Windows based on MS-DOS.

UNIX and Linux™ UNIX was one of the first operating systems ever written. It was designed to work on powerful business and scientific computers. Later versions of UNIX have been developed to work on personal computers.

One of these versions of UNIX is a system called Linux. Linux works with an optional GUI and is very fast compared to other operating systems. It is also unique in that it is an open-source operating system, in which the source code used to create it is available to the public. Programmers from across the globe constantly work on Linux to test and improve it. Linux is free and can be downloaded from the Internet, but most users buy it with other features. Though Apple and Microsoft dominate the market of OS for personal computers, Linux is now challenging them for a share of the web client OS market.

Key Terms

- backup utility
- driver utility
- file compression utility
- install
- Plug and Play (PnP)
- reinstall
- uninstall
- versioning

Figure 7.2.1 Use an operating system such as Windows to organize and manage files and folders.

System Utilities: File Management

Utility software is a collection of programs that help you maintain and repair your computer. Today, many types of utilities are built into the operating system. Probably the most important utilities are file managers, which let you work with data stored on your computer.

Organizing Files   The operating system, programs, and data are all stored in files, each with a name. Files can be grouped together into folders. Folders are also called directories. A folder can be divided into subfolders.

Using Files   You can use an operating system's file manager to perform several tasks:

- create new folders or subfolders
- move or copy items between folders or to other disks
- delete files and folders
- launch applications

Finding Files   You can use the file finder utility from your operating system to help you look for a file. This utility can search for a file by its name, type, date, or even by looking for specific data inside the file.

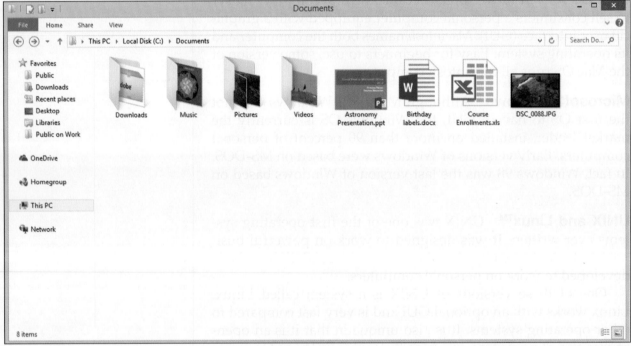

Windows 8, Microsoft Corporation.

System Utilities: Other Jobs

Your operating system probably has utilities that can help with routine maintenance and other jobs.

Driver Utilities A **driver utility** contains data needed by programs to operate input and output devices such as a mouse and printer. Operating systems that have **Plug and Play (PnP)** capability can automatically detect new PnP-compatible devices. Otherwise, you can download the files from the device manufacturer's Web site, or use the installation CD/DVD.

Program Utilities Before you can use a program, you must **install** it on your hard drive. In Windows, you can use the Add/Remove Programs utility to ensure that your program installs properly. You can use the same utility to **uninstall**, or remove, a program you no longer need, or to **reinstall** a program that is not working the way you want.

Backup Utilities **Backup utility** programs automatically copy data from the computer's hard drive to a backup storage device, such as an external hard drive or a CD. Businesses and individuals routinely use backup utilities to ensure data is not lost if a computer or disk drive fails. You, too, should regularly back up your computer data. By maintaining a regular back up schedule, and by keeping incremental versions of backed up files, you minimize the risk of losing data. Some operating systems, including Windows and Mac OS, have **versioning**, which automatically saves previous versions of files that you change. This is another way of avoiding data loss.

File Compression Utilities **File compression utilities** are programs that reduce the size of files without harming the data. These programs make it easier to copy and send files.

Global Settings Operating systems also manage global settings for features such as privacy and storage. For example, global settings may be used to control access from outside sources, such as whether an online game can store a score on your computer.

Figure 7.2.2 Microsoft Windows comes with utilities for backing up and restoring data and programs.

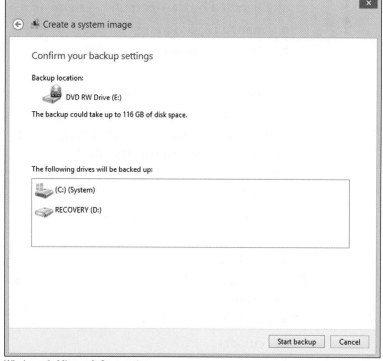

Windows 8, Microsoft Corporation.

Use the Vocabulary

Directions: *Match each vocabulary term in the left column with the correct definition in the right column.*

_____ 1. interface
_____ 2. crash
_____ 3. graphical user interface
_____ 4. desktop
_____ 5. icon
_____ 6. driver utility
_____ 7. Plug and Play
_____ 8. backup utility
_____ 9. file compression utility

a. area on a computer screen where you perform work

b. to stop working

c. program that controls input/output devices

d. picture that represents something on a computer

e. on-screen tools that let you use the computer

f. program that copies a file onto another medium

g. lets you use a mouse to work with the computer

h. capable of detecting compatible devices

i. reduces file size without harming data

Check Your Comprehension

Directions: *Determine the correct choice for each of the following.*

1. Which of the following is NOT usually handled by the operating system?
   a. managing programs
   b. dealing with input/output devices
   c. publishing Web pages
   d. interacting with the user

2. Which kind of computer operating system usually requires the least amount of user interaction?
   a. real-time systems
   b. single-user/single-task systems
   c. single-user/multitask systems
   d. multi-user systems

3. Which of the following is a key part of a graphical user interface?
   a. command words
   b. cursors
   c. memory
   d. icons

4. Which operating system is found most often on large business and scientific computers?
   a. Microsoft Windows
   b. Mac OS
   c. UNIX
   d. Linux

5. Which of the following do operating systems, application programs, and user data have in common?
   a. They are all system utilities.
   b. They are all Windows-based.
   c. They are all created by the user.
   d. They are all stored in files.

6. What kind of utility is used to reduce the size of a file?
   a. driver utility
   b. program utility
   c. backup utility
   d. file compression utility

Think Critically

Directions: *Answer the following questions.*

1. What are the major functions of an operating system?

2. What effect do you think the development of graphical user interfaces had on the number of people using computers? Why?

3. Pick one operating system component such as disk operations, GUI, or hardware drivers and explain its purpose.

4. Why might you install an operating system update?

5. Why is it a good idea to back up your important files?

Extend Your Knowledge

Directions: *Choose and complete one of the following projects.*

A. Go to Help in a Microsoft Windows operating system. Find out how it is organized, but make no changes to the system settings. Follow the same process on a Macintosh computer. Which Help section was easier to use? Provide reasons for your preference. Discuss your conclusions as a class.

B. Find ads in computer magazines or on the Web that are sponsored by companies that sell backup and file compression utilities. Make a chart to summarize the features of three products in each category. Note which operating system each product works with and its price. Create a word-processing document in which you summarize your findings. Name and save the document using proper file management techniques. With your teacher's permission, print the document. Read it out loud with a partner or to the class.

C. With your teacher's permission, use the Internet to research two or three operating systems for mobile devices. As you work, take notes and keep track of your sources. Evaluate the information you find and only use it if it is accurate, relevant, and valid. Create a column chart comparing and contrasting the operating systems. Share the chart with a partner or with the class.

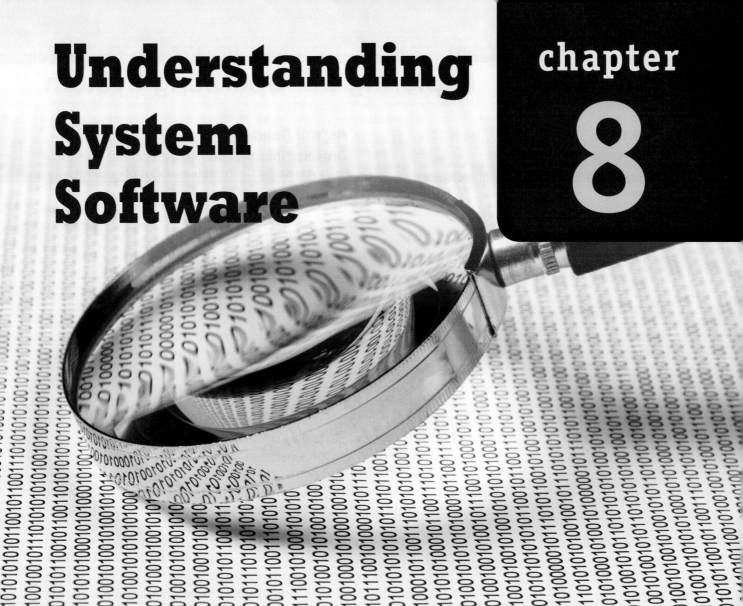

Understanding System Software

What Is the Purpose of an Operating System?

When you use a computer program, most of the activity you see on the screen is conducted by the operating system. An application, such as a word processor, asks the operating system to perform actions, such as opening a file, printing a document, or showing a list of recently used documents.

To fulfill these requests, the operating system needs to know how to handle different **file formats**, or standards used to save data on a disk. Those formats determine how text documents, graphics, audio, and video files are stored and used. In this chapter, you will learn more about what the functions that the operating system and its utilities perform, and how you use them.

Chapter Outline

Exploring the Operating System

Objectives

- Summarize the boot process.
- Describe the features of a graphical user interface.
- Explain how operating systems can be configured and changed.

As You Read

Organize Information   Use a concept web to help you collect information about operating systems as you read.

🔑 Key Terms

- boot
- CMOS
- hibernate mode
- pop-up menu
- power-on self test (POST)
- pull-down menu
- Ribbon
- screen saver
- sleep mode
- system administrator
- user account
- user rights
- window

Loading the Operating System

The operating system, or OS, controls the computer and manages its work. The OS also provides an interface which enables you to interact with the computer.

The Boot Process   When you turn the computer on, you **boot** it. That is, you start the computer, and it responds by loading the operating system. If your computer is set to show it, the first thing you see is the BIOS screen. As you learned earlier, *BIOS* stands for basic input/output system, and it manages and configures the computer's hardware. This means that the computer will be able to accept input from the keyboard and display information.

The Power-On Self Test   As a computer boots, it performs a series of tests called the **power-on self test**, or **POST**. During POST, the BIOS or UEFI checks the major components of the system, such as its memory, keyboard, and hard drive. It does this in part by reading information stored on the **CMOS** chip. CMOS, which stands for Complementary Metal-Oxide Semiconductor, is a battery-powered memory chip on the motherboard that stores information about the computer components.

If there is a problem during start up, a written message or a sound alerts you. If this happens, the computer may need repair. If no problem is detected, parts of the operating system are loaded from storage into memory and take control of the computer.

The Login   As the operating system starts, you may see a screen that asks you for a username and password. This is called the login screen. Businesses and schools often use this process to control who has access to the computer.

Exploring the GUI

When the operating system is loaded into RAM, it displays the desktop provided by the graphical user interface, or GUI. The desktop is where all work is done, including opening and closing programs, modifying system settings, and managing files. Icons on the desktop allow you to launch programs by clicking or double-clicking them. You also can click Start (on a PC) or Finder (on a Macintosh®) and then the name of the program you want. A taskbar on the desktop identifies which programs or files are open. To switch back and forth among applications, just click what you want to work on next.

Using Windows   The operating system in today's PCs and Macintosh computers displays documents in **windows**, or rectangular, on-screen frames that can be opened, closed, resized, and rearranged to view programs or documents. Each window provides commands and options. Some programs have **pull-down menus** that list commands when you select an item from the menu. Sometimes menus have submenus with additional commands. In Microsoft Office, the window provides commands on the **Ribbon**, a series of tabs at the top of the window. Each tab has a group of related commands for specific tasks. A command may display a dialog box that lets you set several options at the same time.

Pop-up menus, or lists of shortcut commands that appear when an area of the screen is clicked or right-clicked or the mouse button is held down, can appear anywhere in a window. Pop-up menus can be context-sensitive, providing options that relate to tasks you are doing at that moment.

Figure 8.1.1 Many programs have dialog boxes you use to select options, such as number formats in a spreadsheet.

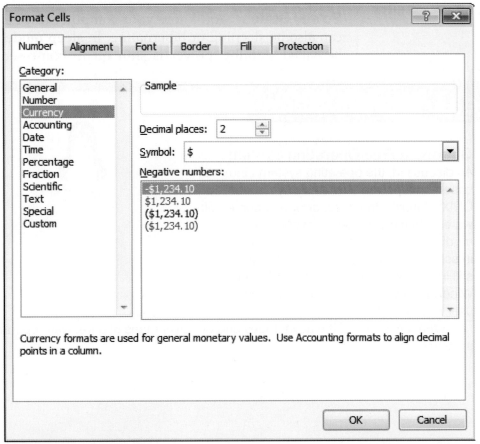

Excel 2013, Microsoft Corporation

The Arts CRT monitors can be damaged if the same image stays on the monitor for an extended period of time. A screen saver is a utility designed to protect the monitor by continuously changing the image it displays. Most screen savers use an animated effect, such as flying graphics or product logos, or imaginative shapes that build themselves piece by piece on the screen. On LCD monitors, screen savers are used for fun instead of for protection.

Screen savers are created by talented artists, using sophisticated digital drawing and animation tools. These artists need to know more than just how to draw; they need to know how to create effective, small-scale animations that will work under a specific operating system.

Exploring Configuration Options

Computer systems come in many different configurations. In order for an operating system to work correctly on every computer it must be flexible. The two most common tools an operating system uses to adapt to different requirements are drivers and system preferences.

- Drivers let the OS work with different devices and peripherals. Some basic drivers for common devices such as a keyboard and a mouse are built into the operating system. Other drivers you install when you connect a device.

- System preferences let the user select options for controlling and customizing options, such as the appearance of the user interface or how the computer will shut down. In Windows, you use the Control Panel to access the customization options. On a Mac, you use the System Preferences command.

Power Options You can usually set options to control the way a computer uses power. This is particularly important when you use a system such as a tablet or notebook that relies on a battery. Using more power might increase performance, but it also drains the battery faster and costs more on your energy bill. Some operating systems, such as Windows, have built-in power plans designed for maximum performance, maximum energy conservation, or a balance.

Power States You know your computer can be on or off. It can also be sleeping or hibernating. In **sleep mode**, which may be called standby, power is shut off to non-essential compo-

Real-World Tech

Offering a Free Operating System

As discussed, the operating system Linux® is based on a powerful scientific system called UNIX®. Linux is freeware, or open-source software, which means programmers can freely modify its code. To help expand computer use in schools in Mexico, Miguel de Icaza, while still in his 20s, developed GNOME, one of the Windows-based, easy-to-use desktop graphical user interfaces for Linux.

What are some of the advantages and disadvantages of a freeware operating system?

nents. Some power is used and data remains in RAM. In **hibernate mode**, data from RAM is saved to the hard disk and then power is shut down.

Most operating systems let you select options for entering sleep mode or powering down the display after a set period of inactivity. On a tablet or notebook, you might also be able to change the function of the Power button. Options include doing nothing, powering down, sleeping, or hibernating. Some operating systems automatically lock the system after a set period of inactivity. You must enter a password or PIN number to unlock the system to regain access.

Changing system settings lets you customize your computer, but it also cause your computer to malfunction. Most operating systems have a feature that lets you restore settings to a previous configuration.

Desktop Changes   Your operating system lets you change the desktop display. Among your choices are these:

- change the background appearance of the desktop, sometimes called the wallpaper
- change the **screen saver**, a utility program that changes the screen display after a preset period of nonuse
- add or eliminate desktop icons for various programs
- display or hide the taskbar
- change the language used to display menus, Help, and other system communication
- enable accessibility options such as a narrator to read screen text out loud and a magnifier to increase the size of content on the screen

Real-World Tech

See It on the Big Screen   One fascinating task that computers do is create some of those dramatic special effects you see in movies. The Linux operating system, authored by Linus Torvalds (pictured at right), has been especially influential in this area in recent years. Linux was used in the filming of *Titanic* to make a model of the ship look real; in *The Fellowship of the Ring* to make human actors look small and a computer-generated troll look huge; and in *Shrek* to combine models and animation with startlingly lifelike effects.

What movie have you seen recently in which the special effects caught your attention?

Managing User Accounts

Since computers are used for many different tasks, from playing games to writing reports and calculating numbers, businesses may want to restrict the use of some programs and files to designated users. This may also be true in schools, homes, and other settings where several people can use the same computer.

Usernames and Passwords One way to protect data is to set up **user accounts** that identify who can access a computer. Each user is assigned a username and a password that he or she must provide in order to gain access. User accounts are set up using a system tool provided by the operating system. The **system administrator** is the person responsible for maintaining the computer system and for setting up user accounts. He or she has permission to customize and configure all aspects of the system for all users.

User Rights User accounts may also have specific **user rights** assigned to them to limit or allow access, including:

- file access rights that specify which files a user can access and whether he or she can only read files or has access to read and write (edit) them
- installation rights that specify whether a user can install or remove programs
- hardware rights that specify whether a user can add or remove hardware
- configuration rights that specify whether a user can change operating system settings
- group policy rights that specify configuration and policy settings for a group of users on computers and mobile devices

Logging On and Off To access your account, you log on to the system. When you are finished, you should always log off so no one else can access your data and account information. Most operating systems also let you switch users without logging off. This closes your account and switches to the account for the other user.

Exploring System Utilities

Objectives

- Analyze file names and file formats.
- Explain cross-platform compatibility issues.
- Identify and discuss system maintenance utilities.

As You Read

Draw Conclusions Use a chart to help you draw conclusions about system utilities as you read.

Managing Files and Folders

Among the most important system utilities is the file manager, called Explorer in Windows and Finder in Mac OS. This utility allows you to organize, view, copy, move, rename, and delete files. You can even use it to create certain types of files.

Directories and Folders Most operating systems manage file storage using a multilevel, or **hierarchical**, filing system called a **directory**. The directory looks like the roots of a tree. At the top is the main storage location, called the **root directory**. Within the root are **subdirectories** called folders, which may contain other folders, called subfolders, and files. You navigate through the hierarchy by expanding and collapsing the folders to show or hide their contents. Most operating systems come with some folders already set up. For example, Windows comes with Documents, Pictures, Control Panel, and so on. You can create new folders and subfolders as needed.

Naming Files and Folders When you create a new file or folder, you give it a **file name**. Using descriptive names helps you identify the contents and keep your data organized. For example, the name *2013 Annual Report* is more descriptive than *Report*. It also helps keep you from accidentally deleting or overwriting files and folders that have the same name. Most operating systems have specific file and folder naming conventions. They usually let you use file and folder names with up to 255 characters, including spaces and punctuation. You cannot use <. >/ :. ", /, \, |, ?, or *.

Key Terms

- corrupted
- cross-platform compatibility
- directory
- disk scanner
- file extension
- file format
- file fragmentation
- file name
- hierarchical
- malware
- quarantine
- root directory
- subdirectories
- virus

Common File Type Extensions	
Extension	**File Type**
.doc/.docx	Microsoft Word Document
.txt	Text Document
.xls/.xlsx	Microsoft Excel Document
.ppt/.pptx	Microsoft PowerPoint Presentation
.wav	Waveform Audio File
.mp3	MP3 Audio File
.jpg	JPEG Image File
.mov	Quicktime Video File
.zip	Compressed File
.html	HTML File
.csv	Comma Separated Values Document

File Type Some operating systems, such as Windows, automatically add a period and a file extension to file names. A **file extension** is a short series of letters that indicate the application used to create the file and the **file format**. The file extension determines the file type. For example, a Microsoft Word document has the extension .doc or .docx. You can set options to display file types when you view a file list. By default, the operating system uses the program associated with the file type to open the file. So, a file with an .xlsx extension opens in Microsoft Excel and a file with a .wmv extension opens in Windows Media Player.

Figure 8.2.1 You can display file types when viewing files with Windows.

Name	Type	Size
Current Science Projects	File folder	
Article.docx	Word 2007 Document	18 KB
Astronomy Presentation.pptx	Microsoft Office PowerPoint 2007 Presentation	3,793 KB
Book Report Presentation.ppt	Microsoft PowerPoint 97-2003 Presentation	6,857 KB
Drawing.gif	GIF image	222 KB
Invitation Back.pub	Microsoft Publisher Document	113 KB
Invitation Front.pub	Microsoft Publisher Document	148 KB
Lion.jpg	JPEG image	200 KB
Mayans.docx	Word 2007 Document	27 KB
Scanned Image.tif	TIF File	1,970 KB
Schoolwork Compressed.zip	Compressed (zipped) Folder	10,571 KB

Spotlight on...

STEVE JOBS

At age 21, Steven Jobs and his friend Stephen Wozniak founded Apple Computer Company in the Jobs' family garage. A year later, Apple released the first mass-market personal computer. In 1984, Apple released the Macintosh computer, the first personal computer to use a GUI. Jobs, who passed away in 2011, was considered a visionary for anticipating the demand for devices such as the iPod music player, iPhone smart phone, and iPad tablet computer.

Using Files on Different Operating Systems

The two most widely used operating systems are Microsoft Windows on PCs and Mac OS on Apple Macintosh computers. Many times, a file created on one OS can work on another. This is because the OS associates files with specific programs.

Cross-Platform Compatibility   Sharing files across operating systems is called **cross-platform compatibility**. There are two keys to compatibility. First, both operating systems must have the same program installed in a compatible version that has been written for each operating system. Second, the application must allow its file formats to be shared across different operating systems. There are some programs that allow you to run a second operating system on a computer. For example, Apple's Boot Camp allows Windows and Windows programs to run on a computer with Mac OS.

Using System Maintenance Utilities

Like any machine, a computer needs routine maintenance. System maintenance utilities do these jobs and more.

Disk Management   Computer files can be **corrupted**, or damaged to the point at which data is unrecoverable, in different ways. One way is by being stored on a damaged part of the hard drive. Running a utility called a **disk scanner**, which checks magnetic disks for errors, can fix this problem. A disk scanner looks for and tries to correct irregularities on a disk's surface. You can use a disk cleaner utility to identify files such as cookies, offline Web pages, and temporary files that you can delete to make more disk space available.

Disk Defragmenter   As you add, move, and delete files on your computer, parts of files end up saved in different areas of the hard drive. **File fragmentation** occurs when a file is broken into pieces that are saved in different places on a hard drive.

File fragmentation reduces disk efficiency because the read/write head must travel longer distances to retrieve parts of a file that are scattered across a disk than if the files were stored close together. A disk defragmentation program can gather all the file pieces and place them together, thus improving the efficiency of the disk or hard drive.

Virus Detection   Viruses and malware can enter your system through infected e-mail messages, programs, and files. **Malware** is any type of software designed to damage or disable your computer system or data. A **virus** is a type of malware that can replicate, or copy, itself. Antivirus and antimalware utilities constantly monitor your system for viruses and malware programs that can slow down processing or damage your data and devices. Once there, they can destroy or corrupt data.

Antivirus programs check your computer's memory and disks looking for virus code. Most programs can also check e-mail and files as they are downloaded to your computer from the Internet. If the program discovers a virus, it alerts you and then attempts to **quarantine**, or disable, and remove the virus.

Because new viruses and malware are introduced every day, it is important to install antivirus and antimalware program updates automatically whenever they become available. Most programs can be set to automatically check your system on a schedule, automatically install updates, and automatically remove or quarantine an infected file.

Figure 8.2.2
Virus protection programs look for different types of viruses and malware that have infected your computer system.

Use the Vocabulary

Directions: *Match each vocabulary term in the left column with the correct definition in the right column.*

_____ **1.** boot
_____ **2.** POST
_____ **3.** window
_____ **4.** pull-down menu
_____ **5.** pop-up menu
_____ **6.** screen saver
_____ **7.** file extension
_____ **8.** cross-platform compatibility
_____ **9.** disk scanner
_____ **10.** file fragmentation

a. to start the computer and load the operating system
b. option that appears when an item is selected from the menu bar
c. utility that looks for errors in magnetic media
d. changes the display on the desktop
e. two to four letters that identify a file's format
f. series of tests run during the boot process
g. ability to share files across operating systems
h. shortcut command that appears anywhere in a window
i. frame that displays a document or file
j. having parts of files stored on different areas of a disk or hard drive

Check Your Comprehension

Directions: *Determine the correct choice for each of the following.*

1. Which of the following indicates that the computer can accept input from the keyboard and display information on the monitor?
 a. POST
 b. BIOS screen
 c. GUI
 d. cross-platform application

2. At what point in the boot process can users be asked their username and password?
 a. at the control panel
 b. in a screen saver
 c. in a file manager
 d. at login

3. If a pop-up menu is context-sensitive, what is it related to?
 a. file format
 b. printer settings
 c. what you are doing
 d. operating system

4. Which of the following is NOT a system change most users should attempt?
 a. moving the operating system
 b. adding a scanner
 c. changing mouse settings
 d. removing a program

5. Along with the data itself, which of the following is saved with a file?
 a. login procedure
 b. code for the application that created it
 c. icon that describes it
 d. maintenance utility

6. Which of the following is one way that a file can be corrupted?
 a. by deleting it
 b. by appearing on the desktop
 c. by moving it to a new folder
 d. by storing it on a damaged disk

Directions: *Answer the following questions.*

1. List at least one program that you run on a personal computer but wouldn't run on a mobile device?

2. What is a file type and why is it important? Give at least three examples of file types, including the associated file extension and program.

3. Why do most operating systems let users make system changes?

4. Suppose some of the reporters and photographers for your local newspaper work from home and are networked. What is an example of one application that would allow them to work without concern for the operating system they use?

5. What are system management tools and how are they used? Give an example.

Extend Your Knowledge

Directions: *Choose and complete one of the following projects.*

A. With a partner, interview three adult computer users: one who uses Microsoft Windows, one who uses a Macintosh, and one who has experience with both operating systems. Prepare written questions related to ease of learning the operating system, ease of use, availability of programs, and overall satisfaction with the operating system, and take notes to record the answers. Add your findings to your own experiences and write a conclusion about the user preferences of the two major operating systems. Share your conclusion with a partner or with your class.

B. Explore the desktop on your computer. Identify the icons on the desktop and explain what each launches. Use the taskbar to identify files or programs that are open and the file formats they are in. How does the desktop help you manage your work on the computer? Using a text editor, word-processing application, or on paper, write a paragraph explaining the concept of a computer desktop. Then, write step-by-step instructions that someone could use to arrange items on the desktop. With your teacher's permission, print or publish the document and exchange it with a classmate. Read your classmate's work. As a class, discuss why step-by-step instructions are useful.

DIRECTIONS: *You will use your operating system to navigate to a storage location where you will create a folder. You will then create, copy, move, rename, and delete files and subfolders. You will also display file properties and change the folder view.*

1. Start your computer, and log in to your user account, if necessary.
2. Use your operating system to navigate to the location where your teacher instructs you to store the files for this activity. For example, plug a flash drive in to a USB port, and display the contents of that drive in a program window.
3. In the storage location, create a new folder named **OS-1_folder1_*xx***. Replace *xx* with your own initials or name, as directed by your teacher.
4. In the same storage location, create a new text document named **OS-1_text1_*xx***.
5. Copy **OS-1_text1_*xx*** in to **OS-1_folder1_*xx***.
6. In **OS-1_folder1_*xx***, rename **OS-1_text1_*xx*** to **OS-1_text2_*xx***.
7. Navigate back to the original storage location.
8. Rename **OS-1_folder1_*xx*** to **OS-1_folder2_*xx***.
9. Move **OS-1_text1_*xx*** in to **OS-1_folder2_*xx***.
10. Open **OS-1_folder2_*xx*** and, if not already selected, change the folder view to Large Icons.
11. Maximize the folder window, and then, on your keyboard, press the key combination to capture an image of the folder window on the screen. For example, press ALT + PRTSC .

12. Start a graphics or paint program, such as Paint, and paste the screen capture image in the program window. It should look similar to Illustration A.
13. Save the file in the default graphics file format as **OS-1_image1_*xx*** in **OS-1_folder2_*xx***.
14. With your teacher's permission, print the file, and then exit the program.
15. In **OS-1_folder2_*xx*** , change the folder view to Content.
16. Change the folder view to Details.
17. Display the properties for **OS-1_image1_*xx***, and then close the Properties dialog box.
18. Delete **OS-1_text2_*xx***.
19. In **OS-1_folder2_*xx***, create a new folder named **OS-1_folder3_*xx***.
20. Copy **OS-1_text1_*xx*** into **OS-1_folder3_*xx***.
21. With your teacher's permission, make a backup copy of **OS-1_folder3_*xx*** and then delete the folder.
22. Navigate to the original storage location, and close it.
23. If necessary, safely remove or eject the storage device.
24. With your teacher's permission, log off and/or shut down the computer.

Illustration A

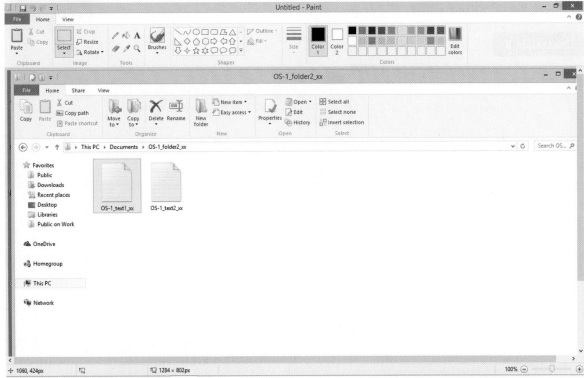

Windows 8, Paint, Microsoft Corporation

DIRECTIONS: *You will explore the features of your operating system. You will identify storage devices, network components, and installed printers, and you will locate information about the amount of installed RAM and processor speed for your system. To complete this activity, work in teams or small groups.*

1. Start your computer, and log in to your user account, if necessary.
2. Create a new text document named **OS-2_wp1_xx** in the location where your teacher tells you to store the files for this activity.
3. Start a text editor or word-processing program, and open **OS-2_wp1_xx**.
4. Maximize the program window, if it is not already maximized.
5. Type your name and today's date in the file, and save the changes.
6. Minimize the program window.
7. Use your operating system to display available storage devices.
8. Count the number of available storage devices.
9. Make the text editor or word-processing program window active.
10. Arrange the two open windows side by side. Your desktop should look similar to Illustration B.
11. Cascade the two open windows.
12. Maximize the text editor or word-processing program window.
13. In the text document, press Enter to start a new line, type **Storage Devices:**, and then type the total number of available devices you counted in step 8. Save the changes.
14. Restore down the program window.
15. Make the PC window active.

16. Display the contents of a storage device. For example, double-click Local Disk (C:) or a removable device.
17. Display the components of your current network.
    ☐ *In the Windows Navigation pane, click Network.*
18. Close all File Explorer windows, leaving the word-processing program open.
19. Display a list of available printers.
20. Count the number of available printers.
21. Make the text document active, press Enter, type **Printers:**, and then type the total number of available printers you counted in step 20. Save the changes.
22. Display system information, including the amount of installed RAM and processor speed.
23. Switch to the text document, press Enter, type **RAM:**, and type the amount of installed RAM.
24. Press Enter, type **Processor speed:**, and type the processor speed. Save the changes.
25. Close all Control Panel windows.
26. With your teacher's permission, print **OS-2_wp1_xx**, then close it and exit the program.
27. Close all open windows. With your teacher's permission, log off and/or shut down the computer.

 Illustration B

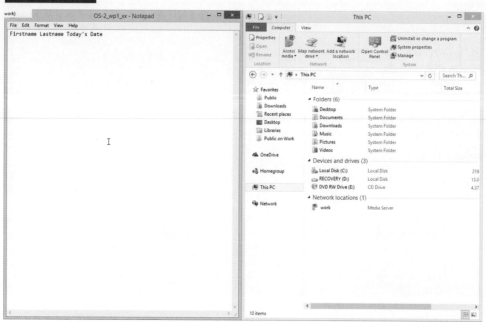

Windows 8, Microsoft Corporation.

DIRECTIONS: *You will personalize your operating environment by customizing desktop icons and by changing the theme, desktop background, and window colors. You will capture an image of the desktop and paste it into a graphics file. Finally, you will reset all options to the previous configuration.*

1. Start your computer, and log in to your user account, if necessary.
2. If necessary, display the Desktop, and change the desktop display to show large icons.
3. Sort the icons on the desktop by name.
4. Sort the icons on the desktop by item type.
5. Personalize the desktop using a built-in theme. For example, if you are using Windows 8, apply the Flowers theme.
6. Personalize the desktop by applying a different picture to the background.
7. Personalize the desktop by changing the color of window borders.
8. Display options for adjusting the date and time display.
9. Synchronize the clock with Internet time.
10. Select to display an additional clock, showing the time in Beijing, China. Name the clock **Beijing**.
11. Make sure the Beijing clock is displayed. (In Windows 8, rest the mouse pointer over the clock/calendar in the taskbar to display a ScreenTip.) Then, capture an image of the desktop.

12. Start a paint or graphics program, such as Paint, and paste the captured image into the new blank file. Scroll the window so you can see the clock. It should look similar to Illustration C, depending on the options you select in step 7.
13. Save the file as **OS-3_image1_*xx*** in the location where your teacher tells you to store the files for this activity.
14. With your teacher's permission, print the file, and then close it and exit the program.
15. On the desktop, create a shortcut to the **OS-3_image1_*xx*** file, and then use the shortcut to open the file.
16. Resize the program window so it is about 4" high by 4" wide.
    □ *If the window is maximized, you must restore it before you can resize it.*
17. Close the file, and exit the program.
18. Mute the speaker volume.
19. Restore the desktop settings, clock, and speaker volume to the way they were at the beginning of this activity.
20. With your teacher's permission, log off and/or shut down the computer.

Illustration C

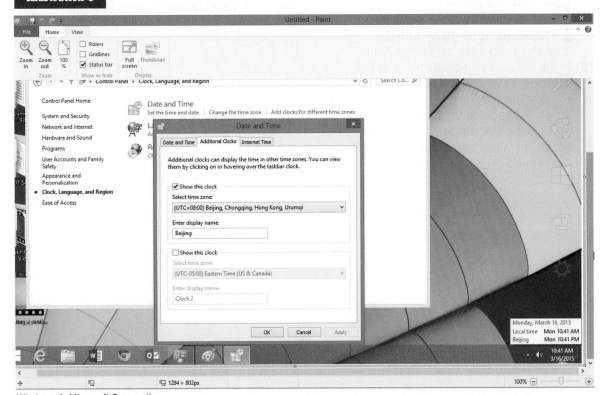

Windows 8, Microsoft Corporation.

Operating System Activities

DIRECTIONS: *You will use your operating system to set up an electronic portfolio. You will read about how to create a useful and effective portfolio, and then you will create a folder with subfolders where you can store items you select to include. You will convert printed items into digital files, and you will copy or move digital files into the portfolio.*

1. Open the .pdf file **OS-4_Portfolio**, from the data files for this course. This file contains information about electronic portfolios.
2. Read the information to learn about electronic portfolios.
3. In your operating system, navigate to the location where you want to store the electronic portfolio.
4. Create a new folder, and name it **OS-4_Portfolio_xx**.
5. In the folder, create one subfolder named **Academic Achievement**, a second named **Personal Information**, and a third named **Career Information**.
6. Select an application that you can use to create a list of artifacts and other items you will include in your portfolio. This might be a word-processing program, a spreadsheet program, or a database program.
7. Use the application to create a new file. Save the file in the **Personal Information** subfolder, with the name **OS-4_List of Artifacts_xx**.
8. In the file, list the name and a description of each artifact and item you want to include in the portfolio. (Refer to the information in the **OS-4_Portfolio.pdf** file.)
9. In the file, include whether each artifact already exists, is on-going, or if it is something you will create in the future.
10. In the file, also include the name of the subfolder in which you will store the artifact. For example, you might store a resume and list of references in the **Career Information** folder and an example of a word-processing document you typed and formatted in the **Academic Achievement** folder.

11. Save the file. You can modify it and refer to it as you develop your portfolio.
12. Locate existing artifacts and items you have stored in digital format and copy or move them into the appropriate subfolder in your **OS-4_Portfolio_xx** folder.
13. Locate printed artifacts and items, and use appropriate technology, such as a scanner or digital camera, to convert them into digital files. Store them in the appropriate subfolder in your **OS-4_Portfolio_xx** folder.
14. Select an application, and use it to create new items to include, such as a contact information sheet, a personal academic plan, and guidelines for assessment. Store the items in the appropriate portfolio subfolders.
15. Select an application, and use it to create reflections for your artifacts. Store the reflections with the artifacts in the portfolio.
16. Select an application, and use it to create a table of contents for your portfolio. Format the items as hyperlinks that link to the digital artifacts and items.
17. Practice presenting the portfolio to your class.
18. Continue to review, update, and add new artifacts and items to your portfolio on a regular basis.

DIRECTIONS: *You will use your operating system to capture images of different program windows and insert the images into a word-processing file. You will then print the file and label the elements on each image.*

1. Start your computer, and log in to your user account, if necessary.
2. Start a word-processing application, such as Microsoft Word or Google Documents.
3. Save the default blank document with the name **OS-5_wp_xx** in the location where your teacher instructs you to store the files for this activity.
4. Maximize the application window.
5. On the first line of the word-processing file, type your first and last names and today's date.
6. Press Enter to start a new line.
7. Capture an image of the screen.
8. Paste the image from the Clipboard into the word-processing document.
9. Save the document, and then minimize the application window.
10. Capture an image of your computer desktop.
11. Restore the word-processing program window.
12. Press CTRL + ENTER to start a new page.
13. Paste the captured image into the word-processing document.

14. Save the document, and then minimize the application window.
15. Start a spreadsheet application.
16. Maximize the spreadsheet application window.
17. Capture an image of the spreadsheet application window.
18. Exit the spreadsheet application.
19. Make the word-processing application window active.
20. In the word-processing document, press CTRL + ENTER , to start a new page.
21. Paste the captured image into the word-processing document.
22. Save the word-processing document.
23. With your teacher's permission, print the word-processing document and label the parts of all three screens. Alternatively, use drawing tools to insert callouts or text boxes in the word-processing document to label the parts of the screens. Page 1, the word-processing screen, might look similar to Illustration D.
24. Close the word-processing document, saving all changes, and exit the application.

Illustration D

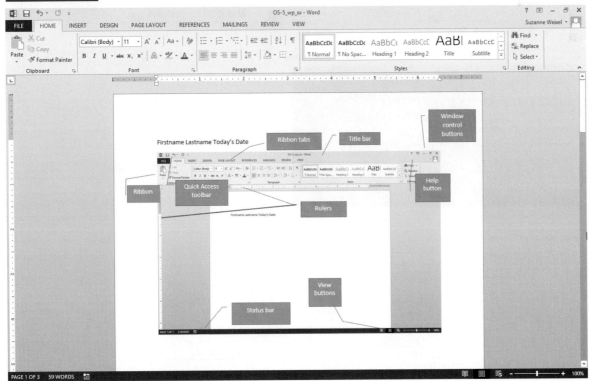

Word 2013, Microsoft Corporation.

DIRECTIONS: *You will use a Help program to locate and review security settings. You will also access the command prompt and display a directory.*

1. Start your computer, and log in to your user account, if necessary.
2. Start your operating system's Help program, and maximize the window.
3. Search for **managing security settings**.
4. Click a link for information about protecting your PC from viruses.
5. Read the information, scrolling down in the window until you reach the end.
6. Click the Back button to return to the previous window.
7. Search for information about antivirus protection. For example, in Windows, search for **Windows Defender**.
8. Click a link for more information, such as the link *Turn Windows Defender on or off*.
9. Click a link to open the program. If you are using an operating system other than Windows, click a link to open the window where you can view security settings.
10. With your teacher's permission, use the tabs on the page to view information about your antivirus program.
11. Close the window.
12. Close the Help program window.
13. If you are on a Windows OS, search for and open the Command Prompt. If you are on a Mac OS, skip to step 21.
14. Type **dir**, and press [ENTER] to display a directory list of files.
15. Capture an image of the command prompt window.
16. Start a paint or graphics program and paste the screen capture into the file. It should look similar to Illustration E, although the actual directory contents depend on the contents of your system.
17. Save the file as **OS-6_image1_*xx***.
18. Close the Command Prompt window.
19. With your teacher's permission, print **OS-6_image1_*xx***.
20. Close the file, and exit the program.
21. With your teacher's permission, log off and/or shut down the computer.

Illustration E

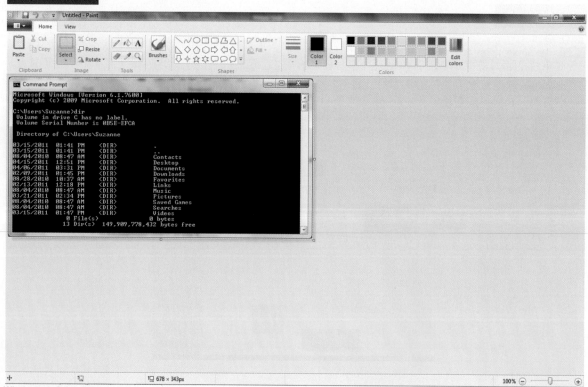

Windows 8, Paint, Microsoft Corporation.

part 2

Applications

Application Basics

What Is Application Software?

Application software is a type of program, such as word-processing or spreadsheet software, that directs a computer to perform one or more tasks. Think about all the things a computer can help you do. You can write letters and reports. You can look up information, record songs, play games, chat with friends, and more. Application software makes it possible for your computer to perform such tasks.

There are many different types of application software (sometimes called applications), each best suited for a certain purpose. Some programs perform specific jobs. Others do many different tasks. Once you become familiar with application software, you can make choices to help your computer work faster and more efficiently.

Chapter Outline

 Lesson 9–1

Selecting Application Software

 Lesson 9–2

Obtaining Application Software

 Lesson 9–3

Getting Started with an Application

Selecting Application Software

Objectives

- Identify widely used types of application software.
- Compare and contrast three types of application software.
- Decide what kinds of applications will work best for you.

As You Read

Compare and Contrast   Use a three-column chart to compare three different types of application software. Write each type as a column header and list the features below the header.

🔑 Key Terms

- application software
- apps
- integrated software
- personal information manager (PIM) program
- productivity suite
- stand-alone program

Why Use Application Software?

Application software performs a specific job or task. For example, some applications help astronomers research stars. Others help doctors care for their patients. It is important to choose applications that can do the jobs you want done. The most common types of application software include:

- word processors for writing letters and reports
- spreadsheets for working with numbers and doing math
- databases for storing and finding information
- presentation graphics for creating slide shows
- desktop publishing for creating printer-ready publications such as brochures, newsletters, and invitations
- telecommunications for using the Internet and e-mail
- **personal information manager (PIM)** programs for storing phone numbers and addresses and creating schedules

Types of Application Software

Application software falls into three basic categories: stand-alone programs, integrated software, and productivity suites. These forms differ in their features (the tasks they do) and in cost. Wise computer users choose the type of software that best fits their needs, their computers, and their budgets.

Why Use Application Software?

Application	Purpose
Word-processing	Create text-based documents such as reports and letters
Spreadsheet	Display and analyze business, personal, or financial data
Database	Store and organize information
Presentation	Create and deliver multimedia slide shows
Desktop-publishing	Create publications such as brochures and invitations
E-Mail	Create, send, receive, and organize electronic mail messages

Stand-alone Programs   Software that specializes in one task is called a stand-alone program. Because each program—such as a word processor, database, or spreadsheet—is dedicated to just one application, **stand-alone programs** can have many useful and advanced features. However, stand-alone programs may cost more than other forms of application software.

Because they focus on one kind of job, stand-alone programs usually have many very specialized features. Word processors, for example, give users tools to print labels and envelopes.

Integrated Software   Buying multiple stand-alone programs might require too much memory in your computer or may cost too much. You might want to do more with the software than a stand-alone program is capable of handling.

Integrated software programs combine the basic features of several applications into one package. They are not as powerful or as complete as their stand-alone counterparts, nor do they specialize in one application. However, integrated software usually is less costly and is fairly easy to use. These programs let you do basic work in several applications such as word processors, databases, spreadsheets, graphics, and more.

People use integrated software programs because the applications work in similar ways. That is, you often can use many of the same commands. You also can use data from one program in another.

Spotlight on...

APPS FOR ALL

With its iPhone, Apple Computer pioneered the development of **apps**, third-party software programs developed specifically for smart phones, tablet computers, and other handheld devices. Apps are purchased from app stores, which are online portals where you select and download the programs. Basic versions of these apps are often free, although premium apps offering more features may cost anywhere from $2.00 to $200.00. Some so-called "free" games are designed so that the consumer can advance in the game faster if he or she pays a fee. These "free-to-play" games originally cost nothing but a player who is not careful can end up spending large amounts of money. Apps take up very little storage space—usually around 6–10 megabytes.

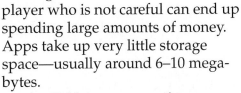

Available apps range from popular games like "Angry Birds," to practical apps that let you locate restaurants or count your calories.

Productivity Suites   What if you need to use the advanced features of several stand-alone programs? You might select a productivity suite. Although one suite may differ from another, in general **productivity suites** combine several programs such as word-processing, spreadsheets, databases, and graphics. Like integrated software, the programs in productivity suites have a common look and feel. But productivity suites contain more than the basic software found in integrated programs. They contain the actual stand-alone programs with all their features.

Productivity suites generally cost more than integrated software, but usually they are cheaper than buying the stand-alone programs separately. Some common productivity suites include:

- Microsoft Office (with Word, Excel, PowerPoint, Outlook, and Access in the Windows version)
- Corel WordPerfect Office (with WordPerfect, Quattro Pro, Paradox, Corel Presentations, and Corel CENTRAL)
- Adobe Creative Suite Design Premium (with Photoshop, Illustrator, InDesign, Dreamweaver, and Flash)

New Types of Applications

Like most technology, new types of software are always emerging, and existing software is always evolving. Current trends include applications that reside on Internet servers and applications that give everyday objects computing power.

Software as a Service   Some companies are now making applications available for use online. For example, Microsoft offers a version of its Microsoft Office suite online, and Google offers Google docs. For free or a subscription fee, users can access the applications using an Internet connection instead of installing the program on their own computer.

Pervasive Computing   Now that so many objects have embedded computer chips, applications are emerging that let users interact with their things. For example, applications make it possible for you to use voice activated telephone calling in your car and to program your dishwasher to alert you when it is full.

Which Type of Software Is Right for You?

The type of application software you choose depends on what you want it to do, how much you are willing to spend, and how easy the programs are to learn. It also depends on whether the software will work on your computer and how much space each program will take up on your hard drive. You might want to match the software you use at home with the programs you use at school so you can work on documents in both locations.

While most computers are sold with some application software installed, your computer may not have the software you need. Your needs will also change over time. Consider how problems could arise if you use the wrong software product when you try to complete a specific task—like attempting to perform advanced mathematical calculations using a word-processing program. Whether you consider upgrading your existing software, buying new programs, or downloading free software from the Internet, you should consider the following:

- Reviews of the software. Consumer reviews are usually a great source of information.

- User-friendliness. What kind of support is available? Is there live help included?

- Licensing agreements (see Lesson 9–2). Can you agree to the licensing requirements? Remember that copying a friend's program is piracy.

Figure 9.1.1 Computing devices usually come with some applications installed, and you can purchase more to meet your needs.

Obtaining Application Software

Objectives

- Explain why computer hardware and software must be compatible.
- Identify sources for obtaining application software.
- Explain the difference between proprietary and open-source software.
- Summarize the best way to install or uninstall application software.
- Analyze how piracy affects makers and users of computer software.

Key Terms

- Cloud apps
- commercial software
- freeware
- open-source software
- proprietary software
- public domain software
- shareware
- single-seat license
- single-user license
- site license
- software license
- system requirement
- volume license
- Web apps

As You Read

Organizing Information   Make an outline of the lesson. Use Roman numerals for main headings. Use capital letters for subheadings, and use numbers for supporting details.

Minimum System Requirements

Each software program has minimum **system requirements**. The computer must meet the minimum hardware and software needs of the program for it to work properly.

To get the most from your computer, it is important to choose software that will work with the following:

- your type of computer (Macintosh or PC compatible)
- microprocessor speed
- operating system (such as Linux, MAC OS X, or Windows)
- available amount of memory (RAM)
- available hard drive space
- special equipment, such as a DVD drive

Software that is not compatible with your system will not work. Worse, trying to install incompatible software may damage your computer. To avoid compatibility problems, double-check the system requirements before buying or installing any software program.

Obtaining Application Software

Some application software is usually loaded on new computers. You can also obtain additional software in multiple forms.

Commercial Software   Companies own the copyrights to the application software they sell to the public. This prevents you from illegally copying it to sell it to others, giving it away, or sharing it. **Commercial software**, which may also be called **proprietary software**, is copyrighted software that you must buy before using it. Usually, you must agree to or sign a license, as well. With commercial software, you are paying for the right to use the software, not necessarily for the right to the software's code. Software where the user doesn't gain access to the program's code is also called closed-source software.

Shareware Proprietary software that you can use on a try-before-you-buy basis is called **shareware**. If you decide to keep using it, you must pay a registration fee. You are also allowed to copy shareware and give it to your friends. They must follow the same process to acquire the software.

Freeware Some companies give away their copyrighted software for free. This is known as **freeware**. The companies allow users to install the program as long as they do not resell it.

Open-source Software Open source software is a program, like propriety software, and you may have to pay for it. However, unlike proprietary software, this kind of software makes the source code available to the public. The idea is that the software will improve and benefit from the innovations of users, who troubleshoot weak points and expand features. Critics, however, say that developers are not fairly compensated for their work (open source is not automatically "free") and also that the software development suffers if there is no central organizer.

Creative Commons A creative commons license lets software copyright holders open some of their work for public use while letting them hold onto other parts of their work. As with open-source software, there are critics who complain that creative commons licenses eat away at intellectual property rights. Yet, several million pages of Web content are "brought to you" by Creative Commons licenses, such as The Library of Public Science, Garageband.com, and Flickr, the photo sharing site.

Public Domain Software On occasion, program authors allow you to use programs, share them, give them away, or even

Technology @ Work

Shareware companies make money by collecting fees for the products they send out on a free trial basis.

Think About It!
Shareware has many advantages for its producers. Identify each benefit of shareware listed below as either true or false.

➤ A user might try shareware rather than opting to buy a commercial program.

➤ Shareware companies do not have to pay for distribution.

➤ Users who do not like the product still have to pay for it.

Real-World Tech

Authoring Shareware California-based Tenadar Software develops adventure games and distributes them as shareware. To play the game more than once, you send the requested royalty to the copyright holders. Who are they? Tenadar employees are all between 10 and 12 years old. What started as a fifth-grade project has grown into a business of several employees offering a variety of computer games for the Macintosh. The company's motto is "Great Software for Kids, by Kids."

If you were to create shareware, what might you choose to develop?

Application Basics • 113

alter them to meet certain needs. This is called **public domain software**. Beware: the quality of these programs can vary widely, and they may contain more errors than other types of software.

Installing, Reinstalling, and Uninstalling Programs

Application software must be installed, or prepared to run on a computer, before it can be used. You must copy it from a location such as an installation disk or download it from the Internet to the computer's hard drive.

Most programs come with an installation, or setup, program that prompts you to load the software onto the computer. Companies that make commercial software often provide printed or online guides, telephone support, or online help to solve installation problems.

To delete a program from the computer, you must run a special removal program to properly uninstall it. Otherwise, parts of the program can remain on the computer and may interfere with its operation. You can reinstall the program if you need it again, or to repair a problem.

Using Web Apps
Web apps, which are sometimes called **Cloud apps,** are applications that are stored on cloud servers so you do not have to install them on your computer. Usually, you must register with a Web site to use a Web app. Some common Web apps include online e-mail services such as Gmail and Yahoo mail, social networking sites such as Facebook and Twitter, and productivity suites, such as Google Docs and Office 365. Businesses may have a cloud-based customer relationship management (CRM) system for managing customer data and interactions.

Using Software Legally

Buying proprietary, copyrighted software comes with a **software license**, which allows the buyer to use and install the program, and sometimes entitles the buyer to receive free or reduced cost support and updates. Individuals might buy a **single-user license** for one copy of the program, or a **single-seat license** to install the program on a single computer. Organizations such as schools or businesses usually buy a **volume** or **site license** which lets them install on multiple systems or a network for multiple users. Network licensing generally costs less per user and allows users to share resources.

Software Piracy
People who copy copyrighted software to install on other computers, give away, or sell are guilty of violating federal copyright laws and stealing, called software piracy. Violating a copyright and pirating software are both morally wrong and illegal. These activities discourage the authors of good software from writing new and better programs because they may not get paid for their work. Pirated software cannot be registered, so users do not get the support services they may need.

Figure 9.2.1 Most software programs come with a license agreement, like the one shown here for Windows 8.1 Pro.

MICROSOFT SOFTWARE LICENSE AGREEMENT

WINDOWS 8.1 PRO

Thank you for choosing Microsoft Windows 8.1 Pro. This is a license agreement between you and Microsoft Corporation (or, based on where you live, one of its affiliates) that describes your rights to use the Windows 8.1 Pro software. For your convenience, we've organized this agreement into two parts. The first part includes introductory terms phrased in a question and answer format; the Additional Terms and Limited Warranty follow and contain greater detail. You should review the entire agreement, including any linked terms, because all of the terms are important and together create this contract that applies to you. You can review linked terms by pasting the forward link into your browser window once the software is running. **The Additional Terms contain a binding arbitration clause and class action waiver. If you live in the United States, these affect your rights to resolve a dispute with Microsoft, so you should read them carefully.**

By accepting this agreement or using the software, you agree to all of these terms and consent to the transmission of certain information during activation and for Internet-based features of the software. If you do not accept and comply with these terms, you may not use the software or its features. Instead, you should return it to the retailer for a refund or credit, if any.

Windows 8, Microsoft Corporation.

Getting Started with an Application

Objectives

- Describe how to launch a program.
- List common features of application software windows.
- Explain how to maximize and minimize a program window.
- Explain how to create, open, save, and close a file.
- Explain how to exit an application.

As You Read

Draw Conclusions Use a conclusion chart to help you understand how to use application software as you read.

Launching an Application

To get started with an application program, you open it using the operating system on your computer. Most applications use similar commands to accomplish basic tasks, such as starting, exiting, and saving. Once you learn these tasks in one program, you can easily transfer the knowledge so you can use other programs, too.

Starting a Program When a computer is turned on, it typically starts its operating system. You can then **launch**, or start, any application installed on the computer. You can launch an application in two ways: a menu or an icon.

- Menu—In Windows 7 or earlier, clicking the Start button displays a list of programs installed on the computer.
- Icon—Icons, which may be called tiles, are on-screen symbols that stand for a computer function or program. Because they are shortcuts to programs, it is helpful to customize your desktop or Start screen to include icons for the programs you use most often.

Exploring Application Windows

A launched application appears in a frame called a window. You can work in any size window, but it is usually best to **maximize** the window, or make it as large as it can be. Sometimes you will want to use another program without closing the first one. You can resize it or **minimize** it to make it as small as possible so it remains out of the way while you use the other program.

Key Terms

- command
- groups
- launch
- maximize
- menu bar
- minimize
- Ribbon
- scroll
- tab
- title bar

Figure 9.3.1 The Windows 7 Start menu.

Windows 8, Microsoft Corporation.

The largest portion of an application window is the space for your work. The rest of the window contains tools that you use to develop your files.

Title Bar   The top row of an application window is called the **title bar**. The title bar shows the program's name and, in some cases, the name of the document you are working on.

The Ribbon   In Microsoft Office, the **Ribbon** is the control center for using the application. The Ribbon has three parts:

- **Tabs.** Each **tab** contains important tasks you do within an application. For example, the Home tab in Excel offers formatting and formula options.
- **Groups.** Each tab contains **groups** of related tasks. For example, in Excel, the Number group on the Home tab offers number formatting options.
- **Commands.** A **command** is a button, a box for entering information, or a menu. For example, the % button in a spreadsheet program formats a number as a percentage. Click a command to select it or use a shortcut key combination. For example, press and hold Alt and then press the shortcut key identified in the command name.

The Menu   A **menu bar** lists sets of commands. On a Macintosh, it appears at the top of the screen. In Windows applications, the menu generally appears under the title bar.

Figure 9.3.2 Applications in the Microsoft Office software suite share these basic elements.

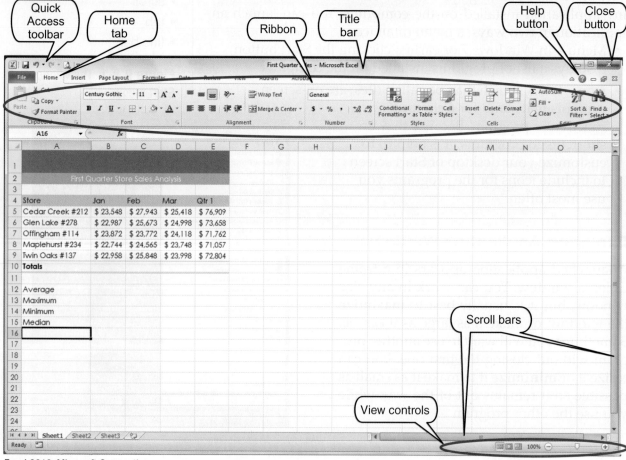

Excel 2013, Microsoft Corporation.

Creating, Opening, Saving, and Closing

Application software lets you create new documents, save them for future use, or work on documents you have saved. You can close the application when you are done working. Most applications have a File menu (see below)—though the 2007 version of Microsoft Office has an "Office" button—which includes these commands:

- New—creates a file into which you can enter data
- Open—finds a document that was previously saved as a disk file and displays it in a window
- Save—saves the document in the current window to a disk file
- Save as—saves the document as a new file with a new name, in a different location, or in a different format
- Close—closes an open file
- Exit or Quit—closes the application and removes its window from the screen

Moving in the Application Window

Some tools allow you to **scroll**, or move from one part of a window to another. The scroll bars usually appear at the right side of the window and at the bottom. Boxes appear in these bars to show whether you are at the beginning or end of the file or somewhere in the middle. You can move from one place to another by either dragging these scroll boxes or clicking the scroll arrows at each end of the scroll bars.

Technology @ Work

Many jobs have been created in the computer industry. Thanks to the way we rely on computers, many companies hire staff who have computer skills but possess degrees in other fields, such as history or science.

Earning a certificate in a computer-skill area is one way to show today's companies that you have computer training. MOS (Microsoft Office Specialist) certification confirms the user is proficient with Microsoft Office programs such as Word, Excel, PowerPoint, or Access.

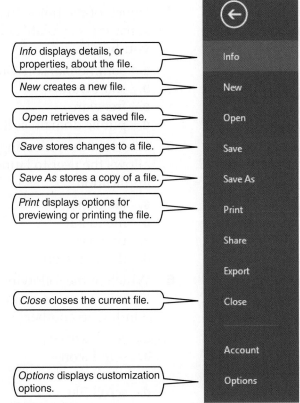

Info displays details, or properties, about the file.

New creates a new file.

Open retrieves a saved file.

Save stores changes to a file.

Save As stores a copy of a file.

Print displays options for previewing or printing the file.

Close closes the current file.

Options displays customization options.

Figure 9.3.3 In Microsoft Office, use the File menu in Backstage view to access commands for creating, saving, printing, and managing documents.

Word 2013, Microsoft Coporation.

Use the Vocabulary

Directions: *Match each vocabulary term in the left column with the correct definition in the right column.*

_____ **1.** personal information manager	**a.**	software that you can try before purchasing
_____ **2.** integrated software	**b.**	uncopyrighted software that is given away without cost
_____ **3.** productivity suite	**c.**	software that stores phone numbers and creates schedules
_____ **4.** shareware	**d.**	combines several full-featured programs in one package
_____ **5.** freeware	**e.**	third-party software programs developed specifically for certain smart phones
_____ **6.** public domain software		
_____ **7.** uninstall	**f.**	to delete a program from the computer
_____ **8.** maximize	**g.**	combines basic features of several applications into one package
_____ **9.** apps	**h.**	move from one place in a window to another
_____ **10.** scroll	**i.**	to make a window as large as possible
	j.	copyrighted software that is given away without cost

Check Your Comprehension

Directions: *Determine the correct choice for each of the following.*

1. Which of the following items is NOT an example of application software?
   a. spreadsheet
   b. database
   c. operating system
   d. word processor

2. Which of the following types of application software combines the basic features of several applications?
   a. stand-alone program
   b. integrated software
   c. productivity suite
   d. personal information manager (PIM) program

3. Which of the following types of software must be purchased in advance?
   a. commercial software
   b. shareware
   c. freeware
   d. public domain software

4. Which of the following types of software is available on a try-before-you-buy basis?
   a. commercial software
   b. shareware
   c. freeware
   d. public domain software

5. Which of the following features allows the user to launch an application?
   a. Help menu
   b. menu bar
   c. title bar
   d. desktop icon

6. Which of the following tools allows the user to move from one part of a window to another?
   a. scroll arrows
   b. scroll icons
   c. scroll menu
   d. scroll file

Directions: *Answer the following questions.*

1. Compare and contrast open source and proprietary software. Why might a programmer choose to release software as open-source instead of as proprietary?

2. Why should you check a program's system requirements before purchasing it?

3. Why is it important to uninstall a program you no longer use?

4. What is the difference between the New and Open commands on the File menu?

5. Why does an application window include tools such as scroll bars, scroll boxes, and scroll arrows?

Extend Your Knowledge

Directions: *Choose and complete one of the following projects.*

A. The computer desktop shows many different types of icons. Icons can represent applications, files, or file folders. Experiment with a Macintosh or Microsoft Windows operating system. Make a three-column chart of the icons that appear on the desktop. Include a description of what happens when each icon is clicked, and identify what type of file or program the particular icon represents.

B. Several types of application software are listed in this chapter. They include word processors, spreadsheets, databases, presentation graphics, telecommunications, and personal information managers. Using the Internet or other resources, prepare a report that evaluates, compares, and contrasts at least two types of application software that you may use based on their appropriateness for a task, licensing agreements, and available support. As you work, take notes and keep track of your sources. Include a list of sources or bibliography with your report. Evaluate the information you find and only use it if it is accurate, relevant, and valid. Share your report with the class.

Understanding Applications

How Can an Application Help You?

Application software provides the tools you need to get a job done. When you select the right program for the job, you can accomplish the task quickly and efficiently.

Applications are designed to meet different needs. Some are designed for one specific purpose, such as managing medical records or product inventory. Some are designed for multiple purposes, such as creating presentations on any subject.

In this chapter, you examine application software more closely. You learn more about types of applications and how to use an application program to complete a task.

Chapter Outline

 Lesson 10–1

Examining Types of Application Software

 Lesson 10–2

Application Documentation and Versions

 Lesson 10–3

Using Application Software

Examining Types of Application Software

Objectives

- Compare and contrast horizontal and vertical applications.
- List examples of horizontal and vertical applications.
- Describe the role of beta versions in the software-testing process.

As You Read

Organize Information   Use an outline to organize information about application software as you read.

Key Terms

- beta version
- copy protection
- horizontal application
- personal productivity program
- premium apps
- time-limited trial
- vertical application

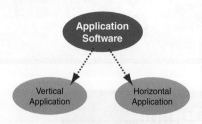

Figure 10.1.1 Vertical application software is very specific—such as the computer-aided design programs used by architects—and horizontal application software—such as Microsoft Word—can be used by all types for everyday computing tasks.

Which Direction Is Right for You?

Application software can be classified as a stand-alone, integrated, or productivity suite program. These types of software differ in the number of tasks they perform. Another way to classify application software is based on whether it is developed for a few users with very specific needs or whether it appeals to many users with shared needs.

Vertical Application   A **vertical application** is designed for a very limited purpose, such as restaurant management or medical billing. Although the software is very useful to one field or business, it is of little interest to others.

Horizontal Application   A **horizontal application** is a general-purpose program that meets the needs of many different users. It can be applied to many tasks. It also tends to be less expensive. It is likely that you will use horizontal, not vertical, applications for schoolwork you do on the computer. Horizontal applications are also used in many households to track finances and prepare tax forms.

Types of Horizontal Applications

Horizontal applications can be divided into several categories depending on the focus of the program.

Personal Productivity Programs   The most popular horizontal applications are known as **personal productivity programs**. They help people work more effectively and include common applications such as word processors and database systems.

Multimedia Applications Some horizontal applications combine text, graphics, video, and sound. These include:
- desktop publishing—to combine text and graphics to produce newsletters and brochures
- graphics—to create and edit pictures
- Web page design—to create Web pages using sound, graphics, animation, and text

Internet Applications Some horizontal applications help computer users communicate over the Internet, including:
- Web browsers—to access data from the World Wide Web
- e-mail—to send and receive electronic messages

Online or Mobile Apps Applications designed for use online are called online apps, Web apps, or Cloud apps, while those designed to download and use on a smart phone or tablet are called mobile apps. They are available for thousands of uses, from productivity suites to games. Some are free, and some, called **premium apps**, must be purchased.

Apps have a range of uses from playing music to helping improve productivity. Some apps even track a user's health and exercise. Apps that use the Internet can connect to a web browser, a user's e-mail, or social media sites, such as Facebook and Twitter. There are also reference apps you use to search for information; creation apps for drawing or creating images; and content apps for organizing data, like the contacts on your phone. Like computer applications, apps are written to run on a specific operating system so not all apps run on all mobile devices.

Testing Software

Beta versions, or early working copies of application software, are often sent to selected users to test the program. They use it for a period of time and report errors or problems to the developer. Beta versions help ensure that the final software will work correctly and offer customers the best tools possible.

Limited Trials To protect their work and guard against illegal copying, companies may set their beta software to expire after a certain date. These **time-limited trials** stop working after a certain number of uses or days.

Copyright Concerns Developers sometimes add **copy protection**, a physical device or software tool to keep users from making unauthorized copies of the beta software. These copyright safeguards can protect the sellers' property from illegal copying—a serious crime. Copy protection prevents beta software, which is still in development, from being widely distributed.

Real-World Tech

Protecting Digital Media Copy protection extends beyond software. Any form of information that is stored digitally is at risk of being illegally copied, including CD music and DVD movies. An early attempt by Sony Corporation to copy-protect CDs sold across Europe failed. It turned out that consumers could defeat the copy-protection method too easily.

Why do you think companies continue to research new and better ways to copy-protect their work from unethical and illegal duplication?

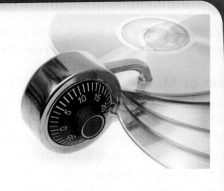

Application Documentation and Versions

Objectives

- Compare and contrast types of documentation.
- Explain the purpose of versions and version numbers.
- Describe why it is important to register your software.

As You Read

Cause and Effect   Use a cause-and-effect chart to help you understand the results of various software elements.

Software Documentation

Most software packages provide directions on how to install the program, to use the application, and to **troubleshoot**, or correct, problems. These instructions, called **documentation**, are typically available in three forms:

- printed tutorials and reference manuals
- electronic help screens in the program or on CD-ROM
- information available on the publisher's Web site

Printed Documentation   Installation instructions may be a single sentence printed on the software disk or CD. Other instructions may take the form of a booklet. Some programs include encyclopedia-type references that detail the software features.

Electronic Help Screens   Application software frequently provides reference materials in electronic form as part of the program or on a separate CD or DVD. Opening the program's Help menu lets you troubleshoot problems as they happen and find out how to perform certain operations or tasks.

Key Terms

- documentation
- knowledge base
- maintenance release
- product key
- troubleshoot
- version

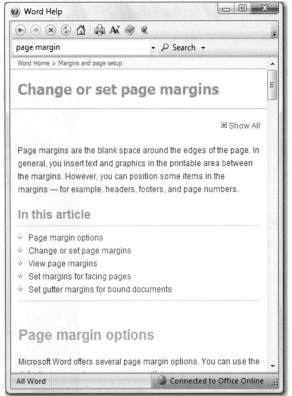

Figure 10.2.1 Most software programs provide help screens, like this one.

Word 2013, Microsoft Corporation.

Technology @ Work

There is a gradual but steady shift in most companies away from outputting files in hard copy (printed) to outputting soft copy (digital or electronic files). Digital output includes any information displayed on a computer, including application files, e-mail, e-mail attachments, and Web pages.

Think About It!

Outputting files electronically is convenient, fast, and can save costs related to printing and mailing. It also poses some risks. Which of the following issues do you think poses the greatest risk to companies and individuals?

> lack of hard copy documentation

> risk of unauthorized access to data

> risk of loss or damage to data

> inability to open or read incompatible files

Web Sites Software documentation sometimes may be found on the software publisher's Web site. These sites often include answers to users' frequently asked questions (FAQs) and give other helpful hints. Files, sometimes called patches, may be available to fix, or patch, problems with the software. More so than other types of support, Web documentation can be updated quickly by the publisher and shared with users who need it.

Other Sources If you need more information than is provided by the software's documentation, telephone or online support may be an option. Many software companies maintain an online **knowledge base** that users can search to find information and get help. In addition, many helpful application software references and tutorials are available in libraries, online, or at bookstores.

Versions of Software

Successful software can lead to multiple **versions**, or releases. Companies typically identify their new software with a version number. A version can be identified by the year it was released, such as Microsoft Word 2013. Sometimes the version number is a whole number followed by a decimal or a letter, such as 5.D or 6.22. Smaller numbers such as 1.2 or 1.2a indicate a **maintenance release**—a minor revision to correct errors or add minor features. A larger number indicates that the software has significant revisions with new features.

The version number may not be obvious when an application launches. However, most software manufacturers locate the version number in the Help menu, where you can select the About command. This will open a window with useful information about the software—including its version and revision number.

Figure 10.2.2 In most programs, you can find the version number and other information through the Help menu.

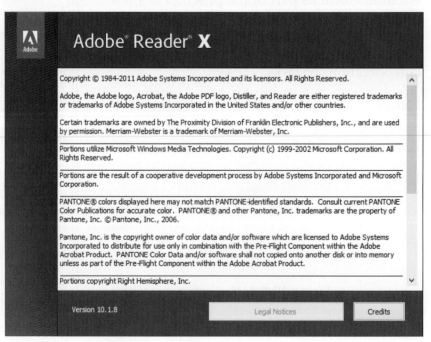

Software Registration and Protection

When you install software, you are typically asked to register, or be recorded as the owner of your copy, with the publisher. You can register by faxing or mailing a printed form that comes with the package or by completing an online form that can be sent to the software manufacturer. Sometimes registration is part of the program activation. To activate the program, you usually enter a license number, called a **product key** or product code, and agree to an End User License Agreement (EULA).

Registration allows you to use the software legally. Since the software company knows you have a legal copy of its product, it may offer services such as free technical support. The company may also send notices of new version releases or upgrades offered at no cost or at a discounted price.

Organizations that have many computers—such as schools, businesses, or government agencies—may purchase a site license instead of registering individual copies of the software. A site license, which may be called a multi-user or volume license, usually includes one product key for all users, and gives permission to install the software on a specific number of computers for the organization's internal use only. On the other hand, a single-user or single-seat license, provides one key per copy.

One type of software sees seasonal increase in sales. Every spring, many families purchase tax preparation software to assist in preparing annual federal tax returns to send to the Internal Revenue Service by April 15, the filing date.

Think About It!

Some revisions in tax preparation software are out of the control of the programmers. Of the reasons listed below for a revision, which do you think developers could not have predicted?

➤ bugs in the program

➤ changes in tax laws

➤ changes in the data user's input

Spotlight on...

NORAH SCHOLL

She was the fastest typist in sixth grade. Why is that so special? Well, Norah Scholl cannot use her hands. She was born with arthrogryposis, an incurable condition that prevents her from using her arms or hands and limits the mobility of her legs.

She was the youngest person ever to master the special software and hardware provided by Easter Seals that allowed her to speak into her computer to operate it. Despite her physical challenges, Norah was able to graduate from high school and college and pursue a graduate degree in community counseling. Advancements in technology continue to help people with handicaps achieve alongside their non-handicapped peers.

Lesson 10–3   Using Application Software

Objectives

- Identify and describe common features of application software.
- Explain how default settings can be changed to suit a user's needs.
- Explain the benefits of multitasking.

As You Read

Summarize Use a chart to summarize the purpose of each common feature of application software as you read.

 **Key Terms**

- application workspace
- command button
- default
- menu
- multitask
- preference
- Print Preview
- status bar
- tab
- toolbar
- zoom

Working in an Application's Window

There are several common features you are likely to find in your application windows. You use a mouse or keyboard to navigate in the window, to make selections, and input commands.

Application Workspace The largest area of a program's window is called the **application workspace**. It displays the file in which you are working. You can enter text, graphics, or other data into the workspace. You also can locate and open a saved file into the application workspace. The workspace looks different depending on the application. For example, a word-processing application workspace looks like a page; a spreadsheet workspace looks like a grid of columns and rows.

Title Bar The title bar usually displays the name of the application and the name of the file you are in. If this is a new document, you will see a placeholder name, such as *Untitled* or *Document 1*.

Toolbar and Command Buttons Most applications have a **toolbar** or **command buttons** that you use to select a command. A toolbar is a row of icons or buttons. Clicking a toolbar icon or command button tells the application to execute that command.

Word 2013, Microsoft Corporation.

Figure 10.3.1 The Ribbon in Microsoft Office programs provides easy access to commands. Other programs may use toolbars or menus.

Some applications have more than one toolbar. Many toolbars can be dragged to a different location, if desired, or even "floated" in the application workspace.

Menus and Tabs   **Menus** and **tabs** give you access to the program's commands. They present a list—or menu—of choices so you can select the one you need.

Viewing a Document   Many programs let you change how a document is displayed in the application workspace. Changing the view can help you accomplish specific tasks. For example, you might change to **Print Preview** to see how a file will look when it is printed, or change to Draft view when you do not need to see features such as graphics or columns.

Adjusting the Display   You can adjust the display of the data in the workspace by using the **zoom** control. This option magnifies the view of the document. You typically can set it to any size you prefer between 10 percent and 500 percent. Zoom options do not affect the printing size, only how you see your document on the screen. A 100 percent magnification shows the document at the same size that a printed copy will be.

Protected Mode   Some programs automatically open certain files in protected mode, or protected view, which means most editing functions are disabled. For example, Microsoft Office programs open files downloaded from the Internet or received as an e-mail attachment in protected mode. Protected mode can help protect your computer from viruses and other malware. You can click the Enable Editing button to exit protected mode.

Read-Only View   Most programs let you set properties to open a document or file in read-only view, which means you can read it but not edit it.

Figure 10.3.2 The same document displayed in Draft view (left) and Page Layout view (right) in Microsoft Office.

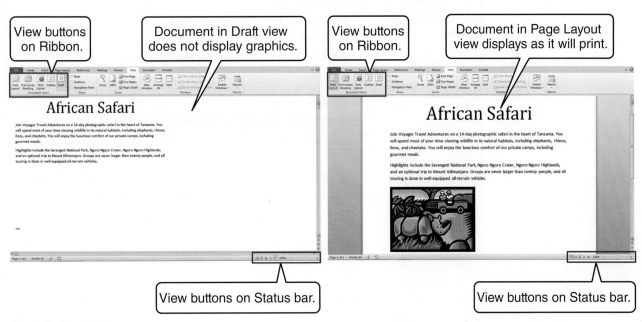

View buttons on Ribbon.

Document in Draft view does not display graphics.

View buttons on Ribbon.

Document in Page Layout view displays as it will print.

African Safari

African Safari

View buttons on Status bar.

View buttons on Status bar.

Word 2013, Microsoft Corporation.

Figure 10.3.3 Changing default Display settings in Adobe Reader.

Checking Your Status Many software programs display a **status bar** below the application workspace. A status bar shows information about the program and other useful messages. For example, the status bar in Word displays the current page number, total page count, and the number of the line on which you are currently typing.

Setting Options and Preferences

Software applications start using **default** settings. These are options preset by the software maker, based on what most users prefer. You can customize the program for the way you want to work by selecting **preferences** or options. Changing an option or preference replaces the default setting.

You can change such features as how the screen looks, how the spelling checker works, and the preferred location for saving documents. You can choose to apply a preference to a current document only, or save it in the computer as a new default setting. Many programs also allow you to reset the revised default settings back to their original settings. To set options in a Microsoft Office program, click File and then click Options.

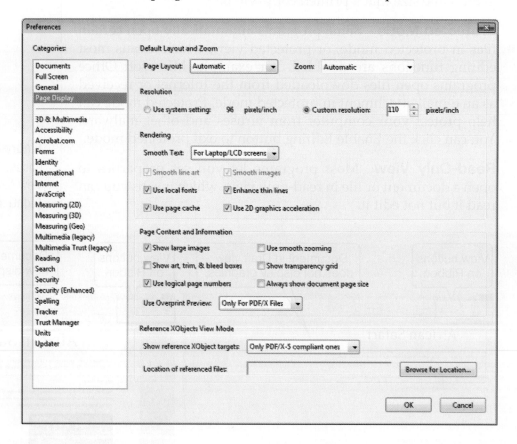

Common Application Features

Most application programs have many of the same features. For example, most programs include cut, copy, and paste commands for moving and copying text and objects. Text formatting commands are similar in almost all programs, as are commands for inserting, moving, and resizing objects, such as pictures. Most include a spelling checker that you can use to identify and correct spelling errors. Other common features including the Print command for printing a file, Undo and Redo commands for undoing changes, and a Search, or Find and Replace command for locating specific information within the file. Most programs also have a built-in Help program you can use to look up information about how to use the program or to solve problems. Usually, you can press the F1 key or click a Help icon to start Help.

Working with Two or More Programs

The term **multitasking** means working with more than one computer application at the same time. Computer operating systems allow you to multitask by giving sections of memory to each application that is running. You can then switch among them as needed.

To multitask, open the desired programs, such as a word processor and a spreadsheet. Each application appears in a separate window. Select one window by clicking its button on the taskbar, and begin to work. You can move from one window to another. If you create a chart in a spreadsheet, you can cut or copy and paste it into the word processor. When you are done, exit each application to close your programs.

Figure 10.3.4 Multitasking means using more than one program at a time.

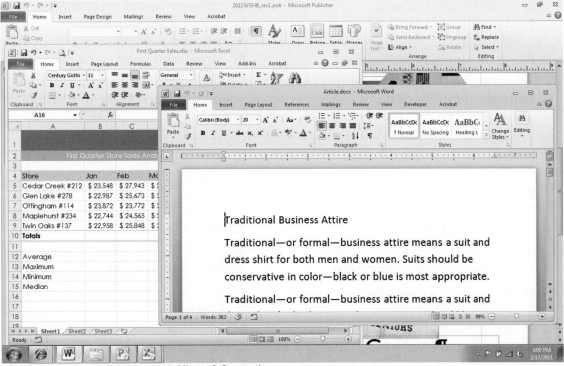

Excel 2013, Word 2013, Publisher 2013, Microsoft Corporation.

Use the Vocabulary

Directions: *Match each vocabulary term in the left column with the correct definition in the right column.*

_____ 1. vertical application
_____ 2. horizontal application
_____ 3. beta version
_____ 4. copy protection
_____ 5. documentation
_____ 6. version
_____ 7. site license
_____ 8. application workspace
_____ 9. zoom
_____ 10. preference

a. permission to install software on multiple computers
b. main area of a program window
c. a program designed for a limited purpose
d. a general-purpose program that can be used by a variety of users
e. tool that keeps a user from making unauthorized copies of software
f. instructions that make using software easier
g. to change the size of the data on the screen
h. test copy of software that companies use to find errors
i. setting defined by the computer user
j. copy of software that may have new features

Check Your Comprehension

Directions: *Determine the correct choice for each of the following.*

1. Which of the following is an example of a vertical application?
   a. an Internet browser
   b. a library card catalog
   c. a popular personal information manager
   d. an inexpensive spreadsheet

2. Which of the following is NOT an example of multitasking?
   a. switching from one program to another
   b. moving data to a different document
   c. keeping your desktop clear
   d. working in three or four applications at once

3. Software documentation can help you do which of the following?
   a. troubleshoot problems
   b. obtain a site license
   c. make an application vertical
   d. create a new version

4. Which of the following is NOT a characteristic of a maintenance release?
   a. minor revisions to existing features
   b. minor features added
   c. letter added to the version number
   d. significant improvements

5. Changing the zoom controls allows you to do which of the following?
   a. change the font of the data on the screen
   b. adjust the size of the data on the screen
   c. change the order in which the data is displayed on the screen
   d. adjust the document's margins

6. Which of the following menus would a word processor most likely have?
   a. Calculate
   b. Message
   c. Sound Controls
   d. Edit

Chapter Review and Assessment

Think Critically

Directions: *Answer the following questions.*

1. What are some consequences of violating copyright laws to both software companies and to users?

2. In what ways do beta versions help improve new software applications?

3. Why is good documentation important?

4. Why might a user choose to upgrade to a newer version of a particular software application?

5. How are the terms *default* and *preferences* related?

Extend Your Knowledge

Directions: *Choose and complete one of the following projects.*

A. Horizontal applications are popular types of software, such as word processors and Internet browsers, with which most computer users work. Vertical applications are designed for more specific activities. Interview two adults who use computers for their jobs. Identify the types of applications they use at work. What programs do they use that are specific to their careers or businesses? How do they use popular applications differently? For both types of software, to what extent do licensing agreements and customer service/ technical support influence their purchasing decisions? Create a Venn diagram comparing your findings.

B. Several types of documentation are listed in this chapter, including printed material, help screens, and Web sites. Using the Internet or other resources, prepare a report that discusses documentation. Discuss the purpose of each type of documentation. How and when might you need to use each—now and in the future? What are some of the different features available in each type of documentation? Share your reports with the class.

Chapter Review and Assessment

Word-Processing Basics

What Is Word Processing? In 1968, IBM first used the term *word processing*. The term described machines that could be used to type a document, remember the typist's keystrokes, and produce more than one copy. With this new tool, workers saved time.

That was just the beginning. Today's word-processing programs do much more. Suppose you were writing something by hand and made a mistake or changed your mind about what you wanted to say. If you were using a pen, you would probably cross out the words you wanted to change. Doing that leaves the page messy, though. With word-processing software, you can change the text and still create neat pages. You can even save what you typed and use it again a day, a week, or even a year later.

Chapter Outline

Creating a Document

Objectives

- List the four basic functions of word-processing programs.
- Name two tools used to navigate a word-processing document.
- Summarize four key features of word-processing programs.
- Identify three standards for word-processing documents.

🔑 Key Terms

- AutoCorrect
- autosave
- insertion point
- pagination
- word-processing program
- word wrap

As You Read

Organize Information Complete a spider map to help you organize basic facts about word processing as you read.

Functions of Word-Processing Programs

Word-processing programs are used for creating and printing text documents. These programs have four functions:

- writing—entering text and symbols into a document
- editing—revising or reorganizing the text
- formatting—changing how the text looks on the page
- printing—producing a printed copy

These tasks do not need to be done all at once or even in the order shown here. Whatever the order, these four functions are at the heart of word processing.

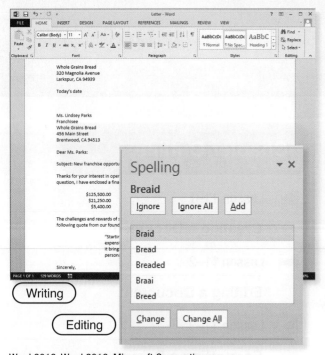

Writing

Editing

Word 2013, Word 2016, Microsoft Corporation.

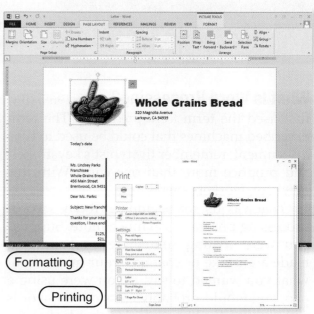

Formatting

Printing

Word 2013, Microsoft Corporation.

Figure 11.1.1 The four main functions of a word-processing program.

Uses of Word Processing

Word-processing programs can be used to create almost any kind of printed document, such as letters, reports, and brochures. They can also be used to create calendars, return-address labels, and labels for homemade CDs. It is no surprise that word-processing software is the application that people use more than any other application.

Working with a Word-Processing Document

A new, blank word-processing document looks like a blank piece of paper on the screen. The program is ready for you to start writing. You can create another document at any time. For example, in Microsoft Word you create a new document by clicking the File tab, clicking the New command, selecting Blank Document, and clicking the Create button. Most word-processing programs allow you to create a new document using shortcut keys. For example, in a Windows-based program press Ctrl+N (hold the Ctrl key and press N). In Mac OS, press Command+N.

Click File > Save As to use the Save As command to save a new document. When the Save As dialog box opens, name your document, select a storage location, and click Save.

Insertion Point The **insertion point** shows where the text you type will appear. It moves as you type.

Scrolling As you write, you might want to reread or change something you wrote earlier. That is made easy by scrolling—using the mouse or keyboard to move through the document.

Technology @ School

Some students sharpen their word-processing skills by writing to pen pals in other countries.

Think About It!

Before writing a letter, think about the topics you could cover. Which items listed below would you discuss in a pen-pal letter?

➤ your family

➤ your school

➤ your hometown

➤ your math class

➤ your favorite movie

Figure 11.1.2 All word-processing programs share basic features, but commands may be located on a different toolbar or menu.

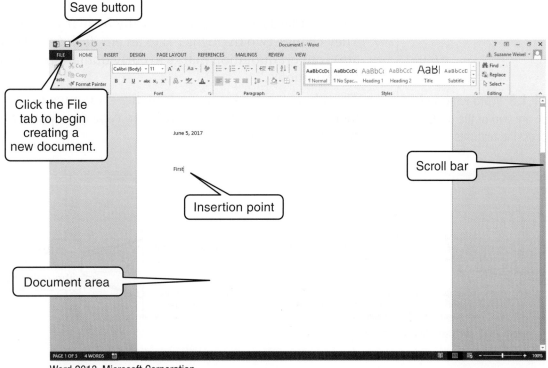

Save button

Click the File tab to begin creating a new document.

Scroll bar

Insertion point

Document area

Word 2013, Microsoft Corporation.

Copy Editor Copy editors check documents for correct spelling, grammar, and consistency of style. Although some copy editors work on hard copy, or paper, many edit soft copy, or electronic files. Among the problems they look for are inconsistent or wrong formats, such as incorrect em dashes, en dashes, and spacing, or unacceptable hyphenation generated by the word processor.

You can scroll up or down by using the mouse to click the scroll bar or drag the scroll box at the right of the document window. Many mouse devices have scrolling wheels. You can also use the Up and Down arrow keys or the Page Up, Page Down, Home, and End keys to move around in the document.

Basic Features

Most word-processing programs have these features to help you write, edit, and save your work.

- With **word wrap**, the program automatically starts a new line, or "wraps" the text, when the current line is full. If you wish to force text onto a new line, press Enter or Return.

- When a page is full, the **pagination** feature automatically starts a new page. You can also force a new page by inserting a special character, called a page break.

- The **AutoCorrect** feature fixes common spelling mistakes as they are typed. You can turn off this feature or modify it to accept unusual words that you often use.

- The AutoRecover or **autosave** feature automatically saves a document as often as you want. If the computer shuts down accidentally, you can retrieve the most recently saved version.

- The spelling checker identifies spelling and grammar errors and suggests corrections. You can select a suggestion, ignore the error, or type the correction yourself.

Typing Standards for Word-Processing Documents

As you write, keep in mind three standards of style to make your work look professional.

- Two standards are met automatically by many programs. They change two hyphens (--) to an em dash (—). They also convert quotation marks to curly quotation marks, or "smart quotes."

- The other standard is not automatic—you have to remember to do it. This standard is to type one space, not two, between sentences.

Figure 11.1.3 Word wrap and pagination are two of the basic word-processing features.

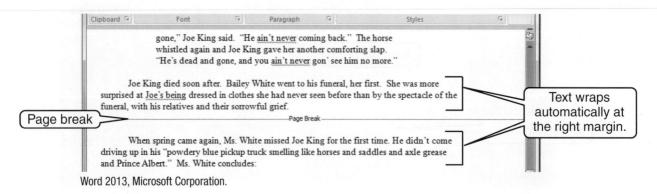

Word 2013, Microsoft Corporation.

Editing a Document

Objectives

- Explain how to identify document files in a list of files.
- Describe the benefits of selecting text.
- Contrast different editing tools, such as the Cut and Copy commands, and the Undo and Redo commands.

As You Read

Identify Cause and Effect Complete a cause-and-effect chart to help you identify what happens when word-processing functions are applied as you read.

Opening a Document for Editing

Editing can take place at any time after you have created the document. You can go back and edit text you recently entered, or you can edit a document you created, saved, and closed. To do so, you open the file so you can work on it again.

You can use a word-processing program's Open command to open a file, or you can use your operating system's file management features to find files on a disk. In Windows, file names have extensions, such as .txt, .rtf, .docx, or .wpd, although these extensions may be hidden from view. On a Macintosh computer, documents are simply listed by file name.

Word-processing programs make editing easy. You can add words simply by typing them. You can delete characters by pressing the Delete or Backspace keys. Powerful features in these programs help you do even more.

Selecting Text

To change text already entered in a document, you must **select** it. Then you can delete it, move it, copy it, or change its formatting.

To select text, click and drag over the text you want. Most programs also let you select text by using the keyboard. You hold down the Shift key while you use the arrow keys and other keys to select the text. Selected text is highlighted on the screen; that is, it appears with a different background color. To help you select just the text you need, use the Show/Hide command to display nonprinting characters, such as paragraph marks, tabs, and spaces.

🔑 Key Terms

- Clipboard
- Copy
- Cut
- data source
- mail merge
- Paste
- Redo
- select
- Undo

Cutting, Copying, and Pasting

Two common reasons for selecting text are cutting and copying. Both actions place the text in the Clipboard.

The Clipboard The **Clipboard** stores cut or copied text while you work. Once you close the program or shut down the computer, items on the Clipboard are no longer available. Some programs store only one item at a time, so cutting or copying new text replaces what was held before. Some programs can hold many items on the Clipboard.

- The **Cut** command removes the selected text from a document and places it on the Clipboard.
- The **Copy** command places a duplicate of the selected text on the Clipboard.

Pasting Use the **Paste** command to insert an item copied or cut to the Clipboard. Simply place the insertion point where you want the item to appear. Then, click the Paste icon on the Clipboard group of the Home tab or press Ctrl+V. The copied item or text appears where you want it.

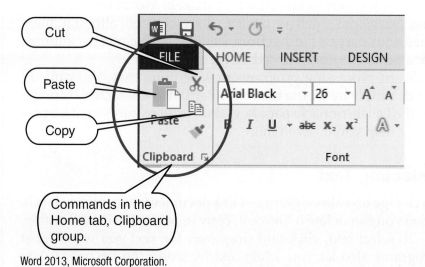

Word 2013, Microsoft Corporation.

Figure 11.2.1 The Cut, Copy, and Paste buttons are located in the Clipboard group in Microsoft Word.

Moving   Moving a sentence from the middle of a paragraph to the beginning can be done by selecting and dragging it. You can use Cut and Paste to move that sentence farther—for example, to another page—or to move text or a graphic from one document to another. You can even open a new window, paste the text you cut from another document, and save the pasted text as a new document.

Copying   Copying and pasting saves time when you need to repeat some text. You can also copy and paste to bring a graphic from one document into another.

Undoing and Redoing

Word-processing programs have commands that can undo or cancel an edit. If you delete a word by mistake, you can use the **Undo** command to put it back. Many programs also have a **Redo** command. You can use this feature to put a change back in effect after cancelling it with Undo.

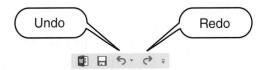

Word 2013, Microsoft Corporation.

Figure 11.2.2 The Undo and Redo commands are on the Quick Access toolbar in Microsoft Office programs.

Merging

Most word-processing programs have a **mail merge** feature you can use to generate customized form letters, mailing labels, envelopes, and even e-mails. You create a word-processing document that includes the content you want everyone to receive and then merge it with a **data source** of customized information, such as names and addresses.

The Copy command isn't suitable if the copied text will change.

Think About It!

Think about what the Copy command does. For which items below would the copy command be useful? For which would it not be useful?

➤ the delivery address for letters to different people

➤ the cook's name on the top of recipe cards

➤ the title of a CD in a list of CDs

➤ a paragraph to appear in two different letters

Formatting a Document

Objectives

- Explain what default formatting is.
- Identify four parts of any document that can be formatted.
- Summarize the advantages of dividing a document into sections for formatting.
- Compare portrait and landscape orientation.

As You Read

Summarize Complete a summary chart to help you identify different features that can be formatted as you read the lesson.

🔑 Key Terms

- default
- page formatting
- sans serif font
- section
- serif font

Figure 11.3.1 Dialog boxes like these let you change all sorts of formatting options.

Appearance Is Important

A document's formatting—its appearance—is sometimes as important as its contents. This is why word-processing programs have so many tools to format documents.

Word-processing programs include many preset formats, called **defaults**. The program applies these formats automatically, unless you change them. For example, many word processors use Times New Roman as the default font. Microsoft Word, however, uses Calibri, but you can change to a different font whenever you want.

You can format four distinct parts of a document: characters, paragraphs, sections, and pages.

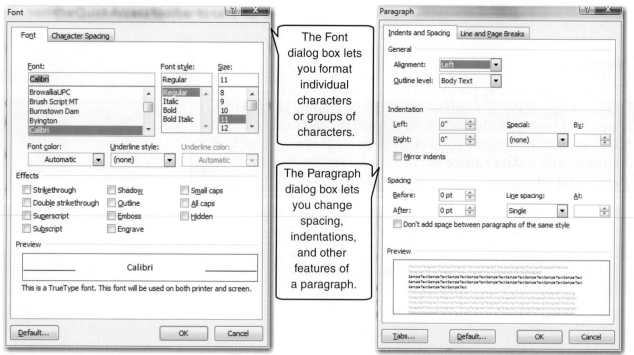

The Font dialog box lets you format individual characters or groups of characters.

The Paragraph dialog box lets you change spacing, indentations, and other features of a paragraph.

Word 2013, Microsoft Corporation.

Word 2013, Microsoft Corporation.

Formatting Characters

Character formatting lets you change the look of letters. Three primary formats are applied to characters:

- The font is the family of characters used. A font is a named set of characters that have the same appearance.
- Font size is the height of characters, measured in points. One point equals 1/72 inch.
- Font styles are characteristics such as boldface and italic.

There are four general categories of fonts. **Serif fonts**, such as Times New Roman, have serifs, or lines projecting from the ends. They are easy to read and are often used for document text. **Sans serif fonts**, such as Arial, do not have serifs, and are often used for headings. Script fonts are used to simulate handwriting. Decorative fonts have embellishments such as curlicues.

Categories of Fonts

Category	Description	Example
Serif	Serifs, or decorative flourishes, project from the ends. Easy to read in print. Often used for paragraph text.	Times New Roman Cambria
Sans Serif	No serifs. Often used for headings. Easy to read on a screen.	Arial Tahoma
Script	Simulate handwriting. Characters appear connected or almost connected. Formal script fonts usually neat and flowing. Informal script fonts usually messy and more natural.	Edwardian Script ITC Mistral
Decorative	Artistic. May have embellishments, such as curlicues. Also called ornamental or display fonts.	Jokerman Chiller

Formatting Paragraphs

A paragraph is any text that ends with the press of the Enter key. Whenever you press Enter, you create a paragraph. You can change many paragraph formats, including:

- Alignment—This is the way a paragraph lines up between the page's left and right margins.
- Line spacing—This is the amount of space between the lines of text in a paragraph.
- Indentation—This is added space between a margin and the text.
- Tabs—These are stops placed along a line. Pressing the Tab key moves the insertion point to the next stop. Tabs can be used to align text in tables or columns.

You can apply these paragraph formats through dialog boxes, but you also can apply some of them by using ruler settings. In Word, for example, you can create a tab stop by clicking the horizontal ruler at the point where the tab stop should be. You can change a paragraph's indentation by dragging indent markers, which normally are found at each end of the ruler. Ruler settings apply only to the paragraph that contains the insertion point, or to selected paragraphs.

Figure 11.3.2 A key feature of a word-processing program is the ability to align and position text on the page.

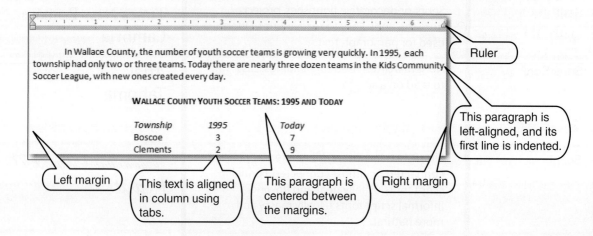

In Wallace County, the number of youth soccer teams is growing very quickly. In 1995, each township had only two or three teams. Today there are nearly three dozen teams in the Kids Community Soccer League, with new ones created every day.

WALLACE COUNTY YOUTH SOCCER TEAMS: 1995 AND TODAY

Township	1995	Today
Boscoe	3	7
Clements	2	9

Ruler

This paragraph is left-aligned, and its first line is indented.

Left margin

This text is aligned in column using tabs.

This paragraph is centered between the margins.

Right margin

Formatting Sections

In some word processors, a **section** is part of a document that contains specific format settings. A document begins as one section, but you can insert section breaks to divide the document into more than one section. You can format each section in its own unique way. For example, in a most newsletters, the first section is one column, so the title spans the width of the page, but the next section is two columns, allowing more articles to fit on the page.

Formatting Pages

Page formatting affects how and where text is positioned on the page. The main features in page formatting are:

- Paper size—Various sizes of paper can be used to create documents.
- Orientation—Text can be printed in one or two directions, or orientations. In portrait orientation, text is printed down the page's long edge, creating a page that is taller than it is wide. In landscape orientation, text is printed down the page's short edge, creating a page that is wider than it is tall.
- Margins—This is the space between the four paper edges and the text. This open space frames the page and can make the text easier to read.
- Headers and footers—This is special information placed at the top of the page—headers—or at the bottom—footers. These areas can show page numbers, the date, or the document's title.
- Graphics—These include drawings, photographs, or other images. Some graphics, like charts and graphs, are informative. Others are decorative. Many word-processing programs let you create or add graphics.

Did You Know?

Although many files are output electronically, most word-processing documents are designed for printing. Blurry or faded text, uneven margins, or incorrect paper size are just some of the printing problems that can ruin your final document.

Think About It!

How can you avoid the following printing problems before they occur?

- ➤ misaligned print heads causing uneven printing
- ➤ low ink or toner causing faded or missing text
- ➤ uneven margins causing the document to look unbalanced
- ➤ incorrect paper size causing the text to overflow the page
- ➤ incorrect paper size causing too much white space

Figure 11.3.3 Word-processing programs let you print documents in portrait and landscape orientations.

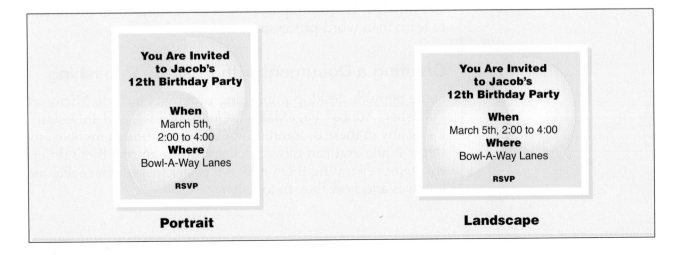

Portrait

Landscape

Basics of Desktop Publishing

Objectives

- Describe the benefits of creating documents in a desktop-publishing program.
- Compare word-processing and desktop-publishing programs.
- Summarize the basic steps in desktop publishing.

As You Read

Organize Information Complete a sequence chart to help you organize basic facts about desktop publishing as you read the lesson.

 Key Terms

- crop
- desktop-publishing
- frame
- layout
- master page

Publishing from a Desktop

Desktop-publishing (DTP) programs are used to create high-quality publications that look as if they were produced on a printing press. They can be used to do some of the same tasks as word-processing programs, but they greatly expand design options so you can create high-quality documents.

Word-processing and DTP programs complement each other. In fact, they are often used together. Text is frequently created and edited in a word processor, and then that text is brought into a DTP program to be formatted for publishing.

Benefits of DTP Desktop-publishing software gives you tools you can use to produce the files and fonts for large projects, such as books, magazines, and other complex printed materials. DTP software also gives you more control over the final product than you would have if you hired a professional contractor or other "outside" source.

Drawbacks of DTP Desktop publishing is not without its problems. Often it is a team effort, which means that the work of writers, editors, artists, and layout specialists has to be carefully coordinated. These complex programs can also be more difficult to learn than word-processing software.

Creating a Document with Desktop Publishing

Some popular desktop-publishing programs include Microsoft Publisher, Adobe® PageMaker®, QuarkXPress®, and InDesign®. Using any of these programs to publish a document involves six steps. While you can move back and forth among these different steps, separating them makes it easier to see what each one involves and how they fit together.

Designing the Layout The most important task—and the one that is done first—is designing the document's **layout**. A designer plans how each page will look by creating a **master page**. This provides the pattern for all the pages to follow and sets the basic features of the document's look, including:

- page size and margins
- number of columns, width of columns, and space between columns
- type font, size, and treatment for all the major elements that will be repeated in the document, such as titles, headings, text, and headers and footers
- rules that will be followed in placing, sizing, and treating images

The columns on the master page create areas called **frames**. Frames are simply empty containers that will eventually hold text or graphics. They will be filled as you add text and images to the document.

Entering Text Text can be placed in the frames by typing it, but desktop-publishing software is not well suited to entering text. Therefore, text is usually created and edited in a word-processing program. Then, that text is automatically placed in the DTP frames, filling as many pages as needed.

If the writer has formatted the text by using styles in the word processor, the DTP software may be able to use those styles to identify and format different parts of the document automatically.

Comparing Word-Processing and Desktop-Publishing

Word-Processing Programs	Desktop-Publishing Programs
Emphasizes content—the text	Emphasizes appearance—layout and the mix of text and graphics
Can import many kinds of graphics	Can import many kinds of graphics
Can format text in many ways	Has more tools for formatting text and for combining text and graphics
Can produce relatively simple documents, such as brochures and newsletters	Can produce very complex documents, including magazines and books
Effective at black-and white documents; not effective with full-color documents	Effective with both black-and-white and full-color documents
Prints on standard office machines such as laser and inkjet printers	Prints on high-quality printers

Workers who do desktop publishing are called graphic designers. There are about 200,000 graphic designers in the United States. Most work for companies, but about one third work for themselves.

The Bureau of Labor Statistics says that in the next few years the number of jobs for desktop publishers will grow by a huge amount—about 67 percent.

Interested students can take courses in design at some colleges and professional schools. Of course, experience in using computers is a great plus!

Importing Graphics   After the text has been imported, images can be added. A location for each image is found. The text then wraps around the art.

Laying Out the Document   A DTP user then formats the document by adjusting the size of art and the use of space to make the page attractive and easy to read. Program tools make it easy to change an image's size or shape or rotate it. Other tools can be used to **crop** the image, or trim it to focus only on certain parts.

Checking and Revising   DTP documents are often printed several times before they are finished. Editors review these versions, called proofs, to make sure that no text has been lost and that the text reads correctly. Designers check design elements. Then DTP users make changes to the document.

Printing   After the document is final, it is printed. Sometimes, DTP documents are published on the Web or are printed on powerful color laser printers. Items such as books and magazines are sent to printers who print and bind finished copies. For color documents, the DTP program can prepare color separations, which are separate versions of the document's pages. Each version contains a specific set of colors; each of which is applied in a separate pass through the printer. When the colors are combined, the full-color document is finished.

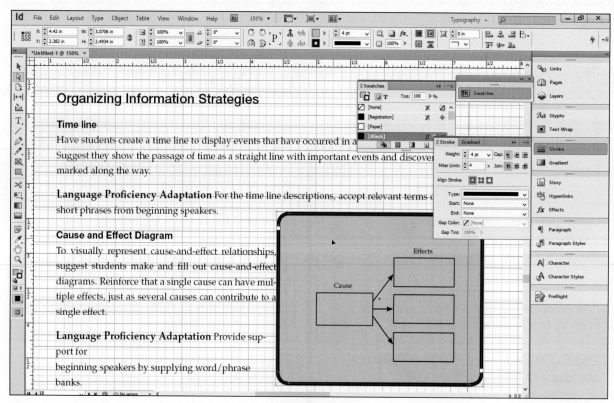

Figure 11.4.1 Designing a page in a desktop-publishing program.

Use the Vocabulary

Directions: *Match each vocabulary term in the left column with the correct definition in the right column.*

_____ 1. insertion point
_____ 2. word wrap
_____ 3. pagination
_____ 4. AutoCorrect
_____ 5. select text
_____ 6. Clipboard
_____ 7. default
_____ 8. section
_____ 9. page format

a. features that identify how and where text is positioned

b. a separate part of a document with its own formatting

c. area where cut or copied text is temporarily stored

d. fixes common spelling mistakes as they are typed

e. shows the place in a document where text will be added or deleted

f. automatically moves text to a new line

g. the automatic division of a document into pages

h. action made on a block of text before changing it

i. preset formats

Check Your Comprehension

Directions: *Complete each sentence with information from the chapter.*

1. The four functions of word processing are writing, editing, _____, and printing.

2. The _____ feature protects you from losing work because you forgot to save.

3. One standard of word processing is to have only one space after each _____.

4. Some programs add extra characters, called a(n) _____, to a file name.

5. The _____ command lets you restore a change that you have just undone.

6. You can repeat a sentence in more than one location in the same document—or in other documents—by using the _____ and Paste commands.

7. _____ programs are used to create high-quality publications that look as if they were produced on a printing press.

8. One _____ equals 1/72 inch.

9. Indentation refers to the _____ between a margin and the text in a paragraph.

10. An example of a(n) _____ is a page number that appears at the bottom of every page in a report.

 **Think Critically**

Directions: *Answer the following questions.*

1. What is the difference between a serif font and a sans serif font? Give examples of each.

2. Why is selecting text an important function in word processing?

3. Why are there both mouse and keyboard methods for performing actions such as selecting, cutting, copying, and pasting?

4. What is the difference between landscape and portrait orientation?

5. Why might a student type his or her name and the class period in the header of a homework assignment?

Extend Your Knowledge

Directions: *Choose and complete one of the following projects.*

A. Open a word-processing program and type these directions in full. Add the heading *Formatting Sample* above the first line of text. Then do the following: (1) Copy your text and paste the copy below the first paragraph; (2) Format the text by changing fonts and type size; (3) Change the page to landscape orientation; (4) Apply a page background; (5) Add a header; and (6) Print your document. Remember to save your file.

B. Open a word-processing program. Choose one of the menus on the menu bars or Ribbon tabs. Write down the items listed on the menu or the groups listed on the tab. Choose two of the menu items or one of the groups. Look up the commands in the Help system. Take notes on what you read. Make a presentation to the class describing which actions result from choosing each command. Identify a way that someone could use the commands in working on a document.

C. With your teacher's permission, conduct research on different word-processing programs. Record your findings in a chart so you can compare and contrast the available features. Use critical thinking skills to select the program you think would be best for creating documents for business communication. Explain your selection to a partner or to the class.

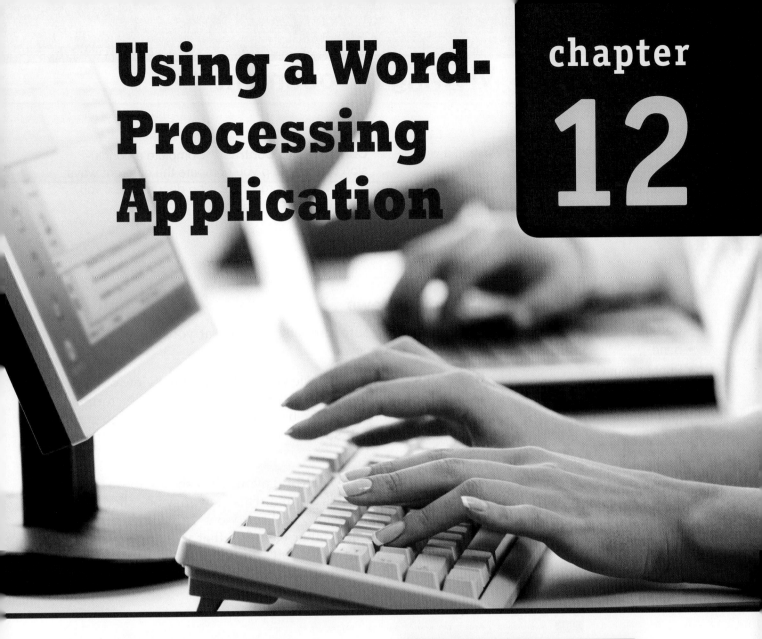

Using a Word-Processing Application

chapter 12

What Does Word Processing Do? In 1875, Mark Twain sent his publisher a historic manuscript. It was the first time that an author submitted a manuscript that had been written using a typewriter. Now, more than 125 years later, word-processing software does far more than a typewriter ever could. As discussed in Chapter 11, you can format text, add graphics, and even print documents in color.

In this chapter, you learn more about the word-processing tools you can use to create neat and professional documents. You learn how to select a view, how to insert pictures and symbols, and how to prepare a document for printing. Finally, you explore the options for collaborating with others to improve your work.

Chapter Outline

 Lesson 12–1

Viewing a Document

 Lesson 12–2

Enhancing a Document

 Lesson 12–3

Formatting and Printing

 Lesson 12–4

Making and Tracking Edits

Viewing a Document

Objectives

- Compare different document views in a word-processing program.
- Describe the benefits of using split windows.
- Explain how to use a document map to move through a document.

As You Read

Compare and Contrast Complete a conclusion chart to help you compare the different ways of viewing a word-processing document as you read.

Key Terms

- document map
- pane
- Print Layout view
- Web Layout view

Changing Views

Word-processing software lets you look at your documents in several different views.

Basic View The most basic view, called Normal view or Draft view, shows text in the correct font and has character formatting like bold and italic. The basic view does not display certain parts of a document, such as margins, headers and footers, or columns.

Print Layout View The **Print Layout view** shows how a document will look when it is printed. This view may be called Page Layout view, Layout view, or Page view. It includes all text, graphics, margins, and other elements that will appear on the printed page. In this view, you can edit headers and footers, change margins, and work with columns and graphics.

Figure 12.1.1 A Word document in Print Layout view.

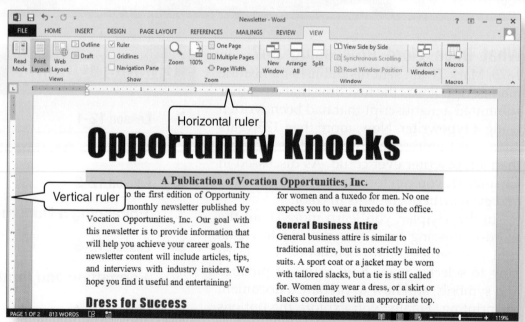

Word 2013, Microsoft Corporation.

Web Layout View Some word-processing programs have a **Web Layout view**, which shows how a document will appear when published on the World Wide Web.

Outline View An Outline view reveals the structure of a document. It breaks down the document into its major headings, subheadings, and text. You can choose to view only the main headings, both the headings and subheadings, or everything, including the entire text. This view is useful when editing a large document. Some programs let users rearrange large amounts of text simply by dragging outline headings from one place to another.

Ruler Settings Some views display a horizontal ruler—a guide at the top of the document window, showing you where each paragraph's tab stops and indents are located. In Word's Page Layout view, you also see a vertical ruler on the left side of the screen. You can use rulers to set margins, tabs, indents, and other paragraph formats.

Changing Views It's easy to change from one view to another. Just go to the View menu and select the option you want. Some programs also have small icons representing different views near the status bar. Clicking an icon changes the view.

Zooming In and Out

The Zoom feature changes the size of the text displayed on the screen. While larger text is more readable, smaller text allows you to see more at once. But only at 100 percent will you have an accurate picture of the text as it will appear when it is printed. At this percentage, you get the benefit of a program's WYSIWYG (What You See Is What You Get) display, which means that the screen shows how the printed page will look.

Connections

Language Arts A writing style is a set of guidelines for the language, punctuation, and formatting of a document. There are a number of accepted styles, but many teachers prefer the Modern Language Association (MLA) style. Some examples of MLA style rules include double-spaced lines, 1" margins on all sides, and in-text citations of sources. Other commonly used styles include the *Chicago Manual of Style*, which does not require in-text citations, and American Psychological Association (APA) style, which is usually preferred for papers written about the social sciences. Before writing a research paper, ask your teacher which style you should use.

Figure 12.1.2 Use Zoom controls to change the magnification of a document display.

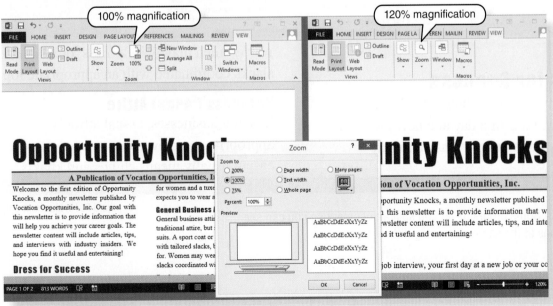

Word 2013, Microsoft Corporation.

Career Corner

Multiple Views of the Same Document

Some word-processing programs allow you to split the document window into two sections, or **panes**. This split screen lets you view two parts of a document at the same time. You can scroll through each pane separately to display any part of the document. This feature makes it easy to move or copy text from one part of a large document to another. You can also use this feature to compare discussions of the same topic in two different parts of a document.

Mapping the Document

Some programs also split the screen by showing text in one pane and a list of the document's headings in the other. This list is called a **document map** or navigation pane. You can use the document map to move about in the document simply by clicking a heading or by using a search feature. In some programs, you can change the display in the navigation pane to show thumbnails or icons representing each page. You can click a page to display it in the main document area.

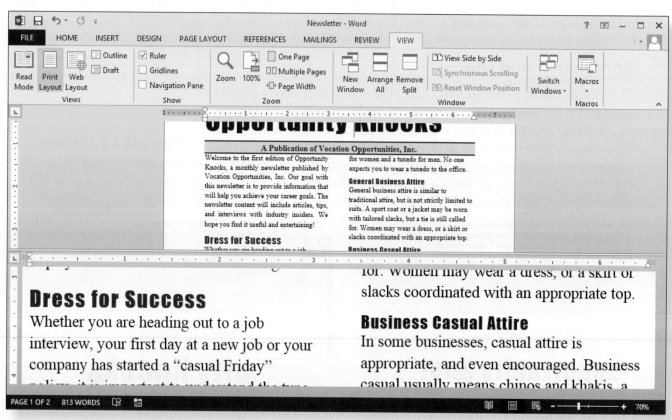

Figure 12.1.3 Some programs let you split a document so you can see different sections at the same time using different views.

Word 2013, Microsoft Corporation.

Enhancing a Document

Objectives

- Identify the advantages of using keyboard shortcuts.
- Explain how to insert special characters or symbols.
- Describe the process for adding clip art.
- Describe uses for the find and replace features.

As You Read

Organize Information   Complete a spider map to help you organize details about different editing features as you read.

Keyboard Shortcuts

Usually, you move the insertion point and select commands using the mouse. Sometimes you may find it easier and faster to keep the fingers of both hands on the keyboard. You may be able to use the keyboard to type, issue commands, and select options quicker than you can move a mouse through a series of menus.

Most programs offer **keyboard shortcuts**, combinations of keys that can carry out some actions. Usually, issuing these commands requires pressing the Control (Ctrl) key in Windows or the Command key in Macintosh in combination with some other key. Ctrl + C, for example, is a Copy shortcut on Windows computers. Some of the shortcuts use a **function key**, one from the row of keys at the top of the keyboard that are labeled F1, F2, and so on.

Key Terms

- find and replace
- function key
- keyboard shortcut

Common Keyboard Shortcuts

Command	Windows	Macintosh
Boldface	Ctrl + B	Command + B
Italic	Ctrl + I	Command + I
Underline	Ctrl + U	Command + U
Cut	Ctrl + X	Command + X
Copy	Ctrl + C	Command + C
Paste	Ctrl + V	Command + V
Undo	Ctrl + Z	Command + Z

Using Special Characters and Symbols

Most word-processing programs allow you to insert special characters and symbols. These are symbols and characters that cannot be created simply by pressing one key. Common symbols can be made using a combination of keys. For example, in some programs you can type (c) to make the copyright symbol ©.

There are too many special characters to have keyboard shortcuts for all of them. Many word-processing programs provide a dialog box that displays all the characters they offer. In Word, to choose a symbol, click the Insert tab and click the Symbol command in the Symbols group.

Adding Art

Suppose you are making a birthday card and want to add a piece of art to decorate it. Many word-processing programs make that easy by providing a collection of ready-to-use drawings called clip art. Most programs have an Insert command for inserting pictures and other media files from as many as three different places:

- the computer's hard drive
- a CD or DVD
- a Web site

Once you insert a picture into a document, you can resize it, move it, and even crop out parts you don't want to show. You can rotate it around an axis point. You can also add effects such as shadows or change the colors. You can also insert other types of graphics, including pictures, shapes, charts, and diagrams.

Figure 12.2.1 Most word-processing progams like Microsoft Word provide access to online clip art galleries.

Finding and Replacing

Suppose you had written an essay about President George Bush. After finishing, you realized you had to make clear that you were writing about George W. Bush and not his father, George Herbert Walker Bush, who also had been president. You can use a powerful word-processing feature to search your essay for every time the name *George Bush* appears. You can even use the program to automatically replace every occurrence of *George Bush* with *George W. Bush*.

Using Find and Replace The **find and replace** (or search and replace) feature lets you:

- locate a word or combination of words
- change those words to other words
- search for text characters, including spaces, punctuation, and symbols
- search for text that is formatted a certain way

In most programs, you select the command for Find and Replace, and then use a dialog box to enter the text to find and the replacement text.

Cautions Use the search and replace feature very carefully. The feature looks for a specific set of letters, not just the word containing that set of letters. Suppose you type *his* as the search term and *hers* as its replacement. Since the program will replace every instance of *his* with *hers*, it will change *history* to *herstory* and *this* to *thers*.

You can avoid this problem by making sure you search for the word *his*, not just the letters *his*. The dialog box typically has an option for searching only for the whole word. Be sure to choose this option to avoid such errors.

Some businesses mail the same letter to many different customers. In these letters, all the text is exactly the same. Only the name and address changes.

Think About It!

Think about a word-processing feature that automatically makes the changes needed in these letters. Which features listed below would be useful for this purpose?

- ➤ changing document views
- ➤ formatting text
- ➤ inserting special characters
- ➤ find and replace
- ➤ merge

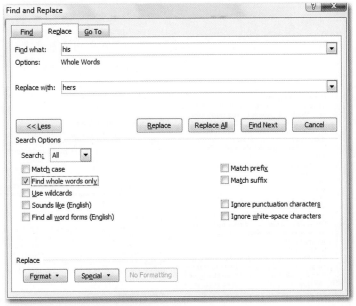

Word 2013, Microsoft Corporation.

Figure 12.2.2 The Find and Replace feature can locate text anywhere in a document and replace it with different text.

Formatting and Printing

Objectives

- Explain how to use styles to format a document.
- Describe how tables can be used to display information.
- Describe the benefits of previewing a document.
- Compare print options.

As You Read

Outline Information Complete an outline to help you identify different ways of creating a professional-looking word-processing document.

🔑 Key Terms

- paragraph
- Print Preview
- style
- style sheet

Applying Styles

A **style** is a set of formats that is applied all at once. You can apply styles to text and to objects. For example, you can apply a style to a heading to quickly format the heading with a set of formats, such as bold, large font size, and an underline. You can apply a style to a picture to change the border or shape, or to add effects. Using styles to apply consistent formatting gives your document a professional look.

Using Styles Styles can be applied to selected characters or to **paragraphs**. Character styles include font formatting, such as font, font size, and font style. Paragraph styles include font formatting and paragraph formatting, such as alignment, line spacing, and tabs.

To apply a paragraph style, place the insertion point in a paragraph, and select the style.

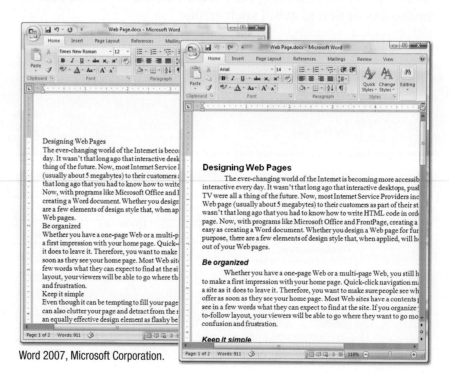

Figure 12.3.1 A document before and after styles were applied.

Word 2007, Microsoft Corporation.

Some programs display each style in the correct font and type size so you can quickly see what it looks like. You simply choose the style you want for the selected paragraph. The program then assigns a set of formats to the paragraph.

Modifying Styles   You can easily change the look of all paragraphs that have the same style. For example, to make all main headings larger, simply edit the *Heading 1* style and change the type size. The program automatically changes the size of all those headings.

Using Style Sheets   Most programs provide a standard **style sheet**, a collection of predefined styles that go together. For instance, there are styles for text, headings, page numbers, headers, lists, and so on.

You can probably find styles you want to use in the standard set of styles. If not, you can modify existing styles or even design new ones.

Presenting Information in Tables or Lists

Suppose you wanted to show the batting averages of the players on your school's baseball team. You could do this by writing a paragraph, but tables let you compare this information more easily by placing it in columns and rows. Columns run down the table; rows go across.

In some programs, you insert tables by using the Insert menu. Others have a special Table menu. In Word, the Tables group is on the Insert tab. These methods make it easy to add a table to your document and format it. You can even add color and shading so different parts of the table stand out.

When you don't need multiple columns, you can format text as a bulleted or numbered list. Use numbers when the order matters, like for directions. Use bullets when the order does not matter. Most programs have commands that quickly apply list formatting.

Printing a Document

Although some documents are designed to be viewed on a monitor, people usually print the reports, greeting cards, letters, and posters they create.

Print Preview   Before printing a document, you can see how it will look by selecting the feature called **Print Preview**. Print Preview shows everything in a document—margins, graphics, headers, page numbers, and text. If you change margins and edit text while in Print Preview, you will immediately see these changes on your document.

Technology @ School

Tables and clip art aren't the only graphics that can be brought into documents. Word processors can bring in or create charts and graphs.

Think About It!

Think about the kinds of graphics you could use in school assignments. Which items listed below would be good ways to use charts, graphs, and tables at school?

➤ graph showing students' results with an experiment in science class

➤ chart for a book report in English class

➤ graph showing economic growth for social studies class

➤ chart of number of calories in different foods for health class

➤ graph of the popularity of different colors in art class

Figure 12.3.2 Many programs let you select options for printing in a Print dialog box or on a Print tab.

Print Options   To print, you typically go to the File menu and then select Print. This opens a dialog box or tab that gives you several options:

- Printer—If the computer is connected to more than one printer, you can choose which one to use.
- Page range—You can choose to print every page in the document, the current page, or a group of pages.
- Number of copies—You can print one copy of the document, hundreds of copies, or any number in between.
- Print quality—You may be able to print in a faster "draft" mode or in a slower, high-quality mode.
- Orientation—You can select Portrait (the height of the page is greater than the width) or Landscape (the width of the page is greater than the height).
- Paper Size—You can select from a list of standard paper sizes, such a 8.5" x 11", or you can set a custom size.
- Margins—You can select from standard margin widths or set custom margins. You may also be able to select and set gutter widths. Gutters are used in bound publications. The gutter is the margin along the side of the page closest to the binding.

Depending on your printer, you might have other options. For example, if you have a color printer, you may have the option to print documents in black-and-white or grayscale modes. Most printers let you choose to print Collated which means printing multiple copies in 1, 2, 3, order; or Uncollated, which means printing all copies of one page, then all of the next, and so on. You can also usually scale pages to print multiple copies per sheet. If your printer can print in duplex (using both sides of the paper), you can set options to control this feature, too.

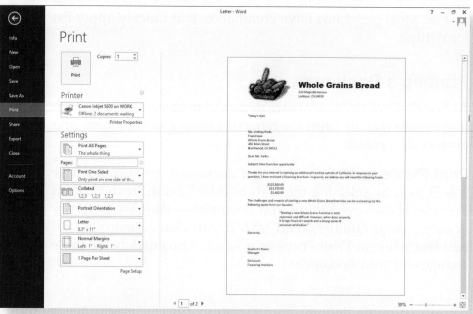

Word 2013, Microsoft Corporation.

Making and Tracking Edits

Objectives

- Explain how to check spelling, grammar, and style.
- Describe the benefits of tracking editing changes.
- Outline the steps for adding comments to a document.

As You Read

Organize Information Complete a chart to help you organize basic facts about checking tools and workgroup editing functions in word-processing programs.

Tools for Correcting Errors

Most word-processing programs offer tools to help with your writing. These tools check spelling, grammar, and writing style.

Spelling Checker The **spelling checker** matches each word in the text against a word list built into the program and gives you options for correcting a misspelling. You can accept one of the spellings or ignore the suggested change. You can also add a word to the word list so the program will accept it in the future. You can use the spelling checker in two ways:

- Check spelling as you type. The program highlights possible errors as they occur. In some programs, you can click the error to find different spellings and then quickly choose one.

- Check a word, a selection, or a whole document. As each possible spelling error is displayed, you decide whether to keep the original spelling or change it.

Spelling checkers are useful, but they accept words as long as they are spelled correctly—even if they are used incorrectly. You need to proofread your documents carefully even if you use the spelling checker.

Key Terms

- grammar checker
- spelling checker
- style checker
- Track Changes

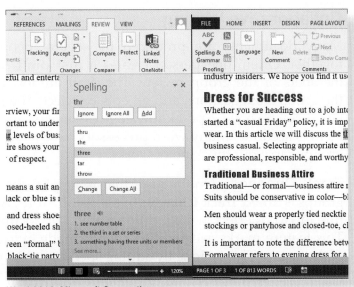

Word 2013, Microsoft Corporation.

Figure 12.4.1 Use the spelling checker to check spelling in a document.

Some programs can connect users to Web translation services. There, a computer program will translate text from one language into another. One word-processing program that has links to this kind of service cautions that "important or sensitive documents" should be translated by a person.

Think About It!

Think about situations in which the translation feature might be used. Which examples listed below do you think could safely be translated by computer?

➤ a government document

➤ a movie review

➤ a newspaper article

➤ a letter from a lawyer

➤ a person's medical records

Grammar and Style Checkers You can run grammar and style checks as you type, or you can check a selection or the entire document at once. Either way, the program highlights potential errors. You can examine each one and accept or ignore the suggested correction.

Grammar checkers look for problems such as errors in the use of verb tenses, pronouns, punctuation, and capitalization. For instance, the program would suggest fixing the sentence "He had ran yesterday." The grammar checker also finds sentence fragments (incomplete sentences) and run-on sentences (two sentences joined together incorrectly).

Style checkers suggest ways to improve the writing style in a document. They let you know whether a sentence is unclear or too wordy or long. They offer alternatives to the use of contractions or language that is too informal.

Most programs also include a Thesaurus feature that lets you look up definitions, synonyms, and antonyms for words. You can use a thesaurus to improve your writing by replacing overused or boring words.

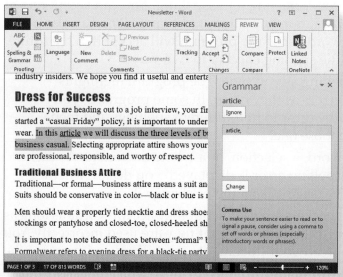

Word 2013, Microsoft Corporation.

Figure 12.4.2 Checking grammar in a document.

Collaborative Writing

Many documents are produced by several people working together. Often, one person creates a first draft, which other members of the group review. The draft author then reviews the group's suggestions and accepts or rejects them. This way, workers who have expert knowledge can make sure that a document is accurate. Many word processors have features that help groups carry out this kind of work.

Track Changes One feature that is helpful for working in groups is called **Track Changes** in Microsoft Word. A similar feature in WordPerfect is the red-line method of document review. This feature marks each editing change made by each member of the group. This is done by adding specific marks to the document at the point where the changes were made.

- Inserted text is shown in a specific color assigned to each group member.
- Deleted text is not removed but appears in the assigned color with a line running through the words.
- In some programs, special boxes name the person who made the change.

When the original author reviews the document, he or she can choose to accept or reject each suggested change.

Comments   Some programs let group members add notes to a document without changing the document's text. Microsoft Word does so using the Comment feature. In most programs, including Microsoft Word, to insert a comment, click Review and then click New Comment. A special pane appears at the bottom or edge of the screen, ready for you to type your comment.

Several people can add comments to a document, and the program tracks each person's comments. That way, the author can see who added what remarks to the document. Comments can be hidden or deleted, and a comment's text can be formatted and edited just like normal text.

Document Protection   Most programs let you protect a document from unauthorized changes. Protection options range from allowing users to read but not edit or format a document to allowing only those with a password to open the document.

Technology@School

Tools that check spelling and grammar as you type are useful for correcting errors, but what if you use alternative methods to input text?

Think About It!

You can help yourself create error-free documents by practicing enunciation and reading skills for use with speech-recognition programs, and digital penmanship for use with handwriting-recognition programs. Work with your teacher to create a plan for developing these skills. It will help you improve academically in all areas.

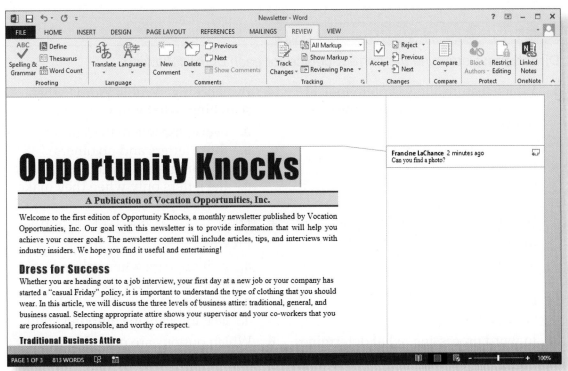

Word 2013, Microsoft Corporation.

Figure 12.4.3 Comments can appear in small boxes in the document's margins.

Use the Vocabulary

Directions: *Match each vocabulary term in the left column with the correct definition in the right column.*

_____ **1.** Print Layout view
_____ **2.** Web Layout view
_____ **3.** pane
_____ **4.** document map
_____ **5.** keyboard shortcut
_____ **6.** function key
_____ **7.** find and replace
_____ **8.** paragraph
_____ **9.** style sheet
_____ **10.** Print Preview

a. text in a document up to a forced new line

b. screen that shows a document's text and a list of its headings

c. feature that finds a word and puts another in its place

d. document display that shows how page elements will look when published on the Web

e. print feature that shows everything in a document as it will look when printed

f. holds formats for all elements in a document

g. document display that shows how page elements will look when printed

h. a special key labeled F1, F2, and so on

i. combination of keys that carry out an action

j. partial window seen in split screen

Check Your Comprehension

Directions: *Determine the correct choice for each of the following.*

1. Which feature allows you to look at two parts of a document at the same time?
   a. side-by-side pages
   b. split screen
   c. Document view
   d. Outline view

2. Which of the following keys is used in many keyboard shortcuts?
   a. Backspace
   b. Delete
   c. Escape
   d. Control

3. In word processing, what determines the end of a paragraph?
   a. 20 lines of text
   b. 400 words of text
   c. a forced new line
   d. a forced new page

4. By choosing "Whole Word" when searching, what will you replace?
   a. every case where the letters appear
   b. those letters and no others
   c. all paragraphs with those letters
   d. the letters only when they make a word

5. How does a document look in Print Preview?
   a. as it appears when printed
   b. as it appears on the Web
   c. as it appears on the monitor
   d. as it appears in computer code

6. Which options are provided in the Print dialog box?
   a. bold or italic type
   b. number of copies
   c. size of paper
   d. inserting graphics

Think Critically

Directions: *Answer the following questions.*

1. Why is the document map feature useful for editing large documents?

2. What is the difference between using the mouse to carry out basic commands and using keyboard shortcuts? Which do you think is easier? Why?

3. How do you insert special characters?

4. What do you need to do to bring clip art from a CD into a word-processing document?

5. Suppose you want to create a table to keep track of your test scores in math class. How would you design your table?

Extend Your Knowledge

Directions: *Choose and complete one of the following projects.*

A. Open a word-processing program and create a new document. Locate the AutoCorrect settings and add a word to the list. Input any two paragraphs from this chapter. After you input the text, change the font of the paragraphs. Create a left tab setting for the paragraphs and indent the first lines using that setting. Type "Formatting Practice" as the title at the top, and center that line. With your teacher's permission, record a simple macro to change the document margins, and then run the macro. Alternatively, adjust the page setup to use different margins. Add a header at the top of the page that displays your name and the date. Check and correct the spelling. Review and save your document. Then, print it for your teacher to review.

B. Working with a partner or small group, develop and conduct a survey you can use to learn how many of your classmates use the following computer programs at home: word processing, spreadsheet, database, graphics, e-mail, games, and Web browser. Create a word-processing document. Type the first program type, press Tab and type the number of classmates who use that program. Press Enter and repeat for each of the program types. Select all of the information and convert it to a 2-column table. Sort the table into alphabetical order by program name. Format the table with a table style. With your teacher's permission, print the document.

Word-Processing Activity 1: Writing an Advertisement

DIRECTIONS: *You will use a word-processing program to make changes to the text of an advertising poster.*

1. Start your word-processing program.
2. Open the data file **WP-1_Board**, and save it as **WP-1_Board_xx** in the location where your teacher instructs you to store the files for this activity. Replace *xx* with your own initials or name, as directed by your teacher.
3. Insert a footer that includes your full name and today's date and time. Read the advertisement. Notice that it contains several typographical and grammatical errors.
4. Correct the capitalization error in the first line of text.
5. Use the program's Search feature to locate the incorrect adjective, *Better*, in the second line of text, and replace it with the correct adjective, *Best*.
6. Insert an exclamation point after the word *Difference* at the end of the third line of text.
7. Locate and correct the spelling error in the fourth line of text.
8. The fourth line of text contains a singular noun that should be plural. Locate and correct the incorrect noun usage.
9. The last line of text—the address—is missing punctuation. Identify and insert the correct punctuation.
10. Change the page orientation to landscape.
11. Format the font in the first line of text in 48-pt. bold Impact and apply a Fill - Blue, Accent 1, Shadow effect, if available.
12. Format the font in the second line of text in 26-pt. Arial Black.
13. Select lines three through six of text, and apply 14-pt. Arial Black font formatting.
14. Select lines four through six of text, and apply bullet list formatting with a checkmark as the bullet.
15. Change the font of the last line of text on the page to Arial.
16. Select all text in the document, and center it horizontally.
17. Insert a clip art picture of a skateboarder at the beginning of the third line of text.
18. Size the picture approximately 2.5" high by 2" wide.
19. Set the text wrap to Top and Bottom and center the picture horizontally.
20. Add the button for checking spelling to a toolbar. For example, add the Spelling & Grammar button to the Quick Access Toolbar.

21. Create a new menu, toolbar, or tab named **PRINTING** that contains the Page Setup, Preview and Print, and Quick Print commands. The customized toolbars and/or menu should look similar to Illustration A.

Illustration A

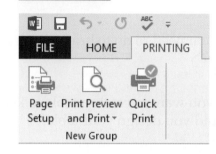

Word 2013, Microsoft Corporation.

22. Working with a classmate or peer editor, use the button on the customized Quick Access Toolbar to check the spelling and grammar and correct errors.
23. Using the customized toolbar and/or menu, preview the document. Make modifications to the text and formatting as necessary.
24. Use your program's Print feature to preview the document. If necessary, adjust the page size, margins, and orientation so the advertisement looks good on the page. With your teacher's permission, print the advertisement.
25. Restore the toolbar and/or menu to their default configuration.
26. Use the Word Count feature of your program to determine the number of pages, words, and characters in the document. Compare these values with a classmate to see if they are the same.
27. With your teacher's permission, use your program's translation feature to translate the document text into another language, and then translate it back into English.
28. Save the document, then close it, and exit your word-processing program.
29. As a class, discuss how language can be used to influence someone's actions and thoughts. List the places where you see advertisements, and discuss what makes some ads more effective than others.

DIRECTIONS: *You will examine the results of a survey. Then, you will use a word-processing program to create a summary of the survey results.*

1. Start your word-processing program.
2. Open the data file **WP-2_Survey**. Save it as **WP-2_Survey_xx** in the location where your teacher instructs you to store the files for this activity. Replace *xx* with your own name or initials, as instructed by your teacher.
3. Read the survey, and then minimize the **WP-2_Survey_xx** document.
4. Open the data file **WP-2_Summary**. Save it as **WP-2_Summary_xx** in the location where your teacher instructs you to store the files for this activity. Replace *xx* with your own name or initials as instructed by your teacher. This document contains a paragraph summarizing the results of the survey. You will use tabs and a table to insert some of the survey results data in the document.
5. Insert a footer that includes your full name and today's date.
6. Move the insertion point to the last blank line in the document, and press Enter twice. Set a center tab at the 3" mark.
7. Tab to the tab stop, and type **Student Survey**. Reveal the formatting of the heading at the top of the page, and then apply the same formatting to the text *Student Survey*.
8. Press Enter.
9. Turn off bold formatting, then insert a table with three columns and three rows.
10. Type **Question**, press Tab, type **Yes**, press Tab, and then type **No**.
11. Move to the left cell in the second row and type **Do you plan to go to college after high school?**. Press Tab.
12. Arrange the two word-processing documents so you can see them both at the same time.
13. Make the **WP-2_Survey_xx** window active.
14. Increase the zoom magnification, then count the ticks under Yes for question 1, and then count the ticks under No.
15. Make the **WP-2_Summary_xx** window active, and type the correct number of Yes responses in the Yes column. Press Tab, and

type the number of No responses in the No column.
16. Move to the left cell in the third row.
17. Type **Do you plan to live in the same state after you finish school?**. Press Tab.
18. Go to the **WP-2_Survey_xx** window. Count the ticks under Yes for question 2, and then count the ticks under No.
19. Return to the **WP-2_Summary_xx** window, and type the correct number of Yes responses. Press Tab, and enter the number of No responses.
20. Check the spelling and grammar, and correct any errors you find.
21. Apply the Grid Table 5 Dark - Accent 1 Table style to the table, if available. If not, apply the formatting of your choice.
22. Exchange documents with a classmate. Proofread your classmate's document carefully and mark spelling and grammar issues using basic proofreader's marks, or as instructed by your teacher. Insert comments to offer constructive criticism and praise.
23. Exchange documents back, and edit your document based on the proofreader's marks.
24. Add the following tag properties to the file: **college plans**; **survey**; **staying in state**. For example, in Word, click the Info tab in Backstage view, click Tags in the right pane, and type the tag text.
25. Use your program's Print feature to preview the document. If necessary, adjust the page size, margins, and orientation so the content looks good on the page. With your teacher's permission, print the document.
26. Close both open documents, saving all changes, and exit your word-processing program.
27. As a class, discuss the survey results. If possible, use the survey questions in your class and compare the results with the sample used in this activity.

DIRECTIONS: *You will use a word-processing program to create a table that lists whether an action is legal or illegal under current copyright laws.*

1. Start your word-processing program.
2. Open the data file **WP-3_Copy**. Save it as **WP-3_Copy_xx** in the location where your teacher instructs you to store the files for this activity. Replace **xx** with your own name or initials as instructed by your teacher. This is a two page document that contains information about copyright laws.
3. Insert a footer that contains your full name and today's date. Read the entire document, and then scroll up to the top of page 1.
4. In the first paragraph, select the sentence that best describes the main idea and apply the underline format.
5. Repeat step 4 to identify and underline the sentence that best describes the main idea in the remaining body paragraphs.
6. Save the changes. Preview the document, and, with your teacher's permission, print it.
7. Open the data file **WP-3_Legal**. Save it as **WP-3_Legal_xx** in the location where your teacher instructs you to store the files for this activity. Replace **xx** with your own name or initials as instructed by your teacher. This document lists examples of how different individuals use copyrighted materials. Some of the examples are legal and some are illegal.
8. Insert a footer that contains your name and the current date.
9. In the title at the top of the page, insert the copyright symbol (©) after the word *Copyrighted*.
10. Select the five paragraphs of text and remove the numbered list formatting.
11. Move the insertion point to the last blank line of the document, and insert a table with 2 columns and 3 rows.
12. Type **Legal** in the first column of the first row, and center the text in the cell. Press Tab, type **Illegal** in the second column of the first row, and center the text in the cell.
13. Format the text in the first row in 14-pt. bold. The table should look similar to Illustration B.
14. Read the first example in the list. Use the information you learned reading the **WP-3_**

Copy_**xx** document to determine whether this example describes a legal or illegal use of copyrighted materials.
15. Select the text in the first example and cut it to the Clipboard. If necessary, display nonprinting characters in order to see the paragraph marks on-screen.
16. Paste the selection into the appropriate column in the second row of the table.
17. Repeat steps 14 through 16 to move the text from the second example into the appropriate column in the table.
18. Continue cutting and pasting each example until all of the items in the list have been moved to the table. Insert new rows in the table as needed.
19. Delete the extra paragraph marks that remain in the document above the table.
20. Check the spelling and grammar in the document, and then preview it with a partner or peer editor. Make changes and corrections as necessary.
21. Use your program's Print feature to preview the document. If necessary, adjust the page size, margins, and orientation so the content looks good on the page. With your teacher's permission, print the document.
22. Protect the document by applying the password **!copyright?** and then close it.
23. Open the document by entering the password.
24. Save a copy of the document as **WP-3_Legal2_xx** in the location where your teacher tells you to store the files for this activity.
25. Remove the password from the version of the document named **WP-3_Legal2_xx**.
26. Format the table in **WP-3_Legal2_xx** to enhance its appearance and make it easier to read. For example, apply a table style, or apply borders and fills. Delete unnecessary columns and rows.
27. With your teacher's permission, print the **WP-3_Legal2_xx** document. Close all open documents, saving all changes, and exit your word-processing program.
28. As a class, discuss why it is important to respect the copyright laws.

Illustration B

Legal	Illegal

DIRECTIONS: *You will create and format a letter about the stages of the water cycle.*

1. Start your word-processing program, and create a new document. Save it as **WP-4_Water_xx** in the location where your teacher instructs you to store the files for this activity.
2. Set the document margins to .75" at the top, and 1" for the left, right, and bottom.
3. On the first line of the document, insert the date in *month dd, yyyy* format. Do not set the date to update automatically.
4. Set line spacing to single and paragraph spacing to 0 points before and after, or apply a No Spacing style. Insert three blank lines, and then enter the following name and address using an available input device and software that converts words into digital text. For example, you may type on a keyboard, use voice-recognition software, or use handwriting-recognition software.
   Dr. Sandra Phipps
   Science Department
   Watertown University
   1 Watertown Blvd.
   Anytown, MI 48000
5. Press Enter twice to leave a blank line and type the salutation, **Dear Dr. Phipps:**. Press Enter twice, and save the document.
6. Insert the text from the data file **WP-4_Letter**. If necessary, in the inserted text, adjust the line spacing to single and the paragraph spacing to 0 points before and after.
7. Identify the headings and descriptions of the four stages of the water cycle—Evaporation, Condensation, Precipitation, and Runoff and Groundwater—and format them as a multilevel list. The name of each stage should be a top level. The two sentences that describe each stage should be formatted as a second level (refer to Illustration C).
8. Read the paragraph following your multilevel list. Click at the beginning of the third sentence in the paragraph (*If this is so . . .*), and press Enter to start a new paragraph. Then, click at the beginning of the second sentence (*Isn't all of . . .*) in that new paragraph, and press Enter.
9. Select the two new paragraphs and apply number list formatting using numbers followed by a period (refer to Illustration C).
10. Replace the line *Your Name* with your own name and replace the school name and address with your school's name and address.
11. Exchange documents with a classmate according to your teacher's instructions. For example, you might send it electronically by e-mail, share it on a wiki or other collaborative software tool, or print it. Proofread your classmate's document carefully. Check the spelling and grammar and insert comments to offer constructive criticism and praise.
12. Exchange documents back, and respond to your classmate's comments.
13. Select the inside address in the letter and create an envelope. Enter your school's address as the return address.
14. Add the envelope to the document. Do not save the return address as the default.
15. With your teacher's permission, print the document.
16. Close the document, saving all changes, and exit your word-processing program.

My science class is currently studying the water cycle. We learned that there are four steps in the cycle:

1) Evaporation
   a) During evaporation, sun heats up water in lakes, rivers, or oceans and turns it into vapor or steam.
   b) The vapor or steam then enters the atmosphere.
2) Condensation
   a) During condensation, water vapor in the air cools.
   b) As it cools, it turns back into liquid, forming clouds.
3) Precipitation
   a) During precipitation, the condensed liquid becomes too heavy for the air.
   b) Water falls back to Earth in the form of rain, sleet, snow, and hail.
4) Runoff and Groundwater
   a) Some of the precipitation runs off along the surface of the ground.
   b) Some soaks into the soil to become groundwater.

Because of the water cycle, Earth constantly recycles the same water to be used over and over again. Our teacher told us that this cycle has been going on for millions of years and that the amount of water on Earth has remained fairly constant over that entire time.

1. If this is so, why should we conserve water?
2. Isn't all of the water on Earth eventually reused as part of the water cycle, whatever we do with it?

Illustration C

DIRECTIONS: *You will create a newsletter by writing three articles about recent events in your family or community. You will revise and edit your work and arrange it in a newsletter format.*

1. Open the .pdf file **WP-5_News**. With your teacher's permission, print the Data Record Sheet. Close the file, and exit the pdf reader program.

2. Use the space provided on the Data Record Sheet to plan a newsletter. Write a name for your newsletter in the space for the title. Think of three articles about upcoming special occasions, recent vacations, family outings, or any other exciting news you might have. Write a headline and text for each article.

3. Think of a photograph or an image that relates to one of the articles. Write a description of the image or sketch it in the space provided on your Data Record Sheet.

4. Determine the best method for creating or obtaining the image, and then do so. For example, you could use clip art, scan an existing photograph, take a new photograph with a digital camera and then import it, or create an image file using drawing tools. Save the image file with the name **WP-5_Images_xx** in a format that is compatible with your word-processing program (such as .jpg), in the location where your teacher instructs you to store the files for this activity. Add appropriate tags to help identify the image.

5. Start your word-processing program, and create a new document using a Newsletter template. Alternatively, you may choose to use a desktop-publishing program. Save the file as **WP-5_Newsletter_xx** in the location where your teacher instructs you to store the files for this activity.

6. Insert a header that includes your full name and today's date. Insert a page number in the footer.

7. If available in your word-processing program, apply a theme and a style set.

8. Replace the template title with your newsletter title.

9. Replace the sample article text and headlines with the three articles from your Data Record Sheet. Be sure to use one space after punctuation, smart quotes instead of straight quotes, and en dashes and em dashes as needed.

10. Format the paragraphs with single line spacing, first-line indent, and justified alignment.

11. Read the articles and revise them as necessary. Look for places to add transition words to improve the flow of the text. Use the thesaurus to select interesting and descriptive words that improve the text.

12. Modify or apply formatting, such as styles and fonts. For example, use a style to format headlines, or apply a larger font size to make headlines stand out.

13. If not already in the template, insert a section break below the title and format the second section of the newsletter into two columns.

14. Insert the image file that you created earlier to replace a sample image in the template. Format it so that text will wrap around it.

15. Resize and position the image to create an attractive layout for your newsletter, and format it using a style or other formatting options.

16. Insert a simple text box, and copy and paste a key sentence from one of your articles into it. Format the text in the text box to stand out. Format the text box so that text will wrap around it. Resize and position it on the page so it looks good and is easy to read.

17. Create a SmartArt graphic in the newsletter, if the feature is available.

18. Adjust the zoom so you can see the entire page on the screen, and make any changes or adjustments necessary to improve the page layout and design.

19. Save the document, and then exchange documents with a classmate according to your teacher's instructions. For example, you might send them electronically as an attachment to an e-mail message, or you might print them and exchange the printed copies. Check the spelling and grammar in your classmate's document and use your program's revision tracking feature to mark any errors that you find. Insert comments to make suggestions or praise good work.

20. Exchange documents to get your own back, and accept or reject changes to incorporate the suggestions, and delete or respond to comments, as necessary.

21. Use your program's Print feature to preview the document. If necessary, adjust the page size, margins, and orientation so the content looks good on the page. With your teacher's permission, print it.

22. Save the document in .pdf format with the name **WP-5_Newsletter_xx** in the location where your teacher instructs you to store the files for this activity.

23. Close all open files, saving changes, and exit all open programs.

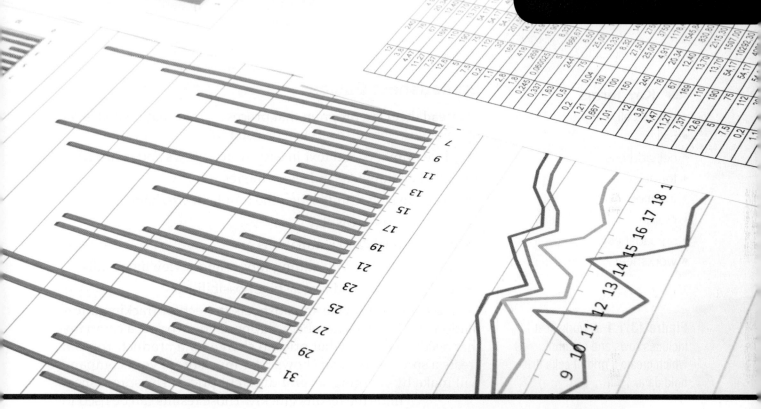

Spreadsheet Basics

chapter 13

What Is a Spreadsheet? Suppose you wanted to keep track of all your grades in one of your classes so you could figure out your final average for the class. Spreadsheet programs are the perfect software for doing this kind of work.

Spreadsheets are set up like tables with information running across rows and down columns. You could enter your assignments in one vertical column. Then you could enter the grade or score you received on each assignment in the next column. The spreadsheet could add up all the scores and calculate your average. When an assignment is returned to you, you could add it to the spreadsheet, and your average would be updated automatically. Just think how long it would take you to do this if you did it by hand!

Chapter Outline

Exploring Spreadsheets

Objectives

- Explain the purpose of spreadsheet software.
- Identify and describe parts of a worksheet.
- Summarize key features of spreadsheet software.

As You Read

Organize Information Use a concept web to help you organize basic facts about spreadsheets as you read the lesson.

🔑 Key Terms

- active cell
- cell
- cell address
- formula
- function
- merge
- spreadsheet
- worksheet

Figure 13.1.1 A worksheet includes rows and columns, which create a grid of cells that hold data.

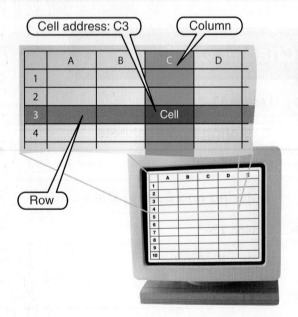

Spreadsheet Basics

A **spreadsheet** is a program that processes information that is set up in tables. Spreadsheets can be used to:

- place numbers and text in easy-to-read rows and columns
- calculate numbers and show the result
- calculate new results when the numbers are changed
- create charts to display data
- create models and simulations
- make predictions by adding inputs and reviewing results
- analyze trends and forecasting possibilities

These features make spreadsheets perfect for tracking information that involves numbers. Suppose you work at a company that needs to decide what price to charge for a product. You can create a spreadsheet that shows how much profit your company will make by charging several different prices. The spreadsheet finds the results quickly. Those results can be used to set a price.

Understanding Worksheets When you use a spreadsheet program, your data goes into a special kind of document called a **worksheet**, a grid made of vertical columns and horizontal rows. Columns are labeled with letters, and rows are labeled with numbers.

Each column and row meets to make a box called a **cell**. Each cell in the grid is identified by a unique name—its **cell address**. The address is made simply by taking the letter of the column and the number of the row that meet to make the cell. For example, column C and row 3 create the cell address C3.

Parts of a Worksheet

Most worksheets look similar. The parts of a worksheet include:

Frame   The frame forms the top and left borders of the worksheet. It includes the column and row headings.

Active Cell   The **active cell** is the cell currently in use. A rectangle appears around this cell to highlight it and make it easy to spot.

Cell Identifier   Located in the upper-left corner, just above the frame, the cell identifier is an area that shows the cell address of the cell that is active.

Formula Bar   The formula bar displays what you type. This data will be entered into the active cell when you are done. The formula bar is like a one-line word-processing program. Pressing Enter, Return, or Tab completes the entry and places the data in the cell.

Scroll Bars   Scroll bars appear on the worksheet's right and bottom edges. You can click on the arrows or slide the scroll box to see another part of the worksheet.

Worksheet Tabs   On the same line as the horizontal scroll bar are tabs that show the other worksheets that belong to the same spreadsheet file. If you click on one of these tabs, you switch to that worksheet.

Status Bar   The status bar appears below the scroll bar at the very bottom of the worksheet. Messages from the program are displayed here.

Figure 13.1.2 All spreadsheet programs share basic elements.

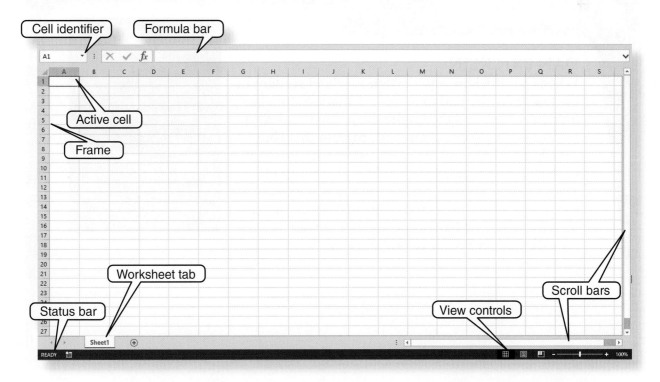

Working with a Spreadsheet

Spreadsheet programs share many features. You can perform many similar actions, regardless of the program.

Navigating   Use the Home, End, Page Up, and Page Down keys, along with the scroll bars, to move large distances within the worksheet. Use the Tab key to move one cell to the right or the arrow keys to move one cell at a time in any direction. Use the Go To command to jump to any cell, or use the Search or Find feature to locate a cell with specific content.

Selecting Cells and Entering Data   To make a cell active, click on that cell. Then, type to enter data in the cell. Data can be text, numbers, dates, or formulas.

Formulas   **Formulas** are mathematical expressions. In a spreadsheet, most formulas reference the data entered in one or more cells. A simple formula might add the numbers in two cells. The formula appears in the formula bar but not in the active cell. The active cell shows the result of the formula. **Functions** are built-in formulas for performing calculations, such as addition, in a table.

Formatting the Worksheet   You can change the look of a worksheet in many ways. You can add or remove rows or columns or change their size. You can change the font or type size of the data. You can also add color, borders, or shading and change how the data is aligned in the cell. You can even **merge** two or more cells which means combine them into one. Most programs have a Merge and Center command that lets you merge selected cells and center the data at the same time.

Spotlight on...

DAN BRICKLIN

When Dan Bricklin was a business school student in the late 1970s, he had to do his calculations for class on a calculator and then write them down. Bricklin wanted to develop a computer program that could calculate and display the work automatically. He and his friend Bob Frankston created such a program. They called it *VisiCalc*®—short for visible calculator. It was the first computer spreadsheet. Although VisiCalc is not sold anymore, today's spreadsheets are all based on Bricklin's original idea.

Objectives

- Describe types of data you can enter in a worksheet.
- Compare and contrast values and labels in a worksheet.
- Describe ways to edit and format data in a worksheet.
- Use a spreadsheet to create a chart.
- Evaluate the benefit of printing options.

As You Read

Sequence Steps Use a sequence chart to help you sequence the steps in working with spreadsheets as you read the lesson.

Entering Data

In addition to formulas, you can enter three types of data in a worksheet: values, labels, and dates and times.

Values A **value** is a number, such as a whole number, a fraction, or a decimal. The program automatically formats values to align to the right in a cell. If a value is too large for the width of the cell, you may see a set of symbols such as ###### or *******. You can change the column width so that the full number shows. Click the right edge of the column heading and drag it to the right.

Labels A **label** is text or a combination of numbers and text. Labels are typically used for headings or explanations. By default, labels are aligned to the left in a cell. Labels that are too wide will overlap into the next cell to the right—if that cell is empty. If that cell already has text, the long text in the first cell will appear cut off. Again, you can widen the column to show the entire label.

🔑 Key Terms

- chart
- filter
- label
- print area
- sort
- value

Figure 13.2.1 If data doesn't fit in a cell, it might not display correctly.

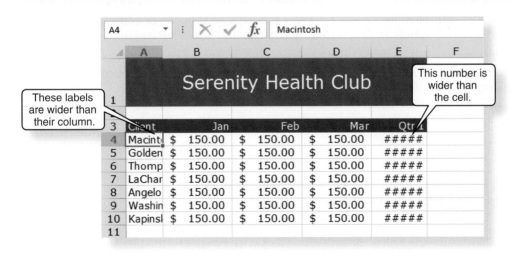

These labels are wider than their column.

This number is wider than the cell.

Many people use spreadsheets at home to track monthly income and expenses. They can set up a worksheet to show regular monthly costs. Then, they only need to copy and paste it on other blank worksheets to create budgets for other months.

Think About It!

Before you set up a budget, think about which expenses arise each month. Which items listed below do you think would be a regular monthly expense?

➤ housing payment

➤ vacation

➤ telephone

➤ holiday presents

➤ food magazine subscription

Editing Data

You can easily change data to correct an error or reflect new information in a spreadsheet.

Editing Cell Data To edit data, click the desired cell. Then click within the formula bar to place the insertion point where you want to make the change. Press Backspace or Delete to remove characters, or type to add them. Press Enter to place the edited information in the cell.

Moving or Copying Data To move information from one cell to another, select the cell and drag its contents to the new cell, or use the Cut and Paste commands. To copy information, go to the Edit menu, and select Copy. Click the new location, and then go to the Edit menu and select Paste. As an alternative to the Edit menu, use command buttons found on the Ribbon or a toolbar.

Removing Data To remove data, select the cell and press Delete. You can also go to the Edit menu, and select Delete. A dialog box will ask if you wish to delete the entire row or column or just those cells.

Formatting Data You can change the appearance of the data in the cells. You can show data in bold or italic type and change its type size. You can also change the format of numbers.

Filtering and Sorting Data You can **sort** data to list rows alphabetically or numerically, and you can **filter** data to show only the rows that match the criteria you select. For example, you might filter an address list to show only records for Texas, and then sort it alphabetically by city.

Program	Click	Then click	Next step
Excel	Home tab	Number group	Click the desired format button or activate the Format Cells dialog box and select the desired format.
Quattro Pro	Format menu	Selection	Select the Numeric Format tab and select the desired format from the dialog box.
iWork Numbers '09	Inspector button	Cell format drop-down	Select the desired format.

Figure 13.2.2 The steps for formatting data in spreadsheet programs vary slightly depending on the software you are using.

Creating a Chart

With a spreadsheet program, you can create **charts**, which are also called graphs. Charts show data in ways that are visually more interesting than tables, and make it easier to analyze trends such as changes over time. Simply select the cells that have data you want to graph. Then, choose the command for creating a chart.

Next, you select a type of chart. Bar charts compare different amounts, such as how many students there are in each grade in a school. Pie charts show how parts relate to the whole. For instance, a pie chart would show what percentage of all students are in each grade. Line charts show change over time, such as the number of students in a grade each year. Once you have chosen the type of chart to create, dialog boxes help you through the rest of the process. After you have made a chart, you can copy it and paste it into another document.

Previewing and Printing a Worksheet

Before you print, preview your worksheet to make sure the data displays the way you want. Most spreadsheets have special features for printing. For example, you can specify a portion of a worksheet called a **print area** before you instruct the program to print. Headings for columns and rows normally only print on the first page, but you can choose to print the headings on every page. You can also add headers and footers, change the page margins, and switch from portrait to landscape orientation.

Physical education teachers in one school are taking advantage of the spreadsheet's ability to make graphs. They chart students' performance on basic fitness tests. Then, they make graphs showing students' progress over time.

Think About It!

Think about other ways graphs could be used at school. For which items listed below do you think graphed test results would be useful?

➤ to show parents how well their children are doing

➤ to show students which skills they need to work on

➤ to compare students by athletic ability

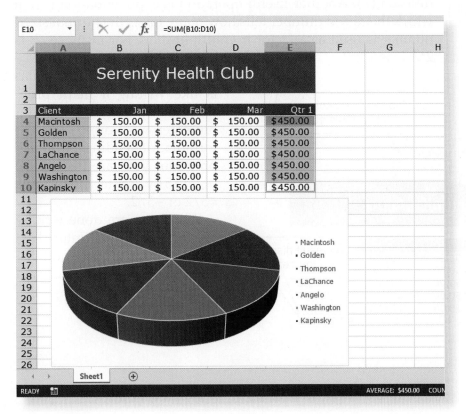

Figure 13.2.3 Creating a chart from data in a worksheet.

Using Formulas

Objectives

- Construct a simple formula using one or more operators.
- Explain the importance of the order of evaluation.
- Evaluate the benefit of building formulas using cell references.

As You Read

Enter Information   Use a concept web to help you enter formulas in a worksheet as you read the lesson.

Key Terms

- cell reference
- order of evaluation

Entering Formulas in Worksheets

The power of a spreadsheet is its ability to use formulas to represent data in different cells.

Entering Formulas   To enter a formula, click the cell where you want the result of the formula to appear, and type the formula in the formula bar. You need to begin the formula with a symbol to signify that you are typing a formula. In Excel and AppleWorks, that symbol is an equal sign (=). In Quattro Pro and Lotus 1-2-3, formulas start with a plus (+) or minus (–) sign.

Simple Formulas   Many formulas use the basic arithmetic operations of addition (+), subtraction (–), multiplication (*), and division (/). Another useful operation is exponentiation (^), in which the raised number tells how many times the normal sized number is used as a factor in multiplication. For instance, 2^2 is 2*2; 2^3 is 2*2*2.

Figure 13.3.1 Using a formula in a worksheet.

Entering simple formulas is like writing a math problem. To add 5 and 2, you simply enter =5+2 or +5+2 as the formula, depending on which program you are using. To divide 5 by 2, enter the formula =5/2 or +5/2.

When you are done writing the formula, press Enter. That completes the formula and displays the result in the selected cell.

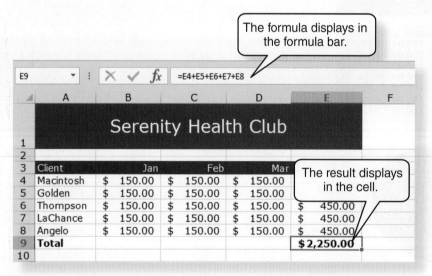

The formula displays in the formula bar.

The result displays in the cell.

Complex Formulas

You can enter more complex formulas as well. Formulas can include many numbers, such as =1+2+3+4+5. They can also include more than one mathematical operation. For instance, suppose you owned a store that sold 50 copies of a game one month and 56 copies the next. You want to know by what percentage your sales of that game increased. You could find out by writing this formula: =(56–50)/50. In this formula, you subtract 50 from 56 to find the number of additional games you sold. Then, you divide the result by 50, the number of games sold the first month, to find the percentage increase. The answer is .12, or 12 percent.

Working with Complex Formulas Many formulas, like =(56–50)/50, have two or more operations. How does the program know which one to do first? It uses the **order of evaluation**. This rule tells the program to do the most important operation first. Then, it does the others in order, from most to least important.

Ranking Operations Operations within parentheses are the most important. Exponentiation comes next, followed by multiplication or division, then addition or subtraction. Use the sentence, "Please excuse my dear Aunt Sally" to remember the order. The first letter of each word (P-E-M-D-A-S) matches the first letter of each operation in the right order.

Using Order of Evaluation Suppose you want to write an Excel formula to average the numbers 29, 34, and 27. The formula =(29+34+27)/3 is correct. The parentheses tell the program to add the three numbers first. The sum, 90, is then divided by 3 to find the average, which is 30.

The formula =29+34+27/3 is not correct. In this case, the program would first divide 27 by 3 because division is performed before addition. It would then add the result, 9, to 29 and 34 for an answer of 72.

Some formulas have more than one operation with the same importance, such as addition and subtraction. In this case, those operations are done in the order in which they appear from left to right.

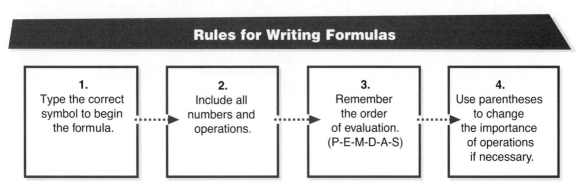

Rules for Writing Formulas

1.	2.	3.	4.
Type the correct symbol to begin the formula.	Include all numbers and operations.	Remember the order of evaluation. (P-E-M-D-A-S)	Use parentheses to change the importance of operations if necessary.

Statistician People who work with statistics, or facts expressed as numbers, are called statisticians. They study information about the number and ages of people in a population, the economy, the number of people who tune in to radio and television shows, and so on.

Statisticians rely heavily on computers, as the information they work with can be very complex. Spreadsheets are very useful for them because of their power to store and process numbers.

Figure 13.3.2 Examples of a formula and a function in a worksheet.

Using References, Not Values

The formulas discussed so far have used values. But formulas can also use **cell references**, or cell addresses. For example, suppose you wanted to multiply 5 times 3. If the value 5 is entered in cell A1, and the value 3 is entered in cell B2, you could enter the formula =A1*B2. It is better to use cell references for the two reasons listed below.

Avoiding Errors You might accidentally type the wrong value and not realize it, as the formula does not always show in the cell. If you insert a cell reference, however, the formula will always use the correct value.

Reflecting Changes A value in a formula never changes. The formula =5*3 will always produce 15. But if you use a cell reference, the formula uses whatever value is entered in the cell. If the cell value changes, so will the result calculated by the formula. By using cell references, you make sure that your worksheet remains up-to-date even if data changes.

Functions

Spreadsheet programs come with built-in functions, which are formulas used to perform common tasks. For example SUM is the function used to find a total and AVERAGE is used to find the average of a range. Using a function can make it easier to enter formulas. Using functions is covered in Lesson 14–4.

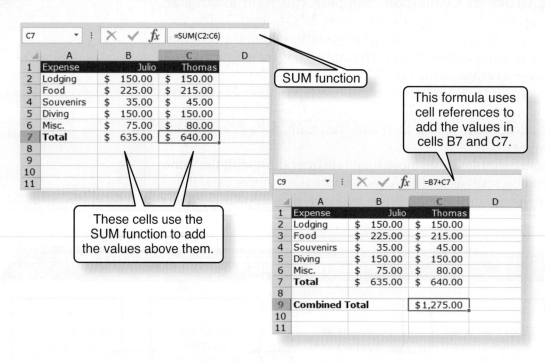

SUM function

This formula uses cell references to add the values in cells B7 and C7.

These cells use the SUM function to add the values above them.

Sharing Data Among Programs

Objectives

- Explain benefits of sharing data among programs.
- Contrast embedding and linking data.
- Summarize how to import data from a word-processing program into a spreadsheet.

As You Read

Compare and Contrast Use a Venn diagram to compare and contrast ways to share data as you read.

Sharing Data

Many spreadsheet programs are not used alone. In fact, many are part of a productivity suite—a set of separate programs that are similar in look and are sold together as a package. As a result, the programs have features that allow them to export data, or send it to other programs in the package. They can also import data from other programs that are not in the package.

Using Strengths By sharing data, you let each program perform its strengths. For example, suppose you are writing a report about the American economy. You want to include a chart that shows the growth of the economy in one period. It makes sense to use a spreadsheet to create the chart because spreadsheets have powerful charting features. Then, you can import that chart into your word-processing document.

Saving Time Importing data from another program also can save you time. Suppose you had created a worksheet containing the data on American economic growth before you started writing your report. Instead of typing the data again, it is much easier to simply copy it from the spreadsheet into the other application.

Key Terms

- destination file
- embed
- link
- source file
- parse

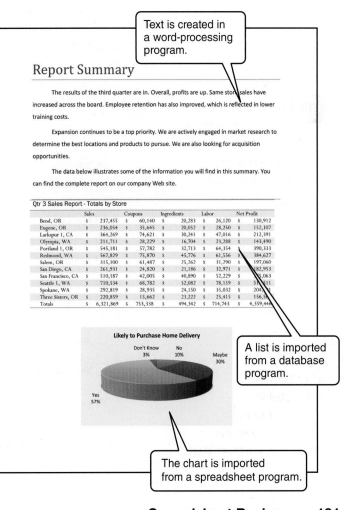

Text is created in a word-processing program.

A list is imported from a database program.

The chart is imported from a spreadsheet program.

Figure 13.4.1 A single document can include data from several different applications.

Financial Analyst Spreadsheets are vital tools for financial analysts. These analysts look at financial information and make judgments on a company's financial health. They also make recommendations to people about how to invest their money wisely.

Financial analysts often create spreadsheets to support their recommendations. They can export those spreadsheets to word-processing reports that they give to clients.

Ways to Share Data

There are two basic methods of sharing data between applications. In one you **embed** the data. In the other, you **link** it. In both, the file that contains the original data is called the **source file**, and the file where you place the shared data is called the **destination file**.

Embedding The simplest way is to copy the data in the source file and paste it into the destination file. This process is called embedding. For example, you could select a chart in a spreadsheet, and choose the Copy command. Then, position the insertion point in a word-processing document, and choose the Paste command.

Embedding is useful if you do not need to keep the pasted data up-to-date. Even if the data in the spreadsheet changes, the data pasted in the document will not change.

Linking There is a way to export data that keeps objects up-to-date. This is called linking. To link data, you begin in the same way—by copying the data from the source. However, instead of using the Paste command in the destination, you use Paste Special.

When you choose the Paste Special command, a Paste Special dialog box appears. In that box, click the button for Paste Link. Then, select the type of object you want. When you click OK, the object displays in your destination file. Any changes you make to the source data will be updated in the destination file as well.

Figure 13.4.2 In Windows applications, you can use the Paste Special command and this dialog box to link data between documents or applications.

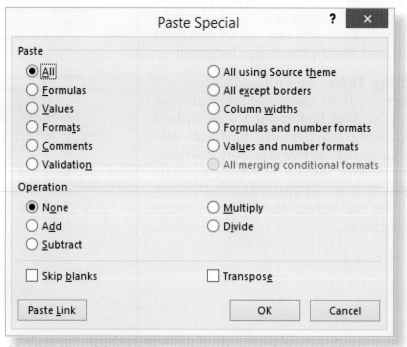

Excel 2013, Microsoft Corporation.

Importing Data into Spreadsheets

You can use embedding and linking to copy data from other files into a spreadsheet. If the data is in a table format, it is pasted into the spreadsheet cells. However, when text from a word-processing file is pasted into a spreadsheet, the continuously flowing text is split into chunks that fit in the columns. The spreadsheet breaks up the file using its **parse** feature.

Importing text files works best if the text is formatted in a way that lets the spreadsheet program identify where to break for each column. You can do this using tabs. For example, suppose that you had a word-processing document with a list of addresses. Entries might read as follows ("[Tab]" stands for a tab entered between address parts):

Kim [Tab] Chang [Tab] 4444 Adams Street [Tab] Springfield [Tab] AR

Austin [Tab] Sinclair [Tab] 522 Jefferson Street [Tab] Springfield [Tab] AZ

Maria [Tab] Torrez [Tab] 111 Washington Street [Tab] Springfield [Tab] TX

Tempest [Tab] Withers [Tab] 3567 Madison Street [Tab] Springfield [Tab] TX

Another way to format text so it can be imported into a spreadsheet is to use comma separated values. Entries might read as follows:

Kim, Chang, 444 Adams Street, Springfield, AR

Austin, Sinclair, 522 Jefferson Street, Springfield, AZ

To import the data into Excel, go to the Data tab, click the Get External Data command, and select From Text. The program lets you choose how to break up the data. In this example, it would convert the tabs into column breaks. The result would be a spreadsheet with data in five columns—one each for the first name, the last name, the address, the city, and the state.

Spotlight on...

HOOD RIVER, OREGON

Teacher Stephanie Perkins in Hood River proves that computers and Physical Education classes really do go together. Physical fitness progress reports are sent home with report cards several times a year in this Oregon school district. Spreadsheet data is input by the students to create the charts and graphs that reflect their fitness progress. The data is then interpreted to help students improve their level of fitness and set goals.

Use the Vocabulary

Directions: *Match each vocabulary term in the left column with the correct definition in the right column.*

_____ **1.** cell
_____ **2.** cell address
_____ **3.** active cell
_____ **4.** formula
_____ **5.** function
_____ **6.** value
_____ **7.** label
_____ **8.** destination
_____ **9.** print area
_____ **10.** order of evaluation

a. rules followed for carrying out the order of more than one mathematical operation
b. mathematical expression that might link numbers in cells
c. part of a spreadsheet to which printing can be limited
d. place where a column and row meet
e. number in a cell
f. file where you paste shared data
g. highlighted cell in use, where data or a formula will be entered or edited
h. text or text and numbers in a cell
i. shortcut to a formula that is used frequently
j. identifies each individual cell

Check Your Comprehension

Directions: *Determine the correct choice for each of the following.*

1. Tables in spreadsheets are better than tables in word processors because they
   a. use numbers only
   b. will have unchanging formats
   c. can be easily updated
   d. have accurate data

2. All changes to values, labels, or formulas in a spreadsheet are made in the
   a. formula bar
   b. cell
   c. frame
   d. function line

3. Values, by default, are aligned
   a. to the left
   b. to the right
   c. centered in the cell
   d. at the top of the cell

4. How does an Excel spreadsheet know that =10/12 is a formula and not the date October 12?
   a. The equal sign (=) signals it.
   b. The division (/) sign signals it.
   c. Dates cannot be shown that way.
   d. It would not know.

5. Operations are carried out in the following order:
   a. A-D-E-M-P-S
   b. M-D-E-P-S-A
   c. P-M-D-A-S-E
   d. P-E-M-D-A-S

6. It is best to write formulas using cell references so that a spreadsheet
   a. has no hidden information
   b. has all correct values
   c. can be updated easily
   d. can be more easily graphed

Think Critically

Directions: *Answer the following questions.*

1. How do values and labels differ in the way they treat data that is too wide for the cell?

2. If you were preparing a budget for a business, how would you indicate that the numbers represent dollar amounts in the worksheet?

3. Describe the function of a comma separated value (.csv) file.

4. What type of graph would be best for showing how much a child grew in inches over the years? Why?

5. Look at the formulas =B1/B2+B3 and =B1/(B2+B3). Would these formulas give the same result? Why or why not?

Extend Your Knowledge

Directions: *Choose and complete one of the following projects.*

A. Open a spreadsheet program and create a new worksheet. Place the title "Cupcake Café Sales" in cell A1. Enter the days of the week in cells A2 to A8. Enter the following values in cells B2 to B8: $10,000; $11,500; $13,000; $9,500; $12,000; $13,000; $8,000. Write a formula that places a total in B9. Create a chart that compares sales for each of the seven days. Save the file, and, with your teacher's permission, print it. Then, save it in comma separated value (.CSV) format.

B. Think of three ways spreadsheets could be used. Identify one use that is suitable for each of the following people: a 12-year-old student; a 35-year-old businesswoman; and a 70-year-old man. Describe each use, and explain how it is suitable to the person's age. If possible, create one of the spreadsheets using made-up data.

C. Open a spreadsheet program and create a new worksheet. Create a custom ribbon tab or command group. Import the data from the worksheet you created in project A. Practice manipulating the cells, columns, and rows. For example, merge and split cells, hide and unhide columns, rows, and titles, insert and delete columns and rows, and create and apply a new cell style. Try applying different number formats, such as currency, date, and percentage. Use Undo to remove the format, Redo to reapply it, and then Undo, again. Insert a hyperlink from one cell to another cell in the same worksheet. Finally, use a PivotTable to summarize the worksheet data. Save the file, and with your teacher's permission, print it.

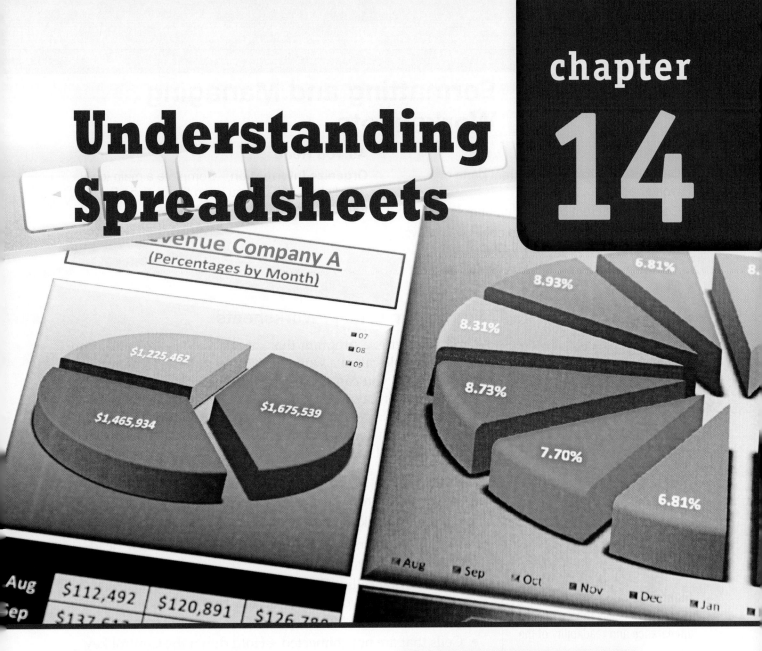

Understanding Spreadsheets

What Do Spreadsheets Do? For many years, businesses tracked financial data on large pieces of paper called ledgers. For instance, a business owner might list each worker's weekly pay, then add the numbers to find the total weekly payroll. The process could take many hours. If there were any changes, a lot of work would have to be redone.

Today's businesses use spreadsheet programs to do this work automatically, and to act as a simple database for storing information. They enter information into an electronic table. Then, the spreadsheet program makes the calculations. If information changes, as when a new employee is added, the program creates a new result. These programs can save hours of work, and the calculations are often more accurate than those done by hand.

Chapter Outline

 Lesson 14–1

Formatting and Managing Worksheets

 Lesson 14–2

Creating Effective Spreadsheets

 Lesson 14–3

Automatic Spreadsheet Features

 Lesson 14–4

Using Functions in a Worksheet

Formatting and Managing Worksheets

Objectives

- Describe how to select different parts of a worksheet.
- Compare different data and number formats.
- Explain how to add or delete columns or rows.
- Explain how to name, add, delete, and move multiple worksheets in the same spreadsheet file.

As You Read

Organize Information Complete a main idea/detail chart to help you learn the options for formatting spreadsheets as you read.

🔑 Key Terms

- range
- worksheet tab

Formatting Data in Worksheets

A spreadsheet is a program that displays data—text and numbers—in a table called a worksheet. After you have entered data and formulas, you can make a worksheet look better by changing various formats. You can also create a spreadsheet based on a template. Spreadsheet templates include formatting, functions, and formulas for common spreadsheets such as budgets, invoices, and lists.

Selecting Cells to Format The first step in formatting is to select the cells to format. To select:

- One cell—Click the cell.
- An entire column or row—Click the column or row heading in the frame.
- Neighboring cells—Click a cell and drag the mouse over additional cells you want to select. This defines a **range**, a group of cells next to each other.
- Cells that are not connected—Hold down the Control key while you select each cell.

Figure 14.1.1 Apply formatting to worksheet cells to improve the appearance and readability of the data.

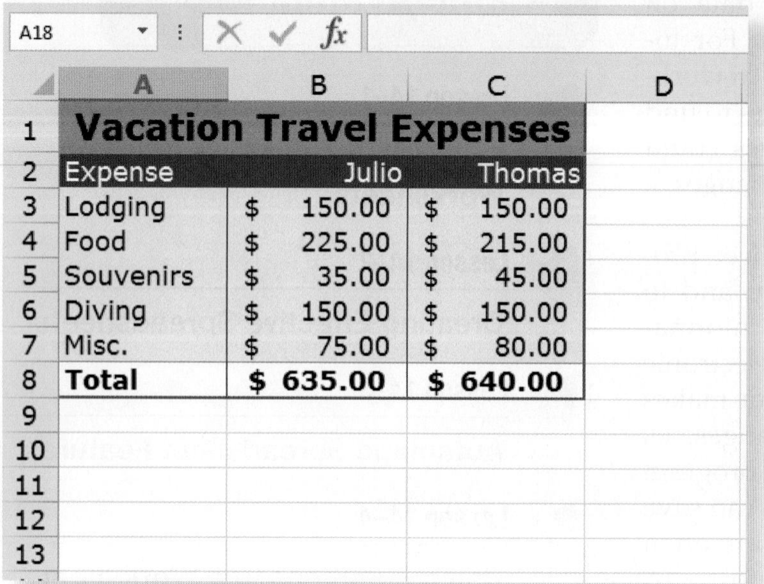

A18	▼	⁝	✗ ✓	fx		
◢	**A**	**B**	**C**	**D**		
1	**Vacation Travel Expenses**					
2	Expense	Julio	Thomas			
3	Lodging	$ 150.00	$ 150.00			
4	Food	$ 225.00	$ 215.00			
5	Souvenirs	$ 35.00	$ 45.00			
6	Diving	$ 150.00	$ 150.00			
7	Misc.	$ 75.00	$ 80.00			
8	**Total**	**$ 635.00**	**$ 640.00**			
9						
10						
11						
12						
13						

How to Format

In some programs, such as Excel or iNumber, you make formatting changes by clicking a button on a toolbar or Ribbon. In some other spreadsheet programs, you click the Format menu, click Selection, and make your choice.

Data Formats You can change the look of either labels (text and numbers) or values (numbers used in calculations) in the selected cells. You can adjust these features:

- Font—the typeface used
- Point size—the size of the font
- Font style—effects such as bold and italic applied to the font
- Color—whether the font is black or another color
- Alignment—where data is positioned in the cell

Number Formats Number formats, such as percent, currency, decimal, or fraction, affect the way numbers display. You have several options:

- General—presents numbers as they are typed
- Currency—adds a dollar sign, a comma to numbers over 1,000, and two decimal places
- Comma—shows two decimal places and a comma for numbers over 1,000
- Percentage—multiplies the number in the cell by 100 to calculate the percentage and adds a percent symbol to the result
- Negative numbers—adds a minus sign or places numbers in parentheses or in red
- Decimals—includes number of decimal places chosen

Cell Formats You can also change the look of one or more cells. You can give them color backgrounds or highlight the cell borders using lines of different styles and thickness. Most programs include cell styles which quickly apply a set of formats to the cell.

Adjusting Columns and Rows

To add columns or rows, go to the Insert menu and select Column or Row. The existing columns will move to the right of the active cell, and rows will move down to make room for the new column or row. To delete a column or row, click the heading in the worksheet's frame. In the Edit menu, select Delete.

You can also make columns wider or narrower or rows taller or shorter to fit data. To change column width, drag the right edge of the column's heading left or right. To change row height, drag the lower edge of the row's heading up or down.

Using Multiple Worksheets in a File

In most spreadsheet programs, a file holds several worksheets. They are arranged like pages in a book. In fact, a file is often called a workbook.

Figure 14.1.2 You can insert new rows and columns into a worksheet.

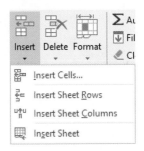

Some Windows spreadsheet programs give you the chance to see worksheets from different files at the same time. Simply open the files and select Arrange in Excel or Tile Top to Bottom or Tile Side to Side in Quattro Pro.

Think About It!

Think about the advantages of viewing worksheets from different files at the same time. For which examples listed below would this feature be useful?

➤ move data from one file to another
➤ work on a worksheet on a different tab
➤ insert cell references in another file
➤ copy cells from one part of a worksheet to another

Each worksheet is represented by a **worksheet tab** in the lower-left corner of the screen. Clicking one of these tabs opens that worksheet. Having these extra worksheets is like working in three dimensions; you can store data not only in columns and rows but also on different sheets.

Naming Worksheets The program labels the tabs with letters ("A," "B") or numbers ("Sheet 1," "Sheet 2"). You can change the names on those worksheet tabs by double-clicking the tab and typing a new name. Suppose you were creating a year's budget. You could name each tab for each month of the year and put a month's budget on each worksheet.

Adding and Deleting Worksheets To add another worksheet to a file in Excel, right-click on a worksheet tab, and select Insert from the pop-up menu. A new tab appears on the screen. To delete a worksheet, right-click on the tab, and select Delete from the pop-up menu.

Moving Worksheets You can move worksheets within a file or from one file to another. There are two ways to do this:

- Pop-up Menu—Select the sheet that you want to move by clicking the sheet tab. Then, right-click to display the pop-up menu and select Move or Copy Sheet. A dialog box asks you to select the file (or workbook) and the new location.

- Click and Drag—First, click the sheet tab and then drag it to its new location in the same file or in a new one. To move a worksheet to a different file, that file must be open. As you drag, the mouse changes to a small sheet and an arrow guides you.

Figure 14.1.3 You can copy or move a worksheet within the same file or to another file.

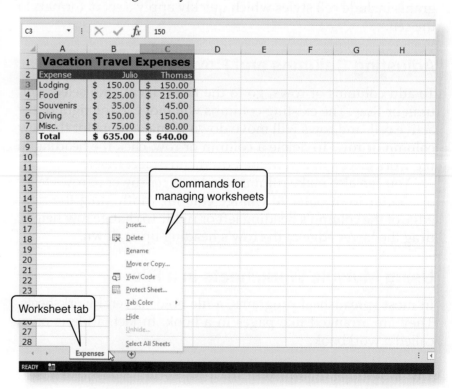

Creating Effective Spreadsheets

Objectives

- Outline the steps in designing an effective spreadsheet.
- Identify strategies to avoid spreadsheet errors.
- Explain reasons for using protection in spreadsheets.
- Describe how to hide cells and columns.

As You Read

Summarize Information Complete a summary chart to organize ways to create effective spreadsheets as you read.

Planning Is Important

Almost anyone can create a worksheet. But someone who simply enters labels, values, and formulas might create a worksheet that contains errors. Effective worksheets require careful planning before any data is entered.

Here are some suggestions to help you create an effective and error-free spreadsheet:

Identify the Purpose of the Worksheet What are you trying to accomplish by creating the worksheet?

Think About the End Product What results do you want to report? What individual values do you expect in columns or rows? Do you need summary statistics such as totals or averages?

Identify What Data Is Needed What information will you need? How will it be gathered? Who will put it into the worksheet? How will its accuracy be checked?

Think About What Formulas Are Needed How will you convert your input data into final results? Do you want intermediate results to appear in the worksheet or only final answers? What formulas or functions will you need? How will you test the accuracy of the formulas?

Use Cell References in Formulas How will you write formulas? Remember that it is better to write formulas that refer to cells rather than to values.

Identify Cells to Protect from Replacement What data and formulas should not be changed? You want to protect these cells from being replaced.

 **Key Terms**
- password
- protect

Imagine a spreadsheet that cooks can use to see if the temperatures they are using are adequate to kill different germs found in food. Cells in the spreadsheet allow cooks to input their cooking temperatures for comparison.

Think About It!

Which type of cell listed below do you think should be protected in the spreadsheet described above?

➤ column headings

➤ data

➤ formulas

➤ labels

Plan How to Enhance the Worksheet   Which cells are most important? Use formatting—typefaces, alignment, border, shading, and color—to make those cells stand out.

Protect Data and Formulas   You can prevent errors in spreadsheets by **protecting** cells. This process blocks accidental changes.

Levels of Protection

Spreadsheet programs let you lock one or more cells, a worksheet, or all the worksheets in a file. Some programs also allow you to assign a **password**, or coded access word. Then, only people who know the password can open the file or save changes to it.

Using Protection   Often users protect an entire worksheet and unlock only the cells they allow to be changed. These might include cells that will hold the values that formulas use or data like names and addresses. The rest of the worksheet remains locked until protection is removed.

How to Add Protection   Programs differ in how protection is added to a worksheet. In Excel, select the Review tab, Changes group, and choose the Protect Sheet command. In Quattro Pro, you select Sheet from the Format menu. In Apple's Numbers click on the Inspector button and then use options in the document inspector to apply password protection.

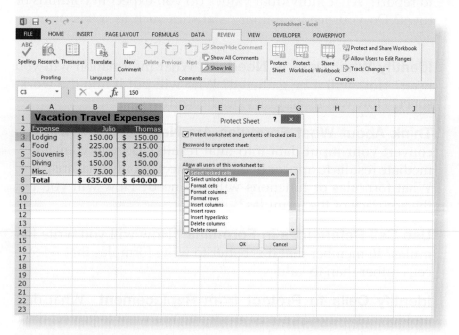

Figure 14.2.1 You can protect an entire worksheet or just certain parts of it.

Hiding Cells and Columns

Another feature that can help protect data and formulas is the Hide option. By hiding certain cells or columns in a worksheet, you discourage other users from changing the information in them.

Automatic Spreadsheet Features

Objectives

- Explain how to use the automatic entry feature.
- Differentiate between series increments and decrements.
- Identify advantages of using the automatic fit and formatting features.
- Compare different types of charts.
- Summarize the advantages of using macros.

As You Read

Organize Information Complete a concept web to identify and organize information about automatic features of spreadsheets as you read the lesson.

Automatic Data Entry

With the automatic data entry feature (often called **AutoFill**), you can enter many kinds of data series in a set of cells. A **data series** is a set of data that changes by a constant value. The series *2005, 2006, 2007, 2008* increases by one. The series *10, 8, 6, 4* decreases by two. The number by which each value increases is called the **increment**. If a series decreases, the value by which it becomes smaller is called the **decrement**. Some data series are text, such as the days of the week. Numbers and dates can also be entered as series.

To use AutoFill, you only need to enter the first one or two values in the series. Then, move the mouse to the lower-right corner of the first cell until a small plus sign or arrow appears. Drag across a row or down a column until you reach the last cell in the series. The data in the series appears in the cells.

Some programs also have a feature called AutoComplete. With AutoComplete, the program automatically completes a cell entry as you type, based on the data already entered in the column. For example, if you have entered the text *Yes* in a cell, and then start typing *Yes* in another cell in the same column, your program enters *Yes*. You can press Enter to accept the entry, or keep typing to change it.

Key Terms

- AutoFill
- data series
- decrement
- increment
- macro

Figure 14.3.1 Use AutoFill to automatically fill in a series of months.

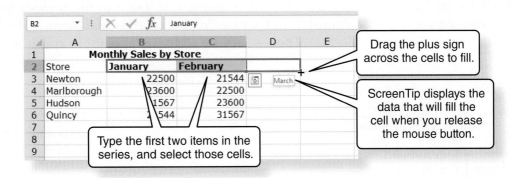

Type the first two items in the series, and select those cells.

Drag the plus sign across the cells to fill.

ScreenTip displays the data that will fill the cell when you release the mouse button.

Figure 14.3.2 Use the SUM function to total numbers in a worksheet.

Automatic Summing

A very common calculation in spreadsheets is adding a series of numbers. The automatic sum function—called SUM or Auto-SUM—makes this action easy. A toolbar button with the symbol ⎵ controls the function. Use the following steps:

• Choose the Location—First select the cell where you want the total to appear and make it active. If you are totalling a column, choose the cell below the last number. If you are totalling a row, choose the cell to the right of the last number.

• Insert the Function—Click the ⎵ button.

• Complete the Formula—In some programs, the total automatically appears. In others, a formula appears and you have to press Enter or Return to accept it. Once you do, the total appears in the cell.

Automatic Formatting

Some automatic features affect the appearance of the worksheet. They include automatic fit and formatting features.

Fitting Data in a Cell   As discussed in Chapter 13, if the data in a cell is too large for the column, you can change the column width by dragging the right edge of the column border in the frame. But, suppose you enter other data that requires you to repeat this step several times. You can choose the program's automatic fit feature to automatically adjust the column to fit the longest data in that column. Simply double-click the right edge of the column heading in the frame and the column resizes itself, or apply the AutoFit command.

Formatting Worksheets   You can make many formatting enhancements to worksheets. Some spreadsheet programs offer an automatic formatting feature. This feature allows you to apply preset formats to an entire worksheet or to a selected part of a worksheet.

To use the feature, select two or more cells that you want to format, and then select the AutoFormat command. For example, in Excel 2010, click Format as Table in the Styles group on the Home tab. In Quattro Pro, click the Format menu and select Speed Format. Then, select the format you want to apply. Most spreadsheets also let you apply conditional formatting, which formats cells in which the data meets certain criteria. For example, you might apply shading to cells with a value greater than 100.

Function in formula bar

IF | ✕ ✓ *fx* | =SUM(B3:B6)

	A	B	C	D	E	F
1		Monthly Sales by Store				
2	Store	January				
3	Newton	$ 22,500.00				
4	Marlborough	$ 23,600.00				
5	Hudson	$ 31,567.00				
6	Quincy	$ 21,544.00				
7	Total	=SUM(B3:B6)				
8		SUM(**number1**, [number2], ...)				
9						

Cells to total

Function in cell

Automatic Charting

A powerful automatic tool of spreadsheet programs is the chart-creating feature. The program takes the data from a worksheet and transforms it into a chart. Use these four steps to create a chart:

- Define the data—Select a range of cells to chart.
- Select the command—Click the chart icon on the toolbar or select the Insert Chart menu command.
- Choose a chart type—A dialog box will offer several different chart types as options. The dialog box explains the uses of the major types of charts.
- Finish the chart—Add or edit elements to enhance the chart, such as a title and labels.

Using Macros

A **macro** is a set of mouse actions, keystrokes, or commands that you can record and put into action again and again. Once a macro is recorded, you can use it whenever you want to repeat the task. Macros save the time and effort of repeating a series of instructions. The program carries out the macro much faster than you could perform the task yourself. Also, using macros ensures that steps are done exactly the same way each time.

Technology@School

The formatting features of spreadsheets offer many options. Some social studies teachers have their students research details and statistics on the countries or time periods they study. By creating charts from the data they collect, students can compare information.

Think About It!

Some spreadsheet data may be easier to analyze in a chart than on a worksheet. Which topics below would be easier to interpret in a chart?

- area of forest
- population of cities
- climate by month
- forms of government
- main products grown in different states

Comparing Types of Charts

Chart type	Use	Example
Column	Uses vertical bars to show changes over time emphasizing fixed points in time.	Compare the number of people in a country in five different years.
Bar	Uses horizontal bars to show different amounts of the same item.	Compare the number of people in five different countries.
Line	Uses lines to show changes over time on an ongoing basis.	Show the sales of several different products over the period of twelve months.
Pie	Uses segments of a circle to show different parts in relation to the whole.	Show the percentage of a country's population in different age groups.

Using Functions in a Worksheet

Objectives

- Explain what functions are.
- Write a spreadsheet function using the correct syntax.
- Summarize how to copy a function.
- Contrast relative and absolute references.

As You Read

Summarize Information Use a summary chart to help you summarize information about using functions in a worksheet as you read the lesson.

🔑 Key Terms

- 3-D reference
- absolute reference
- argument
- keyword
- nest
- relative reference
- syntax

Spreadsheet Functions

As you learned in Chapter 13, a function is a commonly used formula built into a program. Spreadsheets offer many different functions. Some are general, like the functions to add or average a range of numbers. Some have specialized uses, like those designed for engineering, statistics, or financial work.

Some of the most commonly used spreadsheet functions are:

- Average—averages a group of numbers
- Count—counts the number of cells that contain values
- Maximum—finds the largest value in a set of values
- Minimum—finds the smallest value in a set of values
- Sum—adds a group of numbers and displays the total

Entering Functions Each function has its own **syntax**, or rules of wording, that specifies how it must be entered. Functions have three parts:

- An identifier, which is a symbol (such as an equal sign or the @ symbol) that identifies the entry as a formula or function.
- A **keyword**, which is the function's name, such as SUM or AVERAGE.
- An **argument**, which is data the function must use. This is often a reference to a cell or a range of cells but may be a number, date, or other data. A function's arguments are usually enclosed in parentheses.

Conditional Functions Most spreadsheets let you create formulas using an IF function. These formulas perform a calculation only *if* certain criteria are met. For example, you could apply a 10% discount if the total is less than 100, and a 15% if it is greater than 100. Using IF functions is useful for forecasting, because you can compare one possible outcome with another.

Lookup Tables Lookup functions let you locate information in a table column or row based on specific data, such as the cost of a product.

Nesting Functions You can even **nest** functions. When you nest a function, you include it within another function.

Using a Range in a Function Often the argument includes a cell range, or a group of cells. A range can include cells from one column or one row, but it also can combine cells from more than one of either.

To add a cell range to a function—or to any formula—you don't need to name every cell in the range. Instead, name the cell in the range's upper-left corner, and then name the cell in the range's lower-right corner. Depending on the program you use, you must separate the ranges' cell addresses with either a colon (:) or two periods (..).

For example, using the SUM function to add the values in cells B4, B5, and B6 would look like this: =SUM(B4:B6). This is the same as entering: =B4+B5+B6. Multiple cells or ranges can be separated in the formula with commas. The SUM of B4, B5 and D5 through D8 can be entered as: =SUM(B4:B5,D5:D8).

Relative and Absolute References

Usually, formulas (including functions) use relative cell references. A **relative reference** automatically changes when it is copied or moved so that it uses cell addresses that are specific to its new location. That means you only need to enter the formula in one location, and then copy or move it to use it someplace else.

Figure 14.4.1 Use the Average function to find the average of a series of numbers.

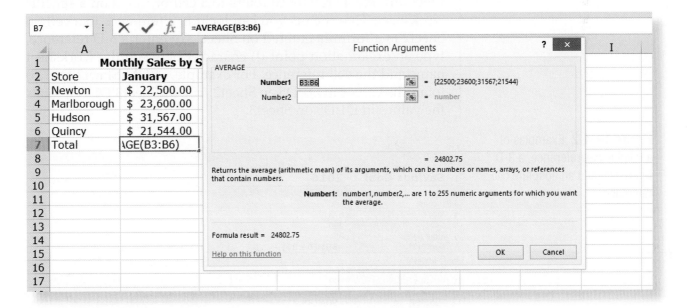

Math Spreadsheets are handy for doing conversions. Suppose you need a table that shows how ounces convert to grams.

In a worksheet, type the word Ounces in cell A1, and type Grams in cell B1. Type the numbers 1 through 10 in cells A2 through A11. In cell B2, type the formula =A2*28.35 and press Enter. Because one ounce equals 28.35 grams, the answer 28.35 appears in cell B2. Copy the formula into cell B2 and paste it into cells B3 through B11. The spreadsheet automatically converts the rest of the list for you!

Formulas can use a different kind of cell reference, called an absolute reference. An **absolute reference** does not change if you copy or move it to a different cell. You should use this type of reference when your formula or function must refer to a specific cell or range. To enter an absolute reference, you type a dollar sign ($) character to the left of the column letter and/or row number.

Suppose, for example, in cell D6 you enter the function =SUM(D1:D5). If you move the function to cell E6, the relative references change and the function becomes =SUM(E1:E5). If you want the function to use the values in cells D1:D5, no matter where you move it, you enter =SUM($D$1:$D$5); the absolute references will not change.

You can create three kinds of absolute cell references by typing a dollar sign in front of the column letter, the row number, or both, as follows:

- $A$1 uses absolute references for both column and row; neither changes when the formula is copied or moved.

- A$1 uses a relative reference for the column and an absolute reference for the row; only the column changes if the formula is copied or moved.

- $A1 uses an absolute reference for the column and a relative reference for the row; only the row changes if the formula is copied or moved.

3-D References

In a 3-D spreadsheet—one that uses multiple worksheets in the same file—you can include a **3-D reference** in your formulas and functions. A 3-D reference refers to a cell or range on a specific worksheet. That means you can include a reference to a cell on Sheet2 in a formula entered on Sheet1. To enter a 3-D reference, type an exclamation point (!) character between the worksheet name and the cell reference. For example, =SUM(Sheet2!D1:D5) totals the values in D1:D5 on Sheet2; =SUM(Sheet3!D1:D5) totals the values in D1:D5 on Sheet3.

Figure 14.4.2 Examples of a relative cell reference, a 3-D reference, and an absolute cell reference.

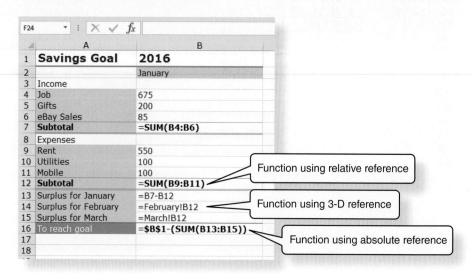

Use the Vocabulary

Directions: *Match each vocabulary term in the left column with the correct definition in the right column.*

_____ **1.** range
_____ **2.** worksheet tab
_____ **3.** data series
_____ **4.** increment
_____ **5.** decrement
_____ **6.** syntax
_____ **7.** keyword
_____ **8.** argument
_____ **9.** relative reference
_____ **10.** absolute reference

a. function name

b. set of data that changes by a constant value

c. rules for writing a function

d. value by which numbers in a series decrease

e. value by which numbers in a series increase

f. cell reference that does not change

g. cell reference that does change

h. lets you access worksheets in a spreadsheet file

i. group of cells that might include cells from different columns and rows

j. reference to cells or range to be acted on by a function

Check Your Comprehension

Directions: *Complete each sentence with information from the chapter.*

1. To select a column, click on the _____.

2. In a spreadsheet, to record results for a race timed to the second and the tenth of a second, use the format _____.

3. To delete a column or row, highlight it, go to the _____, and choose Delete.

4. The automatic fit feature helps you when making a spreadsheet by automatically _____ a column.

5. The _____ feature formats spreadsheets so the data is clear and easy to read.

6. Both a(n) _____ and a line chart can display changes in data over time.

7. Column charts use _____ to display data.

8. _____ are ready-made formulas built into a spreadsheet.

9. A(n) _____ reference is automatically updated to reflect its new location if you move it.

10. The cell reference _____ shows an absolute reference for the column A1.

 **Think Critically**

Directions: *Answer the following questions.*

1. Suppose you wanted to track the statistics of the basketball players for different teams. What spreadsheet feature would help you keep the teams separate from one another? How?

2. What values would you have to enter to use the automatic entry feature for a data series that started with 16 and increased by 3.5?

3. How would you write a reference to the cells in columns U through W and rows 17 through 25?

4. How would you write a function to add values in the cells D7 to D20? What built-in function could you use?

5. Compare and contrast sorting, searching, and filtering data in a spreadsheet.

Extend Your Knowledge

Directions: *Choose and complete one of the following projects.*

A. Open a new workbook. Title it "Town Population Growth" in cell A1. Use the AutoFill feature to fill in the years from 2011 to 2020 in cells A2 to A11. Enter these values in cells B2 to B11: 15,000; 15,700; 16,500; 17,200; 18,000; 18,700; 19,300; 20,300; 21,700; 22,900. If you make an error, use the Undo command and try again. Create a line chart of the data. Save the file, and, with your teacher's permission, print it. Copy the data from B2:B11 to C2:C11. Change the value in cell C5 to 17,000. Delete row 2. Create a column chart of the new data. Insert a new column A. Apply the Long Date format to cell A1 and enter today's date. Apply the Time format to any blank cell and enter the current time. Save the file, and, with your teacher's permission, print it. Which type of chart is more effective for this data? Explain.

B. Use the Internet or the library to learn how spreadsheets have changed the way people do business. In what ways are spreadsheets used in businesses today? Was the same work done in the past? How is it different to do the work now? As you work, take notes and keep track of your sources. Evaluate the information you find and only use it if it is accurate, relevant, and valid. Prepare and deliver a presentation to summarize your findings. Include a slide that lists your sources.

Spreadsheet Activity 1: Budgeting

DIRECTIONS: *You will use a spreadsheet to complete a basic budget worksheet. You will insert formulas for calculating income and expenses, create a chart so you can analyze trends, and you will format the data so it is easy to read.*

1. Start your spreadsheet program and open the file **SS-1_Budget**. Save the file as **SS-1_Budget_xx** in the location where your teacher tells you to store the files for this activity. Replace *xx* with your own name or initials as directed by your teacher.
2. Use the Fill Series command to enter the names of the months from July through December in cells H3:M3.
3. Copy and paste the data in cells B5:G6 to H5:M6, and the data in cells B9:G12 to H9:M12.
4. In cell B7, use the SUM function to total the values in cells B5 and B6. Fill the formula across through cell M7.
5. In cell B13, use the SUM function to total the values in cells B9:B12. Fill the formula across through cell M13.
6. Insert a blank row between rows 7 and 8.
7. Insert a blank row between rows 5 and 6.
8. Cut the data from cells A13:M13 and paste it in cells A6:M6.
9. Delete row 13.
10. In cell B15, enter a formula that subtracts the monthly expense subtotal (B14) from the monthly income subtotal (B8), and then fill the formula across through cell M15.
11. Insert a blank row between rows 14 and 15.
12. Merge and center the data in cell A1 across columns A through M. Format it for a heading.
13. Apply bold to the cells with the labels in row 3 and column A, and apply a light blue fill.
14. Format cells B5:M16 with the Accounting number format with two decimal places.
15. Select the range B3:M3 and the range B16:M16, and insert a 3-D clustered column chart based on the selection.
16. Move the chart below row 16 and resize it to approximately 3.5" high by 9" wide.
17. Hide the chart legend and add the chart title **Monthly Budget Surplus**, and format it with bold.
18. Change the value in cell F6 to **15**.
19. Display formulas in the worksheet.
20. Check and correct the spelling.
21. Insert a custom header with your first and last names on the left and today's date on the right and return to Normal view.
22. Change the orientation to Landscape and scale the worksheet to fit on one page. It should look similar to Illustration A.
23. With your teacher's permission, print the worksheet.
24. Close the spreadsheet, saving all changes, and exit your spreadsheet program.
25. As a class, discuss how a spreadsheet can help you set and achieve savings goals. What other tools could you use to analyze trends?

Illustration A

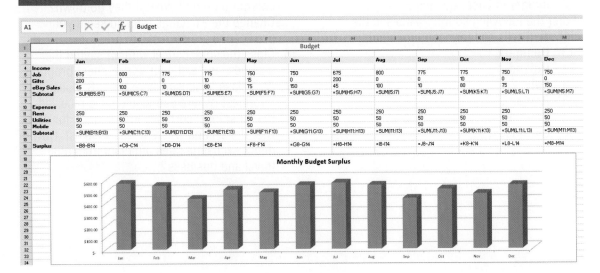

DIRECTIONS: *You will research the currencies of several European countries and their current exchange rates. You will then use formulas to calculate how much of each type of currency you would receive in exchange for dollars.*

1. Open the .pdf file **SS-2_Exchange**. With your teacher's permission, print the Data Record Sheet. Close the file and exit the pdf reader program.

2. With your teacher's permission, use the Internet to research the currency used and the current exchange rate compared to the U.S. dollar for each of the countries listed on the Data Record Sheet.
   a. Using a search engine Web site, search using keywords or phrases such as **exchange rates** or the currency name. You might also try a Boolean search such as **exchange rates AND the currency name**.
   b. When you find a Web site with useful information, bookmark the site, or with your teacher's permission, print the pages.
   c. On the Data Record Sheet, write the source information for each site and fill in the currency and exchange rate information.

3. Start your spreadsheet program. Create a new spreadsheet file, and save it as **SS-2_Europe_xx**, replacing *xx* with your own name or initials, as instructed by your teacher.

4. In cell A1, enter the title **European Vacation Budget**. Center and merge the title across columns A:E.

5. Enter the following labels in the specified cells and format them in bold:
   A2 - **Country**
   B2 - **Currency**
   C2 - **Exchange Rate (U.S. $/foreign currency unit)**
   D2 - **Budget in U.S. Dollars**
   E2 - **Budget in Local Currency**

6. Enter the following country names in the specified cells and format them in bold:
   A3 - **Denmark**
   A4 - **Ireland**
   A5 - **Italy**
   A6 - **Romania**
   A7 - **Belarus**
   A8 - **Ukraine**

7. Referring to your Data Record Sheet, in columns B and C fill in the data for each country.

8. In column D, enter the following information for each country:
   Denmark - **$200**
   Ireland - **$300**
   Italy - **$100**
   Romania - **$100**
   Belarus - **$200**
   Ukraine - **$200**

9. In cell E3, enter a formula to multiply the budget amount in D3 by the exchange rate in C3. The result will be the amount of local currency you will receive in exchange for your dollars. Apply the Comma format and then copy the formula to cells E4:E8.

10. Apply the Currency number format to all values that display U.S. dollars. Apply cell styles, or borders and fills to make the spreadsheet look good and be easy to read. Adjust column widths and row height so you can see all of the data.

11. Sort the data in A3:E8 in descending order by the Country column.

12. Preview the worksheet. If necessary, change the margins and orientation so the data fits on one page.

13. Insert a footer with your first and last names on the left and today's date on the right.

14. With your teacher's permission, print the worksheet and then save it.

15. What do you think would happen to the values in column E if the exchange rates in column C go up? What if they go down? Change the exchange rates to see if your predictions are correct.

16. Close the spreadsheet without saving the changes, and exit your spreadsheet program.

17. As a class, discuss where the U.S. dollar was strongest (where you would have received the most local currency in exchange for each U.S. dollar) and where it was weakest. How might exchange rates affect international travel and business?

DIRECTIONS: *You will use conditional formatting to complete a worksheet analyzing client activity for a landscape service company.*

1. Open the spreadsheet file **SS-3_Landscape**. Save the file as **SS-3_Landscape_xx** in the location where your teacher tells you to store the files for this activity. Replace **xx** with your own name or initials as directed by your teacher.
2. Insert a header that has your first and last names on the left, today's date in the center, and the worksheet name on the right.
3. Sort the data in A5:D32 in ascending order based on column D (Paid) and then by column B (Service).
4. In cell G5, use the SUM function to display the total of all fees that have been paid.
5. In cell G7, use the SUM function to display the total of all Aeration fees that have been paid.
6. In cell G8, use the SUM function to display the total of all Mowing fees that have been paid.
7. In cell G9, use the SUM function to display the total of all Other fees that have been paid.
8. In cell G10, use the SUM function to display the total of all Trimming fees that have been paid.
9. Ignore the errors in cells G5, G7, G8, G9, and G10.
10. Apply conditional formatting to the Fee column that highlights values over $100 with a light red fill and dark red text.
11. Use Find and Replace to replace the Customer name Tayson with Tyson.
12. Adjust column widths and row height to fit the data.
13. Set page layout options so the worksheet will print in Portrait orientation with 1 inch margins on each side. It should look similar to Illustration B on the next page.
14. Protect the sheet so unauthorized users can select locked and unlocked cells but cannot make any changes. Do not use a password.
15. With your teacher's permission, print the worksheet.
16. Close the file, saving all changes, and exit your spreadsheet program.

Spreadsheet Activities

Fry Landscape Services
Client Activity

Customer	Service	Fee	Paid
Renfro	Mowing	$100	No
Nodine	Mowing	$100	No
Fanson	Mowing	$100	No
Erland	Mowing	$100	No
Hoover	Other	$150	No
Carson	Other	$275	No
Fiver	Trimming	$ 50	No
Allen	Aeration	$100	Yes
Welty	Aeration	$100	Yes
Guertler	Aeration	$100	Yes
Walton	Aeration	$100	Yes
Tyson	Aeration	$100	Yes
Hoover	Mowing	$ 75	Yes
Tyson	Mowing	$ 75	Yes
Keeger	Mowing	$ 50	Yes
Poland	Mowing	$ 75	Yes
Tyson	Mowing	$ 50	Yes
Molton	Mowing	$200	Yes
Olson	Mowing	$ 75	Yes
Reece	Mowing	$125	Yes
Branson	Mowing	$ 75	Yes
Friend	Other	$ 65	Yes
Tyson	Other	$ 85	Yes
Manders	Other	$125	Yes
Davis	Other	$100	Yes
Anders	Other	$200	Yes
Jackson	Trimming	$ 60	Yes
Stilson	Trimming	$ 60	Yes

Amount Collected	$1,995
Aeration Paid	$ 500
Mowing Paid	$ 800
Other Paid	$ 575
Trimming Paid	$ 120

DIRECTIONS: *You will keep track of how much time you spend on various activities during a typical week. You will use a spreadsheet program to record your data. Then, you will create charts to visually represent the information.*

1. Open the .pdf file **SS-4_ChartingTime**. With your teacher's permission, print the Data Record Sheet. Close the file and the pdf reading program.

2. For one week, use the Data Record Sheet to record the amount of time you spend on different activities. Note that there are blank columns where you may add activities, such as sports and homework. Record the hours in decimals; for example, 1.5 for one-and-a-half hours. Round the hours to the nearest quarter hour.

3. When your table is complete, start your spreadsheet program. Create a new spreadsheet file using a template, if possible, and save it as **SS-4_DailyLog_xx** in the location where your teacher tells you to store the files for this activity. Replace *xx* with your own name or initials as instructed by your teacher.

4. Apply a theme or design of your choice.

5. In cell A1, enter the title **Daily Activity Log**, and apply formatting appropriate for a title, such as the Title cell style, or a font, font size, and font style that makes the data stand out.

6. Enter the information from your Data Record Sheet into the worksheet, including labels.
   a. In cell B3, enter the label **Activities**.
   b. In cell B4, enter **Sleeping**, then continue across row 4 entering the labels for the remaining activities.
   c. In cell A5, enter **Monday**, and then use the AutoFill feature to fill in cells A6:A11.
   d. Enter the actual times you spend on each activity, per day.
   e. In cell B12, use the COUNT function to count the number of cells in which you entered values.

7. Apply appropriate formatting to make the data easy to read. For example, apply heading style formatting to headings and labels, or apply cell borders and fills.

8. In cell I4, enter the column heading **Total Hours**. In cell I5, use the AutoSum function to calculate the number of hours you spent on each activity on Monday. The result should be 24. Copy the formula from cell I5 to cells I6:I12.

9. Delete the data from cell B12, and then, in cell A12, enter the row heading **Total Hours**.

In cell B12, use the AutoSum function to calculate the total hours you spent sleeping during the week. Copy the formula from cell B12 to cells C12:H12.

10. In cell A13, enter the row heading **Average**. In cell B13, use the AVERAGE function to find the average amount of time you spent sleeping. Do not include the Total Hours value in the average. Copy the formula from cell B13 to cells C13:H13.

11. In cell A14, enter the row heading **Minimum**. In cell B14, use the MIN function to find the minimum amount of time you spent sleeping. Copy the formula from cell B14 to cells C14:H14. Make sure the range includes the data for the days of the week only.

12. In cell A15, enter the row heading **Maximum**. In cell B15, use the MAX function to find the maximum amount of time you spent sleeping. Copy the formula from cell B15 to cells C15:H15.

13. Format the data to make it appealing and easy to read. For example, show numbers with only two decimal places, and use cell styles to add color, borders, and fills. Set the text in row 4 to wrap, and then adjust column widths. Merge and center the label *Activities* across the data.

14. Check and correct the spelling in the worksheet.

15. Select A4:H11 and identify the selected range as a table. Name the table **Log**.

16. Filter the Screen Time column to show days when you spent more than 3 hours on this activity. Clear the filter. Convert the Log table back to a range.

17. Create a 3-D Stacked Bar chart based on the data in the table. Position the chart over cells A17:E31.

18. Add the chart title **Daily Activity Log**.

19. Create a 3-D Pie chart to show the percentage of time you spent on each activity during the week.
   ⬜ *Hint: Select B4:H4 (the activities) and B12:H12 (the total hours), insert the chart, then switch the Row/Column data.*

20. Title the pie chart **Weekly Activity Time**, and display data labels as percentages. Position the pie chart over the range A32:F45. Position the legend for each chart on the right.

21. Delete row 2.
22. Preview the worksheet. Set the margins to Narrow (Top and Bottom 0.75" and left and right 0.25"), and add a footer with your name on the left and today's date on the right.
23. With your teacher's permission, print the worksheet. It should look similar to Illustration C.

24. Look at the data in the pie chart. On what activity do you spend the most time? On what activity do you spend the least time? Does looking at the pie chart help you think of ways you might better spend your time?
25. Close the file, saving all changes, and exit your spreadsheet program.

Illustration C

Daily Activity Log

Column1	Sleeping	Eating	Being at School	Screen Time	Sports	Homework	Reading	Total Hours
Monday	7.50	1.00	8.00	2.00	2.00	2.00	1.50	24.00
Tuesday	8.00	1.00	8.00	2.00	2.00	3.00	0.00	24.00
Wednesday	7.75	1.00	8.00	2.00	2.00	3.25	0.00	24.00
Thursday	7.50	1.00	8.00	2.00	2.00	2.50	1.00	24.00
Friday	8.50	1.50	8.00	4.00	2.00	0.00	0.00	24.00
Saturday	10.00	1.25	0.00	7.75	4.50	0.00	0.50	24.00
Sunday	11.00	1.50	0.00	7.00	2.00	2.50	0.00	24.00
Total Hours	60.25	8.25	40.00	26.75	16.50	13.25	3.00	168.00
Average	8.61	1.18	5.71	3.82	2.36	1.89	0.43	
Minimum	7.50	1.00	0.00	2.00	2.00	0.00	0.00	
Maximum	11.00	1.50	8.00	7.75	4.50	3.25	1.50	

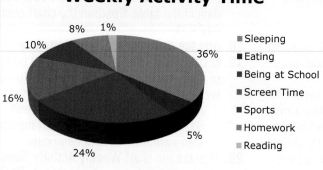

Firstname Lastname

Today's Date

DIRECTIONS: *You will insert formulas for calculating a price markdown in an existing spreadsheet. You will predict what might happen if the markdowns change, and test your prediction. Then, you will use the spreadsheet as a data source for a merge to generate price labels.*

1. Open **SS-5_Discount**, and save it as **SS-5_Discount_xx** in the location where your teacher instructs you to store the files for this activity. Replace **_xx** with your own name or initials as instructed by your teacher.

2. In cell D2, enter a formula that calculates the price after applying the discount.

    ☐ *Hint: Multiply the regular price by the discount. Then, subtract the result from the regular price.*

3. Fill the formula down through cell D16.

4. Insert a footer with your first and last names on the left and today's date on the right.

5. With your teacher's permission, print the spreadsheet, and then save the changes.

6. What do you think would happen to the new prices if the store increased the discounts by 5%? What if it decreased the discounts?

7. To test your predictions, use Find and Replace to change all 20% discounts to 25% and all 40% discounts to 35%.

8. Filter the data to display only items with a 35% discount. Clear all filters.

9. Close the spreadsheet without saving the most recent changes, and exit your spreadsheet program.

10. Start your word-processing program and save a new blank document as **SS-5_Labels_xx** in the location where your teacher instructs you to store the files for this activity.

11. Use the program's merge feature to start a merge for labels. For example, with Microsoft Word, click the Mailings tab, click Start Mail Merge, and click Labels.

12. Select a label that is 1" high by 2.63" wide, such as Avery 5160 Easy Peel Address Labels.

13. Select to use an existing data source. For example, in Word, click Select Recipients and then click Use Existing List.

14. Select Sheet 1 in the **SS-5_Discount_xx** spreadsheet as the data source.

15. In the **SS-5_Labels_xx** document, click in the first cell of the table and insert the **Item** merge field.

16. Press **Enter**, type **Regular Price: $** and insert the Regular_Price merge field.

17. Press Enter, type **Discounted Price: $** and insert the New_Price merge field.

18. Update the labels, and preview the result.

19. Check the spelling, and correct any errors. Adjust the spacing, if necessary.

20. Update the labels and preview the results. Then, with your teacher's permission, print the labels. Close the document, saving all changes, and exit your word-processing program.

21. As a class, discuss other ways you might use merge to integrate data from a spreadsheet program with a document.

DIRECTIONS: *You will use a spreadsheet template to create a project planning schedule for a team or group project.*

1. Meet with your team or group to discuss the project. Identify and write down the project goals, and the tasks that will need to be accomplished to achieve those goals. Set a timeline so you know when each task should be complete. Agree on who will be responsible for each task.
2. Start your spreadsheet program and create a new workbook based on a simple schedule template. For example, in Excel 2013 you might use the Weekly Chore Schedule. If necessary, with your teacher's permission, search online for an appropriate template.
3. Save the file as **SS-6_Schedule_xx** in the location where your teacher instructs you to store the files for this activity. Replace **xx** with your own name or initials as instructed by your teacher.
4. Insert a footer with the first name of each team member and today's date.
5. Replace the sample title in the spreadsheet with the name of your project, and replace the sample date in cell C4 with today's date.

6. Replace the sample task items with the tasks you identified in step 1, adding or removing rows, as necessary.
7. Replace the sample names in the spreadsheet with the name of the team member responsible for the task.
8. If necessary, add or delete dates to include all the dates necessary for completing the project.
9. Save the changes to the spreadsheet. A sample schedule is shown in Illustration D.
10. With your teacher's permission, print the spreadsheet.
11. As you work on the project, use the spreadsheet to mark each task that is completed as Done, so you can make sure you are progressing on schedule to achieve your goals.
12. As a class, discuss how project and time management tools can help you succeed in school, at home, and in a career.

Illustration D

Colony Report

TASK	FOR THE WEEK OF: 2/28/2016		SUN 28		MON 29		TUE 1		WED 2		THU 3		FRI 4		SAT 5	
		WHO	DONE	WHO	DONE	WHO	DONE	WHO	DONE	WHO	DONE	WHO	DONE	WHO	DONE	WHO	DONE
Select Colony			☐	All	☑		☐		☐		☐		☐		☐
Research Founders			☐		☐		☐	David	☐		☐		☐		☐
Research Hardships			☐		☐		☐	Jane	☐		☐		☐		☐
Research Economy			☐		☐		☐	Dakota	☐		☐		☐		☐
Organize Sources			☐		☐		☐		☐	LeShawn	☐		☐		☐
Obtain Images			☐		☐		☐		☐	David	☐		☐		☐
Type Report			☐		☐		☐		☐	Jane	☐		☐		☐
Format Report			☐		☐		☐		☐	Dakota	☐		☐		☐
Insert Images			☐		☐		☐		☐		☐	LeShawn	☐		☐
Create Bibliography			☐		☐		☐		☐		☐	David	☐		☐
Proofread and Correct Report			☐		☐		☐		☐		☐	All	☐		☐
Edit HTML File			☐		☐		☐		☐		☐	Jane	☐		☐
Publish to Web			☐		☐		☐		☐		☐	Dakota	☐		☐

Spreadsheet Activities

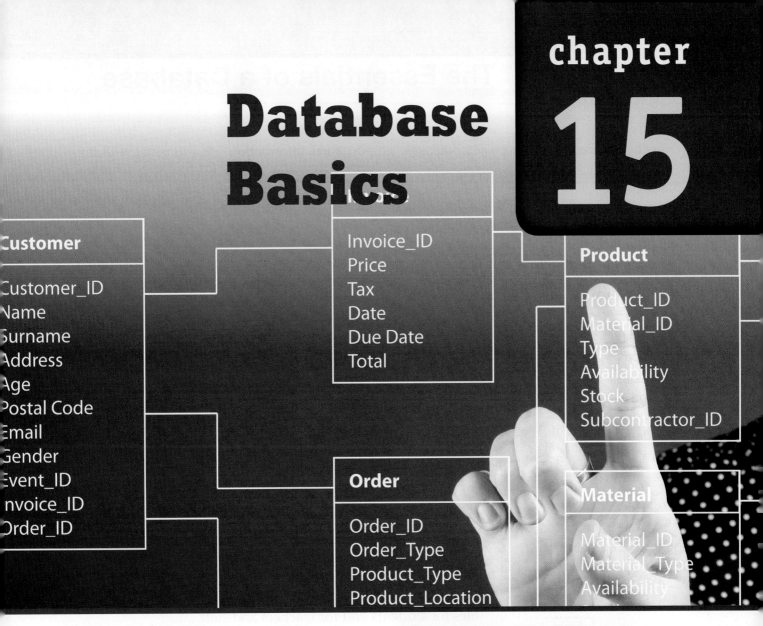

Database Basics

Customer

Customer_ID
Name
Surname
Address
Age
Postal Code
Email
Gender
Event_ID
Invoice_ID
Order_ID

Invoice_ID
Price
Tax
Date
Due Date
Total

Product

Product_ID
Material_ID
Type
Availability
Stock
Subcontractor_ID

Order

Order_ID
Order_Type
Product_Type
Product_Location

Material

Material_ID
Material_Type
Availability

What Is a Database? What do the following things have in common: an address book, a telephone directory, a list of family birthdays, and a catalog of DVDs? For one thing, each can be stored in a **database**, or an organized collection of information. Databases can exist on paper or on a computer. Computerized databases can be huge, containing information on millions of items. A computerized database is an ideal tool for making use of huge amounts of existing data.

Databases make it easy to store, add, organize, and retrieve information. Suppose a worker has to find the account number for a customer. Imagine how much time that worker saves if he or she can find the information simply by typing the customer's name instead of searching through piles of paper!

Chapter Outline

The Essentials of a Database

Objectives

- Describe the basic organization of a database.
- Summarize advantages to using database software.
- Define GIGO, and explain how it relates to the quality of a database.

As You Read

Organize Information As you read the lesson, use a concept web to help you organize basic facts about databases.

Key Terms

- database
- data mining
- data type
- field
- garbage in, garbage out (GIGO)
- metadata
- record
- table

Figure 15.1.1 Databases are made of tables, fields, and records.

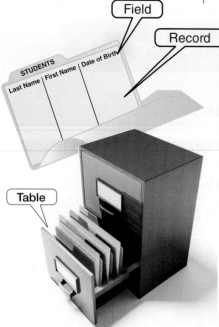

Database Organization

What makes up a database? How is it organized? Picture a file cabinet. One drawer might hold information on a company's customers, and another might have data on the company's products. Within each drawer are folders. Each folder is dedicated to a particular person or product. Finally, each folder stores different bits of information about that person or product.

A computerized database is also structured in three parts:

- tables
- records
- fields

Tables A database has one or more **tables**, just as a file cabinet may have one or more drawers. Each table contains a collection of related data. Although databases can store data in one large table, it is more typical to divide databases into smaller tables. For example, your school's database might contain separate tables for students and for teachers and staff.

Records The data in each table is further split into smaller units that contain related information about one individual or item. Each of these units is called a **record**. For your school's database, each unit of information, or record, is about an individual student or teacher.

Fields Each separate piece of data that is stored in a record—a student's last name, first name, and so on—is called a **field**. Each field is set up so that only a certain type of information, called the **data type**, is permitted in that field. For example, a field for date of birth allows only dates to be entered.

Advantages of a Database

While smaller databases might just as easily be kept on paper as on a computer, computerized databases make it easier to do the following:

Enter Information   Most databases let you input data using a table or a form. Often, rules restrict the type and amount of data you can enter, which helps minimize errors. For example, you can only enter a date in a date field, or a select an entry from a drop-down list.

Store Large Amounts of Information   If you want to keep track of 20 or 30 phone numbers, you can easily use an address book. A computerized database, however, can hold thousands, or even millions, of telephone numbers.

Find Information Quickly   A computerized database can save you time in finding information. Powerful **data mining** tools let you search through large amounts of data to find what you need quickly, and then let you easily change your requirements to find something else.

Organize Information in Different Ways   Paper filing systems can limit your ability to arrange information. For example, should you organize your personal phone book by listing each person's phone number, cell phone number, or e-mail address first? With a computerized database, you can easily sort, resort, and filter the data into any order you need.

Technology @ Home

A database is a useful tool for organizing information at home. For example, you can create a database to organize your CD or video game collection.

Think About It!

Fields are the groups of information that are included for every table in a computerized database. Which fields listed below do you think would be useful for a database of your CDs?

➤ type of music
➤ artist
➤ movie title
➤ stars
➤ CD title
➤ director

Real-World Tech

Preserving Ancient Art   Databases are often put to unexpected uses. Because databases can record and store large amounts of information, organizations have come up with creative ways to use them.

For example, at New Mexico State University, CD-ROMs store aerial views of 1,500-year-old American Indian rock art to preserve a natural art form that is vanishing due to erosion and vandalism.

How might you use a database to record information about the culture of your family or your community?

Update Information Database software makes it easy to change or update data. Think about adding a new name to your address book. It would be difficult to re-alphabetize the list if it existed only on paper. Think about how messy the book might look after just a few changes. With a computerized database, names and numbers can be added, deleted, or changed easily and quickly. After making these changes, you have an easy-to-read, updated version of the database.

Describing the Data

Specific items of information entered in database fields are called **metadata**. Metadata, which is sometimes called properties, is data about the data. For example, when you look at a list of stored files, you see information such as the file name, file type, file size, and date the file was last modified. Metadata describes the information stored in the database. It also makes it easier and faster to search through a database to find the specific record you need, and helps you keep your database organized.

It's All About the Data

Databases can be useful tools at home and at work. They also have many different uses at school. Administrators can use them to track student performance, payroll, and supplies. Teachers can use them to record students' test scores and attendance. Students can use them to organize their grades or search for information for a project.

However, databases are useful only if they are accurate. In other words, databases are only as good as the data they contain. The acronym *GIGO* explains this principle. **GIGO** is short for "**garbage in, garbage out.**" It means that if the information placed in a database is wrong, anyone using that information will get the wrong results. When adding information to a database, it is very important to do so accurately and to check your entries.

Figure 15.1.2 Businesses can use databases to keep track of their customers' contact information.

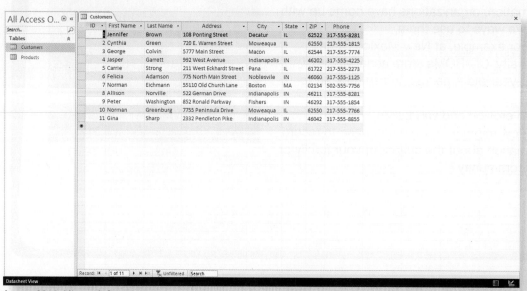

Access 2016, Microsoft Corporation.

Objectives

- Summarize the purpose of a database management system.
- Compare and contrast types of database management programs.
- Evaluate the characteristics of a well-designed database.

As You Read

Outline As you read the lesson, use an outline to help identify types of database management systems and characteristics of good design.

Database Management Systems

A database management system, or **DBMS**, is software used to manage the storage, organization, processing, and retrieval of data in a database. There are several kinds of database management programs, including flat-file databases, relational databases, object-oriented databases, and multimedia databases.

Flat-File Databases   A **flat-file database** allows you to work with data in only one table. A computerized address book is one example. In flat-file databases, records can be retrieved randomly. That is, you can look for just one name on a list. You can also retrieve an entire table and **sort** the data, or arrange it in a different order. You might sort to find all the people living in the same town, for example.

Flat-file databases have a limitation. The data in one table cannot be linked to the data in another table. That might not be a problem with a simple address book. However, many businesses and other large organizations use databases in more complex ways, and they need added flexibility.

Relational Databases   A **relational database** can use data from several tables at the same time. This is because the tables are linked by a **key field**, a field that is found in each of the tables. A relational database is more complex than a flat-file database program. It also requires more skill to use and costs more. However, its greater power makes it more popular.

Think about a relational database a school might have. One table might hold all students' schedules. Another might have all their grades. Yet another table might include their addresses and phone numbers. All the tables can be linked by a key field: each student's name or student identification number. By using key fields, administrators can find data about a particular student from any available table.

🔑 Key Terms

- database management system (DBMS)
- flat-file database
- key field
- object-oriented database
- relational database
- sort

Businesses can link their relational databases by customer names and numbers. Companies use these databases for many purposes, including storing customer information, such as name, address, and telephone number; seeing where to ship goods the customer buys; issuing bills for purchases and receipts for payments made; and tracking what customers have bought over time and using that information to tailor ads and promotions.

Object-Oriented Databases Another type of DBMS is called an **object-oriented database**. These databases store objects, such as documents, video clips, and audio clips. Each object contains both that data and the program needed to display that data, including showing a graphic or playing a sound.

Object-oriented databases are not yet widely used. Some experts believe that they will replace relational databases in the future.

Multimedia Databases Traditional databases can store all kinds of text and numerical data. Today's computers also often deal with pictures, sounds, animation, or video clips. Multimedia professionals use databases to catalog media files, such as art, photographs, maps, video clips, and sound files. Media files themselves generally are not stored in databases because they are too large. Instead, a multimedia database serves as an index to all the separately stored files. Users can search through the index and then locate the particular file they want.

Figure 15.2.1 Databases are everywhere in our wired world. For example, at supermarkets, they store information about the products we buy. On our cell phones, they store information about the people we contact.

Well-Designed Databases

For databases to be effective, they need to be planned carefully. Following are three characteristics of good database design:

Ensuring Data Security   The same features that make databases efficient tools make them vulnerable to invasions of privacy. Personal information can be misused. Requiring users to input a password before they can access data is one way of keeping a database secure.

Preserving Data Integrity   The accuracy and validity of the information gives a database its data integrity. Errors make the database less accurate and less useful.

Avoiding Data Redundancy   Repeating the same data in many tables wastes space by requiring a computer to store the same information more than once. It also increases the amount of work needed to update records because the data needs to be changed in more than one place. That, in turn, increases the chance of errors and slows down searches for data. Storing data in only one table and then linking the table to others enables the data to be used in various ways.

Career Corner

Database Administrator   One key to good database design is testing the design to make sure it works the way it is supposed to. That testing is part of the work of database administrators. They also maintain the security of the database and write manuals that explain how to use the database.

Figure 15.2.2 Protecting the database with a password.

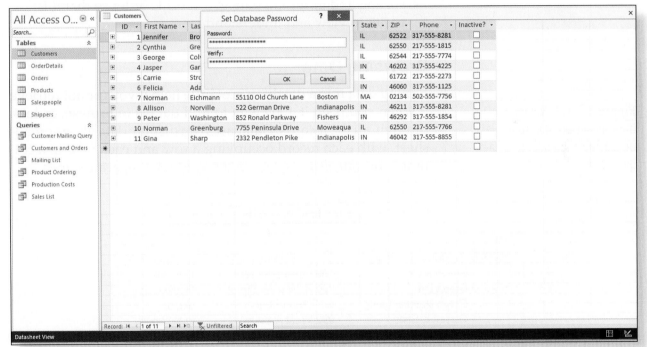

Access 2016, Microsoft Corporation.

Database Techniques

Objectives

- Give examples of how to manage information in databases.
- Compare and contrast browsing, sorting, and querying data in a database.
- Describe the features of a report template.

As You Read

Summarize As you read the lesson, use a chart to help you summarize techniques for using databases effectively.

🔑 Key Terms

- ascending order
- browse
- descending order
- information overload
- report
- report template

Figure 15.3.1 Navigation buttons allow users to move quickly through a large database table.

Information Management

Computers can produce too much information, or **information overload**. Database creators can help manage data by:

- summarizing information so that database users are not overwhelmed by details
- filtering data in reports to include only what is necessary to meet specific user needs
- sorting and grouping data in a specific order so that it is easier to view and understand

Browsing Data

Putting data into a database is of little help if you cannot retrieve it when you need it. One way to find data is to **browse**, or look through, all the records. Databases can display data like a spreadsheet, with each record occupying a row and each field in a column. You can also display each record on a separate screen.

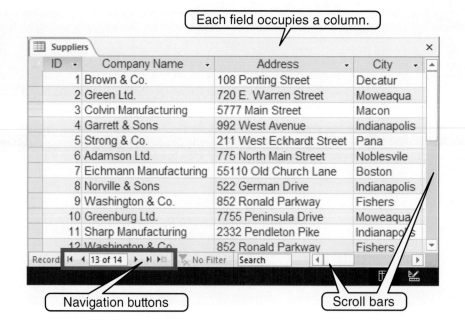

Each field occupies a column.

Suppliers				×
ID ▾	Company Name ▾	Address ▾	City ▾	
1	Brown & Co.	108 Ponting Street	Decatur	
2	Green Ltd.	720 E. Warren Street	Moweaqua	
3	Colvin Manufacturing	5777 Main Street	Macon	
4	Garrett & Sons	992 West Avenue	Indianapolis	
5	Strong & Co.	211 West Eckhardt Street	Pana	
6	Adamson Ltd.	775 North Main Street	Noblesvile	
7	Eichmann Manufacturing	55110 Old Church Lane	Boston	
8	Norville & Sons	522 German Drive	Indianapolis	
9	Washington & Co.	852 Ronald Parkway	Fishers	
10	Greenburg Ltd.	7755 Peninsula Drive	Moweaqua	
11	Sharp Manufacturing	2332 Pendleton Pike	Indianapolis	
12	Washington & Co.	852 Ronald Parkway	Fishers	

Record I◄ ◄ 13 of 14 ► ►I ►▣   No Filter   Search

Navigation buttons

Scroll bars

Many database programs provide keyboard commands and other tools, such as scroll bars and navigation buttons, that help users browse quickly through records. You can also limit the browsing so that the program displays only certain records and fields. This can greatly reduce the time it takes to locate or review specific records.

Sorting Data

Another way to save time is to sort the data. Sorting lets you locate information quickly.

Types of Sorting Databases can sort data in three ways:
- Alphabetical sorting of letters and symbols
- Numerical sorting of numbers and values
- Chronological sorting of dates and times

Data can be sorted in **ascending order**, in which values increase, such as A, B, C or 1, 2, 3. It can also be sorted the opposite way, in **descending order**. In this order, values decrease. Letters are listed C, B, and A, and numbers are sorted 3, 2, and 1.

Single and Multiple Sorts The easiest kind of sort uses a single field, such as name. Databases can also sort data using more than one field, such as last name and first name. When two records are identical in the first field, they are sorted again based on the next field. In this case, a database would list "Williams, Serena" before "Williams, Venus."

Querying Data

Databases can speed up the process of browsing information by finding only records that match specific criteria. A query is a user-created direction that tells the database to find and display specific records.

Figure 15.3.2 Sorting lets you organize data so it best suits your needs.

ID No.	Last Name	Birthday
1	Rodriquez	10-13-89
2	Goldstein	06-03-88
3	Smith	05-15-88
4	Hernandez	11-01-87
5	Abdullah	04-21-89
6	Chung	01-03-87

Sort by ID Number

ID No.	Last Name	Birthday
5	Abdullah	04-21-89
6	Chung	01-03-87
2	Goldstein	06-03-88
4	Hernandez	11-01-87
1	Rodriquez	10-13-89
3	Smith	05-15-88

Sort by Last Name

ID No.	Last Name	Birthday
1	Rodriquez	10-13-89
5	Abdullah	04-21-89
2	Goldstein	06-03-88
3	Smith	05-15-88
4	Hernandez	11-01-87
6	Chung	01-03-87

Sort by Birthday

Creating Reports

With a database program you can create a report to show the information in a table or a query. A **report** is an ordered list of selected records and fields in an easy-to-read format. Reports can display data in columns, as labels, or as single records. Reports are usually printed on paper so people can read them and interpret the data.

Reports are really just a format and a layout; the data is stored in the database. When you generate the report to view or print, the program uses the data currently available. If you save the report and generate it again later, the data will show updates made to the database.

Designing a Report Template   In most databases, users design a **report template**, a pattern that controls how data will be displayed. This template typically has several main features:

- a report header that appears at the beginning of a report, such as the report title
- a report footer that appears at the end of a report, such as summary totals or averages
- a page header that appears at the top of each page, such as field headings
- a page footer that appears at the bottom of each page, such as the date the report was printed and the page number
- the arrangement of the data that you want the report to include

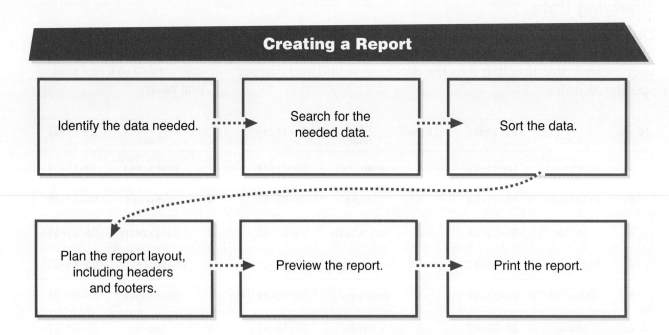

Creating a Report

Identify the data needed. ⟶ Search for the needed data. ⟶ Sort the data.

Plan the report layout, including headers and footers. ⟶ Preview the report. ⟶ Print the report.

Use the Vocabulary

Directions: *Match each vocabulary term in the left column with the correct definition in the right column.*

_____ **1.** database
_____ **2.** record
_____ **3.** field
_____ **4.** data type
_____ **5.** GIGO
_____ **6.** database management system
_____ **7.** flat-file database
_____ **8.** relational database
_____ **9.** key field
_____ **10.** ascending order

a. smallest part of a database; holds an individual piece of data

b. term that stresses the importance of inputting accurate data

c. examples are A, B, C and 1, 2, 3

d. organized collection of information stored on computer

e. database that allows you to work with data in only one table

f. part of a database that holds data about a particular person or item

g. software used to manage the storage, organization, processing, and retrieval of data in a database

h. database in which shared key fields link data among tables

i. limited kind of information that can be entered into a field

j. element that links tables

Check Your Comprehension

Directions: *Complete each sentence with information from the chapter.*

1. Some databases have only one _____, but others can hold several, each containing a set of related data.

2. Database programs are superior to paper databases in part because the information can be _____ in different ways.

3. GIGO is a reminder that a database is of poorer quality if the _____ is not accurate.

4. The kind of database that stores and opens programs for images, video clips, and audio clips is a(n) _____.

5. A multimedia database is similar to a book _____.

6. Protecting sensitive data by requiring users to input a(n) _____ is one way to aim for data security.

7. Data _____ is usually undesirable because it wastes space and introduces the possibility of errors.

8. One way that databases can be used to reduce information overload is to _____ information so that users are not overwhelmed by details.

9. Dates and times are sorted in _____ order.

10. You can create multiple _____ to tailor the reports generated from a database.

 **Think Critically**

Directions: *Answer the following questions.*

1. Suppose you wanted to create a database of your school's DVD collection. What fields might you include?

2. Based on efficiency, which kind of database software would you choose to create a database in which you needed to link information? Why?

3. What can you do to try to ensure the accuracy of the data you enter into a database?

4. Identify and explain the purpose of fields in a database.

5. Identify and explain the purpose of records in a database.

Extend Your Knowledge

Directions: *Choose and complete one of the following projects.*

A. Select a magazine in your school library, and create a database of the articles featured in that issue. Include such fields as author, title, topic, and starting page number. Add another field for date of the issue, and add some records from another issue of the same magazine. Create a report that displays the data you input. With your teacher's permission, print your report. Then, find another way of presenting the data, and, with your teacher's permission, print that report. Save your database.

B. In small groups, make an appointment to visit a local business. Interview the owner or a key employee about the databases that the business uses. Find out what tables, records, and fields the databases have. Ask how the databases are used. Prepare a brief report summarizing your findings. Present it to the class. Read your report out loud to a partner and listen while your partner reads his or her report out loud to you.

Understanding Databases

What Makes Information Valuable? Just because information can be stored in a database does not make it valuable. Information by itself has little worth. To be valuable for decision making, information needs to have these traits:

- accessibility—easily located and retrieved
- accuracy—free of errors
- relevancy—related to your purpose
- completeness—does not omit anything relevant
- economy—costs less to use than to create
- reliability—available when you need it
- security—unauthorized people denied access
- simplicity—clear and understandable
- timeliness—up-to-date
- verifiability—can be confirmed by another source

Chapter Outline

 Lesson 16–1

Creating an Effective Database

 Lesson 16–2

Maintaining Efficient Databases

 Lesson 16–3

Using Queries and Filters

Creating an Effective Database

Objectives

- Describe the parts of a data structure.
- Explain how the structure of a database influences its effectiveness.
- Sequence the steps in creating a data structure.
- Compare and contrast data types.

As You Read

Identify Details   As you read the lesson, use a main idea chart to help you identify important details for creating databases.

🔑 **Key Terms**

- binary large object (BLOB)
- data structure
- field name
- field width

Creating a Data Structure

All structures have an underlying frame that determines their size, shape, and general appearance. Databases also have a framework, called a **data structure**. It defines the fields in the database, and thus defines what each record will contain.

Parts of a Data Structure   A data structure has four parts:

- The field sequence is the order in which the fields will appear in each record.
- The **field name** is a unique identifier for each field, such as "Last Name" or "Class."
- Data type specifies the kind of information the field will contain; for example, numbers, date, text, or hyperlink.
- The **field width** is a limit on the size of the field, which is typically the number of characters in the largest expected data value. For example, a field width for a U.S. state in an address might be two characters. The field for a phone number might be 10 or 14 characters.

Customizing Data Structure   Most database programs in use today allow you to design a data structure from scratch and define your fields. Many programs also have predesigned database structures that can be customized.

Benefits of Good Design   Well-designed data structures can improve database effectiveness. They set up the proper amount of space for the data you will collect. They also enable you to gather the data you need and organize data so that it can be searched efficiently. Poorly designed data structures result in databases that take up unnecessary disk space. They might exclude data that you need. These problems make it more difficult to retrieve the data you need in a meaningful way.

Designing the Data Structure

Generally, a database is used by many people—not just the person who designed it. Good design is important for this reason, too. Users should find the database easy to understand and its tools easy to use. The database should be set up to encourage accurate, efficient data entry and to provide reliable results when running queries and reports. A data structure is usually designed in four steps:

1. Identify the database. You can choose an existing database in which to place the tables or you can create a new database that will contain all the tables, forms, and reports you specify.

2. Create the tables. Create each new table to be included in the database.

3. Identify each field. As you create a table, specify the name, data type, and field size of each field that will exist within the table. Many database programs give other options for fields:

   • Default values are used automatically if no data is entered in the field.

   • Input masks are formats that standardize the way data looks, such as dashes between the different parts of all phone numbers.

   • Prompt captions are messages that appear on-screen to help the person entering data understand the content of the field.

   • Validation rules are limits that determine what data is acceptable for a field. For instance, a field for test scores could be limited to values between 0 and 100.

4. Save the data structure. You can always modify a structure later, if you wish. You can add or delete fields, rearrange their order, or modify the data type or width. You can also add new tables and make changes to existing ones.

Career Corner

Librarian   Librarians work with many different databases. Some catalog books, videos, and reference materials. Librarians assign numbers to the items they are cataloging based on the subjects of the items.

Reference librarians help users find the information they want in databases. Some librarians work for private companies doing this research. They have job titles such as researcher and database specialist.

Steps in Designing a Database

Identify the database.	→	Create each table.	→	Identify each field within each table.	→	Save the data structure.

Did You Know?

Four of the United Kingdom's busiest airports, including London's Heathrow International and Manchester Airport, are using a database with a very unusual data type—eye scans. Nicknamed IRIS for "Iris Recognition Immigration System," the high-tech machines scan passengers' eyes as soon as they check in. Airport security officials hope that IRIS will make it much more difficult for illegal immigrants and criminals—particularly terrorists—to get into the country.

Common Data Types

Many databases allow you to select a data type for each field. This prevents users from typing numbers in a field that is supposed to hold names, for instance. There are several common data types:

- Text—letters, numbers, and special characters. This is used for a name or an address, for example.
- Number—numeric data that can be used in calculations, such as values that are totaled or averaged.
- Logical—data with only two possible values, such as "yes/no" or "true/false." This might be used to indicate whether a student is male or female.
- Currency—consists of number fields with special formatting to reflect the fact that they represent sums of money. This could be used for billing information.
- Date/time—used to indicate a date or time of day.
- Memo—allows for an unlimited amount of text information. This type is used for notes.
- Autonumber—automatically assigns a number to each record in the table. This could be used for assigning an identification number to each student, for instance.
- Object—any nontext object. This type is used for an image, sound, or video.
- Hyperlink—connects to a Web address.

Some database programs allow you to specify a data type to handle very large objects. This data type is known as a **binary large object (BLOB)**.

Figure 16.1.1 Assigning data types in a table of order information.

Orders

Field Name	Data Type	Des
Order ID	AutoNumber	
Order Date	Date/Time	
Customer	Number	Numeric because it is related to
Shipper	Number	Numeric because it is related to
Salesperson	Short Text	

Maintaining Efficient Databases

Objectives

- Describe techniques for maintaining data.
- Compare two methods of processing records.
- Explain how adding and deleting data contributes to the efficiency of a database.

As You Read

Outline As you read the lesson, use an outline to help you organize basic information about maintaining databases.

Data Maintenance

As with any tool, a database needs to be well maintained. You can make sure that a database continues to operate efficiently by performing regular **data maintenance**. This includes tasks such as adding new records, modifying existing records, and deleting those you no longer need.

You can modify databases in other ways, too. You might change the reports the database uses. You also might update the structure of the database to reflect your needs.

Keeping a Database Current

Databases typically provide for two methods of updating data: batch processing and transactional processing.

People choose a processing method based on how important it is for the data to be completely up-to-date. Batch processing was more common in the past. Most databases today use transactional processing.

Batch Processing In **batch processing**, the data is recorded as events take place, but the database itself is not updated until there is a group, or batch, of data ready to process. Each batch is processed all at once, typically when the computer is idle, such as in the late evening—this frees up memory for more extensive programs and also speeds up productivity.

Batch processing is used for tasks where updating a large database might take several hours. For example, credit card companies store customers' transaction data to be sent out in batches at the end of the month; otherwise, you'd get a paper bill for every single transaction. Batch processing is not appropriate, however, in situations where data must always be kept as current as possible.

Transactional Processing Databases that require immediate updating of data use **transactional processing**. In this method, the database is updated as events take place. For example, airline reservation systems cannot wait hours to have their records updated. They must have each new reservation entered right

Key Terms

- batch processing
- data maintenance
- form
- online analytical processing (OLAP)
- online transactional processing (OLTP)
- transactional processing

Technology @ Work

Businesses want their databases to be kept up-to-date so they can be more efficient. Suppose a business sends bills to all its customers. If some are sent to the wrong address, payments may be delayed.

Think About It!

Which reasons listed below would require a company to access up-to-date database records?

➤ send bills

➤ check inventory

➤ send catalogs

➤ pay employees

➤ ship goods

away. A form of transactional processing called **online transactional processing**, or **OLTP**, provides for immediate approval of Internet credit card purchases 24 hours a day.

Analytical Processing Some databases use analytical processing to compare information from multiple sources at the same time. To analyze many types of data, queries are made using multiple dimensions. For example, when you compare two sets of data, such as the price of different types of pens and the number of pens sold, you are using two dimensions. If you include the total profit made from selling each set of pens, you are adding a third dimension. A form of analytical processing called **online analytical processing**, or **OLAP**, is often used in business. OLTP databases are used for storing current information, like airline reservations, while OLAP databases are used for storing large amounts of historical information to be used for business analysis, such as profits over multiple years.

Adding, Modifying, and Deleting Records

Databases manage the many changes made to records as they are updated.

Adding Data Adding records to a database is a common action. When new students enroll at a school, for example, their records must be added to student tables.

Modifying Data Data already held in records can also be modified or edited to reflect changing conditions or to correct a data entry error. For instance, when a student moves, the school's database can be updated to reflect the new address. If a grade

Spotlight on...

JEFF BEZOS

Amazon.com opened its Web site worldwide on July 16, 1995. A whole new way of selling had been launched. Bezos developed his site by first hiring a programmer who developed an easy-to-use system of searching CD-ROM databases of all books in print. That system gave Bezos—and the world—the first widely used "e-commerce" company. Customers search the company's databases to find what they want. Then, Amazon.com ships their purchases.

is entered incorrectly, the student's record must be corrected. Records in a database table can be added or modified on-screen much like entering data in a spreadsheet program. The corrected data is entered and then saved.

Using Forms to Change Data Often, databases contain forms. A **form** is a window that makes it easier for users to view, enter, and edit data. A form typically shows all the data for a given record at one time. It might also include questions or prompts to make updating the data easier. Forms also allow users to pull data from more than one table—a big advantage. A data access page, which is similar to a form, stores data in HTML format so you can view data in a Web browser.

Often, the form shown on-screen looks like the printed paper form used to gather the data. For example, a personnel form might look like a company's job application. This makes entering the data faster and more accurate because the person entering the data can look in the same place on both forms for information.

Deleting, Moving, and Linking Records Sometimes a record is removed from a database. For instance, a customer might cancel an account with a business. Although you can remove records that are no longer needed, records are typically moved from an active table into an inactive table. For example, when you graduate, your records will probably not be deleted from your school's database but will be moved to a graduate table. The main database might retain only your name, ID number, and graduation date. These will be linked to the complete record in the graduate table.

Linking is done for two reasons. First, it keeps the information available in case it is needed again. Second, it reduces the space and processing time needed when using the active records in the database.

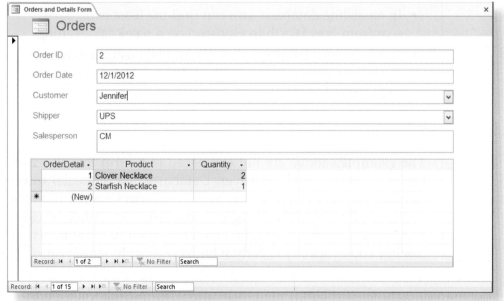

Figure 16.2.1 A database form lets you view, add, or change the data in a single record.

Using Queries and Filters

Objectives

- Explain how queries make a database easier to use.
- Compare and contrast SQL and QBE.
- Compare and contrast a query and a filter.

As You Read

Summarize   As you read the lesson, use a chart to help you summarize details about queries.

Key Terms

- filter
- query
- Query by Example (QBE)
- query language
- Structured Query Language (SQL)

Looking for Data

In a large database, it is inefficient to look through every record to find what you need. Many database programs have a search feature that lets you quickly locate only those records that match your search. To carry out this search, you create a query. A **query** is a question that you ask a database.

Queries are powerful tools that make databases much more efficient. You can create a query and use it once, or you can save it to use again. Queries can also be used to maintain databases. For example, you may be able to use a query to update or even delete records in the database. A query looks a lot like a table, but it is very different. You use a table to enter, store, and validate data. A query is a tool for finding, displaying, and manipulating the data stored in one or more tables.

Examples of Queries   You can write queries constructed to find the following information:

- In a database of collector series baseball cards, you can find all new players whose careers started between 2001 and 2003 by including the word *rookie* in the query.
- In an airline database, you can find the least expensive seat from Fort Worth to Houston on a weekday evening.
- In a business database, you can find all customers who have not purchased anything in more than two years and then move these names to an inactive table.

Query Languages

The examples above are not expressed in a form that the database can understand, however. Databases use a special **query language** in which queries are written in ways similar to mathematical equations. This language uses precise syntax, or rules, to correctly combine specific elements, such as statements, allowing you to specify exactly what you want to search for.

SQL A popular database query language is **Structured Query Language**, or **SQL**. SQL is written using elements, including queries, expressions, clauses, predicates, and statements. Most SQL queries start with a SELECT command. This tells the database to identify selected records that match given criteria. The SQL query also identifies the files and fields from which the data is to be selected.

For example, an SQL query to find the names and class schedules of all students in the seventh grade who have an average better than 85 looks like this:

SELECT	Name, Class
FROM	Student
WHERE	Average>85
AND	Grade=7

QBE Many database programs allow users to avoid typing SQL queries by providing a **Query by Example**, or **QBE**, feature that lets you provide an example of what you are seeking. You typically identify a field and then type the condition that explains the acceptable data limits. For example, the query for the student list might look like this:

FIELD	Name	Class	Average	Grade
FILE	Student	Student	Student	Student
SHOW	✓	✓		
CRITERIA			>85	=7

Real-World Tech

Seeing Stars One use for databases is to learn more about the stars and planets. Using a special computer program, astronomers can send queries into a database that holds pictures of the sky taken by the Hubble Space Telescope and by an earthbound observatory. By putting the information together, they can quickly find all records of objects in the same position in the sky. Then, they can study the images taken over many years to learn more about the objects. There are many other high-tech ways that scientists, government agencies, and other organizations use databases.

What databases can you think of that your local government agencies maintain?

Figure 16.3.1 Creating a query in Microsoft Access.

Options Queries can search by complete data fields or parts of them. Database programs typically offer these search options:

- *Whole field* queries allow you to look for items that match the entire data value. For example, you can search for all records with a first name of "Martin."
- *Part of field* is a query that allows you to look for data that matches any part of a data value. For example, you can search for a date that includes March 2005 or a city that starts with "New."
- *Sounds like* queries allow you to look for data values that are similar to the search word. For example, if you look for "Smith," you might also find "Smyth" or "Smythe."
- *Match case* is a kind of query in which you look for data that matches the capitalization exactly as written. In this case, a search for "PowerPoint" would not find "Powerpoint," "POWERPOINT," or "powerpoint."

Filters

A **filter** helps reduce the quantity of data to be reviewed by temporarily hiding some records from view. It makes the database seem much smaller and speeds up processing.

For example, if you plan to review or edit only the records of seventh-grade students, you could filter the school's database to display only that grade. Any queries or editing would be done on this smaller record set rather than the entire database. When you no longer need the filter, you can simply cancel it to return the database to its full status.

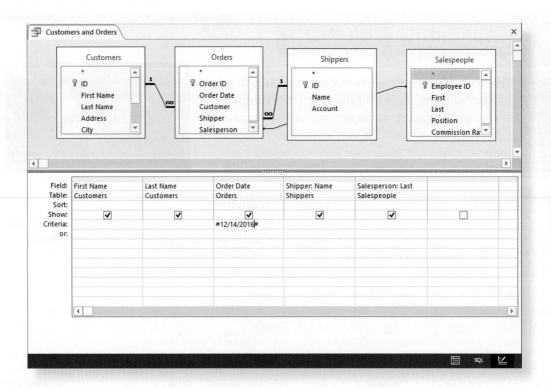

Use the Vocabulary

Directions: *Match each vocabulary term in the left column with the correct definition in the right column.*

_____ 1. data structure
_____ 2. field name
_____ 3. field width
_____ 4. batch processing
_____ 5. transactional processing
_____ 6. online transactional processing
_____ 7. form
_____ 8. query
_____ 9. query language
_____ 10. filter

a. special way of phrasing queries

b. provides approval of Internet credit card purchases

c. request to search for data

d. way of limiting records being searched

e. the way a database is organized

f. identifier for each field

g. maximum number of characters in a field

h. on-screen window in which users view, enter, and edit data

i. way of changing databases that automatically keeps them up-to-date

j. way of changing databases that delays updates for a time

Check Your Comprehension

Directions: *Complete each sentence with information from the chapter.*

1. Creating a good _____ makes it easier to use a database because it promotes efficient searching.

2. In creating a data structure, you need to identify the database, create the tables, and then _____.

3. In a bank database, the bank account would have a(n) _____ data type, but the balance in the account would be shown by a currency data type.

4. If a company sends weekly bills to clients, it would be reasonable for the company to use _____ processing.

5. Records can be modified in a table or by using a data _____.

6. Moving outdated information into a(n) _____ file keeps the database smaller and easier to use.

7. Making a(n) _____ is an efficient way to find complex information in a database.

8. A query made with _____ tries to identify selected records that meet particular criteria.

9. To limit a query to only those records that match the entire value, you would choose the _____ option.

10. _____ work by temporarily hiding some records from a search.

Think Critically

Directions: *Answer the following questions.*

1. What is the role of data structure in designing a database?

2. How do data types for each field affect a database?

3. Identify and explain the purpose of a query language.

4. Identify and explain at least two elements of a query language.

5. Describe the process of constructing a query to find the records for all freshmen in a school. Then, describe the process for finding records for all freshmen whose last names begin with the letter M.

Extend Your Knowledge

Directions: *Choose and complete one of the following projects.*

A. With your teacher's permission, use the Internet to research the new-car inventory of an auto dealership. Review the dealer's database, or plan one of your own on paper that could be used to store information about the new cars in stock. Define or identify the fields and the report layout. Write a sample query, and share it with your class.

B. With your teacher's permission, use the Internet to learn about database security issues. As you work, take notes and keep track of your sources. Evaluate the information you find and only use it if it is accurate, relevant, and valid. Prepare a brief written summary of the problem and possible solutions. Include a list of sources or a bibliography. Read your summary out loud to a partner and listen to your partner read his or hers out loud to you.

C. Spreadsheets and databases are similar in many ways. For example, they both organize data in columns and rows. Create a spreadsheet file and enter contact information for at least five people. Include Firstname, Lastname, and E-mail address. Save the spreadsheet. Start a database program and import the spreadsheet records to create a new table. Write a paragraph comparing the two programs, and discuss it with a partner or as a class.

DIRECTIONS: *You will create a database about landforms that glaciers make as they move. You will create a table for the information, and use a form to enter records. You will also create a report to present the data.*

1. Open the .pdf file **DB-1_Landforms**. This file contains information about glaciers and the landforms they create. With your teacher's permission, print the file. Close the file, and exit your pdf reader program.

2. Start your database program and create a new, blank database file, and save it as **DB-1_Glacier_ xx** in the location where your teacher instructs you to store the files for this activity. Replace **xx** with your own initials or name, as directed by your teacher.

3. Create a new table named **tblGlacial Landforms**.

4. Add the following two fields to the table:

Field Name	Data Type	Field Size
Landform	*Text*	*50*
Description	*Text*	*250*

5. Do not specify a primary key.

6. Save and close the table. Keep your database program open.

7. Create a form based on **tblGlacial Landforms**.

8. Save the form as **frmGlacial Landforms**.

9. Refer to the .pdf file **DB-1_Landforms**, and enter the data from the pdf into the database using the **frmGlacial Landforms** form.

10. Review each record carefully to be sure you enter correct information, and proofread your work for typing errors.

11. Save and close the form.

12. Open **tblGlacial Landforms**.

13. If necessary, increase the column width of the table columns so you can see the entries.

14. Sort the table in A to Z order by Landform.

15. Save the changes to your table.

16. Preview the table, and change the orientation to landscape. The table should look similar to Illustration A.

17. Show your table to your teacher as directed.

18. Create a tabular report based on the table, including all fields. Name the report **rptGlacial Landforms**.

19. Preview the report and adjust the page layout and design as necessary. For example, change to landscape orientation and increase the height of the Description field so all data displays.

20. With your teacher's permission, print the report.

21. Close the database file, and exit the database program.

Illustration A

tblGlacial Landforms	
Landform	**Description**
Arete	An arete is a sharp ridge separating two cirques.
Cirque	A cirque is a bowl-shaped hollow eroded by a glacier.
Drumlin	A drumlin is a long mound of till that is smoothed in the direction of the glacier's flow.
Fiord	A fiord forms when the level of the sea rises, filling a valley once cut by a glacier in a coastal region.
Glacial lake	Glaciers may leave behind large lakes in long basins eroded by plucking and abrasion.
Horn	When glaciers carve away the sides of a mountain, the result is a horn, or a sharpened peak.
Kettle lake	A kettle lake forms when a depression left in till by melting ice fills with water.
Moraine	A moraine forms where a glacier deposits mounds or ridges of till.
U-shaped valley	A flowing glacier scoops out a U-shaped valley.

Database Activities

DIRECTIONS: *You will collect and organize information relating to the climates of the United States and Canada. You will enter this information in a database, and then sort and query it to compare climates in both countries, and create a report to present your data.*

1. Open the .pdf file **DB-2_Stats**. With your teacher's permission, print the Data Record Sheet. Close the file, and exit your pdf reader program.
2. With your teacher's permission, use the Internet or use a textbook to research the climate in at least ten states—including your home state—and three Canadian provinces. Write down all source information as you work.
   a. If you are using the Internet, use a search engine Web site, and search using keywords or phrases such as **climate** or the name of a state or province, or use Boolean search strategies. For example, you might search for the **[name of a state] AND climate**. Find at least two sources for each fact. When you find a Web site with useful information, bookmark the site, or with your teacher's permission, print the pages.
   b. Record useful information on your Data Record Sheet. If you need more space, use the back of the sheet, or a separate piece of paper. When you have completed your research, close your Web browser.
3. Start your database program, create a new database, and save it as **DB-2_Stats_xx** in the location where your teacher instructs you to store the files for this activity. Replace **xx** with your own name or initials as directed by your teacher.
4. In a new table, change to Design View and save the table as **tblClimate Stats**.
5. In the table, include a primary key that automatically assigns a unique value to each record.
6. Create four text fields matching those in the **DB-2_Stats** Data Record Sheet: **State, Province, or Territory**; **Country**; **U.S. Region**; **Climate(s)**.
7. Save the table, and change to Datasheet view.

8. Referring to your Data Record Sheet, enter records for each of the states or provinces you researched. Fill in all of the information for each field in the table. If a state, province, or territory has multiple climates, separate the climates with commas. Adjust column widths, as necessary.
9. Sort the data in A to Z order by Country. Delete one record.
10. Check the spelling in the table, and correct any errors.
11. Preview the table, and adjust the page layout as necessary so the data displays properly and is easy to read. For example, change to Landscape orientation.
12. Filter the records to show only your home state. Then, remove the filter and close the table.
13. Create a new Select query based on **tblClimate Stats**. Include all fields except the Country field. Save the new query as **qryClimate Stats**.
14. Modify the query to show only records for states, provinces, or territories that have the same climate as your home state. To do this, enter the climate of your home state as the criteria for the Climate field. Save the new query as **qryClimate Home State**.
15. Sort the query in Ascending order by U.S. Region. Run the query.
16. Preview the query, and adjust the page layout so the data displays properly and is easy to read.
17. Compare tables and queries with a partner or peer editor. Correct errors.
18. Create a report based on the **qryClimate Home State** query. Name the report **qryClimate Home State**.
19. With your teacher's permission, print the report.
20. Close all open objects, saving all changes.
21. Close the database, and exit your database program.

DIRECTIONS: *You will search the Web to find ten species in your state that are on the endangered or threatened species list, as well as the reasons why they are. You will create a database to organize the information, and then design a report based on specific criteria.*

1. Open the .pdf file **DB-3_Species**. With your teacher's permission, print the Data Record Sheet. Close the file, and exit your pdf reader program.

2. With your teacher's permission, use the Internet to research ten endangered species in your state. Write down all source information as you work.

   a. If you are using the Internet, use a search engine Web site, and search using keywords or phrases such as **endangered species**, or use Boolean search strategies. For example, you might search for the **[name of a state] AND parks and wildlife**. Find at least two sources for each fact. When you find a Web site with useful information, bookmark the site, or with your teacher's permission, print the pages.

   b. Write useful information on your Data Record Sheet. If you need more space, use the back of the sheet, or a separate piece of paper. As you conduct your research, think about problems that might occur when animals become extinct or endangered. When you have completed your research, close your Web browser.

3. Start your database program, create a new database, and save it as **DB-3_Species_xx** in the location where your teacher instructs you to store the files for this activity. Replace **xx** with your own name or initials as directed by your teacher.

4. Create a table with field names similar to the column headings on the Data Record Sheet: **Name of Species**; **Type**; **State Status**; **Federal Status**; **Reasons for Endangerment**; **Population Numbers**; **Location in State**; **Interesting Fact**. Be sure to define the data type for each field and to set field properties as necessary. You do not need a primary key.

5. Save the table as **tblEndangered Species**.

6. Referring to the information from the Data Record Sheet, enter records for each species you researched. (You may use the abbreviations **T** for threatened and **E** for endangered in the State Status and Federal Status fields.)

7. Check the spelling, and adjust column widths to display all data.

8. Sort the table by Type. Preview the table and adjust the page setup as necessary. For example, change to Landscape view.

9. Sort the table in A to Z order by Name of Species, and then by State Status.

10. Create a Select query to find the records that have both a State Status and a Federal Status.

11. Save the query as **qrySpecies Status**.

12. Create a report based on the **qrySpecies Status** query, named **rptSpecies Status**.

13. Preview and modify the design of the report to improve the appearance and make the data easier to read.

14. Preview the report and adjust the page setup as necessary. With your teacher's permission, print the report.

15. Close all open objects, saving all changes.

16. Close the database, and exit your database program.

17. As a class, discuss why some species may be endangered at one government level but not at another. Discuss ways governments and individuals can protect and preserve wildlife.

DIRECTIONS: *You will create a database to track products for a garage sale and predict the possible income you could earn. You will design a query that calculates sales of each item, and then you will generate a report that groups and summarizes the data.*

1. As a class, discuss organizations that could benefit if you donated proceeds from a garage sale. Select one, and plan a garage sale.
2. Open the .pdf file **DB-4_Money**. With your teacher's permission, print the Data Record Sheet. Close the file, and exit your pdf reader.
3. Choose five categories of items you might be able to gather from classmates to sell at a garage sale. Categories might include clothing, toys, entertainment, home goods, and sporting goods. List these in the wide columns in the top (gray) row of the table on the Data Record Sheet. In the rows under each category, list at least ten items you might sell. In the narrow column to the right of each item, enter the price you would charge.
4. Start your database program, and create a new database named **DB-4_Managing_Money_xx** and save it as instructed by your teacher.
5. Create a table with the following fields: **Category**, **Item Name**, **Quantity**, **Sale Price**, and an ID AutoNumber field as the primary key. Set data types appropriate for each field.
6. Save the table as **tblGarage Sale**.
7. Use the information on the Data Record Sheet to create a record for each garage sale item. Illustration B shows a sample table with records.
8. After entering the data, check and correct the spelling.

9. Create a query based on the table, and save it as **qrySales Total**.
10. Add a calculated field named **Sales Total** to the query that multiplies the quantity of each item by the sale price.

    ☐ *Hint: Enter **Sales Total: [tblGarage Sale]! [Quantity]*[tblGarage Sale]![Sale Price]**.*
11. Run the query.
12. Create a report based on the query that groups the records by Category, sorts them by Sale Price, and sums the Sales Total for each group and the grand total for all groups. Save the report as **rptSales Report**.
13. Apply a dollar currency format to the totals.
14. Adjust the design and formatting of the report to improve its appearance and make it easier to read.
15. With your teacher's permission, print the report.
16. Close all open objects.
17. Close the database, and exit your database program.
18. As a class, discuss how you could use the database to find ways to increase your earnings from the sale. For example, could you sell more items, or charge more per item? Brainstorm other opportunities for students to earn money.

Illustration B

ID	Category	Item Name	Quantity	Sale Price	Click to Add
1	Toys	Lego Set	1	$2.50	
2	Clothing	Sweater	3	$1.75	
3	Clothing	Blouse	2	$0.75	
4	Entertainment	Books	10	$0.25	
5	Entertainment	Music CDs	15	$1.00	
6	Entertainment	DVDs	5	$2.00	
7	Sporting Goo	Roller Skates	1	$5.00	
8	Sporting Goo	Baseball Glov	2	$2.00	
9	Home Goods	Glasses	8	$0.25	
10	Home Goods	Vase	2	$0.25	
*	(New)				

Record: I◄ ◄ 1 of 10 ► ►I ►⊞ No Filter Search

Database Activities

DIRECTIONS: *You will collect information on several different breeds or types of pets. You will create a database to organize and sort the information. You will copy the data to a spreadsheet so you can analyze the information, perform calculations, add a picture, and print the information.*

1. Open the .pdf file **DB-5_Costs**. With your teacher's permission, print the Data Record Sheet. Close the file, and exit your pdf reader program.

2. With your teacher's approval, select a type of pet that you want to research, such as dogs, cats, birds, rabbits, or reptiles, and write it in the space provided on the Data Record Sheet. In column 1 on the Data Record Sheet, list five breeds or types of your selected pet.

3. With your teacher's permission, use the Internet or the library to research the pet and record the facts and statistics about the average life expectancy, adult weight, and estimated annual costs for feeding, health care, and grooming in the appropriate columns on the Data Record Sheet. Look for photos or other images of the animals. Record all source information as you work.

   a. If you are using the Internet, use a search engine Web site, and search using keywords or phrases such as the type or breed, or use Boolean search strategies. For example, you might search for **[type of pet] AND life expectancy**.

   b. Be sure to evaluate each Web site you visit for accuracy and validity. When you find a credible Web site with relevant information, bookmark the site, or with your teacher's permission, print the desired pages. When you have completed your research, close your Web browser.

4. Start your database program, and save a new database as **DB-5_Comparing_Costs_xx** in the location where your teacher instructs you to store the files for this activity.

5. Change to Design view and create, and save a table as **tblPet Costs**. Define fields matching the columns on your Data Record Sheet, assigning the appropriate data type to each field. You do not need a primary key.

6. Referring to the information from the Data Record Sheet, enter records for each breed or type of pet you researched.

7. When all data is entered, check and correct the spelling, adjust column widths, and then save the table.

8. Select all of the records and copy them to the Clipboard.

9. Close the database, and exit the database program.

10. Start your spreadsheet program, and save a new file as **DB-5_Comparing_Costs_SS_xx**.

11. Select cell A2 and paste the database records into the spreadsheet.

12. In cell G2, enter the label **Total Annual Cost**.

13. In cell G3, use the SUM function to enter a formula that calculates the total annual cost of pet maintenance for the first pet. Copy this formula down to cell G7.

14. In cell H2, enter the label **Cost for Life**.

15. In cell H3, enter a formula that multiplies the life expectancy by the total annual cost. Copy this formula down to cell H7.

16. Sort the data in rows 3 through 7 in descending order based on **Cost for Life**.

17. In row 1, enter the title **Comparing Pet Costs**. Merge and center it across columns A through H.

18. Apply formatting such as number formats, styles, borders, files, and font formatting to make the data appealing and easy to read.

19. Correct any errors that occur, such as numbers stored as text, or narrow column widths.

20. Insert a picture that illustrates your work and center it under the spreadsheet data.

21. Check and correct the spelling in the spreadsheet.

22. Preview the spreadsheet. Change the orientation to landscape and add a footer with your name on the left and today's date on the right. A sample worksheet is shown in Illustration C on the next page.

23. With your teacher's permission, print the spreadsheet.

24. Close the file, saving all changes, and exit the spreadsheet program.

25. As a class, discuss what you learned from the database information. What were you able to do with the data in the spreadsheet that you could not do in the database?

Illustration C

Comparing Pet Costs							
Breed or Type	Life Expectancy	Average Weight	Feeding Costs/Year	Health Care Costs/Year	Grooming Costs/Year	Total Annual Cost	Cost for Life
Cocker Spaniel	16	20	$300.00	$200.00	$250.00	$750.00	$12,000.00
Toy Poodle	16	5	$300.00	$200.00	$200.00	$700.00	$11,200.00
Golden Retriever	10	80	$500.00	$200.00	$150.00	$850.00	$8,500.00
Siberian Husky	12	70	$500.00	$200.00	$0.00	$700.00	$8,400.00
Labrador Retriever	10	85	$600.00	$200.00	$0.00	$800.00	$8,000.00

Firstname Lastname

Today's Date

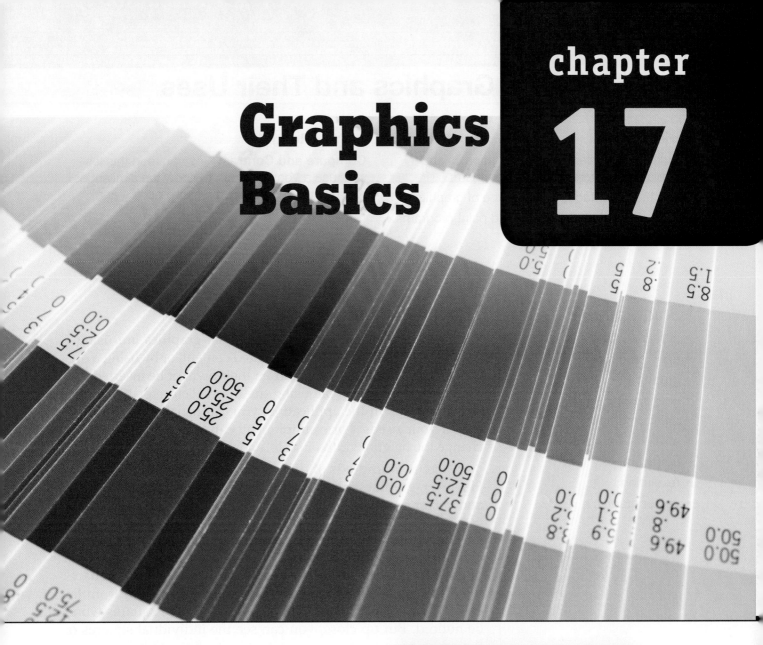

Graphics Basics

chapter

17

What Is a Graphic? In day-to-day speech, people use the word *graphic* to refer to any visual image or object. A family photo, a road map, and a stick figure drawn on a chalkboard are all examples of graphics.

When people talk about a computer graphic, they usually are referring to an image. Images include drawings, painted backgrounds, and photographs. Computer graphics can be displayed in a variety of ways. They can appear on the screen as a background, or they can be placed into a document to add color and information. Thus, in the broadest sense of the term, *computer graphic* could refer to anything that can be seen on the computer screen.

Chapter Outline

 Lesson 17–1

Graphics and Their Uses

 Lesson 17–2

Exploring Graphics Programs

 Lesson 17–3

Working with Graphics

Graphics Basics • 239

Graphics and Their Uses

Objectives

- Identify two different types of graphics and explain the differences between them.
- List the advantages of each type of graphic.
- Differentiate between draw and paint programs.

As You Read

Compare and Contrast   As you read this lesson, use a Venn diagram to show the similarities and differences between raster graphics and vector graphics.

 Key Terms

- bitmapped graphic
- draw program
- graphic
- image editor
- paint program
- pixel
- raster graphic
- resolution
- vector graphic

Types of Graphics

The most common ways to create digital **graphics** are using a graphics program, by scanning printed content, or by using a digital camera. Graphics may stand on their own, or be inserted into a different application file using the Insert Picture or Insert Clip Art command. In the application, you can usually modify them to suit your needs. For example, you can crop unwanted areas, change the height, width or scale, and position them on the page.

There are hundreds of different uses for computer graphics. However, graphics fall into only two categories: raster graphics and vector graphics.

Raster Graphics   A **raster graphic**, which is commonly called a **bitmapped graphic** or bitmap, is an image formed by a pattern of dots. Imagine a sheet of graph paper with each of its squares filled in with a certain color to make a picture. If seen from far enough away, the picture will look clear, and the squares won't be noticed. But up close, you can see the individual squares of the graph paper.

Raster graphics are composed of tiny dots of different colors. Each single point in the image is a **pixel**, short for "picture element." The smaller the pixels in the image, the smoother it will look. The more colors in the image, the brighter and sharper the image will look.

Some common raster file formats include:

- Graphics Interchange Format (GIF)
- Joint Photographic Experts Group (JPG)
- Portable Network Graphics (PNG)
- Windows Bitmap (BMP)

Some formats are used for images on Web pages, while others are used for icons and images in the operating system. In Windows, these same abbreviations are used as the file extensions. A file ending in *.gif*, for example, is in the GIF file format.

Raster graphics are preferred for some types of images. They often are used for photos or images that require backgrounds.

Vector Graphics A **vector graphic** is an image that is created using paths or lines. A vector image tells the computer where a line starts and where it ends. It allows the computer to figure out how to connect the two points. The lines can form shapes, which may be filled with a color or pattern.

Encapsulated PostScript, or EPS, is one of several formats commonly used for vector art. EPS files contain the information that a printer needs in order to print a graphic correctly. The information is combined with a small sketch of what the graphic should look like. The sketch inside an EPS file allows you to preview an image on-screen. This way, you can be sure the image is correct before printing it.

Size, Resolution, and Dots Per Inch

Two basic qualities affect how every raster image will appear. Size, the height and width of the graphic, is normally measured either in pixels or in inches. **Resolution** tells how many pixels are in a certain piece of an image. Resolution also determines the quality of the computer image. Resolution is usually measured in dots per inch, or dpi. An image that is 1 inch square at 72 dpi will contain a total of 5,184 pixels (72×72). Generally, the higher the resolution, the sharper the image will look.

Vector graphics are created using lines or paths rather than pixels. Thus, the number of dots per inch is not a concern when changing the size of vector graphics. If a raster image is enlarged to twice its normal size, it will look fuzzy and jagged. A vector image can be enlarged to any size and keep its quality.

Figure 17.1.1 When viewed on the screen, vector graphics look sharper than raster graphics.

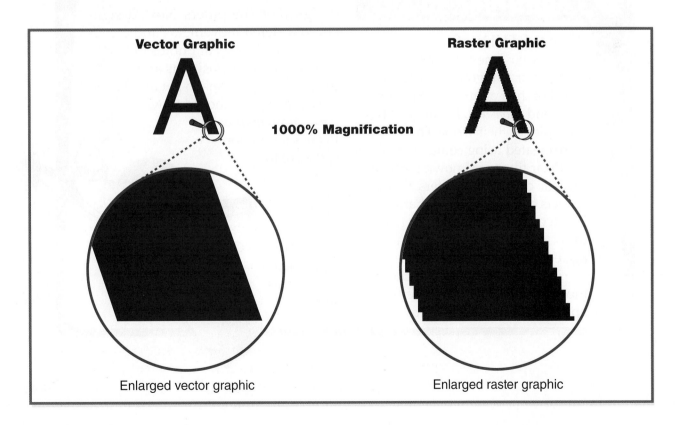

Vector Graphic   Raster Graphic

1000% Magnification

Enlarged vector graphic   Enlarged raster graphic

Technology @ Work

Multimedia designers develop Web sites and CDs using some of the same programs you use. Their jobs vary, but they often create images for programs.

Think About It!

Using the right design program is important for designers. Consider the following tasks. Which would need to be completed by a draw program?

➤ view a raster image

➤ add color to a vector image

➤ add effects to a raster image

➤ change the size of a vector image

Graphics Programs

Different programs allow you to create, edit, and view different graphic file types. Choosing the right program depends on which type of graphic you are working with and what your needs are.

Paint Programs   A **paint program** allows you to create a new raster image. Paint programs also allow you to open a raster image, view it on-screen, and make changes to it. Microsoft Windows comes with a paint program called Paint.

Draw Programs   A program that allows you to create and edit vector images is called a **draw program**. Since draw programs focus on vector images, they make editing easy. You can change the size of an image or add color to it.

Many application programs including Microsoft Word and PowerPoint come with built-in basic drawing tools. More complex programs, such as Adobe® Illustrator® and CorelDRAW®, allow you to do more.

Image Editors   An advanced paint program is called an **image editor**. Image editors are designed for editing raster images. They are also often used for adding special effects to photographs. Adobe® Photoshop® and Adobe® Photodelux® are examples of popular image editors. You can also use built-in picture editing tools in some programs, including Microsoft Word and PowerPoint.

 Spotlight on...

PIXAR STUDIOS

You may have never heard the name *Pixar*, but you've probably heard of their animated films. *Toy Story* and *Monsters, Inc.* are just two examples of their work. These films were created using computers.

Pixar films are known for their realistic cartoon characters. Some aspects of creating these characters involved technology similar to the draw and paint programs and image editors discussed in this lesson.

After final drawings or clay models of the characters were approved, 3-D models were designed on computers. Next, designers considered movements and expressions. They looked at photos of live actors in various positions and with different expressions to get an idea of how each figure should move. Animators then used Pixar's animation software to make the images come to life with movements and expressions.

Exploring Graphics Programs

Objectives

- Identify the main sections of a graphics application window.
- List the different tools available in paint and draw programs.
- Determine when to use the tools in a paint or draw program.

As You Read

Summarize Information Make a table that lists tools used in paint and draw programs on the left. On the right, include the type of program(s) each tool is used in.

Exploring the Application Window

Paint and draw programs vary from one to another, but most include a workspace, toolbars, and color palettes.

Workspace Most of the screen is devoted to the **workspace**, the blank, white area which contains the graphic. This area is sometimes called the drawing area.

Toolbars A toolbar is a bar across the top or down the side of a window. It contains icons that link to the program's tools. By clicking an icon, you can create, edit, add, or remove information within the graphic. Toolbars usually appear, or are docked, on the edges of the screen. They also can be moved around, or floated, to fit your preferences.

Color Palettes The display of color options in paint and draw programs is called the **color palette**. These options allow you to choose colors for an image. Most programs also allow you to change the color palette.

Key Terms

- color palette
- Eyedropper
- graphics tablet
- Selection tool
- stylus
- workspace

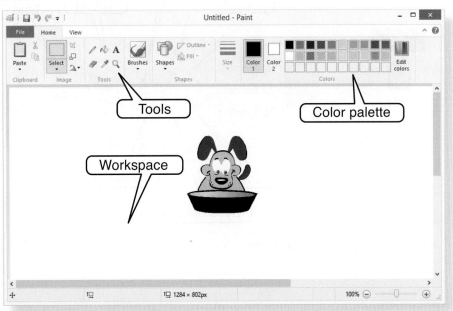

Figure 17.2.1 Paint and draw programs share several basic tools, such as a workspace, toolbars, and color palettes.

Windows 10, Paint, Microsoft Corporation.

Figure 17.2.2 Some tools are commonly found in Paint programs. The toolbar shown here is from Microsoft Paint.

Paint Program Tools

In paint programs, the following tools are used to place and remove color in the workspace.

Pencil The Pencil tool is used for freehand drawing. Clicking and dragging this tool across the workspace leaves a trail of the selected color. This tool is used to draw fine details. Only the color or thickness of the line drawn can be changed.

Brush The Brush tool works like the Pencil tool, but it makes a broader stroke of color. Often, the shape of the brush can be changed to create different shapes of colors. For instance, the brush can be large and square or small and circular.

Line and Shape The Line tool allows you to draw a line and use the toolbar to change its color and width. Various shapes, such as rectangles and ovals, also can be drawn using tools on the toolbar. Shape tools allow you to create shapes in three different forms: Outline, Filled With Outline, and Filled Without Outline.

Eyedropper The **Eyedropper** tool allows you to work with a specific color from an image. You place the eyedropper over the desired color in an image and click. That color becomes the selected color and can be used elsewhere in the image.

Eraser The Eraser tool removes color from an image. It is used by clicking the tool and dragging the eraser across the image. The area touched with the eraser becomes the background color.

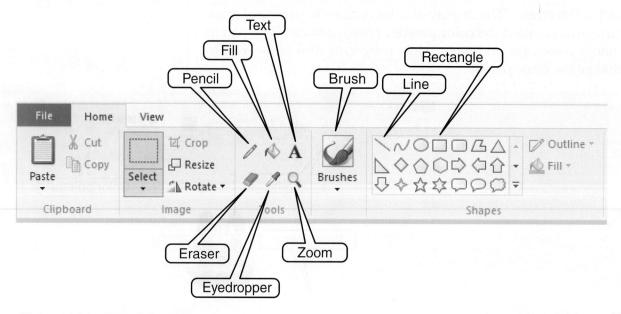

Windows 10, Paint, Microsoft Corporation.

Draw Program Tools

The Line and Shape tools in draw programs are similar to those in paint programs, but with one important difference. In a draw program, you can change an image's lines and shapes without changing nearby ones. In paint programs, it is hard to change one part of an image without altering other parts that are close to it. A **Selection tool** allows you to select a portion of an image to be enlarged, moved, or edited.

Interacting with the Program

A variety of different input tools allow you to work easily with a graphics program. A mouse is used to select part of an image or to activate tools on the toolbar. By dragging, releasing, or double-clicking the mouse, a tool's function is performed.

A **graphics tablet** is a piece of hardware used for drawing or inking. The user moves a **stylus** or pointing device over the drawing surface. The tablet senses the movement of the stylus and moves the cursor on-screen. As the cursor moves, it creates on the screen the image that is being drawn on the tablet. The skills for writing with a stylus on a tablet are quite different than writing with a pen and will take some time to master. Some tablet computers combine the features of a graphics tablet with the functions of a personal computer.

Figure 17.2.3 An interactive pen display combines the capabilities of a graphics tablet with an LCD monitor, so you can draw and choose commands directly on the screen by using a special pen.

Real-World Tech

Using Graphics Tools   The tools in paint and draw programs have many uses. As you might expect, they often are used by newspaper and magazine publishers. What you might not expect is that students your age are using them, too.

For example, at Centennial Middle School in Boulder, Colorado, students publish an online newspaper called *The Vocal Point*. To create and edit the images in the newspaper, students rely on graphics programs.

How might you use draw and paint programs at school?

Lesson 17–3

Working with Graphics

Objectives

- Explain how to modify an image with special effects.
- Compare the processes for combining vector or raster graphics.
- Explain how to work with clip art.
- Describe how graphics can be converted from one format to another.

🔑 Key Terms

- alignment
- balance
- clip art
- color
- emphasis
- export
- group
- harmony
- import
- layer
- line
- proportion
- proximity
- repetition
- shape
- space
- texture
- trace
- ungroup
- unity
- variety

As You Read

Organize Information As you read this lesson, make an outline. Use Roman numerals for main headings. Use capital letters for subheadings, and use numbers for supporting details.

Adding Effects to Graphics

To create a new graphic, start with a blank workspace (sometimes called the background or canvas). If you are creating the graphic in a paint program, use the paint tools to add color and form to the image. If you are creating the graphic in a draw program, use the Line and Shape tools to add information to the image.

Special effects can be used to modify an image. Flipping an image turns it upside down. Mirroring the image makes it flip from left to right, as if it were being viewed in a mirror. Stretching makes the image appear longer in one direction than the other, as if it were drawn on a sheet of rubber that was stretched out. Skewing tilts the image horizontally or vertically.

Inverting reverses the colors in the graphic. In a black-and-white graphic, all the white dots will turn black, and all the black will turn white. In a color graphic, each color will change to its "opposite" color. For example, yellow will become dark blue.

Understanding the Principles of Design

An effective graphic uses the basic principles of design, including contrast, balance, and proportion.

- **Contrast**—Contrast uses differences in shape and color to create a comparison. Different sized objects and opposite colors can distinguish one part of the graphic from another.
- **Balance**—The way objects are arranged is called balance. Symmetrically arranged objects are evenly balanced, while asymmetrically arranged objects are unevenly balanced.
- **Proportion**—The size and location of one object in relation to other objects in the graphic is called proportion.

Other principles of design include **repetition** in which a color, shape, or pattern is repeated throughout the graphic; **emphasis**, which creates a focal point; **proximity**, in which the closeness between objects indicates a relationship; **unity**, in which objects in the image establish a connection through style or color; **harmony**, which is when the elements of the graphic come together as a complete idea; **alignment**, which is the placement of text and objects so they line up within a space, and **variety**, which creates visual interest by using different colors and shapes.

Understanding the Elements of Design

Many different elements are present in an effective graphic, including color and shape.

- **Color**—The use of color has a direct effect on the appearance of a graphic. Each individual color has its own hue, value, and saturation. Hue is the base color, like blue or red. Value is the color's brightness; adding black or white to the color changes the value. Saturation is the colors intensity. Colors are also related to each other. If they are complementary colors they are on opposite sides of the color wheel.

- **Shape**—Graphics are made up of many shapes, such as triangles and circles.

Other elements of design include **lines** that create form, perspective, and shapes; **space**, which is the distance between objects in a graphic or on a page; and **texture**, which is the quality of the surface of shapes, causing them to look smooth like glass or rough like sand.

Combining Images

Bringing information, such as a graphic, into a file from another file is called **importing**. Once imported, the image can then be modified or expanded.

Exporting is when data is saved in a format that can be used in another application. When you export a graphic, you must consider how it will be used, and select an appropriate format that balances quality and file size.

Layering Images   Raster graphics use layers, or stacks of information, to create a graphic. A powerful process known as **layering** stacks each level of an image on top of another. Imagine three or four sheets of wax paper, each with a different part of a drawing. When all of them are stacked, the complete picture is visible. You can edit each layer separately. Changes only affect the layer you are working on.

The default layer is the background. You can add or delete layers as needed. The layer you're working with is usually highlighted in a color. You can hide a layer you're not using to see other parts of the image.

Career Corner

Graphic Artist A graphic artist creates the design and layout of different products, such as advertisements, brochures, Web sites, and CD-ROMs/DVDs. They design or acquire images and choose and edit text features to communicate a message.

An art degree, courses in graphic arts or design, and recent experience using related software are important qualifications for this career.

Grouping Images Grouping is the process of combining separate vector images into one image. Once the images are grouped, they can be moved or resized as a single unit. To group images, select all of the desired items and then select the Group command. **Ungrouping** is the process of separating combined images into individual images. To ungroup an image, select a grouped image and then select the Ungroup command.

Working with Clip Art

It is not always necessary to create an image from scratch. Instead, you can start with **clip art** (graphics files that come with a program, or that you download from the Internet).

Raster Clip Art Clip art in a raster format (such as GIF, JPG, or PNG) can be imported into a paint document. The art then can be edited like any other raster graphic.

Vector Clip Art Vector art can be imported in a draw program and modified. If the image is complex, it can be ungrouped. Its individual parts can then be edited or moved.

Converting Graphics

If you want to use a graphic that is in a format your program does not support, you may have to convert it. You can use a file conversion program, or open the file and use the Save As command to save it in a different file format. File conversion is also required if you want to change a vector graphic to a raster graphic, or vice versa.

Vector-to-Raster Graphics Vector graphics must be changed to pixels before the image can be edited in a paint program.

Raster-to-Vector Graphics Converting raster graphics to vectors requires a special process called **tracing**. Tracing requires special software and can be complicated when an image has a lot of color and detail.

Figure 17.3.1 Vector clip art may look sharper than raster clip art and can be edited like any vector graphic.

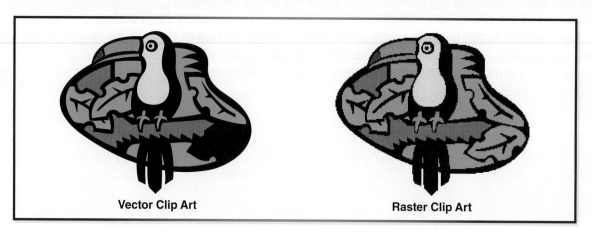

Vector Clip Art   Raster Clip Art

Directions: *Match each vocabulary term in the left column with the correct definition in the right column.*

_____ **1.** raster graphic

_____ **2.** vector graphic

_____ **3.** resolution

_____ **4.** paint program

_____ **5.** color palette

_____ **6.** Eyedropper

_____ **7.** graphics tablet

_____ **8.** import

_____ **9.** layer

_____ **10.** clip art

a. the number of pixels in a certain image that affects its visual quality

b. images that can be downloaded for use in a graphics program

c. images created using lines or paths

d. tool that captures and uses color from one portion of an image in another

e. input device for creating graphics

f. stacks of information on top of one another to form a more complete image

g. image created using pixels, or series of dots

h. allows you to modify raster graphics

i. brings information into a file from another file

j. the display of color options in paint and draw programs

Check Your Comprehension

Directions: *Complete each sentence with information from the chapter.*

1. Sets of dots that make up an image are called _____.

2. A(n) _____ allows you to create and edit vector graphics.

3. Advanced paint programs that allow you to edit and add effects to a raster graphic are _____.

4. The area of the screen where images are created and edited is the _____.

5. The set of color options in a particular paint or draw program shown in small boxes on the screen is called the _____.

6. In a draw program, a(n) _____ allows you to pick a certain portion of an image to work on.

7. A common input device in a graphics program is the _____.

8. The process of formatting data so that it can be used in another application is _____.

9. Combining separate images to form a single image is called _____.

10. The process of converting pixels to lines or paths is known as _____.

Think Critically

Directions: *Answer the following questions.*

1. What are two differences between a raster graphic and a vector graphic?

2. When editing graphics, why is it important to consider the file format in which an image is created?

3. How do toolbars in draw and paint programs help you to edit and add effects to images?

4. Why are exporting and importing important functions for working with graphics?

5. How are layering and grouping similar? How are they different?

Extend Your Knowledge

Directions: *Choose and complete one of the following projects.*

A. Create a comic strip using vector or raster graphics. You may create your own images or edit clip art. Your comic strip should have at least four frames. Be sure to use the different tools and colors in the program. With your teacher's permission, print your comic strip to show to the class, or show it on a monitor or with a projector.

B. Newspapers and magazines often use graphics to capture the readers' attention or to make a point. Find three graphics (including photos with special effects) in newspapers or magazines. Next, create a three-column chart. On the chart, paste each image, identify each source and page number, and categorize the graphic as raster or vector. Present your chart to the class.

Understanding Graphics

Graphics in the Real World Graphics make up everything you see on your computer screen. The images and even the letters in a word-processing document are kinds of graphics.

When working with computer graphics, there are many things to keep in mind. How many colors will an image need? How will those colors look? Will the image appear fuzzy and bumpy or smooth and sharp? How much space will it take to store the image on the computer? Can it be viewed on the Internet? How fast will images be transmitted? Graphics software helps computer users create, change, and refine the words and images we see on-screen.

Chapter Outline

Preparing Computer Graphics

Objectives

- Compare and contrast lossless and lossy compression.
- Explain the effect of color on computer memory.
- Name and describe the four basic color modes.

As You Read

Organize Information As you read this lesson, create an outline to help you organize the information.

🔑 Key Terms

- color depth
- compress
- lossless compression
- lossy compression

File Compression and Graphics

Graphics files can be very large. When they are stored on the computer, the images are often **compressed**, or saved in a format requiring less space. This saves disk space and decreases the time it takes to send images via the Internet.

When a file is compressed, the program performing the compression replaces certain pieces of information with shorter codes. This makes the file smaller.

Lossless Compression In **lossless compression**, information is removed in such a way that all of it can later be fully restored without introducing errors. This process results in a perfect copy of the file that is about one third of the original size. Lossless compression is a good choice for reducing files with graphics, text, or computer code.

Lossy Compression In **lossy compression**, some information is permanently removed from the file in such a way that it cannot be restored to its original state. Lossy compression can reduce a file to one fiftieth or less of its former size. It is best for reducing the size of video and audio files.

Figure 18.1.1 After lossy compression an image may look fuzzy or out of focus.

Color Depth

The more colors or shades of gray an image contains, the sharper and more detailed it will look. The number of colors that can be displayed on a monitor at one time is the **color depth**. Most modern computer monitors can display millions of colors. Because the computer must store more bits of information for each color pixel, more memory is needed to store colors than to store black and white alone.

Color Modes

Color modes determine which and how many colors are available for creating computer graphics.

Bitmap Mode When it comes to color modes, bitmap refers to a 1-bit, or black-and-white, image.

Grayscale Mode When working in grayscale mode, the computer can display 256 different shades of gray to represent the colors, shades, and textures in an image.

RGB Mode Look closely at a television picture, and you may notice that it is made up of tiny clusters of dots. Each cluster has one red, one green, and one blue dot. When these three colors are combined in various ways, they produce different colors.

RGB mode allows each of these three colors to have 8 bits of information, resulting in 256 different shades each of the colors red (R), green (G), and blue (B). Color computer monitors use RGB color to display graphics, so RGB mode is used to design on-screen graphics such as those for the Internet.

CMYK Mode In CMYK mode, a combination of four colors in different densities produces other colors. Variations of cyan (greenish-blue), magenta (purplish-red), yellow, and black (known as K) are combined to produce new colors.

Figure 18.1.2 An image's color mode determines how many colors appear.

| Bitmap | Grayscale | RGB | CMYK |

CMYK mode is used to design graphics that will be printed on a printing press. Each of the four color values in a CMYK graphic is assigned to one of the four inks. These inks are then used on the printing press to print a full-color piece.

But what if you wanted to display a CMYK graphic on a monitor? To view a CMYK graphic on the screen, the computer has to convert it to RGB. This is why printed graphics may look different from an on-screen preview of the image.

Resolution Issues

When creating or modifying graphics, it is important to work with the proper resolution. A graphic's resolution should be determined by how that graphic will be displayed—the output.

If a graphic is to be viewed on-screen only, the resolution need not be higher than 72 dpi or 96 dpi. A 300-dpi graphic looks the same on-screen as a 72-dpi version of the same file. Increasing the dpi does not improve on-screen appearance. Because a 72- or 96-dpi file is smaller, it will display more quickly.

If a graphic will be printed, the resolution should be as high as the device on which it will be printed. For an image to look its best on a 300-dpi printer, it should be created at 300 dpi.

Real-World Tech

Offset Printing The printing technique known as offset printing involves spreading ink on a metal plate with etched images on it. The plate is then pressed against another surface, often a rubber sheet. This transfers the ink onto the new surface, but the image now appears backward. Finally, the new surface is pressed against paper. This reverses the ink image from the surface onto the paper.

The equipment used and the cost of setting up the printing press are quite expensive. Therefore, offset printing is usually done to print a large quantity, or print run.

What types of printed materials that you read might have been printed using an offset process?

Exploring Image Editing Programs

Objectives

- Identify two different ways to bring existing images into a computer.
- Summarize how filters improve the look of an image.
- Compare and contrast image editor selection tools.

As You Read

Identify Key Concepts As you read this lesson, use a concept web diagram to help you identify tools used to edit images.

Input Devices for Graphics

While it is possible to create graphics from scratch using paint or draw programs, there are many times when images from the "real world" need to be imported into the computer. There are two main input tools that let you digitize images so you can import them into the computer: scanners and digital cameras.

Scanners As discussed in Chapter 3, a scanner is a device that copies and changes a printed image into a digital format—one the computer can process and store. A scanner divides the image into boxes and assigns each box a value representing its "darkness" or color. One type of scanner is called a flatbed scanner. Its reader—the part that actually "sees" the image—sits underneath a pane of glass, much like a copy machine. Flatbed scanners are now routinely included in All-in-One printers. The reader moves back and forth to scan the image. Another type of scanner is a handheld scanner. It is moved across an image to digitize it.

Digital Cameras A digital camera stores images digitally instead of on film. A computer chip in the camera changes light patterns from the captured image into pixels, which the camera can store. The image, or photo, can then be downloaded to the computer for storage or for printing.

 **Key Terms**
- filter
- Lasso
- Magic Wand
- Marquee

Figure 18.2.1 A scanner (above) lets you digitize printed documents, such as photos. Digital cameras (below) store images digitally instead of on film.

Technology @ Home

Filters are useful tools to use on home-computer projects. You can touch up images for holiday cards, party invitations, and even personal photographs.

Think About It!

The right filter is needed to gain a desired effect. For each of the following items, determine whether an image should be edited with a Sharpening tool, a Blur tool, or a Noise tool.

➢ make edges look crisp

➢ soften hard edges

➢ remove a pattern of dots

➢ add a textured look

Filters in Image Editors

Image editors are used to edit raster images—often, high-resolution images such as digital photographs. Image editors usually contain **filters**, preset features that alter images in a certain way. Many filters are designed to improve photos. Common filters include sharpening, blur, and noise filters.

Sharpening Filters   Image editors often contain several sharpening filters. One type of sharpening filter more clearly defines the edges of an image. It does this by finding a line of pixels that runs together as one color and is next to other pixels of other colors. The filter increases the color differences between the line of pixels of one color and those of nearby colors, making the edges more distinct.

Blur Filters   There are also many kinds of blur filters. A blur filter softens the look of an image by making hard edges look blurrier. They can be used to apply this effect to all or part of an image.

   Using both sharpening and blurring techniques at the same time can add depth to an image. One way to do this is to apply sharpening effects to the area of an image that extends toward the viewer. Then, blur the areas farther away from the viewer. This produces a three-dimensional, or 3-D, effect.

Noise Filters   Filters designed to add or remove roughness from an image are called noise filters. Two types of noise filters are the despeckle and median filters. They determine the edges of an image and leave them alone. Then, they smooth out other areas with less difference in color. This is often done to remove moiré patterns, or unwanted patterns of dots, that show up in some scanned photos.

Figure 18.2.2   A blur filter was used on the left image to create the "softer" or blurred effect seen in the right image.

Image Editor Selection Tools

One powerful feature of an image editor is its ability to work with certain pixels in an image while leaving other pixels unchanged. This is done using a selection tool, a graphics tool that allows you to choose one part of an image or the objects that make up an image. For instance, you can use a selection tool to choose eyes in an image of a face. Three common selection tools are:

- Marquee tool
- Lasso tool
- Magic Wand tool

Marquee The rectangle selection tool is sometimes called the **Marquee** tool. It works just like the Rectangle tool that allows you to draw a box in Word. But instead of drawing a box, the Marquee selection tool highlights a simple shape.

Lasso The **Lasso** tool in an image editor is used to select complex, or freehand, shapes. It is well suited for selecting images that share colors with nearby pieces of an image.

Magic Wand Perhaps the most powerful selection tool is the **Magic Wand**, which selects all touching pixels of a similar color. If you select a red pixel, then all red pixels that are connected with it will automatically be selected. The Magic Wand can be adjusted for small or wide ranges of color. For instance, if set for a small range, the wand will select only exact matches. But if set for large ranges, it will select similar shades of red.

Technology @ School

Selection tools can be useful when working on images for the school paper or to touch up yearbook photos.

Think About It!

For the following shapes, identify the right tool to use to highlight an image of each—Marquee tool, Lasso tool, or the Magic Wand.

➤ shape of a tree outside a classroom window

➤ color blue in a textbook cover

➤ lunchbox

➤ red stripes in the American flag

Figure 18.2.3 The Lasso tool is often used to select complex shapes.

Draw and Animation Features

Objectives

- Describe four advanced tools in draw programs.
- Summarize the process of computer animation.
- Explain how animation is viewed on a computer.

As You Read

Show Cause and Effect   Use a cause-and-effect chart to help you understand how advanced drawing tools create graphics.

Key Terms

- Align
- Distribute
- frame
- frame rate
- Grid
- Order
- player software
- tween

Advanced Draw Program Tools

Draw programs provide a number of tools to help you work with images.

Align Tool   The **Align** tool moves parts of an image and determines how the parts will be placed in relation to one another. It can be helpful for lining up objects of different sizes. To use this tool, select several objects in the graphic—such as lines or shapes—and then open the tool. You can arrange objects to make the tops, bottoms, sides, or middles of the objects align with one another.

Distribute Tool   The **Distribute** tool moves objects to distribute, or space, them from each other. The two kinds of distribution are fixed amount and within bounds. Fixed amount distribution puts a uniform distance between objects. For instance, you might want to put an inch of space between several objects. Within bounds distribution leaves the outermost objects exactly where they are and evenly spaces all the other selected objects between them.

Figure 18.3.1 Use the advanced drawing tools to work with images.

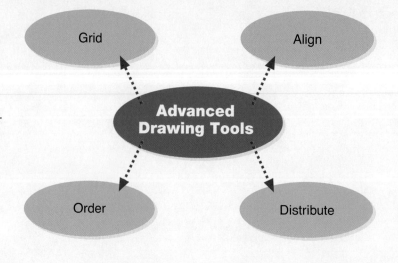

Order Tool Sometimes objects in an image overlap, or lay partially on top of one another. When this happens, certain objects may be blocked from view. The **Order** tool changes the position in which objects are stacked and rearranges them to avoid this problem. Objects can be moved to the bottom, the top, or the side of a stack.

Grid Tool Many graphics programs offer a **Grid** tool to align images properly. Grids work just like a sheet of graph paper, by showing squares on the computer screen. For objects to align, they must begin in the same column on the grid.

Many graphics programs offer a feature called snap-to-guides or snap-to-grids. When this feature is turned on, objects are automatically moved to the nearest grid line. This helps ensure that every object is in a perfectly aligned position.

Animating Images

When two or more graphics are displayed one after the other, they can appear to be in motion. Animation is the process of quickly showing many images of an object to make it appear as if it is moving.

Animating by Hand Before computers, animation was done by hand or with cameras. Sometimes, artists drew by hand each **frame**, or individual still image in a sequence. The frames would then be flipped to simulate motion. Other times, sophisticated film cameras took one still picture at a time and sequenced them quickly to mimic movement. The more frames displayed per second, the more convincing the animation looked. The speed at which a frame moves, measured in number of images per second, is called the **frame rate**.

Animating on Computer In computer animation, frames are created and then rapidly displayed to create the impression of motion. There is, however, a key benefit to computer animation. **Tweening** is the ability of a graphics program to determine in-between frames, so you do not need to draw every one. You just draw the starting and ending frames, and the computer draws those in-between frames in sequence.

Figure 18.3.2 Rapidly displayed frames simulate motion.

Technology @ Work

Player software converts animated graphics into images. Many companies are now using this technology to advertise their products on the Internet.

Think About It!

Circle the items you think would benefit from advertising with player-software technology.

- socks
- cartoons on television
- remote-controlled airplanes
- fans

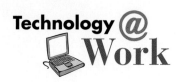

Software for Viewing Animation

Player software, a program that interprets the information in an animation file, must be installed in order to view animated graphics on a computer monitor. Player software usually can tell the computer how to interpret and convert animated graphics into images it can display.

Flash™ Player Made by the Adobe company, Flash Player is player software that allows a Web browser to view vector animation. Because vector animation downloads quickly, Flash movies have become common on the Web.

QuickTime® Player Created by Apple Computer, QuickTime is commonly used for bitmapped animation. It provides the continuous flow of information needed to display movies, live action, and animation. QuickTime was created by Apple for Macintosh computers, but versions for Windows PCs have been available for several years.

RealPlayer® First used for streaming audio, RealPlayer® has added support for both vector and bitmapped animation.

Name ▲	Size	Type
Car chase.avi	65 KB	AVI Video
The Da Vinci Code.gvi	2,704 KB	Google Video file
dog cartoon.mov	65 KB	QuickTime Movie
Grand Canyon hike.mpg	65 KB	MPEG Video
my dance audition.mp4	65 KB	MPEG-4 File
A tree grows in Plymouth.rm	65 KB	RealAudio / RealVideo

Figure 18.3.3 There are many file formats used for displaying streaming video, animation, or live action. These various formats can be played on a variety of player software.

Use the Vocabulary

Directions: *Match each vocabulary term in the left column with the correct definition in the right column.*

_____ **1.** compress
_____ **2.** lossless compression
_____ **3.** color depth
_____ **4.** filter
_____ **5.** Marquee
_____ **6.** Magic Wand
_____ **7.** lossy compression
_____ **8.** frame
_____ **9.** tween
_____ **10.** player software

a. color selection tool

b. compression format in which all information is kept

c. compression format in which some information is permanently removed

d. saved in format that uses less space

e. one individual image in an animation

f. image editor feature that changes appearance of an image

g. program that converts animation files for viewing

h. colors shown on a monitor at one time

i. to generate middle frames of animation by computer

j. rectangle selection tool

Check Your Comprehension

Directions: *Determine the correct choice for each of the following.*

1. Which color mode is based on a combination of three colors to make new colors?

  a. bitmap
  b. grayscale
  c. RGB
  d. CMYK

2. If a graphic is to be printed, how high should its dpi rating be set?

  a. 72 dpi
  b. higher than output device
  c. lower than output device
  d. same as output device

3. Which filter will make an image's edges look softer?

  a. sharpen
  b. blur
  c. noise
  d. despeckle

4. Which tool is good for selecting complex shapes of whatever color you point out?

  a. Marquee
  b. Lasso
  c. Magic wand
  d. Distribute

5. Which tool is used to move objects so they line up in a certain way?

  a. Align
  b. Distribute
  c. Order
  d. Grid

6. Which player software views vector and bitmapped images?

  a. Flash Player
  b. RealPlayer
  c. QuickTime Player
  d. Vector Player

 **Think Critically**

Directions: *Answer the following questions.*

1. Why do graphics files often need compression?

2. Why is RGB mode used to design computer graphics?

3. What input devices allow graphics in other formats to be digitized?

4. How has tweening changed the animation process?

5. What is one advantage of vector animation?

Extend Your Knowledge

Directions: *Choose and complete one of the following projects.*

A. Experiment with the toolbars in an image editor to see what each tool does. Then, use a scanner or digital camera to capture an image and save it on your computer. Edit the image, using several of the tools. With your teacher's permission, print the images and present both your original and edited images to the class. Explain which tools you used to achieve the effects shown.

B. Several tools for working with graphics are discussed in this chapter. Research other tools for applying special effects to graphics, such as tools that let you create drawings that look like they were created using actual ink, watercolor, acrylic, or oil paint. Create a chart identifying these tools and explaining how they are used. Use a graphics program to create drawings or shapes using the tools to illustrate your chart. Read your chart out loud to a partner and listen while your partner reads his or hers out loud to you.

C. As a class, discuss how graphics can be used both to make a publication look better but also to help convey a message. Select a topic that interests you and have it approved by your teacher. Then, use graphics software to create an image that could be used on a Web page about your topic. Make sure the image would both enhance the appearance of the page and convey a message about the topic. As a class, display and discuss the images.

DIRECTIONS: *You will use drawing tools to design a billboard for a city zoo. You will include clip art, text, and colors to create an attention-getting design for your billboard.*

1. Start the program your teacher instructs you to use for this graphics activity. For example, you might use a presentation program, a paint program, or a word-processing program that has graphics capabilities.
2. Save the file as **GR-1_Zoo_xx** in the location where your teacher tells you to store the files for this activity. Replace **xx** with your own initials or name, as directed by your teacher.
3. Size the page to 10" wide by 7.5" high, and display the rulers and the gridlines. If you are working in a presentation program, change the layout of the title slide to blank.
4. In the blank file, insert a footer that includes your first and last names and today's date.
5. Insert a clip art photo of a baby elephant.
6. Crop the photo as close to the elephant as possible, and resize the picture to approximately 3.0" high by 4.0" wide.
7. Align the picture in the middle of the page vertically, with its left border about 1" from the left edge of the page.
8. Insert a clip art photo of tiger cubs.
9. Crop the photo as close to the cubs as possible, and resize the picture to approximately 2.5" high by 4.0" wide.
10. Align the picture in the middle of the page vertically, with its right border about 1" from the right edge of the page.
11. Insert a text box approximately 1.5" high by 9" wide above the pictures.

12. Set the font in the text box to Arial, bold, 48 points, and type **Come See Our New Arrivals!**
13. Center the text in the text box.
14. Center the text box horizontally.
15. Draw a rectangle with rounded corners below the other objects, centered horizontally. Size it to approximately 1.0" high by 5.0" wide.
16. Add text to the rectangle, and, using 26-point Arial Black, type **Townsville City Zoo**, centered in the text box.
17. Draw another text box below the rounded rectangle, with no border or fill, and centered horizontally. Size it to approximately 0.5" high by 5.0" wide.
18. Set the font to 20-point Arial and type **123 Elm Street—Open 7 days a week!**, centered in the text box.
19. Apply a solid light green background to the slide or canvas.
20. Select the rounded rectangle and the text box within it, change the font color to black, and apply a green fill and a black outline.
21. Check the spelling and grammar, and correct any errors that you find.
22. Display the file in Print Preview. It should look similar to Illustration A. If necessary, adjust the alignment and position of objects.
23. With your teacher's permission, print the file.
24. Close the file, saving all changes, and exit the program.
25. As a class, discuss the different programs available for creating graphics. Why might one be better than another?

Illustration A

DIRECTIONS: *You will use drawing tools to create a poster illustrating geometric solids. You will insert and format shapes and text boxes, and apply text effects (or WordArt). Refer to Illustration B to see a sample poster.*

1. Start the program your teacher instructs you to use for this graphics activity. For example, you might use a presentation program, a paint program, or a word-processing program that has graphics capabilities.
2. Create a blank file and save it as **GR-2_ Geometry_xx** in the location where your teacher tells you to store the files for this activity.
3. Display the rulers and the gridlines. If you are working in a presentation program, change the layout of the title slide to blank.
4. In the blank file, insert a footer that includes your name and today's date.
5. Set the workspace to a good size for a poster, as instructed by your teacher. As you work, size and position shapes so they are appropriate for the size poster you are creating.
6. Insert a text box and type **What Is A Solid?** Position the text box 1.5" from the top of the page. Center the text in the text box and center the text box horizontally on the page.
7. Format the text box using a fill and border.
8. Insert another text box and type **A solid is a three-dimensional shape such as a cylinder, cube, or pyramid.** Center the text in the text box, and center the text box horizontally on the page.
9. Format the text box using a fill and a border.
10. Position the top of the second text box so it overlaps the first text box but does not block the text. Group the two text boxes.
11. Draw a cube shape.
12. Draw a cylinder shape.
13. Draw a pyramid shape.
   ▢ *If your program does not have these shapes as part of its shape gallery, you may draw a square, rectangle, and triangle and use 3-D effects to create the solids.*

14. Format the shapes using fills, borders, and effects such as shadows.
15. Size and position the three shapes so they look good on the page. Take into consideration the blank areas, or white space, on the page when determining how to position the shapes.
16. Insert a text box next to each shape and enter the shape name. Format, size, and position the text boxes to coordinate with the shapes.
17. Group each shape with its text box.
18. Centered along the bottom of the page, use a feature such as WordArt to create a text object using the text **Geometry**. Format the object with effects such as 3D, shadow, border, and fill. You might try changing the shape and spacing to see how it looks. Use Undo and Redo as necessary, as you work.
19. Insert other objects that you think will enhance the poster, and apply a background, page, or canvas color.
20. With a partner or peer editor, preview your file. A sample is shown in Illustration B on the next page.
21. Check the spelling and grammar, and correct any errors that you find. If necessary, adjust the alignment and position of objects and the formatting to improve the effectiveness of the poster.
22. With your teacher's permission, print the file.
23. Close the file, saving all changes, and exit the program.
24. Create a display of the posters in your classroom.

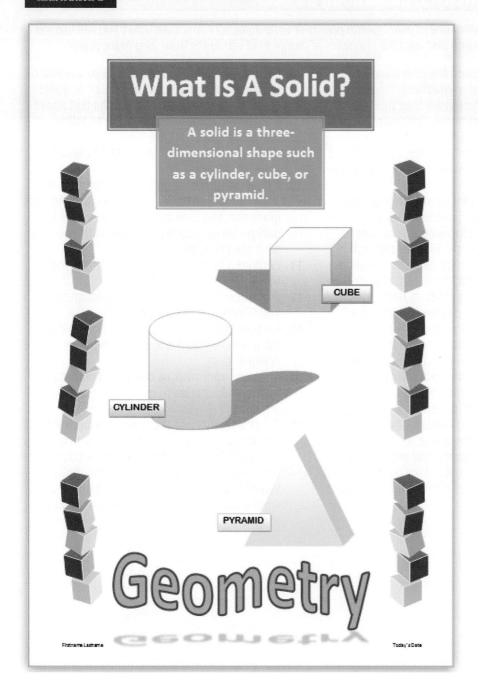

What Is A Solid?

A solid is a three-dimensional shape such as a cylinder, cube, or pyramid.

CUBE

CYLINDER

PYRAMID

Geometry

Firstname Lastname

Today's Date

DIRECTIONS: *You will select one of your favorite poems or write a poem of your own. Then, you will use the computer to create a drawing that uses the principles of design to illustrate the main idea of the poem.*

1. With a partner, research the principles of design as they relate to graphics.
2. Select a poem that you have read this year, either in school or at home. Ask your teacher to approve your selection.
3. Research the copyright for your selection and determine whether you can legally reproduce all or part of it.
4. Start a program that includes drawing tools, and create a new file. Save it as **GR-3_Poem_xx** in the location where your teacher instructs you to store the files for this activity. Replace **xx** with your own name or initials as instructed by your teacher. Insert a header with your full name and today's date.
5. With the principles of design in mind, use the drawing tools to draw a picture that illustrates the poem. Be sure to use different tools and colors as you create your drawing. Try using tools to demonstrate the digital use of inks, watercolors, acrylics, and oils.
6. Preview the drawing frequently, looking for ways to improve it and to apply the principles of design. For example, move or resize shapes to develop balance and proportion. Apply formatting and effects for contrast.
7. When you are satisfied with the drawing, save the changes.

8. Use the program's text tool to type the title of the poem, the poet's name, and all or some lines from the poem. Position the text above or below your drawing. Be sure to follow copyright laws.
9. Apply font formatting to the text to enhance your illustration.
10. Review your file carefully with a partner or peer editor. Correct any errors in spelling and grammar, and look for ways to improve the design. When you are satisfied with your file, save the changes.
11. With your teacher's permission, print your file.
12. Close your file, saving all changes, and exit your word-processing program.
13. Present your illustration to the class. Read the poem out loud and explain why you selected it.
14. Combine your printed document with those of your classmates to create a class book of poetry.
15. As a class, discuss the difference between creating a work of art electronically and manually. What advantages does a computer program have over using real art supplies? What limitations does the program have? In what situations would you use a computer program?

DIRECTIONS: *In this activity, you will design a DVD case for a movie based on a story or book you have read.*

1. Open the .pdf file **GR-4_Case**. With your teacher's permission, print the Data Record Sheet. Close the file, and exit your pdf reader program.
2. Select a story or a book that you have read for which you will design the DVD case.
3. Research the copyright for your selection and determine whether you can legally reproduce all or part of it. As you develop your project, be sure to abide by the copyright laws.
4. Complete the Data Record Sheet by sketching a design for the front of the case. Define space for at least one image and the areas where you want to display text. Write a summary of the plot, and include the names of actors who would play the main roles.
5. Use one of the following methods to obtain or create the image: scan an original drawing; take a photo with a digital camera; draw the image using drawing tools; or, with your teacher's permission, download and save an image from the Internet.
6. Start your word-processing program, and create a new document. Save it as **GR-4_Case_xx** in the location where your teacher instructs you to store the files for this activity. Replace *xx* with your name or initials as directed by your teacher.
7. Change the right margin to 3" to simulate the size of a DVD case. Insert a header that includes your name and today's date.
8. Draw a text box, and type the title of the story or book at the top of the page. If necessary, remove the fill and border from the text box.
9. Draw a second text box, and type a sentence introducing the actors and the parts they will play in the film. Again, remove the fill and border from the text box if necessary.
10. Draw a third text box, and type a brief statement describing the film. Format the text box without a fill or border.
11. Draw a fourth text box, type **Based on the story by**, and then type the author's name. Format the text box without a fill or border.

12. Referring to the sketch on your Data Record Sheet, size and position the text boxes on the document page the way you want them to appear on the front of the DVD case.
13. Apply font formatting effects to the text.
14. Insert your image file in the document. Size and position the image as you want it to display on the DVD case cover.
15. Use the drawing tools in the word-processing program to draw a rectangle with no fill color around the content on the page to indicate the front of the DVD case, and then save the document.
16. Insert a page break below the rectangle so you can define the back of the DVD case.
17. Draw a text box, and type the summary you wrote on your Data Record Sheet. Format the text box without a fill or border.
18. Insert text boxes and type any other information you would like to include on the back of the DVD case.
19. Format the text on the back cover.
20. Use the drawing tools in the word-processing program to draw a rectangle around the content on the page to indicate the back of the DVD case.
21. Proofread the text on both pages and make corrections. Then, run a spelling and grammar checker and correct all errors.
22. Preview the document. If necessary, adjust the size and position of the objects on the pages. Change or apply colors and font formatting or text effects to make the text more readable and interesting.
23. Preview the document again, and, with your teacher's permission, print the document.
24. Close the document, saving all changes, and exit your word-processing program.
25. Display your work for the class. Discuss your design and why you think it effectively illustrates the story or book.

DIRECTIONS: *You will measure different rooms in your home or school and use a spreadsheet to calculate their scaled measurements. Then, you will use drawing tools to draw scale versions of these rooms. You will use text tools to label these shapes and then export the graphics in .pdf format so you can embed them in a Word document.*

1. Open the .pdf file **GR-5_Rooms**. With your teacher's permission, print the Data Record Sheet. Close the file, and exit the program.
2. Working with a partner, measure the floor space of four different rooms in your school or home. Record the actual dimensions of each side of each room in the tables on the Data Record Sheet. Record all measurements in feet, and round to the nearest foot.
   ☐ *Use the spaces labeled Side 5 and 6 if you are measuring a room with more than four sides. Leave those spaces blank if your rooms have only four sides.*
3. Start your spreadsheet program. Create a new spreadsheet file, and save it as **GR-5_Scale_xx** in the location where your teacher instructs you to store the files for this activity.
4. In cell A1, enter the name of the first room you measured.
5. Starting in cell A2, and moving down to cell A7, enter the following row headings: **Side 1**, **Side 2**, **Side 3**, **Side 4**, **Side 5**, and **Side 6**.
6. Starting in cell B1 and moving across to cell D1, enter the following column headings: **Length in Feet**, **Length in Inches**, and **Scaled at 1/250**.
7. Starting in cell B2 and moving down the column, enter the measurements in feet of each side of the first room from your Data Record Sheet.
8. In cell C1, enter a formula that multiplies the number of feet by 12 to convert the value to inches. Copy the formula down the column for the remaining room sides.
9. In cell D1, enter a formula that divides the length in inches by 250. Copy the formula down the column for the remaining sides.
10. Format the measurements to show four decimal places. The worksheet should

look similar to Illustration C, although your measurements will depend on the actual measurements of your room.
11. Starting in cell A9, repeat steps 4 through 10 to enter and calculate the measurements for the second room you measured. Repeat the process for the remaining two rooms.
12. Save the spreadsheet file.
13. Select and start the program you want to use to create your scale drawings, and save a new file as **GR-5_Scaled Rooms_xx**.
14. Enter the title **Scaled Room Drawings**. Insert your name and today's date as the subtitle or as a footer.
15. Referring to the data on your spreadsheet printout, draw a scaled version of each room. Use one page or slide for each room. Use gridlines and rulers to aid you in drawing.
16. Insert a title above each drawing to identify the room, and a text box next to the drawing in which you enter the room's original measurements and its scaled measurements. Explain that the drawing has been scaled by a factor of 1/250.
17. Proofread the text and correct errors, and then export the graphics in .pdf format. Exit the program, saving all changes.
18. Create a new word-processing document named **GR-5_Scaled Rooms_xx**. Write a paragraph explaining your project. Embed the .pdf of the graphics in the file, and set the text to wrap around it.
19. Copy the spreadsheet data and paste it into the document to show the measurements.
20. With your teacher's permission, print the document. Then save the file and exit all programs. Share your document with a partner or with the class.

Illustration C

D5		✕ ✓ f_x	=C5/250	

	A	B	C	D	E
1	Bedroom	Length in Feet	Length in Inches	Scaled at 1/250	
2	Side 1	8	96.0000	0.3840	
3	Side 2	5	60.0000	0.2400	
4	Side 3	8	96.0000	0.3840	
5	Side 4	5	60.0000	0.2400	
6	Side 5				
7	Side 6				

Presentation Basics

chapter 19

What Are Presentations? A presentation is a visual or multimedia display. Every day, presentations are shown on overhead screens in classrooms and at meetings. They help people teach ideas, sell products, and share information with others.

Before computers, creating a professional presentation took a lot of time and involved many people. First, an artist would create graphics. Next, the graphics and wording would be organized for logical flow and visual appeal. Then, this information was transferred onto transparencies or slides.

Now, thanks to presentation software, many people create presentations more quickly. Knowing how to use presentation software is an important skill in today's world.

Chapter Outline

 Lesson 19–1

Exploring Presentation Software

 Lesson 19–2

Creating Presentations

 Lesson 19–3

Previewing Presentations

Exploring Presentation Software

Objectives

- Identify the benefits of presentation software.
- Identify two options for creating a new presentation.
- Describe six views in PowerPoint.

As You Read

Organize Information   Use a concept web to help you organize ways to create and view presentations as you read.

🔑 Key Terms

- AutoContent wizard
- Master views
- Normal view
- Notes Page view
- presentation software
- Reading view
- slide
- Slide Show view
- Slide Sorter view
- template
- thumbnails
- wizard

Introducing Presentation Software

Presentation software allows you to organize and display information visually so it can be viewed by a group of people. In most cases, this information—called a presentation—consists of both graphics and text, and may also include audio, video, and animation. Information in a presentation is organized into separate pages in an order the audience can follow easily. Each page is called a **slide**. Each slide can contain one or more main points. Information about each main point is organized into a list of short, easy-to-read key points. There are a host of good programs such as Microsoft PowerPoint, Corel Presentations and Apple's Keynote that are specifically designed for creating, saving, editing, and producing presentations.

Creating a New Presentation   The most common presentation software is Microsoft PowerPoint. With PowerPoint, you have two options for creating a new presentation:

- template
- blank presentation

Template   Work on a presentation may begin by selecting a **template**, or a preformatted version of a certain type of document. After choosing a template, you type in your information. You can also change the look and feel of the template by adjusting its settings.

Blank Presentation   This option starts by providing a plain blank slide. While this option may require more work than using a template, it does have benefits. For instance, you can create a new presentation from scratch to make your work more original by selecting your own color scheme, art, fonts, and other design elements.

AutoContent Wizard Earlier versions of PowerPoint let you use the AutoContent Wizard to create a new presentation. A **wizard** is a series of dialog boxes that guides you through a step-by-step procedure. The **AutoContent wizard** provides the steps for creating a presentation. It asks questions about the goals and purpose of your presentation. Once its questions are answered, the wizard creates a format for the presentation. To complete the presentation, you enter the words and images into the wizard's format.

Exploring Presentation Views

While working, you can select to view a presentation in many ways, depending on the task at hand. Each view has its own strength. Depending on the program you use, you may be able to choose from these views:

- Normal view
- Slide Sorter view
- Notes Page view
- Slide Show view
- Reading view
- Master views

Figure 19.1.1 Most presentation programs let you choose a theme or template to quickly apply coordinated formatting to your slides.

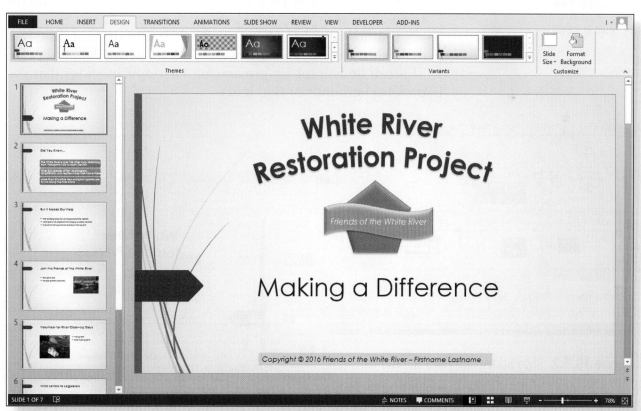

PowerPoint 2013, Microsoft Corporation.

At work, employees may be asked to make presentations to inform others about company policies, to show the results of the company's latest research, or to sell a new product.

Think About It!

Using the right view in presentation software can make creating a presentation a little bit easier. Which views listed below would help you organize your slides?

➤ Normal view

➤ Slide Sorter view

➤ Notes Page view

➤ Slide Show View

➤ Reading View

➤ Master Views

Normal View Text and graphics can be added, removed, or edited in **Normal view**. Normal view splits the screen to show a Slide view and a Navigation pane.

Slide Sorter View **Slide Sorter view** displays **thumbnails** of all of the slides in a presentation. This view allows you to change the order of the slides by dragging them to different locations.

Notes Page View In **Notes Page view**, part of the screen displays the slide and the rest of the screen shows a text box. You can type notes in the text box to use during a presentation or to print as handouts. Notes do not appear in the presentation that is shown to the audience.

Slide Show View The primary on-screen method of previewing and displaying slides during a presentation is called **Slide Show view**. Slides are displayed full-screen, one after another, in order. A slide-show presentation can be set to automatically advance slides or to wait until you—the presenter—advances the slides manually.

Reading View **Reading view** is similar to Slide Show view, except the slides are not displayed full-screen.

Master Views Many programs let you use **Master views** to make universal style changes to every slide, notes page, and/or handout pages.

You may also be able to use Black and White and/or Grayscale views to see how slides will look if printed without color. This can be helpful for previewing handouts of slides that use dark backgrounds or thin fonts.

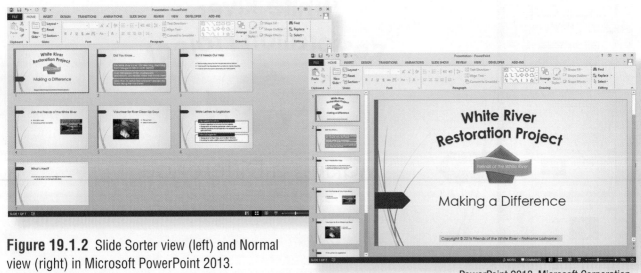

Figure 19.1.2 Slide Sorter view (left) and Normal view (right) in Microsoft PowerPoint 2013.

PowerPoint 2013, Microsoft Corporation.

Creating Presentations

Objectives

- Explain how placeholders are used in presentation software.
- Identify five steps in designing presentations.
- Summarize techniques for adding content.

As You Read

Sequence Information Use a sequence chart to help you order steps for creating presentations as you read.

Designing Presentations

Following these five steps will help you plan, design, and save an effective presentation.

1. Decide How Your Slides Will Be Formatted To begin designing a presentation, choose an option for creating it. Choose either a blank presentation or a template. If none of the templates is exactly what you want, select the one that is closest. You can change much of its graphic content, format, and text. Graphics can be resized or deleted. Placeholders can be added, removed, or resized as well.

2. Choose the Slide Layout Every slide in a presentation can be formatted in a preset layout. These layouts already have placeholders in position. This allows text and graphics to be added immediately. Some examples of slide layouts include bulleted lists, tables, grids, and flowcharts. Since each slide in a presentation can have a different layout, select a layout for each new slide you add.

3. Work with Placeholders A **placeholder** is an area within a slide layout designed to hold data such as text or pictures. A placeholder automatically applies a format based on the type of content. For instance, selecting a text placeholder will change the cursor to the Text tool. Selecting a picture placeholder will bring up a prompt asking which image to insert. Placeholder prompts guide you and are overwritten, or replaced, as you enter data.

4. Insert Graphics and Sound Make your presentations come to life. Insert sound, video, clip art, drawing tools, or imported images to support or illustrate a slide's text. But, be sure that the additions don't distract from the content.

 Key Terms

- animation
- AutoShapes
- placeholder

Some teachers use interactive multimedia software to help them teach. This software allows students to control the pace of the instruction.

Think About It!

Using interactive multimedia in the classroom has advantages and disadvantages. Which of those listed below could present a disadvantage for schools?

➤ expensive

➤ uses images

➤ uses sounds

➤ only some subjects available

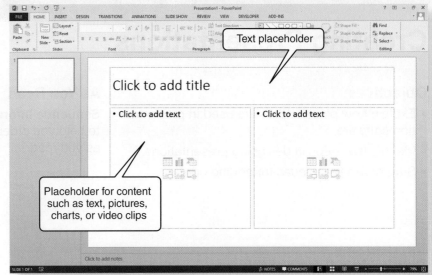

PowerPoint 2013, Microsoft Corporation.

Figure 19.2.1 A Two Content slide layout in Microsoft PowerPoint 2013.

5. View and Organize the Presentation Once information has been added to the slides, save it, and then preview the entire presentation using the Slide Show view. Make any changes to the order of the slides in Slide Sorter view. Typos and text changes can be handled in Outline view or Normal view.

Adding Content to Presentations

When you create a new presentation, you must use the Insert Slide command to add the slides you need to display your content. You can also use the Delete command to remove slides you don't need.

Each new slide in a presentation has a layout with placeholders for adding content. For instance, a layout might contain a placeholder where you can add a title. Click (or, in some programs, double-click) the placeholder and begin typing. The program automatically formats the text to fit the area with a preselected font and alignment.

Adding Graphics You can insert many types of graphics including clip art, pictures, drawings, charts, diagrams, and tables. In PowerPoint, use the buttons on the Insert tab of the Ribbon, or click the appropriate icon in a Content placeholder. PowerPoint drawing tools also include ready-to-use shapes, called **AutoShapes**. The list includes banners, arrows, borders, frames, and more. Save the file after every change.

You do not need a placeholder to insert graphics. Select the desired tool and use it in a blank area of the workspace.

Adding Animation and Sound A multimedia presentation combines text and graphics with sound and **animation**. Both sound and animation, or moving images, are inserted using menu commands. For example, in PowerPoint you can choose to insert video or audio clips using buttons in the Media group on the Insert tab.

Adding Text To add text, you simply type in a placeholder or in an outline. Text on a slide is often formatted as a bulleted list, which is a neat and effective way to present information.

Career Corner

Software Production Manager
Have you ever wondered who oversees the process of developing presentation or multimedia software? That is the job of software production managers. These are some of their job responsibilities:

➤ oversee people working on a project
➤ work with clients to develop features for the software
➤ oversee testing of the new software

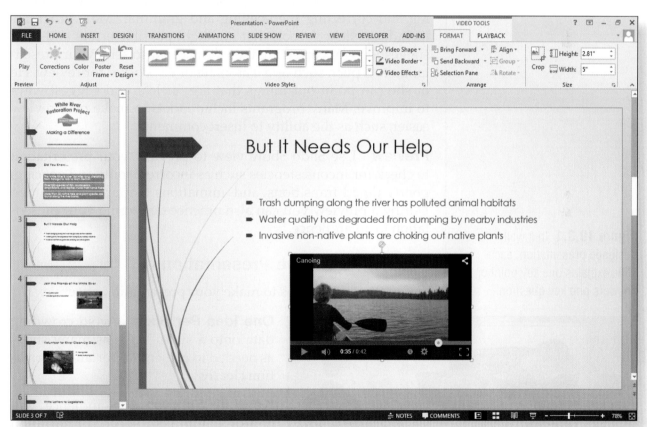

Figure 19.2.2 Previewing a video that has been inserted on a slide.

PowerPoint 2013, Microsoft Corporation.

Previewing Presentations

Objectives

- Identify reasons for reviewing and previewing a presentation
- Summarize seven tips for creating effective presentations.

As You Read

Organize Information   Use a main idea/detail chart to help you create useful presentations as you read.

Previewing a Presentation

Before finalizing a presentation you should review it and preview it.

Review   Reviewing your presentation should include checking and correcting the spelling and grammar. Most programs include spellcheck tools that highlight possible errors and offer suggestions for correcting them. You can also send your presentation to a peer, such as a classmate or co-worker for review. He or she can point out things that are unclear and suggest ways to improve. Many programs include tools to make peer review easier, such as the ability to insert comments.

Preview   Use Slide Show view to preview your presentation to check for inconsistencies such as incorrect fonts and spacing, poorly timed transitions, and animations that are out of order. During a preview you can also practice delivering your presentation to an audience.

Creating Effective Presentations

Apply these seven tips to make your presentation effective.

One Idea Per Slide   Avoid crowding data onto a slide. Make as many slides as needed to present important information clearly.

Keep It Simple   The audience will be listening to your speech or narration while viewing your slides. Use simple words to make key points. Include clear transitions from one topic to another.

Figure 19.3.1 In a well-designed presentation, each slide explains one key point or answers one key question.

Display Key Facts Your slides should serve as an outline for the audience. Your speech will fill in the gaps in that outline. Displaying too much information can make a presentation hard to follow.

Mix It Up Vary the layouts and content of your slides to help hold the audience's attention. For instance, switch between lists that appear on the right-hand and left-hand side and break up text with illustrations.

Use Color Cautiously Select colors that are pleasing to the eye. For instance, bright pink lettering on a bright blue background will be difficult to read. Avoid using too many colors on a slide.

Watch the Fonts Do not use more than two fonts on a single slide. This helps prevent a presentation from becoming too distracting to read. Also, be sure to use fonts that fit the tone. A presentation about the Civil War, for example, would not use fonts that seem playful or humorous.

Make It Readable Choose readable font and color combinations. Check that your text and images can be seen from the back of the room so your presentation can be viewed by your entire audience.

 Spotlight on...

DISTANCE LEARNING

Can you imagine creating presentations to show people who live hundreds of miles away? Distance learning teaches people at remote, or off-site, locations from the teacher. These students aren't seated together in a single classroom. Companies that develop distance-learning materials must create presentations students understand. It also means these presentations must keep students' interest.

Distance learning is offered by a large number of schools, colleges, and universities. Many people are

now earning college degrees through distance learning by taking classes online. Some schools also offer classes that combine some face-to-face instruction with online presentations.

Use the Vocabulary

Directions: *Match each vocabulary term in the left column with the correct definition in the right column.*

_____ **1.** presentation software
_____ **2.** slide
_____ **3.** wizard
_____ **4.** template
_____ **5.** Slide Show view
_____ **6.** placeholder
_____ **7.** AutoShapes
_____ **8.** animation
_____ **9.** thumbnail
_____ **10.** Slide Sorter view

a. preformatted version of a certain type of document

b. list of ready-to-use drawing tools

c. allows you to change the order of slides by dragging them to different locations

d. single page in a presentation

e. creates and displays visual information

f. miniature versions of each slide image

g. area in a presentation that holds data

h. can automatically show a presentation in the correct order

i. images that show movement

j. a series of dialog boxes that provides a step-by-step guide

Check Your Comprehension

Directions: *Complete each sentence with information from the chapter.*

1. Graphics designed using _____ usually are accompanied by text.

2. Using _____ view lets you make universal style changes to every slide, notes page, and/or handout pages.

3. The _____ view provides information that only the presenter can see during a presentation.

4. An on-screen method of previewing a presentation's slides is called the _____.

5. Animation can be added to some PowerPoint presentations using the _____.

6. Bulleted lists, flowcharts, and grids can be included in a slide's _____.

7. You can create a multimedia presentation with _____.

8. In a presentation, only the most _____ should be included on slides, not everything you plan to say.

9. A(n) _____ presentation combines text and graphics with sound and animation.

10. To prevent a presentation from becoming too distracting, do not use more than two _____ on a single slide.

Directions: *Answer the following questions.*

1. Which option for creating a new presentation works best for you? Explain.

2. What are disadvantages to adding clip art to PowerPoint presentations?

3. Why is it important to limit each slide in a presentation to a main concept or idea?

4. Why is it important to preview your presentation from the back of the room?

5. Which of the seven tips for creating effective presentations was the most meaningful to you? Why?

Extend Your Knowledge

Directions: *Choose and complete one of the following projects.*

A. In addition to PowerPoint, other software is available to create professional-looking presentations. Conduct research online or in software catalogs to find one other presentation program. Create a Venn diagram to compare and contrast the features of this program to those of PowerPoint.

B. Work in small teams, taking turns acting as team leader. Assign each team member one of the PowerPoint presentation views described in this chapter. Have each person create slides in his or her assigned view, summarizing the content of this chapter. As a team, present your slides to the class and watch their slides. Discuss the effectiveness of each view.

C. Work in small teams, taking turns acting as team leader. Plan and create a presentation that might be used in business, such as for training, marketing, or sales. Have each team member create at least one business-related element to include in the presentation, such as a table, embedded spreadsheet, chart, graph, organizational chart, or flow chart. Animate the elements, if appropriate. Package the presentation for CD delivery or to be viewed online.

Enhancing Presentations

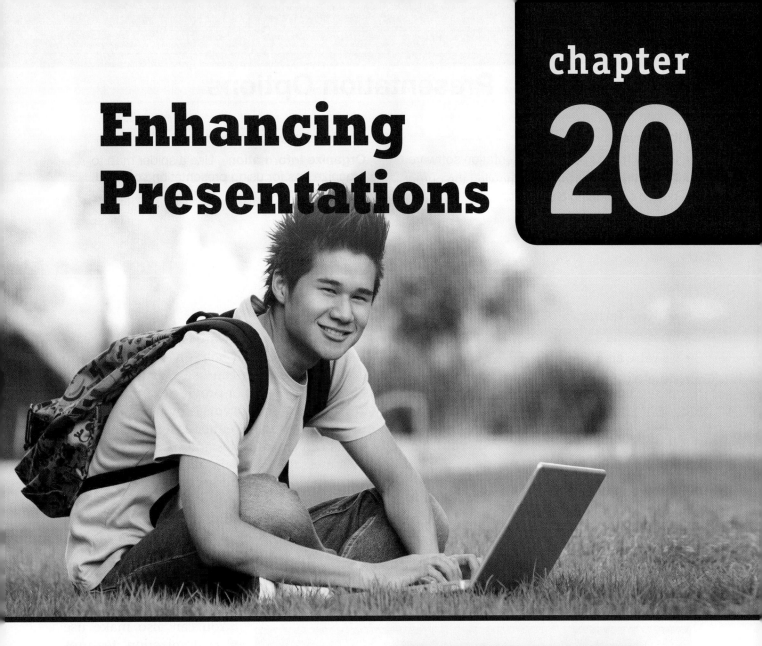

The Big Moment You have worked hard to assemble all the necessary tools and information. The stage is now properly set. The colors and lighting are perfect, and the script is well written. The show is about to begin.

Is this a Hollywood production? Is it a stage play? No, it's a computer presentation. Presentation software allows you to create a presentation with graphics, audio, text, animation, and more. Today, your computer screen is the stage. On other days, your show may be viewed on a large screen or on the Internet. The text, images, and sounds are your actors and props.

Learning to use presentation software is an important skill for school and work. Learning to use it effectively will benefit you for years to come.

Chapter Outline

 Lesson 20–1

Presentation Options

 Lesson 20–2

Developing Presentations

 Lesson 20–3

Enhancing and Finalizing Presentations

Presentation Options

Objectives

- Identify the purpose of presentation software.
- Explain the importance of knowing the output before developing a presentation.

As You Read

Organize Information Use a spider map to organize tips for using presentation software effectively as you read.

 Key Terms

- master slide
- viewable area
- visual aid

Figure 20.1.1 Depending on which profession you choose, you may see a lot of presentations.

Using Presentation Software

The main purpose of presentation software is to provide speakers with **visual aids**, or graphics that help give information to an audience. For example, a teacher can use a chalkboard, flip chart, or handouts to illustrate ideas or provide examples.

Another way to present these concepts is by using presentation software to introduce key points either as text or images or to clarify details. Users can create slides and handouts to teach a concept or convey a message. They also can deliver presentations on-screen in an office, in a conference room, and on the World Wide Web.

Most presentations use default settings suitable for creating and displaying a full color slide show to an audience on a monitor or screen, controlled by a live presenter. You can change the presentation options. For example, you can create a self-running presentation that does not require a live presenter, or that can be controlled by an individual.

You can also make use of customization features such as designs and masters to create consistent and professional-looking presentations. For example, you can apply a design template to your presentation to give it a uniform look and color scheme.

Working with Masters

Programs such as PowerPoint let you work with Slide, Notes, and Handout masters. Masters are default templates; changes you make to a master are applied to the components based on that master.

A **master slide** is a default template that is applied to all slides of a certain type. There are two different types of master slides in a presentation program such as PowerPoint:

- Slide Master
- Title Master

By editing a master slide, you are able to change fonts, sizes, colors, and layouts for all of the slides of that type throughout a presentation. For instance, the Slide Master controls the format for the slides. A Title Master controls the appearance of the title and subtitle of a title slide.

For example, suppose you want to change the font used for the main heading at the top of each slide. You can open the master slide, select the heading placeholder, and make your change. When you close the master slide, all the slide headings in the presentation will have changed to match the new format.

Technology @ School

When preparing a presentation for school, it may be a good idea to use Speaker Notes to help you remember what you want to say to the audience.

Think About It!

Entering notes can help remind you of details you want to share about your slides. For which of the ways listed below can Speaker Notes help you do this?

- ➤ help presenter remember dates and details
- ➤ organize layout of the slide show
- ➤ show thumbnails of the presentation
- ➤ prompt the punchline to a joke

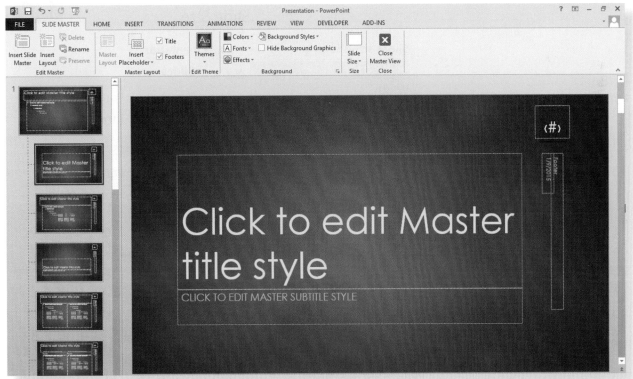

PowerPoint 2013, Microsoft Corporation.

Figure 20.1.2 Like PowerPoint 2013, most presentation programs let you use a master slide to control the look of an entire presentation.

Consider the Output

Presentation software programs offer options for optimizing the settings for printing the presentation and for displaying the slides onscreen or as 35-mm slides. Other issues to consider are printer output and displays.

Printer Output If a presentation is to be printed and provided as a handout, the page setup should match the capabilities of the printer. A solid black background with green lettering might look fine on a computer screen. However, printing a colored background on every page for every person in the audience uses a lot of ink. In addition, simple color graphics lose their effect if they are printed in black. Also, dark backgrounds can make text hard to see on a printed page.

Displaying the Output For each presentation, it is important to anticipate the display's **viewable area**, or portion of the screen where an image can be shown. Different displays have different viewable areas. For instance, if the computer uses a television as an output device, some of the information may not be visible. This is also true when using an LCD (liquid crystal display) monitor to project computer-screen images for large audiences. It is important to adjust the page setup so that all of the presentation can be viewed on-screen by the audience.

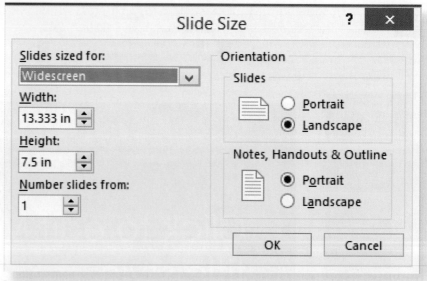

PowerPoint 2013, Microsoft Corporation.

Figure 20.1.3 In Microsoft PowerPoint 2013, use the Slide Size dialog box to optimize settings for slide size and orientation. Other options may be found in the PowerPoint Options dialog box.

Developing Presentations

Objectives

- Explain the use of a presentation outline.
- Identify slide layout options.
- Explain the benefit of designing the content of a slide before choosing the layout.
- Summarize the editing process that should occur after a draft presentation is complete.

As You Read

Sequence Information Use a sequence chart to sequence the steps to organize a presentation as you read.

Using a Presentation Outline

In most presentation programs you can use an outline to develop your presentation. You can type the outline to create slide titles and bullet items, or you can import an outline from a program such as Microsoft Word.

Typing an Outline When you type a presentation outline, the first line you type displays as the slide title. From the title, you press Ctrl+Enter to start a bulleted list, or Enter to create a new slide. From the bulleted list, you press Enter to continue the bulleted list, or Ctrl+Enter to start a new slide. You can format and rearrange outline text and increase or decrease outline levels to change the way the text displays on the slide.

Importing an Outline If you have an existing outline in a file created with a program such as Microsoft Word, you can import it into your presentation program. Each heading 1 level in the outline becomes a slide title, and the subheadings become bulleted lists.

Key Terms

- transition effect
- self-running presentation
- rehearsed presentation

Figure 20.2.1 PowerPoint lets you work with a presentation outline.

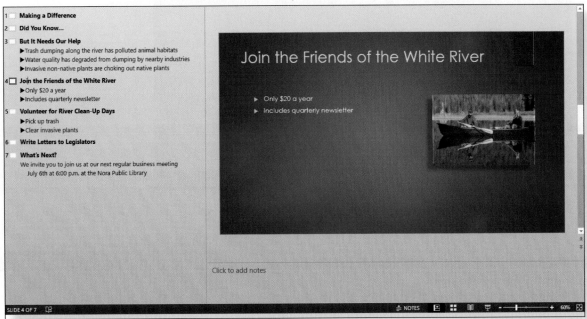

PowerPoint 2013, Microsoft Corporation.

Technology @ Work

Large companies often use organizational charts to identify the structure and responsibilities of employees. PowerPoint offers a template layout to help generate this information.

Think About It!

Which items listed below would be valuable to an organizational chart for a business?

➤ detailed job descriptions

➤ names of department heads

➤ telephone extensions

➤ work schedules

Figure 20.2.2 Checking the spelling in a presentation.

Choosing a Slide Layout

Each slide in a presentation can have its own layout. Consider the content of a slide before you choose a layout. By deciding the slide's key points first, you can then select the most appropriate layout for it.

The first slide in a new blank presentation usually has the Title Slide layout, with placeholders for entering a title and a subtitle. By default, new slides you add have the Title and Content layout, with placeholders for a title and content such as a bulleted list, clip art, picture, chart, table, or media clip. Other layout choices include Two Content, Comparison, Title Only, Blank, Content with Caption, Picture with Caption, and Section Header.

Editing Your Presentation

Good presenters edit drafts of their work. Be sure to fix the errors you find, reorganize the sequence of the slides, and improve the flow of ideas. If a slide is in the wrong location, use Slide Sorter or Outline view to move it. To revise the flow of text, use Outline view to adjust it.

Checking Errors   Presentation software can check spelling as you type text in a placeholder. If a red, wavy line appears under a word, it might be spelled incorrectly. If so, in Windows, right-click the word to open the suggested-spellings list and see other spelling choices, or run a spelling checker.

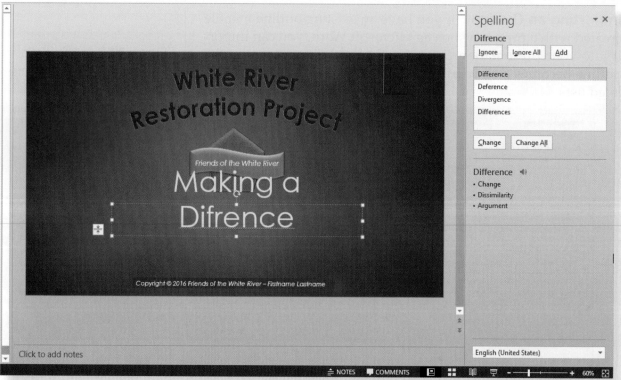

PowerPoint 2013, Microsoft Corporation.

Enhancing a Presentation

Inserting Images   Text-only presentations can be dull. Insert clip art, photos, and other images to clarify and enhance key points. Use charts, shapes, and drawings to help your audience better understand the information in your slides.

Adding Animation, Video, and Sound   Sound, animation, and video can make a presentation more informative and interesting. Most presentation software can import and use standard animation formats, including animated .gif clips. You can also animate objects and text on a slide. For example, you can have a title slide in from the left, or set a picture to fade out or blink.

Some presentation programs, including PowerPoint, include the ability to embed video clips or a link to a video from your presentation. You can insert sound files, such as music or recorded narration. When you insert sounds or video, an icon displays on the slide. You can hide the icon during a presentation, or set it so the clip only plays when a viewer clicks it.

Adding Transitional Effects   A **transition effect** is a multimedia feature that adds visual interest as your presentation moves from one slide to the next. For example, one slide might suddenly appear to fade out as the next slide appears. A new slide can move into view from one side of the screen as the previous slide disappears from sight.

Adjusting the Timing   You can adjust the timing of slide shows. In **self-running presentations**, each slide stays on the screen for a specified period of time. Timings are usually set by entering the number of seconds you want a slide to display. In a **rehearsed presentation**, you set the program to record how long you spend presenting a slide; the program automatically sets the timing based on your rehearsal.

Palm Island
Your Vacation Getaway

Figure 20.2.3 Graphics can make slides more informative or more appealing.

Enhancing and Finalizing Presentations

Objectives

- Identify strategies to enhance a presentation.
- Summarize choices for presentation output.

As You Read

Draw Conclusions   Use a conclusion chart to draw conclusions about finalizing a presentation as you read.

🔑 Key Terms

- digital projector
- on-screen presentation
- webcast

Making Powerful Presentations

Presentation programs are effective tools for generating high-interest, engaging presentations. Here are ten tips for finalizing presentation slides so that they are easy to understand and help you meet your presentation goals.

Remember your goal.   Keep your goal, and your main message, in mind as you outline your presentation. When finalizing your presentation, review your slides and the information they convey to ensure that your goal has been met.

Support your main idea.   Start by stating your main idea or topic sentence. Follow it with details that are simply presented and that clarify or support your main idea.

Know your audience.   Fewer words on a slide mean fewer words your audience has to read. However, make sure that you do not oversimplify the content on your slides or you run the risk of boring your audience. Finally, rehearse in clear language and make sure your slides are also clear to others.

Preview and review.   A preview slide introduces the presentation for an audience. This slide usually appears after the presentation's title slide and before the first slide that addresses a point.

A review slide usually restates the presentation's main points and may be identical to the preview slide. Used together effectively, a preview and review slide can help your audience remember the most important points of your presentation.

Figure 20.3.1 The more planning you do, the better your presentations will be.

Stay on point. The purpose of slides is to highlight key facts, so it is fine to leave out supporting details. Keep your text lively but to the point.

Select and apply a consistent design. Too many different designs or too many colors and fonts can distract or confuse an audience.

Be smart with art. Use clip art, tables, charts, icons, and animations wisely to enhance a point. Don't add illustrations that do not contribute to your message.

Proofread your text. Use the spelling checker to help you eliminate typos from your work. Then, print your slides and ask someone to proofread them.

Check the output. Make sure the hardware on which you plan to display your work will be able to run your slide show. Incompatible machines can ruin your presentation.

Watch the clock. Rehearse your presentation with a timer. Make sure any timed slides are sequenced with your verbal message.

Figure 20.3.2 Badly designed slides make it hard to understand your message.

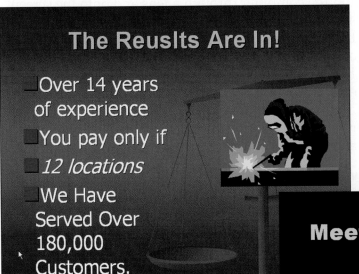

Figure 20.3.3 Well-designed slides make your message memorable.

Choosing a Delivery Method

There are a number of ways to deliver a presentation to an audience, including:

- on-screen delivery, with or without a speaker
- interactive presentation at a kiosk or booth
- Internet broadcast
- published in a variety of file types, such as pptx, pdf, jpg, show, or png

Choose the best delivery method to meet the needs of your audience, using the available technology.

On-screen Presentations Sometimes two or three people can comfortably gather around a single computer to view a slide-show presentation. In other cases, large groups may view a presentation on an overhead or video monitor, a presentation projector, or a "jumbo" screen. This is called an **on-screen presentation**, or a screen display of the slides.

In the past, overhead projectors were commonly used for on-screen presentations, especially in classrooms. Today, **digital projectors** are used. Overhead projectors worked by shining light through transparencies. Digital projectors project an image directly from the computer through a lens and onto the screen.

Large-format displays require special hardware, such as a digital light projector that takes the computer's output and projects it onto a wall or other large surface. Large-scale monitors are available but are expensive and difficult to move. In large settings, other equipment is often required, such as a microphone, amplifier, and speakers, which allow the audience to hear the speaker and any sound that plays during the presentation. The projector and speakers connect to your computer with cables.

Interactive Presentations PowerPoint allows users to add interactivity to a presentation. To help promote a product at a conference sales booth or a shopping mall kiosk, for example, you can set animation effects to play when a customer clicks a specific object on-screen. Depending on the object selected, the customer is routed to a specific part of the presentation and receives different information.

Internet Delivery If the audience is in a remote place, the presentation can be exported for broadcast on a Web site. The user can then view the slide show at any time through a Web browser. This method is useful for long-distance education. Group size is not an issue, and interactivity and animation are both possible presentation features. When the presentation is live and controlled by a presenter over the Internet, it is called a **webcast**.

Audience Handouts You can help your audience remember important or complex information by providing audience handouts. These handouts may be printouts of your slides or a summary of your main ideas.

Use the Vocabulary

Directions: *Match each vocabulary term in the left column with the correct definition in the right column.*

_____ 1. visual aid
_____ 2. digital projector
_____ 3. master slide
_____ 4. viewable area
_____ 5. transition effect
_____ 6. self-running presentation
_____ 7. rehearsed presentation
_____ 8. on-screen presentation

a. device used to display an image directly from a computer through a lens and onto a screen

b. changing the format of this slide changes all slides of this type

c. automatically switches from one slide to the next

d. uses a counter to help determine how long a slide should stay on the screen

e. graphic that is used to assist in communicating a topic

f. a display of slides on a monitor or screen

g. technique for switching from one slide to another during a presentation

h. portion of a screen on which an image can be seen

Check Your Comprehension

Directions: *Determine the correct choice for each of the following.*

1. What is the overall purpose of presentation software?
   a. show images to large audiences
   b. provide visual aids for speeches
   c. provide a way of creating art
   d. replace human presenters

2. Which color combination is best for printed handouts?
   a. white background with black letters
   b. black background with green letters
   c. dark blue background with red letters
   d. pale yellow background with white letters

3. Which slide usually restates the presentation's main points?
   a. title slide
   b. master slide
   c. review slide
   d. blank

4. Which slide layout is best for adding a two-column bulleted list?
   a. Title and Content
   b. Blank
   c. Two Content
   d. Picture with Caption

5. What kind of presentations are timed in a specific sequence?
   a. self-running
   b. rehearsed
   c. transition effect
   d. slide sorter

6. Which presentation delivery method is useful for long-distance education?
   a. on-screen delivery with a speaker
   b. Internet broadcast
   c. interactive presentation at a booth
   d. printed handouts

 **Think Critically**

Directions: *Answer the following questions.*

1. Why are the master slides valuable to someone using presentation software?

2. Why should you know your method of output before giving a presentation?

3. What choices does a presenter have for adding a graph, table, or spreadsheet to a slide?

4. How can the use of colors, fonts, font styles, and font sizes affect the design of a presentation?

5. Identify the functions of presentation software.

Extend Your Knowledge

Directions: *Choose and complete one of the following projects.*

A. There are many ways to add graphics to a presentation. You can download images from the Internet; export images from digital files or paint or draw programs; or use clip art stored on your compute or on CD. Access to premade images makes adding images to slides easy. Start a presentation program and create and save a new presentation file. Set up Slide Masters for a title slide and for a presentation slide that will display text and one image. Using the masters, create a title slide and three presentation slides. On each of the presentation slides insert an image captured in a different way, and a text description. Modify the masters to change the presentation format and design. Present your slides to the class, and explain the process you followed to create them. Document your sources.

B. Design, create, and distribute a survey to ten people of different ages to find out what kinds of presentations they have seen in the past 12 months. In your survey, include questions about the type of delivery method and the effectiveness of the presentation. Draw conclusions from the results of your survey about the use of presentation software to convey information to an audience. With a partner compare and discuss the results of your surveys and your conclusions.

DIRECTIONS: *You will prepare a presentation that defines the basic parts of speech, lists examples of each, and includes a sample sentence using one of the examples. You will format the presentation, apply transitions, and prepare the presentation for viewing.*

1. Open the .pdf file **PR-1_Speech**. With your teacher's permission, print the Data Record Sheet. Close the file, and exit your pdf reader program.

2. In the second column of the Data Record Sheet, write a definition of each part of speech listed in column 1. Use a dictionary, textbook, Internet, or other reference to gather the information. In column 3, enter three examples of words that fall into that category of speech. Then, in column 4, write a sentence using one of the three examples.

3. Start your presentation program, and save a new presentation as **PR-1_PartsofSpeech_***xx* in the location where your teacher instructs you to store the files for this activity. Replace *xx* with your own initials or name, as directed by your teacher.

4. On the title slide, type the title **Parts of Speech**. Include your full name as the author of the presentation in the subtitle, along with today's date.

5. Referring to the Data Record Sheet, prepare a slide for each part of speech listed in column 1, for a total of 8 slides. On each slide, include a title that identifies the part of speech, a text box in which you enter the definition, and a bulleted list for the three examples. A sample slide is shown in Illustration A.

6. In the Notes pane on each slide, enter the sentence from the usage column in the Data Record Sheet.

7. Insert clip art or teacher-approved Internet images on at least three of the slides, sizing and positioning them so they enhance the appearance of the slide.

8. Add a slide at the end for listing source information, including the Web address of any downloaded images you use.

9. When you have finished entering the slide and note text, proofread each one carefully with a partner or peer editor, checking spelling and grammar and correcting any errors that you find.

10. Apply a theme or design to the presentation that you think helps make the content easy to read and the presentation appealing.

11. View the presentation and look for ways to improve it. For example, you might decide to change the theme colors and/or fonts, or modify the slide backgrounds.

12. Apply transitions to all slides and set timings to advance automatically after 10 seconds or on a mouse click.

13. If possible, record narration for the presentation.

14. Set the presentation so it can be browsed at a kiosk.

15. With your teacher's permission, print the notes pages for yourself, and print handouts with three slides per page for the class.

16. Close the presentation, saving all changes, and exit your presentation program.

17. As a class, set up a computer or workstation to display your presentations. Politely discuss the effectiveness of each presentation. What were the strengths and weaknesses? Use critical thinking skills to evaluate the presentations for design, content, delivery, purpose, and relevancy to the assignment.

Noun

A noun is the part of speech that is used to name or identify a person, place, thing, quality or action.

▸ Athlete
▸ Stadium
▸ Basketball

Illustration A

Presentation Activities

DIRECTIONS: *You will use presentation software to create a slide show about a book you have read, including information about the book's characters, setting, conflict, and theme.*

1. Open the .pdf file **PR-2_Report**. With your teacher's permission, print the Data Record Sheet. Close the file, and exit your pdf reader.
2. Select a book you have read recently, have it approved by your teacher, and then use the Data Record Sheet to record information about the book.
3. Start your presentation program. Create a new presentation based on a template, and save it as **PR-2_Book_*xx*** in the location where your teacher instructs you to store the files for this activity. Replace *xx* with your own name or initials as instructed by your teacher.
4. Apply a theme or design to your presentation.
5. On the title slide, type a title for your presentation. Use the book's title and the author's name as the presentation subtitle. Insert a footer on this slide only that reads: **Prepared by [your full name]**, along with today's date. See Illustration B for a sample.
6. Insert a new slide with placeholders for a title and content.
7. Title this slide **Characters**.
8. Insert a table on the slide with two columns and one row for each character. List the character names in the left column and a description of the character in the right column. Format the table so it is attractive and easy to read.
9. Create slides for the Setting and Conflict using the information from your Data Record Sheet. For example, the next slide should be titled **Setting**, and should include information about the setting of the story. The slide after that should be titled **Conflict**, and should describe elements of the conflict in the story.
10. Insert a new slide with a title only layout.
11. Type the title **Plot** on the slide. Insert a flowchart diagram or use the drawing tools to create a flowchart that illustrates the major events in the book. Refer to your Data Record Sheet. If there are many events, consider extending the diagram to another slide.
12. Improve the appearance and readability of the diagram by resizing and positioning the drawing objects and by formatting the shapes in the illustration using colors, outlines, and fills. Format the text using font formatting such as

color and font styles.
13. Add one more slide to the presentation. Title the slide **Theme**, and type a bulleted list explaining the theme of the story.
14. Insert graphics to illustrate your slides.
15. Proofread each slide carefully with a partner or peer editor, checking spelling and grammar, and correcting any errors.
16. View the presentation, and look for ways to improve it. For example, you might want to change the theme colors and/or fonts to enhance the appearance of the slides.
17. Add transitions and animations, and view the presentation again.
18. Add speaker's notes that you can refer to while delivering the presentation.
19. With your teacher's permission, print the notes pages for yourself, and print handouts with three slides per page for the class.
20. Rehearse the presentation.
21. Use a projection system to show your presentation to the class and respectfully watch the presentations of your classmates.
22. Close the presentation, saving all changes, and exit the presentation program.
23. As a class, discuss the effectiveness of each presentation, including the use of graphics, fonts, themes, and other elements. What features caught your attention the most? What were the strengths and weaknesses of the presentation? Use critical thinking skills to evaluate the presentations for design, content, delivery, purpose, and relevancy to the assignment.

Illustration B

DIRECTIONS: *You will explore a career that interests you. You will conduct research to find out about duties, training, and salary associated with that career. You also will investigate how technology is used in the career, and how changes in technology have impacted the field. Then, you will create a presentation about the career.*

1. Open the .pdf file **PR-3_CareerResearch**. With your teacher's permission, print the Data Record Sheet. Close the file, and exit your pdf reader program.

2. Use the Internet or library resources to research a career that interests you, recording all source information as you work.

   a. If you are using an online catalog, search for the keyword **careers**. With an Internet search engine, you might search for words or phrases such as **"career information for teens"**. Be sure to include quotation marks around the keywords. Evaluate each Web site you visit for accuracy and validity. When possible, find at least two sources for each fact. When you find a Web site with useful information, bookmark the site, or with your teacher's permission, print the pages. Check copyright and fair use guidelines to make sure you can legally use the information.

   b. Write useful information on your Data Record Sheet. If you need more space, use the back of the sheet, or a separate piece of paper.

   c. If you locate any images or photographs related to your chosen career, ask your teacher for permission to download and save them as files so you can use them in your presentation. Again, make sure you can legally use them.

   d. When you have completed your research, close your Web browser.

3. With the information from your Data Record Sheet, draw a storyboard to map a presentation of at least six slides. Use project- and time-management skills to be sure you complete the presentation by the due date. You may want to use the schedule from Spreadsheet Activity 6.

4. Start your presentation program. Create a new, blank presentation or create a presentation based on a template, and save it as **PR-3_Career_xx**, in the location where your teacher instructs you to store files for this activity. Replace **xx** with your own name or initials as instructed by your teacher.

5. Apply a theme or design to your presentation.

6. Create the first slide as a title slide. Type an appropriate title that reflects the career you chose. The subtitle might include a phrase about the career that will grab your audience's attention. Insert a footer on this slide only that reads: **Prepared by [your full name]**, along with today's date. The title slide should look similar to the one shown in Illustration C on the next page.

7. Insert a new slide using a layout that has placeholders for a title and a bulleted list. Type **Job Duties** as the title. Using your Data Record Sheet, type bulleted items listing the job responsibilities. If there are too many items, either modify the layout to include two columns, or continue the list on a new slide.

8. Create slides for the Required Training, Average Salary, and Job Outlook rows on your Data Record Sheet. Use a slide layout that works best with the information you have and insert any images or clip art you want to include.

9. Using your research, create at least one slide that summarizes how technology is used in your chosen career, and how technology is changing or impacting that career.

10. When you have finished entering the slide text, proofread each one carefully with a partner or peer editor, checking the spelling and grammar and correcting any errors.

11. View the slide show and make any changes that you think will improve the presentation value, or make the presentation more effective. For example, split crowded slides into two slides, change the theme colors and/or fonts, or modify the slide background.

12. Add transitions and animations, and view the presentation again.
13. Add speaker's notes that you can refer to while delivering the presentation.
14. With your teacher's permission, print the notes pages for yourself, and print handouts with three slides per page for the class.
15. Rehearse the presentation.
16. Show your presentation to the class and respectfully watch the presentations of your classmates.

17. Close the presentation, saving all changes, and exit the presentation program.
18. As a class, discuss how changes in technology affect employment and the way people work. How do you think it impacts worker productivity? How does it influence how workers are trained? How has it changed the traditional office structure?

Illustration C

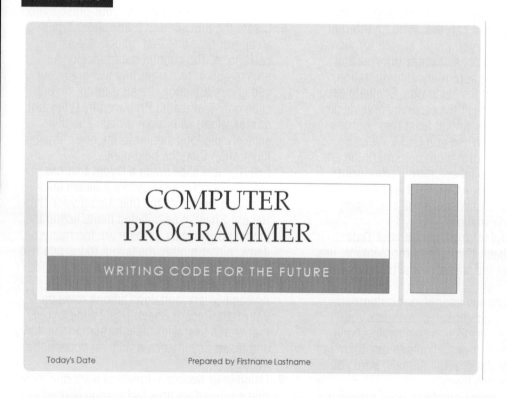

DIRECTIONS: *You will conduct research to learn about technology trends. Then, you will create a slide presentation to display your findings.*

1. Open the .pdf file **PR-4_Trends**. With your teacher's permission, print the Data Record Sheet. Close the file, and exit your pdf reader program.

2. With your teacher's permission, open a Web browser and navigate to a search engine. Search for sites that offer information about technology trends as well as evolving and emerging technologies. Try to identify at least five trends. For example, you might research wireless networks, tablets, touch screens, smart phones, satellite technology, nano technology, or smart devices.

   a. Try searching for words or phrases such as **technology trends**, or use a Boolean search such as **Technology AND Trends**. Review each Web site you visit for accuracy and validity. When possible, find at least two sources for each fact. When you find a Web site with useful information, bookmark the site, or with your teacher's permission, print the pages. Check copyright guidelines to make sure you may legally use the content. When you have completed your research, close your Web browser.

   b. Use the Data Record Sheet to record the information that you find. Include the name of each trend and a description.

   c. If you locate any images or photographs related to the trends, ask your teacher for permission to download and save them as files so you can use them in your presentation. Again, make sure you can use them legally.

   d. Record your source citation information on the Data Record Sheet.

3. With the information from your Data Record Sheet, draw a storyboard to map a presentation of at least eleven slides. Use project- and time-management skills to be sure you complete the presentation by the due date. You may want to use the schedule from Spreadsheet Activity 6.

4. Start your presentation program. Create a new presentation, and save it as **PR-4_Trends_xx** in the location where your teacher tells you to store the files for this activity. Replace **xx** with your own name or initials as instructed by your teacher.

5. Apply a theme or design to the presentation.

6. Format the first slide to contain a title and a subtitle. Type **What's New in the Computer World?** as the title. Type **Latest Technology Trends** as the subtitle. Insert a footer on this slide only that reads: **Prepared by [your full name]**, along with today's date.

7. Develop your presentation, creating 1-2 slides for each trend listed on your Data Record Sheet. Select an appropriate slide layout, enter a title, and insert the content. For example, you might type a bullet list, or insert a table, chart, or image. Include a slide listing ways the trends and emerging technologies impact individuals and businesses. On another slide, create a chart that compares and contrasts the trends and technologies.

8. When you have finished creating your slides, insert a footer on all but the first slide with the date, time, and page number, then proofread each slide carefully with a partner or peer editor. Correct any errors in spelling, capitalization, punctuation, or usage.

9. View the slide show and make any changes that you think will improve the presentation value, or make the presentation more effective. For example, split crowded slides into two slides, change the theme colors and/or fonts, or modify the slide background.

10. Add transitions and animations, and view the presentation again.

11. Add speaker's notes that you can refer to while delivering the presentation.

12. With your teacher's permission, print the notes pages for yourself, and print handouts with three slides per page for the class.

13. Rehearse the presentation.

14. Show your presentation to the class and respectfully watch the presentations of your classmates.

15. Close the presentation, saving all changes, and exit the presentation program.

16. As a class, discuss some of the more interesting trends you discovered during your research. What other types of emerging and evolving technology do you expect to see within the next ten years? In what new ways do you think computers and/or technology will be used in the future? How are these technology trends relevant to daily living, lifelong learning, and future careers?

DIRECTIONS: *You will use a presentation program to create a photo album for displaying photographs on a computer.*

1. Select a topic for a photo album and have it approved by your teacher. Then, collect at least five photographs that you can use in your album. If the photographs are not already in a digital format, convert them as necessary. For example, scan printed photos. With your teacher's permission, locate images online to download and save, recording all source information you will need according to copyright laws.
2. Start your presentation program. Create a new presentation.
3. Create a new photo album in your presentation program. Use the Help button to learn how, or ask a classmate or your teacher. If your software does not have a photo album feature, then create a blank presentation.
4. Select the pictures to insert, and create the album.
5. Save the album as **PR-5_Album_*xx***, in the location where your teacher instructs you to store files for this activity. Replace *xx* with your own name or initials as instructed by your teacher.
6. On the title slide, type a title and make sure your name displays correctly.

7. Insert a footer with your name and today's date on the title slide.
8. Insert a text box on each slide, and type a description of the picture.
9. Apply a theme or design to your presentation.
10. Check the spelling and grammar in the presentation, and correct any errors.
11. Set the slides to advanced on a mouse click, or automatically after 10 seconds. Set up the show to be browsed by an individual and to loop continuously.
12. View the album. (A sample album displayed in Slide Sorter view is shown in Illustration D.)
13. With your teacher's permission, publish the album to the Web, a slide library, or a shared site so others may view it and comment on it.
14. Close the presentation, saving all changes, and exit the presentation program.
15. As a class, discuss different ways of sharing photos using technology. Discuss the benefits—such as staying in touch and keeping up-to-date with family and friends—and drawbacks—such as privacy issues.

Illustration D

PowerPoint 2013, Microsoft Corporation.

Multimedia Basics

chapter 21

Different Media Offer Powerful Choices

For centuries, people have shared their thoughts and ideas by speaking, drawing pictures, or using written words. When you talk or write words on paper, you use one medium, or means of expressing information. Today, however, computers allow people to use many different media (the plural of *medium*) at the same time.

When you play a video game, watch a movie, or visit a Web site, you see many kinds of media, such as text, graphics, audio, video, and animation. A few years ago, it took expensive equipment and a lot of experience to combine these different media. Today, ordinary PCs and inexpensive software tools allow anyone to create entertaining and useful presentations, Web pages, interactive programs, games, and more using a combination of media types.

Chapter Outline

Introducing Multimedia

Objectives

- Define multimedia and compare multimedia and interactive multimedia.
- Explain how multimedia is used in various fields.
- Identify tools used to work with audio and video.

As You Read

Organize Information Use a main idea/detail chart to help you identify details about multimedia applications as you read.

🔑 Key Terms

- frame rate
- interactive multimedia
- multimedia
- sound card
- video capture board
- video editor

Defining Multimedia

A medium is one way to communicate information or express ideas. Talking is a medium, as is writing or drawing. Different media can be combined together in many ways. An animated cartoon, for example, combines moving graphics (one medium) with sound and music (other media). This is what is meant by the term **multimedia**—combining different media to express information or ideas. A multimedia event can include text, graphics, sound, video, and animation.

Because multimedia can take so many forms and be used in so many ways, terms such as event or experience are often used to describe it. A multimedia event can be many things. Movies and television programs are common examples, but now watching videos on YouTube or Hulu, listening to an audio podcast, or using a social networking site, like Facebook, are just as common. And while many kinds of computer programs use multimedia, from games to encyclopedias, a teacher displaying slides or using a low-tech chalkboard is also creating a multimedia event.

Many, though not all, examples of multimedia are interactive. **Interactive multimedia** allows the user to make choices about what is displayed. Computer and video games, educational computer software, and some Web sites—which let you decide what you see and how you interact with information—are all examples of interactive multimedia.

To be interactive, a multimedia event must provide more than audio or video. It must also give the user a way to control the action and make choices that determine what happens next. Think of a video game that lets you direct an avatar through a series of passages and then go back again. Or think of multimedia social networking Web sites that let you update your "status," watch videos posted by others, and comment on them.

Using Multimedia

Multimedia applications are widely used today in business, education, and entertainment.

Business Multimedia technologies help businesses communicate with their customers and employees. Many corporate Web sites, for example, use sound, video, or animation to demonstrate products to customers.

Businesses also use multimedia to train employees. For example, many companies create custom multimedia programs that workers can access via CD-ROM, a network, or online. These programs use audio and video to demonstrate products and explain procedures. These programs can be interactive, which allows workers to jump to different areas of the content at will or take tests that provide feedback about their knowledge.

Education Multimedia can make learning more fun for students and provides extra tools for teachers. Interactive software can teach lessons, present quizzes, and give students immediate feedback to help them see how well they are doing.

Multimedia programs offer audio and video to enhance learning in ways that printed text alone cannot. For instance, instructional software may use audio to teach languages. Multimedia encyclopedias can play video clips from historical events.

Entertainment Video and computer games are multimedia programs. Flight simulators use rapidly changing graphics and sound to put the player "inside the cockpit" of a plane. Action games use realistic graphics and color to create the experience. But interactivity is what gives these games their true appeal. Using a game controller or keyboard, you can direct the action from start to finish. Multimedia technologies are used in many products besides games. Movies use 3-D animation and computer-generated effects. Concerts, documentaries, and television programs also incorporate multimedia.

Technology @ School

The sales catalogs that are sent to schools these days don't just include books. They also offer a large number of multimedia programs that can be used in teaching various subjects.

Think About It!

Which benefits listed below might a school gain from purchasing multimedia programs?

- easier material

- providing immediate feedback to students

- capturing students' attention

- making an actual teacher unnecessary

- matching students' learning styles to material (whether they learn best through sight or sound)

Figure 21.1.1 Many schools and libraries use multimedia programs to teach all kinds of subjects to people of all ages.

Tools for Working with Audio and Video

Audio (sound) and video (movies and animations) are essential components of multimedia. You will need these three components to create multimedia.

Sound Card As you learned earlier, a **sound card** is a special expansion board that allows the computer to input, edit, and output sounds. Audio—whether voices, music, or sound effects—is entered into the computer through the input jacks on the sound card. Once audio is captured on the computer's hard drive, you can edit and work with it. You can then play it through the computer's speakers or headphones, or save it to a disc. You can also send it to another audio device using the sound card's output jack. Full-featured cards even include optical inputs and outputs for digital sound and special software for mixing sound.

Video Capture Board Video signals, such as those from television programs or movies, have to be converted into a format that computers understand. This is done with a **video capture board**, a special card that plugs into a computer. You can transfer video to the capture board from video cameras, digital cameras, and other sources.

Video Editor After video and audio are saved to the computer's hard drive, you can combine them in new ways. You do this work with a video editor. A **video editor** is a program that allows you to cut and paste sound and video segments and change the order in which segments appear. Video editors also allow you to define the **frame rate**, or how many still images are displayed in one second, and specify the speed at which video should be displayed.

Figure 21.1.2 Today's multimedia products use several kinds of data, from simple text to sound to video.

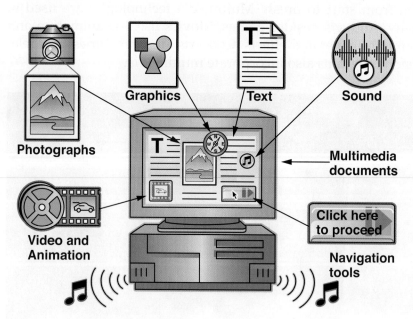

Graphics

Text

Sound

Photographs

Multimedia documents

Video and Animation

Click here to proceed

Navigation tools

Multimedia File Formats

Objectives

- Identify video file formats.
- Summarize audio file formats and the platforms on which they run.
- Identify programs used to play multimedia programs on a computer or the Internet.

As You Read

Outline Information   Use an outline to help you understand multimedia tools as you read.

Video File Formats

Multimedia can combine text, audio, graphics, video, and animation. To do such complicated work, designers choose from a number of file formats, each suited for a specific task.

MPEG   MPEG is a family of formats developed by the Moving Picture Experts Group. Web sites and CD-based products commonly use MPEG to display video such as movie clips, animations, and recorded television broadcasts. MPEG files offer full-motion video; thus, they give a very realistic effect.

Different versions of the basic MPEG format have been developed. MPEG-2 is used for regular television, DVDs, and high-definition television (HDTV). The MPEG-4 format is used for interactive graphics and interactive multimedia on the Internet.

QuickTime™   Designed by Apple Computer, QuickTime is the basic file format for showing animation and video on Macintosh computers. QuickTime videos also can be viewed on Windows computers, but a special player must first be installed. The QuickTime format is often used for high-quality movie trailers shown on Web sites. It is also used for the video feeds from Web sites that provide news and weather information.

AVI   Audio Video Interleave, or AVI, is another name for Microsoft Video for Windows format. Some AVI videos are not of the best quality, but they can be played on any Windows computer. Many businesses create their multimedia in AVI format to tap into the huge market of Windows users.

 Key Terms

- encoder
- synthesize

Did You Know?

It is a crime to create a duplicate CD or DVD and then sell it for profit. This type of piracy, called intellectual piracy, is theft because the original artists and producers do not make the money they deserve from their work.

Audio File Formats

While formats like MPEG, QuickTime, and AVI capture both pictures and sound, other formats can be the best choice when sound quality is a priority.

MP3 MPEG audio layer 3 (MP3) files are very common today, thanks to the ease of downloading music from the Internet. The MP3 format takes a large audio file and makes it very small. It does this using regular compression methods and also by removing data from the music file that the human ear cannot hear. This results in a much smaller file, with little or no loss of sound quality.

WMA WMA is the music format of Microsoft. It stands for Windows Media Audio®. WMA files are also compressed from larger audio files but do not have information removed. WMA files can be converted back to the original uncompressed files while MP3s can only be uncompressed into approximations of the original files.

AU AU, or audio, is the standard format for audio files for the UNIX operating system.

WAV The waveform audio (WAV) format is built into the Microsoft Windows operating system. WAV files can be played on almost any computer system. WAV and WMA files can be converted into MP3 files using a hardware device or special software programs called **encoders** that convert the files from one format to another. Unlike MP3 and WMA files, WAV files are not compressed.

MIDI Musical Instrument Digital Interface, or MIDI, is a standard that allows a computer to control a musical instrument. MIDI sounds are **synthesized**. This means that sounds imitative of musical instruments are generated by the computer when they are played; no actual recorded sound is stored in the file.

Name	Size	Type
A Hard Rain's A-Gonna Fall.mp3	3,998 KB	MP3 Audio
Angel Eyes.mp3	2,684 KB	MP3 Audio
Avalon.mp3	4,012 KB	MP3 Audio
Dance Away.mp3	3,512 KB	MP3 Audio
Do The Strand.mp3	2,218 KB	MP3 Audio
In The Midnight Hour.mp3	2,948 KB	MP3 Audio
Jealous Guy.mp3	4,604 KB	MP3 Audio
Love Is The Drug.mp3	3,824 KB	MP3 Audio
More Than This.mp3	3,912 KB	MP3 Audio
Oh Yeah.mp3	4,318 KB	MP3 Audio
Over You.mp3	3,234 KB	MP3 Audio
Pyjamarama.mp3	2,696 KB	MP3 Audio
Same Old Scene.mp3	3,712 KB	MP3 Audio
Sign Of The Times.mp3	2,316 KB	MP3 Audio
Slave To Love.mp3	4,030 KB	MP3 Audio
These Foolish Things.mp3	4,522 KB	MP3 Audio
Virginia Plain.mp3	2,786 KB	MP3 Audio

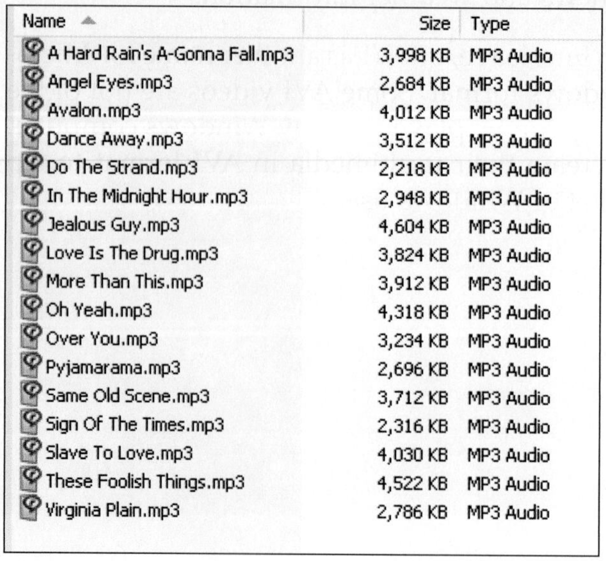

Figure 21.2.1 MP3 files are one type of common music format.

Multimedia Players

You use a media player program to play multimedia content on your computer, media device, or on the Internet. This can be a stand-alone media player or a browser plug-in that you download for free from the Internet.

Windows Media, QuickTime, and RealPlayer™ Cloud These three players are very popular for playing streaming audio and video—that is, content that is broadcast in a continuous feed from Web sites. They are also useful for playing content from some disc-based multimedia products.

All of these players can handle a wide variety of audio and video formats, although each one has its own unique format. You can use any of these players to listen to music broadcast by online radio stations, watch news and weather reports, check out movie trailers and music videos, and enjoy many other kinds of multimedia content. Many people have all three of these players installed on their computer.

Adobe Flash™ and Shockwave® Players Multimedia developers can use special file programs called Shockwave and Flash to create interactive multimedia content, such as animated games. These programs can accept user input, use high-quality audio and graphics, and are very small so they can be downloaded quickly from a Web site or disk. To view content created in these programs you need the Flash Player and the Shockwave Player, both of which are free.

 Spotlight on...

GEORGE HARRISON

George Harrison is best known as a member of the Beatles, the music sensation of the 1960s and 1970s. But Harrison was a musical innovator in his own right. His 1969 release *Electronic Sound*, for example, led to more experimentation by other musicians and, ultimately, to the rave generation of music.

Introducing Virtual Reality

Objectives

- Explain what virtual reality is and describe some methods of presenting it.
- Discuss computer and video games.

As You Read

Organize Information   Use a concept web to help you organize details about virtual reality as you read.

 Key Terms

- augmented reality
- Cave Automatic Virtual Environment (CAVE)
- head-mounted display (HMD)
- virtual reality (VR)

Forms of Virtual Reality

The terms **virtual reality**, **VR**, or Virtual Environment, VE, are used interchangeably to describe three-dimensional computer-generated environments that you can explore by using special hardware and software. Such environments simulate spaces, such as the flight deck of an airliner or the inside of an underwater cave. The purpose of all VR environments is the same: to let users explore and also manipulate every aspect of the space, moving in any direction, just as if that space or the things within it were real.

Sophisticated hardware and software are needed to create large-scale, detailed VR environments. Users can explore such environments in several different ways.

HMD   A **head-mounted display**, or **HMD**, is usually a helmet or a set of goggles that wraps around the head, blocking out light. A tiny computer monitor is located in front of each eye. Using these two separate monitors gives the illusion of three dimensions. HMDs often have headphones to provide audio to the user.

In advanced HMDs, tiny sensors can tell when the user's head tilts in any direction. The image on the monitors then shifts accordingly, in order to create a convincing illusion of being part of the action, rather than a spectator of it. HMDs can use liquid crystal display monitors to display images.

Figure 21.3.1 A head-mounted display is a portable, relatively inexpensive way to experience virtual reality.

CAVE2 The **Cave Automatic Virtual Environment2**, or CAVE2, is an expensive and advanced form of VR. Images of a virtual world are displayed using LCD panels on the walls of a room. Visitors wear special goggles that create the illusion of three dimensions. The result is so realistic and so convincing that most "explorers" cannot tell where reality ends and virtual reality begins without reaching out and touching something.

In many CAVEs, users wear special gloves (called data gloves) or hold special wands, either of which can detect hand movements. These devices allow users to interact with objects in the virtual world, by opening doors, for example, or picking up the pieces in a virtual chess game.

Augmented Reality An emerging category of virtual reality is called **augmented reality**. Cameras in mobile devices are used to layer virtual information onto real information. One example is a smart phone app for translation. When you point your phone at foreign language text, the English translation displays on the screen

HMDs that allow for images to be superimposed over real-world images allow a computer to interact with the physical world. These HMDs have lenses that use optical mixers to display digital images without blocking real-world images. Google Glass is an HMD that allows for mixed reality, or the combination of the real world and digital information.

Connections

Science Many educators believe virtual reality is having a major impact on science classrooms. Students can now "visit" and explore various ecosystems—take a stroll in a rain forest, for example, or shiver on the Alaskan tundra. Students studying anatomy can get a 3-D view of the respiratory system, the digestive system, and so on. Students opposed to dissecting animals can cut apart a virtual frog, making that experiment less distasteful.

Real-World Tech

Strolling Through Comet Tails A new virtual reality deep vision display wall at Boston University will let students and professors stroll through comet tails, walk through the sun's weather, observe an earthquake, and study how air flows around airplanes. Two IBM supercomputers and 24 projectors fill a 15 × 8-foot screen with a high-resolution stereo image. The images change as the visitors move through the room.

What other phenomena could usefully be explored in a room like this?

Technology @ Home

While board games like Monopoly™ and Boggle™ remain popular, electronic games have become a major part of the game industry.

Think About It!

Have you tried all three types of electronic games? Sequence each kind of electronic game using a scale of 1 (lowest) to 3 (highest) to indicate which you enjoy most.

➢ game consoles

➢ computer games

➢ multiplayer online games

Computer and Video Games

The first electronic games displayed only simple, two-dimensional images with limited sounds. Today, because of virtual reality, you can choose from hundreds of games with detailed graphics, lifelike characters, and realistic environments.

Computer Games Today's PCs, with their fast processors, powerful sound and graphics cards, and large displays, let you get the most from your games. Games for PCs can be installed using compact discs or downloaded from the Internet.

Game Consoles A game console is a device that uses a television to display a game. You interact with the game by using one or more controls, which are connected to the console. The most popular consoles in recent years have been the Nintendo Wii U®, Microsoft Xbox One®, and Sony Playstation 4®. While consoles used to be just dedicated to game playing, now some are used to stream videos from the computer to the TV. Consoles now have games, like Sony's Just Dance, that track the users physical movements using sensors.

Online Games Many PC games, such as World of Warcraft (WoW), are available on the Internet and allow multiple players to compete in real time while keeping score. To have the best gaming experience, you often need a high speed Internet connection, a PC with multimedia features, and a new model game console. Sometimes players need to pay a monthly fee to play, and all multiple player games require you to abide by a set of rules, called an End User Licensing Agreement (EULA). These rules prevent conflicts between players, and players who violate them are banned from playing.

Figure 21.3.2 Many computer and video game controllers are motion-sensitive.

Use the Vocabulary

Directions: *Match each vocabulary term in the left column with the correct definition in the right column.*

_____ 1. multimedia
_____ 2. video capture board
_____ 3. video editor
_____ 4. frame rate
_____ 5. encoder
_____ 6. synthesize
_____ 7. virtual reality
_____ 8. head-mounted display
_____ 9. CAVE2
_____ 10. interactive multimedia

a. allows the user to make choices about what is displayed
b. very realistic form of virtual reality that is displayed in a room
c. hardware that lets a computer work with video data
d. software that changes a WAV file into MP3 format
e. using more than one medium to express information or ideas
f. program that lets users manipulate sound and video
g. realistic, but simulated, 3-D world
h. number of still images displayed in one second
i. helmet or goggles used to display a virtual reality environment
j. the process in which a computer generates sounds

Check Your Comprehension

Directions: *Determine the correct choice for each of the following.*

1. What kind of multimedia lets users make choices about the direction a program may take?
   a. graphic multimedia
   b. animated multimedia
   c. interactive multimedia
   d. technical multimedia

2. What hardware allows a computer to input, edit, and output audio?
   a. a sound card
   b. a video editor
   c. AU
   d. 3-D

3. Which audio file format does a computer use to produce synthesized sounds?
   a. CAVE
   b. CD-ROM
   c. MIDI
   d. AVI

4. Which of the following file formats allows you to view interactive multimedia games on your computer?
   a. MPEG-2
   b. Shockwave
   c. video capture board
   d. Net video

5. Where are the monitors in an HMD located?
   a. on the wall
   b. in a helmet or a set of goggles
   c. in a room
   d. online

6. Which of the following layers virtual information with real information?
   a. CAVE
   b. virtual 3-D
   c. World of Warcraft
   d. augmented reality

 **Think Critically**

Directions: *Answer the following questions.*

1. For what purpose might a business want to hire a computer specialist who knows QuickTime and AVI?

2. What equipment and software would you need to develop your own multiplayer online game?

3. What two file formats are commonly used for interactive games found on Web sites?

4. Why is a virtual reality simulation used to train fighter pilots an example of interactive multimedia?

5. What is an example of how an electronic textbook might make use of VR technology?

Extend Your Knowledge

Directions: *Choose and complete one of the following projects.*

A. In groups of four students, work cooperatively to choose a topic you are studying in language arts, social studies, science, math, art, or music. Plan a two-minute multi-media presentation on that topic that includes at least one example of each of these media: audio, video, text, and graphics. Assign one medium to each member to complete. Use groupware or collaborative software to review one another's work. Then, use a video editor to combine the pieces into a smooth, logical sequence.

B. Electronic games can be a lot of fun, but some people believe that youngsters spend too much time playing them. Conduct online or library research to identify some specific objections that people have to these games. Then, debate the pros and cons of electronic games, using your research and your own gaming experiences as resources. Which argument was the most persuasive? Why?

C. With a partner, plan a one minute audio advertisement on a topic approved by your teacher. Write a script that delivers the desired message. Rehearse and record it. Use audio editing software such as Audacity to edit it to the desired length. Share it with the class.

Understanding Multimedia

Using Your Senses Human beings are sensory creatures—that is, we operate not just through what we know but through what we see and hear and feel. Reading about something brings us understanding, but our senses of sight, hearing, and touch deepen that understanding.

Multimedia—combinations of words, sounds, images, video, and animation—can provide that sensory input. Multimedia productions can take many forms, including an encyclopedia CD-ROM, a television commercial, a full-length movie, a short video within a presentation, or an animated introduction to a Web site.

Multimedia techniques are also used to create virtual worlds for us to explore, worlds that can test medical procedures, preview new buildings, and tap our imagination.

Chapter Outline

 Lesson 22–1

Exploring Multimedia

 Lesson 22–2

Developing Online Multimedia

 Lesson 22–3

Exploring Virtual Reality

Exploring Multimedia

Objectives

- Describe the forms of multimedia.
- Identify specialized tools used to produce multimedia.

As You Read

Outline Information Use an outline to help you organize details about multimedia as you read.

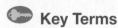 **Key Terms**

- information kiosk
- pen-based graphics tablet

Forms of Multimedia

Multimedia combines text, graphics, video, animation, and sound. Television programs and movies are one-way multi-media—you are a passive viewer. Interactive multimedia lets you interact with the computer-generated content.

CDs and DVDs Both CDs and DVDs offer a rich opportunity for multimedia experiences. Watching a movie on DVD is no longer a passive activity because you can choose whether to view the film in letterbox or standard television format. You decide what language to hear it in. You can skip to or replay your favorite parts. Many DVD movies include interactive features such as games.

CDs and DVDs also offer educational experiences and adventures. A multimedia encyclopedia offers videos and animations that bring subjects to life. A mountain-climbing DVD lets you choose your view of the mountain and your route to the top. A DVD used with a stationary bike and your computer can give you 18 different "rides" and check your speed and heart rate while you pedal.

Information Kiosks An **information kiosk** uses an automated system to provide information or training. In effect, this is a PC-in-a-box, usually with a touch screen allowing input. At the Museum of Science in Boston, Massachusetts, for example, you can create artificial fish and watch how they behave when you release them into a simulated fish tank.

Games Computer games, home video game consoles, gaming apps, and arcade games offer dramatic examples of multimedia. They create an interactive experience that uses many different media. Many computer games, or video games, create immersive worlds in which the player has clear objectives to complete. The games can be educational, like a typing training program, or for entertainment, like a flight simulator or a fantasy adventure. Many video games involve an online component. Online gaming allows players to interact with each other in real time. Video games can be run on multiple platforms from PCs to smart phones.

Multimedia Development Tools

Certain tools are used to create and make use of the elements of a multimedia presentation including the following:

Pen-Based Graphics Tablets   When creating still or animated graphics for use in a multimedia program, many artists find it easier to draw and sketch using a **pen-based graphics tablet** rather than a mouse. To use the tablet, you move a stylus, or electronic pen, across a sensitive touchpad or a touchscreen, and your movements are recorded by your graphics software. The images can then be saved and edited.

Microphones   Audio can be recorded into a conventional recording device and then imported through a sound card. Audio can also be recorded directly into the computer using a microphone. Most sound cards have a special plug for a microphone. Using the software that comes with the sound card, you can assign a file name, click "record," and start speaking into the microphone. The sounds will be recorded to a new audio file.

Digital Cameras   Digital cameras and camcorders are an easy way to acquire images and video for use in multimedia. These cameras don't require film. Images and video are stored in the camera and can then be transferred to the computer through a special cable or disk. Once on the computer, the pictures and video can be edited and used in presentations, movies, Web sites, and other applications.

Career Corner

Online Reporter   Some online news services are affiliated with newspapers, magazines, or radio and television networks. Others exist only online. Online reporters need traditional reporting skills. But they must also be familiar with collecting news and photos in a variety of formats, including multimedia, and with presenting information and graphics effectively on a screen. The top candidates have good communication skills, work quickly and accurately, and understand how to use high-tech tools.

Figure 22.1.1 Microphones let you use a computer by talking. This student is using a PC and microphone to practice a foreign language.

Developing Online Multimedia

Objectives

- Describe how to access online multimedia.
- Explain the term "authoring" as it relates to multimedia.
- Discuss the use of authoring tools.

As You Read

Organize Information   Use a spider map to help you categorize information about online multimedia as you read.

🔑 Key Terms

- authoring tool
- rip
- stream

Accessing Online Multimedia

Multimedia presentations aren't limited to files stored on your computer's disks. With an Internet connection, you have access to an unlimited number of multimedia experiences. Many multimedia Web sites can **stream** video and audio data—that is, transmit it across a network without interruption. You don't have to wait until the entire file is downloaded to your computer for it to play. The file begins playing as soon as it starts to download from the Web site to your PC.

Net Radio   Internet radio is a method for listening to music, talk, and information over the Internet. Net radio doesn't actually use radio waves. Instead, audio programs are converted to digital format and streamed across the Internet. Streaming radio places a temporary audio file on your hard drive. This is what is heard—not the actual stream. The audio stream replenishes the file on the hard drive, continually updating the data as it plays.

Net Video   Like Net radio, Net video uses streaming, but it delivers pictures as well as sound. News sites use online video to deliver the latest news. Movie sites preview upcoming releases and offer short films and animations. Subscription video sites, like Netflix and Hulu, stream TV shows and videos. In the business world, Net video is used for videoconferencing. In a videoconference, small cameras are used to allow people in different places to see and hear one another. Live streaming is when content is put onto the Internet live.

Ripping   If your computer has a CD-ROM drive, you can also copy music for your personal use from audio CDs onto your hard drive. This process is called **ripping**, and it requires special software. Once audio is ripped to the hard drive, it can be converted to MP3 format, which creates a much smaller file than a regular audio file.

Creating Multimedia

Authoring is the term used to describe the creation of multimedia programs. To combine audio, video, graphics, and text, you use software called **authoring tools**.

Using Authoring Tools Authoring tools let you choose which sounds, video clips, animations, text, and graphics will appear. You also control timing, transition effects, and volume. Authoring tools let you respond to questions such how long each image will appear on-screen, how will one clip transition into the next, and how loud should sound play.

Most authoring tools save data in a format for use only by the software developers and authorized users. You use a media player program to view the finished piece.

Choosing Authoring Tools The authoring tool you choose depends on how complex your project will be, the type of computer system you have, and how much time you have to spend learning the program. Some sophisticated authoring tools are for media professionals; others are simple enough that they can be used by anyone who wants to create their own multimedia CDs, videos, and presentations.

The professional version of QuickTime and some high-end desktop publishing programs include a small set of multimedia authoring tools. Adobe offers several popular products, like Director, Director/Student Edition, and Studio MX. Programs, like Audacity, can be used to record and edit audio. Presentation programs such as Microsoft PowerPoint includes tools for inserting audio and video and for animating slides. Microsoft is currently developing the program Sway to allow for presentations containing multiple types of multimedia to be viewed across many devices from personal computers to tablets and smart phones. Many PCs come with software such as Muvee Reveal by Muvee Technologies for creating movies that include video, images, and sound.

Technology @ School

Think about the ways your school could inform the public about school activities. Sequence each medium from 1 (lowest) to 5 (highest) to show which you think would be most effective.

➤ CD

➤ video for cable television

➤ information kiosk

➤ local newspaper article

➤ Web page

Figure 22.2.1 Authoring programs let you create and edit multimedia projects.

Exploring Virtual Reality

Objectives

- Explain what is meant by immersive virtual reality.
- Identify virtual reality equipment and language.
- Discuss real-world uses of virtual reality.

As You Read

Organize Information Use a concept web to help you understand the practical applications of virtual reality as you read.

🔑 Key Terms

- data glove
- simulations

The Technology of Virtual Reality

Virtual reality works by making a computer-generated scene feel as it would in the real world. It does this by using three-dimensional, or 3-D, graphics, color, texture, and sound.

In some cases, VR worlds are displayed on regular computer screens. A 3-D video game is one example. Another example is a flight simulator, which is valuable in training pilots.

Virtual reality's main potential, however, lies in immersive technologies that surround a viewer with the VR world. With immersive VR, the user feels part of the virtual environment. For example, gaming consoles such as Microsoft's Kinnect for Xbox let the player use his or her body as the controller; some museum exhibits project moving images on walls around the viewer; and arcade games let you steer a race car or ski down a mountain.

VR Gadgets In addition to a head mounted display, virtual reality often uses a device called a **data glove**. A data glove is a basic glove equipped with sensors that measure movements of the hand and fingers. One use of the data glove is to operate equipment from a distance.

VR Language To create virtual worlds on the Internet, programmers use a language called X3D. X3D allows programmers to describe objects that appear in the virtual world, such as shapes, buildings, landscapes, or characters.

Figure 22.3.1 A head-mounted display is an important tool in immersive virtual reality.

Practical Applications of Virtual Reality

Virtual reality has become very useful for **simulations**. Simulations are virtual reality programs that mimic a specific place, job, or function. Virtual reality is used in many design and architectural businesses. It is also used in the military to train fighter pilots and combat soldiers without the risks of live training.

In medicine, virtual reality is used to simulate complex surgery for training surgeons without using actual patients.

Easing Pain At the University of Washington's Harborview Burn Center, virtual reality is being used to help severe burn victims deal with their pain. Patients are immersed in a virtual reality environment. There, they imagine that they are flying through icy canyons and cold waterfalls, building snowmen, and throwing snowballs. By focusing on things that are pleasant and cold, patients can focus less on their pain.

Overcoming Fear A study by Walter Reed Army Hospital and Emory University School of Medicine showed that patients placed in virtual reality flight simulators overcame their fear of flying as successfully as patients treated using other techniques. But the VR method offers additional benefits: It is cheaper and easier than taking the patients on real airplane flights.

Technology @ Work

VR applications can help in many fields. CAD software, for example, is used by architects and building supply stores to show customers how a kitchen might look with new cabinets.

Think About It!

Think about which professions might benefit from using virtual 3-D worlds. Which professions listed below do you think would find this technology useful?

➤ museum exhibit organizer

➤ landscape designer

➤ art teacher

➤ flower arranger

➤ construction worker

Real-World Tech

Exploring Virtual Therapy For many years, psychology resisted technology. Online therapy seemed to lack the necessary closeness between patient and therapist. At the 2002 meeting of the American Psychological Association, however, therapists saw virtual reality equipment that can help people overcome fears or generate a group of "virtual" people with whom a patient can interact.

What practical applications of virtual reality at middle schools can you think of?

Today, people can use their computers to get help for all kinds of problems, including those that are personal, psychological, financial, and medical.

Think About It!

Think about how people might sensibly and safely use their computers to seek help. Which of the strategies listed below do you think will lead to useful advice?

- searching for factual information on the Web

- joining an online support group

- e-mailing friends about the problem

- finding an online advisor

- describing the problem on a personal Web site

Saving Lives Heart surgeons often need to replace portions of a heart and its valves with artificial pieces. Designing replacement valves is very tricky, because even minor flaws can cause major problems.

Scientists at the University of Sheffield in England have developed a way to use virtual reality to test new heart valves before they are manufactured, using a computer to simulate how blood will flow through them. This software lets doctors predict whether or not the valve will work properly after it is in the body.

Virtual reality is also used to train doctors to perform surgery. Software can simulate open heart surgery, for instance, allowing doctors to practice without the risk of harming a patient. Virtual reality programs allow for doctors to control robots to perform surgery. Someday, doctors using virtual reality interfaces may be able to operate on actual patients halfway around the world!

Figure 22.3.2 Using specialized VR systems, doctors can master surgical procedures without practicing on a real patient.

Use the Vocabulary

Directions: *Match each vocabulary term in the left column with the correct definition in the right column.*

_____ **1.** information kiosk
_____ **2.** pen-based graphics tablet
_____ **3.** stream
_____ **4.** rip
_____ **5.** simulation
_____ **6.** authoring tool
_____ **7.** data glove

a. copy music from an audio CD to a computer hard drive

b. computer program that mimics a specific place, job, or function

c. transmit audio or video data across the Internet without interruption

d. equipment with sensors that measure hand movements

e. automated system used for information or training

f. equipment that lets users draw images for animation and multimedia

g. software that helps in the production of multimedia

Check Your Comprehension

Directions: *Determine the correct choice for each of the following.*

1. Which input device is usually used on an information kiosk?
   a. DVD
   b. data glove
   c. keyboard
   d. touch screen

2. Which device allows you to input your voice directly into a computer?
   a. digital camera
   b. microphone
   c. CD-ROM drive
   d. media player

3. What kind of Internet video starts playing as soon as you start to download it?
   a. graphic video
   b. virtual video
   c. streaming video
   d. ripping video

4. Which of the following is NOT accomplished using authoring tools?
   a. fading one video clip into the next
   b. setting the length of time an image will display on-screen
   c. setting the price of a multimedia program
   d. setting the volume for an audio clip

5. Which of the following CANNOT be produced using an authoring tool?
   a. Web page
   b. head-mounted display
   c. multimedia presentation
   d. CD-ROM

6. Which VR application is sometimes used in pain-control therapy?
   a. simulations
   b. X3D
   c. CAD
   d. Net video

 **Think Critically**

Directions: *Answer the following questions.*

1. What special effects might you create for a multimedia presentation if you use a stylus and a digital camera?

2. What are three ways your computer can offer you interactive multimedia experiences?

3. Why might a business want to hire someone who is skilled in using authoring tools?

4. What piece of VR equipment might be useful in training surgeons? Why?

5. How might landscapers use VR technology to plan their work and attract customers?

Extend Your Knowledge

Directions: *Choose and complete one of the following projects.*

A. Digital video cameras are popular consumer items. Also popular are easy-to-use home-movie editing programs like iMovie® for Macintosh computers. Conduct research in the library, at a store, or online to find several cameras in the same price range, and compare their features. Repeat this process with several home-video editing programs. Create a chart in which to record your findings. Then, conclude which camera and which editing program you would recommend.

B. In small groups, use basic video production equipment and video editing software to create a one minute video on a topic approved by your teacher. Use a storyboard to plan the shots. Use proper lighting. Edit the video, inserting, cutting, and erasing frames as necessary to achieve the desired message and length. Upload the completed video to a class Web site or social media page. As a class, discuss the video production process, and the qualities of effective communication in a video.

DIRECTIONS: *Working in teams or small groups, you will select the appropriate program for creating a multimedia slogan. You will then design a slogan using graphics and text objects. Finally, you will animate the slogan.*

1. Using a dictionary, look up the word *slogan*. As a class, brainstorm a list of slogans you are familiar with, such as slogans for fast food restaurants or other businesses.

2. As a class, discuss the types of programs installed on the school computers that you could use to design a multimedia slogan. For example, you might consider a presentation program, animation program, or an image editor.

3. With your team, work cooperatively to make a plan for completing this activity. Assign team roles to each team member and set a schedule so the work will be completed on time. Brainstorm ideas for an original slogan for your time and write them on a piece of paper. As a team, select the one you want to use.

4. When you are ready, start the program you selected and save a new file as **MM-1_ Slogan_xx** in the location where your teacher instructs you to store the files for this activity.

Replace the initials *xx* with your own name or initials, as instructed by your teacher.

5. Create your slogan by inserting shapes, images, and/or text objects. A sample slogan created using WordArt and a shape in Power Point is shown in Illustration A.

6. Use the program's animation tools to animate the slogan. You might choose to animate the entire slogan as a group, or animate the individual parts of the slogan. For example, you might have each word fly in separately, or have the entire slogan shrink and grow.

7. Apply color to the background or canvas.

8. Preview the multimedia slogan. Make any adjustments necessary so that all transitions and animations are smooth and effective.

9. Show your slogan to the class, and respectfully watch your classmates' slogans.

10. Close the file, saving all changes, and exit the program.

Illustration A

DIRECTIONS: *You will use the United States Department of Agriculture Web site to learn about the Choose MyPlate system of nutrition. You will then use the information to create a multimedia educational presentation explaining the importance of eating a healthy balance of foods every day.*

1. With your teacher's permission, log on to the Internet and go to the Web address www.choosemyplate.gov.

   a. Using the Navigation bar and other links on the page, navigate to and read information about the food groups, including what foods are in each group, how much you should eat, what the health benefits are, and any tips. Record the information that will be useful for your presentation on paper or in a word-processing file.

   b. Locate the list of links under Printable Materials & Ordering and click on MyPlate Images. With your teacher's permission, download the JPG version of any full-color MyPlate graphic. Save it as **MyPlate.jpg** in the location where your teacher instructs you to save files for this activity.

2. Start your presentation program. Create a new presentation. Save it as **MM-2_MyPlate_xx** in the location where your teacher instructs you to store files for this activity.

3. Apply a theme or design to your presentation.

4. Insert a footer on all slides that displays your name and today's date.

5. On the slide 1 title slide, type the title **Nutrition and You**. In the subtitle placeholder, type your full name.

6. Also on slide 1, insert or create a graphic that illustrates the theme of your presentation. Use at least two different shapes that you combine using tools such as layering and grouping. Apply formatting such as fills, borders, and effects to the shapes.

7. Develop the presentation to show how someone can use MyPlate guidelines to choose healthy, delicious foods.

   a. Insert slides with the following slide titles: **What Is ChooseMyPlate?**; **Grains**; **Vegetables**; **Fruits**; **Milk**; **Meat and Beans**; **Oils**; and **Summary**.

   b. On each slide, enter content that explains and illustrates the title. Use the information from your research.

   c. Insert the MyPlate graphic on at least three slides, and other appropriate images on at least two slides.

   d. Between the Vegetables and Fruits slides, insert a slide titled **Types of Vegetables**. On that slide, use a feature such as SmartArt to create a flowchart or other diagram to list types of vegetables and examples of each. Refer to Illustration B to see a sample slide.

   e. Insert an appropriate clip art video on the title slide, such as an animated .gif of fruit or vegetables.

   f. Insert an appropriate audio clip on the title slide. Set Playback options so it starts automatically, plays across slides, loops until stopped, and plays in the background. Hide the audio icon during the slide show.

8. When you have finished entering the slide content, proofread each slide carefully with a partner or peer editor, checking for consistency in sentence structure, spelling, and grammar, and correct any errors you find.

9. View the slide show and make any changes that you think will improve the presentation value, or make the presentation more effective. For example, split crowded slides into two slides, change the theme colors and/or fonts, or modify the slide background.

10. Add transitions and animations, and view the presentation again.

11. With your teacher's permission, print handouts with three slides per page for the class.

12. Ask your classmates to view the presentation.

13. Close the presentation, saving all changes, and exit the presentation program.

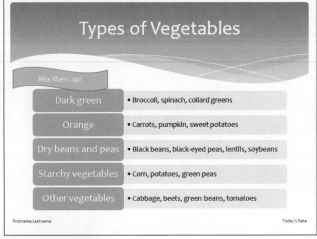

Illustration B

DIRECTIONS: *You will use text, images, audio, and video to create a multimedia slide show promoting tourism for a city or state.*

1. Open the .pdf file **MM-3_Tourism**. With your teacher's permission, print the Data Record Sheet. The sheet includes a chart to help you record information for your tourism presentation. Close the file, and exit your pdf reader program.

2. Select a city or state and have it approved by your teacher. Then, use the Internet (with your teacher's permission) to find information about your selected city or state's climate, special events, outdoor recreation, and tourist attractions.

3. To use the Internet, open a Web browser and navigate to a search engine. Search for sites by typing the keywords **[your state] tourist information**. You might also try a Boolean search such as **[your state] AND tourism**.

4. When you find a Web site with useful information, bookmark the site, or with your teacher's permission, print the pages. Check all copyright requirements to make sure you are authorized to use the information.

5. Use your Data Record Sheet to record relevant information you find.

6. If you locate any images or photographs related to tourism in your state, identify whether or not they are available for use by students free of charge. If they are, download them and save them as files so you can use them in your presentation. If possible, you might use a digital camera to take digital photographs that you can use in the presentation, as well.

7. Record your source citation information on a separate sheet of paper, including the sites from which you download images.

8. When you have finished your research, exit the Web browser.

9. Start your presentation program. Create a new presentation, and save it as **MM-3_Tourism_xx** in the location where your teacher tells you to store the files for this lesson.

10. Apply a theme or design to the presentation.

11. On the title slide, type your city or state name as the title. For the subtitle, enter a catchy slogan. Insert a footer on this slide only that reads: **Prepared by [your name]**, along with today's date.

12. Add a slide using a layout with placeholders for a title, bulleted list, and graphics.

13. Type **Climate** as the title of the slide.

14. In the bulleted list, type information about the climate of your selected city or state.

15. Insert a related photograph you downloaded from the Internet or took with a digital camera. Check the image in a photo editing program first and make any necessary adjustments or improvements. For example, you might crop or rotate the image, or adjust the brightness or contrast. If you do not have a photograph, use an appropriate clip art image. Position and size the image to enhance the slide.

16. At the bottom of the slide, insert a text box where you credit the source of the image, if necessary. Be sure to include the name of the site, its URL, and the date you visited the site. A sample slide is shown in Illustration C on the next page.

17. Repeat this process to create a slide for Special Events, Outdoor Recreation, and Tourist Attractions. Use information from your Data Record Sheet, and insert pictures and other images to illustrate the slides.

18. Insert a new slide 2 that has the title **Contents** and a bulleted list of all the slide titles in order. Insert hyperlinks from each bullet to the corresponding slide.

19. At the end of the presentation, add a slide that identifies the ideal times of year to visit your state. Enter the slogan you used on the opening slide as the slide title.

20. Insert a video clip on the last slide that illustrates tourism in your state. You may use a video from clip art, or a free Internet clip that you download or link to. Or, with your teacher's permission, you may use digital video equipment , such as a camcorder or smart phone, and video-editing software to create your own video to insert.

21. Insert an audio clip in the presentation. You may insert music that plays during the entire presentation, or an audio clip that plays when a certain slide is displayed. (Be sure you are authorized to use the clip.) Or, with your teacher's permission, you may use digital recording equipment and an audio-editing program such as Audacity to record and edit an appropriate audio clip to insert.

22. In the lower-right corner of all but the title slide, insert an icon or image of a house, or a text box, in which you type **Home**. Format it with a hyperlink to display the title slide.

23. When you have finished entering the slide content, proofread each slide carefully with a partner or peer editor. Check the spelling and grammar in the presentation. Revise and edit your work as necessary.

24. Add transitions and animations to the presentation.

25. Preview the presentation, checking to be sure the slides adhere to good design principles and that they effectively convey your message. Make any final modifications.

26. Rehearse the presentation and then show it to the class. Be sure to demonstrate the hyperlinks. Alternatively, record narration and set the show to be browsed by an individual or at a kiosk.

27. Close the presentation, saving all changes, and exit your presentation program.

Illustration C

Climate

- Four seasons
- Cold winters
- Moderately warm summers
- Average annual precipitation ranges from 39 to 46 inches

Home

Image courtesy of elen_studio/shutterstock

DIRECTIONS: *You will create a multimedia presentation on an environmental problem. You will conduct research to identify specific actions that affect the environment in both positive and negative ways. You will present your findings in a presentation enhanced with audio and animation effects.*

1. Open the .pdf file **MM-4_Effects**. With your teacher's permission, print the Data Record Sheet. The sheet includes diagrams to help you identify cause and effect. Close the file, and exit your pdf reader program.
2. Use the Internet (with your teacher's permission), library resources, or a textbook to search for information on an environmental problem, such as water pollution, drought, or ozone depletion.
3. To use the Internet, open a Web browser and navigate to a search engine. For the search, type the environmental problem plus the word **causes** as the keywords. For example, you might type **water pollution causes** as your keywords. Or, use Boolean search strategies. For example, you might search for **"water pollution" AND causes**.
4. When you find a Web site with relevant information, bookmark the site, or with your teacher's permission, print the pages. Check the copyright laws to make sure you have permission to use the content.
5. In the Causes list in the first diagram on the Data Record Sheet, record three causes of the environmental problem you selected. Record the effect(s) the causes have in the Effect(s) circle.
6. Then, conduct research to identify three things that people can do to reduce the environmental problem you selected. Type **"ways to protect the environment"** as your keywords, making sure that you include the quotation marks. Look for sites that list specific actions people can take to reduce the problem.
7. In the Causes list in the second diagram on the Data Record Sheet, record three things people can do to reduce the environmental problem, and the effect(s) of the action in the Effect(s) circle.
8. Record your source citation information on a separate sheet of paper.
9. When you have finished your research, exit the Web browser.
10. Start your presentation program. Create a new presentation, and save it as **MM-4_Environment_xx** in the location where your teacher instructs you to store the files for this activity.
11. Apply a theme or design to the presentation.
12. On the title slide, type **People and the Environment** as the title, and then type **By** followed by your own name as the subtitle. Insert a footer with today's date and your name on all slides.
13. Insert a slide using a title only slide layout.
14. Type the title **Main Idea**.
15. Draw a text box in the space below the title, and type a sentence that states the main idea of your presentation.
16. Insert a video clip on the slide that illustrates the main idea. You may use a video from clip art, or a free clip downloaded from the Internet. Or, with your teacher's permission, use digital video recording equipment and video-editing software to create your own video to insert.
17. Insert another slide using a title only slide layout, and type the environmental problem you researched as the title.
18. In the space below the title, use the program's pre-drawn diagrams or its drawing tools to create a cause-and-effect diagram like the one on your Data Record Sheet.
19. Type the causes and the effect(s) in your diagram.
20. Duplicate this slide and edit the text to match the causes and effect(s) you listed in the second diagram on your Data Record Sheet.
21. When you have finished entering the slide content, proofread each slide carefully with a partner or peer editor. Check the spelling and grammar in the presentation. Revise and edit your work as necessary.
22. Insert an audio clip in the presentation. You may insert music that plays during the entire presentation, or an audio clip that plays when a certain slide is displayed. Or, with your teacher's permission, use digital audio recording equipment and sound-editing software such as Audacity to record an appropriate audio clip to insert.
23. Add transitions and animations to the presentation. For example, animate the cause-and-effect diagrams.
24. Preview the presentation and make any final modifications.
25. Rehearse the presentation, and then deliver it to your class.
26. Close the presentation, saving all changes, and exit your presentation program.
27. As a class, discuss ways people can work to protect the environment.

Multimedia Activities

DIRECTIONS: *You will write an article on how to use technology to better prepare for college and career pursuits, develop new skills, and stay informed about the changing world around you. You will publish the article in html format and then enhance it with a graphic, a video, and an audio clip.*

1. Open the .pdf file **MM-5_TechOutline**. With your teacher's permission, print the Data Record Sheet. The sheet includes an outline to help you prepare your article. Close the file, and exit your pdf reader program.

2. Use the Internet (with your teacher's permission), library resources, or information from your school's guidance counselor or career center to research the importance of technology to college and career readiness, lifelong learning, and daily living.

3. To use the Internet, open a Web browser and navigate to a search engine. Search for sites by typing keywords or phrases such as **using technology to prepare for college**. You might also try a Boolean search such as **technology AND "lifelong learning"**.

4. When you find a Web site with relevant information, bookmark it, or with your teacher's permission, print the desired pages. Make sure you can legally use the information.

5. Use your Data Record Sheet to record relevant information you find. Support each point in the outline with facts and details.

6. If you locate any images or photographs related to your research, ask your teacher for permission to download them and save them for use in your report. Select a file format optimized for quality and size for online use. Again, check copyright or fair use guidelines to make sure you can legally use them.

7. Record your source citation information on a separate sheet of paper, including the sites from which you download images.

8. When you have finished your research, exit the Web browser.

9. Start your word-processing program. Create a new document, and save it as **MM-5_Technology_xx** in the location where your teacher instructs you to store the files for this activity.

10. Insert the title of the article, along with your name and today's date. Using the outline on your Data Record Sheet, write your article.

11. When finished, check the spelling and grammar and proofread it carefully with a partner or peer editor.

12. With your teacher's permission, print the document.

13. When you have finalized the document, save it in html format. Name the file **MM-5_Technology_Web_xx**. Assign an appropriate page title.

14. Close the file, and then open it in your html or WYSIWYG editor. (Refer to Chapters 29 and 30 for more information.)

15. Keeping the principles of design in mind, change the color of the title using a hexadecimal value, and adjust the font and font size so the title will look good when opened in a Web browser. Insert and format subheadings, too.

16. Insert at least one image file or photograph on the page. Use the principles of design to make sure it is in the best size and position to improve the appearance of the page.

17. If your editor supports video, insert a video file related to the article. Or, insert an animated .gif that illustrates the article's topic.

18. Insert an audio file that reflects the tone and mood of your article.

19. For both the audio and video, set properties so viewers can turn them off if they choose.

20. Preview the page in your Web browser, and then close it and exit your Web browser. If necessary, go back and make changes and adjustments to optimize, correct, or improve the Web page.

21. Close your html file, saving all changes.

22. With your teacher's permission, publish the document to the class Web site. Create a table of contents page with hyperlinks that viewers can use to navigate to and from the class pages.

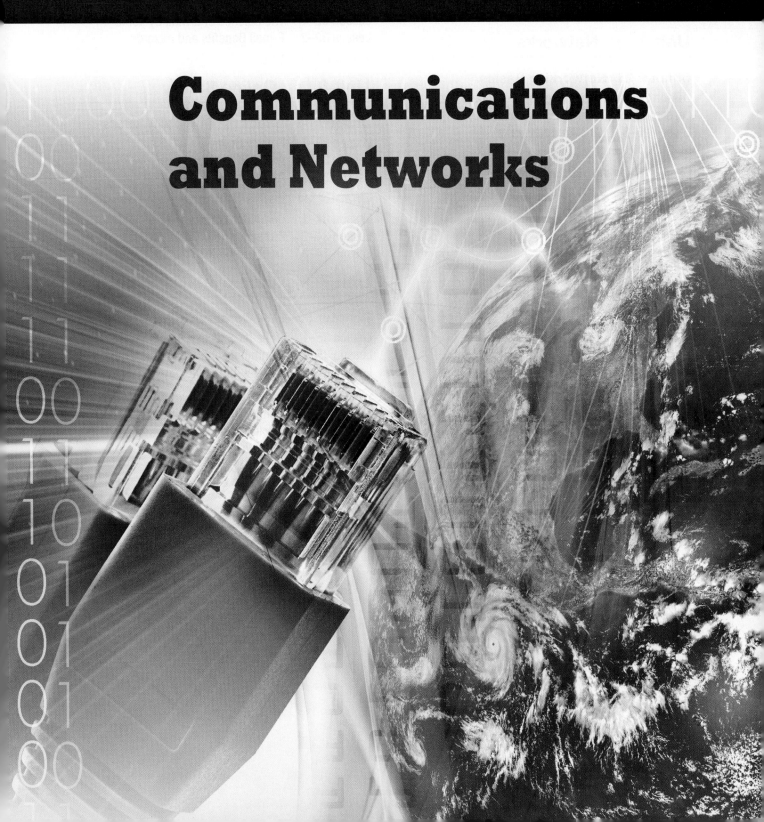

part **3**

Communications and Networks

Communications Basics

chapter 23

Why Are Telcommunications Valuable?

Telecommunications is a word that means "messages exchanged over distances." The most common telecommunications device is the telephone. Think of how important the telephone is to you. Wired and wireless technology makes it possible to have conversations, send text messages, pictures, and even video.

Another important telecommunications device is your computer. You connect to the Internet through a phone or cable line, and you send and receive e-mail messages, use instant messaging, surf the Web, and even talk face-to-face.

These ways of sending and receiving messages and information are valuable to individuals, businesses, communities, and schools. All these forms of communication rely on networks.

Chapter Outline

 Lesson 23–1

The Telephone System

 Lesson 23–2

Using Telephone Communications

 Lesson 23–3

Exploring High-Speed Telecommunications

Communications Basics • 329

The Telephone System

Objectives

- Explain how local and long-distance telephone calls are made.
- Compare and contrast analog and digital connections.
- Identify the technologies that handle telephone calls.

🔑 Key Terms

- analog
- Bluetooth
- circuit
- digital
- duplex
- fiber-optic cable
- half-duplex
- infrared
- local loop
- microwave
- telecommunications
- twisted pair
- Wi-Fi

Figure 23.1.1 Today, telephones are so common and easy to use that we take them for granted.

As You Read

Organize Information Use a spider map to help you organize ways in which the telephone system operates as you read.

Communicating by Telephone

The first telephone message was sent in 1876 over a line connecting two rooms. Eventually telephone cables were connected to a central office. Operators in the office could connect calls to anyone on the network. Today's equipment can connect telephones anywhere in the world.

Telecommunications Formats Sending information over a telephone network is called **telecommunications**. Telecommunications has grown due to the demand for instant communication. Telecommunications can be **duplex** or **half-duplex**. With duplex communications the people on both sides can communicate at same time, like on a phone call. In half-duplex communication only one side can communicate at a time, like through walkie-talkies. Today, people use many forms of telecommunications to rapidly relay information:

- telephones
- cell phones
- pagers
- e-mail
- Internet
- fax machines

Making Telephone Calls

In the past, only a few companies provided telephone services in the United States. Today, people can choose from among many phone companies that offer both local and long distance service.

Public Switched Telephone Network Many phone calls are made through the Public Switched Telephone Network (PSTN). This network is built from copper wires and other cables and forms a **circuit** between the caller's telephone and another telephone.

Local Calls   For local calls, your phone company provides directly wired services between the homes and businesses that belong to the local network. Within your neighborhood, telephones connect to a common network for telephone service. This common network, called the **local loop**, connects to the phone company's central office. Much of the local loop is an **analog** system. An analog system sends electrical signals that carry voice and other sounds.

Long-Distance Calls   Outside the local loop, the long-distance telephone system today is mostly digital. **Digital** connections use computer code and can carry voice, data, and video on a single line. When you dial a long-distance number, computers figure out how to complete your call. To connect analog and digital networks, special equipment changes analog signals into digital signals.

Contrasting Analog and Digital Communications   People often confuse the terms "analog" and "digital" when they are talking about communications or computers. The difference is important but easy to understand. In analog communications, sounds (such as a person's voice or music) start as waves or vibrations in the air. The vibrating air varies in frequency or pitch (how high or deep the sound is) and strength or loudness. A small microphone in the telephone converts the sound waves into varying patterns of electrical signals or radio waves. The pattern of electrical signals or radio waves is similar to the pattern of the sound waves. These signals are converted back into sound waves by a small loudspeaker in the receiver. In digital communications, sounds are converted into binary data (a series of 1s and 0s) at the caller's end. The stream of 1s and 0s is transmitted without any variation in the pattern of electrical or radio waves. The receiver converts the binary data back into sound waves.

The Wired—and the Wireless—World

Wires connect the phone jack in your wall to an interface box outside. Outside wires may be above or below ground. Wires also connect your local loop with distant places.

Parts of a Telephone Number

1	214	555	7804
Long Distance	**Area Code**	**Prefix**	**Line Number**
Finds the country code (1 is the code for the United States.)	Finds a geographic area (214 is the code for Dallas, Texas.)	Finds a local-rate area	Finds a specific phone line

Home appliances are among the upcoming targets of wireless communication. Appliances with *picoradios*—very small, very low-power radios built into the appliance—can communicate with one another.

Think About It!

If customers are going to be interested in them, picoradios must be useful. Which item(s) listed below would be *unlikely* to be useful?

▷ a bedroom clock that can start a coffeemaker

▷ a sensor that can close a refrigerator door

▷ a faucet that can turn on a light

Twisted Pair At first, the entire telephone system depended on twisted pair technology. **Twisted pair** refers to a pair of copper wires that are twisted together to reduce interference, or outside noise. In the United States today, most homes and business buildings still have twisted pair wiring. Twisted pair wiring can be either shielded (STP) or unshielded (UTP). Twisted pairs may be shielded to prevent electric interference from other sources.

Fiber-Optic Cables **Fiber-optic cables** are strands of fiberglass that transmit digital data by pulses of light. These cables can carry large quantities of information. They work faster and more efficiently than copper wires. As they get lower in price, fiber optic cables will eventually replace copper.

Wireless Wireless communication frees users from traditional telephone lines. Messages are sent on radio or infrared signals. Cell phones use radio signals. Wireless networks, or **Wi-Fi**, use radio signals to connect computers. **Bluetooth** technology is a wireless technology that works over short distances. It uses radio signals to allow communication between devices. Bluetooth allows cellular telephones to work through wireless earpieces and car radios. **Infrared** signals are light waves that cannot be seen by the human eye. Remote control devices for TVs, VCRs, and DVD players use infrared signals.

Before fiber-optic cables, high-frequency radio waves called **microwave** signals were used to relay long-distance telecommunications. Microwaves are broadcast from repeater tower to repeater tower in a straight line.

Satellites orbiting Earth also transfer voice and data. Satellites provide an efficient means to handle large amounts of phone calls and data.

Spotlight on...

CORNING, INC.

A 161-year-old company that made its name making glass casserole dishes is at the forefront of telecommunications technology. In 1970, a team of Corning scientists developed a technology that would revolutionize telecommunications—though its impact wouldn't be felt until three decades later. Scientists Peter Schultz, Donald Keck, and Robert Maurer spun optical glass into thin strands that could transmit electrical impulses and light. The Corning Glass researchers are credited with making optical fi-

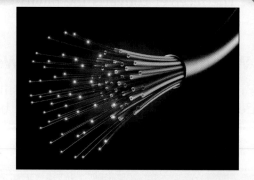

ber—capable of carrying 65,000 times more information than traditional copper wire—a practical reality. Now more than 90% of the U.S. long distance traffic is carried by optical fiber, almost all of it using the design of Schultz, Keck, and Maurer.

Using Telephone Communications

Objectives

- Sequence the steps in a modem transmission.
- Explain how fax machines operate.
- Summarize how modems and fax machines have affected the ways people communicate.

As You Read

Compare and Contrast Use a Venn diagram to help you compare and contrast modems and fax machines as you read.

Using Modems

Back in the early 1990s, when the Internet was still "new," most people used phone lines to connect to it. Your computer is a digital device. The local loop that connects you to the telephone system, however, is analog. A device called a **modem** makes it possible for your computer and telephone lines to communicate, and for your computer and TV cables to communicate.

The word *modem* actually names the work the device does: ***mod**ulation* and ***dem**odulation*. Through modulation, the modem changes the digital signal of the computer to the analog sounds used by telephones. Then, the data—in the form of pictures, audio, or video—can travel over the telephone wires. When the data gets to its destination, the receiving modem changes the analog signals back to digital. This process is called demodulation. The early dial-up modems were usually internal, housed inside the computer. Today's modems for use with DSL and cable (discussed later) are usually external.

Key Terms

- bits per second (bps)
- demodulation
- fax machine
- modem
- modulation

Figure 23.2.1 A 56K modem, like the one show here, is a hardware device that enables a PC to send and receive data through a standard telephone line.

The Arts Can a fax machine create art? Artist and lecturer Margaret Turner of Australia thinks so.

To demonstrate a connection between human emotions and computers, Margaret borrowed handkerchiefs—plain and fancy, white and patterned. The handkerchief represented a human element becoming art through an electronic medium.

She scanned the handkerchiefs into a computer and manipulated the images. Then, she faxed the resulting images to a gallery for a special exhibit called "Electric Hankie."

Drawbacks of Dial-Up Today only 10% of U.S. households connect to the computer using the local phone line loop, but dial-up service is still a worthwhile backup. One problem with using dial-up was that you could not be on your computer and use your telephone simultaneously, so the computer modem required a dedicated phone line. Another larger drawback was slow speed.

Modem speed is measured in **bits per second**, or **bps**, which is the amount of data that can be sent in one second. Dial-up modems can only transmit 56,600 bps, which has been surpassed by newer, speedier technologies.

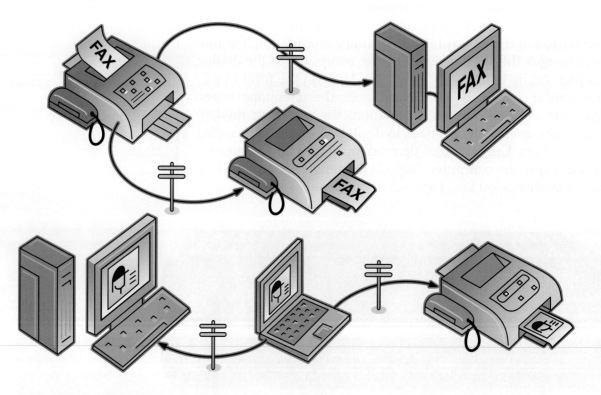

Figure 23.2.2 Fax machines can send and receive documents using standard telephone lines.

Sending Faxes

While dial-up is usually a thing of the past, there is one machine that still uses telephone lines to send printed messages or visual images. A facsimile machine, or **fax machine**, is a device that allows you to send pages of information to a fax machine anywhere in the world. Fax machines can send hand-written documents, printed text, pictures, blueprints, or anything else on a page. Yet, even these machines are largely being replaced by e-mail, by which you can send documents and scanned pages over the Internet as attachments.

How Fax Machines Work As a document enters a fax machine, a sensor scans it. The data becomes a digital signal. An internal modem in the fax machine (or in an All-in-One printer with fax capability) changes the digital signal to an analog signal. The receiving fax machine accepts the analog signal, changes it back to digital, and prints a copy of the original document.

Many stores now use special scanners at the checkout counters. These scanners read the Universal Product Code on a package and record the product and price on the sales receipt.

Think About It!

Think about the advantages store scanners offer. Which item(s) listed below would be an advantage, and which would not?

▷ Price changes can be entered in a central computer rather than stickered on a package.

▷ The computer prevents clerks from entering mistakes.

▷ The computer tracks the number of products sold.

▷ The computer cuts down on the need for employees.

Figure 23.2.3 In businesses, fax machines are still important for transmitting important documents, particularly those that have or require personal signatures.

Exploring High-Speed Telecommunications

Objectives

- Explain the importance of bandwidth.
- Identify alternatives to analog systems.
- Predict advances in telecommunications.

As You Read

Organize Information Use a chart to help you identify various new technologies as you read.

🔑 **Key Terms**

- bandwidth
- broadband
- Voice over Internet Protocol (VoIP)

Introducing Bandwidth

People always want faster, better, and less expensive telecommunications choices. Twisted pair copper wiring in many homes and businesses in the United States at first made it hard to increase bandwidth. Then telephone, cable, and satellite television companies began to compete in offering higher speed communications. Now, more than eight out of ten homes and businesses are using high-speed connections for Internet access.

Understanding Bandwidth Bandwidth is the amount of data that can be sent through a modem or network connection. The more bandwidth, the faster the connection. It is usually measured in bits per second (bps) or in Megabits per second (Mbps). The more bandwidth, the more information can be transferred in a given amount of time.

Imagine several people on different computers connecting to the Internet to visit Web pages, participate in video chats, or send e-mail. These users need a lot of bandwidth. That's why there is always a race to find a technology that offers services that transmit data faster. Currently the fastest technology is broadband transmission.

Working with Broadband Transmission

Broadband is the general term for all high-speed digital connections that transmit at least 1.5 megabits per second (Mbps), though current broadband services transmit between 10 and 30 Mbps. Mobile phones use mobile broadband which transmits around 10 Mbps. Current phones use the fourth generation of technology, or 4G. Broadband technology is able to send multiple signals at the same time through the medium. Unlike broadband, baseband technology uses the entire bandwidth to send one signal. Several broadband technologies are available, and more are always on the drawing board. This high transmission speed is required for videoconferencing, video-on-demand, digital television services, and high-speed Internet connectivity in general.

When broadband uses twisted pairs, the twisted pairs are categorized by the amount of data the wires can carry. Category 3 wires (Cat 3) are used in Ethernet at about 10 Mbps. Cat 5e wires can support 1 Gigabit Ethernet.

DSL Digital Subscriber Line, or DSL, uses the same copper wires telephones use, but it transmits data in digital form rather than analog. Voice calls and DSL can exist simultaneously on copper lines, because each service has its own frequency band. Unlike the old dial-up, DSL allows for very fast connections to the Internet and features an "always-on" connection. DSL service also requires a modem, which translates the computer's digital signals into voltage sent across phone lines to a central hub. There is one drawback to DSL: A user must be within a few miles of a local telephone switching station for a connection to be made.

Different companies offer DSL at different levels of service and price. For instance, asymmetric DSL (ADSL) allows download speeds of up to 1.5 Mbps and upload speeds of 128 kilobits per second (Kbps). This means you can receive data (download) faster than you can send it (upload) with ADSL. Subscribers to a Symmetric Digital Subscriber Line (SDSL) can send data at the same speed at which they receive it. These are used usually by businesses that need to send large files, data, and programs.

SONET Telephone companies that offer DSL and other Internet connection methods rely on a digital network called SONET. SONET stands for *Synchronous Optical Network*. It uses fiber optics to provide faster connections and greater bandwidth—from 52 Mbps to up to a whopping 40 gigabits per second (Gbps).

Technology @ School

With all the ways that schools use technology these days, they need a lot of bandwidth to send and receive information electronically.

Think About It!

Think about who in your school might benefit from increased bandwidth. Which tasks listed below could use bandwidth?

➢ students participating in a class teleconference

➢ a teacher researching Mars

➢ a librarian helping a student find a book

➢ a counselor checking student records

➢ a principal answering e-mail

Figure 23.3.1 In a video-conference, users in different locations transmit and receive audio, video, and computer data in real time. This kind of activity requires a great deal of bandwidth.

Sales and Service Technician

Cable and satellite companies hire many sales and service technicians. These employees sell broadband services to customers and try to get current customers to upgrade their existing service. They also install and test the equipment.

Experience with technology is desirable, as is hands-on training specific to this industry. As more homes accept cable and satellite offerings, the need for sales and service technicians will grow to meet the demand.

Cable and Satellite TV Connections   Most cable and digital television companies offer high-speed Internet connection through a cable modem. Satellite television companies also offer a similar service with signals sent through the customer's satellite dish. A cable modem connects your computer to the local cable TV line and supports data transfer rates of up to 30 Mbps—over 500 times faster than the old dial-up modem. However, this number can be misleading, because most Internet Service Providers (ISPs) cap subscribers' transfer rates to less than 6 Mbps to conserve bandwidth. However, this is more than enough for the average home computer user.

Voice over Internet Protocol   Just as you can use your telephone to send and receive messages over the Internet, you can use the Internet to send and receive messages over the telephone. **Voice over Internet Protocol (VoIP)** technology allows you to have a telephone connection over the Internet. VoIP uses data sent digitally, with the Internet Protocol (IP), instead of analog telephone lines. People use VoIP to talk to each other from across the globe, sometimes without having to pay a cent. With Webcams callers can also see each other during their calls.

The Future of Bandwidth

The demand for bandwidth is growing. People want increased bandwidth for video-on-demand, meetings via the Internet, and Web-based learning. Thus, telephone and other high-tech companies continue to look for new ways to improve telecommunications services and data transmission.

Real-World Tech

Making Communication Possible   It's not just governments and huge companies that put communications satellites into orbit. Students are doing it, too.

In 2001, for example, six students at the U.S. Naval Academy built a satellite with equipment anybody could buy: A tape measure was used as the antenna, and 24 AA batteries provided the power. Both a sailor in the Atlantic Ocean and some hikers in New Zealand used signals from the students' satellite to contact family at home.

How might students fund the cost of their experiments?

Use the Vocabulary

Directions: *Match each vocabulary term in the left column with the correct definition in the right column.*

_____ **1.** telecommunications
_____ **2.** analog
_____ **3.** digital
_____ **4.** fiber-optic cable
_____ **5.** microwave
_____ **6.** modulation
_____ **7.** demodulation
_____ **8.** bits per second
_____ **9.** bandwidth
_____ **10.** broadband

a. the measure of how much data can be sent through a network connection

b. system using computer code to carry different kinds of data

c. changing digital signals to analog

d. system using electrical signals that match the human voice and other sounds

e. high-frequency radio waves that carry data

f. strand of fiberglass that transmits data by pulses of light

g. using a telephone network to send information

h. high-speed digital connection of at least 1.5 Mbps

i. measurement of the speed at which data can be sent in one second

j. changing analog signals to digital

Check Your Comprehension

Directions: *Complete each sentence with information from the chapter.*

1. The _____ consists of the local loop and long-distance lines that handle data and voice communications.

2. The _____ part of your telephone number identifies the area of the country you live in.

3. In the long-distance telephone system, _____ largely have replaced twisted pair copper wire.

4. Radio and infrared signals make _____ communication possible.

5. Within a neighborhood, telephones connect to a common network called the _____.

6. One issue DSL users face is that it is _____ to send information than to receive it.

7. A fax machine sending a document transmits data into a(n) _____ signal and changes it into a(n) _____ signal.

8. _____ offers a way for people across the globe to call each other over the Internet free of charge.

9. *DSL* stands for _____.

10. The demand for _____ will continue to grow.

Think Critically

Directions: *Answer the following questions.*

1. Why is a modem needed to access the Internet?

2. Why is faxing an order to a company an example of telecommunications in action?

3. For what types of documents might a fax machine be a better method of transmission than e-mail?

4. What challenges do you think telecommunications companies face in the near future?

5. Why might it be important for a home-office computer to have Internet service that offers a lot of bandwidth?

Extend Your Knowledge

Directions: *Choose and complete one of the following projects.*

A. With your teacher's permission, research, compare, and contrast full-duplex and half-duplex communications. Take notes and keep track of your sources. Only use information from reliable and accurate sources. Present your findings to a partner or to the class.

B. Divide into two groups and have one group research VoIP service packages offered by Vonage and the other research the same service offered by Skype. Write up your findings and discuss the differences.

C. With your teacher's permission, research, compare, and contrast different methods for network connectivity such as broadband, wireless, Bluetooth, and cellular. Take notes and keep track of your sources. Only use information from reliable, and accurate sources. Make a table showing your findings and present it to a partner or to the class.

Understanding Communications

How Do You Use Cell Phones? People all over the world rely on cellular, or cell, phones to communicate. Cell phones allow for instant access to families, friends, and—on a smart phone—the Internet. They're great for emergencies, sending messages, chatting on the go, and, for many people, they have replaced traditional landline phones.

When you're home you may call someone with your analog telephone system, your cell phone, or even your computer. Many businesses you call—or who call you—use telephones and computers together.

Cell phones and computer technology promise great things for the future. You can expect even faster access to information, better communications, and more choices of ways to stay in touch with family and friends.

Chapter Outline

 Lesson 24–1

Using Cell Phone Technology

 Lesson 24–2

Choosing Digital Options

Using Cell Phone Technology

Objectives

- Explain how cellular telephones make and receive calls.
- Identify advantages of cell phones to subscribers.
- Compare and contrast local and long-distance cell phone calls.

As You Read

Organize Information   Use an outline to help you organize the information in the lesson as you read.

 Key Terms

- cell
- cellular phone
- cell site
- leased line
- personal digital assistant (PDA)

Figure 24.1.1 Primarily due to their flexibility and ease of use, cell phones are replacing wired telephones as the communication system of choice.

What Are Cell Phones?

A cell phone actually is a type of radio. In fact, that's the definition: **cellular phones** are mobile phones that use radio waves to communicate. Early cellular phones were called radiotelephones and were used in ships at sea and in police cars. Radiotelephones were very useful during World War II, when they were used to send military information.

For a while after that war, only a few people in a city could use radiotelephones at one time. New technology, however, soon increased the number of possible callers by adding more radio frequencies within each city.

What Does "Cellular" Mean?

When you use a traditional landline phone, the call is connected through a wire. The wire from your house is connected to a telephone pole or buried cable in the local loop and from a local office to long-distance wires. Cell phones bypass part of the wired system, using a cellular system instead.

Locating Cells   Cell phone systems are divided into **cells**, or geographic areas to which a signal can be transmitted. Each cell has a **cell site**, also called a base station, for all the cellular phones in that area. Each cell site has a radio tower that receives radio signals from other towers and sends them on to still other towers. As a caller moves from one area to another, a new cell site automatically picks up the call to keep the signal strong and clear. Ultimately, the signal gets to individual cell phones.

Managing Locations   Each geographic area is assigned to a central base station, or Mobile Telephone Switching Office (MTSO). It, in turn, is connected to the standard Public Switched Telephone Network

(PSTN) telephone system. The MTSO has several responsibilities:

- directs cellular activities at base stations
- locates cellular users in the area
- tracks users as they roam, or move, from cell to cell
- connects cellular phones to land-based phones

Providing Services Of course cell phones provide many services in addition to completing phone calls—most for an additional service fee. You can pay for sending and receiving text messages and for data service. With data service, you can access the Internet, send and receive e-mail, and stream audio and video. Most cell phones and other mobile devices can be set to automatically sync with cloud-based services so that your data and apps are always up-to-date.

Cell phones, and most landline services, include voice mail which allows callers to leave a spoken message if you do not answer after a set number of rings. You can record an outgoing voice mail message instructing the caller that you are not available. The caller's message is recorded and stored until you delete it. You can then listen to the message by accessing the voice mailbox.

Most cell phones and other devices display notifications when an event occurs. You can configure the settings on the device regarding when, where, and how to display notifications. For example, you might want to have a sound play when you receive a text, or you might want the device to vibrate.

Technology @ Work

Communicating with cell phones can pose a major security risk. Wireless communication can be monitored by outsiders, who can intercept and overhear what is being said. Some employers, including the U.S. Department of Defense, prohibit the use of most wireless devices for company communication.

Think About It!

How might eavesdroppers use information collected from wireless communications to harm a company? Can you think of other risks posed by using cell phones?

Spotlight on...

RICHARD FRENKIEL AND JOEL ENGEL

Two of the reasons people today have cell phones are Richard Frenkiel and Joel Engel. They worked on a team of more than 200 engineers at AT&T's Bell Labs in the 1960s and 1970s. As part of this team, they helped to increase the number of mobile phones that could operate at once in a city. This was accomplished by dividing a city into small "cells" that could reuse radio channels many times and by creating the technology to "handoff" calls from cell to cell without losing the signal.

In 1987, Frenkiel and Engel were awarded the Alexander Graham Bell Medal for their contributions to the advancement of telecommunications. In 1994, President Bill Clinton awarded the partners National Medals of Technology.

Retired from Bell Labs, Frenkiel and Engel now consult for the telecommunications industry.

How Cell Phones Work

When you turn on a cellular phone, it searches for a signal from the service provider's base station in the local area. When you place a call, the MTSO selects a frequency for your phone and a tower for you to use and identifies the tower you are using. Each tower sends and receives signals to and from the individual cell phones within its cell. The MTSO is connected to the local telephone network, usually by telephone cable. Cell phones are connected to the telephone network through the cell site.

Receiving a Phone Call When someone calls your cell phone, the cellular service provider locates the phone by cell. Moving from one cell into another, the phone transmits this information to the service provider's base station. The base station reports this information to the MTSO so it knows where to find you.

Placing Long-Distance Calls If you dial a long-distance number from your cell phone, the MTSO connects the call through a **leased line**. A digital leased line is a permanent connection allowing the MTSO to interact with long-distance providers.

Using Wireless Networks

Many cellular telephone companies now use Wi-Fi to transmit calls through the Internet. By using Wi-Fi, cellular calls can be made in areas with Internet access but without cell towers. Access to the Internet though wireless networks allows phones to run online apps, as well.

What Else Does Cellular Technology Offer?

A **personal digital assistant**, or **PDA**, such as the Palm Tungsten E2, is a small, highly portable handheld computer. Smart phones are cell phones offering advanced capabilities that are able to function as both personal computers and cell phones. The main difference between the two is that smart phones are oriented more to mobile phone features while PDAs are heavy on the business/organizational features and do not necessarily include phone/fax service.

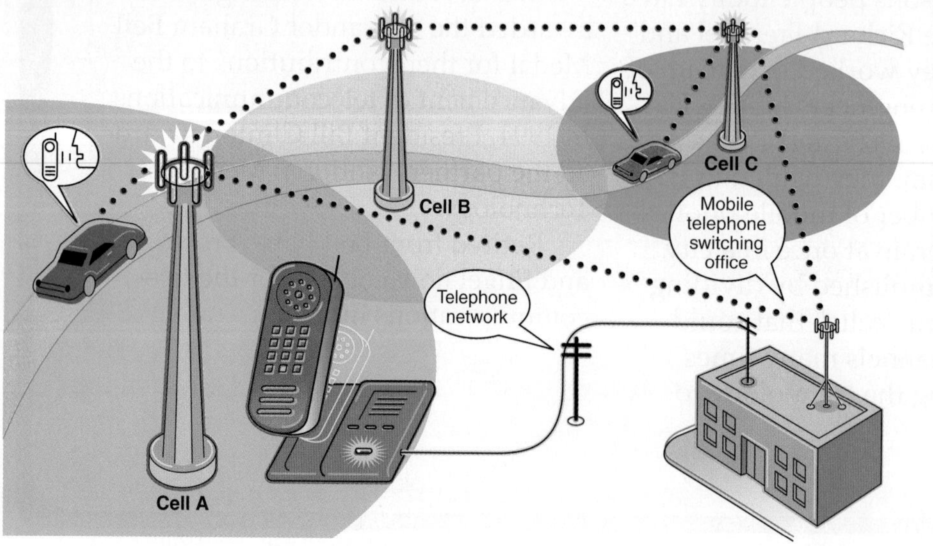

Figure 24.1.2 Because the cellular system stores information about your phone, it can track your location as you move. Cells often overlap, so users do not lose service if they move from one cell to another.

Cell B

Cell C

Mobile telephone switching office

Telephone network

Cell A

Choosing Digital Options

Objectives

- Identify advantages of computer telephony integration.
- Identify competitors for business in the telecommunications market.

As You Read

Draw Conclusions   Use a chart to help you draw conclusions about the information in this lesson as you read.

Using Computer Telephony Integration

By working together, computers and telephones can increase the power of communications. Linking computers to telephone systems is called computer telephony integration (CTI). While uses of CTI have expanded in recent years, one of the most traditional uses is when the computer takes the place of a human and acts as a **call center**, a central place where an organization's inbound and outbound calls are received and made. A call center CTI helps businesses and other organizations become more efficient. Suppose you call your favorite pizza restaurant for a delivery order. If this restaurant uses CTI, the modem and computer software work together to identify your name and your last delivery order. It will locate your house on an area map. Many organizations use CTI including the following:

- emergency response centers in police and fire stations
- hospitals
- telemarketers (who conduct surveys or sell products or services by telephone)
- voicemail services
- banks, manufacturers, and small businesses

 Key Terms

- cable modem
- call center
- download
- upload

Figure 24.2.1 The 911 emergency telephone system is a great example of how computers and telephone systems can be integrated.

Technology @ Home

Many of us use a combination of technologies to communicate at home. We use phones, computers, and televisions to send and receive messages.

Think About It!

Conduct a class survey to identify how many of each tool below your class uses at home. Write your own answers and then compare your responses with those of your classmates. What conclusions can you draw?

➤ analog telephones

➤ cell phones

➤ ISDN or DSL connections

➤ digital satellite systems

➤ cable systems

➤ wireless networks

➤ other

Competition Brings Choices

Most landline telephones are analog-based and rely on twisted pair technology. For more than 100 years, telephone service was provided only by telephone companies. The Telecommunications Act of 1996, however, introduced competition into the telecommunications market. Now, satellite companies, cable television companies, and businesses offering wireless services compete with telephone companies to provide high-bandwidth digital telecommunications. This competition has created new, affordable methods for transferring voice, video, and data.

People are no longer bound to a single choice for their telecommunications needs. Think of the different choices available to consumers at home and at work for sending and receiving voice, text, and images quickly and reliably. In addition to analog phones and DSL services, choices include:

- digital satellite systems
- cable systems
- wireless networks

Communicating Without Analog

Some people use the Internet to bypass some or all analog phone wires. Some communicate through a purely digital network that links one computer to another. Others connect a computer to a telephone or a telephone to a computer.

Many people today talk with others without using a telephone. A computer with a sound card, a microphone, speakers, and the right software allows this type of communication to take place with ease.

Direct Broadcast Satellites   If you have satellite television, your family subscribes to a digital satellite system, called a Direct Broadcast Satellite (DBS) service. Satellites receive signals from a central broadcast center here on Earth and then rebroadcast them around the globe. In many areas of the country, DBS systems are now offering Internet access and data transfer services. Because satellites can only transmit data to a subscriber, a modem and telephone line are needed to send data, such as a pay-per-movie request, to the provider.

Cable Connections   If your family has cable television, the cable that brings in your favorite television shows may also let you access your favorite Web site. There's plenty of bandwidth on the cable for both television programs and data. Connections usually are fast and reliable—unless too many subscribers share bandwidth in a specific area.

To connect your computer to a cable service, you need a **cable modem**. Like analog modems, cable modems can be internal or external. Cable modems catch the downstream signal from the Internet, called **downloading**, and pass it on to your computer. Some cable modems can also send information upstream, or **upload**, data from your computer back to the Internet. Not all cable modems allow two-way communication. Some two-way communications work at different speeds. For example, downloading information may be faster than uploading. Like DBS, they require an analog phone line and an analog modem.

Wireless Networks   Cell phones are one form of wireless communication. In addition, wireless networks allow computers to communicate through radio signals. Many hospitals, college campuses, businesses, hotels, and even cafes use wireless networks or "Wi-Fi." Wi-Fi is a short range network with high-bandwidth for data transfer. Multi-computer households may also use wireless networks, allowing family members to share equipment and exchange data. Wireless networks can be secured or unsecured. An unsecured network can be accessed by anyone within range, which puts information at risk. You can secure a wireless network by using an encryption protocol such as Wired Equivalent Privacy (WEP) or Wi-Fi Protected Access2 (WPA2).

With the advent of smart phones there is need for networks designed for use with cell phone technology. These networks, called 3G or 4G, provide layered transmission of data, allowing for increased network capacity, a wider range of services, and faster upload and download speeds.

Career Corner

Telematics   Blending telecommunications technology with computers to control the electric, electronic, and mechanical tools we use is a relatively new field known as telematics.

Requirements for success in this industry include programming, engineering, and telecommunications training and experience.

Telematics professionals will find a growing demand for their services as the field develops.

Real-World Tech

Finding Your Way by Satellite

Some of the satellites that circle Earth can pinpoint any spot on the ground or at sea. Using signals from these satellites, a Geographic Positioning System (GPS) receiver can show maps and directions on a screen. GPS is widely used by the military, but it is also used by drivers, boaters, hikers, hunters, and others who may rely on directions.

How is GPS used in cars?

Use the Vocabulary

Directions: *Match each vocabulary term in the left column with the correct definition in the right column.*

_____ 1. cellular phone
_____ 2. cell
_____ 3. cell site
_____ 4. leased line
_____ 5. personal digital assistant
_____ 6. cable modem
_____ 7. download
_____ 8. upload

a. permanent connection for long-distance cell phone calls

b. handheld computer

c. geographic area to which radio signals are sent

d. phone that uses radio waves to communicate

e. base station for handling cell calls

f. to send a file from your computer to another computer

g. to receive a file from another computer

h. device that enables a computer to access the Internet through a cable television connection

Check Your Comprehension

Directions: *Complete each sentence with information from the chapter.*

1. A cell phone is a type of _____.

2. Cell phones use _____ to communicate.

3. A problem with early cell phones was a lack of _____ for making calls.

4. The central base station manages activities in assigned _____.

5. As a caller moves from one point to another, a new _____ relays the signal from MTSO to MTSO.

6. Linking computers and telephones to work together is called _____.

7. A wireless network, which may be called _____, is a short range network with high-bandwidth for data transfer.

8. DBS service relies on _____ for its transmission signals.

9. All cable modems allow downloading of data, but not all offer the ability to _____ information through the cable television connection.

10. _____ allow computers to communicate with each other without being physically connected.

Think Critically

Directions: *Answer the following questions.*

1. Why are mobile phones called cell phones?

2. What fairly common communications tools do you think use CTI to send and receive information?

3. Why do you think so many companies offer telecommunications services?

4. How are cell phones like wireless networks?

5. Which telecommunications choice do you think will offer more options to consumers in the future?

Extend Your Knowledge

Directions: *Choose and complete one of the following projects.*

A. Some states and industries have developed policies to guide cell phone use. Select one of the following topics: (1) states that have banned or restricted drivers from using handheld cell phones or (2) airlines that restrict cell phone calls at certain times. With your teacher's permission, conduct online research to identify the reasons for the rules or laws, using appropriate strategies to locate the information on the Internet. Then, conclude whether or not the desired results have been achieved.

B. Some people complain that cell phone towers are unsightly. Others are concerned about possible harmful effects of the microradiation that comes from them. With your teacher's permission, conduct online or library research to find out more about these topics, and then conduct a class debate on the issues.

Networking Basics

What Is a Computer Network? In the simplest terms, a computer network is a group of computers and devices connected to each other so they can exchange data. The smallest network may only connect two computers; the largest—the Internet—connects millions.

In this chapter you are introduced to the concepts and terminology associated with computer networks, including the difference between local area networks and wide area networks.

Chapter Outline

 Lesson 25–1

Introducing Computer Networks

 Lesson 25–2

Local Area Networks

 Lesson 25–3

Wide Area Networks

Introducing Computer Networks

Objectives

- Explain what a computer network is.
- List media commonly used in networks.
- Identify three key benefits of using a network.
- Discuss how computers communicate.

As You Read

Organize Information Complete a chart to help you identify the details that support the main idea of the lesson.

 Key Terms

- gateway
- network
- network interface card (NIC)
- network traffic
- node
- open protocol
- physical media
- proprietary protocol
- protocol
- protocol suite
- synergy
- terminal
- Transmission Control Protocol/Internet Protocol (TCP/IP)
- workstation

Introducing Networks

If your family owns two computers, can they both use the same printer? They can if your computers are networked.

A computer **network** is two or more computers connected to one another to share resources. Networks allow users to access files and programs. They also let users share printers and other equipment. They allow people to work together, too. A network may be small, with just a few computers, or it may be large, with thousands of workstations. The network functions the same way, no matter how many workstations are connected.

Physical Media To create a computer network, each workstation and device must be able to communicate with the network. This requires establishing the physical connection using **physical media**. The medium can be any type of telecommunications connector: twisted pair telephone lines, coaxial cable, fiber-optic cable, or a microwave, radio, or infrared system.

Working together, the network media and the computers determine how much data can be sent through the connector. Wireless networks usually aren't as fast as wired networks.

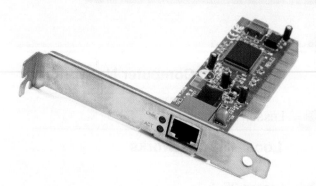

Network Interface Cards Some computers are designed with the ability to connect to networks. Others need a **network interface card**, or **NIC**, which handles the flow of data to and from the computer in both wired and wireless networks. If the network is put together by actual cables, those cables connect to the NIC. NICs often have a light that blinks green and amber to alert you to activity it's experiencing.

Figure 25.1.1 Network interface cards enable PCs to connect to a network.

Organizing Users

If you have more than one computer at home, you probably identify them by each user's name—your computer, Mom's computer, and so on. In businesses, schools, and other organizations, a network is organized into workstations, each with its own name and address. In both home and larger networks, pieces of equipment connected together must be able to understand one another.

Network Members A **workstation** is a computer connected to a computer network. It is often set up with the same operating system, applications, and access to resources as the other computers in the network. Workstations are where individuals do their day-to-day work.

In a large network, a workstation is also called a **node** by the people who take care of the network. A node is anything connected to the network—a workstation, a printer, a fax machine, or any other piece of equipment. A **gateway** is a node on your network that enables communication with other networks, such as the router on a home network that lets you connect to the Internet.

Network Alternative Sometimes network users work at a **terminal**, which usually includes a keyboard, a monitor, and a mouse. A terminal can feel as if the computer is local, but it's not. Users are actually sharing time on a central computer, with their own work displayed on their terminal's monitor. (This kind of network is sometimes called a timesharing system.)

Terminals can save on the cost of purchasing workstations. They are also useful in situations with limited need for a workstation, such as a public computer in a library.

Ensuring Communication

Once a network is created, the computers and other connected equipment can communicate with one another. The communication on a network is called **network traffic**. Network traffic is the electronic pulses of information sent by the network cards to carry data through the network wires to its destination. Specifically, computers communicate with languages called protocols.

A **protocol** sets a standard format for data and rules for handling it. There are many different protocols available to use on networks. For computers to speak with one another, they must use the same protocol.

Kinds of Protocols There are two protocol categories: open and proprietary. An **open protocol** is available for anyone to use. For example, the most common open protocol is the **Transmission Control Protocol/Internet Protocol (TCP/IP)**, which is used by computers on the Internet.

Technology @ School

If your school is networked, it will enjoy the same benefits all networks do—hardware, software, and people benefits.

Think About It!

Think about the benefits of a network. Sequence the value of each possible benefit using a scale of 1 (lowest) to 4 (highest). What conclusions can you draw?

➤ one expensive printer shared among 20 computers

➤ one version of a program installed on all computers

➤ a school newspaper file to which each computer user can contribute

➤ a joint science experiment conducted by two schools

Figure 25.1.2 Computers in different locations can communicate as long as they use the same network protocols.

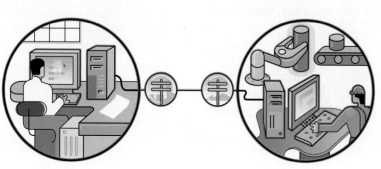

A **proprietary protocol**, however, is not open to everyone. Instead, only people who buy certain equipment, services, or computers can use it. Some personal digital assistants, digital cameras, and even dial-up Internet services use proprietary protocols. Overall, however, open protocols are more common. Both manufacturers and consumers benefit from open protocols that allow a broad range of connections.

A Stack of Protocols The protocols networks use to communicate are often called a **protocol suite**. A protocol suite is the stack, or collection, of individual protocols that determines how the network operates. For example, TCP/IP is not just one network language, but many smaller ones. Each small protocol in this suite has a specific job to do in a specific order. Working together, protocols allow computers to communicate.

Working with Others

Everyone on a network has the ability to access programs and data stored anywhere on the network. You might use an application like Google docs which is stored on a network rather than on your own computer, or you might print a document on a printer that is located on a different floor than your computer. Of course, for security, you can specify sharing levels for folders to control who can access the stored data. Publicly shared folders allow anyone access. Shared folders may be shared only with authorized users. Sometimes, shared folders are accessed using shared links. That means you send a link to someone to allow them to access the folder.

Networks also let people work together in new and exciting ways. People on a network can collaborate more easily than those working on standalone systems. **Synergy** is the effect a group effort can create. People working together on a network can accomplish more than people working alone on unconnected computers.

Using a Network

The steps you use to access network resources are basically the same as those you use to work on your own computer. Your actions may seem simple enough, but behind the scenes, the network's hardware and software are performing complex tasks.

Some tasks you can accomplish using a network include:

- Scheduling a meeting
- Instant messaging
- Sending e-mail
- Video conferencing
- Exchanging documents
- Playing games.

Local Area Networks

Objectives

- Describe how local area networks work.
- Define how local area networks allow information sharing.
- Compare peer-to-peer and client/server networks.

As You Read

Organize Information   Complete a spider map to help you identify the basics of networking as you read the lesson.

Introducing LANs

A school lab with its ten computers networked together is an example of a **local area network**, or **LAN**. A LAN is a network in which all the workstations and other equipment are near one another. LANs can be set up in any defined area, such as a home, a school, an office building, or even a cluster of shops.

A LAN can have just a few or several hundred users. Small or large, a LAN lets its members share equipment and information, resulting in lower costs. There are three key ways to share information: sharing files, using collaborative software, and sharing peripherals.

Sharing Files   Through a computer's operating system, people connected to a LAN can participate in **file sharing**. File sharing is making files available to more than one user on the network. The file is stored on a network server so anyone with permission rights may access the file from any location.

Using Collaborative Software   **Collaborative software** enables the network to help people work together more closely. With collaborative software, users can share calendars, work on a document together, or even hold meetings through the network. Collaborative software is also called **groupware**.

Sharing Peripherals   In addition to sharing files and software, a LAN allows users to access **remote resources** such as printers, fax machines, or any other equipment that is not connected directly to your computer, but is connected to the network.

Using a Peer-to-Peer Network

Your peers are your equals. In a **peer-to-peer network (P2PN)**, all the computers are equals. Peer-to-peer networks are usually small, made up of two to ten computers.

Key Terms

- client
- client/server network
- collaborative software
- file server
- file sharing
- groupware
- local area network (LAN))
- network operating system (NOS)
- peer-to-peer network (P2PN)
- remote resource

Shared files and databases are extremely useful in many office situations. If the office is networked, any employee on the network can access the data.

Think About It!

Think about what information might be useful at a magazine publishing house. Which databases below do you think should be networked for any employee to access? Which should not?

➤ a collection of photographs of famous people

➤ a list of employees' salaries

➤ a directory of all the subscribers and their addresses

➤ a dictionary and a thesaurus

➤ a series of notes on recent historical events

Sharing Files   In a P2PN, each user decides whether any files on his or her computer will be shared. You can share the files with your neighbor, a few of your neighbors, or everyone on the network. The reverse is true, too. Other workstations may have files you'd like to access through the network—and you can if you have permission.

Creating a P2PN   A P2PN is an easy network to create, since all of the workstations are equals. The operating system of each computer typically has built-in file-sharing abilities. The workstations are connected to each other through the network cable. In some systems, the network cables all connect to a central device called a hub. A hub handles the flow of traffic from computer to computer.

Evaluating P2PNs   A peer-to-peer network is ideal for small offices and homes. In a large business, however, peer-to-peer networking has some drawbacks:

• Security problems can arise.

• Data can be hard to back up.

• With many users, file sharing can become difficult.

• Finding shared files can be difficult.

• Managing resources can be complicated.

These problems arise because resources are scattered across many computers. If one computer fails or is turned off, its resources are no longer available to the network.

Figure 25.2.1 An ethernet switch with many ports can be used to set up a local area network.

Using a Client/Server Network

Large businesses usually use a **client/server network**. With this system, one powerful computer provides information and management services to the workstation computers, the **clients**.

Creating a Client/Server Network   The main computer in a client/server system is called the **file server** or the server. It contains the network operating system, other programs, and large data files. The **network operating system**, or **NOS**, manages and secures the entire network. It controls access, permissions, and all aspects of network use, and provides a directory, or list, of all resources available on the network. Only those who provide a username and a password can use the network. It centralizes and protects data and controls what users can do with files. Thus, a client/server network is far more secure than a P2PN.

Evaluating a Client/Server Network   For a large office, file servers are better than peer-to-peer networks, for several reasons:

- They offer a central location for files.
- Data is easy to back up and easy to recover.
- Servers are faster than workstations.
- Servers usually are powered on.
- Security is easier to maintain.

Figure 25.2.2 In a client/server network, users can share files stored on the file server and access a common printer, too.

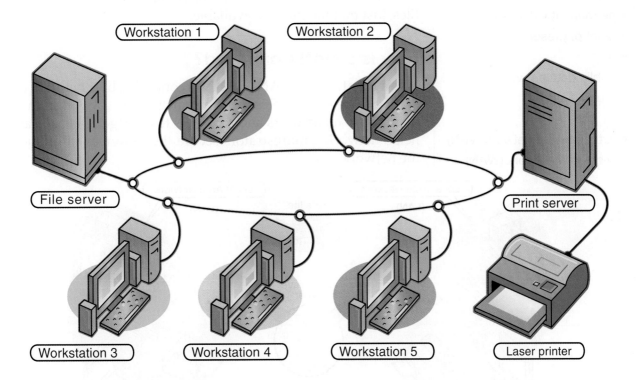

Wide Area Networks

Objectives

- Identify the purpose and components of a wide area network.
- Compare methods organizations use to connect to a point of presence.
- Compare and contrast packet-switching networks and circuit-switching networks.
- Describe three types of WANs.

As You Read

Organize Information   Complete an outline to help you note key facts about wide area networks as you read the lesson.

🔑 Key Terms

- backbone
- circuit-switching
- congestion
- firewall
- frame relay
- metropolitan area network (MAN)
- packets
- packet-switching
- permanent virtual circuit
- point of presence (POP)
- port
- public data network
- router
- T1 line
- virtual private network (VPN)
- wide area network (WAN)

What Is a WAN?

A **wide area network (WAN)** connects computers and other resources that are miles or even continents apart. A business with offices in many places can use a WAN to link its LANs in different cities. Then, users from any of the locations can, with the proper permissions, access the network. Each user can access files, printers, and other resources as if they were local. As far as users are concerned, a WAN "feels like" one giant LAN.

Once a WAN is created, users may not even realize the files they are sharing are remote. And that's the way it should be. Users should not worry about the physical location of the shared files, just that the files are available.

How Is a WAN Controlled?

Like a client/server LAN, a WAN is controlled by a network operating system. A NOS is especially helpful on a WAN because there are so many users and resources to manage. The NOS also helps network administrators secure the resources throughout the network.

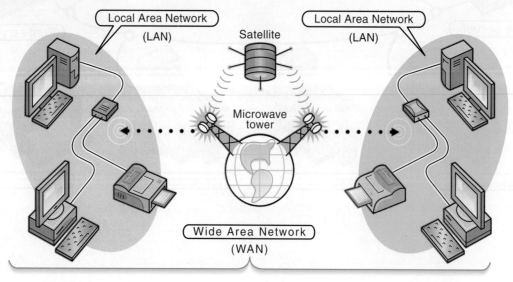

Figure 25.3.1 A WAN can link distant LANs through telephone lines or microwave signals.

Creating WANs

To create a WAN, LANs are connected through high-speed data lines called **backbones**. Organizations attach to the backbone at a **point of presence (POP)**. But how do they get to the POP? There are several options.

ISDN and DSL These technologies use ordinary telephone lines to attach to the backbone. Special adapters or modems provide ways to deal with digital data.

Leased Lines Some companies rent a private end-to-end connection, called a leased line, from a telecommunications company. Leased lines allow data to be sent at 56,000 bps.

T1 Lines Larger companies and many school districts lease **T1 lines**. T1 lines can be either copper or fiber optic, and they allow data to be sent at more than 1.5 million bps.

Permanent Virtual Circuits A **permanent virtual circuit (PVC)** allows multiple users' data to travel the line at once. Thus, they are cheaper than private lines. Most PVCs use a technology called **frame relay**. Frame relay allows voice, data, and video to travel on the same line and at the same time.

Sending Data Long-Distance

Packet-Switching Networks Most networks use **packet-switching** technology. The sending computer divides information into tiny segments called **packets**. Each packet is marked with a delivery address, so packet transfers are quick and accurate. When you transfer a file, send an e-mail, or even browse a Web site, you're sending and receiving packets.

Circuit-Switching Networks Some WANs use circuit-switching technology to transmit messages. **Circuit-switching** happens on a real, end-to-end connection between the sending computer and the receiving computer, which make up the circuit. There's no delay on circuit-switching networks, so they are ideal for sending voice messages and for teleconferencing. A telephone network uses circuit-switching.

Routers are network devices or programs that choose the best pathway for each packet. If there is **congestion**, or too much traffic, on the network, the router can delay some of the packets. The receiving computer puts the packets back together in the right order.

Types of WANs

Businesses and other organizations use three types of WANs.

Public Data Network   A **public data network** allows a company to set up its own network. Telecommunications companies own the public data network and charge fees for the use of the network.

Private Data Network   Some companies set up a private data network that cannot be accessed by outsiders. Having a private data network costs more than using a public data network.

Virtual Private Network   A **virtual private network (VPN)** is a private network set up through a public network. VPN users connect to an Internet service provider (ISP) to access the network.

Metropolitan Area Network   A **metropolitan area network (MAN)** is a network that covers a large area, such as a university campus or a city.

Real-World Tech

Networking the Navajo Nation   The Navajo Nation spreads across 26,000 square miles in Arizona, New Mexico, and Utah. The Nation's Diné College has seven campuses that are hundreds of miles apart. Only about half of the Nation's households have phone lines. How could the educational system take advantage of the Internet? The solution was to create a WAN using a variety of technologies. Small satellite dishes receive information while phone and dedicated data lines send messages out. The Navajo Nation's wide area network has expanded to overcome the wide open spaces in which its people live.

What group or institution do you think would benefit from a WAN? Why?

Network Security

A network can be secured or unsecured. On an unsecured network, there are no barriers to access and anyone within the network can access information. These networks allow for free flow of information but leave little protection from hacking for the individual computers. Secured networks, however, limit access and protect the computers and users. One way secured networks prevent unauthorized access is by requiring users to enter an ID and password.

Computing in a network can be private or public, as well. When you use the computers in your local library, you are on a public network that anyone can access. The networks in your school or home, however, are private and usually require an ID and password for access.

There are also public and private IP addresses. Public IP addresses are used by all computers connected to the Internet by a modem, including your home network computers. Private IP addresses are used on internal networks, such as a company intranet. Private IP addresses cannot be contacted directly over the Internet the way a computer with a public IP address can be. This provides an extra layer of security for the internal network.

Networks also use firewalls as a level of security. A **firewall** is a filtering system that opens or blocks programs and **ports** to keep outside data from entering the network. Firewalls are usually located on a gateway, such as a router that lets a network access the Internet. From that location the firewall can examine the packets trying to get into the network and determine whether or not to let them through. Some firewalls are built into a computer's operating system, such as Windows. You, or the system administrator, can control what the firewall blocks and what it lets through by maintaining lists of allowed or blocked programs and ports.

Figure 25.3.2 Use the Windows Firewall Allowed Apps settings to allow or block programs and ports.

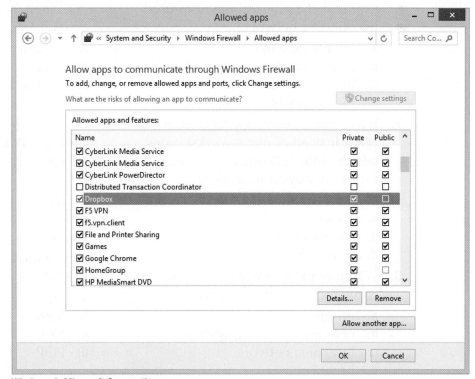

Windows 8, Microsoft Corporation.

Use the Vocabulary

Directions: *Match each vocabulary term in the left column with the correct definition in the right column.*

_____ 1. network
_____ 2. workstation
_____ 3. protocol
_____ 4. local area network
_____ 5. collaborative software
_____ 6. peer-to-peer network
_____ 7. file server
_____ 8. backbone
_____ 9. point of presence
_____ 10. virtual private network

a. network in which all computers are equal

b. computer connected to a network

c. local connection to a WAN

d. standard format and rules

e. set up on a public network

f. two or more computers linked together

g. program that lets people work together closely

h. high-speed line that carries network traffic

i. network set up in a limited area

j. the central computer in one kind of network

Check Your Comprehension

Directions: *Determine the correct choice for each of the following.*

1. Which of the following is NOT an example of a physical medium used to connect a network?

   a. telephone wires
   b. electric cords
   c. fiber-optic cables
   d. radio signals

2. If a company buys one large computer instead of many workstations, which of the following will it supply for its employees to work on?

   a. a file server
   b. nodes
   c. a point of presence
   d. terminals

3. Which of the following is another name for collaborative software?

   a. groupware
   b. network operating system
   c. local area network
   d. backbone

4. Which of the following do users of a client/server network have to provide?

   a. a client
   b. a file
   c. a protocol
   d. an access control

5. Which of the following is used to control a WAN?

   a. NIC
   b. VPN
   c. NOS
   d. POP

6. Which of the following is used to provide a local connection to a WAN?

   a. NIC
   b. VPN
   c. NOS
   d. POP

Directions: *Answer the following questions.*

1. How are a LAN and a WAN similar? How are they different?

2. Why might a P2PN be a good choice for a small network? Why might a client/server model be a good choice for a large network?

3. Why is the Internet an example of a WAN?

4. What kinds of wires and wireless lines can be used as the backbone of a WAN?

5. Why are protocols important to LANs and WANs?

Extend Your Knowledge

Directions: *Choose and complete one of the following projects.*

A. With your teacher's permission, research, compare and contrast a server, workstation, host, and client. Take notes and keep track of your sources. Create a chart showing your findings and share it with a partner or with the class.

B. Conduct research in the library or, with your teacher's permission, on the Internet to find more details about different types of networks. Compare the advantages and disadvantages of coax, Cat 3, Cat 5, fiber optic, UTP (unshielded twisted pair), and STP (Spanning Tree Protocol), and wireless networks, and the conditions under which they are appropriate. Present your findings in an illustrated chart. Compare the details you discovered with those your classmates found.

C. With your teacher's permission, research the differences, advantages, and disadvantages of standard protocols. Take notes and keep track of your sources. Only use information from reliable and accurate sources. Use the information to create a chart and present it to a partner or to the class.

Using Networks

Can Computers Work Together? From the workstations in your classroom, to the PC at the library, and lately even in the interface on your cell phone, computers are everywhere. Today, thanks to networking, these devices can become even more useful.

Networks, and the science of network design, are becoming more important in our lives than ever before. People at home, in schools, and at work are all exploring how they can use networks in their daily activities.

In this chapter, you learn about the different designs used to create networks, and how networks are used by businesses and individuals.

Chapter Outline

 Lesson 26–1

Connecting Computers

 Lesson 26–2

Creating Local Area Networks

 Lesson 26–3

Connecting Remote Networks

Connecting Computers

Objectives

- Explain what is meant by network architecture.
- Explain OSI.
- Summarize how networks are designed.

As You Read

Organize Information Use a main-idea chart to help you identify the details that support the main idea of the lesson.

 Key Terms

- collision
- contention
- network architecture
- network layer
- topology

Network Architecture

To design a network for your school, you would consider the number of students, the placement of your servers, Internet access, and more. Designing a network for a large company raises different issues.

Setting Up a Network **Network architecture** is the science of designing a network. In many cases, a systems engineer is hired to find out what the network will be used for and to design a network the operating system can handle.

Real-World Tech

Networking the Home For some homeowners, it's not enough to buy a house. They want a smart house—a networked house. It offers benefits such as wireless security systems and baby monitors, central control of heat and lighting, high-tech control of home entertainment systems, and more. The retail world is changing as more and more companies are able to turn houses into smart houses!

Which high-tech feature would you most like to have in your home?

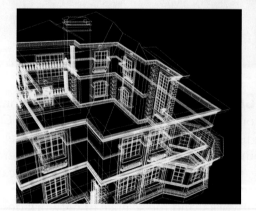

Small networks are fairly easy to create. The network administrator first connects the network card of each work-station to the network cable and usually connects the cable to a hub. The administrator also has to make sure the operating system of the computer is set up to participate in the network. On larger networks, however, the job becomes more complicated.

Following Rules Recall that all network communication, large or small, is based on and must follow common rules, called protocols. These rules were developed by the International Standards Organization, or ISO.

The rules specific to computer networks are called the Open Systems Interconnection, or OSI, model, which has seven layers. These rules define what happens at each step of a network operation and how data flows through it. Each layer communicates with the layer above and below it to ensure that networking takes place. Sometimes, layers 1, 2, and 3 are called the lower layers. They define rules for how information is sent between computers over a network. The upper layers, or layers 4, 5, 6, and 7, define how applications interact with the network.

On the sending computer, data flows from the application layer, down through each layer in the model, and out through the network. Then, it flows back up through the model on the receiving computer. Each layer has a job to do to prepare outgoing data for the network and incoming data for the operating system. All layers are important, but the **network layer** deserves special attention.

Career Corner

Systems Engineer Systems engineers have enormous responsibility in working with networks. They design and install them, but they also continue working to improve the network and troubleshoot to solve problems. Systems engineers aim for maximum performance and security in the networks they deal with. They are knowledgeable about both hardware and software.

Layers of the OSI Model

Layer	Purpose
7. Application	Communicate with the operating system to do an actual job
6. Presentation	Package data from the operating system so the lower layers can understand it
5. Session	Create and end communication between two devices on the network
4. Transport	Manage the flow of data within the network and check for errors
3. Network	Route and address data traffic
2. Datalink	Choose the right physical protocols for the data
1. Physical	Define the actual network hardware, such as cabling and timing

The word *contention* has more than one meaning. It can mean a state of rivalry or a statement that one supports.

Think About It!

Think about the various meanings of the word *contention*. Which sentence(s) below do not use the word correctly?

➤ Sally and Tom are in contention for the job of manager.

➤ Ralph did not apply for that position because he feels contention in his present job.

➤ It is Sally's contention that her skills are ideal for the job.

Network Design

If you were to create a map of your neighborhood, you might include streets, lakes, and hills. A map of a network shows the physical structure of the network, including servers, workstations, and other network devices. The network's layout is called the network **topology**.

Topology isn't only concerned with where to put equipment, however. The design of a network must also solve another problem: Only one computer on a network may speak at a time. When two computers try to access the network at the same time, they're in **contention**. If both sent their data at once, there could be a **collision**, and the data could become all mixed together.

To avoid such collisions, each computer divides its data into very small, fast-moving packets. Network equipment or software transmits these packets. Users typically are not affected by the tiny delays this system causes as each computer must wait its turn to transmit data.

Figure 26.1.1 Like the traffic signals used on roads, networks use special means to prevent data from colliding.

Creating Local Area Networks

Objectives

- Compare and contrast LAN topologies.
- Identify network types.
- Describe the operation of an Ethernet.

As You Read

Organize Information   Use an outline to help you identify types of LANs as you read the lesson.

Choosing a Network Topology

Each LAN can have a different combination of computers, printers, and other equipment. The LAN designer chooses a network type to connect the components. Each type of network can be described by its topology: bus, ring, star, and star bus.

Bus Topology   An older network design, **bus topology** is rarely used now. In a bus, devices are connected to a single network line like a string of holiday lights. When one network device fails, the entire network fails, and adding new devices to the network can also be tricky.

Key Terms

- bus topology
- Ethernet
- hub
- mesh topology
- ring topology
- star bus topology
- star topology
- token

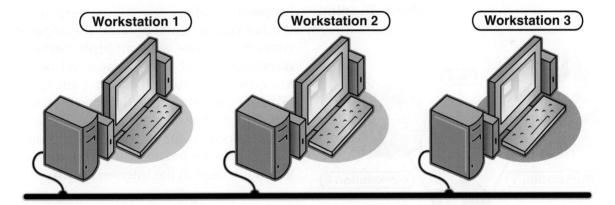

Figure 26.2.1 In a bus topology, all computers connect to a single cable.

Technology @ School

Which topology would you use if you were in charge of networking a classroom with five computers, one printer, and one scanner?

Think About It!

Sequence the value of each topology below using a scale of 1 (lowest) to 5 (highest) to indicate which you believe would be best in the classroom.

➤ bus topology

➤ ring topology

➤ star topology

➤ star bus topology

➤ mesh topology

Ring Topology As its name suggests, **ring topology** connects all the network devices in a circle. To control collisions, such networks pass **tokens**, or special units of data, around the ring. Only the workstation that has control of the token can send other data onto the network. Because of the token-passing technique, these networks are also called token rings, or, if the network is wireless, wireless token rings. Like bus topology, one fault can disrupt a ring network, but this network type has the advantage of not requiring a network server.

Star Topology **Star topology** design connects each network device to a central hub. A **hub** is a connection point for all the computers, printers, and other equipment on the network.

Adding and removing devices to a star network is easy. If the hub loses power or fails, however, the network devices will not be able to communicate. Star topology avoids collisions by using strategies that manage contention.

Star Bus Topology **Star bus topology** connects multiple star networks along a bus. It is the most common design used in LANs today.

Suppose each classroom in your school had its own network with its own hub. The hub in each classroom could then be connected to a common line, called a backbone. A backbone is a fast network medium that provides communication among all of the networks. It links all the hubs in the school, for example, expanding the reach of each network.

Mesh Topology In **mesh topology** the components are all connected directly to other components. Because this topology connects devices with multiple paths, redundancies exist. But, because all devices are cross-connected, the best path can be taken at any time. The drawback to mesh topology is that needing at least one and a half connections for each computer makes it very expensive to construct. This topology is usually used in the Internet structure.

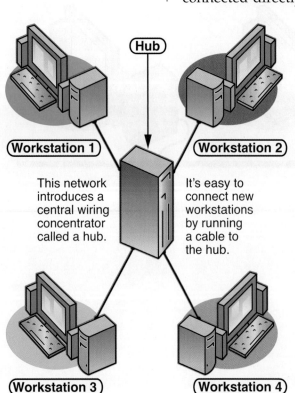

Hub

Workstation 1

Workstation 2

This network introduces a central wiring concentrator called a hub.

It's easy to connect new workstations by running a cable to the hub.

Workstation 3

Workstation 4

Figure 26.2.2 A star topology.

Exploring Ethernet

Ethernet is the most common networking technology used on LANs. To create the network, Ethernet cables plug into Ethernet ports on computers, LANs, and cable or DSL modems. Ethernet and star bus topology work together to ensure fast data transfers, logical network design, and fewer collisions. Ethernet uses a rule called Carrier Sensing Multiple Access/Collision Detection, or CSMA/CD. This protocol governs how network devices communicate and what happens if they break the rules.

Ethernet Communications Like a well mannered conversation, CSMA/CD requires each network device, also called a node, to take turns speaking. The node first listens to hear whether anyone is using the network, and then it transmits the data. When a node transmits data, every workstation on the network receives the data. However, only the device the data is intended for actually accepts it.

Ethernet Collisions If two nodes speak at the same time, a collision occurs. In that case, each of the conflicting nodes waits a random number of milliseconds and then attempts to speak again. The random waiting time helps prevent another collision.

Star bus topology expands a network's reach. As more nodes are added to a single network and as more networks are connected, the chance of multiple collisions increases. To solve this problem, Ethernet often uses bridges, switches, or routers. These devices divide the network into segments. To reduce congestion, messages are routed to the proper segment rather than to the entire network.

Spotlight on...

ROBERT M. METCALFE

In the 1970s, Xerox® wanted a system that would let all the computers at a research center share a laser printer—the world's first laser printer, in fact. When Robert Metcalfe and his assistant, David R. Boggs, came up with Ethernet, the problem was solved.

Later, Metcalfe founded his own company, 3Com Corporation, which stands for *computers*, *communications*, and *compatibility*.

Connecting Remote Networks

Objectives

- Summarize the purpose of WANs.
- Specify WAN technologies.
- Identify common uses for WANs.
- Explain the use of intranets.

As You Read

Organize Information   Complete a concept web to help you identify different WAN applications.

Key Terms

- cloud computing
- electronic data interchange (EDI)
- extranet
- intranet
- point-of-sale (POS)
- telecommute

Figure 26.3.1 WAN networks allow people spanning a large geographic area to share resources and communicate.

Overview of WANs

Recall that a wide area network, or WAN, is just what its name suggests: a network that links resources that are far apart from one another. Often, a WAN connects two or more LANs into one large network. Suppose a company has networks in Chicago, Illinois; Indianapolis, Indiana; and St. Louis, Missouri. A high-speed data line between Chicago and Indianapolis can connect those two networks. From Indianapolis, another high-speed data line is connected to St. Louis. Now, all three networks are connected, and the company has a WAN.

Protecting a WAN   In the example network described above, the company has a problem. If the data line between St. Louis and Indianapolis fails, users in St. Louis cannot communicate beyond their LAN. Companies can solve this problem by adding more high-speed lines. For example, a data line between St. Louis and Chicago would ensure connectivity to resources in all three LANs even if one line fails.

WANs in the Business World

The introduction of WANs allowed individuals on each network to communicate, access resources, and collaborate on projects. And as people got used to networking, they developed new forms of personal and business communications.

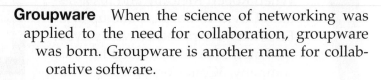

Groupware   When the science of networking was applied to the need for collaboration, groupware was born. Groupware is another name for collaborative software.

EDI Companies can also use WANs for **electronic data interchange**, or **EDI**. EDI is a business-to-business WAN. For example, a company can use EDI to order equipment from a supplier quickly and accurately. It helps the supplier, too, because it automatically creates a bill and sends it to the buyer. Though EDI is expensive to set up, it saves both buyers and suppliers money: It saves paper and employee time, and it helps companies avoid having to stock large inventories.

WANs in Your World

You are likely exposed to WANs every day. Many of the retail stores you visit, such as grocery stores, shoe stores, or video stores, use WANs to track sales, inventory, and profits. You are also involved with WANs every time you use the Internet.

The POS System One example of a WAN in action is a **point-of-sale** system. Here's how it works:

- The cashier at a retail outlet, such as a grocery store, scans the bar code on the item you purchase. That bar code is linked to a central database.

- The POS system allows the store to order more of the product automatically, learn which day of the week customers are likely to buy the item, and compare its sales with other stores.

- Once a store has collected information on its sales, it can predict trends. Knowing these trends lets the store managers stock the shelves and set prices sensibly.

The Internet The Internet is the most common example of a WAN. You and others access the Internet through an Internet service provider (ISP). The ISP is connected to a backbone in order to reach other networks where Web servers are located.

Cloud Computing

A recent network trend is **cloud computing.** Cloud computing is the use of remote network servers to store data and resources, such as applications. Cloud resources are shared, so users do not actually own them. Instead, they pay to use server space. Cloud computing is a cost-effective option for many businesses, because they do not have to build and maintain their own network.

With cloud computing, users with access to the cloud can retrieve data from multiple computers. Multiple users can also retrieve the same information, allowing for easy collaboration. Another benefit is that cloud-based applications such as Microsoft Office 365 and Adobe Creative Cloud are updated automatically. Users always have access to the most current software.

Technology @ Home

Often, an employee who is connected to the office through a network can work from home, or telecommute.

Think About It!

Think about the advantages and disadvantages of telecommuting for the company. Which items below do you think are advantages? Which are disadvantages?

➤ You do not have to dress up to go to work.

➤ You do not travel to get to work.

➤ You can avoid people very easily.

➤ You can work at your own pace.

➤ You can take breaks whenever you want.

Social Studies Who was that man? What made that woman famous? History examines many stories of people who made a difference. And the Internet is making a difference in how you can learn about people in history. Specialized networks and networks maintained by universities, scholarly groups, and professional organizations provide rich sources for historical and biographical information.

Check out www.biography.com for tons of biographical information about all types of famous people.

What Is an Intranet?

Many companies,universities, and other organizations install intranets. An **intranet** is a private network that uses the same TCP/IP protocol as the Internet.

Comparing Intranets and the Internet Intranets offer many of the same services the Internet does, such as e-mail and Web sites. Intranets are different from the Internet in that they are not meant for public use. Firewall software prevents outsiders from accessing the intranet.

Creating an Extranet An intranet can also be converted to an **extranet**, which allows for limited public access. Companies often use extranets so employees can access the network while they travel or **telecommute**, which is when employees work from home while linked to the office by computer. Extranets are also used to share information with other businesses.

Figure 26.3.2 Company intranets enable employees to access information such as human resources forms, shared databases, and information about company policies.

Use the Vocabulary

Directions: *Match each vocabulary term in the left column with the correct definition in the right column.*

_____ **1.** network architecture

_____ **2.** topology

_____ **3.** contention

_____ **4.** bus topology

_____ **5.** hub

_____ **6.** token

_____ **7.** star topology

_____ **8.** firewall

_____ **9.** cloud computing

a. science of designing a network

b. network designed around a hub

c. software that prevents outsiders from accessing an intranet

d. layout of a network

e. two messages trying to travel at once on a network

f. use of a remote network for data storage

g. unit of data that prevents collisions in ring topology

h. network connected to one line

i. a connection point for all the computers, printers, and other equipment on the network

Check Your Comprehension

Directions: *Determine the correct choice for each of the following.*

1. All networks follow rules developed by the _____.

  a. ISO

  b. POP

  c. EDI

  d. LAN

2. The OSI model defines how data travels through _____.

  a. a collision

  b. backbones

  c. seven layers

  d. groupware

3. Early LANs were designed with _____.

  a. bus topology

  b. ring topology

  c. star topology

  d. star bus topology

4. Ethernet deals with contention by _____.

  a. storing messages in the session layer

  b. assigning messages to a POP

  c. dumping messages that collide

  d. delaying messages that collide

5. Groupware makes all of the following possible EXCEPT _____.

  a. videoconferences

  b. e-mail

  c. electronic bulletin boards

  d. protocol stacks

6. A _____ topology is used in the Internet structure, and it is the most expensive.

  a. tree

  b. star bus

  c. mesh

  d. ring

Think Critically

Directions: *Answer the following questions.*

1. How does the existence of protocols such as the Open Systems Interconnection model make the job of designing a network easier?

2. What equipment do you think employees need to telecommute?

3. For what purposes might a big bank use both LANs and a WAN?

4. Do you think LANs and WANs will become more or less standardized in the future? Why?

5. How has networking changed the way many companies do business?

Extend Your Knowledge

Directions: *Choose and complete one of the following projects.*

A. Work with a partner to find out more about Ethernet, which many schools use in their networks. With your teacher's permission, use a search engine and the keyword *Ethernet* to research three Web sites that describe this technology. Take notes and keep track of your sources. Next, outline and create a chart to help you evaluate the three sites. Identify the source of each. Then develop a scale and rank each on completeness, clarity, organization, and overall value.

B. With your teacher's permission, research the characteristics of backbones and segments. Take notes and keep track of your sources. Only use information from sites that are reliable and accurate. Compile the information into a report and present it to a partner or to the class.

C. With your teacher's permission, select, research and analyze the directory services of two or three major network operating systems. Take notes and keep track of your sources. Only use sources that are reliable and accurate. As part of the research, identify clients that work well with each of the network operating systems and their resources. Write a paragraph summarizing your findings, and include a chart. Read your paragraph to a partner or to the class.

chapter 27

Internet Basics

A Network of Networks The Internet connects people all over the world through a huge network of computer systems. The U.S. government and university researchers began the Internet to share information. Since then, it has turned into one of the most exciting inventions in history.

As more and more people use the Internet, the demand for user-friendly online services has also grown and created new business opportunities. Additionally, electronic mail and instant messaging services have changed the way people meet and stay in touch with one another. People online can work together on projects in different locations, sharing information as if they were in the same office.

Chapter Outline

What Is the Internet?

Objectives

- Compare and contrast LANs, WANs, and the Internet.
- Describe how the three main parts of the Internet work together.
- Explain the advantages and disadvantages of the organization of the Internet.
- Identify organizations responsible for setting standards for the Internet.

As You Read

Organize Information Use a spider map to organize information about the Internet as you read.

🔑 Key Terms

- Internet
- Internet client

Figure 27.1.1 Like many networks, the Internet is made up of connected client and server computers, which use protocols to communicate.

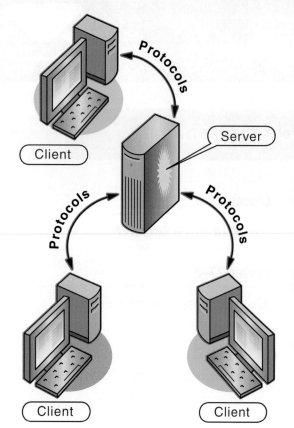

Organization of the Internet

The **Internet** is a global WAN, a network of networks. It connects everything from single computers to large networks. The Internet can even connect computers that run different operating systems. This ability to share information with almost any computer makes the Internet a powerful tool for communication. The Internet is made up of three important parts: servers, clients, and protocols.

Servers Internet servers are the computers that provide services to other computers by way of the Internet. These services include processing e-mail, storing Web pages, or helping send files from one computer to another.

Clients and Protocols Internet clients are the computers that request services from a server. When you connect to the Internet, the computer you use is considered a client. Like other networks, the Internet uses protocols—the sets of rules that allow clients and servers to communicate.

Is the Internet a WAN?

There are three key differences between the Internet and other WANs.

Type of Access The Internet is public, while WANs are typically private.

Degree of Security While the Internet is becoming more secure, it is still not as secure as a private WAN connection. As data travels through the Internet, snoops and eavesdroppers on the public networks through which the data moves sometimes try to access it. A private WAN is more secure because it is more likely that only the organization that owns it has access to it. Internet users must take security measures on their own, such as installing firewalls and using antivirus and antimalware programs.

Types of Information On the Internet, information is transmitted in the form of Web pages and other types of files. A WAN is used for more than just browsing Web pages. It provides access to network resources, such as printers, file servers, and databases.

Inventing the Internet

In the 1960s, people were working on ideas that later became the Internet. In 1969, the first four major computer centers in the United States were linked. By 1973, the network was international. In 1983, the Internet protocols went online for the first time. Two major groups worked on the development of the Internet: the United States military and university researchers.

United States Military In the 1960s, the United States government wanted to find a way to communicate in the event of a disaster or military attack. The military began to work on a system that would operate even if some communication connections were destroyed. The Defense Advanced Research Projects Agency (DARPA) of the U.S. Department of Defense focused on computer networking and communications. In 1968, this research led to a network of connected computer centers called the Advanced Research Projects Agency Network (ARPANET).

University Researchers With the military's leadership and funding, DARPA formed computing research centers at universities across the United States. From 1969 through 1987, the number of computers on the network increased from 4 to more than 10,000. These connections created the networks that became the Internet.

Technology @ Home

Staying current with changing technology is not always easy.

Think About It!

Listed below are other technologies invented since research for the Internet began in the mid-1960s. Which item(s) listed below do you have in your home?

- food processor
- VCR
- cellular phone
- video game
- DVD

Figure 27.1.2 Today, the Internet includes millions of servers and connections all over the globe.

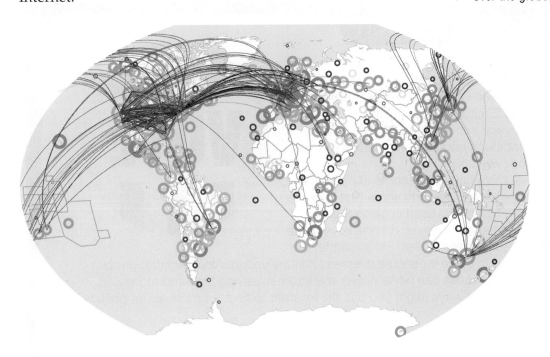

Internet Management

Who owns the Internet? The truth is, no specific organization or government does. Many organizations are responsible for different parts of the network. Here are some examples:

- The World Wide Web Consortium (W3C) issues standards related to the World Wide Web.

- Internet Engineering Task Force (IETF) is a large international community of network designers, operators, vendors, and researchers. This group is concerned with the future structure and smooth operation of the Internet. Like many organizations that set computing standards, the IETF is "open," meaning any interested person can participate.

- Internet Corporation for Assigned Names and Numbers (ICANN) is a nonprofit corporation with a variety of responsibilities, including the management of domain names.

- Web Standards Project (WaSP) is a coalition that supports standards for simple, affordable access to Web technologies.

Freedom of the Internet   One advantage to the open quality of the Internet is the ability to share information. Anyone can make an idea or opinion accessible to anyone else.

Pitfalls of the Internet   However, there are pitfalls to this open organization. People can post whatever point of view or information they want, even if it can sometimes be misleading or false. It is up to the users of the Internet to think critically about the information they find. If you have a question about anything you find on the Internet, ask an adult you trust about it.

Real-World Tech

Voting on the Internet?   According to the Federal Election Commission, the Internet is not ready for U.S. citizens to vote on it. Safeguarding the privacy, security, and reliability of the voting process is important to ensuring a free democratic election.

While there have been some experiments with Internet voting, experts agree that it will be a long time before it is used in general elections. The Internet, however, can improve some parts of the election process. For example, the technology is in place for secure overseas military voting. Also, registration databases and vote totals can be sent over the Internet, saving time and money.

In what other ways might you use the Internet to find out more about politics?

Connecting to the Internet

Objectives

- Identify ways to connect to the Internet.
- Compare and contrast Internet Service Providers and online services.
- Categorize access methods by temporary or permanent IP address.
- Compare and contrast the connection speed of a modem to DSL and to a fiber-optic line.

As You Read

Outline Information   Use an outline to organize information about how the Internet works as you read.

Accessing the Internet from Home

There are different ways to connect to the Internet. The reasons for various options are availability, location, speed, and price.

Dial-up, ISDN, and DSL Access   The least expensive way to get online is to use a dial-up connection between a standard phone line and a modem. These connections are called "dial-up" because your computer must connect to the Internet by using a telephone number to contact a server. Only 10% of households in the United States still use dial-up access. This type of access uses a modem and a standard phone line to connect to the Internet with **Point-to-Point protocol (PPP)**. Aside from the slow speed, a drawback of dial-up is that your computer is assigned a temporary IP address; you can't run server software without a permanent IP address. When the session is over, the connection is broken.

Some Digital Subscriber Lines (DSL) require a special telephone line. Integrated Services Digital Network (ISDN) lines require a special ISDN adapter and modem. As a result, both services cost more than regular phone service. Furthermore, DSL and ISDN are not available in all areas. One drawback of DSL is that service does not extend more than a few miles from telephone switching stations, so this service is unavailable in some areas.

Cable and Satellite   Cable television companies offer Internet access through cable modems. This access is at speeds much faster than dial-up modems. You need a network card in your computer, a cable modem, and cable access. Satellite access is also very fast for downloading files to your computer, but it requires a phone line and a modem for sending files to outside users.

Key Terms

- Internet service provider (ISP)
- navigate
- online service
- Point-to-Point protocol (PPP)
- username

Accessing the Internet from Work

Access needs of large organizations may differ from those of home Internet users.

LAN Access   If your school or library has a local area network (LAN) that is connected to the Internet, you access the Internet through the network. LAN access is generally much faster than dial-up access because LANs usually access the Internet via a high-speed connection. But the performance you experience depends on how many LAN users are trying to access the Internet at the same time. In most cases, you have a permanently assigned IP address on a LAN.

Fiber Optics   An organization that needs a high bandwidth might use a T1 line (which stands for trunkline) for Internet access. Internet service providers, who are responsible for maintaining backbones, need even faster connections, such as a T3 line. T1 and T3 lines use fiber-optic cables that are capable of handling huge amounts of data. This technology is popular for Internet backbones and LANs.

To get an idea of just how fast a modern backbone is, compare the speed of an old-fashioned dial-up modem to the speed of different types of fiber-optic lines. At one time, home computers came equipped with a 56K modem, which could transmit about 50,000 bits per second, or approximately 5,000 characters per second. The following table illustrates the amount of data that can travel across DSL, cable, and fiberoptic lines. A computer's connection speed can be found in the Network and Sharing Center in Windows or the Network Utility on Mac OS.

Common Connection Problems

There are some common problems that can interfere with an Internet connection. Typical problems include loose connections, a power outage, interference from other devices, blocking from a firewall, and ISP service problems. You can try basic troubleshooting steps to isolate and solve the problem, including resetting devices, reconnecting cables, and temporarily turning off the firewall.

Type of Line	Transmission Speed
ADSL (Asymmetric digital subscriber line)	16 to 640 kilobits per second sending data 1.5 to 9 megabits per second receiving data
SDSL (Symmetric digital subscriber line)	Up to 3 megabits per second
T1	1.544 megabits per second
T3	43.232 megabits per second

Getting Online

After you have access to the Internet, you must select a way to get online. Choices include Internet service providers and online services.

Internet Service Providers An **Internet service provider (ISP)** is a company that provides a link from your computer to the Internet. For a fee, an ISP provides its subscribers with software, a password, an access phone number, and a username. A **username** identifies who you are when you access the Internet. An ISP does not guide you through the Internet—it only provides an easy-to-use connection to it. You can use either a local ISP or a national ISP.

Online Services An online service connects your computer to the Internet. **Online services** are businesses that provide tools to help you **navigate**, or move to different parts of, the Internet. Online services are not the Internet. These services are now almost all free. When you register for them on the Internet, special software is downloaded onto your computer. The software makes the connection to the service, which then guides you through content and activities. Three popular online service providers are Microsoft Network (MSN), AOL, and Google. The functions of online service providers, Internet portals, and search engines, which you'll read about soon, will likely overlap. Also, the term online service provider has broadened to include any business that offers services over the Internet—from Amazon.com to banks offering online banking to entertainment sites, like youtube.com.

You can use your operating system to check whether or not your computer is correctly connected to the Internet. On most systems, a network or connectivity icon displays on the status bar. If there's a problem, it might be marked with an X or an exclamation mark. Right-click the icon to display a menu of options, including Troubleshoot problems and Open Network and Sharing Center.

You can also check connectivity by opening your browser and trying to access a site such as Google or Amazon. If you can access the site, your computer is connected to the network.

Figure 27.2.1 Microsoft Network (MSN) is a popular online service provider with millions of subscribers.

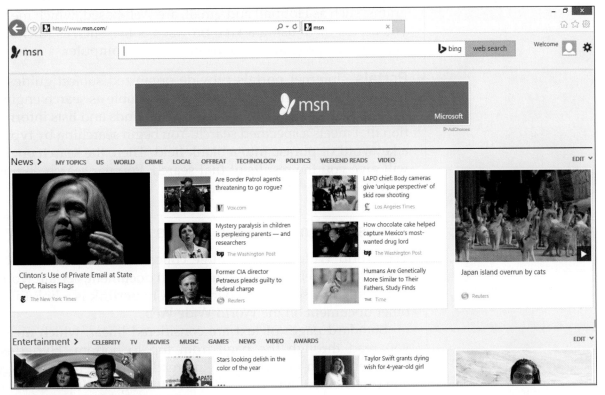

Microsoft Network, Microsoft Corporation.

Comparing Internet Services

Objectives

- Identify and describe types of Internet services.
- Summarize how to access information on the Web.
- Analyze the usefulness of e-mail in daily living.
- Explain File Transfer Protocol.
- Discuss issues related to transferring files.

As You Read

Identify Main Idea/Details Use a main idea/detail chart to identify the main idea and details of popular Internet services as you read.

Key Terms

- download
- e-mail
- file compression
- hyperlink
- hypertext
- portal
- search engine
- uniform resource locator (URL)
- upload
- virus
- Web browser

Internet Services

When you send an **e-mail** message to a friend, you use one kind of Internet service. Browsing the World Wide Web is done through another type of service. Different Internet services are used for accessing the World Wide Web, sending and receiving electronic mail, and conducting file transfers.

Internet Software

The protocols for delivering an e-mail message are not the same as the protocols for displaying a Web page. Typically, there is different software for each Internet service. You use a **Web browser** to view Web pages. Popular Web browsers are Mozilla Firefox, Google Chrome, and Microsoft Internet Explorer. You use a mail program to send and receive e-mail messages. Some mail programs, such as Hotmail and gmail, are Web-based, which means you access them using a Web browser. Some, such as Microsoft Outlook, are programs you install on your computer.

Portals Internet **portals** provide organized subject guides of Internet content, and they are likely to double as search engines as well. A **search engine** is software that finds and lists information that meets a specified search. You begin searching by typing a keyword or phrase into a blank field. Then, the search engine will give you the results of that search. Popular search engines include Google, Yahoo, and Bing.

Accessing Information on the World Wide Web

The World Wide Web is a huge collection of hypertext documents called Web pages. In a **hypertext** document, certain words or pictures can serve as hyperlinks. A **hyperlink** is a link to another document on the World Wide Web.

Standard pages of text are considered linear, which means you read through the page from top to bottom. Hypertext, however, is non-linear. As you are reading through a web page, you can click on hyperlinks to move through multiple layers of information.

Hyperlinks Usually hyperlinks appear underlined, in a different color, or highlighted. Sometimes there are buttons or images that can be clicked. When you move your mouse over a hyperlink, the pointer changes to an icon of a hand. You can click this hyperlink item to be transferred to another document.

URLs When you click a hyperlink, the Web browser retrieves and displays the document connected to that hyperlink. How does this work? Every document has a unique address, called a **uniform resource locator (URL)**, which tells exactly where the document is located on the Internet. A hyperlink instructs the browser to go to the URL for that document.

Electronic Mail

For many Internet users, electronic mail, or e-mail, has replaced traditional mail and telephone services. E-mail is fast and easy. If you organize your e-mail addresses into groups, you can broadcast, or send, a message to a group in just one step.

E-mail Pros and Cons E-mail is not free, and it's not instantaneous. However, you do not pay to send each e-mail, as you would a letter. The cost of your e-mail service is included in the fee you pay your Internet service provider or online service provider. In most cases, it takes minutes or more for an e-mail message to reach its destination. But it costs the same and takes approximately the same amount of time to send a message to someone in your own city as it does to send a message halfway around the world.

Spotlight on...

TIM BERNERS-LEE

In the 1980s, Tim Berners-Lee turned what was a system for keeping track of his random notes into a system for linking the work of scientists anywhere in the world.

Berners-Lee designed the URL, or a scheme for locating Internet addresses; developed HTML, or a language for encoding hypertext; created HTTP, or a system to link hypertext documents; and built the first browser. Few people in history have had a greater impact on the way we communicate than Berners-Lee.

Figure 27.3.1 The File Download - Security Warning from Windows. If you trust the source of the file, you click Run or Save.

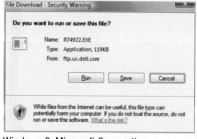

Windows 8, Microsoft Corporation.

Transferring Files

File Transfer Protocol (FTP) lets you transfer files on the Internet. With an FTP client, you can transfer files from an FTP server to your computer in an operation called **downloading**. In **uploading**, you transfer files from the client to the server.

FTP can transfer both text files and binary files. Binary files are program files, graphics, pictures, music or video clips, and documents. Once you've stored a file on an FTP server, you can share the URL so that others can download the file from the server, as well. The file remains on the server until you delete it. When you transfer a file as an e-mail attachment you must save the file on your computer or it will be deleted when you delete the message. E-mail is considered a more secure method, however, because only the recipient of the e-mail message has access to the attached files.

Telnet is an older protocol which lets users access files on remote computers. Telnet has largely been replaced by SSH and SSH2, which are encrypted, and therefore more secure than Telnet.

Of course, when you upload or download files you are transferring them between your computer and an Internet, or cloud, server. Most Web sites have buttons or links to make it easy to upload and download files, or you may use your browser's File > Open and File > Save As commands.

File Transfer Issues

Computer Viruses It's important to exercise caution when downloading files from the Internet, especially program files. Files are commonly used to transmit viruses. A **virus** is a program created to damage computers and networks. The damage caused may be minor or serious, such as altering or destroying data. It's a good idea to check all downloaded files for viruses before saving them. Most antivirus programs will do this for you automatically. You should update your antivirus program regularly to be protected from the newest viruses. The Windows operating system helps by giving a security warning when a download is about to begin. You may want to review the advice provided by clicking the *What's the Risk?* link.

File Compression The larger a file is, the more time it takes to travel over a network. **File compression** is a way of reducing file size so it can travel more quickly over a network. If you are sending a large file, it is important to compress it. It can also be convenient to compress multiple files into one when you are sending them to someone in an e-mail attachment. Some compressed files are set to decompress automatically. Others must be decompressed using decompression software. The most widely used compression software for a Windows system is WinZip®. Macintosh computers use a program called StuffIt™ to compress files and a utility called StuffIt Expander to decompress files.

Use the Vocabulary

Directions: *Match each vocabulary term in the left column with the correct definition in the right column.*

_____ **1.** Internet
_____ **2.** Internet client
_____ **3.** Internet service provider
_____ **4.** username
_____ **5.** search engine
_____ **6.** portal
_____ **7.** hyperlink
_____ **8.** uniform resource locator
_____ **9.** download

a. highlighted text or graphic in a Web site that directs browser to another URL

b. software that finds and lists information that matches criteria

c. computer that requests services from a server

d. identification while on the Internet

e. address of documents on the Web

f. vast network of connected computers

g. a company that provides access to the Internet

h. to transfer a file from a server to a client

i. Internet service that provides a guide to Internet content

Check Your Comprehension

Directions: *Complete each sentence with information from the chapter.*

1. A network that covers a large area is called a(n) _____.

2. The three main parts of the Internet are _____, servers, and protocols.

3. The two main groups responsible for inventing the Internet are the U.S. military and _____ .

4. A(n) _____ is the least expensive way to access the Internet.

5. _____ are businesses that provide special software to guide users through Internet content and activities.

6. A(n) _____ enables someone to search for a Web site with a keyword.

7. In a(n) _____ document, certain words or pictures serve as hyperlinks.

8. File _____ is a way of reducing file size.

9. A(n) _____ is used to view Web pages.

10. You can send a(n) _____ to someone by attaching it to an e-mail message.

 **Think Critically**

Directions: *Answer the following questions.*

1. Why did the U.S. Department of Defense begin to research computer networking and communications?

2. Why do you think it is important to think critically about the accuracy and validity of information you find on the Internet?

3. Why might someone use an online service rather than an Internet service provider?

4. Compare and contrast methods such as e-mail, telnet, ftp, and a browser, by which information may be accessed and transmitted over the Internet.

5. Explain problems that might interfere with network connections. Select one of the problems and describe the troubleshooting steps you would take to solve the problem.

Extend Your Knowledge

Directions: *Choose and complete one of the following projects.*

A. Because the Internet is so easily accessible, it is important to learn how to protect yourself when you are online. With permission from your teacher, conduct research using the Internet to compile a list of Web safety tips. Be sure to evaluate the information you find and only use that which is accurate, relevant, and reliable. Include information about any acceptable use policy your school may have. Publish your findings, with permission from your teacher, on your school's Web site.

B. With your teacher's permission, research and evaluate the wireless standards, protocols, and procedures for configuring a wireless device to a network. If possible, set up and configure a network—such as a home network—using standard protocols. Describe the experience to a partner or to the class.

C. With permission from your teacher, in small groups, conduct online research using keyword and Boolean logic strategies to learn what kinds of Internet access are available in your area. Find out how much the services cost and the benefits of each. If possible, get information from companies competing for the same services so you can compare prices. Compile your research in a chart. Then, summarize your findings as a class.

Using the Internet

Expanding Our Horizons Are you interested in Japanese animation? Hiking trails in the Australian Outback? Sending pictures of your family to a pen pal in another country? Each day more resources are available on the Internet. The ability to send data faster and faster allows people to more easily share ideas, information, and entertainment with people all over the world.

Every day more people connect to the Internet, using whatever form of technology is available to them. As demand for Internet access increases, even remote areas of the globe will be able to connect to the Internet and contribute to the ever-changing, diverse collection of information and services that can be found there.

Chapter Outline

Internet Structure

Objectives

- Compare and contrast the Internet and the telephone system.
- Sequence how information travels through the hierarchy of networks on the Internet.
- Summarize the advantages of a cross-platform network

As You Read

Identify Key Information Use a concept web to help you identify six key phrases to describe what the Internet is as you read.

🔑 Key Terms

- cross-platform
- platform

Organization of the Internet

You can pick up a phone, dial a number, and, within a few seconds, communicate with any other person on a phone connected to the telephone system. This is similar to the Internet, in that any computer can communicate with any other computer on the network.

Internet Versus Telephones The Internet, however, does work on different principles than the phone system does. Rather than a telephone number, every computer on the Internet has an Internet address, also called an IP address. It can contact any other computer on the Internet by "dialing" the other computer's address.

Another difference is that the Internet works on packet-switching technology rather than the circuit-switching technology of the telephone system.

Real-World Tech

The Internet of Things Today the Internet affects much more than just computers. Smart objects are everyday objects that are connected to the Internet. Your phone, television, car, and even household appliances may be connected to the Internet. For example, you can install a smart thermostat in your home and then set the temperature using an app on a tablet or smart phone. The connection of all these devices to the Internet is called the "Internet of Things."

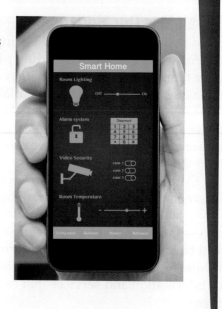

Internet Infrastructure

When you use your computer to connect to the Internet, the computer is called a client. A client uses a browser to request access to a Web page stored on an Internet server computer. Your request travels by local connections to your Internet service provider's (ISP) local point of presence (POP). From there, your ISP sends your request to a regional backbone, which uses high-speed lines that connect your city to a larger metropolitan area. Your request then travels to a network access point, or NAP.

On the Internet, dozens of large ISPs connect with one another at NAPs in various cities. Trillions of bytes of data flow between the individual networks at these points. This is how your computer at home connects to another computer in a completely different region.

Cross-Platform Network

One amazing thing about the Internet is that you can exchange information with computers that are different from your own. When you connect to the Internet, you may connect to an Internet server on a Macintosh, a Windows PC, a Linux PC, a UNIX machine, or a mainframe computer.

Connections

Science Vinton Cerf, one of the developers of TCP/IP protocol, is working with scientists on parcel transfer protocol, which will send data to other planets and spacecraft. It is hoped that this new technology will help pave the way for manned missions to Mars by 2099. The plan for wiring Earth to Mars includes using an existing international antenna system, a six-satellite constellation around Mars, and a new protocol for transferring data between the planets.

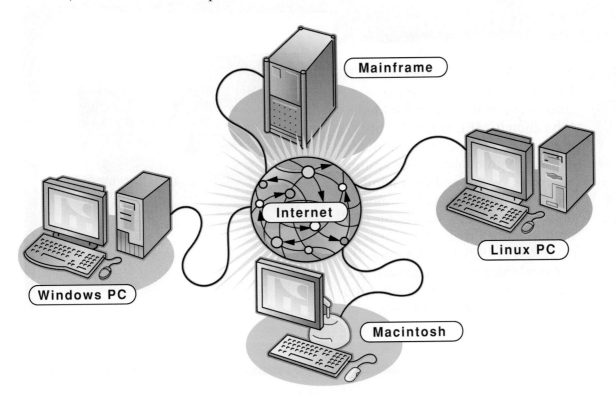

Figure 28.1.1 All kinds of computers can communicate with one another through the Internet, as long as they use the same protocols.

In the United States, one employment benefit on the rise is telecommuting, or working from home on a computer.

Think About It!

Networks are needed to allow employees to work efficiently between their home and their office. Which type(s) of networks listed below would a telecommuter likely use to conduct work from home?

➤ LAN

➤ WAN

➤ Internet

A **platform** is a kind of computer that uses a certain type of processor and operating system, such as an Intel-based Windows PC. Software or hardware is said to have **cross-platform** capability when it can run the same way on more than one platform. When you are using the Internet, you don't know which type of computer platform you are accessing, and it doesn't matter. This is because all computers on the Internet use TCP/IP protocols. As a result, they all look and behave the same way online, regardless of their platform.

Compatibility   Cross-platform compatibility is one of the major reasons for the increasing popularity of private intranets. Many organizations, such as schools, use computers that run on different platforms. They may use computers running the Macintosh operating system in one part of the school and computers running Windows in another. Yet, they still need to share information. After the computers are connected with the Internet's TCP/IP protocols, the computers can exchange data and even control one another's operations. For instance, someone could create a file on a Macintosh computer and then send it to a printer connected to a computer running Windows.

Spotlight on...

KATHRYN C. MONTGOMERY

Dr. Montgomery is one of the cofounders of the Center for Media Education (CME). This nonprofit organization focuses on creating a safe and high-quality online culture for young people and their families. Montgomery's work helps frame national public policy, such as the Children's Online Privacy Protection Act (COPRA) of 1998. COPRA states that personal information requested of children under 13 years of age online must be limited and necessary.

Accessing Data on the Internet

Objectives

- Distinguish between Internet Protocol addresses and domain names.
- Explain how the domain names are organized.
- Identify the different parts of a URL.
- Describe how to locate the owner of a domain name.

As You Read

Outline Information   Use an outline to organize information about how the Internet works as you read.

Accessing Data

The Internet has revolutionized access to data. Anyone with an Internet connection can find information on virtually any topic. Many local governments insure access to all citizens by making Internet access available at public locations such as libraries. That means even those who are disabled or disadvantaged have the same access as everyone else.

Requesting Data on the Internet

To understand how a data request is sent on the Internet, it might be helpful to compare the process to taking a road trip. Recall that when you request a Web page through your Web browser, the request travels by local connections—like streets in a town—to your ISP's local POP. From there, your ISP sends your request to a regional backbone—a type of data highway.

Your Web page request then travels to a NAP, which is like a freeway. As your request nears its destination, it moves off the information freeway. It travels back through other regional highways and local roads until its trip is complete and the Web page you requested is displayed on your computer screen.

Domain Names

Each computer that connects to the Internet has to be uniquely identified. To do this, every computer is assigned a four-part number separated by periods called the **Internet Protocol (IP) address**. For example, the IP address for your computer might be 123.257.91.7. The administrator of the network to which your computer connects assigns your IP address. You can locate your computer's IP address by looking at its network settings.

🔑 Key Terms

- domain name
- domain name system
- Internet Protocol (IP) address
- Software as a Service (SAAS)
- top-level domain
- WHOIS database

Alex Jarrett started a nonprofit organization called the Degree of Confluence Project to have people visit each of the latitude and longitude markers in the world. They then send his company pictures of each location to post on the Web.

Think About It!

If a company has Internet access, it can start its own Web site. But first it has to get a domain name. Which top-level domain name(s) listed below do you think would be most appropriate for Jarrett's company?

➤ .org
➤ .gov
➤ .edu
➤ .com
➤ .mil

A **domain name** identifies one or more IP addresses and is used to locate information on the Internet. For example, an Internet server computer's domain name might be whitehouse.gov, but its numeric IP address might be 206.166.48.45. The domain name and the IP address are simply two ways to identify the same computer on the Internet.

Top-Level Domains   Every domain name has a suffix that tells which type of organization registered the name. The most common domains are .com (commercial), .edu (education), .org (nonprofit organizations), .gov (government), .mil (military), and .net (network organizations). These are called **top-level domains**. New top-level domain names such as .biz (business) and .museum (arts and culture) are coming online to meet the growing demand for new classifications. Top-level domain country codes are two letter codes that identify the country where the site is located. For example, us is the country code for the United States.

Acquiring a Domain Name   A special server called a **Domain Name System (DNS)** server matches the domain name to the correct IP address. To get a domain name, you or your ISP must contact a registering organization, which then contacts InterNIC. InterNIC is a service organization that maintains a central database of domain names in the United States. Other countries maintain their own network information centers.

When you register a domain name, you pay a fee to keep it in the database of domain names. If you do not pay the renewable registration fee, the domain becomes available for someone else to register in his or her name.

Figure 28.2.1 .com might be the most common top-level domain, but there are many others, including .edu and .org.

Domain Names and WHOIS Searches

Within the Domain Name System, each computer on the Internet must have a unique name, or the browser would not know to which server to go.

The InterNIC The organization responsible for maintaining the list of the registered domain names is the InterNIC. When you register a domain name, you pay an accredited registrar to insert an entry into a directory of all the domain names and their corresponding computers on the Internet. An Accredited Registrar Directory provides a listing of accredited domain name registrars available on the InterNIC Web site.

The central database of domain names is called the **WHOIS database.** You can look up information about the owner and servers of a certain domain on this database.

Software as a Service

In the past, people and companies would purchase software programs and install them on their local computers or networks. Now, more and more applications are stored on cloud servers and can be accessed on the Internet. Instead of purchasing a program outright, you purchase a subscription that allows you to log in and use the software. Accessing applications this way is called **Software as a Service (SAAS).** With SAAS, the applications are kept on the software company's network instead of on the client computer, leaving more storage space available on the client. The software company maintains the software and keeps it up-to-date. Customers can log in from any location making it possible for them to work at the office, at home, or while traveling.

Career Corner

Branding Consultant Branding consultants work with businesses to define their image to their target customers. Everything from the colors on a logo to the domain name communicate a company's personality to a customer. Brand consultants use both research and creativity in the building of a company's brand.

Lesson 28–3

Internet Communications

Objectives

- Identify different ways to communicate online.
- Identify advantages and disadvantages of electronic communication.
- Discuss the future of the Internet.

🔑 Key Terms

- alt newsgroup
- blog
- channel
- chat room
- hierarchy
- instant messaging (IM)
- Internet 2 (I2)
- Internet Relay Chat (IRC)
- newsgroup
- podcast
- social networking
- Usenet
- Web feed
- wiki

As You Read

Organize Information   Use a spider map to help you organize key details about Internet services as you read.

Communicating Online

The Internet is fast becoming the main means by which people communicate over distances. If you have an Internet connection and an account with a communication service, there are many ways to communicate. Communication can be formal, through e-mailing and **newsgroups**, or it can be more informal, through online chat channels or forums, instant messaging, and social networking sites.

Newsgroups

The **Usenet** is a discussion system computer users can access through the Internet. It has thousands of newsgroups on many subjects and contains messages newsgroup users have posted. Usenet newsgroups are organized into categories called **hierarchies**.

These hierarchies are divided into subcategories: 1) standard newsgroups or world newsgroups, which feature high-quality discussions on any topic; 2) biz newsgroups, which are devoted to discussing commercial uses of the Internet; and 3) **alt newsgroups**, which can be created by anyone to discuss a specific topic and often feature odd or offensive discussions. Usenet servers are not required to carry alt newsgroups.

Online Television

Most people access television over the air or by using cable or satellite services, but a growing number are using the Internet. Some smart TVs come equipped for Internet access, and others use devices such as Roku, Inc.'s Roku or Apple, Inc.'s Apple TV to provide streaming services. Usually, you pay a subscription fee to access channels, and then you can watch the programs you want, when you want. Some web sites also stream television programs and broadcasting companies often post TV shows online for free after they have aired.

Communicating on the Internet

There are a variety of ways to communicate with others online, ranging from instant messaging with friends to expressing yourself on social networking sites and blogs, and sharing photos and video clips.

Internet Relay Chat (IRC) is an Internet service that enables users to join chat groups, called **channels**, and enter into live, or real-time, conversations. In addition to IRC channels, most ISPs offer chat forums as well. Chat channels can also be found within online video games. Sometimes **chat rooms** are not friendly places, but they are not entirely without rules. Every channel has a moderator who can remove a sender from the channel for any reason. The standards of behavior differ from channel to channel, so it is best to practice respectful online behavior.

Instant Messaging (IM) **Instant messaging** is when you send real-time messages to another Internet user. Instant messaging is like a chat room, except you get to choose your chat partners. For most young people, instant messaging, or chatting, along with texting on their cell phones, has replaced phone calls as the quickest, most satisfying way to communicate in real time. Chat features are built into programs and Web sites. Google+ Hangout and Google Chat allow you to instant message while logged in to your Google+ account, Windows comes with Windows Live Messenger, AOL Instant Messenger (AIM) is available from AOL, Inc., and Facebook has a messaging window. There are even apps such as ICQ that notify you when your contacts are online.

Photo and Video Sharing Photo and video sharing is using the Internet to send digital photos or video clips to another Internet user. These photos and videos can be shared privately or publicly on Web sites and apps, such as Instagram and Youtube.

Social Networking Sites such as Facebook and LinkedIn let you connect family, friends, and business colleagues by linking your own personal profile to those of others. Most social networking sites are free, although you have to register an account. On Facebook, as with other social networking sites, you can tailor your profile to add as much or as little personal information as possible, as well as uploading photos, posting messages, and linking to other sites. Twitter, another popular social networking site, lets you create 140-character messages, called "tweets," to keep others up-to-date on what you are doing or thinking about. You upload messages to the Twitter.com Web site, where they can be read by anyone who is interested. When using social networking you must remember that everything you do and say is online for others to see. Always think about what you are going to write before you post it. You do not want to post content that may embarrass you or hurt another's feelings.

Podcasts A **podcast** is an audio or video file that is created for downloading to an iPod or an MP3 player. Many radio stations create podcasts of popular programs or parts of them. College teachers create podcasts and upload them to a special Apple Web site called iTunes U or to other Web locations. Students can download the podcasts to their iPods or MP3 player, or they choose to listen to them on their own computers.

Technology @ School

Some services safeguard students on the Internet at school. For example, some allow teachers to create password-protected Web pages that include secure chat rooms and discussion forums.

Think About It!

Participating in online communities can be a great way to gain information, but it is not without risks. Circle the suggestions below that can help you to stay safe online.

➤ Chat only on monitored channels.

➤ Refuse to give out any personal information.

➤ Practice good netiquette (Internet etiquette).

Web Feed A **Web feed** is a service that automatically downloads Web page content that a user has signed up for. The content may include the text of news or opinions or audio/video files. A site that offers a Web feed has a symbol such as RSS to indicate that a feed is available. When a browser detects a feed on a Web page, it may also display a special Web feed icon. When you click on the button, the site asks the user to indicate how and where the content is to be downloaded.

Blogs and Wikis A **blog**—or Weblog—is a type of Web page diary. People create blogs to share their thoughts and opinions. A blog is stored on a Web server, like a Web page, and the owner usually updates it on a regular basis. Anyone with access to the Internet can read the blog. Blogs are not restricted to only text. Photo blogs consist solely of digital photographs. Often, blogs provide a way for readers to comment on the blog content. A **wiki** is a collaborative Web page. Anyone can edit or create content on the page. The most notable wiki is Wikipedia.org, an encyclopedia Web site with user-generated content. It is important to keep in mind that blogs and wikis reflect the opinions of the people who write or edit the content; they may not always be accurate or up-to-date.

Advantages and Disadvantages Electronic communication helps create and maintain bonds between people. It is also available around the clock, making it possible to communicate at any time of day. These same advantages also cause problems. Constant electronic communication can get in the way of face-to-face communication and hurt personal relationships. It also leaves room for misunderstandings. Electronic communication allows for large digital social networks to be formed, introducing people to new ideas and perspective. However, it is important to keep in mind that electronic communication should not be a replacement for real life interactions.

Internet Growth

Over the next decade, millions of new users will connect to the Internet. Can the Internet handle this kind of growth? Internet experts say that improvements must take place to make certain the Internet doesn't become overwhelmed by its own success.

More Internet Addresses IP protocol allows for about 4 billion IP addresses. Surprisingly, that is not enough. One solution lies in a new version of the Internet Protocol called IPv6. However, the problem with this solution is that existing Internet equipment must be modified to work with the new protocol.

More Bandwidth With growing Internet use, new technologies to increase bandwidth must be developed. The **Internet 2 (I2)** project will develop and test high-performance network and telecommunications techniques. These improvements will eventually find their way to the public Internet, allowing faster access for all users.

Use the Vocabulary

Directions: *Match each vocabulary term in the left column with the correct definition in the right column.*

_____ **1.** domain name
_____ **2.** IP address
_____ **3.** social networking
_____ **4.** WHOIS database
_____ **5.** Usenet
_____ **6.** wiki
_____ **7.** Domain Name System
_____ **8.** channel
_____ **9.** platform
_____ **10.** Internet 2 (I2)

a. domain name lookup
b. a special server that matches a domain name to the correct IP address
c. project that tests new network technologies
d. an individual IRC chat group
e. identifies one or more IP addresses and is used to locate information on the Internet
f. virtual communities that offer real-time chatting options
g. hosts thousands of newsgroups
h. a kind of computer that uses a certain type of processor and operating system
i. a four-part number separated by periods used to identify a computer connected to the Internet
j. a webpage where anyone can write or edit content

Check Your Comprehension

Directions: *Complete each sentence with information from the chapter.*

1. After your Web page request goes to your ISP's POP, it goes to a(n) _____.

2. Software or hardware is said to have _____ platform capability when it can run the same way on more than one platform.

3. The _____ domain identifies which type of organization registered the domain name.

4. _____ is a service organization that maintains a central database of domain names in the United States.

5. When you use your computer to connect to the Internet, the computer is called a(n) _____.

6. The _____ of the network to which your computer connects assigns your IP address.

7. In the Domain Name System, each name has to be _____.

8. You can search the _____ database for the owner and servers of a particular domain.

9. By using _____ people can effectively create their own personal chat channels.

10. In the future, the Internet will need to increase bandwidth and create more _____.

 **Think Critically**

Directions: *Answer the following questions.*

1. How is licensing software with SAAS beneficial for software programmers?

2. Compare and contrast the telephone system with the Internet.

3. Why is it important to have no duplication of domain names? How is this goal accomplished?

4. What are advantages and disadvantages of communicating through social media?

5. How might the increasing popularity of the Internet become a problem?

Extend Your Knowledge

Directions: *Choose and complete one of the following projects.*

A. With your teacher's permission, use Internet research, including keyword searches, and personal observation to find out about some interesting technology-related projects students are conducting in schools across the country. Create a Web page describing these projects. Add links to any relevant sites. Publish the Web site on the Internet. Be sure to check the page on multiple computer platforms to be sure it displays properly and adjust it, if necessary.

B. Work in small groups to simulate a chat room. Hold a conversation about a topic you are studying by writing messages to each other in random order on one sheet of paper. Pass the paper to anyone who has something to say. Do not speak, and only write one message at a time. After five minutes, discuss your experiences. What advantages and disadvantages did you find to this form of communication?

C. With your teacher's permission, use the Internet to locate a Web site with a URL that includes an international country code. Copy the URL to a word-processing document. Write a brief paragraph explaining the parts of the URL, including the country code. Share your paragraph with a partner or the class.

World Wide Web Basics

chapter 29

A Global Source of Information   Think about a comprehensive source of information—one that grows by thousands of new documents every day. Such a resource would contain a wealth of information.

Actually, you don't have to suppose such a resource into existence. It already exists—it's the World Wide Web. You can turn to the World Wide Web to check out products, get help with schoolwork, find out about current events, and do many more tasks.

However, along with offering a lot of wonderful information, the Web is also home to some inaccurate and potentially harmful information. It is up to you to evaluate the information you find on the Web.

Chapter Outline

 Lesson 29–1

Understanding the Web

 Lesson 29–2

Web Browsing

 Lesson 29–3

Introducing E-commerce

Understanding the Web

Objectives

- Explain the creation of the World Wide Web.
- Contrast the Internet and the World Wide Web.
- Explain the parts of a URL.

As You Read

Organize Information Use a summary chart to help organize details as you read.

🔑 Key Terms

- Cascading Style Sheets (CCS)
- graphical browser
- home page
- Hypertext Markup Language (HTML)
- hypertext transfer protocol (HTTP)
- style sheet
- tag
- Web page
- Web server
- Web site
- World Wide Web

Creating the Web

As early as 1980, a few people were trying to connect documents stored on different computers by means of a private network or the Internet. These connected documents, it was thought, could someday create a "web" of information that would be instantly available to anyone.

In 1989, Tim Berners-Lee developed a way to retrieve one computer's Internet address while working on another computer. (See the Spotlight on . . . feature on page 385.) The resulting programs and protocols led to the creation of the World Wide Web, which is now a widely used part of the Internet. Berners-Lee made this new technology freely available to everyone and pleaded with other researchers to help develop ways to expand the **World Wide Web**, or the Web, as it is commonly called.

In 1992, Marc Andreesen and other students at the National Center for Supercomputing Applications (NCSA) developed a Web browser called Mosaic®. Recall that a browser is a program that enables users to navigate the Web and locate and display Web documents. Mosaic was the first **graphical browser** that could display graphics as well as text.

In 1994, Andreesen introduced Netscape Navigator. A year later, Microsoft released Internet Explorer, and that same year the Web was opened up to public and commercial use. Navigator and Explorer soon became the most popular Web browsers.

The Internet and the Web

Many people use the terms *Internet* and *World Wide Web* as synonyms. In fact, the World Wide Web is just one part of the Internet. Recall that every computer on the Internet has a unique IP, or Internet Protocol, address and that every document on the Web has a unique address, too, called its uniform resource locator, or URL.

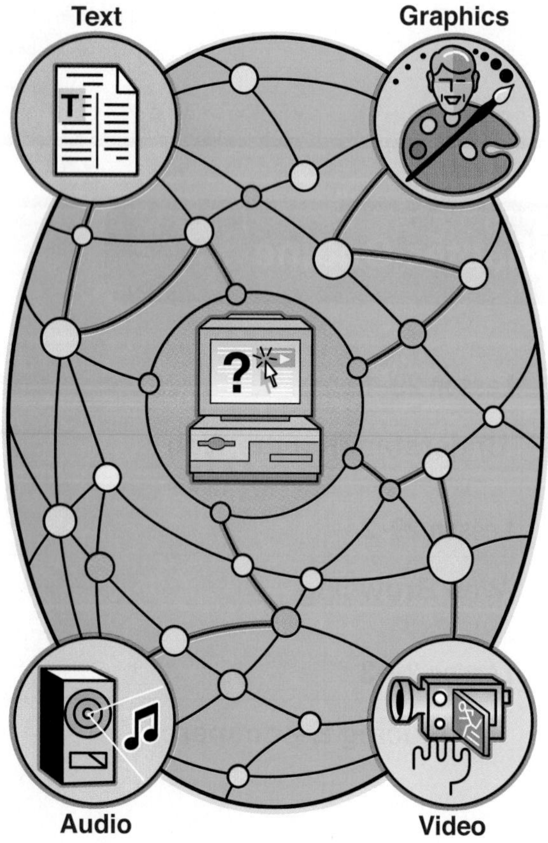

Text **Graphics** **Audio** **Video**

Figure 29.1.1 The Web gets its name from the web of connections it creates between computers all over the planet.

Like e-mail, newsgroups, and file transfer, the Web is a service supported by the Internet. Although these services share the Internet and many of its resources, each is different, with its own set of protocols and applications.

A Web of Documents The World Wide Web is a huge collection of documents linked by hypertext. Writers format documents and add the hyperlinks by using **Hypertext Markup Language**, or **HTML**. People all over the world create and format Web documents by using standardized HTML codes called **tags**. These documents are saved, or "published" to a server on the Internet. When you use a Web browser program to access a Web document, each portion—text, images, sound, or animation—appears with its intended formats.

Formatting the Web The graphical appearance of web sites is one of the key features of the World Wide Web. Web designers take care to make the pages appealing and easy to read. Every page on a web site may have a consistent appearance, such as the background color or the size and font of the titles.

Instead of setting HTML tags for every element on every page, programmers use **style sheets.** A style sheet is a separate document that describes rules used to define how the elements of the pages in a web site will look. **Cascading Style Sheets,** or **CCS,** are style sheets that are used for HTML. CCS are called *cascading* because they describe a hierarchy of style rules. Rules with a higher priority will be applied over rules with a lower priority. This insures that the formatting will be consistent.

Career Corner

Web Designer Web design is a growing field. Web designers consult for individuals and small businesses, work for companies with a strong presence on the Web, and plan and teach programs in Web design. Strong candidates in this field develop skills in fine art, such as photography, filmmaking, and animation; computer graphics; digital video and audio; design software; and design languages such as HTML or Java.

Spotlight on...

MARC ANDREESEN

Web browsers existed before Marc Andreesen's work on linking documents. The graphical browsers he helped develop, however, were a real breakthrough. With graphical browsers, Web documents could include illustrations, photos, animation, sounds, and videos. Through his work on Mosaic and Netscape Navigator, Andreesen greatly contributed to the growth of the World Wide Web.

Technology @ Work

Companies and organizations try to obtain a domain name that will easily lead people to their Web site's home page. The address of specific pages is not as important because the home page can provide navigation aids, such as a row or column of subject buttons.

Think About It!

Below are the parts of the URL of the popular PBS (Public Broadcasting System) program Nature. Sequence from 1 (first) to 4 (last), the order in which the parts of the URL should be listed.

➤ www.pbs.org

➤ /index.html

➤ http://

➤ wnet/nature

Understanding Web Sites

A **Web page** is a document on the Web. A **Web site** is a collection of related pages, which are connected using hyperlinks. You click a hyperlink to browse, or move, from one page to another. When you type a URL or click a link in your Web browser, it sends a request to the computer on the Internet that contains the page identified by the URL. That computer is called a **Web server**. It stores Web pages and responds to requests from Web browsers. When the server receives your request, it sends the document to your computer, and your browser displays the page on your screen.

Most Web sites have a primary page called the **home page** or index page which appears when you first enter the site's URL. A URL can also identify a specific page on a Web site.

Protocol   The first part of a URL specifies the protocol required to access the document. Web documents use http://, indicating that the file should be retrieved using **hypertext transfer protocol (HTTP)**. Some URLs might have other protocols, such as ftp, which shows that the file should be retrieved with file transfer protocol. Another protocol, telnet, allows for access to remote computers. Still another protocol, mailto, lets you click an e-mail address link on a Web page to automatically start your e-mail client with the address entered in the To: field.

Domain Name   The next part of a URL, such as www.fbi.gov, is the domain name of the server that stores the Web site. This part of the URL usually takes you to the site's home page.

Path   The remainder of a URL, if any, defines the path to the document's location on the Web server. Like any computer, a Web server stores files in folders, so the path lists the folder and subfolders, if any, containing the desired document. Thus, a URL such as http://www.fbi.gov/employment/ identifies a folder named "employment" on the site's Web server.

Resource File Name   At the end of a URL, you may see the name of a file—the specific Web resource for which you are looking. The resource may be an HTML document or a Web page, a video clip, a text file, or another type of resource. The file name extension identifies the type of resource.

Figure 29.1.2 The parts of a URL.

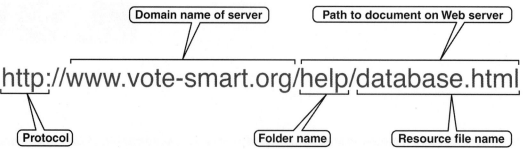

Web Browsing

Objectives

- Explore Web navigation tools.
- Describe how to customize a Web browser.
- Explain the difference between a subject guide and a search engine.

As You Read

Organize Information   Use an outline to organize ways of accessing and evaluating Web pages as you read.

Browsing the Web

You use a Web browser application to display Web information on your computer. Most Web browsers, including the popular Mozilla Firefox, Google Chrome, and Microsoft Internet Explorer, share some common features. By default, most browsers display Web pages in separate tabs so you can have more than one page open at a time. You can enable or disable this feature, if you want. They also share common navigation tools. Like any application, browsers and Web sites use mouse clicks and double-clicks to select options and links. With a touchscreen, there may be a delay before the browser registers the click. Some Web sites program in a hover action so when you hover, or rest the mouse over an object, it triggers an event such as a pop-up window.

Navigation Buttons   Located on the browser's toolbar, **navigation buttons** let you perform certain operations quickly. When you click Refresh or Reload, the browser again downloads the page you are viewing. When you click the **Back button**, the browser reloads the previous page. The **Forward button** moves ahead to pages previously viewed before Back was activated.

Address Box   If you type a URL in the Address box and press Enter, the browser will display the Web page located at that URL in a new tab. In some browsers, if you type a search phrase and press Enter, the browser displays a page of search results. Click a link in the search results to open that page.

Key Terms

- Back button
- cookie
- Forward button
- knowledge base
- navigation buttons
- tracking

Figure 29.2.1 All popular browsers feature navigation buttons, an Address box, and tools for creating a list of frequently visited Web sites.

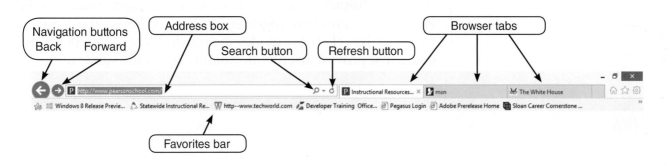

Navigation buttons Back Forward | Address box | Search button | Refresh button | Browser tabs

http://www.pearsonschool.com/

Favorites bar

Favorites, Bookmarks, and History   The Favorites feature in Internet Explorer and the Bookmarks feature in Google Chrome and Mozilla Firefox let you create a list of frequently visited Web pages. Then, rather than retyping the URL, you can return to any bookmarked or favorite page by clicking its name in the list. Some browsers let you sync your bookmarks across all of your devices. You can delete a page from the Bookmark or Favorites list when you no longer need it. Browsers also track your browsing history. Display the History list to quickly find pages you visited in the past. Clear the History list to remove a record of sites you have visited.

Customizing a Web Browser

Browsers start with default settings, but usually you can customize the settings to suit your preferences. Most customization options can be found in a dialog box such as Internet Options in Internet Explorer.

Changing the Start Page   You can customize your browser by making any Web page your start page. You can also set your browser to display a blank page when it launches, so you don't have to wait for a start page to load before you begin to work.

Security and Privacy   You can select different levels of security and privacy. For example, set a high security level to disable all Internet file downloads, or a high privacy level to block **cookies**—small files that store identification information—from being automatically stored on your computer. Most browsers include options for preventing **tracking**, which is when a Web site gathers information about your Web browsing activity.

Organizing Favorites or Bookmarks   You can use the browser's organization tools to create folders and subfolders to organize your preferred links. You can also add and remove sites to your Favorites or Bookmark list.

Finding Information on the Web

The Web is an amazing tool for acquiring information, but because it is so vast, it can be hard to locate the information you need. Subject guides and search engines can help.

Subject Guides   Many Web sites offer subject guides to the Web, pages grouped together under headings like Careers, News, or Travel. These guides include links only to articles and pages that provide useful information about the subject.

Knowledge Base A **knowledge base** is a searchable collection or database of information related to a specific subject. For example, a law library might have a knowledge base of law articles, cases, and other relevant information. Companies often maintain a knowledge base of help information that customers can use to solve problems on their own.

Search Engines A search engine is a program or Web site designed to search the Web looking for documents that match specified criteria, such as keywords. In a matter of moments, the search engine displays a list of links to pages that match. General search engines, such as Google, Yahoo, or Bing, search throughout the Web to find matches. Some search engines are customized for a certain topic. For example, the Web site www.fedworld.gov, maintained by the U.S. Department of Commerce, lets you search U.S. government documents.

Some search engines support advanced searches that let you search for files based on file type, size, category, and other properties. For example, you can search for picture files, videos, or music.

Figure 29.2.2 Search engines and search tools help users find information on specific topics.

Bing, Microsoft Corporation.

Introducing E-commerce

Objectives

- Compare and contrast methods of e-commerce.
- Identify reasons for the success of online shopping.
- Discuss how e-postage works to deliver postage across the Internet.

As You Read

Organize Information   Use a spider web to help you organize ways to use e-commerce as you read.

 **Key Terms**

- e-commerce
- online banking

Electronic Commerce

Electronic commerce, or **e-commerce**, is the use of telecommunications networks or the Internet to conduct business. E-commerce is not new; companies have used wide area networks, or WANs, to do business for years.

Thanks to the Internet and affordable computers, e-commerce has become accessible to anyone who has an Internet connection and a Web browser. More and more Internet users are researching products, shopping, opening bank accounts, and trading stocks online. Many businesses realize that they may lose customers if they do not have an online presence.

Online Banking

In **online banking**, customers use a Web browser to access their accounts, balance checkbooks, transfer funds, and pay bills online.

Personal Finance Programs   Programs such as Microsoft Money or Intuit's Quicken® have features that can help you budget your money, analyze your spending habits, balance your checkbook, and make account transactions. One drawback to these programs is that you can access your online account only from the computer on which you keep your Microsoft Money® or Quicken data. Another potential problem is that anyone with access to that computer and your password can view this data.

Web-based Banking   Web-based banking allows users to access their accounts in financial institutions. All the data is stored on the bank's computer, not your own, so you can access your account from any computer that has an Internet connection. You can learn about different types of services and interest rates, transfer funds, check your statements, reconcile your accounts, or even pay bills online. This service allows you to set up accounts for the businesses you want to pay. When you receive a bill in the mail, you log on to your bank account, enter the amount to be paid, and pay online instead of writing a check and mailing the payment.

Online Shopping

When many people think of e-commerce, they think of shopping online. Online shopping has grown in popularity due to security features built into popular Web browsers.

The Buyer's Point of View The World Wide Web is an excellent resource for researching products, services, and prices. At many sites, buyers can read product reviews posted by other buyers. At other sites, they can find vendors and product ratings.

The Seller's Point of View One of the main advantages of online business is low startup cost. For a small investment, a vendor can open a Web storefront and sell products online to a wider variety of customers than one physical location offers.

Amazon.com, for example, was launched by Jeff Bezos in 1995. Rather than visit a bookstore that stocks from 10,000 to 40,000 titles, consumers around the globe can log on to Amazon.com and search a database of millions of titles. What started out as "The Earth's biggest bookstore," has morphed into the Earth's biggest store—period. The Web site not only offers millions of books, music, and movies, but it also sells everything from auto parts, toys, and electronics to cosmetics, prescription drugs, and groceries. In 2010 the company had sales of $13 billion.

Almost anyone with financial resources can set up a checking or savings account at an online bank.

Think About It!

Think about the advantages an online bank account offers. Which statements listed below would be an advantage?

▷ lets you check your account any time
▷ lets you make deposits anytime
▷ helps you avoid math mistakes
▷ helps you plan your spending
▷ prevents overspending

Figure 29.3.1 E-commerce Web sites have benefits for both shoppers and sellers.

Government Web Sites

The United States government makes services available online through web sites using the top-level domain .gov. On government web sites you can find important information about government function and policies. There are government web sites for all levels of government, from the legislative and executive branches of the national government to your state and local governments.

Government agencies have web sites as well. On the Internal Revenue Service's web site you can find information about paying taxes. Through your state's department of motor vehicles website you can find information about registering a car or obtaining a diver's license. There are also sites for other permits and licenses, such as those for hunting or entering national parks.

The United States Postal Service website allows you to renew your Passport and purchase stamps. You can even buy e-stamps that you can print at home, saving a trip to the post office.

Figure 29.3.2 You can take an interactive tour of the White House at www.whitehouse.gov.

Directions: *Match each vocabulary term in the left column with the correct definition in the right column.*

_____ **1.** graphical browser
_____ **2.** HTML
_____ **3.** Web server
_____ **4.** Web page
_____ **5.** Web site
_____ **6.** navigation button
_____ **7.** cookie
_____ **8.** e-commerce
_____ **9.** tracking
_____ **10.** style sheet

a. tool that lets users perform routine operations with a browser
b. a small file that stores identification information
c. computer that houses Web sites and sends documents to users
d. a collection of related documents on the Web
e. document that describes rules used to define how the elements of the pages in a web site will look
f. conducting business through a network on the Internet
g. Web navigation program that shows pictures and text
h. when a Web site gathers information about your Web browsing activity
i. single document on the Web
j. markup language used to format Web documents

Check Your Comprehension

Directions: *Determine the correct choice for each of the following.*

1. Which was the first browser that could display graphics as well as text?
   a. Explorer
   b. Mosaic
   c. Firefox
   d. Chrome

2. Which of the following is NOT part of a complete URL address?
   a. protocol
   b. server
   c. path
   d. author

3. Which of the following browser tools will most easily help you revisit a Web site you enjoyed?
   a. Favorites or Bookmarks
   b. Forward
   c. Refresh or Reload
   d. Address box

4. By which of the following does a search engine search?
   a. URL addresses
   b. Favorites
   c. Bookmarks
   d. keywords

5. Which of the following has contributed the most to the growth of e-commerce?
   a. traditional stores
   b. advanced Web browsers
   c. affordable computers
   d. personal finance programs

6. Which of the following is the language used to create Web pages?
   a. FTP
   b. HTTP
   c. HTML
   d. LINUX

Chapter Review and Assessment

 **Think Critically**

Directions: *Answer the following questions.*

1. Why is the URL of a page describing a particular book available on Amazon.com more detailed than the URL of the company's home page?

2. Explain the difference between the Internet and the World Wide Web.

3. Which Web browser features or tools do you find most useful? Why?

4. Identify the protocol, domain name, path to the document on the server, and the resource file name in the following URL: http://www2.ed.gov/nclb/choice/index.html

5. Explain the purpose of the HTML elements tags, style sheets, and hyperlinks.

Extend Your Knowledge

Directions: *Choose and complete one of the following projects.*

A. Browsers provide other features and functions in addition to those listed in this lesson. For example, as you begin to type an address, most browsers reveal a list of sites you've already visited that begin with the same letters. With your teacher's permission, work with a partner and explore the functions of a browser. Position the mouse over other buttons to see what appears. Click the buttons to see what happens. Visit the online Help feature to find out more about it. Create a chart in a word-processing program and enter your findings.

B. Work with a partner or small group. With your teacher's permission, use a Web browser to view the Web sites of one online-only retailer and retailer that also has stores. Create a chart comparing and contrasting the two sites. Are they visually appealing? Are they easy to navigate and use? Share your chart with another team or the class.

C. The Web has been praised for the wealth of knowledge it provides for users around the world. It is also criticized for the dangers it makes possible and for the temptation it offers some people. With your teacher's permission, conduct online or library research to learn the praises and objections people have for the World Wide Web, and take notes. For your search, use effective Internet search strategies such as keywords and Boolean logic. Be sure to evaluate the information you find and only use it if it is accurate, relevant, and valid. Participate in a debate on the advantages and disadvantages of the resource.

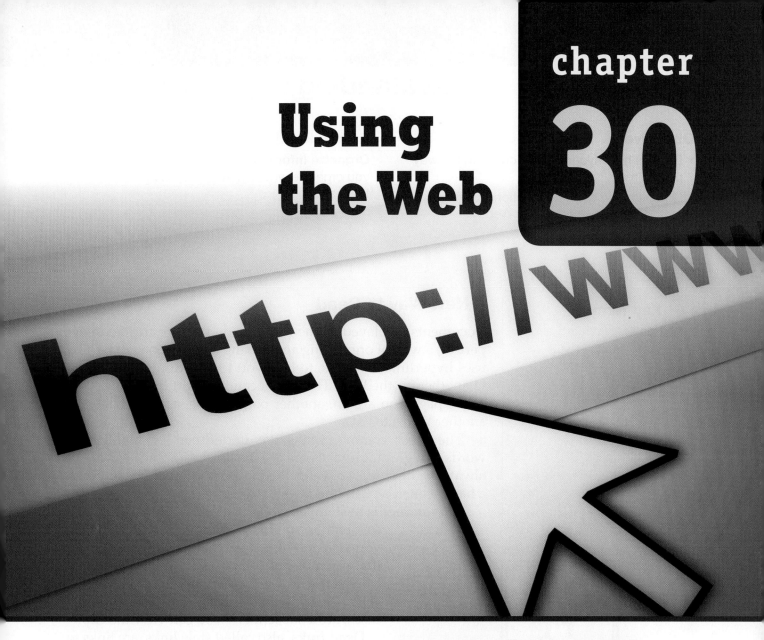

Using the Web

Finding Your Way Around the Web The World Wide Web is fast becoming the preferred source for information on news, weather, products, and much more. Knowing how and where to find this information is the key to successfully using the Web.

As a student, you probably search for information to help with schoolwork, to learn more about things you are interested in, or to decide which products you want to own. Others seek information about careers, about places they might want to live in or travel to, or about the issues in an election. At home, people track their finances, pay bills, and make investments online.

Learning how to find your way around the World Wide Web will prepare you to take advantage of the variety of resources it offers.

Chapter Outline

 Lesson 30–1

Understanding Hypertext

 Lesson 30–2

Designing for the Web

 Lesson 30–3

Working on the Web

 Lesson 30–4

Conducting Business Online

Understanding Hypertext

Objectives

- Discuss how hypertext has changed the way people read.
- Compare and contrast traditional writing methods and writing for the Web.

As You Read

Organize Information Use a table to help you organize what hyperlinks do as you read the lesson.

Key Terms

- add-on
- authentication cookie
- breadcrumbs
- dead link
- hypermedia system
- plug-ins
- Web cache
- widgets

A New Way to Read

Documents displayed on the World Wide Web are created in hypertext, a way of organizing and linking information. Hypertext uses hyperlinks, or links, to take you to and from one location to another on the Web. The new location might be another part of the page you are on, another page on the same Web site, or another Web site.

The most common links are underlined or highlighted words, but graphic images can also be links. Graphic links aren't always highlighted, so watch the mouse pointer. If it changes to a hand icon, it's positioned over a hyperlink.

A **hypermedia system** lets you retrieve multimedia resources, such as sounds and videos. The next time you visit an online news site, look for any icons that resemble videotapes. Clicking one of these icons retrieves a video clip. If you have the right software loaded on your system—and, in some cases, are a subscriber—you can view the clip.

Dead links, also called stale links, are links to pages that have been moved or deleted from the Internet. If you click a dead link, you may see a message that the page no longer exists in that location or you may reach a page that obviously is not one you want. Click the Back button to return to the document you were reading.

A New Way to Write

Well designed Web pages usually are not crammed with information. Authors break their documents into smaller pieces. Then they create

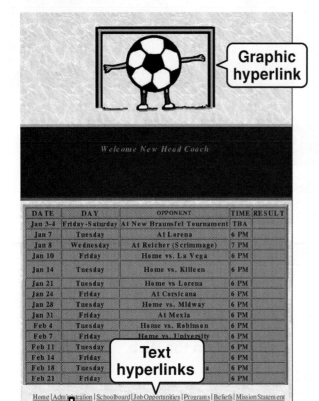

Figure 30.1.1 On a Web page, text and graphics can be used as hyperlinks.

a master document in hypertext that lets them create links to the pieces.

Using Links for Explanation   Hypertext authors don't have to explain everything on one page. Instead, they can define links to other documents containing additional information. If readers want to know more about the topic, they can click the links. When they're done exploring the new page, they can jump right back to the original document.

Using Links for Reference   Have you ever had to write a research paper using footnotes? Web page authors cite references differently. Rather than identifying the source at the bottom of a page, they set up a link to the original source. Likewise, bloggers include links to related pages on their posts.

Browsers Navigate the Web

Hypertext allows for documents to be linked through the Web, but your browser software program is the tool you use to move from one document to the next. In order to help you effectively navigate the Web, your browser has many functions. You can enter an Web page address and the browser displays that page. Most browsers let you search for a page if you don't know the address, and you can use navigation buttons to move forward and back through pages you have been looking at. Browsers also maintain a History list of sites you have visited in the past, and you can create your own Favorites or Bookmarks list of sites you visit frequently.

Spotlight on...

MAKONNEN DAVID BLAKE HANNAH

At age 13, Makonnen David Blake Hannah began acting as an official advisor for Jamaica's Web site. He got the job while visiting the office of the Minister of Technology with his mother. The nation's Web site needed updating and this student came to the rescue.

Makonnen researches ideas, uploads information, and makes suggestions for expanding computer education in Jamaica.

Someday Makonnen would like to have his own computer-game design company. But, he says, "I have many goals. I would like to change the world—especially Jamaica."

Many browsers now also use **breadcrumbs** for navigation. Breadcrumbs are links that help you keep track of what page you are viewing in a Web site or on a server by displaying the path you followed to get there. Usually, breadcrumbs are near the top of the browser window or in the address bar, displaying links back to each previous page you viewed while navigating to the current page. Each link is separated by a greater-than symbol, like this: Home Page > Topic Page > Subtopic Page. You can click any link to go directly to that page.

When you open a Web page, your computer temporarily stores the document in a **web cache** on a storage device, such as a hard disk. The cache allows you to quickly display pages you have already viewed. You might notice that when you click the Back button in your browser, the Web page loads much faster than it did originally. That's because it is being loaded from the cache on your storage disk, not from an Internet server.

Web pages also interact with your computer. Some sites store data on your computer called cookies. One type of cookie, called an **authentication cookie**, is a piece of data that allows your computer to log in to a secure Web site through a secure account.

Many Web sites have interactive elements such as pop-up windows, buttons, and pull-down windows. These components are called **widgets**. You use widgets to perform a function or access a service, such as checking the weather in your home town, or viewing a Twitter feed.

Similar to widgets are **plug-ins**. Plug-ins are mini programs embedded in a Web site to add a feature or function, such as a search engine or video player. One of the most well-known plug-ins is Adobe Flash Player. Plug-ins are complete programs and can even be installed on computers or other devices without a browser. An **add-on**, however, is code designed specifically to add a feature to a Web browser, modify a Web page, or integrate your browser with other services. For example, you might use an add-on to share or sync your list of bookmarked pages across different browsers, or display a button you can use to link directly to your Twitter account. Add-ons may be called browser extensions.

There are some risks with using add-ons. Hackers can use them to track your online movements and even collect personal information. They may also slow down your system performance. In most browsers you can view, enable, and disable add-ons.

Figure 30.1.2 The Manage Add-ons dialog box in Internet Explorer.

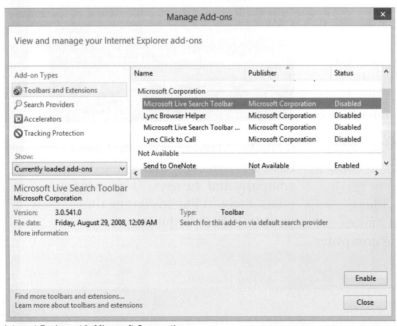

Internet Explorer 10, Microsoft Corporation.

Designing for the Web

Objectives

- Discuss Web page design tools.
- List six major steps in creating a Web site.
- Identify advanced design and browser tools.

As You Read

Organize Information Use an outline to help you organize details about Web page design as you read.

Choosing Web Page Design Tools

To publish documents on the Web, you must use Hypertext Markup Language, or HTML, to format the text and define links to other documents. Each section of text is enclosed in tags that mark it as a heading, a paragraph, a link, and so on. Several kinds of programs allow you to work with HTML tags. You may use other programming languages, like JavaScript, along with HTML while programming a Web site.

Text Editors Programs like Notepad and SimpleText are simple tools you can use to enter both text and codes. Using these programs can be tedious, though. If you want your Web page to include a menu, for example, you have to write the HTML code for each detail of that menu.

HTML Editors These programs feature text editing and an easier way to add HTML tags. Examples include HomeSite™ and BBEdit™. These kinds of programs require the user to do most or all of the HTML coding manually.

Word-Processing Programs You can use a word-processing program to create a Web page. However, it must be a program, such as Microsoft Word 2010, that allows you to save your work as an .htm or .html file.

WYSIWYG Web Page Editors WYSIWYG stands for "What You See Is What You Get." Often called GUI editors, these sophisticated editing programs let you create a page without entering tags yourself. They are almost as easy to use as a word processor and feature many of the same kinds of editing and formatting tools. The difference, however, is that these programs automatically handle the HTML coding for you. You set up the page to look the way you want, including graphics or hyperlinks. Adobe® Dreamweaver® is an example of a program that automates the process of formatting documents for the Web.

Content Management Systems (CMS) These programs let you create blogs and simple Web sites. Sometimes called a Web Management System, they are software or a suite of tools

Key Terms

- applet
- Dynamic Hypertext Markup Language (DHTML)
- storyboard
- Web host
- Webmaster
- WYSIWYG

Technology @ School

Today, many schools have their own Web sites, with a Webmaster who makes the site useful for students, teachers, and families.

Think About It!

If your school or school district has its own Web site, which features listed below does it offer? If your school does not have a Web site, which features listed below do you think would be helpful in your school community?

➤ school calendar
➤ a showcase for student work
➤ bulletin board for school-related discussions
➤ homework schedule for each class
➤ lunch menus
➤ campus tours

Figure 30.2.1 A finished Web page (right) and its underlying HTML code (left).

and applications that allow an individual or organization to create, edit, review, and publish electronic text. Most of these systems provide a Web-based GUI, which allows you to use a Web browser to access the CMS online. Examples of CMS are Tumblr and Wordpress.

Creating a Web Site

Are you interested in having your own Web site? You'll need a **Web host**, a company that provides space on a Web server for Web sites, either for free or for a small monthly fee. The following list describes the main steps for creating a Web site:

1. Plan the Web site. Some designers use a **storyboard** for this. A storyboard is a map or plan that defines the layout, organization, and navigational structure of the site. Think about your purpose and audience. Consider that the purpose of the Web site may influence the domain you will use. For example, if you are creating a Web site for your school, you will probably use an .edu domain. If you are creating a Web site for a business, you will probably use the domain .com.

2. Choose your design tools. Do you want to learn HTML and code the site manually, or can you access software that will walk you through the process?

3. Design and create the Web site. A fast way to build a Web site is to use a pre-coded template that includes titles and navigation bars. You can insert text, graphics, and links based on your storyboard or map.

4. Upload the Web site. To put your Web site on the Internet, you have to upload, or publish, your files to the server of your Web host. This is usually done through a utility program provided by your Web host.

5. Test the Web site. This means viewing your pages in a Web browser to see if they look and work as you intended.

6. Maintain the Web site. Don't just build a Web site and forget about it. You are the **Webmaster**, the person responsible for the look and maintenance of the site.

Web Site Design

The principles of design and color theory used in graphics are also an important part of Web page design. Successful Web pages use design principles such as balance, unity, scale, contrast, and harmony. The entire page should have a unified theme, helping viewers to recognize and respond to the page content. To emphasize different parts of the page, there must be contrast between images, colors, titles, and text. Design elements such as typeface, color, and space help you make sure the text is easy to read. Imagine trying to read green text on a Web page with a black background! It is also important to use the space on the Web page wisely. Design elements such as shape, texture, space, and form help you create a page that is appealing and easy to use.

Web pages should be easy to navigate. That means designers must consider the types of links and where they will be located. The content should be easy to read and links clearly marked. Many sites have a header or footer with important links and information. For example, Home is almost always a link to the site's home or main page. Some site use Navigation bars to list links to the major topics or sections, including a Contact Us page listing the information viewers need to contact the business behind the Web site. Some larger sites include Site Maps, which usually display an alphabetical list of links to all pages in the site, and some have built-in search engines so users can more quickly find the content they are interested in.

Exploring Advanced Tools

To create some of the dramatic effects you see on the Web, designers use advanced design tools and upgraded browsers to display the pages as they intended.

Advanced Design Tools   Designers can use **Dynamic Hypertext Markup Language**, or **DHTML**, to add interactivity to Web pages. You might see butterflies flying across a screen or a personal greeting when you visit an online store. Some designers use JavaScript, a cross-platform programming language, to create **applets**, or small applications for the Web.

Advances like DHTML, JavaScript, and others have made it possible to have internal search engines, animation, downloadable audio and video clips, and streaming audio and video on the Web.

Advanced Browser Tools Web users may like to access splashy features, but their browsers must be able to process them. Browsers can be upgraded with plug-in programs— small, downloadable programs that add new features to an application. RealPlayer® and Windows Media® Player play streaming media. Shockwave®/Flash™ supports interactive documents and animation. Sometimes sites are created all in Adobe® Flash, but the main drawback is that they are not as searchable and take longer to load than sites done in HTML. Finally, Adobe® Acrobat® Reader makes it possible to view documents on-screen in the same format as they appear when printed.

Spotlight on...

WIREDWOODS

WiredWoods is a summer camp program for middle school students designed to foster in them a lifelong interest in technology. Campers learn how to create their own Web pages, use HTML animation, and work with digital cameras. The result? One example is the creative online brochure of the camp created by 12-year-old Tyneshia. Her work includes photos of the camp and streaming video of various activities.

Working on the Web

Objectives

- Demonstrate how to use inclusion or exclusion operators and wildcards to find information on the Web.
- Explore methods to critically evaluate information found on the Web.

As You Read

Identify Information Use an outline to help you identify effective ways to use the Web as you read.

Getting More from Web Searches

Search engines index keywords in Web pages and maintain a database of those words. You can search for Web sites by typing one or more key words in the search engine; the engine then displays a list of pages that contain your keyword or words.

You can improve search effectiveness by using advanced search tools. For example, you could use an exact-phrase search by enclosing the text you want to find in quotation marks. Some search engines accept complete sentences in the form of a question, such as "How do hurricanes form?" You might also try a **Boolean search**, which lets you use special terms and characters called Boolean operators.

Inclusion Operators An **inclusion operator** is a plus sign (+) or the word AND. It indicates that you want to find only pages that contain a match for all the specified words. Searching for *dog+husky* finds only pages that contain both words.

Exclusion Operators An **exclusion operator** is a minus sign (-) or the word NOT. Use it to find pages that contain certain words but not others. Searching for *"dog+husky-sled"* returns a list of pages with the words *dog* and *husky* but not *sled*.

Key Terms

- Boolean search
- hashtag (#)
- inclusion operator
- exclusion operator
- proximity operator
- wildcard

Figure 30.3.1 Conducting a search using the Boolean operators + and -.

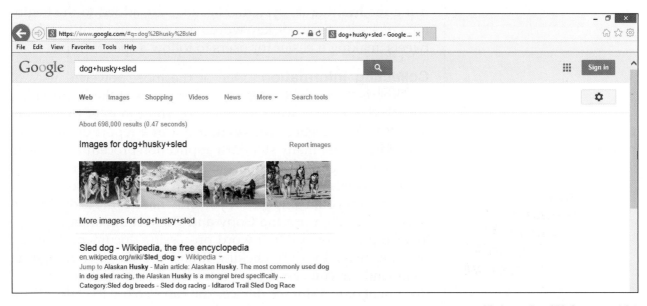

Many younger workers know more about the Web than their older colleagues. Can they use their skills to help their co-workers find information on the Web?

Think About It!

Which of the online tasks listed below could you teach a co-worker to perform?

➤ use a search engine

➤ conduct a keyword search

➤ use a hyperlink

➤ comparison-shop online

➤ make an online purchase

Proximity Operator Use the operator NEAR to search for words that appear close together in a document.

Exact Phrase Search Use quotation marks around a phrase to find the phrase exactly as typed. For example, searching for "*Austin, Texas*" finds only pages that contain the exact phrase. It won't find pages with just *Austin*, or just *Texas*.

Parentheses Use parentheses to nest one expression within another. For example searching for (*growth OR increase*) NEAR (*Internet OR Web*) find documents that mention the words *growth* or *increase* within a few words of *Internet* or *Web*.

Wildcards Many search engines let you use **wildcards**, or symbols that stand for other characters. The most common wildcard is the asterisk (*). A single asterisk can represent one or more characters. If you search for *harvest**, you get pages with variations on the word, such as *harvests* and *harvester*.

Another common wildcard is the question mark (?). A single question mark represents a single character. If you search for *to?*, you get pages containing words such as *top* or *toy*.

Advanced Searches Many popular search engines feature special pages with tools for advanced searches. These pages often appear as forms; instead of constructing complex keyword searches yourself, you can use the form's text boxes and options to create very sophisticated searches. Nearly all such advanced search pages support Boolean operators, special symbols, and wildcards. You can also search for files by type, category, size, date, or other properties.

Searching on a Web Page You can use your browser's Find command to search an open Web page for specific information. In most browsers, press Ctrl + F to display a search box, or select the command on the Edit or Customize menu. Type the search term and press Enter to highlight each occurrence of the term on the page. On Twitter, you can search for related subject threads using the **hashtag (#)** system. Hashtags are added to the beginning of search terms or key words in a tweet to identify related tweets, making it easier for users to follow a specific topic.

Collecting Information One of the most powerful uses of the Web is to conduct research. Once you find the information you need, you may want to save it so you can refer to it again, or, if you have legal permission, use it in a report or presentation. You can use many standard application procedures to save, copy, and paste information from a Web page. For example, you can use the File > Save As command in you browser to save the Web page on your computer. If you only need some text, you can select it and then use the Copy and Paste commands or drag-and-drop to copy it into a word processing document. You can save an image by right-clicking it and use the Save Image As command, or you can drag it from the Web page into an open document or to a storage device. You can also use the File > Print command in your browser to print a Web page.

Evaluating Information on the Web

Whether you're doing schoolwork or pursuing your own interests, it is important to use critical thinking to evaluate the information you find on the Web for accuracy before you use it. Many sites may cover the same information but you are responsible for determining which sites are more accurate. One example is news. Before the Internet, most news was covered by news organizations such as newspapers and television. With the Internet's easy access and global reach, citizen journalists have emerged. Citizen journalists are not professional journalists, but instead they are just everyday people who take the time to post articles online on sites other than those run by major media outlets, or to upload photos and videos. These journalist can often give accurate reports of world events and fact-check the news at newspapers. However, they can also make things up. Unofficial reporting must be evaluated by the accuracy of the information given. When evaluating information on the web consider these criteria:

Author The author should be identified in the site. If you can't locate this information, there may be a reason the author chooses to remain anonymous. If you do locate a name, conduct a search to find out more about the person or organization responsible for the content in the site.

Language and Purpose Evaluating whether the information is well-written and presented in a balanced, factual manner or if it is biased or argumentative and filled with spelling and grammatical errors can help you determine the author's purpose.

Content Validity Does the author indicate the sources of the information? Do those sources appear to be respected, valid, and authoritative? Run a search on the references or other sources to see what you can learn. Determine if the information given is fact or just opinion.

Relevancy Most search engines list results in the order of hits received. Thus, search engines sometimes place popular sites before relevant sites. Don't be fooled into thinking that a page is relevant simply because it appears at the top of a list of results. Also, commercial search engines allow advertising and sponsored links, which are paid for by companies hoping to get your business. Don't assume the first link on a results page is the best. It might just be for the company that pays the most.

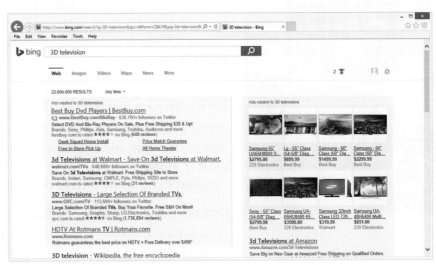

Figure 30.3.2 Searching for 3D television returns a list that's almost all advertisements.

Bing, Microsoft Corporation.

Figure 30–4

Conducting Business Online

Objectives

- Analyze online shopping.
- Compare and contrast online and traditional stores.
- Explain the process of securing online transactions.

As You Read

Organize Information   Use a chart to help you organize main ideas and details about e-commerce as you read.

 **Key Terms**

- click-and-mortar store
- encryption
- e-tailer
- secure electronic transaction

Figure 30.4.1 Clothing is one type of merchandise that sells successfully online.

Online Shopping

The World Wide Web has become a global market. Most things are available for sale online.

What Sells Online   Merchandise that sells successfully online ranges from clothing to jewelry, electronics to vacations, and furniture to homes and cars. Amazon.com is a successful, high-profile company that started out selling books and moved into many other product lines. The company tries out new products in a "test" store to see if they will sell well. If they don't, that link is shut down.

Many popular Web sites offer shopping channels to help you locate items and check the latest prices. Buyers can also access a directory of online vendors, or **e-tailers**, organized by category.

Challenges of Selling Online   Not every business can successfully sell products online, and some face unique challenges. For example, there are very few successful online knitting and yarn stores, because knitting and crochet enthusiasts like to see and feel the yarn. Companies that sell perishable items, such as fresh fruit or baked goods, must have a system in place that lets them deliver products quickly and safely. A book can travel for days without suffering any quality problems, but red velvet cupcakes must be delivered before they become stale. While grocery store consumers like to talk to the butcher or squeeze the melons to see if they are ripe, some online grocers have found a niche by tailoring their offerings to hurried consumers who don't want to take the time to shop.

Click-and-Mortar Versus Bricks-and-Mortar

A traditional retail outlet is known as a bricks-and-mortar store. Businesses that also sell products online are called **click-and-mortar stores**. Some online businesses have bricks-and-mortar counterparts, while others only sell online.

Online-only Stores   Online shopping sites like eBay and Amazon.com do not sell in traditional stores. This saves the company money on salaries and overhead, so prices can be lower.

Although online shopping is convenient, if you have a problem with your purchase, you can not talk to someone about it face-to-face. If you want to return something, you have to ship it back and sometimes pay for shipping costs, too.

Click-and-Mortar Online stores that also have bricks-and-mortar locations have an advantage over companies that do business only online. If you are not satisfied with a product, you may be able to take it back to a store location for a refund or replacement. You can speak with someone face-to-face and get the problem resolved right away.

Online shopping is similar to in-store shopping in many ways. When you are buying a pair of jeans in the mall, you are able to browse from store to store comparing the prices at different locations. You might also shop at a store your friends recommend. Online, you can browse many different retail Web sites to find the best deals. You can also read reviews to learn if a site is respectable and secure. Most sites have rating systems or customer comments that you can use to learn about other consumers' experiences with the seller. These reviews can help you make an educated decision on which Web sites to use. When you shop online, you are giving your personal and financial information to a third party. It is important to be savvy and responsible while shopping online.

Secure Electronic Transactions

One of the keys to the growth of e-commerce is **secure electronic transactions**. Originally a standard that relied on digital

Connections

The Arts Like stores, museums and art galleries may offer both bricks-and-mortar and click-and-mortar locations.
Google's Art Project (www.googleartproject.com) offers visitors an online tour of seventeen of the world's most famous art museums. Visitors can view hundreds of works of art in the privacy of their own homes, tour the museums, and even create and share their own collection of masterpieces.

Real-World Tech

E-pinionated Online Shoppers Word-of-mouth spreads fast on the Internet. In fact, when it is unstoppable, we say that a product, a video, or phenomenon has gone "viral." One way to get reliable word-of-mouth opinions of products you want to purchase online is to go to Epinions.com, which offers unbiased reviews of products and services. They are written by average people—even teens—so you can review your latest electronic gadget or piece of clothing. Most e-commerce sites, however, offer customer reviews and a five-star rating system for all products.

Check them out before you put items into your virtual shopping cart.
What would prompt you to write a product review online? A good or a bad experience and why?

Schools, too, can place orders for merchandise online.

Think About It!

Which item(s) listed below do you think your school might order online?

➤ costumes for a school play

➤ school supplies

➤ textbooks

➤ electronic equipment

➤ athletic equipment

signatures, secure electronic transaction now refers to a variety of measures **e-tailers** use to secure online transactions so customers can bank and shop online without worrying that their private information will be misused, lost, or stolen, which could result in identify theft and fraud.

Secure Sites   A secure Web site uses **encryption**—coding—and authentication standards to protect online transaction information. That means your personal information including debit card numbers and personal identification numbers (PINs) are safe when you shop online. You can tell that you are viewing a secure Web site because the letters "https" display to the left of the Web site name in the Address bar of your browser. On an unsecured site, there is no "s." Also, a small lock icon displays in your Web browser's status bar. You can double-click the lock icon to display details about the site's security system.

Secure Payment Services   PayPal®, which started out as a service for eBay buyers and sellers, is now the most popular secure online payment service. It is used by millions of buyers and sellers on thousands of e-commerce sites. PayPal lets you avoid repeatedly entering your credit card number and other personal data when making transactions online. Instead, you can designate an amount to be used for PayPal purchases, and, when you make an online purchase, the money is deducted directly from your bank account. To use PayPal, or any other secure online payment service, you sign up directly and provide your payment information only once. The service keeps your records secure and handles payments to online vendors for you, using only secure methods. Apple also has a payment service called Apple Pay that lets you use an iPhone, iPad, or Apple Watch to pay in stores and online.

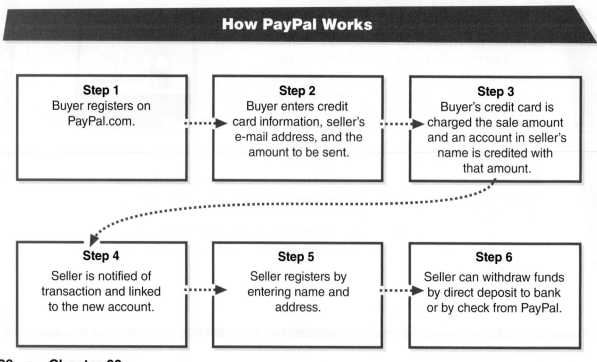

How PayPal Works

Step 1
Buyer registers on PayPal.com.

Step 2
Buyer enters credit card information, seller's e-mail address, and the amount to be sent.

Step 3
Buyer's credit card is charged the sale amount and an account in seller's name is credited with that amount.

Step 4
Seller is notified of transaction and linked to the new account.

Step 5
Seller registers by entering name and address.

Step 6
Seller can withdraw funds by direct deposit to bank or by check from PayPal.

Use the Vocabulary

Directions: *Match each vocabulary term in the left column with the correct definition in the right column.*

_____ **1.** hypermedia system
_____ **2.** dead link
_____ **3.** WYSIWYG
_____ **4.** e-tailer
_____ **5.** encryption
_____ **6.** cookie
_____ **7.** exclusion operator
_____ **8.** wildcard
_____ **9.** web cache
_____ **10.** Web host

a. lets users retrieve audio and video online
b. symbol that stands for another character
c. sophisticated Web-page editing programs
d. temporarily stored Web pages on a personal computer
e. someone who primarily uses the Web to sell goods or services
f. data a Web site stores on a personal computer hard drive
g. connection to a document that no longer exists or has been moved
h. minus sign or the word NOT
i. coding used to protect data
j. a company that provides space on a Web server for Web sites

Check Your Comprehension

Directions: *Determine the correct choice for each of the following.*

1. Which of the following indicates that a particular graphic on a Web page is actually a link?

  a. The mouse pointer turns into a hand.
  b. The mouse pointer changes color.
  c. The graphic moves across the screen.
  d. The graphic is underlined.

2. Which of the following can you use to upgrade a browser to add new features to an application?

  a. plug-in program
  b. cookie
  c. DHTML program
  d. WYSIWYG program

3. Which of the following is NOT an indicator that a Web site is an accurate source?

  a. author is identified on the site
  b. information is balanced and factual
  c. the link displays at the top of a list of search results
  d. spelling and grammar are correct

4. Which of the following might yield a list of pages with *travel, travels, traveled,* and *traveling*?

  a. wildcard
  b. database
  c. inclusion operator
  d. exclusion operator

5. What term is used to describe a traditional retail outlet that does not sell products online?

  a. online stores
  b. test stores
  c. bricks-and-mortar stores
  d. click-and-mortar stores

6. Which of the following is a secure payment service that consumers can use to complete online transactions?

  a. eBay
  b. Secure Payment Service
  c. PayPal
  d. ASCII

Think Critically

Directions: *Answer the following questions.*

1. Identify at least five design principles and explain how their use can help you create an effective Web page.

2. What does a hyperlink do?

3. What are several ways to find information quickly on the Web?

4. Identify at least six design elements and explain how their use can help you create an effective Web page.

5. Compare and contrast writing HTML with a text editor and developing a Web page using a GUI editor.

Extend Your Knowledge

Directions: *Choose and complete one of the following projects.*

A. Find out what differences there are between the bricks-and-mortar store and the click-and-mortar store for the same company. Do they sell the same merchandise? Do they use the same pricing? What are the advantages and disadvantages for the company? For the customer? Write your findings in a report and share it with a partner or with the class.

B. With your teacher's permission, with a partner, try using several Web browsers. Look for and test features such as opening and closing multiple tabs, History and the Bookmarks or Favorites list. Explore customization options such as how to enable or disable multiple tabs, plugins, and add-ons. Discuss the advantages, disadvantages, and features of each. Then, create and complete a Venn diagram to summarize your preferences.

C. With a partner or small group, plan, design, develop, and publish a Web site for a business. Look at available templates and use storyboarding techniques to help with the planning, navigation, and design. Select the tools you will use to develop the site. For example, will you use HTML, DHTML, or XML editors? Will you need to convert from one to another? When you are ready, select an available template to use to create the site. Insert text, graphics, and links. Use the principles of design and color theory to make sure the pages in the Web site are consistent, appealing, and readable. Modify the Web site template to achieve your design goals, if necessary. Optimize, edit, and test the pages, and then publish the Web site using ftp, or as instructed by your teacher.

DIRECTIONS: *You will search the Internet to learn about what types of information are protected by copyrights and what you legally can and cannot use. Then, you will use a word-processing program to make a top-ten list of facts about copyright laws*

1. Open the .pdf file **Web-1_CopyrightInfo**. With your teacher's permission, print the Data Record Sheet. The sheet includes a K-W-L chart and forms for recording source information. K-W-L stands for What I **K**now, What I **W**ant to Know, and What I **L**earned. Close the file, and exit your pdf reader program.

2. Working with a partner, in the K-W-L chart, fill in the K column with what you already know about copyright laws, creative commons, public domain, and open source regulations, and fill in the W column with what you want to know.

3. With your teacher's permission, open your Web browser and navigate to a search engine.

4. Use the search engine to find information about copyright laws. Search for keywords from the W column of your K-W-L chart. Use Boolean search strategies such as AND, NOT, or OR to fine-tune the search results list. Look for sites that explain what information you can and cannot use according to copyright laws. Research illegal acts such as software piracy, as well as patent and trademark infringement. Find sites that explain the consequences of violating these copyright laws in simple, easy to understand language.

5. Evaluate each site you visit for accuracy and validity.

6. Write the source information about each Web page that you use on the bottom portion of the Data Record Sheet, on the back, or on a separate piece of paper.

7. With your teacher's permission, print relevant information from the Web sites you find most helpful. You may want to copy the information from the Web page into a word-processing or notes program, along with the page's URL, and then print it.

8. Using your browser's History list, go back to one of the sites that explained the consequences of copyright violations.

9. Mark the site as a favorite or bookmark it.

10. When you have finished your research, exit your Web browser.

11. Read the information you printed. As you read, use a highlighter to identify the main ideas of each article.

12. Use your findings to write ten facts about copyright laws, creative commons, public domain, and open source regulations in the "What I Learned" column of the K-W-L chart.

13. Start your word-processing program, and create a new document. Save it as **Web-1_Copyrights_xx**. Replace **xx** with your own initials or name, as directed by your teacher. Insert a footer that includes your full name and today's date.

14. At the top of the document, type the title **Ten Things to Remember About Copyrighted Materials**. Increase the font size of the title to 18 points, center it, and make it bold, or apply the Title style.

15. Leave a blank line below the title, change the font style to Normal, and type the ten facts you learned from the K-W-L chart. Format the items as a numbered list.

16. Insert a blank line below the last fact, type **Source Sites** and format it in bold with a solid underline.

17. On the next line, remove the bold and underline formatting, and then type a list of the Web sites or other sources you recorded on your Data Record Sheet. Format the sources in a smaller font size than the rest of the document text, and leave one blank line between sources. Remove all hyperlink formatting.

18. Proofread the document carefully. Check the spelling and grammar, and correct any errors.

19. Preview the document.

20. With your teacher's permission, print the document.

21. Close the document, saving all changes, and exit your word-processing program.

22. As a class, brainstorm scenarios that do or do not violate copyright laws. Write the scenarios on the board or an overhead transparency. Discuss which scenarios are legal under current copyright laws.

Web Activities

DIRECTIONS: *In teams or small groups, you will use a search engine to research one of the original thirteen colonies. You will then use a word-processing program to create a written report about the colony, including images. Then, you will save the document as an HTML file so you can publish it on the Web.*

1. Open the .pdf file **Web-2_ColonyInfo**. With your teacher's permission, print the Data Record Sheet. The sheet includes a table where you can record information about a colony and a checklist you can use to make sure you complete your report correctly. Close the file, and exit your pdf reader program.

2. With your group, list the thirteen colonies on a sheet of paper. Then, choose one colony to research. Make a plan for completing the project and write down the steps you will use to achieve your goals, including which group member will be responsible for each step. As you work, cross off each step as it is completed. Alternatively, use a project management schedule such as the one used in Spreadsheet Activity 6.

3. With your teacher's permission, use the Internet to find information about the early history of the colony you chose.

4. To use the Internet, open a Web browser and navigate to a search engine. Search for sites by typing keywords or phrases such as the name of your colony, or use a Boolean search phrase such as AND.

   a. Look for information about the key individuals or groups who helped establish the colony, the basis for the colony's economy, the hardships that colonists encountered, and important dates in the history of the colony.

   b. Locate at least three images related to the colony. The images might include maps, paintings, photographs of artifacts, or portraits of the colony's leaders. When you find the images online, check the copyright information to make sure you can use them, and ask your teacher for permission to download and save them in a compatible format.

5. Evaluate each site you visit for accuracy and validity.

6. When you find a Web site with useful information, bookmark the site, or with your teacher's permission, print the pages.

7. Record the details and facts that you find on the Data Record Sheet, including the source information about each Web site you use.

8. When you have finished your research, exit your Web browser.

9. Start your word-processing program, and create a new document. Save the document as **Web-2_Colonies_xx** in the location where your teacher instructs you to store the files for this activity. Insert a footer on all but the first page that includes your full name, the page number, and today's date.

10. Create a title or cover page that includes a descriptive title for the report, formatted in bold and centered, or apply the Title style. Include your name, today's date, and an appropriate picture that you source from clip art or create yourself using a graphics program. A sample cover page is shown in Illustration A on the next page.

11. Use the information on your Data Record Sheet to write a report on the colony you researched. Your report should be at least two pages and should have headings and subheadings, formatted using styles. Use Outline view and the Document Map, if available, to organize the report and adjust formatting.

12. Insert images to illustrate the report. Select appropriate text wrapping options. Size and position the images so they improve the look of the report and make it easier to read.

13. Insert a caption below each image. You may do this using your program's Insert Caption feature or by inserting a text box in which you type a caption. Format the text box so that text will wrap around it, and format the caption text with a smaller font size than you use in the body of the document.

14. At the end of the report, insert a Works Cited page or Bibliography listing your sources. Insert footnotes or endnotes, if necessary. If appropriate, at the beginning of the report insert an automatically-generated table of contents.

15. Proofread your report carefully. Use your program's thesaurus feature to find interesting synonyms for common words in order to improve your writing. Check the spelling and grammar in the document and correct any errors that you find.

16. Format all paragraphs with a first-line Indent and justified alignment.

17. Preview the document by adjusting the zoom so you can see multiple pages at one time, and make modifications to the page layout, as necessary. For example, you may want to adjust the margin width.
18. With your teacher's permission, print the report.
19. Close the document, saving all changes.
20. Share your report file with another group, according to your teacher's instructions. Use the information on the Data Record Sheet to evaluate your classmates' work. Does the report meet the requirements of the assignment? If not, how can it be improved? Turn on your program's revision tracking and commenting features, or handwrite your comments and edits to provide feedback and corrections. Then, return the report file to your classmates.
21. Accept or reject the revisions to incorporate your classmates' comments and suggestions into your report. Insert a footer on all pages with your name and the field codes for the current date and time.
22. Save the changes to the report.
23. Save the document as a single file Web page.
24. View the document as it will display on the Web. With the principles of design and color theory in mind, open the document in an HTML or WYSIWYG editor and adjust the position and formatting of the text, colors, and images on the page to improve its appearance and readability.
25. Insert hyperlinks from the report page to your source Web sites.
26. With your teacher's permission, publish your Web page on your school or class's Web site so other students can access it.
27. Open your Web browser and view your Web page and those of your classmates. Then, close all open documents, saving all changes, and exit all open programs.

Illustration A

Massachusetts

The Second of the Thirteen Original Colonies

By

Firstname Lastname

Today's Date

Web Activities

DIRECTIONS: *Working in teams, you will use wiki collaboration to develop a multimedia anti-bullying campaign for your school. You will collect information on types of bullying, how bullying impacts victims and perpetrators, and how to respond to it. You will then collaborate with your team to develop the content. You may also choose to publish the information on a class social media page.*

1. Open the .pdf file **Web-3_Bullying**. With your teacher's permission, print the Data Record Sheet. Close the file, and exit your pdf reader program.

2. Working with your team, make a plan for completing the project and write down the steps you will use to achieve your goals, including which group member will be responsible for each step. As you work, cross off each step as it is completed. Alternatively, use a project management schedule such as the one used in Spreadsheet Activity 6.

3. Use the Internet (with your teacher's permission), library resources, or your school's student handbook or code of conduct to locate information about the three main types of bullying: physical, verbal, and cyber.

4. To use the Internet, open a Web browser and navigate to a search engine. Search for words or phrases such as **bullying**, or use Boolean search strategies. For example, you might search for **bullying AND physical** or **bullying AND cyber**.

5. When you find a credible Web site with useful information, bookmark the site, or with your teacher's permission, print the desired pages, or copy the information from the Web page into a word-processing or notes file for saving and printing. Write the source information about each site on a separate piece of paper.

6. Use the information you find to complete the first table on the Data Record Sheet.

7. When you have finished your research, exit your Web browser.

8. Go to the wiki space that your teacher has created.

9. Working cooperatively with your team members, create the following for the wiki:
   - Photo of your school, in the format that provides the best image quality and file size for use online
   - List of the first names of all team members
   - Slogan or title for the anti-bullying campaign
   - Brief introduction to the topic of bullying in text, video, or audio
   - Text, video, or audio summary on each of the three types of bullying—physical, verbal, and cyber—based on the information you recorded on the Data Record Sheet.

10. As a team, develop recommendations on how to respond to each type of bullying. Write your ideas in the second table on the Data Record Sheet.

11. Work with your team members to combine and edit the recommendations on the wiki space.

12. With your teacher's permission, share your wiki with others, and read and comment on other teams' wikis.

13. With your teacher's permission, publish all or parts of the project on a class social media page on a platform such as Facebook, Wimba, or Moodle so others can comment. Use the comments to gauge the reactions of people who view the page.

14. As a class, discuss the different types of bullying, and how you can expand the anti-bullying campaign in your school.

DIRECTIONS: *You will develop a blog on one of your hobbies or interests. You will gather information and statistics on the hobby and create content to post on the blog.*

1. Open the .pdf file **Web-4_Blog**. With your teacher's permission, print the Data Record Sheet. Close the file, and exit your pdf reader program.

2. Use the Data Record Sheet to enter information on a hobby or interest. Be as detailed and informative as possible. Use your own experience, as well as research resources such as Web sites, other blogs, publications, and books.

3. With your teacher's permission, access the designated blogging service. To register with a blogging service, you will typically be required to provide an e-mail address and password. You may then be asked to provide a blog title (which is the title that appears on the published blog) and a blog address, or URL.

4. If available, select a design template for your blog.

5. Using the information on your Data Record Sheet, write a blog post about your hobby or interest. Be sure to use complete sentences, proper subject-verb agreement, and correct verb tense. Also, use only one space after punctuation marks.

6. When you have finished writing your blog post, proofread it carefully with a partner or peer editor. Check the spelling and grammar and correct errors.

7. Preview your post if the blogging service provides that option.

8. When you have finalized the post, publish it, and then view your blog.

9. Edit the blog post by inserting a picture or image that represents your hobby or interest. Make sure the image is in a format that provides the best quality and file size for use online.

10. Publish the post again, and view it.

11. Refer to the information about resources that you listed in your Data Record Sheet. Create a new post that describes at least one of the Web sites you listed where you can obtain helpful information about your hobby or interest. Create a link in the post to the Web site.

12. Publish the post, and view your blog.

13. Share the URL of the blog post with your teacher. Then, with your teacher's permission, print a copy of the blog post.

14. Log out of your blog service when finished.

Web Activities

DIRECTIONS: *You will research a natural disaster and its effects on the surrounding ecosystems. You will use a word processor to write a description of the disaster, and save the document in HTML format. You will edit and format the HTML document using the principles of design. You will also add images that you download from the Web. Then, you will publish your work as a Web page, upload it to your school's network, and bookmark it.*

1. Open the .pdf file **Web-5_EvaluationForm**. With your teacher's permission, print the rubric. The rubric identifies points on which your research will be evaluated. Close the file, and exit your pdf reader program.

2. With your teacher's permission, use the Internet to research a recent natural disaster. Write down questions you would like to answer about how, where, and when the disaster happened. Write down questions you would like to answer about the problems and damage they caused to ecosystems in the area. Find examples of the ecosystems that were disrupted and how they are repairing.

3. To use the Internet, open a Web browser and navigate to a search engine. Search for sites by typing keywords or phrases such as the type or name of the natural disaster, or use a Boolean search to narrow your focus.

4. When you find information about the disaster, carefully evaluate it to make sure it is valid and relevant to the topic.

5. During your research, locate before and after photos of the event. If copyright laws allow, with your teacher's permission download and save the images in a format that provides the best quality and file size for online use.

6. Find at least three helpful URLs, one of which contains a photo, and save them as Favorites or bookmarks in your Web browser.

7. Start your word-processing program, and save a new file as **Web-5_Research_xx** in the location where your teacher instructs you to store the files for this activity.

8. Make your Web browser active and return to the sites you bookmarked. Refresh the pages, if necessary. Select relevant text and images from each site and copy them to the word-processing document for saving or printing. Copy the source URL and type the page title for all content you copy.

9. Save the changes to the word-processing document, and with your teacher's permission, print it.

10. When you have completed your research, exit your Web browser.

11. In your word-processing program, create a new document, and save it as a Web page with the name **Web-5_Ecosystems_xx** and the page title **Ecosystem Equilibrium**, in the location where your teacher instructs you to store files for this activity.

12. Insert a footer on the page that includes your name and the field codes for the current date and time.

13. Apply a theme or design to the page, or apply a page background color.

14. Enter a descriptive title on the page. Use a readable font and center and boldface it. Increase the font size to make it stand out, or apply an appropriate style.

15. Using the information in your **Web-5_Research_xx** document, enter a description in your own words of the natural disaster. Include examples of the ecosystems that were affected and the natural succession, or recovery, which occurred afterward.

16. Apply ½" first line indents to each paragraph.

17. Insert at least one image from your research to your Web page document to illustrate the content. Select appropriate text wrapping options. Size and position the image so it integrates with and enhances the text, but does not overwhelm it.

18. At the end of the document, type a list of URLs hyperlinked to your source pages, so readers can use the links to access the pages for more information.

19. Proofread the document carefully with a partner or peer editor. Check the spelling and grammar and correct any errors that you find. Save the changes.

20. Preview the document as it will look in a Web browser, and test the links. Open the file in an HTML or WYSIWYG editor, and make corrections and modifications to the page layout. Keep the principles of design in mind as you work, and preview the page often to make sure it looks good and is easy to read.

21. When you are satisfied with the results, with your teacher's permission, print the document.

22. With your teacher's permission, publish your Web page on your class Web site so other students can access it.

23. Open your Web browser and view your Web page and those of your classmates. Bookmark your page. Then, close all open documents, saving all changes, and exit all open programs

24. Using the rubric, evaluate your own Web page and the pages of your classmates.

Personal Communications Basics

Staying in Touch How do you stay in touch with friends after school, on weekends, or during school vacations? How do you stay in contact with friends who have moved? You could make phone calls and hope someone answers, or send letters and then wait for a response. Today, however, many people use their computer to stay in touch with friends, family, and co-workers.

Computer technology allows you to stay connected with people who are both close by and far away. You can communicate through text messages. You can chat online with several friends at once. With the right technology, you can even chat face-to-face through a computer network. There's no need to feel out of touch!

Chapter Outline

 Lesson 31–1

Using E-mail

 Lesson 31–2

Avoiding E-mail Problems

 Lesson 31–3

Other Electronic Communications

Using E-mail

Objectives

- Describe e-mail systems.
- Identify the purpose of a unique identifier.
- Explain the parts of an e-mail address
- Identify the key components of an e-mail message.
- Describe the process of creating, sending, and replying to messages.

As You Read

Sequence Information   Use a sequence chart as you read to help you outline the process of receiving a message and responding to it.

Key Terms

- alias
- attachment
- e-mail client
- e-mail server
- mailbox name
- server address

Evaluating E-mail

E-mail, or electronic mail, allows people to send an unlimited number of messages quickly and easily to anyone with an e-mail address. Messages sent through e-mail can be a casual, like a letter to a friend, or formal, like a memo for a business. It is also less expensive than standard mail and voice, fax, and telephone messages. In fact, standard mail is sometimes called "snail mail" because it is so much slower than e-mail. To use e-mail, all you need is a computer, an Internet connection, e-mail software, and an e-mail account.

E-mail also lets you attach files to a message. Anything sent with an e-mail message is called an **attachment**. Common attachments include word-processing documents, spreadsheets, photos, artwork, and movies.

Some e-mail programs, like Outlook, include features for managing a calendar and contact list as well as taking notes and scheduling tasks.

Understanding E-mail Addresses

Figure 31.1.1 Every e-mail address has two basic parts—a mailbox name and a server address.

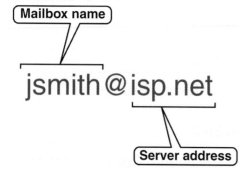

Like a computer on a network, every communication service user must have a unique identifier, usually called a username. The system uses the identifier to differentiate one user from another in order to deliver services, such as mail. For e-mail, the identifier is the e-mail address. All e-mail addresses have two parts. The **mailbox name** is the part of the address before the "at" symbol (@) that identifies the user. The **server address** follows the symbol. It gives the domain name of the e-mail server where the mailbox is stored. An **e-mail server** is a computer, operated by your Internet service provider (ISP), that handles three key jobs:

- accepts incoming messages
- sends outgoing messages
- delivers incoming messages

Sending, Receiving, and Forwarding E-mail

To send or receive e-mail, you use an **e-mail client**, which is a program that lets you create, send, receive, and manage e-mail messages. You may get the program from your ISP, as part of a productivity suite, or with a Web browser. For example, Microsoft Outlook is the e-mail client that comes with the Microsoft Office productivity suite. There are also Web-based e-mail clients, such as Google's gmail and Microsoft's Outlook.com.

Composing E-mail   To compose a new message, you click a button within the e-mail client. The client displays a form for you to complete. The form includes two main parts—the header, which includes places for entering the recipient(s) and the subject, and the body, which is where you type the message.

First, you must specify the message's recipient in the To: line of the message form. Depending on your e-mail client's features, you may select someone's name from an address book. You may also type the e-mail address, which can be a name or a combination of letters and numbers. For example, the e-mail address for Chris Rodriguez might be chris_rodriguez@isp.net or cjr615@ isp.net. Instead of typing a complete address, you may be able to type an alias, or select it from a list. An **alias** is an easy-to-remember nickname for the recipient, such as Chris_R.

If you want to send a copy of the message to other recipients, you can add their names or addresses to the To: line or place them in the Cc: line. (The characters Cc stand for "carbon copy.") To send a copy of message without the recipient's e-mail address appearing in the To: or Cc: line, enter it in the Bcc: line. Bcc stands for "blind carbon copy." Recipients whose addresses are in the To: or Cc: line are not able to see whose address is in the Bcc: line when they open the message.

Next, fill in the Subject line. The Subject line gives the recipient an idea of the message's content and may help the recipient decide whether to open it or delete it. Some e-mail clients will not accept messages with blank Subject lines. When the header is complete, type the text message. You can add attachments by clicking a button and then clicking the name of the file you want to attach to the e-mail. Finally, click Send.

Netiquette are the rules for polite online behavior.

Think About It!

Which of the following online rules help make e-mail more useful?

▷ Type a lengthy description in the Subject line.

▷ Vary fonts and type sizes in the message.

▷ Edit the original message so only the part you are answering appears in your reply.

▷ Don't write in anger.

▷ Be brief, but be polite.

Figure 31.1.2 Creating an e-mail message with Google's gmail.

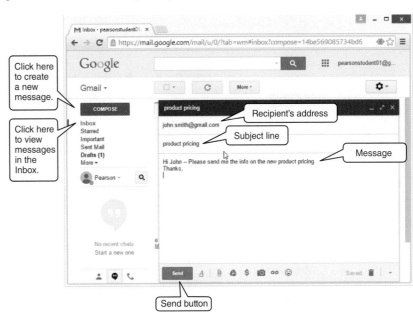

Click here to create a new message.

Click here to view messages in the Inbox.

Recipient's address

Subject line

Message

Send button

Configure Message Options Most programs let you set options such as delivery options before sending a message. You may be able to select when you want a message to send, specify the level of importance or sensitivity, set security options such as encryption, and request a confirmation that a message has been opened or read.

Replying to E-mail You can respond to the person who sent a message by clicking Reply. You can also click Reply All, which responds to all the people who received the original message. Several things occur when a response is prepared:

- The client displays a reply form with the original sender's address shown in the To: field.
- The subject field may show Re: in front of the subject of the original message. (*Re* stands for "regarding.")
- The original message is copied into the body of the reply. Most e-mail programs give you the option of excluding the original text in your reply.
- You can type your reply above or below the original text, and then click Send.

Forwarding E-mail When you receive a message, you can pass it along to someone else. This is called forwarding a message. The Subject line of a forwarded e-mail may include the characters *FW:* before the subject text to show that the message has been forwarded. You can add your comments before the original message's text.

Before you hit "send" on any e-mail, it's good to remember that your e-mail can be forwarded to other people. Don't write anything that you don't want other friends, parents, or teachers to see!

Figure 31.1.3 Replying to an e-mail message.

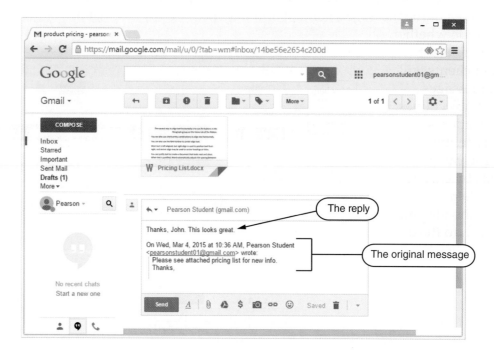

Avoiding E-mail Problems

Objectives

- Examine problems related to e-mail.
- Define bounce messages and spam.
- Explain the use of digital signatures with e-mail.

As You Read

Compare and Contrast Use a Venn diagram as you read to help you compare and contrast various e-mail problems.

Failed E-mail

It is easy to send e-mail messages, but it is also easy to make mistakes. What happens when you make a mistake?

Using the Wrong Address One of the most common e-mail mistakes is entering an incorrect address in the To: field. When you do this, one of two things will happen:

- Your message will go to the wrong person if the incorrect address is someone else's valid address. Unless that person replies, you may never know what happened to your message.
- The e-mail server will return the e-mail to you with a bounce message.

  A **bounce message** is a notice from the e-mail server telling you that your message could not be delivered. Bounce messages are often a result of an incorrect e-mail address. You sometimes see "MAILER-DAEMON@..." as the "From" address of a bounce message. Also, a message may not be delivered if the recipient's mailbox is full. This happens because many ISPs limit the amount of server space available for each user's messages. Never attempt to reply to a bounce message.

Avoiding Bounce Messages If you or your family changes ISPs, your e-mail address will change. In that case, be sure to tell everyone in your address book about your new e-mail address. Otherwise, people sending messages to your former address will receive a bounce message when they write to you.

 **Key Terms**

- bounce message
- digital signature
- spam

Technology @ Work

Bounce messages are a part of e-mail use. But what should you do when you get one?

Think About It!

Suppose you e-mail the school photographer to find out whether your class pictures are ready. However, you get a bounce message. Which actions listed below might then be helpful?

➤ Retrieve the message from your Sent Items folder and check your typing.

➤ Confirm the e-mail address of the photographer.

➤ Resend the message to the same address.

➤ Send a reply to the bounce message asking for help.

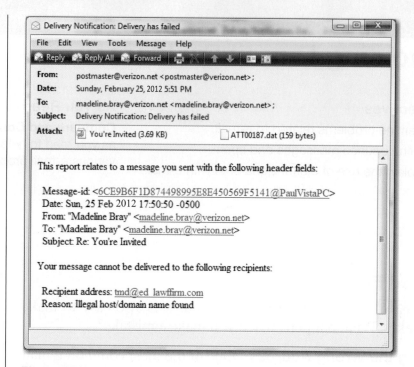

Figure 31.2.1 A bounce message, due to an incorrect e-mail address.

Junk E-mail, or Spam

Many e-mail users complain about the flood of **spam**, a term used to describe unwanted, or junk, e-mail messages and advertisements. Like physical junk mail, spam usually tries to sell something to the recipient. Spam can cause several problems:

- The recipient wastes time reviewing and deleting spam.
- Spam clogs e-mail servers, slowing Internet traffic.
- Spam often contains incorrect or misleading information.

Sometimes you unknowingly generate the spam you get. When you make an online purchase, you might agree to get e-mails from the company about future sales. You might have signed up for e-mail newsletters at many Web sites or joined a group (as in Yahoo Groups) that lets you exchange messages about a topic.

Blocking Unwanted E-mail You can mark unwanted messages as junk, or spam so your program automatically delivers them to the Junk or Spam folder instead of to your inbox. Most newsletters and user groups give easy directions to unsubscribe to the e-mail. For e-mail newsletters, you will usually find an "unsubscribe" link at the bottom of the page in tiny print. Yet, stopping spam from reaching e-mail servers and clients is an ongoing battle. Some servers use technology to block "spammers." Some e-mail clients provide special spam filters that users can configure to automatically delete junk mail. It is worthwhile checking your spam folder regularly, because sometimes personal or important e-mail is mistakenly re-routed there.

E-mail Risks

Because you cannot see who is actually sending you a message, e-mail is often used to commit crimes. Someone can send you a message and pretend it is from someone else. The message could contain a virus or request personal information. Because you trust the person or organization you believe sent the message, you open it or reply.

Using Digital Signatures   One way to secure e-mail messages is by using a **digital signature**—an electronic identifier which verifies that the message was created and sent by the person whose name appears in the From field.

Most current e-mail programs support digital signatures, which you purchase from a vendor, such as Symantec's VeriSign Authentication Services. Once the certificate is installed on your computer, you can use it to "sign" any message you send by embedding the certificate in the message. The signature proves that the message comes from you.

Connections

Language Arts   Did you know you can use e-mail to improve your reading and writing? There are online magazines to which you can submit your work for publication. One of these sites, WritingDEN (www2.actden.com/writ_den), also has language-building exercises on words, sentences, and paragraphs. You complete the exercises, e-mail your answers, and receive your scores shortly.

Real-World Tech

Getting Career Advice by E-mail   What do you think you want to do when you "grow up?" It's not too early to start exploring careers and find out what conduct, dress, and behaviors are acceptable in the workplace. Career advice that appears in newspaper or magazine columns exists online as blogs. Some are geared toward specific careers and some to general career advice, like how to be a good team member, solve problems, or get organized.

Search out some career question-and-answer forums available online. Look for ones that offer general advice on how to dress and behave in the workplace. Remember, as with all online resources, be cautious about where you send e-mail and any information you share.

Other Electronic Communications

Objectives

- Compare and contrast technology-enabled conferences.
- Describe one key advantage of teleconferencing for business.
- Examine the technical aspects of videoconferences.
- Summarize goals of Web-based training.
- Explain distance learning.

As You Read

Organize Information   Use an outline as you read to help you organize information about advanced communications methods.

🔑 Key Terms

- blended learning
- flame
- Learning Management Systems (LMS)
- libel
- slander
- teleconference
- videoconference
- Web-based training

Teleconferencing

While the use of e-mail is convenient, there are times when you need to speak with others directly. Meetings and telephone calls are ideal, but in today's world people are spread over wide areas. You may use a telephone conference to join multiple people into one telephone call, but scheduling a call or a meeting can be difficult, and expensive.

Finding a Solution   A **teleconference** is an online meeting by two or more people. Many teleconferences allow participants to communicate in real time, just as they would if they were sitting together in the same room. In a typical real-time teleconference, each participant sits at a computer. They see messages typed by the other participants and type responses for the others to see immediately. Most teleconferences include voice communication as well.

Teleconferences help companies in several ways:

- They save time and money.
- They are similar to in-person meetings.
- They are convenient.
- They allow all participants to communicate in real time.

Chat Rooms   Not all teleconferences are conducted for business. Informal, public real-time teleconferences in which participants discuss chosen topics are called chat rooms. Unlike business teleconferences where the participants are known to one another, chat-room participants are likely to be strangers to one another. Exercise caution and discretion when revealing personal or confidential information in a chat room. You do not know how someone might use details from your conversation without your knowledge or permission.

Videoconferencing

A **videoconference** is a teleconference that includes video as well as text or audio. Videoconferences require equipment such as cameras, a fast network connection, and video screens or computer monitors. A Web-based videoconference allows participants to connect to a Web server, identify themselves, and then join the meeting.

Types of Videoconferences Videoconferences can serve many purposes. Depending on the goal, they are set up in one of three delivery methods.

- One-to-one videoconferences allow two people to see and talk to each other on their computers. This type of conference is easy to set up through applications such as Microsoft NetMeeting or through using Voice over Internet Protocol (VoIP) with Skype, software that lets you use your computer to make voice or video phone calls.

- One-to-many videoconferences are similar to watching television programs. Many people can watch the presentation, but usually only one person speaks to the group.

- Many-to-many videoconferences are like a face-to-face meeting. Any of the participants can speak and be seen and heard at any time in the conversation.

Videoconferences are useful for collaboration on projects and training. Most Web-based videoconferences allow screen sharing, which means everyone who logs in can view the presenters' screen. In this way, the presenter can demonstrate actions instead of just talking about them. The presenter can also pass control to anyone else on the call.

Learning from a Distance

Distance learning makes use of telepresence to let you to learn anytime, anywhere—as long as you are on a computer connected to the Internet. A **Learning Management System**, or (LMS),

Spotlight on...

TELEMENTORING

The International Telementor Program, or ITP, matches students with workplace mentors who help them complete projects. Students and their mentors communicate online. Students at Eisenhower Middle School in Topeka, Kansas, developed their school's first Web site with help from ITP mentors. And students in Pleasant View School in Baldwin Park, California, worked with mentors to create multimedia presentations on their state's history.

Many students and teachers use distance learning.

Think About It!

Think about some of the ways schools might use distance learning. Which statement(s) listed below identify a sensible use?

➤ Small schools could offer a wider range of courses.

➤ Schools could let individuals or small groups pursue their interests.

➤ Schools could pair a sports team with a coach.

➤ A teacher in one school could share lessons with teachers on other campuses.

is an application designed for education that can manage records, report grades, and deliver subject matter content. You can complete high school courses or even earn a complete college degree online. Many schools offer classes via distance learning, and they use a variety of technologies. In many cases, the instructor provides lectures and displays slides through a one-to-many videoconference, which students can watch on their home computers. Tests and quizzes can be done via the Internet and students can work together via teleconference and e-mail.

Web-based Training   One of the newest methods of distance learning is **Web-based training**. Schools, colleges, and businesses are using the speed and technology of the Internet to deliver educational programs and activities. This method of education offers anytime, anywhere learning, as long as you have an Internet connection.

Blended Learning   Some students find the best method of learning combines traditional classroom education with Web-based education. **Blended learning** offers opportunities for students to interact with others face-to-face and at a distance.

Computer-based Training   Online instruction is one form of computer-based training, or CBT. But the first method for delivering computer-based training—the CD—remains popular among teachers and students. Many companies use CD tutorials to train employees on policies, products, and procedures. The advantage of this type of CBT is that the user can carry it around, and it does not require a network or Internet connection.

Text Messaging

Perhaps the most popular alternative to e-mail is **text messaging**. Texting allows you to use a smart phone to type a brief message and transmit it to the recipient's phone. Since the text messages are brief, text messaging is also know as Short Message Service, or SMS. Text messaging is a popular way to communicate because it is fast and easy. It is important to know when it is appropriate and inappropriate to use text messaging. Because it is informal, texting is not the appropriate means of communicating sensitive or personal information.

Tweeting is a form of text messaging; you send the message to the Twitter Internet site, where any registered user can read it. Twitter allows for short messages to be read by a much larger audience. Digital messages can be sent with photos and videos, as well, using Multimedia Messaging Service (MMS).

Commenting Online

Many Web sites allow you to share and express your views on the site's content by commenting. Usually, once you register you can type a comment which is linked to the content on the site. Others can click the link to read your comment.

For example, you can comment on newspaper articles. Online stores let customers review products or share their experiences using the products or the Web site. Content sharing sites, like YouTube, allow viewers to give feedback on uploaded content and videos. You can upload your own content to these sites, or just comment on something you viewed. Social media sites allow for a great degree of freedom in posting ideas and opinions. Posts can be commented on and then those comments in turn can be commented on, creating full conversations that can include many people from many locations.

Communications Standards

Whatever type of communication you use, it is important to abide by certain standards. Personal communication may be less formal than you use for business, but you should still be polite and respectful. You never know who will read it.

- Use correct spelling. Proofread before sending to make sure there are no errors.
- Using abbreviations may be fine for personal communications with your friends and family but not for professional communications.
- Using all capital letters is considered to be shouting. Be sure to use proper capitalization.
- Don't send messages or images that may embarrass you in the future. Take a minute to think about what you are saying before you send a message.
- Don't forward or send unwanted messages like spam.
- Don't **flame**, or insult, anyone, even as a joke. Sometimes written communication is misinterpreted as being serious, even when if you said it out loud it might be considered funny.
- Don't use electronic communication to bully others.
- Don't make false statements that might hurt someone's reputation. It's called **libel** or **slander**, and it's illegal. You may be sued for damages.

Use the Vocabulary

Directions: *Match each vocabulary term in the left column with the correct definition in the right column.*

_____ 1. attachment
_____ 2. mailbox name
_____ 3. e-mail client
_____ 4. alias
_____ 5. e-mail server
_____ 6. bounce message
_____ 7. spam
_____ 8. digital signature
_____ 9. teleconference
_____ 10. videoconference

a. part of an e-mail address
b. a meeting that provides audio and visual contact for people in different locations
c. a notice that e-mail could not be delivered
d. junk e-mail
e. anything sent with an e-mail
f. a meeting via computers and a network or the Internet, which lets participants talk or exchange text messages
g. an electronic identifier used to verify the identity of an e-mail sender
h. an ISP computer that accepts, sends, and delivers e-mail messages
i. software that lets you create, send, receive, and manage e-mail messages
j. nickname by which an e-mail user is known

Check Your Comprehension

Directions: *Complete each sentence with information from the chapter.*

1. In an e-mail address, the symbol @ represents the word _____.
2. The _____ is an Internet service provider's computer that routes e-mail.
3. In an e-mail message form, the _____ field identifies people other than the main recipient who should receive the message when it is sent.
4. When you _____ an e-mail message you have received, you send it to another person.
5. You will not get a bounce message if you enter an incorrect but _____ address.
6. Some e-mail clients have _____ that you can configure to delete unwanted e-mail.
7. Sometimes, _____ can clog e-mail servers, slowing Internet traffic.
8. Teleconferences and videoconferences save money because people don't have to _____ to attend a meeting.
9. One-to-one _____ allow two people to see and talk to each other on their computers.
10. Many schools now offer classes through the Internet, a practice known as _____.

Think Critically

Directions: *Answer the following questions.*

1. How do an e-mail client and an e-mail server work together to handle e-mail?

2. What steps can you take to avoid receiving junk e-mail?

3. What advantages do e-mail, teleconferences, and videoconferences offer to workgroups in different locations?

4. What is one way to avoid receiving a bounce message?

5. Could distance learning make use of a videoconference? How?

Extend Your Knowledge

Directions: *Choose and complete one of the following projects.*

A. Start your e-mail program. With your teacher's permission, create a distribution list or contact group of people in your class. Create a message and address it to the contact group. Set the importance level as high and request a delivery receipt. With your teacher's permission, send the message.

B. In small groups, brainstorm for the advantages and disadvantages of face-to-face communications, traditional letters, e-mail, telephone calls, teleconferencing, and videoconferencing. Then, create a list of situations for which each of these media might be the most appropriate communications choice.

C. Working with a partner or small group, use the Calendar feature in your e-mail program to schedule a meeting and send a meeting request to your partner or group members. Follow up the meeting request with an e-mail that includes an attachment of an agenda in a document. When you receive the e-mail from someone else, save the attachment and open it in a word-processing program.

Understanding Personal Communications

We Need to Communicate Thanks to technology, today we can stay in touch more easily than ever before. We have many communications options, from speaking face to face or talking on the phone to using computers to exchange ideas and information.

Technology also gives us more freedom in communicating. We no longer have to sit by the phone waiting for a call or stay by a computer to check our e-mail; phone calls and e-mail messages can travel with us.

Advances in science and technology help us communicate anytime, almost anywhere. However, the virus programmers who deliberately interfere with communications systems continue to cause millions of dollars of damage to computers each year.

Chapter Outline

 Lesson 32–1

The Science of E-mail Systems

 Lesson 32–2

E-mail Benefits and Hazards

The Science of E-mail Systems

Objectives

- Describe how e-mail travels through networks.
- Summarize the key e-mail protocols.
- Explain how e-mail can be organized.

As You Read

Organize Information Use a concept web as you read to help you organize ideas about e-mail systems as you read the lesson.

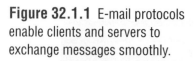

Key Terms

- authentication
- e-mail folder
- message header

What Happens When You Send and Receive E-mail?

When you send and receive e-mail messages, you participate in a client-server network. Your e-mail software is the client. The computer that accepts and forwards messages for its users is the e-mail server. Internet service providers (ISPs), companies and institutions, and other mail services maintain the servers. Because e-mail servers and clients use the same protocols, you can send messages to and receive messages from anyone with an e-mail address, as long as the computers have access to the same network or the Internet.

Sending Messages When you click Send, most messages travel first to your ISP's e-mail server via Simple Mail Transfer Protocol, or SMTP. The e-mail server then examines the recipient's address. If the person you are e-mailing uses the same server you do, the message is delivered instantly. The recipient's e-mail client retrieves the message from the server by using another protocol, called the Post Office Protocol (POP). Most current e-mail programs use a version of POP called POP3, which can work with or without SMTP.

Figure 32.1.1 E-mail protocols enable clients and servers to exchange messages smoothly.

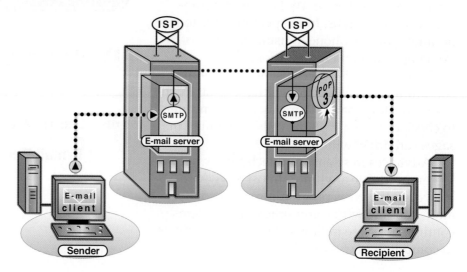

Different Servers Often, however, you and the recipient use different ISP e-mail servers. For example, you may use AOL, while your friend uses Mindspring. In this case, the AOL server, using SMTP, sends your e-mail message to the Mindspring server via the Internet. The Mindspring server then delivers the message to your friend. Attachments to a message are translated by a protocol called Multipurpose Internet Mail Extensions, or MIME.

Receiving Messages What happens to incoming messages sent to you? Usually, your server stores them. When you open your e-mail client and get your mail, the server sends you your messages and, depending on your settings, erases them from the server.

Securing Your Account

To handle your e-mail, your client needs your username and password. The server also uses this information to identify you as a valid user. In a process called **authentication**, the e-mail server confirms that you are a valid user.

Password Protection Guard your username and password, and change your password frequently. It should be easy for you to remember but difficult for others to guess. If someone learns your password, change it. Never allow others to log on with your password.

Organizing Your E-mail

E-mail programs provide you with an address book, where you can store the names and e-mail addresses of frequent e-mail contacts. You may be able to create group contact lists in your address book. If you and several friends are working on a project, you might create a list called Project and add the e-mail address of each group member to the list. This feature lets you send a message to all the contacts at once, saving you the time of typing each address separately.

Storing Messages The list of messages in your Inbox can grow quickly. You should delete unimportant messages after you read them. You can, however, save important messages in folders you create for this purpose. Like a manila folder, an **e-mail folder** stores related messages. For example, you can create a folder to hold messages relating to a specific topic or which come from a certain person. A Folder List identifies the folders you have created. Folders make it easy to find and manage messages.

To retrieve a message saved in the Inbox, click it. To store a message in a folder, drag the message from the Inbox to the desired folder. To open a message saved in a folder, click the name of the folder, and then click the message you wish to read.

Career Corner

Educational Media Technology Specialist Computers and telecommunications are now everyday teaching tools. Schools, museums, and other educational institutions that offer programs to the public have a growing need for educational media technology specialists. Knowledge of effective education practices, hardware, software, and the principles of networking are requirements for applicants in this field.

Technology @ Work

The Electronic Communications Privacy Act of 2000 allows companies to check the e-mail that employees send from office computers.

Think About It!

Think about guidelines employees should follow when sending e-mail on company time. Which statements listed below do you think describe good business "netiquette?"

➤ Use your company address for personal messages.
➤ Make sure the content of your messages is appropriate for your boss to read.
➤ To criticize someone, do it by e-mail.
➤ Use your school e-mail address for personal mail.
➤ Do not open or respond to e-mail from unknown senders.

Figure 32.1.2 Most e-mail programs let you keep your messages organized in folders.

Viewing Messages in the Inbox Incoming messages appear in your Inbox. Depending on your setup, you may see just a list of messages, or you may see the actual contents of the messages, too. At the top of the message is the **message header**. The message header contains information that identifies the sender of the message, other recipients, the date sent, and the subject.

Sorting Messages Most e-mail clients allow you to sort messages—that is, arrange them in a certain order, by senders' names, date received, and so on. To view the messages by sender, click the From heading. To sort by Subject or Date, click either of those headings.

Removing Messages Often you do not want to keep a message in your Inbox. You can move it to another folder, delete it, or archive it. Deleted messages are sent to the Trash or Deleted Items folder and are not actually deleted until you select the command to delete them permanently. Up until you delete it permanently, you can recover a message from the Deleted Items folder.

Archived messages are saved on your computer in the Archive folder. Archiving is a great way to clean up clutter while saving a message with important information, like a phone number or address. Some companies archive all the e-mails of their employees. For legal reasons it is important they have a record of electronic communications.

Configuring E-mail Options All e-mail clients allow you to customize your e-mails. You can usually do this by clicking on the "settings" option. For instance, you can use settings to create a signature that will appear on every e-mail message you create, even with a quote or image you like. When you are out of the office or otherwise not available, you can use an automatic reply, or "away" message to automatically send a reply to incoming

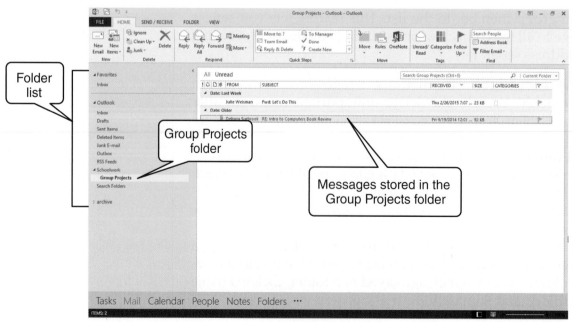

Outlook 2013, Microsoft Corporation.

messages. The reply can politely tell the sender that you are unavailable, and when you will be back. Some systems even let you customize an automatic reply for specific addresses. Other options let you automatically forward messages and set your spam or junk filter to block mail from specific addresses.

E-mail Notifications Many web sites let you set up notifications or alerts that can be sent to you via e-mail. For example, on a social networking site, you can select a setting to send you a notification when someone posts a new picture. On a news site, you can select a setting to send you a notification when there is breaking news about a topic that interests you, such as sports scores or weather.

Using a Digital Calendar

Many communications programs such as Outlook include a Calendar feature that you can use to schedule one-time and recurring events and appointments. There are also stand-alone calendar programs and online calendars.

To schedule a one-time event you create the event and enter details such as the date, time, and location. The event displays on the calendar. You can even set a reminder to display on your screen to remind you about the event. Setting a recurring event is similar but you select the interval that the event recurs, such as every Monday, or the fifth of every month, or even once a year. You can send invitations by text message or e-mail to other people or contact groups that you want to attend the meeting or event and the program will keep track of their replies.

Most programs allow you to maintain more than one calendar, so you can have one for work and one for personal appointments. Use the commands on the View menu to change from one to the other, or display them at the same time.

Many Web sites maintain calendars of events. You can subscribe to these calendars and the Web site will send you notifications when an event is scheduled or changed.

Figure 32.1.3 Use a Calendar to schedule appointments, meetings, and events.

Outlook 2013, Microsoft Corporation.

E-mail Benefits and Hazards

Objectives

- Explain how e-mail attachments work.
- Discuss the hazards of e-mail viruses.
- Assess the value of virus detection software.

As You Read

Organize Information   Use an outline to help you identify the advantages and dangers of e-mail as you read the lesson.

Key Terms

- e-mail virus
- executable file
- macro virus
- replicate

Tapping the Power of E-mail

A useful feature of e-mail is the ability to send attachments. An attachment is a computer file that is added to an e-mail message. The recipient saves the attachment on his or her computer. There are two important issues about attachments that you should be aware of:

- Your recipients may have a different e-mail program or computer platform. They also may not have the program you used to create an attached file. They may not be able to retrieve or use the attachment.

- Large files, such as photo or video files, can take a long time to download. Be sure your recipients want them: Some recipients' e-mail servers or clients may reject large attachments. One way to get larger attachments to your recipients is to use an online database, such as Dropbox. You register at the site and can then store files on its server. You send a link via e-mail, which the recipient clicks to access the file. He or she can leave it online, or download it.

Common Uses of Attachments   What if you are on vacation and want to share photos you took with your digital camera? You can copy them onto your laptop and send them to your friends as e-mail attachments. Are you and your friends working together on a school report? Perhaps you wrote the text for the document and a friend created the artwork, while another created a video explaining the report. Each of you could attach your work to an e-mail message and let the others review your progress.

Business Uses of Attachments   Companies no longer need to print, package, and ship documents. Instead, with just a few clicks, documents can be sent as e-mail attachments. E-mailing attachments can also replace faxing documents to other locations. In both cases, e-mailing documents saves time and money.

Figure 32.2.1 An e-mail message with an attachment.

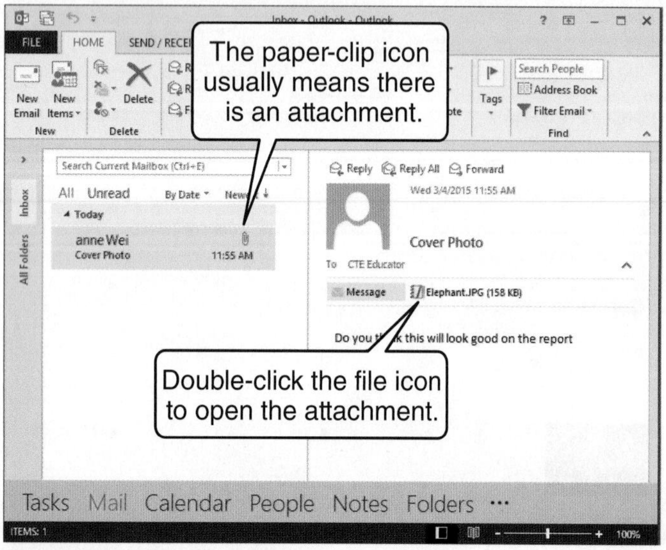

The paper-clip icon usually means there is an attachment.

Double-click the file icon to open the attachment.

Outlook 2013, Microsoft Corporation.

The Dangers of E-mail Attachments

Some attachments can contain **e-mail viruses**—scripts or programs that cause harm, such as changing or deleting files. The worst viruses **replicate**, or copy themselves. They locate your address book and send themselves to every address listed in it. Since your name appears in the message header, the friends and family whom you e-mail do not suspect a problem until they open the message and their computers become infected.

E-mail viruses can do great harm to businesses, too. Imagine that a virus replicated on the computers listed in employees' address books. The e-mail servers would become overloaded, and files would be destroyed.

Executable Files   One way of spreading a virus is through an executable file. An **executable file** is one that carries out instructions that might destroy files on your computer, change its settings, or cause Internet traffic jams.

You can recognize an executable file by the extension at the end of the file name: .COM, .EXE, .VBS, .BAT. If you get an e-mail message that has one of these files attached, beware. You may be asking for trouble if you open it.

Macro Viruses   Another type of virus is called a macro virus. A **macro virus** is a series of commands that takes advantage of the programming language built into everyday application software, such as Microsoft Word. The virus might add words or phrases to documents, or do additional damage.

Real-World Tech

Catching a Virus   Anyone can be vulnerable to viruses—even people who know a lot about the risks. Josh Quittner is a columnist for an online technology magazine. But that didn't protect him when he received an e-mail with an attachment from a friend. He opened it and then watched in horror as his screen began to shimmer. Quittner's computer had been infected by a virus.

What steps can you take to help protect your computer from a virus?

	Reply	Reply Wit
▾	Subject	
:00C	Re: applicatio	
:00C	ILOVEYOU	
:00C	ILOVEYOU	
:00C	ILOVEYOU	
:00C	ILOVEYOU	
:00C	ILOVEYOU	
:00C	ILOVEYOU	

Technology @ Home

Can home computers catch a virus just as business computers can? Of course!

Protecting Yourself

E-mail attachments aren't the only source of viruses. Viruses have been found in:

- files downloaded from the Internet
- files created on public computers, such as those in libraries
- infected media, such as CDs or DVDs

Antivirus Software A good antivirus software program will run all the time on your computer. It looks for any application or script that tries to manipulate the system. Some antivirus software can also scan incoming and outgoing e-mail for viruses.

Automatic Updates Virus programmers continually try to create new viruses and make changes to existing ones, with a primary goal of making viruses more difficult to detect and eliminate. The developers of antivirus software, however, are never more than a step behind the virus programmers. Most good antivirus programs can be updated regularly via the Internet. Some of the programs can update themselves automatically, without the user even knowing about it. By regularly updating your antivirus software, you can protect yourself against the most current viruses.

Figure 32.2.2 Microsoft Windows 10 comes with Windows Defender to help protect your system from malicious software.

Windows 10, Microsoft Corporation.

Use the Vocabulary

Directions: *Match each vocabulary term in the left column with the correct definition in the right column.*

_____ **1.** message header
_____ **2.** authentication
_____ **3.** e-mail folder
_____ **4.** replicate
_____ **5.** executable file
_____ **6.** macro virus
_____ **7.** e-mail virus

a. part of an e-mail that identifies the sender, among other information

b. series of commands hidden in a document

c. to copy or reproduce, as a virus makes copies of itself

d. process by which an e-mail server identifies valid users

e. place to store saved messages

f. can launch a program; sometimes used by viruses

g. a script or program that causes harm

Check Your Comprehension

Directions: *Complete each sentence with information from the chapter.*

1. The _____ helps your e-mail messages reach your e-mail server.

2. With most e-mail clients, you can organize the messages in your Inbox by _____ different headers at the top of the Inbox.

3. Your _____ should be easy for you to remember but hard for someone else to guess.

4. An e-mail folder stores _____.

5. You can send photos with an e-mail message as _____.

6. You can recognize some executable files by the _____ at the end of the file name.

7. _____ software checks for viruses and alerts you to them.

8. An e-mail server uses _____ to confirm that you are a valid user.

9. Incoming messages are listed in your _____.

10. Some e-mail servers or clients may reject attachments that are too _____.

Think Critically

Directions: *Answer the following questions.*

1. What is the overall purpose of SMTP, MIME, and POP3?

2. How can you secure both your outgoing and incoming e-mail?

3. How might your antivirus software help others?

4. Summarize the reasons for organizing e-mail into folders.

5. Explain ways you can customize e-mail options.

Extend Your Knowledge

Directions: *Choose and complete one of the following projects.*

A. Two well-known e-mail viruses are "Here you have" virus, which spread in 2010, and Code Red, which made its way through networks in 2001. Conduct library or, with your teacher's permission, online research to find out what problems each of these invaders caused, how they spread, and how they were defeated. Also, identify a more recent virus and describe its effects and how computer users might have protected themselves from the destruction the virus caused. Present your findings in a report.

B. E-mail is one type of electronic communication, but there are many others, include texting, instant messaging, blogging, and social networking. Compare and contrast the advantages and disadvantages of different types of electronic communication. Summarize your findings in a report and present it to your class.

C. With your teacher's permission, practice using the configuration options for your e-mail program. Learn how to block spam or junk mail, how to create a signature, and how to use automatic replies. Discuss these features with a partner, or as a class.

DIRECTIONS: *You will use e-mail to exchange information about e-mail etiquette. You will create a new contact to which you will send the e-mail. You also will reply to and forward an e-mail message.*

1. Open the .pdf file **EM-1_Etiquette**. With your teacher's permission, print the Data Record Sheet. Close the file, and exit your pdf reader program.
2. Use the Internet (with your teacher's permission), library resources, or your school's acceptable Internet use policy to locate information about e-mail etiquette.
3. To use the Internet, open a Web browser and navigate to a search engine. Search for words or phrases such as **"e-mail etiquette"**.
4. Evaluate each site you visit for accuracy and validity.
5. When you find a Web site with relevant information, bookmark the site, or with your teacher's permission, print the desired pages. Complete the Data Record Sheet. Check copyright guidelines to make sure you can legally use the information.
6. Start your e-mail program.
7. Open your address book or contacts list, and with your teacher's permission, enter the name and e-mail address of a classmate or other recipient.
8. In your e-mail program, create a new mail message. Alternatively, with your teacher's permission, complete this activity using an instant messaging service, social networking site, or other personal communication service.
9. In the To box, select the recipient's e-mail address that you entered in step 7.

10. In the Subject box, type **E-mail Etiquette Guidelines**.
11. In the body of the e-mail message, write a greeting to the recipient, followed by a list of tips or guidelines based on the information you recorded on your Data Record Sheet. In your message, ask the recipient to reply with his or her opinion on your etiquette guidelines. At the end of the message, enter your name or signature. A sample message is shown in Illustration A.
12. Check the spelling and grammar in the e-mail message, and correct any errors.
13. With your teacher's permission, send the e-mail.
14. When you receive the e-mail reply from the recipient, open it and read it.
15. Create a folder where you can store messages relating to the class, and move the reply into it.
16. With your teacher's permission, forward the e-mail with the recipient's reply to your teacher's e-mail address.
17. With your teacher's permission, send a reply to the recipient, thanking him or her for the response.
18. Exit the e-mail program.
19. As a class, discuss the e-mail guidelines. Why do you think it is important to use e-mail etiquette when corresponding with e-mail? Do you think you must use the same guidelines when you communicate with friends as when you communicate with teachers, parents, and other adults?

Illustration A

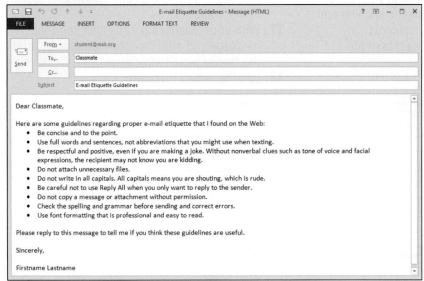

Outlook 2013, Microsoft Corporation.

E-mail Activities

DIRECTIONS: *You will practice using e-mail to send a document. You will write a persuasive essay about an interesting topic in your school or community. You will include specific facts and examples to support your opinion. Then, you will send your essay as an e-mail attachment to the editor of a local newspaper or your school newspaper.*

1. With your teacher's permission, use the Internet to find your local newspaper online. Search the newspaper to find articles about a current issue that relates to your school or community. As you read, formulate an opinion about the issue.

2. Open the .pdf file **EM-2_Outline**. With your teacher's permission, print the Data Record Sheet. Close the file, and exit your pdf reader program.

3. Use the Data Record Sheet to outline a persuasive essay on the topic of the article. List reasons, facts, and details that support your opinion about the issue.

4. Locate the name and e-mail address for the editor of the newspaper you read or for your school newspaper. Write the name and e-mail address on your Data Record Sheet.

5. Start your word processor, and create a new document. Save it as **EM-2_Opinion_xx** in the location where your teacher instructs you to store the files for this activity. Replace the initials **xx** with your own name or initials, as instructed by your teacher.

6. At the top of the page, write a title that makes it clear what issue you are writing about. Format the title appropriately and center it.

7. Using the outline on your Data Record Sheet, write a persuasive essay about the topic. Be sure to use proper keyboarding posture and techniques, including typing only one space after punctuation marks.

8. When you have finished writing your essay, proofread it carefully, check the spelling and grammar, and make improvements.

9. Exchange documents with a classmate according to your teacher's instructions. For example, you may print the document to exchange, copy it to a removable drive, or send it via e-mail. Proofread your classmate's essay by marking errors on the printed page or by turning on your program's revision tracking feature and using comments and revision marks. Return the essay to your classmate.

10. Accept or reject changes to incorporate your classmate's suggestions into your document file.

11. Finalize your essay, close the file, saving all changes, and exit your word-processing program.

12. Open your e-mail program, and create a new mail message.

13. In the To box, type the e-mail address of the newspaper editor that you wrote on your Data Record Sheet. With your teacher's permission, include your teacher's e-mail address in the Cc box.

14. In the Subject box, type a subject related to the issue that is the topic of your essay.

15. Type a brief e-mail message to the editor, explaining that you are attaching an essay that expresses your opinion about the issue. Explain that you are submitting the essay to be considered for publication. Include a respectful greeting at the beginning of the message and your name and school name at the end.

16. Attach the **EM-2_Opinion_xx** file to the message. A sample e-mail message is shown in Illustration B.

17. With your teacher's permission, send the message and attachment. Alternatively, print the message and attachment.

18. Exit the e-mail program.

Illustration B

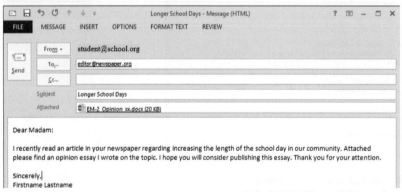

Outlook 2013, Microsoft Corporation.

DIRECTIONS: *You will practice using e-mail to send a spreadsheet as an attachment. You will open an existing spreadsheet, insert a formula to perform a calculation, and create a chart to illustrate the data. You will then create an e-mail message and attach the spreadsheet file before sending.*

1. Start your spreadsheet program and open **EM-3_Survey**. Save the file as **EM-3_Survey_xx** in the location where your teacher instructs you to store the files for this activity.
2. In cell B5, use the SUM function to enter a formula totaling the responses.
3. Select cells A2:B4 and create a 3-D Clustered Column chart.
4. Enter the chart title **Extended School Day Survey Results**.
5. Format the columns (data points) with different colors or gradient fills.
6. Position the chart over cells A7:F21.
7. Insert a footer with your name on the left and today's date on the right.
8. Preview the spreadsheet. It should look similar to Illustration C.
9. With your teacher's permission, print the spreadsheet, and then exit your spreadsheet program, saving all changes.

10. Start your e-mail program, and create a new mail message.
11. In the To box, type the e-mail address approved by your teacher, such as a classmate, a family member, or a teacher.
12. In the Subject box, type **Survey Results**.
13. In the message area, type a greeting and then type: **Attached is a spreadsheet illustrating the results of the survey. Please reply to this message telling me if you think the chart is easy to read.**
14. After the message, type your name.
15. Check the spelling and grammar in the e-mail message, and correct any errors.
16. Attach the **EM-3_Survey_xx** file to the message.
17. With your teacher's permission, send the e-mail.
18. When you receive the e-mail reply from the recipient, open it and read it. Store it in the folder you created for this class.
19. With your teacher's permission, print the e-mail message from the recipient.
20. With your teacher's permission, forward the e-mail with the recipient's reply to your teacher.
21. Exit the e-mail program.

Illustration C

Longer School Day Survey	
Agree with the decision to extend the school day	5
Disagree with the decision to extend the school day	134
Do not have an opinion	12
Total	151

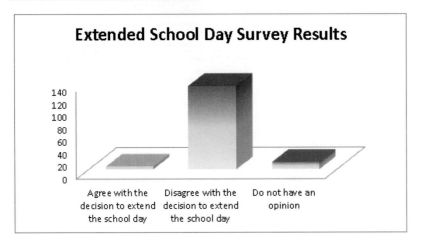

DIRECTIONS: *You will use a word-processing program to compose a cover letter for a job application. You will then copy the text of the letter into your e-mail program to send to a potential employer.*

1. Begin by looking for summer jobs or internships in your area. For example, you might look into being a camp counselor, babysitting in your neighborhood, or any type of employment for students your age. For resources, look in local online newspapers, your school career office, or a local government bulletin board. Identify the name, title, mailing address, and e-mail address of the person responsible for hiring.

2. Start your word-processing program and create a new file based on a simple letter template. Save the file as **EM-4_Cover Letter_xx** in the location where your teacher instructs you to store the files for this activity.

3. Replace the sample text or content controls in the letter to enter the date, your name and address, the recipient's name and address, and the salutation.

4. Replace the sample letter text with two to four paragraphs explaining that you are applying for the position. Be sure to state the position title, where you heard about it, and why you think you are qualified.

5. With a partner or peer editor, proofread the letter carefully and make corrections and improvements.

6. Preview the letter. It should look similar to the one shown in Illustration D (right).

7. Start your e-mail program, and create a new mail message.

8. In the To box, type the recipient's e-mail address. If you do not have an actual employer's address, enter the address of a classmate, family member, or teacher. With your teacher's permission, include his or her address in the Cc box. In the Subject box, type the title of the position for which you are applying, followed by the word **Application**.

9. Arrange the two program windows side by side.

10. Copy all of the text in the **EM-4_Cover Letter_xx** document to the Clipboard.

11. Paste the text into the e-mail message area. A sample is shown in Illustration D (left).

12. Exit your word-processing program, saving all changes.

13. Maximize the e-mail program window. With your teacher's permission, send the e-mail.

14. Exit the e-mail program.

Illustration D

Outlook 2013, Microsoft Corporation.

DIRECTIONS: *You will conduct research about volcanoes. As part of your research, you will send an e-mail message to an expert. You will use the research information to create a presentation, which you will send as an e-mail attachment.*

1. Open the .pdf file **EM-5_VolcanoResearch**. With your teacher's permission, print the Data Record Sheet. You will record notes about volcanoes to create a draft for your presentation. Close the file, and exit your pdf reader program.

2. Use the Internet (with your teacher's permission) to find information about a specific volcano of your choice.

3. Search for terms and phrases such as the name of the volcano. You may also use Boolean searches, such as **volcanoes AND volcanologists**.

4. Compare and evaluate each site you find for its accuracy and validity. Use information from only those sites relevant to your purposes.

5. Locate information about the volcano's location and height, how often it erupts, date of most recent eruption, and at least two interesting or unusual facts about the volcano.

6. Record the information you find on the Data Record Sheet. On a separate sheet of paper, cite sources for all information you use.

7. Search for several photos of the volcano. Check the copyright to be sure you can legally use the photos, and then, with your teacher's permission, download and save them.

8. Locate information about volcanologists. Find information about the following and record it on the Data Record Sheet:
   - How close scientists get to a volcano
   - What precautions they take
   - What kinds of protective equipment they use
   - Which instruments they use to take measurements
   - What kinds of information they gather
   - The e-mail address of a volcanologist or other volcano researcher, such as a professor at a local college or someone at the United States Geological Survey (www.usgs.gov)

9. Start your e-mail program and create a new message. Address it to the researcher. As the subject, type **Volcano Research**. In the message, introduce yourself as a student and request brief answers to the questions in step 8. Check the spelling and grammar in the message and correct errors. A sample message is shown in Illustration E.

10. With your teacher's permission, send the message. If you receive a reply from the researcher, open and read it and then move it into the folder you created for this class. Record any additional notes on the Data Record Sheet.

11. When you have completed your research, close the Web browser.

12. Start your presentation program, and create a new presentation based on a template. Save it as **EM-5_Volcano_xx**.

13. Create the first slide as a title slide, and enter the title for the presentation. Insert a subtitle that includes your name, school name, and school address. Add a footer with your name and today's date.

14. Develop the presentation by modifying the template slides or by inserting new slides. Create slides about the volcano's location, height, and last eruption, interesting facts, equipment used by volcanologists, types of information volcanologists research, and precautions. Include a slide to cite your sources. For each slide, select a slide layout that works best with the information you have and any graphics or clip art you want to include.

15. When you have finished entering the slide text, proofread each one carefully with a partner or peer editor, checking for consistency in sentence structure, and correct any errors you find.

16. Modify or apply a theme or design to your presentation.

17. Modify or add transitions and animations to the presentation.

E-mail Activities

18. Add notes to reference while you deliver the presentation.
19. Preview the presentation, and make any final modifications.
20. With your teacher's permission, print the notes pages for yourself, and print handouts with three slides per page for the class.
21. Rehearse the presentation, and then show it to the class.
22. Close the presentation file, saving all changes, and exit your presentation program.
23. Start your e-mail program and create a new e-mail message. With your teacher's permission, address it to a classmate or to your teacher.

24. In the subject line, type **Volcano Presentation**. Type a brief message explaining that this is a presentation about a volcano. Check the spelling and grammar in the message and correct any errors.
25. Attach the presentation to the message, and then, with your teacher's permission, send it.
26. Exit your e-mail program.

Illustration E

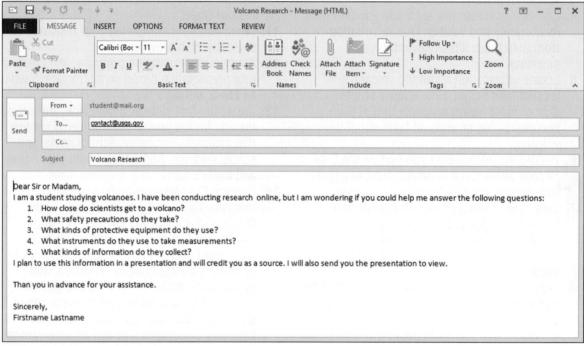

Outlook 2013, Microsoft Corporation.

Issues for Computer Users

Computers and Safety Computers are tools and, like other tools, they are controlled by the person using them. People can use computers to learn, to communicate, and to have fun. However, people can also use computers to snoop into another person's private life or to commit crimes. Careless computer users can pass computer viruses from their machines to those of other users. What can make computers dangerous is the same thing that makes them helpful: They can store vast amounts of data.

When people learn to use tools, they learn to use them with care and to protect themselves and others from harm. Computer users need to learn ways to protect themselves, too.

Chapter Outline

 Lesson 33–1

Privacy Online

 Lesson 33–2

All About Cybercrime

 Lesson 33–3

Avoiding Cybercrime

Privacy Online

Objectives

- Summarize the danger of sharing personal information on the Internet.
- Explain how cookies and global unique identifiers endanger privacy.

As You Read

Organize Information   As you read the lesson, use an outline to help you organize basic information about privacy issues.

🔑 Key Terms

- global unique identifier(GUID)
- infringe

Privacy in Cyberspace

Many consumers share personal information about themselves, their habits, and their finances. Sometimes, however, such information is gathered without a person's knowledge or approval.

How Businesses Obtain Personal Information   Some businesses gather information from public records kept by the government. They may also access information that people volunteer about themselves in several ways:

- Web site registration—Many Web sites require visitors to fill out registration forms.
- Online purchases—Some Web sites gather information about people who buy their goods or services.
- Warranty registration—To take advantage of a product warranty, you usually must register with the manufacturer. Some warranty registrations ask for a lot of personal information.
- Sweepstakes entries—Many people fill out sweepstakes entry forms hoping to win a prize. In doing so, they provide important personal information.
- Social networking sites—These sites gather information about their users from their profiles and posts, including where they live, what they like, and products they use.
- Search engines and messaging services—Some of these sites collect data about users and their online search history to learn what interests them.

Companies that gather personal information often sell it to other organizations, such as marketing companies, whose job is to sell products and services to consumers. As a result, marketing companies have access to enormous quantities of data about people. This information is stored in large computerized databases.

Protecting Privacy   Some people say that individuals should have the right to refuse to provide information about themselves, as well as the right to have information about themselves removed from a database. Although such a guarantee does not yet exist in the United States, you can protect your privacy by being careful to whom you give out personal information about yourself. You can also select privacy settings on Web sites and social networks that limit who can access your personal information or view your posts. For example, you can select to only share your personal information with friends, or set your social networking status to invisible so other people do not know you are online.

Respecting Others' Privacy You also need to make sure not to **infringe** or interfere with the privacy and rights of others. Do not post personal information about others online, via texts, or in e-mails.

Expectations of Privacy Remember that everything you post online or send by e-mail is on record. Employees of a company have no right of privacy for their e-mail when they use their employer's computer system. Although the employer may not say so, every message might be read by someone who alerts management if anything seems amiss. Employees may face serious consequences if they disclose inside information to competitors, threaten or harass other employees, or tell jokes.

In addition, when you apply to a college or university, or to a job, you should expect that the school or potential employer will look for you online. A simple search will let them see a history of what you have posted on almost every Internet site. These are strong reasons why you should always be respectful and polite online, and why you should never post items that may be embarrassing to you in the future.

New Technology and Your Privacy

The Internet has generated new methods for tracking what people do. Even if you do not buy anything online, outsiders can use different hardware and software to learn about your habits and interests. Some people worry that these technologies—and your personal information—can be misused.

Cookies A cookie is a small file that is saved to your hard drive when you visit some Web sites. Cookies give Web sites a way of storing information about you so it is available when you return. Cookies are meant to make your Web experience more pleasurable by personalizing what you see. However, they can also be used to gather data on your browsing and shopping habits without your consent.

If you wish, you can set your browser to reject cookies or warn you about them. Several programs and Web browsers let users see what the purpose of a cookie is. Then you can decide whether or not to accept the cookie.

Global Unique Identifiers A **global unique identifier**, or **GUID**, is a unique identification number that is generated by a piece of hardware or by a program. Companies that place GUIDs in their products generally do not say so openly. Some people worry that GUIDs can be used to follow a person's online activity, invading his or her privacy.

Figure 33.1.1 Most Web-browser programs let you select Privacy settings to control cookies.

Internet Explorer 10, Microsoft Corporation.

All About Cybercrime

Objectives

- Identify techniques that intruders use to attack computer systems.
- Discuss different types of cybercrime.
- Summarize how computer crime costs businesses money.

As You Read

Identify Key Points As you read, use a conclusion chart to help you identify key points about computer-related crime.

🔑 Key Terms

- computer crime
- cybercrime
- downtime
- identity theft
- memory shave
- phishing
- scanning
- software piracy
- spoof
- superzapper
- time bomb
- trap door
- Trojan horse
- virus
- worm

Cybercrime Techniques

Many cybercrimes are based on the ability of people to tap illegally into computer networks. They may create a **virus**, **worm**, or **Trojan horse** program to infiltrate computers and damage or delete data. Or, they may use a variety of other criminal techniques.

Scanning Some intruders develop programs that try many different passwords until one works. This is called **scanning**, or probing. Networks can be blocked from scanners by limiting the number of failed attempts to log onto the system. After three password failures, for instance, the network can refuse access.

Superzapping A program called a **superzapper** allows authorized users to access a network in an emergency situation by skipping security measures. In the hands of an intruder, a superzapper opens the possibility of damage to the system.

Spoofing Some intruders **spoof**, or use a false Internet Protocol (IP) or e-mail address to gain access. Intruders assume the IP address of a trusted source to enter a secure network and distribute e-mails containing viruses.

Phishing **Phishing** criminals try to lure victims into giving them user names, passwords, bank account numbers, or credit card details, usually by using an e-mail that looks like it comes from an official and legitimate source. For example, in a typical phishing scam, a thief sends an e-mail message that looks as if it is from your bank, asking you to verify or update your account information. The thief captures the information you enter and can then steal from your account.

Time Bombs A **time bomb** is a program that sits on a system until a certain event or set of circumstances activates the program. For example, an employee could create a time bomb designed to activate on a certain date after he or she resigns from the company. Although a time bomb is not necessarily a virus, these malicious programs are often categorized or described as viruses.

Trap Doors   Some employees may create a **trap door**, or a secret way into the system. Once they quit working for the employer, they can use this to access the system and damage it. Not all trap doors are viruses, but some viruses are trap doors. Many Trojan horse programs, for example, act as trap doors.

Scams   Some criminals use advertisements and e-mail messages to scam you into sending them money. For example, they might claim you have won a lottery, and if you pay a tax or fee, they will send you the winnings.

Social Engineering   A common criminal tactic is to use social engineering to trick you into clicking a link that will install a virus or capture your personal information. Social engineering is not technical. It relies on human nature and manipulation to convince someone to do something. A common social engineering hack would be an official-looking e-mail notifying you about a problem with your bank account. When you click a link you are sent to a fake bank Web site.

Types of Cybercrime

Crimes using the Internet can take many different forms. They affect individuals, businesses, and government agencies.

Fraud   When someone steals your personal information, he or she can impersonate you and make credit card purchases in your name or access your bank accounts. This is called **identity theft.** The criminal leaves you with bills and a damaged credit rating.

Piracy   **Software piracy** is the illegal copying of computer programs. It is estimated that about one third of all software in use is pirated.

As discussed in Lesson 9–2, most programs that people buy are licensed only to the purchaser. In other words, it is illegal for you to copy such a program and give it to a friend. It is also illegal to accept a copy of software from someone else.

Software piracy affects software publishers. They lose money when people use illegal copies of programs to avoid paying for legitimate copies.

Theft   The vast majority of computer thefts occur "on the inside" (by employees), leaving no signs of forced entry. The hardest crime to detect is **memory shaving**. In this act, a thief steals some of a computer's memory chips but leaves enough so the computer will start. The crime might go unnoticed for days or weeks.

Figure 33.2.1 Identity theft is a growing problem in the United States, and the Federal Trade Commission is taking steps to help consumers avoid this problem.

Vandalism   Some Web servers are not properly secured. As a result, intruders can vandalize a Web site by placing prank material on it.

The High Cost of Computer Crime

The Internet has opened the door to new kinds of crime and new ways of carrying out traditional crimes. **Computer crime** is any act that violates state or federal laws and involves using a computer. The term **cybercrime** often refers specifically to crimes carried out by means of the Internet. Computer crime causes businesses to lose money in the following ways.

Staff Time   Even if intruders steal nothing from a business, they still cost companies money. Staff must make the network secure again and consider how to stop security breaches.

Downtime   Security breaches also cost a company in terms of **downtime**, or a temporary stop to work. System administrators sometimes shut a network down to prevent the loss of data. While the system is down, workers cannot do their jobs. A company can lose business if customers are affected by downtime.

Bad Publicity   When security problems become known, the public image of a company may suffer. Even if no personal information is lost, customers lose confidence that the company's security is trustworthy. Customers then take their business elsewhere.

Fighting Cybercrime

Law enforcement officials are using technology to catch cybercriminals. Several groups have taken part in this effort.

Computer Crime and Intellectual Property Section (CCIPS)
The Department of Justice created a special group known as CCIPS to advise and train federal prosecutors and local law enforcement on cybercrime. They review and propose new laws. They coordinate international efforts to combat computer crime and prosecute offenders.

Computer Hacking and Intellectual Property Project (CHIP)
In the CHIP project, law enforcement officials and prosecutors work closely together to pursue cybercrime. CHIP offices are in areas with a heavy concentration of computer companies.

National Infrastructure Protection Center (NIPC)   In 1998, government officials became worried about terrorist attacks on U.S. computer systems. Staffed by people from intelligence agencies and private companies such as Internet service providers, the NIPC ensures that the nation's computer system could continue to operate in the case of an attack.

Avoiding Cybercrime

Objectives

- Describe ways criminals obtain passwords.
- Discuss ways to protect your computer from being accessed by others.
- Explain the criteria of a strong password.
- Summarize ways to stay safe online.

As You Read

Summarize   As you read the lesson, use a chart to help you summarize ways to protect information on your computer.

Password Theft

Many computer crimes start when an unauthorized user hacks, or gains unauthorized entry, into a computer network. This often happens when the intruder learns the password to access the victim's computer and the network. Following are ways such criminals learn passwords.

Guessing   Too often, computer users choose passwords that are easy for them to remember, such as birthdates, names of pets, names of celebrities, and names of family members. Unfortunately, these passwords are also easy for intruders to guess. Surprisingly, the most common passwords used are "password" and "123456," both of which are extremely weak.

Finding   Sometimes people keep passwords written on pieces of paper near their computer. Other times, criminals simply look over someone's shoulder as he or she types the password and use it later. An intruder can also search the trash in the hopes of finding user IDs and passwords.

"Sniffing"   Some criminals may use **packet sniffers**. A packet sniffer is a program that examines data streams on networks to try to find information, such as passwords and credit card numbers.

Pretending   Some intruders pretend to be network administrators. They call network users and ask for their passwords, claiming that the passwords are needed to solve a problem in the system.

Modifying   Network software makes the people who administer a system into superusers. Intruders who have superuser access can modify virtually any file on the network. They also may change user passwords to ones they know.

 **Key Terms**

- packet sniffer

Technology @ Home

One way companies generate mailing lists for spam messages is by checking the addresses of people in chat rooms and in Web discussion groups. If you use these services, you can minimize spam at your primary e-mail address by using a secondary e-mail address for these chats. You can then trash the spam when you want.

Think About It!

Which contacts listed below would you give your secondary e-mail address to?

➤ friend

➤ movie promotional site

➤ Web site from which you ordered a DVD

➤ chat room

➤ Web site where you receive support for your computer

Protecting Your Personal Data

It is in your best interest to protect your computer and its data. Here are some ways to help protect personal information.

Use Strong Passwords Whenever you create a password, don't use things like family names, nicknames, or birth dates. Random passwords are often the strongest, like S3nD3v. Use a combination of at least six upper- and lowercase letters, numbers, and symbols. Often the site will let you know if your password is strong enough. Remember to change your password every so often. Do not keep a record of your passwords on your computer or on a piece of paper near your computer. Never give out your passwords to anyone, and never type a password while someone is watching.

Browse Anonymously When you go online, surf from sites that protect your identity. Anonymizer and IDZap are two sites offering this service.

Use a Different E-mail Address Although you may not be able to do this at school, on a home computer you can sign up for a free e-mail account from a Web site such as Hotmail or gmail. Use that address when you register at Web sites or participate in other public Internet spaces. This will protect you from receiving unwanted mail, or spam, at your primary e-mail address.

Avoid Site Registration Be careful of Web sites that require you to register. Do not fill out a registration form unless the site clearly says that the data will not be shared with other people without your approval.

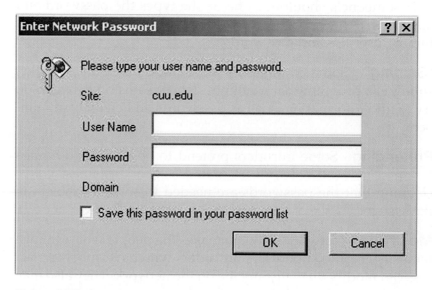

Figure 33.3.1 You may be required to provide a user name and password before accessing a computer network. Be sure to use a "strong" password.

Be Smart Online

You can avoid most computer crime simply by being a smart computer user. You can make sure your Internet browser settings are at the highest level for security and privacy, you can delete e-mail from unknown senders without opening it, and you can be wary of offers that seem too good to be true. Make sure you do business only with established companies that you know and trust. No reputable company or bank will ever ask you to send them your username, password, account information, or social security number. You should never reveal financial or other personal information, even if the request sounds legitimate.

Safe Social Networking   Here are some safety tips for online social networking:

- Do not add just anyone as a "friend." This person will see everything you post, including pictures and status updates.
- Check your settings. If you don't understand how to manage your account, get an adult to help you make sure you maintain your privacy.
- Learn how to change your status to invisible, so others do not know you are online, or visible, so they do know you are online.
- Give your parents or other trusted adult access to monitor your social networking activity.
- Remember that your posts and profiles can be easily tracked online. Don't write or post anything online that you would not want your grandparents or teachers to see or that you would not want posted about yourself.
- Never give out private information such as your phone number or address.
- Never agree to meet a new online friend in person.
- If you feel uncomfortable about an online experience, immediately tell a trusted adult.
- Don't download or install programs without parental permission.

Language Arts   Where did all the unusual names for destructive software come from?

- A computer virus is named for the kind of virus that causes infectious diseases like the cold and the flu.

- A worm is named for a tapeworm, a kind of organism that lives in the intestines of another creature and lives off the food that creature eats.

- A Trojan horse takes its name from an ancient Greek story about soldiers who entered a fortress by hiding inside the body of a giant replica of a horse, which the defenders allowed in. The soldiers hidden inside the horse attacked and defeated the defenders.

Figure 33.3.2 Never give out private information online.

Use the Vocabulary

Directions: *Match each vocabulary term in the left column with the correct definition in the right column.*

_____ **1.** identity theft
_____ **2.** phishing
_____ **3.** global unique identifier
_____ **4.** computer crime
_____ **5.** cybercrime
_____ **6.** downtime
_____ **7.** software piracy
_____ **8.** packet sniffer
_____ **9.** scanning
_____ **10.** spoof

a. using a program to try different passwords until one works
b. using a computer to break the law
c. using the Internet to break the law
d. when workers cannot work because a network is temporarily not available
e. illegal copying of software programs
f. identification number generated by a piece of hardware or by a program
g. use a false IP or e-mail address to gain access to a network
h. impersonating someone in order to commit fraud
i. using an official-looking e-mail to lure victims into providing personal data
j. method of finding another's password

Check Your Comprehension

Directions: *Determine the correct choice for each of the following.*

1. Which of the following should you do cautiously because it could result in sharing personal information without your approval?
   a. buying software
   b. copying software
   c. registering at a Web site
   d. getting warranty protection

2. Which of the following malicious programs is activated by an event or set of circumstances?
   a. worm
   b. e-mail virus
   c. time bomb
   d. Trojan horse

3. Which of the following might cause a business to lose money as a result of computer crime?
   a. faulty product design
   b. downtime
   c. economic recession
   d. fire

4. Which kind of destructive computer program can move from one operating system to another?
   a. macro virus
   b. Trojan horse
   c. virus
   d. worm

5. What is an example of a password that is easy to guess?
   a. a combination of numbers and letters that makes no sense
   b. a four-letter nickname
   c. ten letters that do not spell a word
   d. eight randomly chosen numbers

6. Which of the following is NOT a law enforcement group for fighting cybercrime?
   a. CCIPS
   b. FDA
   c. CHIP
   d. NIPC

Directions: *Answer the following questions.*

1. Why is it a good idea to keep personal information confidential?

2. Summarize the components of a strong password.

3. Give examples of computer crime and cybercrime that illustrate the difference between the two terms.

4. What are the consequences of software piracy? How can you help prevent piracy?

5. Which methods of protecting your privacy and your data do you follow?

Extend Your Knowledge

Directions: *Choose and complete one of the following projects.*

A. Create a poster illustrating one way you can be a smart computer user. Present your poster to the class, and then, with permission, display the poster in a public area of your school, such as a hallway or cafeteria.

B. With your teacher's permission, use the Internet to investigate a cybercrime. Write a brief report outlining what happened, what damage resulted, and whether the criminal was caught. If he or she was caught, describe how. State what consequences the criminal must face.

Using Computers Responsibly

Keeping Information Secure In the past, criminals needed to break into a building to steal money or goods. Today, computers offer new avenues to crime. Criminals can steal data stored on a computer without going anywhere near a home or office building. They simply use an Internet connection and special software to cover their tracks. With these tools, they can drain money out of a company's accounts or steal its secrets. They can steal a person's credit card information and use it to generate huge bills that cause severe financial problems for the innocent person.

Some people and many businesses have electronic security systems to prevent break-ins to homes and offices. Fortunately, there are also tools available to protect the data on your computer.

Chapter Outline

 Lesson 34–1

Computer Ethics

 Lesson 34–2

Protecting Your Data

 Lesson 34–3

Troubleshooting Your Computer

Computer Ethics

Objectives

- Explain copyright laws.
- Give examples of rules in acceptable use policies (AUPs).
- Summarize netiquette.

As You Read

Organize Information As you read the lesson, use a chart to help you organize details about privacy and ethics.

🔑 Key Terms

- acceptable use policy (AUP)
- brand
- censor
- citation
- copyright
- cyberbullying
- ethics
- fair use
- filter
- intellectual property
- netiquette
- patent
- plagiarism
- trademark
- troll

Figure 34.1.1 Your school district's AUP provides guidelines for using your school's computers, network, and Internet access.

Ethical Computer Use

How people use computers, including networks and e-mail, can affect other people. People who practice **ethics** behave morally. Ethical computer users respect others, and make sure their actions do not harm anyone.

Acceptable Use Policies

One way you can act ethically is to follow your school district's **acceptable use policy,** or **AUP**. These policies identify the responsibilities of Internet use. They spell out certain rules of behavior and explain the consequences of breaking those rules. Many businesses use AUPs, too, to govern the way workers use company-owned computers. An AUP may include the following ethical guidelines:

- Do not visit Web sites that contain content that does not meet community standards.
- Do not use language, that is profane, abusive, or impolite.
- Do not copy copyrighted material or damage computer equipment belonging to the school.
- Do respect the privacy of other people.

Schools and businesses may restrict the content that users can access from internal computers. For example, they may **censor,** or block, specific sites that they determine are inappropriate.

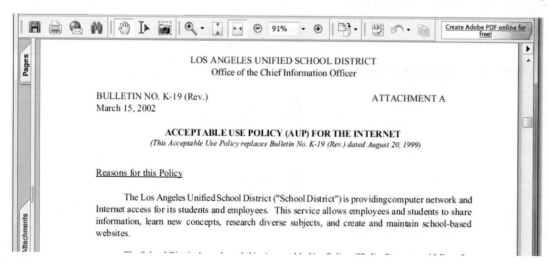

LOS ANGELES UNIFIED SCHOOL DISTRICT
Office of the Chief Information Officer

BULLETIN NO. K-19 (Rev.)   ATTACHMENT A
March 15, 2002

ACCEPTABLE USE POLICY (AUP) FOR THE INTERNET
(This Acceptable Use Policy replaces Bulletin No. K-19 (Rev.) dated August 20, 1999)

Reasons for this Policy

The Los Angeles Unified School District ("School District") is providing computer network and Internet access for its students and employees. This service allows employees and students to share information, learn new concepts, research diverse subjects, and create and maintain school-based websites.

They may also use a **filter** to block access to sites. Disabling the filters or otherwise accessing blocked sites is considered breaking the AUP, and may result in punishment.

Possible Penalties   People who do not follow these rules may face consequences. They might lose privileges or be suspended from school activities. Very serious violations, such as using a school computer to threaten someone, may require police involvement.

Copyright Laws

Federal laws that involve **copyright** protect individuals and companies from the theft or misuse of their **intellectual property**, such as creative, literary, or artistic work. Copyright exists as soon as a work is created, but the creator can register it with the U.S. Copyright Office. It is a crime to copy this kind of work without the permission of the person who owns the copyright to it. Penalties include paying a large fine and possibly jail time.

Cite Your Source   If you use information you find on the Web in your work, you must give credit to the source. You do this by inserting a reference to the source, called a **citation**, in a footnote, endnote, or bibliography. A proper citation gives credit to the source, and provides the tools a reader needs to locate the source on his or her own. Some Web sites have features that automatically generate the citation information for you.

Plagiarism   If you do not cite your sources you are guilty of **plagiarism**, which is the unauthorized use of another person's idea's or creative work without giving that person credit. Plagiarism is equivalent to stealing another person's work and passing it off as your own. The consequences of plagiarism can be quite significant. If you plagiarize work in school, you may have to redo the assignment or lose credit all together. Your school may also take disciplinarian actions, like detention. In the professional world, the consequences of plagiarism are even more significant. A professional who plagiarizes work suffers a loss to his or her reputation and may face legal ramifications, such as a lawsuit.

To avoid plagiarism you just need to properly cite your source. You should insert a citation when you quote, summarize, or paraphrase someone else, use someone else's idea, or reference someone else's work. In a works cited section or footnote, you tell the reader the source of your credited information.

Copyright and Fair Use Doctrine   If the content is protected by copyright, you must have permission from the copyright holder to use the work. However, part of copyright law called the **Fair Use Doctrine** allows you to use a limited amount of copyrighted material without permission for educational

Gestures, facial expressions, and tones of voice—which people use in conversation to add meaning—are missing from e-mail.

Think About It!

Which items listed below do you think would be clearly communicated through the text in an e-mail? Which could be miscommunicated?

➤ fact

➤ sarcasm

➤ anger

➤ question

➤ joy

purposes. For example, you can quote a few lines of a song or a passage from a book. Similarly, an author may issue a creative commons license allowing others to use the work.

Trademarks and Patents   Some intellectual property is protected by trademark or patent. A **trademark** is a symbol that indicates that a brand or brand name is legally protected and cannot be used by other businesses. A **patent** is the exclusive right to make, use, or sell a device or process. Many types of inventions can be patented. Using trademarked or patented property without permission is called infringement. The penalty is usually a large fine and a court order to stop.

Practicing Netiquette

There is an informal set of rules for online behavior called **netiquette**. As an ethical computer user, you have a responsibility to use netiquette at all times. Some ways to practice netiquette include:

- Send e-mails only to people who really need to see a message.
- Keep e-mail messages short.
- Avoid sending extremely large files via e-mail.
- Do not use impolite or rude language online.
- Do not pretend to be someone else online.
- Do not use someone else's work without citing the source.
- Do not share files illegally.

The rules of netiquette are similar to general standards for good behavior. If you go to a search engine and type "netiquette," you will find many Web sites on the topic.

Managing Your Online Identity

Online, people learn about you by what you post and what sites you frequent. You can use your online profile to both promote a positive image, or **brand**, of yourself, and to protect your identity. Building your brand means making sure everything you post or display online supports the reputation and character you want people to associate with you.

You can protect your identity by making sure you effectively manage all of your online profiles, including on gaming sites and on social networking sites such as Twitter, LinkedIn, and Facebook. Be sure to set privacy settings and to never give out your personal information in your profiles. You might also maintain both a professional and a personal identity. For example, you might have two e-mail accounts; one you use for professional and business communication such as a job search, and one you use for personal communication with your friends and family.

Don't Be a Cybercriminal

When you use the Internet it can feel as if no one can identify who you really are. As a result, behavior online can often turn inappropriate, rude, and even illegal. Some users are Internet **trolls**, which means they go on sites specifically to post rude, mean comments intended to upset people. Remember, you can be tracked; someone will figure out who you are.

Whether you are playing a game online or posting a comment on a web site, it is important to behave in the online space as you would in the real world. Always be courteous and respectful. If you post a negative review of a product or service, make sure it is true and accurate and not mean or spiteful. Poor reviews can be damaging to a business. Never insult or bully an individual, or post comments that are untrue. Cyberbullying is a crime.

Sometimes it is not mean comments that can get you into trouble. Many people flirt using electronic communications. Messages can be forwarded or posted on social networking sites for all to see. Sending inappropriate text and pictures electronically is called sexting, and in some circumstances it is illegal.

 Spotlight on...

CYBERBULLYING

With the explosion of tweens and teens using cell phones and social networking sites on the Internet, there has been an explosion of cyberbullying. According to the Cyberbullying Research Center, "**cyberbullying** is when someone repeatedly harasses, mistreats, or makes fun of another person online or while using cell phones or other electronic devices." Cyberbullies hurt their victims by doing things like sending threatening or harassing messages or texts, posting private pictures online or via cell phones, and creating hurtful Web sites, like fake Facebook sites.

Cyberbullying is hard to fight, because it happens anonymously and away from school. However, it has led to many high profile cases of teen suicide, spreading unstoppable rings of grief through whole communities. If you are the victim of cyberbullying, you should tell someone you trust right away, your Internet or mobile phone service provider, your school—or even the police.

Protecting Your Data

Objectives

- Explain how to prevent data loss.
- Describe how to use antivirus programs.
- Discuss ways of backing up data.

As You Read

Organize Information As you read the lesson, use a sequence chart to help you explain ways to protect yourself, your system, and your data.

🔑 Key Terms

- antimalware program
- antivirus program
- full back-up
- incremental back-up
- power surge
- uninterruptible power supply (UPS)
- versioning

Protecting Your Computer

Although corporations and government agencies are far more likely to be targeted than an individual or a school, any system is vulnerable. You should protect your computer now.

Virus and Malware Removal One of the simplest and most important methods of protecting data and keeping your computer running efficiently is to install and use an **antivirus program** or **antimalware program** to discover, quarantine, and remove viruses, spyware, and malware. These programs continually monitor your system for dangerous files. Once they find a virus, they delete it or quarantine it so it can do no harm.

Simply installing an antivirus program is not enough to protect your computer. New viruses are created every day. Software publishers update their antivirus programs to defeat each new attack, and you must make sure you keep the program on your computer up-to-date. The easiest way to do this is to set your antivirus program to update automatically using an Internet connection.

Although every antivirus program is different, the basic steps for identifying and removing a problem file are the same. First, install an antivirus program. Next, set the program to run automatically, update automatically, and to automatically quarantine or remove infected files.

Finally, periodically check the quarantine folder and permanently remove suspicious files. If your program notifies you that it has found and removed a virus, you should shut down your system, restart, and run the antivirus program again.

You can also take steps to prevent viruses:

- Always check files that you download from the Internet for viruses before saving them locally.
- Set your antivirus program to monitor incoming e-mail messages and attachments.
- Always check storage devices you borrow from someone else before connecting them to your computer.

Firewalls To help block unauthorized users from accessing your computer through a network, you can install and activate a firewall. A firewall is a program that restricts unauthorized access. Most operating systems, including Microsoft Windows, come with a firewall, and so do many antivirus programs.

Versioning   One tool for safeguarding your data is maintaining different versions of the files you are working on. **Versioning** is built in to some operating systems and applications, so they automatically save a previous version of a file when you make changes to the current version. If you accidentally damage or delete data in the current file, you can revert to a previous version. For example, in Windows 7 or earlier, the System Restore utility saves previous version of files; in Windows 8 or later, you can configure File History to save previous versions. Mac OS also supports versioning, and many applications, including Microsoft Office programs, automatically save previous versions of both saved and unsaved files.

Public vs. Private Networks Any time you connect your computer to a public network you put your data at risk. A public network is one anyone can access in a public place, such as an airport, coffee shop, or library. A private network is one available to authorized users only, usually through a password. Most devices have a setting that prompts you before you connect to a public network. You also put your information at risk simply by using a public computer, such as one in a library or hotel. When you access the Internet or your social networking sites from a public computer, you enter log in information including passwords, and the computer stores your browsing history. If you do use a public computer, it is a good idea to clear the browsing history and cache before logging out, and never select an option to "remember me on this computer." It is also a good idea to secure your personal wi-fi network using encryption such as WEP or WPA2.

Backing Up Data

A hard drive crash is a problem, but it does not have to be a disaster as long as you have backed up your data. Backing up is simply creating a copy of the data on your hard drive that is stored separately in an offsite or remote location away from the hard drive. You can back up data manually or use a program that performs the back up automatically on a set schedule.

To back up data, you can use an external hard drive, a shared network drive, an online storage service, a flash drive, or a recordable CD or DVD. Online storage, in which data is stored on multiple virtual servers hosted by third parties, is sometimes called cloud storage.

No matter which method you choose, you can back up data to different degrees: **Full back-ups** copy everything stored on your computer. They should be done at least once a month. Versioned or **incremental back-ups** copy only those files that have changed since the last full back-up. These should be made regularly, such as once a week. Some back-up programs, such as Apple's Time Machine, perform them every hour automatically.

Figure 34.2.1 An Uninterruptible Power Supply unit, such as this one from APC, has outlets for all your computer's components, phone, and cable lines. The unit offers surge protection and will prevent a spike in power from damaging your computer. In event of a power outage, the unit will keep your computer running long enough for you to shut it down properly.

Backing up can be done by simply copying files. However, special back-up programs offer advantages. They compress data as they back it up, making the files smaller.

Think About It!

Think about the advantages of compressing data. Which item(s) listed below do you think are an advantage of compressing data in a back-up?

➤ Data will take up less space.

➤ Back-up will take less time.

➤ Labor costs will be lower.

➤ You need the back-up software in order to restore the data.

➤ Back-up programs cost money.

After a crash, the lost data can be restored from the backup. Some programs, such as Microsoft Word and Adobe Acrobat, automatically back-up your files while you work. If the program crashes before you save your current changes, when you reopen it you will be prompted with a message asking if you want to restore your last session. By pressing "yes," you open the latest backed-up version of the document.

Removing Data There may be a time when you want to permanently remove data from your storage devices. Just deleting a file is not enough. Hackers can easily find the deleted files. To make sure information is not left on a drive you must reformat or wipe the drive, which destroys all files. You can clear a smart phone or tablet by resetting it to the factory configuration.

Power-Related Problems Just like any other device that runs on electricity, a computer can be affected by power fluctuations or outages. These problems can lead to the loss of data. A **power surge**, or a sharp increase in the power coming into the system, can destroy a computer's electrical components.

You can help protect your computer from power problems by attaching an **Uninterruptible Power Supply**, or **UPS**, between your computer and the power source. This battery powered device goes to work when it detects an outage or critical voltage drop. It powers the computer for a period of time. A UPS can also protect against power surges by filtering sudden electrical spikes.

Real-World Tech

The Wireless Problem Communicating with wireless devices such as cell phones creates a major security issue. This kind of communication can be monitored by outsiders, who can intercept and overhear what is being said. That is why the U.S. Department of Defense has banned the use of most wireless devices from defense establishments.

Does knowing that other people can overhear cell phone conversations affect whether or not you use a cell phone? Why or why not?

Objectives

- Identify troubleshooting techniques.
- Explain the difference between a hard reboot and a soft reboot.
- Identify the purpose of starting in safe mode.
- Identify how to stay informed about changes and advancements in technology.

As You Read

Identify Key Points As you read the lesson, use a conclusion chart to help you identify key points about troubleshooting.

Simple Troubleshooting Techniques

When your computer is not working properly, you can use diagnosis and **troubleshooting** to identify and fix problems. Diagnosing includes steps for figuring out what is causing the problem, and troubleshooting involves solving the problem.

Check the Connections Many problems occur when cables or wires become loose. When your monitor goes dark or your keyboard won't respond, turn the system off and check to make sure all cables are securely connected. Many computers are plugged in to a power strip. Make sure the power strip is on. When you have reestablished all connections, turn your system back on and see if the problem is resolved.

Platform Compatibility Some software is only designed to run on certain operating systems. Many video games, for example, are only able to run on Windows OS and will be unable to run on Macintosh or Linux systems. Media files such as videos, can only be opened with certain programs. Checking the applica-

🔑 Key Terms

- command prompt
- reboot
- safe mode
- troubleshooting

Figure 34.3.1 You can find troubleshooter utilities for many system components in the Windows Control Panel.

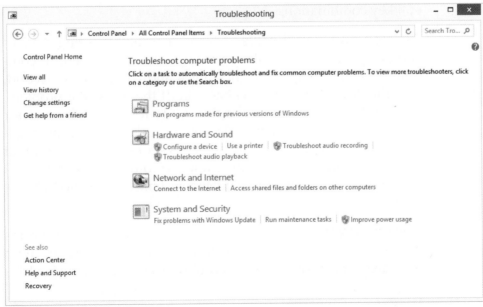

Windows 8, Microsoft Corporation.

tion requirements of programs will allow you to verify that your platform meets the minimum operating criteria for the software. Some software also requires specific hardware devices to run properly. For example, a program may need a Wi-Fi connection or access to the Internet. If your platform is not equipped with the proper hardware, the program will not work.

Refer to the Documentation All your computer products come with product manuals. The manuals may be printed books, or they may be available on the manufacturer's Web site. These manuals will always have a troubleshooting section. In addition, many systems come with built-in troubleshooter utilities. Usually these prompt you through a series of questions to diagnose the problem, and they may offer suggestions for action you should take. For example, you can find Windows 7 troubleshooters through the Control Panel. Click the Start button, click Control Panel, and then click Find and fix problems.

Reboot Many computer problems—such as a program freezing—can be solved by a simple **reboot**. When you reboot your computer, you turn it off and then on again.

There are two kinds of reboots: a *hard reboot* is when you turn off all power by pushing the power button or unplugging your computer. A *soft reboot* is when you use the computer's own software to allow your computer to shut down properly. You can click on the main menu and choose the "shut down" option. If your computer is not frozen, you can try the "restart" option, in which the computer goes through the shut-down sequence and powers back up again. However, if the screen is frozen, a hard reboot may be your only option.

If your computer is unresponsive and you cannot reboot, you may be able to use a key combination to access a troubleshooting menu or restart the computer. On a Windows PC, you can press Ctrl+Alt+Delete. For computers using a Mac OS, you should check your troubleshooting guide, because there are several key combinations.

Devices and Peripherals Steps for troubleshooting devices and peripherals are similar to troubleshooting the entire computer system. First, check the cables and connections. Second, turn the device off and then back on. If there is still a problem, you can look for a troubleshooter utility for the device in your operating system's Help program, or use a device management utility to check that the device is set up properly and that the driver software is installed and up-to-date. In Windows it is called Device Manager; on Mac systems, it is called Profile Manager.

Device Drivers Recall that device drivers are the programs that enable peripherals and devices to communicate with the hardware through the operating system. If a device stops working, you can update the driver, rollback the driver to a previous version, disable the driver, or uninstall and reinstall it. Your operating system can automatically look for and install device drivers, or you can download and install the driver from the manufacturer's Web site.

Firmware Updates Firmware is the permanent instructions stored on read-only memory (ROM) chips that control computer components. ROM does not require a power source, so it is used to boot digital and computer devices. For example, the BIOS or UEFI on your computer is firmware. Firmware stored on flash memory chips can be upgraded. As with software, manufacturers sometimes release firmware updates to fix problems or to update a hardware device. The updates can be downloaded from the manufacturer's Web site. Updating firmware can be risky; if the update is interrupted, it might cause the device to stop working. When you update firmware, follow all instructions carefully.

On most computers you can also use the BIOS or UEFI setup menu to access, update, reset, or repair certain system settings. For example, you may be able to clear your CMOS settings to restore the factory default settings. This can resolve some hardware compatibility problems. These settings, and the methods for accessing them, are different on different systems, so you should always read and follow the instructions for your specific system.

Task and Process Management Most operating systems include a utility for monitoring tasks and processes currently running on your computer. On a Windows system, it is called Task Manager. You open it by pressing Ctrl + Alt + Delete and clicking Start Task Manager. On a Mac, it is called Activity Monitor. You open it from the Applications/Utilities folder. These programs show you the status of programs and processes currently running on your system. You can use them to start and end a program or process; enable or disable startup programs; and to identify and end processes that may be running in the background that you do not need.

Repair Utilities

Most computers come with programs that let you check, diagnose, and repair your computer. The programs may be installed with the operating system, or they may be provided on separate discs.

Figure 34.3.2 On a Windows system, you can use System Restore to restore your computer to an earlier configuration.

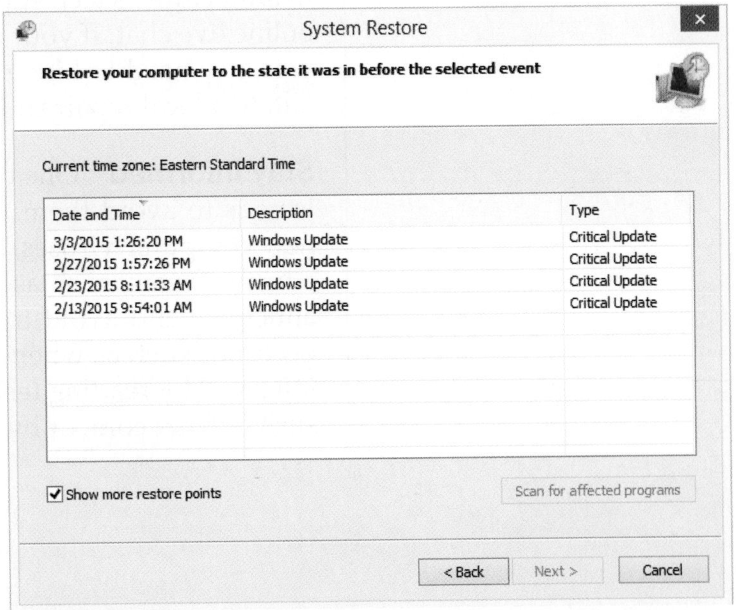

Date and Time	Description	Type
3/3/2015 1:26:20 PM	Windows Update	Critical Update
2/27/2015 1:57:26 PM	Windows Update	Critical Update
2/23/2015 8:11:33 AM	Windows Update	Critical Update
2/13/2015 9:54:01 AM	Windows Update	Critical Update

System Restore

Restore your computer to the state it was in before the selected event

Current time zone: Eastern Standard Time

☑ Show more restore points   Scan for affected programs

< Back   Next >   Cancel

Windows 8, Microsoft Corporation.

Some computer maintenance and troubleshooting should only be done by experienced professionals. If you attempt certain procedures without the required training or knowledge, you could damage the system, or hurt yourself. Hire a professional for the following:

▷ replacing the power supply

▷ replacing processors

▷ replacing or upgrading memory

▷ repairing peripheral devices such as monitors or printers

▷ replacing or upgrading hard drives

▷ recovering data from a damaged storage device

System Restore   You can often use a utility to restore your system to the state it was in before it stopped working. Windows comes with a Restore utility. You select the date and time which you want to revert to, and Windows runs a program to restore that configuration. Changes that occurred since that date and time are undone, including new software installation or modified system settings.

System Recovery   Some computers come with recovery CDs or DVDs that you insert into the appropriate drive before rebooting. You may then select from a menu of options for checking and repairing problems.

Safe Mode   Most computers let you start in **safe mode**, which means they start with only a limited set of files and drivers. Safe mode lets you identify and fix problems with software that is interfering with the operating system and other components. To start a Windows computer in safe mode, restart your computer, and press the F8 key before the Windows logo displays. On the menu, use the arrow keys to highlight the Safe Mode option, and press Enter.

Access the Command Prompt   Before there were graphical user interfaces such as Windows, you typed commands at the **command prompt**. You can still access the command prompt to type commands if necessary. In Windows, the command prompt is available by clicking Run on the Start menu, by clicking Command Prompt in the Accessories folder, or by restarting your computer, pressing F8 before the Windows logo displays, and choosing the Command Prompt option.

Get Help   If you exhaust all basic troubleshooting techniques, you may need to get professional help. If your computer or your software is still under warranty, you can often get help from the manufacturer's tech support team over the phone or through an online live chat. If your computer or software is out of warranty, you may need to hire a computer technician or bring your system to a local repair shop.

Stay Informed   One of the best ways to solve computer problems is to avoid them. Staying informed about issues, such as new computer viruses, changes, such as software updates, and advancements, such as new products or services, can help you anticipate and avoid trouble. It also helps you make informed decisions such as when to purchase new products. You can stay informed by reading technology news articles on reputable sites such as Cnet.com, or by subscribing to technology news feeds.

Use the Vocabulary

Directions: *Match each vocabulary term in the left column with the correct definition in the right column.*

_____ 1. copyright
_____ 2. power surge
_____ 3. fair use
_____ 4. plagiarism
_____ 5. uninterruptible power supply
_____ 6. ethics
_____ 7. reboot
_____ 8. Safe Mode
_____ 9. full back-up
_____ 10. troubleshoot

a. behaving morally
b. unauthorized use of another person's ideas or work without credit
c. a systematic attempt to analyze and diagnose computer or software problems
d. duplicate all files on a hard drive
e. laws that protect creative, literary, or artistic work
f. a sharp increase in the power coming into the system
g. turning a computer system off and then on again
h. device that protects a computer from power problems
i. starting the system with a limited set of files and drivers
j. allowed use of a limited amount of creative work without permission

Check Your Comprehension

Directions: *Determine the correct choice for each of the following.*

1. What is stolen in copyright infringement ?
   a. back-up files
   b. GUIDs
   c. someone's work
   d. someone's identity

2. What should you use to give credit to a source?
   a. citation
   b. plagarism
   c. infringement
   d. netiquette

3. Which of the following is used to identify the responsibilities of a user on an organization's computer system?
   a. copyright laws
   b. Fair Use Doctrine
   c. acceptable use policy
   d. antivirus program

4. Why is copyright infringement a crime?
   a. It is illegal to make back-up copies of your work.
   b. It violates the rights of a software publisher to its work.
   c. It results in identity theft.
   d. It is theft of another's work.

5. Which of the following can help protect your computer system from a power surge?
   a. copyright laws
   b. acceptable use policy
   c. device driver
   d. uninterruptible power supply

6. Which of the following lets you revert your system configuration to a previous date and time?
   a. system restore
   b. system recovery
   c. safe mode
   d. command prompt

 **Think Critically**

Directions: *Answer the following questions.*

1. Explain the consequences of plagiarism.

2. Compare and contrast a full data back-up with an incremental data back-up.

3. Explain the concept of intellectual property laws including copyright, trademarks, and patents. What are the consequences of violating each type of law?

4. Summarize troubleshooting techniques you can use to diagnose and solve computer problems.

5. Explain the process for discovering, quarantining, and removing a virus from a computer.

Extend Your Knowledge

Directions: *Choose and complete one of the following projects.*

A. With your teacher's permission, work with a partner to identify and repair hardware problems. Assemble a system with various components and peripherals. Take turns describing and solving problems such as problem power supplies, projectors, cameras, and other multimedia devices that won't work, and unresponsive input devices.

B. With your teacher's permission, use the Internet to look up a user manual for a hardware device. Locate troubleshooting or problem-solving information and read it. Exit your browser. With a partner, select a problem that someone might encounter using a computer at home. Use a word-processing application to create a document in the manner and style of a user's manual. Provide the necessary information for identifying and solving the selected problem. With your teacher's permission, print or publish the document and discuss it with your class.

C. Review rules your school district may have for computer use as part of its acceptable use policy. Categorize policies based on appropriate use, vandalism or destruction, and consequences of violations. As a class, debate the benefits and drawbacks of items in the policy, such as censorship and filtering.

D. With your teacher's permission, research how to access your computer system's startup, BIOS, CMOS, or UEFI settings menu, and then follow the steps to access and review existing settings. With your teacher's permission, modify a setting. For example, you might reset the computer's clock, or start in safe mode using only the system's basic operational level. Restart the computer and see how the changes affect operation. Discuss the procedure with a partner or the class. Alternatively, explore the options for Windows Update available on your computer. Determine if you can manually install updates, service packs, and patches or if they are done automatically. Check to see which updates have been recently installed.

21st Century Skills

What Skills Do I Need to Succeed?

We live in an exciting, fast-paced, complex world. As the future leaders of our families, communities, government, and workforce, it is critical that you acquire the skills you need to succeed in school, work, and life.

In addition to specific skills for using technology and applications, and for achieving in the specific field you choose to pursue, you will benefit from learning transferable skills that will help you no matter what life path you follow. In this chapter you will explore key transferable skills you can use to succeed.

Chapter Outline

 Lesson 35–1

Skills for Success

 Lesson 35–2

Communicating and Collaborating

 Lesson 35–3

Living with Technology

Skills for Success

Objectives

- Analyze the decision-making process.
- Compare and contrast short term and long term goals.
- Analyze problems and solutions.
- Discuss methods of time management.

As You Read

Organize Information Complete an outline to help you identify key facts about skills for success as you read the lesson.

🔑 Key Terms

- consequences
- decision
- expenses
- goal
- income
- long-term goal
- problem
- process
- resources
- responsibility
- short-term goal
- solution
- time management

Making Decisions

Any time you make up your mind about something, or choose one option over another, you are making a **decision**. Some decisions are simple—what time will I leave for school? Some are more difficult—should I tell my friend I don't like her hair style? The results—or **consequences**—of your decisions affect you in big and small ways.

- If the consequences of a decision are positive and contribute to your well-being, it means you made a healthy—or good—choice.
- If the consequences are negative and interfere with your well-being, that means you made an unhealthy—or poor—choice.

Six Steps to a Decision You can turn decision making into a **process**. A process is a series of steps that leads to a conclusion.

1. *Identify the decision to be made.*
2. *Consider all possible options.*
3. *Identify the consequences of each option.*
4. *Select the best option.*
5. *Make and implement a plan of action.*
6. *Evaluate the decision, process, and outcome.* After you have acted on your decision, you can look back and evaluate it, based on your values and standards.

Thoughtful Decision-Making We all make mistakes. Despite our best intentions, we make poor choices. Most of the time, it doesn't matter too much. If you cut your hair too short, it will grow back. Sometimes, though, we must live with the consequences of our actions for a long time—maybe even our whole lives.

Setting Goals

A **goal** is something you are trying to achieve. Goals help direct your actions and guide your decision-making because they give you something to work toward. They help give your life meaning, because you know that there is a purpose in what you do. When you achieve a goal, you can be proud and express satisfaction.

If all you do is think about a goal, it's just a dream. You make goals real by deciding what you want to achieve and then planning how to get there. While you should set goals that are within reach, there is nothing wrong with challenging yourself to push harder.

Short-Term and Long-Term Goals When you want to achieve something quickly, you set **short-term goals**. You can accomplish short-term goals in the near future—maybe even today. For example, finishing your homework on time is a short-term goal.

A **long-term goal** is something you want to achieve in the more distant future—maybe a year from now, or maybe even more distant than that. Graduating from college is a long-term goal. So is buying a car.

Five Steps to a Goal There's a process you can use to help identify, assess, and set goals:

1. *Identify the goal.*
2. *Assess whether the goal is something you really want.*
3. *Make a plan for achieving the goal.*
4. *Write down your action plan for achieving the goal, being as specific as possible.*
5. *Every once in a while, reevaluate your goals.*

Solving Problems

Any barrier or obstacle between you and a goal is a **problem**. Problems pop up all the time. Mostly, we come up with a solution without thinking too hard. Say you want to go to the movies Saturday night, but your mother says you can't go out until you clean your room.

- The problem: Your messy room is an obstacle between you and the movies.
- The solution: You clean your room.

Some problems sneak up on us over time, sometimes hidden by something else. You might want to do well in Social Studies, but you fall asleep in class every day. Is the problem that your teacher is boring, that your classroom is too warm, or is it that you are staying up late at night playing video games?

Six Steps to a Solution When problems are harder to identify, or harder to solve, you can use the decision-making process to figure out the best **solution**:

1. *Identify the problem.*
2. *Consider all possible solutions.*
3. *Identify the consequences of each solution.*
4. *Select the best solution.*
5. *Make and implement a plan of action.*
6. *Evaluate the solution, process, and outcome.*

Figure 35.1.1 Buying a car is a long-term goal.

Managing Time

Time management means organizing your schedule so you have time to complete tasks and meet your responsibilities. Combining goal-setting with time management is a very effective way to make sure you get things done.

- Create a time journal or log to figure out exactly how you currently spend your time.

- Set specific, realistic, and attainable goals using schedules. Scheduling helps you plan ahead, so you know when you will do something, and you can be ready for it.

- Create to-do lists, and rank list items in order of importance.

- Learn to say no. Some people may ask for too much of your time. They may expect you to take on more **responsibility** than you can handle. It is OK to say no. Be polite and respectful, but explain that your schedule is full.

- Ask for help. If you are having trouble completing tasks that are part of your assigned responsibilities, you will need to find a way to get them done. Ask your teacher, a counselor, a family member, or a friend to help you learn how to organize your time, or find ways to be more efficient.

Calendar programs on your computer and phone are an excellent way to organize your schedule for efficient time management. In the calendar, you can enter a on-time event such as an appointment, or program recurring events, such as a weekly piano lesson. With each event, you can include details such as the location, or enter notes to help you remember important information.

Programs like Google Calendar and Outlook let you invite people to your events and even create group calendars that others can access online. You can even program notifications to remind you of important events, such as family birthdays or the ACTs. You can set up multiple calendars for business and personal use, or subscribe online to calendars for other organizations.

Figure 35.1.2 Showing up on time for appointments, work, and class shows that you are responsible.

Managing Resources Keeping your time and to-do list organized is critical, but if the **resources** you need are not organized, you will not succeed at the task at hand. For example, if you complete the research for a project on time, but cannot find it in order to write the report, you will be unable to complete the assignment. Set up a system of folders—both on your computer and, if you deal with paper, in a filing cabinet—that you keep organized so that you can always find the resources that you need.

One important resource you need to manage is money. Many people track their finances by creating a spreadsheet of the **income** they earn and the **expenses** they spend. There are also financial and banking apps that you can use.

Keeping track of your finances helps you plan your budget and make sure you are not spending more than you are earning. It also helps you understand where and how to spend your money. Budgeting shows you how much you should allocate, or put aside, for necessities like housing and food. Then, you will see how much you have left over to spend on other things, like entertainment. It is also important to remember a portion of your earned income is taxed by the government. This money must be deducted from your budget. Finally, a frugal money manager saves and invests. You need savings for emergencies and eventually for retirement.

Communicating and Collaborating

Objectives

- Explain critical thinking.
- Describe the key features of effective communication.
- recognize the importance of teamwork and leaders.
- Describe bullying.

Key Terms

- active listening
- critical thinking
- effective communication
- nonverbal communication
- verbal communication

Figure 35.2.1 Communicating with people of different backgrounds helps you build global awareness and understanding.

As You Read

Organize Information Complete an outline to help you identify key facts about communication and collaboration as you read this lesson.

Thinking Critically

Critical thinking can help you evaluate your options in many situations. You can use it when you are making decisions, setting goals, and solving problems. When you think critically, you are honest, rational, and open-minded about your options. You consider all possibilities before rushing to judgment.

- Being honest means acknowledging selfish feeling and preexisting opinions.
- Being rational means relying on reason and thought instead of on emotion or impulse.
- Being open-minded means being willing to evaluate all possible options—even those that are unpopular.

Communicating Effectively

Communicating is how people connect with others. Communication prevents misunderstandings. It gives you a way to share ideas. It even makes it easier for you to appreciate and respect other people's opinions.

At its most basic, communication is an exchange between a sender and a receiver. The sender transmits the message with a specific intent. The receiver interprets the message and responds. **Effective communication** is when the receiver interprets the message the way the sender intended. Ineffective communication is when the receiver misinterprets the message.

Sometimes barriers get in the way of effective communication. When you recognize any potential communication barriers, you can take steps to overcome them—both when you listen and when you speak.

Verbal Communication **Verbal communication** is the exchange of messages by speaking or writing. Talking is usually a very effective form of verbal communication. When you speak clearly and use language the receiver understands, he or she almost always gets the message the way you intend it.

Nonverbal Communication Nonverbal communication helps put words into context. This form of communication includes visual messages that the receiver can see, such as a smile when you are talking. It also includes physical messages, such as a pat on the back.

Active Listening Active listening is an important part of effective communication. When you are an active listener, you pay attention to the speaker, and make sure you hear and understand the message. Active listening is a sign of respect. It shows you are willing to communicate and that you care about the speaker and the message. When you listen actively, the other person is more likely to listen when you speak, too.

Cooperating and Collaborating

Any group that works together to achieve a common goal is a team. When you are part of a team, you have access to all the knowledge, experience, and abilities of your teammates. Together you can have more ideas, achieve more goals, and solve more problems. A successful team relationship depends on all team members working together. They depend on each other. They trust one another. If one team member does not do his or her share, the entire team suffers. The challenges of a team relationship come from having different people working together. Even if everyone agrees on a common goal, they may not agree on how to achieve that goal.

Being a Leader Teams benefit from strong leadership. Leaders exhibit positive qualities that other people respect, such as self-confidence. They use skills such as goal setting and critical thinking to make healthy decisions for the benefit of the team.
Being the leader does not mean you are always right. The leader's opinion does not count more than the opinions of the other team members. An effective leader keeps the team on track and focused on achieving its goals.

Being a Team Member While a strong leader is important to the success of a team, team members must also be committed to the group's success. An effective team member helps teammates if they need help, does not blame teammates for problems or mistakes, and offers ideas and suggestions instead of criticism.

Bullying A bully is someone who tries to hurt others on purpose, not just once but over and over. Bullies can be boys or girls, big or small, young or old. Bullies can be found at school, but they can also turn up in other areas of your life, including in your neighborhood, at work, and even at home.

Figure 35.2.2 Cooperating with others makes it easier to achieve your common goals.

Some of the things bullies do include:

- Physically hurting others by tripping, pushing, kicking, pinching, or punching
- Calling people names
- Teasing people about the way they look, the way they act, or their values
- Excluding someone—leaving someone out
- Spreading rumors
- Stealing or breaking personal belongings
- Using threats or violence to make people do things they don't want to do

If you are being bullied, you need to take action right away.

- Tell someone!
- Avoid the bully as much as you can.
- Refuse to do what the bully says.
- Stand up for yourself!

Cyberbullies are bullies who use technology such as the Internet, cell phones, and interactive gaming devices to hurt others. They might:

- Send threatening or harassing messages
- Steal passwords and pretend to be someone else online
- Use blogs or social networking sites to spread rumors
- Send private pictures through e-mail or cell phones
- Create hurtful Web sites
- Distribute someone else's personal information

Victims of cyber bullying may be depressed, anxious, lonely and may consider suicide, while perpetrators, or cyberbullies, often are more likely to be aggressive, skip school, and abuse illegal drugs. Cyber bullying can be tricky to stop, because it is anonymous and takes place away from school. If you are being cyber-bullied you can take many of the same steps you would take with a face-to-face bully.

Figure 35.2.3 The best way to stop a bully is to tell someone about the bullying.

Living with Technology

Objectives

- Identify the impact of technology.
- Compare and contrast the benefits and drawbacks of technology
- Discuss the relevance of technology.
- Recognize the risks of technology.

As You Read

Classify Information   Use a two-column chart to help you compare the benefits and drawbacks of technology as you read this lesson.

Using Technology

Technology is a varied resource that impacts all areas of your life. It makes everyday life easier, more fun, and more rewarding. As with any resource, knowing when and how to use technology can help you be more productive. Using technology just because it's there or seems cool might be fun; it can also end up wasting other resources, such as time, energy, or money.

For example, the Internet is a technology we use all the time. It can provide many benefits when you use it wisely. You can find information to complete a homework assignment, communicate with friends, and research a product before you buy. If you don't use the Internet wisely, you might waste time looking at Web sites that provide incorrect or misleading information. You might spend so much time online that you put your real-life relationships at risk. Or, you might accidentally send personal information to identify thieves.

Critical thinking can help you recognize how best to use technology in your own life. You can decide whether technology will be a resource you use to achieve your goals, or if it will cause new problems.

Impact of Technology   Throughout history technology has had an impact on every aspect of life, including how you learn and what you study. You might use or encounter the following common types of technology.

- Information technology is likely to be the type of technology you use and that impacts your daily life the most. It refers to the use of computers to collect, store, and distribute information.

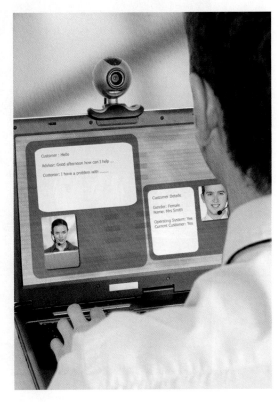

Figure 35.3.1   Videoconferencing is a technology that makes communicating with others easier and more fun.

- Communications technology is part of information technology. It refers to the use of technology to make communication easier and more efficient. It includes cell phones, as well as videoconferencing, voice over Internet protocol (VoIP), and social networking.
- Agricultural technology is the use of technology to control the growth and harvesting of animal and plant products. It includes a wide range of areas, such as soil preparation, harvesting and planting techniques, and the use of chemicals for growth or pest control.
- Medical technology is the use of technology to improve the management and delivery of health care. It includes areas such as medical imaging technology, nuclear medicine technology, and veterinary medical technology.
- Banking technology also stems from information technology. It includes areas such as software for managing online banking, controlling access to accounts, and technology for automated teller machines, as well as debit and credit card readers.

Relevance of Technology Understanding and using technology is important in all aspects of your life. The more you know about technology the more prepared you will be for college, career, daily living, and life-long learning.

- In college you will need technology to research and write papers and communicate with peers and instructors.

Figure 35.3.2 Almost all career fields use some type of technology.

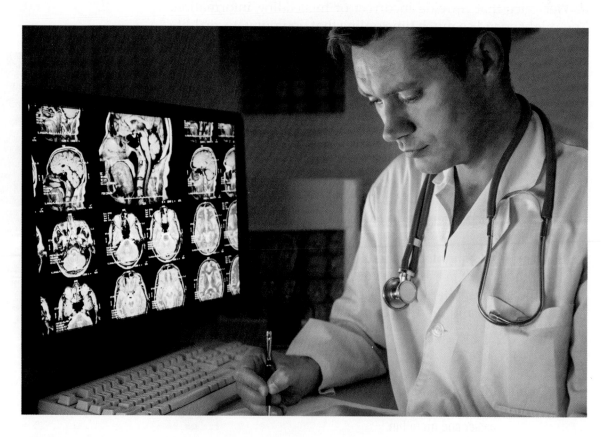

- Whatever career you choose, you will need to use technology. Skills such as using application software and troubleshooting hardware are transferrable to most jobs.

- Throughout your life you can use technology to keep up with current events and stay informed.

- You use technology every day. You will be more productive if you have a basic understanding of how technology works, and what it can do.

Benefits and Drawbacks of Technology   Is it always better to use technology? There are obvious benefits to using technology, but there are also drawbacks. Most new technologies have both positive and negative effects.

- Manufacturing is faster when you use assembly lines, robots, and automated management systems, than when you build products by hand. But, manufacturing processes may release chemicals into the environment causing pollution, and experienced craftsman may lose their jobs.

- Water filtration systems, access to electricity, and advancements in medical care are a few ways technology has improved health and the quality of life. Technology also creates ethical dilemmas, such as testing medical products on animals or genetically modifying food products.

Some newer technologies can help reverse problems caused by older technologies. For example, pollution caused by technology brought some animals to the brink of extinction. Genetic technology is helping animal breeding programs to restore some animal populations. Understanding the positive and negative effects can help you make choices about how best to use technology.

Cyberspace Is a Risky Place   Using the Internet is usually fun. It can also lead to risk. Consider the following:

- How much do you really know about someone online who you've never met? You can't see him.

- How much information do you want everyone to know? Everything you put on the Internet—including messages sent from a cell phone—is public, and it never goes away.

- How much control are you willing to give up? You might send a picture or message to a friend, who forwards it to someone else, who posts it on a social networking site.

Use the Vocabulary

Directions: *Match each vocabulary term in the left column with the correct definition in the right column.*

_____ **1.** goal

_____ **2.** decision

_____ **3.** problem

_____ **4.** process

_____ **5.** solution

_____ **6.** consequences

_____ **7.** responsibility

_____ **8.** income

a. results that happen in response to a decision or action.

b. something people expect you to do or that you must accomplish

c. a series of steps that leads to a conclusion

d. something you are trying to achieve

e. the amount of money you earn for a job

f. the process of choosing one option over one or more alternative options

g. the way to solve a problem

h. a barrier or obstacle between you and a goal.

Check Your Comprehension

Directions: *Complete each sentence with information from the chapter.*

1. _____ can help you evaluate your options in many situations.

2. _____ is when the receiver interprets a message the way the sender intended.

3. The exchange of messages by speaker or writing is called _____ communication.

4. _____ communication helps put words into context.

5. _____ shows you care about the speaker and the message.

6. Combining goal-setting with _____ is an effective way to get things done.

7. Graduating from college is a _____ goal.

8. Finishing your homework on time is a _____ goal.

Think Critically

Directions: *Answer the following questions.*

1. What does it mean if the consequences of a decision are positive? What if the consequences are negative?

2. List the five steps you can use to identify, assess, and set goals.

3. How can you use the decision-making process to solve problems?

4. Why might it be easier to misinterpret a text message or e-mail than a face-to-face conversation?

5. List four areas of study that have been impacted by technology.

Extend Your Knowledge

Directions: *Choose and complete one of the following projects.*

A. Write down three decisions you have faced in the last two days. As a class, discuss the decisions. If more than one of you faced the same decision, discuss the different—or similar—choices you made and why. Compare the outcomes of the choices made by different people.

B. With a partner, practice effective communication skills. Think of something you would like to tell your partner, then use verbal, non-verbal, and active listening techniques to deliver the message, and to receive the message delivered by your partner. Would you use different methods to communicate with people in the workplace such as a co-worker, supervisor, or customer? What if there was a conflict? Try the exercise again pretending to be in a work situation. Discuss the experience with the class.

Career Skills

Why Should I Plan for a Career? Planning for a career is a job in itself. It takes time, energy, and careful management. So why do it? Putting effort into career planning can help you set realistic and attainable goals for education. It can help you identify your strengths and weaknesses, so you focus your resources on finding a career that you will enjoy.

Spending time exploring career opportunities can also be fun and exciting, because you experience new situations and activities. This chapter will help you understand things you can do now that will lead to a successful career in the future.

Chapter Outline

Career Skills • 505

Identify Career Opportunities

Objectives

- Explain the difference between a career and a job.
- Describe the importance of values, interests, and abilities in a self-assessment
- List sources for occupational research.
- Identify non-traditional occupations.

As You Read

Organize Information Use an outline to help you organize information about identifying types of careers as you read the lesson.

🔑 **Key Terms**

- abilities
- career
- interests
- job
- job outlook
- nontraditional occupation
- trend
- values

Figure 36.1.1 The interests and values of a firefighter might be different from those of an architect or chemical engineer.

Identifying Types of Careers

A **career** is a chosen field of work in which you try to advance over time by gaining responsibility and earning more money. Another word for career is occupation. A **job** is any activity you do in exchange for money or other payment. A job does not necessarily lead to advancement.

Even if you have no idea what career you want in the future, you can start now to identify different types of careers and the tasks and duties you would be expected to perform. Learning about careers now will help prepare you to recognize job opportunities and choose the career that is right for you.

Individual Assessment

The first step in identifying a career is self-assessment. That means taking a close, objective look at your **interests, values,** and **abilities**. Knowing this information will help you identify the types of tasks and duties you will find rewarding. You then use that information to select careers or career clusters to investigate further.

Interests Your interests tell what you like to do and what you do not like to do. They are the subjects or activities that attract your attention and that you enjoy doing or learning about. There are six general interest categories: the arts, business, crafts, office operations, science, and social. Knowing your interests helps you identify a career that you will find interesting.

Values A value is the importance that you place on various elements in your life. Knowing what values you feel most strongly about helps you avoid compromising the things that are most important to you. Recognizing your values also helps you prioritize what matters most to you in a career. Money might be more important to you than leisure time. Working with people might be more important to you than what shift you work.

Abilities An ability, or skill, is something you do well. You have many abilities. For example, you may work well with your hands, or you may be very good at mathematics. It is much more pleasant to work in an occupation that uses your abilities.

There are fourteen general categories of abilities: artistic, clerical, interpersonal, language, leadership, manual, mathematical/numerical, musical/dramatic, organization, persuasive, scientific, social, visual, and technical/mechanical. You might have abilities in more than one category.

Occupational Research

Occupational research can help you identify job opportunities and the accompanying job duties and tasks required by a career. It can also help you learn about the education and job skills you would need for career success. By conducting occupational research, you learn details about a career, including tasks performed, duties, the **job outlook**, the education and job skills required, the working environment, the type of experience an employer looks for, and many other things. It requires time and effort to research the occupations that interest you and to prepare for a specific career. Remember, your efforts allow you to find a job that gives you satisfaction.

There are many resources you can use in your research. A good way to get started is to interview individuals who are already working in an occupation that you are interested in.

The Career Clusters The U.S. Department of Education organizes careers into 16 clusters, listed below. The careers in each cluster are in related industries or business areas. Each cluster is organized into pathways. Each pathway leads to a set of specific careers. The careers in a cluster require a similar set of skills and the same core training and education. You can narrow your career search by identifying a cluster that interests you. You can investigate the career clusters and pathways at www.careertech.org.

- Agriculture, Food & Natural Resources
- Architecture & Construction
- Arts, Audio/Video Technology & Communications
- Business Management & Administration
- Education & Training
- Finance
- Government & Public Administration
- Health & Science
- Hospitality & Tourism
- Human Services
- Information Technology

Figure 36.1.2 Careers in information technology are on the rise due to our growing reliance on technology at home and in the workplace.

- Law, Public Safety, Corrections & Security
- Manufacturing
- Marketing
- Science, Technology, Engineering & Mathematics
- Transportation, Distribution & Logistics

Employment Trends Employment trends influence the number of available jobs in a certain industry as well as where the jobs are. A **trend** is a general move in a certain direction. An employment trend is one way the job market is changing over time. Many factors influence employment trends, including economic factors and even cultural trends. For example, a shift from using personal computers to using smart phones impacts employment in the information technology industry.

Technology itself has a strong influence on employment and job outlook. It creates new jobs, replaces old jobs, and changes the way some people perform their existing jobs. Understanding the function and use of technology in the modern workplace is an essential skill in many professions.

- The development of new technology such as mobile phones and handheld devices creates new jobs in areas such as application development, sales, and research and development.
- The trend toward smaller computers has shifted the manufacturing of systems from desktops to notebooks and tablets.
- Improvements in robotics have made it possible to use robots in positions that people once held, such as on automobile assembly lines.
- Electronic record keeping in healthcare has changed the way medical professionals enter patient information, order prescriptions, and access patient records.
- The trend toward storing information and applications on the Internet instead of on local computers has eliminated the need for some information technology managers at large companies.
- The trend toward using video conferencing instead of traveling to meetings impacts travel agents, hotel workers, and people who work in restaurants where travelers might eat.

Figure 36.1.3 More people are finding success in nontraditional occupations than ever before.

A good source for information about employment trends is the Occupational Outlook Handbook, which is published by the U.S. Bureau of Labor Statistics. It describes more than 200 occupations, including responsibilities, working conditions, education requirements, salary ranges, and job outlook. Look it up at www.bls.gov/oco.

Economics Economics and the government also impact job opportunities and the information technology industry. Economics is the study of how people produce, distribute, and use goods and services. An economic system is a country's way of using limited resources to provide those goods and services. In the United States, the free enterprise system encourages people to use their resources to invent products, start companies, and compete for business. The government also imposes regulations and standards that can limit or expand free enterprise.

Nontraditional Occupations A **nontraditional occupation** is any job that a man or woman does that is usually done by someone of the other gender. Try not to rule out a nontraditional career because you associate it with one gender or another; it might be a good match for your skills and abilities. Some nontraditional careers include:

Men:
- Nurse
- Administrative assistant
- Flight attendant
- Hair stylist
- Childcare worker
- Elementary school teacher

Women:
- Construction worker
- Auto mechanic
- Detective
- Architect
- Chemical engineer
- Pilot

Employability Skills

Objectives

- Compare and contrast hard skills and transferrable skills.
- List professional qualities.
- Describe job application materials.
- Explain why education is important.

As You Read

Organize Information   Complete an outline to help you organize information about employability skills as you read this lesson.

🔑 Key Terms

- application form
- cover letter
- employability
- hard skills
- job interview
- lifelong learning
- personal academic plan
- portfolio
- professionalism
- references
- resume
- transferrable skills

Employability Skills

Employability means having and using skills and abilities to be hired and stay hired. Once you recognize the skills that make you employable, you can practice and develop them in school and at home, so you are ready to use them on the job.

Transferable Skills   Employability skills can generally be placed into two groups: **hard skills** and **transferable skills**. Employers often look for people with hard skills to fill specific jobs. For example, a software development company looks to hire people skilled at writing code.

Transferable skills can be used on almost any job. They are called transferable skills because you can transfer them from one situation or career to another. The foundation skills you use to succeed in other areas of your life, such as decision-making and problem-solving, are transferable skills. You can practice and develop these skills in school and at home.

Some computer skills are also transferable. There are very few jobs today that do not require basic computer use. If you have these basic skills, you can take them wherever you go:

- Turn a computer on and start a program.
- Type on a computer keyboard without making many mistakes.
- Access the Internet and navigate from one location to another.
- Use a search engine to do basic Internet research.
- Write and send e-mail.

Figure 36.2.1 Knowing how to present yourself in a positive way is an important employability skill.

Professional Qualities **Professionalism**, or work ethic, is the ability to show respect to everyone around you while you perform your responsibilities as best you can. It includes a basic set of personal qualities that make an employee successful. These qualities include:

- Integrity
- Courtesy
- Honesty
- Dependability
- Punctuality
- Responsibility
- Cooperative
- Positive
- Open-minded
- Flexibility

Professionalism also means you demonstrate positive work behaviors, such as regular attendance. A professional also maintains a clean and safe work environment, performs tasks effectively, shows initiative, and takes pride in his or her work accomplishments. These behaviors lead to advancement at work, in school, and in everyday life.

Professional Appearance A professional appearance is a positive work quality that enhances your employability and can help you advance in your career. Dress standards vary depending on the career that you choose. For example, you wouldn't expect your car mechanic to be wearing a suit and tie, and you wouldn't want your lawyer to be wearing grease-covered clothing. However, good grooming habits are required in all professions. The following are recommendations for maintaining a well-groomed, professional appearance:

- Wear clothes that are clean, neat, and in good repair.
- Wear clean and appropriate shoes.
- Keep your hair neat and clean.
- Brush your teeth at least twice a day.
- Floss daily.
- Use mouthwash or breath mints.
- Bathe daily.
- Use unscented deodorant.
- Keep makeup light and neutral.
- Keep jewelry to a minimum.
- Do not use perfume or cologne.
- Keep nails clean.

Figure 36.2.2 A professional appearance is a positive work quality.

In addition to completing an application form, some employers require applicants to take a test as part of the application process. For example, a personality test might help identify if someone is honest. Other tests are used for specific jobs.

• A cashier might be asked to take a basic math test.

• A customer support representative might be asked to take a problem-solving test.

• A computer technician might be asked to demonstrate a repair.

You can ask a potential employer if you will be expected to take any tests so that you can be prepared.

Career Search Skills

Employability skills also include the ability to prepare and organize the materials you will need for a job search. Every job search requires the following:

• A **resume**, which is a written summary of your work-related skills, experience, and education. It introduces you to the prospective employer by presenting a snapshot of your qualifications. It should be brief and to the point, printed on white paper, true and accurate and have no typographical, grammatical, or spelling errors. A good resume attracts the interest of the reader so he or she wants to learn more about you.

• A **cover letter**, which is a letter of introduction that you send with a resume.

• A list of **references** that includes the names and contact information of people who know you and your qualifications and who are willing to speak about you too potential employers.

You will also be expected to fill out an **application form**—sometimes online and sometimes on paper. Application forms require you to enter specific information about your education and past employment, including dates and locations. As with your resume, it is important to be truthful and accurate.

If an employer thinks you have the qualifications for the job, you will be invited for a **job interview**. A preliminary interview may be by phone but almost all employers will expect a face-to-face meeting. The interview is an opportunity for you and the interviewer to ask questions and decide if the position is right for you. You should prepare for the interview by researching the company and the position and practicing the answers to questions you think the employer might ask. You should also prepare a few questions that you can ask the employer.

After an interview, it is important to write a thank-you note to the employer to show your interest in the position. You should also be prepared to follow-up with a phone call or e-mail.

Figure 36.2.3 Employers value employees who graduate from high school and earn a college degree.

Recognizing the Value of School

Finishing school is an investment in your future. Most companies will not hire an employee who has not graduated from high school, and many will not hire an employee who has not graduated from college. If a company does hire dropouts, it usually pays them less than it pays graduates.

School also provides an opportunity to prepare for a career. Core subjects such as reading, writing, and math are vital for the career search process.

Science, social studies, music, art, technology, and sports all help you gain knowledge and build skills you will need to succeed at work, such as teamwork, leadership, and problem-solving. School clubs and organizations such as SkillsUSA also help you build skills for future success.

Personal Academic Plan A **personal academic plan** is a document that you use to set goals for the things you want to accomplish in school. Some schools call it a personal career plan. Some things that you might put in your plan include:

- Yearly academic goals
- Assessment of your skills, knowledge, and experience
- Assessment of factors that will contribute to your success
- Assessment of factors that might interfere with your success
- Basic skills assessment

Figure 36.2.4 Continuing education can lead to many rewards.

Developing a Portfolio Some academic plans include a portfolio. A **portfolio** is a collection of information and documents that show the progress you make in school and in your career planning. It helps you stay on track to achieve your educational and career goals. A portfolio may be an actual folder that holds printed documents and other materials, or it may be electronic and stored on a computer. Some things to include in a portfolio are examples of achievement such as an essay you are proud of, and awards or certificates of accomplishment.

Lifelong Learning **Lifelong learning** means continually acquiring new knowledge and skills throughout the course of your life. Education and training are not limited to learning new skills for the workplace. You should consider educational opportunities to enrich your life at home, with friends, and in your community. Understanding and using technology can help you achieve lifelong learning. It provides access to online information and helps you stay informed about current events and other topics.

Workplace Environments

Objectives

- Discuss workplace safety.
- Recognize ethical work behavior.
- Analyze workplace rules and procedures.
- Define customer service.

As You Read

Identify Information Use an outline to help you identify aspects of a workplace environment as you read this lesson.

🔑 Key Terms

- customer service
- employee handbook
- organization structure
- work ethics

Workplace Environments

Every workplace is different. Fitting in to a workplace will help ensure your career success. A first step is to understand the **organization structure** of the workplace. An organization structure is the system that assigns work, authority, and responsibility within a company.

The organization structure defines the chain of command, which is the path of authority and supervision among employees. It identifies the responsibilities of each employee, the relationships between employees, and the relationship between departments within the company. By understanding the organization structure of the place where you work, you will better understand your role in the workplace.

Workplace Structure There are many different ways a business can be organized. A business can have one or many owners. A single owner has sole propriety over his or her business. The owner is personally responsible for the business. When more than one person owns a company they are partners in ownership. Large businesses called corporations are owned by shareholders, or people who own a certain portion of the company. The shareholders are not responsible for the corporation. In fact, the corporation is its own legal entity.

Businesses are complex and require many different people with a large range of skills. Within a business there is a hierarchy, or order, to the employees. Not everyone can be in charge, so there is an order of command and responsibility. For example, in a sandwich shop the owner is in charge of the business. He directs the managers who in turn direct the staff. A large business may have multiple departments with varying responsibilities. For example, a large corporation will have administrative, accounting, marketing, and sales departments. If the company is in a large building it may have a mail room, custodial services, security, and human resources, as well.

Safety in the Workplace In 1970, the federal government passed a law called the Occupational Safety and Health Act. This law requires all employers to provide a safe and healthful workplace. Workers must be provided with safe equipment, protective clothing when needed, and education about safety practices. The Occupational Safety and Health Administration (OSHA) was formed to inspect companies and enforce safety laws. Even so, more than 5,000 Americans die from on-the-job accidents every year. As a worker under the Occupational Safety and Health Act, you have the following rights and responsibilities:

- Right to know. You have the right to know about hazards in your workplace, as well as the right to training to learn how to identify workplace hazards and what to do if there is an incident.

- Right to refuse unsafe work. If you have reasonable grounds to believe the work you do or the piece of equipment you use is unsafe, you can stop work immediately. You cannot be laid off, suspended, or penalized for refusing unsafe work if you follow the proper procedures.

- Responsibility to follow safety rules. It is your employer's responsibility to teach you the safety rules; it is your responsibility to follow the rules.

- Responsibility to ask for training. If you feel that you need more training than your employer provides, it is your responsibility to ask for it.

- Responsibility to speak up. It is your responsibility to report incidents and unsafe work practices as well as unsafe conditions.

Real-World Tech

Online Forms Instead of having applicants fill out paper application forms, many businesses use online forms. In many ways, online forms are similar to analog, written forms, in that they are a mechanism for collecting specific information. However, with information entered online, businesses can quickly compile it into a database which makes it easier to organize and manage. Also, information entered in an online form is always clear as there is no illegible handwriting.

Online forms provide fields for entering text. They usually have drop-screen tabs from which the applicant can choose from a menu of options, and check boxes for marking a selection. Online forms may also be easier to use. For example, you can only enter information where you are supposed to, and it is easy to delete an error and enter the correct information.

Part of your responsibility as a worker is to make sure that you keep your work environment safe for yourself and for others. You can practice this at school and at home. You have to take some responsibility for your own safety. That means using equipment properly, according to instructions, and being aware of safety hazards.

Ethics at Work   Ethics are a set of beliefs about what is right and what is wrong. **Work ethics** are beliefs and behaviors about what is right and wrong in a work environment. Ethical behavior includes treating people with respect and also following the law. For example, taking home office supplies is not ethical—it's stealing. Employers value employees who behave ethically at work. It shows that you are honest and respectful, so others with trust and respect you in return.

Behaving ethically at work also means following the company rules, regulations, and processes. Usually, when you start a new job you are given an employee handbook. An **employee handbook** describes company policies and procedures, such as how to request vacation time, and the different benefits that are available. It should also list all rules and policies that you are expected to obey. These might include:

- Maintaining confidentiality of information.
- Respecting copyrights and patents.
- Respecting co-workers' and customers' rights.

Ethics extends beyond the actions and behaviors of individual workers. It also applies to companies and organizations as a whole. A company that ignores the safety of workers, or hides information customers need to make an informed purchasing decision, is not behaving ethically.

Figure 36.3.1 Positive customer service is always good for business.

Customer Service   An important part of the workplace environment is how a business treats its customers. **Customer service** is the way a business meets the needs and wants of each and every customer. A happy customer will return; an unhappy customer will not. And many unhappy customers will post negative comments and reviews about the service, which will impact the business.

If you interact with customers as part of your work responsibilities, your employer will expect you to behave in a polite and professional manner at all times. Even if you do not directly interact with customers, you will be expected to present yourself to co-workers and other businesses in a way that reflects positively on the company.

Use the Vocabulary

Directions: *Match each vocabulary term in the left column with the correct definition in the right column.*

_____ 1. career
_____ 2. job
_____ 3. trend
_____ 4. portfolio
_____ 5. ability
_____ 6. interests
_____ 7. professionalism
_____ 8. personal academic plan
_____ 9. transferable skill
_____ 10. work ethic

a. once you learn this, you can use it at any job

b. things that attract your attention and that you enjoy doing

c. the ability to show respect to everyone around you while you perform your responsibilities to the best of your ability

d. a collection of information and documents that shows the progress you make in school and in your career planning

e. a chosen field of work in which you try to advance over time by gaining responsibility and earning more money

f. beliefs and behaviors about what is proper in a workspace

g. any activity you do in exchange for money or other payment

h. a skill or something you do well

i. a general move in a certain direction

j. a document that you use to set goals for the things you want to accomplish while you are in school.

Check Your Comprehension

Directions: *Complete each sentence with information from the chapter.*

1. Recognizing your _____ helps you prioritize what matters most to you in a career.

2. _____ can help you evaluate your options in many situations.

3. By conducting occupational research, you learn details about a career, including tasks performed, the job _____, the education required, and the working environment.

4. A(n) _____ occupation is any job that a man or woman does that is usually done by someone of the other gender.

5. _____ means having and using skills and abilities to be hired and stay hired

6. Employers often look for people with _____ skills to fill specific jobs.

7. A business with good _____ will meet the needs of its customer.

8. A(n) _____ is a document that you use to set goals for the things you want to accomplish while you are in school.

9. At a(n) _____, the employer asks question to determine if you are right for the job.

 **Think Critically**

Directions: *Answer the following questions.*

1. What is the first step in identifying a career?

2. What is the function of a resume?

3. Describe three ways technology has influenced employment and job outlook.

4. List at least six work behaviors and qualities that enhance employability and job advancement.

5. Select and explain one of the rights and responsibilities a worker has under the Occupational Safety and Health Act.

6. How might planning and time-management skills such as project management and storyboarding help you prepare for and obtain employment?

Extend Your Knowledge

Directions: *Choose and complete one of the following projects.*

A. Use a personal assessment to identify a career that interests you and then record your personal career goals. Use the Internet, library, or your school's guidance resources to learn more about that career, including specific job duties and tasks. Alternatively, interview someone who has that career. Use these career resources to develop a list or database of businesses that hire people in that career and of opportunities for continuing education or workplace experience in that field. Identify the education, job skills, and experience you will need to achieve your career goals. Create a time line showing how you will achieve these goals, and present it to a partner or to the class.

B. Using effective reading skills, find an advertisement for a job opening that interests you. Using effective writing skills, use a word-processing program to prepare a resume, cover letter, and list of references for that position. With a partner, practice filling out an application form and interviewing for the position. During the interview, demonstrate positive workplace behaviors and qualities, such as flexibility and initiative. After the interview, write a thank-you note. With your partner, play-act how you might make a follow-up phone call to find out if you got the job. Remember to demonstrate positive work behaviors and qualities while talking on the phone.

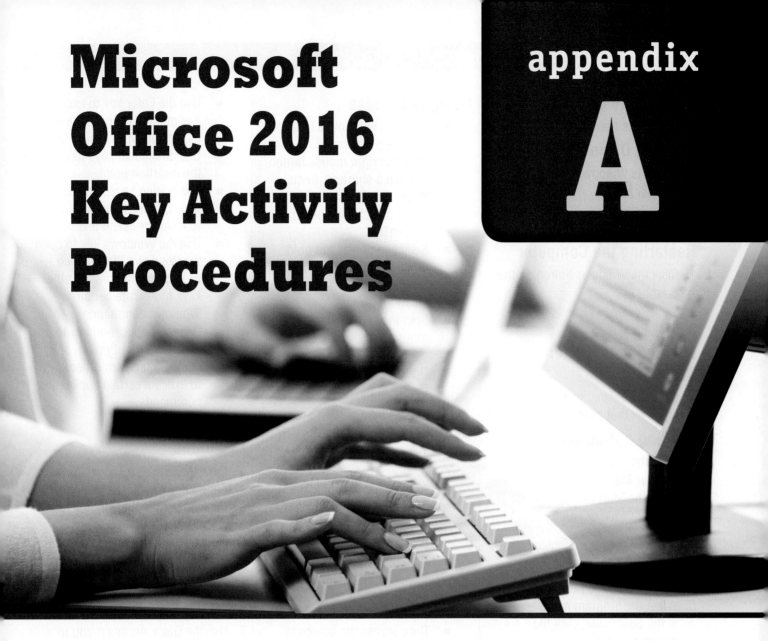

Microsoft Office 2016 Key Activity Procedures

Index to Skills

Starting the Computer

- Press the On switch.

Shutting Down the Computer

1. Click the Windows button on the Taskbar ⊞.
2. Click Power.
3. Click Shut down.

Restarting the Computer

1. Click the Windows button on the taskbar ⊞.
2. Click Power.
3. Click Restart.

Logging in to a User Account

1. Click the desired user account to log in as that user.

Starting a Program

1. Click the Windows button on the Taskbar ⊞.
2. From the Start menu, click the program's tile or name.

OR

1. Click the Windows button on the taskbar ⊞.
2. Begin typing the program name.
3. When the program name appears in the Search list, click the program name.

OR

- Double-click the program icon on the desktop.

OR

- Click the program icon on the Windows taskbar.

Exiting a Program

- Click the **Close** button on the right side of the program's title bar.

Logging off a User Account

1. Click the Windows button on the taskbar ⊞.
2. Click the User Name button near the top left of the Start menu.
3. Click **Sign out**.

Using the Mouse

- Click the left mouse button to execute a command.
- Click the right mouse button to open a shortcut menu.
- Hover the mouse pointer on an object to display a ScreenTip.
- Select an object and hold down the left mouse button to drag the object to another location.
- Spin the scroll wheel on the mouse to move through an open file.
- Double-click the left mouse button to open a file or application.

Using a Touch Screen

- Tap once on an item to open or select it.
- Press down and hold an item to select it, display a ScreenTip, or open a shortcut menu.
- Pinch or stretch an item to display different levels of information or zoom in or out.
- Drag across the screen to scroll.
- Swipe a short stroke to select an item.

Using the Keyboard

- Use function keys as shortcuts for performing specified tasks.
- Use modifier keys (Alt, Shift, and Ctrl) in combination with other keys or mouse actions to select certain commands or perform actions.
- Use the number keypad to enter numeric data.
- Use the Esc key to cancel a command.

- Use the Enter key to execute a command or to start a new paragraph when typing text.
- Use directional keys to move the insertion point.
- Use editing keys such as Insert, Delete, and Backspace to insert or delete text.
- Use the Windows key to open the Windows Start screen or in combination with other keys to execute certain Windows commands.
- Use the Application key to open a shortcut menu, or in combination with other keys to execute certain application commands.

Navigating Storage Locations

1. Click the **File Explorer** icon ▭ on the taskbar.
2. Click an item in the window to select it.
3. Double-click an item to open it.
4. Use the **Back** ← and **Forward** → buttons to move through windows you have opened recently.
5. Use the Quick Access menu to go directly to a window you have recently opened.
6. Click a location in the Address bar to open it.
7. Click an arrow between locations in the Address bar to display a menu, and then click a location on the menu to open it.
8. In the Navigation pane, click a location to display its contents in the window.

Displaying a ScreenTip

- Rest the mouse pointer on a window element.

Controlling Window Size and Position

Minimizing a Window

- Click the **Minimize** button $\boxed{-}$.

Restoring a Minimized Window

- Click the window's taskbar button.

Maximizing a Window

- Click the **Maximize** button $\boxed{\square}$.

Restoring a Maximized Window

- Click the **Restore Down** button $\boxed{\square}$.

Closing a Window

- Click the Close button $\boxed{\times}$.

✓ The Close button may be different in different types of windows but it will always have an X on it.

Resizing a Window

- Position the mouse pointer over the window border, press and hold the left mouse button, then drag the border.

Moving a Window

- Position the mouse pointer over the window's title bar, press and hold the left mouse button, then drag the window to the new position.

Displaying Open Windows Side by Side

1. Right-click a blank area of the taskbar.
2. On the shortcut menu, click Show windows side by side.

Cascading Open Windows

1. Right-click a blank area of the taskbar.
2. Click Cascade windows.

Changing the Active Window

- Click in the window you want to make active.

Capturing a Screen Image

1. Press Prt Scr on your keyboard.
✓ On a notebook computer, you may have to press Fn or the Winkey at the same time.
2. Position the insertion point in the file where you want to insert the image.
3. Click the Paste button $\boxed{}$.

Capturing an Image of the Active Window

1. Press Alt+Prt Scr on your keyboard.
✓ On a notebook computer, you may have to press Fn or the Winkey at the same time
2. Position the insertion point in the file where you want to insert the image.
3. Click the Paste button $\boxed{}$.

Managing the Desktop

Viewing and Arranging Desktop Icons

1. Right-click the desktop and click **View**.
2. Adjust the view of desktop icons in any of these ways:
    - Deselect **Show desktop icons** to hide all icons.
    - Choose to display Large icons, Medium icons, or Small icons.
    - Click **Auto arrange icons** to have Windows arrange the icons, or deselect this option if you want to be able to drag icons to specific locations.
    - Click **Align icons to grid** to snap icons to a grid system so they maintain alignment with each other.
3. Click **Sort by** if desired and select a different sort order for icons.
✓ Icons are sorted by Name by default.

Sorting Desktop Icons

1. Right-click the desktop and click **Sort by**.
2. Click property to sort by.

Creating a Desktop Shortcut

1. Right-click the desktop and click **New**.
2. Click **Shortcut**.
3. Type the path to the program, file, folder, computer, or Internet address, or click **Browse** and navigate to the desired location; click **OK** after selecting the desired object.
4. Click **Next**.
5. Type a name for the shortcut.
6. Click **Finish**.

Creating a Folder or File on the Desktop

1. Right-click the desktop and click **New**.
2. Click the item to create.

Deleting a Folder, File, or Shortcut from the Desktop

1. Right-click the item to delete.
2. Click **Delete**.

Managing Files and Folders

Creating a Folder

1. Navigate to the location where you want to create the new folder.
2. Click the **Home** tab.

Window Group

3. Click the **New folder** button.
4. Type the name of the new folder and press **Enter**.

OR

3. Right-click a blank area of the window.
4. Click **New** and then click **Folder**.
5. Type the name of the new folder and press **Enter**.

OR

4. Click the **New Folder** button on the Quick Access Toolbar.
5. Type the name of the new folder and press **Enter**.

Creating a File

1. Right-click the location in which you want to create the new file.
2. Click **New** on the shortcut menu.
3. Click the file type to create.
4. Type the file name.
5. Press **Enter**.

Copying a Folder or File

1. Navigate to the folder where the item is stored.
2. Right-click the item to copy.
3. Click **Copy**.
4. Navigate to the folder where you want to store the copy.
5. Right-click a blank area of the folder window.
6. Click **Paste**.

OR

1. Navigate to the folder where the item is stored.
2. Click the item to select it.
3. Press and hold down **Ctrl** while you drag the item to the new location.

Renaming a Folder or File

1. Right-click the item to rename.
2. Click **Rename** on the shortcut menu.
3. Type new name.
4. Press **Enter**.

Deleting a File or Folder

1. Right-click the file or folder you want to delete.
2. Click **Delete** on the shortcut menu.
3. Click **Yes** to confirm the deletion.

Moving a Folder or File

1. Navigate to the folder where the item is stored.
2. Right-click the item to move.
3. Click **Cut**.
4. Navigate to the folder where you want to move the item.
5. Right-click a blank area of the folder window.
6. Click **Paste**.

OR

1. Navigate to the folder where the item is stored.
2. Click the item to select it.
3. Drag the item to the folder to which you want to move it.

✓ If you drag files or folders from one drive to another, they are automatically copied. To move them, hold down **Shift** as you drag.

Restarting in Safe Mode

1. Press and hold the Shift key.
2. Click the Power Options button.
3. Click Restart.
4. Click See advanced repair options.
5. Click Troubleshoot.
6. Click Advanced options.
7. Click Windows Startup Settings.
8. Click Restart.

Working with Files

Displaying File Extensions

1. Click **File Explorer** 🔲 on the taskbar.
2. Click the **View** tab.
3. Click the **Options** button 🔻 **Organize** in the toolbar.
4. In the Folder Options dialog box, click the **View** tab.
5. In the Advanced settings list, scroll down if necessary and clear the checkmark from **Hide extensions for known file types**.
6. Click OK.

Opening (Retrieving) a File

1. Click **File Explorer** 🔲 on the taskbar.
2. Navigate to the location where the file is stored.
3. When the desired file displays in the file list, double-click the file to open the file and its application.

Saving a New File

1. Click **File**.
2. Click **Save As**.
3. In the File name box, type a file name.
4. Navigate to the location where you want to store the file.
5. Click **Save**.

Saving Changes to a File

1. Click **File**.
2. Click **Save**.

Printing a File

1. Display the location where the file is stored.
2. Right-click the file.
3. Click **Print**.

Displaying File Properties

1. Click **File Explorer** 🔲 on the taskbar.
2. Navigate to the folder that contains the file.
3. In the file list, right-click the file and click **Properties**.
4. Click **OK** when finished.

Changing the Folder View

1. Navigate to a storage location
2. Click the **View** tab.

Layout Group

3. Click one of the view options:
   - **Extra Large Icons**
   - **Large Icons**
   - **Medium Icons**
   - **Small Icons**
   - **List**
   - **Details**
   - **Tiles**
   - **Content**

Compressing Files

1. On the desktop, click the **File Explorer** icon 🔲 on the taskbar.
2. Click the file you want to compress to select it.
3. Click **Share** and then click the **Zip** button 📎.
4. Enter a new name for the zipped folder if desired.

Adding a File to a Zipped Folder

1. In File Explorer, right-click the file you want to add to the zipped folder.
2. On the shortcut menu, click **Copy**.
3. Display the location containing the zipped folder.
4. Right-click the zipped folder.
5. On the shortcut menu, click **Paste**.

Extracting Compressed Files

1. In File Explorer, click to select the zipped folder.
2. Click the **Compressed Folders Tools Extract** tab.
3. Click the **Extract all** button 📎.
4. If necessary, select the file(s) you want to extract.
5. Click **Extract**.

Modifying Display Properties

1. Right-click on the desktop, and click **Personalize > Themes >Themes settings**.
2. Select from these options:
   - Click **Desktop Background**, select the desired picture, and click **Save changes**.
   - Click **Color**, select a color for window borders from the gallery; then click **Save changes**.
   - Click **Screen Saver**, select a screen saver option, and click **OK**.
   - Click **Display** near the bottom of the left pane to modify Display settings; click **Apply** to apply the changes.
3. If desired, click **Save theme** to name and save personalized settings as a theme.

Displaying System Information

1. Click the Windows button on the taskbar ⊞.
2. Click **Settings**.
3. Click **System**.
4. Click **About**.

Accessing the Command Prompt

1. Click the Windows button on the taskbar ⊞.
2. Type **Command Prompt**.
3. Click **Command Prompt**.

Changing Simple Settings

✓ You may need permission from an administrator to make these changes.

Changing Date and Time

1. Click the Windows button on the taskbar ⊞.
2. Click **Settings**.
3. Click **Time & language**.
4. Click **Date and time**.
5. Toggle automatic options off or on.
6. If Set time automatically is set to off, click the Change button to set the date and time manually.

Changing Audio Settings

1. Click the Windows button on the taskbar ⊞.
2. Click **Settings**.
3. In the Find a setting box in the upper-right of the window, type **Adjust system volume**.
4. Click **Click Adjust system volume.**
4. Drag the sliders to set the volume.

Adjusting Firewall Settings

1. Click the Windows button on the taskbar ⊞.
2. Click **Settings**.
3. Click **Update & security**.
4. In the Find a setting box in the upper-right of the window, type **Windows Firewall**.
5. Click **Windows Firewall**.
6. Adjust settings as desired.

Modifying User Account Control Settings

1. Click the Windows button on the taskbar ⊞.
2. Click **Settings**.
3. Click **Accounts**.
4. Adjust settings as desired.

Adjusting Power Settings

1. Click the Windows button on the taskbar ⊞.
2. Click **Settings**.
3. Click **System**.
4. Click **Power & sleep**.
5. Click **Additional power settings**.
6. Select desired options.

Verifying Network Connectivity

1. Click the Windows button on the taskbar ⊞.
2. Click **Settings**.
3. Click **Network & Internet**.
4. Click **Wi-Fi**.
5. View the current active network connections.

Safely Removing Hardware and Eject Media

1. On the right end of the Windows taskbar, click the **Safely Remove Hardware and Media** icon 📤 .
2. Click the name of the device.
3. Remove the device when the safe to remove message displays.

Displaying a List of Installed Printers and Other Devices

1. Click the Windows button on the taskbar ⊞.
2. Click **Settings**.
3. Click **Devices**.
4. Click **Printers & scanners**.

Converting Content into Digital Files

Acquiring Files from a Camera

1. Connect the camera to the computer, and, if necessary, install the camera's device driver.
2. Follow the prompts in the Camera Wizard to acquire the files.

OR

1. On the desktop, click the **File Explorer** icon 📁 on the taskbar.
2. Double-click the camera device icon.
3. Navigate to the location where the camera files are stored.
4. Right-click the file to copy and click **Copy**.
5. Navigate to the location where you want to store the copied file.
6. Right-click a blank area of the window and click **Paste**.

Searching for Help Information

1. Click the Windows button on the taskbar ⊞.
2. Type a question or a brief description of what you are looking for. For example, type Add a device.
3. In the list of results, click a result. For example, click **Add or remove devices**.

Starting a Microsoft Office Program

- Click the program's icon on the Windows Desktop.

OR

- Click the program's icon on the taskbar.

OR

1. Click the **Start** button ⊞.
2. Click **All apps**.
3. Click the desired application.

Exiting a Microsoft Office Program

- In the program window, click the **Close** button ✕ at the right end of the title bar.

Opening a File

Opening an Existing File

1. Start the application.
2. At the bottom of the Recent list on the left side of the window, click the option to open other files.
3. Click the **Browse** button 📂 and navigate to the file's location.
4. Click the file to select it and then click **Open**.

OR

1. With the application already open, click **File**.
2. Click **Open**.
3. Navigate to the file's location.
4. Double-click the file to open it.

OR

4. Click the file.
5. Click **Open**.

Opening a Recently Opened Document

1. Click **File**.
2. On the Open tab, click the **Recent** option to display a list of recently opened files.
3. Click the file to open it.

Opening Compatible File Types

1. With the application already open, click **File**.
2. Click **Open**.
3. Navigate to the file's location.
4. In the Open dialog box, click the **File Type** button.
5. Select the desired file type.
6. Select the file to open.
7. Click **Open**.

Creating a File

Creating a New, Blank File

1. Click **File**.
2. Click **New**.
3. Click the **Blank *filetype*** icon.

Creating a File Based on a Template

1. Click **File**.
2. Click **New**.
3. Click the desired template.
4. Click **Create**.

Exploring Templates Online

1. Click **File**.
2. Click **New**.
3. Under **New** in the right pane, search for and select the desired template.
4. Click **Create**.

Saving a File

Saving a New File

1. Click **File**.
2. Click **Save As**.
3. Click the **Browse** button 📂 and navigate to the location where you want to save the file.
4. Type the file name in the File name text box.
5. Click **Save**.

Saving Changes to a File

- Click **Save** 💾 on the Quick Access Toolbar.

OR

1. Click **File**.
2. Click **Save**.

Saving in a Compatible File Format

1. Click **File**.
2. Click **Save As**.
3. Click the **Browse** button 📂 and navigate to the location where you want to save the file.
4. In the Save As dialog box, click the **Save as type** button to display a list of file types.
5. Select the desired file type.
6. Type the file name.
7. Click **Save**.

Saving a File as a Template

1. Click **File**.
2. Click **Save As**.
3. Click the **Browse** button 📂 and navigate to the location where you want to save the file.
4. In the Save As dialog box, click the **Save as type** button.
5. Click ***program name* Template**.
6. Click **Save**.

Viewing Application Options

1. With the application open, click **File**.
2. Click **Options**.
3. In the application's Options dialog box, click a category on the left and change options as desired.
4. Click **OK**.

Using the Ribbon

- Click a tab on the Ribbon to display its commands.
- Point to a button on a tab to display its ScreenTip.
- Click a button on a tab to execute a command.
- Click a drop-down arrow on a button to display a gallery or menu of options.
- Click a group dialog box launcher to display a dialog box, task pane, or window where you can select additional or multiple options.

- Hide the Ribbon by clicking the **Collapse the Ribbon** button ⌃.
- Click any tab to expand the Ribbon temporarily.
- Click the **Pin the ribbon** button ⚲ to keep the Ribbon displayed.

Customizing the Ribbon

1. With the application open, click **File**.
2. Click **Options**.

OR

1. Right-click anywhere in the Ribbon.
2. On the shortcut menu, click **Customize the Ribbon**.
3. In the application's Options dialog box, click **Customize Ribbon**.
4. Click options to customize the Ribbon as desired.
5. Click **OK**.

Customizing the Quick Access Toolbar

Adding Buttons to the Toolbar

1. Click the **Customize Quick Access Toolbar** button ▾.
2. On the menu, click a button to add it to the Quick Access Toolbar.

OR

1. Right-click a button on the Ribbon.
2. On the shortcut menu, click **Add to Quick Access Toolbar**.

Removing Buttons from the Toolbar

1. Click the **Customize Quick Access Toolbar** button ▾.
2. On the menu, click a button with a check mark to remove it from the toolbar.

OR

1. Right-click a button on the Quick Access Toolbar that you want to remove.
2. On the shortcut menu, click **Remove from Quick Access Toolbar**.

Moving the Quick Access Toolbar

1. Click the **Customize Quick Access Toolbar** button ▾.
2. Click **Show Below the Ribbon**.

OR

Click **Show Above the Ribbon**.

Scrolling

- Use the directional keys on the keyboard to scroll left and right or up and down.
- Drag a scroll box until you bring the desired portion of the file into view.
- Click a scroll arrow to scroll through the file in small increments.
- If your mouse has a scroll wheel, spin it to scroll up and down.
- If you use a touch screen, swipe to scroll in the desired direction.

Zooming

Zooming Using the Slider

- Drag the Zoom slider to the left to zoom out; drag to the right to zoom in.
- Click the Zoom Out button at the left of the Zoom slider to zoom out; click the Zoom In button to the right of the slider to zoom in.

Zooming Using the View Tab

1. Click the **View** tab.
   - Zoom Group
2. Click the desired zooming options.

OR

2. Click the **Zoom** button 🔍.
3. In the Zoom dialog box, select the desired zooming option.
4. Click **OK**.

Selecting Text

Mouse Selection Commands

- One word: Double-click word
- One sentence: Ctrl + click in sentence
- One line: Click in selection bar to the left of the line
- One paragraph: Double-click in selection bar to the left of the paragraph
- Document: Triple-click in selection bar
- Noncontiguous text: Select first block, press and hold Ctrl, then select additional blocks

Keyboard Selection Commands

- One character right: Shift + →
- One character left: Shift + ←
- One line up: ↑
- One line down: ↓
- To end of line: Shift + End
- To beginning of line: Shift + Home
- To end of document: Shift + Ctrl + End
- To beginning of document: Shift + Ctrl + Home
- Entire document: Ctrl + A

Selecting Noncontiguous Text

1. Select the first block.
2. Press and hold the Ctrl key.
3. Select the next block.

Selecting and Replacing Text

1. Select the text.
2. Type the replacement text.

Canceling a Selection or Command

- Click anywhere outside selected text to cancel the selection.
- Press **Escape** to cancel a command or close a dialog box.
- Click anywhere outside a displayed menu to close it without making a selection.

Moving a Selection

Using Drag-and-Drop

1. Select the text (including paragraph mark, if necessary) to move.
2. Move the mouse pointer anywhere over the selection.
3. Press and hold the left mouse button.
4. Drag to the desired location and release the mouse button.

Using Cut (Ctrl+X) and Paste (Ctrl+V)

1. Select the text (including paragraph mark, if necessary) to move.
2. Click the **Home** tab.
   Clipboard Group
3. Click the **Cut** button ✄.
4. Click where you want to move the text.
5. Click the **Home** tab.
   Clipboard Group
6. Click the **Paste** button 🗋.

Using Keyboard Shortcuts

1. Select the text (including paragraph mark, if necessary) to move.
2. Press **F2**.
3. Click where you want to move the text.
4. Press **Enter**.

Copying a Selection

Using Drag-and-Drop

1. Select the text (including paragraph mark, if necessary) to copy.
2. Move the mouse pointer anywhere over the selection.
3. Press and hold **Ctrl**.
4. Press and hold the left mouse button.
5. Drag to the desired location and release the mouse button.

Using Copy (Ctrl+C) and Paste (Ctrl+V)

1. Select the text (including paragraph mark, if necessary) to copy.
2. Click the **Home** tab.
   Clipboard Group
3. Click the **Copy** button 🗇.
4. Click where you want to copy the text.
5. Click the **Home** tab.
   Clipboard Group
6. Click the **Paste** button 🗋.

Using Paste Options

1. Click the **Home** tab.
   Clipboard Group
2. Click the **Paste** button drop-down arrow 🗋.
3. Click the desired paste option on the menu.

Using Undo (Ctrl + Z), Redo (Ctrl + Y), and Repeat (Ctrl + Y)

- Click the **Undo** button ↶ on the Quick Access Toolbar to reverse a single action or series of actions.
- Click the **Redo** button ↷ on the Quick Access Toolbar to reinstate any action that you reversed with Undo.
- Click the **Repeat** button ↺ on the Quick Access Toolbar to repeat the most recent action.

Applying a Theme

✓ These steps are written for Word and may vary in the other Office applications.

1. Click the **Design** tab.
   Document Formatting Group
2. Click the **Themes** button 🔲.
3. Click the desired theme from the Themes gallery.

Working with Fonts

Applying Font Styles

1. Click the **Home** tab.
   Font Group
2. Click the desired font style, as follows:
   - **Bold** (Ctrl + B) ᴮ
   - **Italic** (Ctrl + I) ᴵ

OR

1. Click the **Home** tab.
2. Click the **Font** group dialog box launcher ⌐.
3. In the Font style list, click the desired style.
4. Click **OK**.

Changing the Font

1. Click the **Home** tab.
   Font Group
2. Click the **Font** button drop-down arrow Calibri (Body) ▾.
3. Click the desired font.

OR

1. Click the **Home** tab.
2. Click the **Font** group dialog box launcher ⌐.
3. In the Font list, click the desired font.
4. Click **OK**.

Changing the Font Color

1. Click the **Home** tab.
   Font Group
2. Click the **Font Color** button drop-down arrow A ▾.
3. Click the desired font color.

OR

1. Click the **Home** tab.
2. Click the **Font** group dialog box launcher ⌐.
3. Click the **Font color** drop-down arrow.
4. Click the desired font color.
5. Click **OK**.

Changing the Font Size
1. Click the **Home** tab.
   Font Group
2. Click the **Font Size** button drop-down arrow [11 ▾].
3. Click the desired font size.

OR

- Click the **Home** tab.
   Font Group
   - Click the **Increase Font Size** button A˄ to increase the font size.
   - Click the **Decrease Font Size** A˅ button to decrease the font size.

OR

1. Click the **Home** tab.
2. Click the **Font** group dialog box launcher ⌐.
3. In the Size list, click the desired font size.
4. Click **OK**.

Applying Font Effects
1. Click the **Home** tab.
2. Click the **Font** group dialog box launcher ⌐.
3. Under Effects, click the desired effect.
4. Click **OK**.

Applying Underlines
1. Click the **Home** tab.
   Font Group
2. Click the **Underline** button drop-down arrow U˅.
3. Click the desired underline style.

OR

1. Click the **Home** tab.
2. Click the **Font** group dialog box launcher ⌐.
3. Click the **Underline style** drop-down arrow.
4. Click the desired underline style.
5. Click **OK**.

Inserting Objects

Inserting a Picture File
1. Click the **Insert** tab.
   Illustrations Group
2. Click the **Pictures** button ⌐.
3. In the Insert Picture dialog box, navigate to and select the picture you want to insert.
4. Click **Insert**.

Inserting Clip Art
1. Click the **Insert** tab.
   Illustrations Group
2. Click the **Online Pictures** button ⌐.
3. In the search box, type the name of the art you want to insert.
4. Click a picture in the task pane and then click Insert to insert it in the document.

Inserting a Shape
1. Click the **Insert** tab.
   Illustrations Group
2. Click the **Shapes** button ⌐.
3. Click the desired shape from the gallery.
4. Click and drag to draw the shape as desired.

Inserting a Text Box
1. Click the **Insert** tab.
   Text Group
2. Click the **Text Box** button ⌐.
3. Click the desired style from the gallery.

OR

1. Click the **Insert** tab.
   Text Group
2. Click the **Text Box** button ⌐.
3. Click **Draw Text Box**.
4. Click and drag to draw the text box as desired.

Inserting WordArt
1. Select the text.
2. Click the **Insert** tab.
   Text Group
3. Click the **Insert WordArt** button 𝒜.
4. Click the desired style from the gallery.

Inserting a SmartArt Graphic
1. Click the **Insert** tab.
   Illustrations Group
2. Click the **SmartArt** button ⌐.
3. Click the desired SmartArt from the Choose a SmartArt Graphic dialog box.
4. Click **OK**.

Formatting Objects

Deleting an Object
1. Click the object to select it.
2. Press **Delete** or **Backspace**.

Resizing an Object
1. Click the object to select it.
2. Drag a sizing handle to adjust the size as desired.

OR

1. Click the object to select it.
2. Click the **Drawing Tools Format** tab.
   Size Group
3. Use the **Shape Height** increment arrows [1"] and the **Shape Width** increment arrows [1"] to adjust the object's size.

Moving an Object
1. Position the mouse pointer over the selected object until the mouse pointer changes to a four-headed arrow ⌐.
2. Drag the object to the desired position and release the mouse button.

Applying a Style to a Picture
1. Click the picture to select it.
2. Click the **Picture Tools Format** tab.
   Picture Styles Group
3. Click the **More** button ▾.
4. Click the desired style in the gallery.

Applying a Style to a Shape
1. Click the shape to select it.
2. Click the **Picture Tools Format** tab.
   Shape Styles Group
3. Click the **More** button ▾.
4. Click the desired style in the gallery.

Applying a Border, Effects, and Layout to a Picture

1. Click the picture to select it.
2. Click the **Picture Tools Format** tab.

Picture Styles Group

3. Click to apply the desired format, as follows:
   - **Picture Border** ✎.
   - **Picture Effects** ◷.
   - **Picture Layout** ▦.

Applying a Fill, Outline, and Effects to a Shape

1. Click the shape to select it.
2. Click the **Drawing Tools Format** tab.

Shape Styles Group

3. Click to apply the desired format, as follows:
   - **Shape Fill** ◭.
   - **Shape Outline** ✎.
   - **Shape Effects** ◷.

Wrapping Text Around an Object

1. Click the object to select it.
2. Click the **Drawing Tools Format** tab.

Arrange Group

3. Click the **Wrap Text** button ▤.
4. Click the desired wrap option from the menu.

Cropping a Graphic

1. Click the graphic to select it.
2. Click the **Picture Tools Format** tab.

Size Group

3. Click the **Crop** button ⊹.
4. Hover the mouse pointer over a cropping handle.
5. When the cropping pointer appears, click and drag to crop out the desired portion of the graphic.
   √ *Use a corner handle to crop from two sides. Use a side or top handle to crop from the corresponding side.*
6. When you're done cropping, click the **Crop** button ⊹ again to complete the crop.

Modifying a Picture

1. Click the picture to select it.
2. Click the **Picture Tools Format** tab.

Adjust Group

3. Click an option to make the desired modification, as follows:
   - **Corrections** ☼ to adjust the contrast and brightness
   - **Color** ▨ to change the color
   - **Artistic Effects** ▦ to add special effects
   - **Compress Pictures** ▣ to reduce the file size
   - **Change Picture** ▤ to change to a different picture, preserving the formatting and size of the current picture
   - **Reset Picture** ▨ ▾ to remove all formatting applied to the picture

Changing the Direction of Text in a Text Box

1. Click the text box to select it.
2. Click the **Drawing Tools Format** tab.

Text Group

3. Click the **Text Direction** button ▥.
4. Click the desired rotation option.

Adding Text to a Shape

1. Right-click the shape.
2. Click **Add Text** on the shortcut menu.
3. Type the text and apply formats as desired.

Grouping Objects

1. Click an object to select it.
2. Hold down **Shift** to select other objects to include in the group.
3. Click the **Picture Tools Format** tab.

Arrange Group

4. Click the **Group Objects** button ▣ ▾.
5. Click **Group** on the menu.

Positioning an Object

1. Click the **Picture Tools Format** tab.

Arrange Group

2. Click the **Position** button ▨.
3. Select the desired position from the gallery.

OR

1. Click the **Picture Tools Format** tab.

Arrange Group

2. Click the **Align Objects** button ▣ ▾.
3. Select the desired alignment option from the menu.

OR

1. Click the object to select it.
2. Press the up, down, left, or right arrow keys to nudge the object in the desired direction.

Rotating an Object

1. Click the object to select it.
2. Position the mouse pointer over the object's rotation handle so it resembles a circular arrow ↺.
3. Drag to rotate the object as desired.

OR

1. Click the object to select it.
2. Click the **Picture Tools Format** tab.

Arrange Group

3. Click the **Rotate Objects** button ◪ ▾.
4. Click the desired rotation option from the menu.

Layering Objects

1. Click an object to select it.
2. Click the **Picture Tools Format** tab.

Arrange Group

3. Click the **Bring Forward** button ▥ or the **Send Backward** button ▤ to layer it with other objects.

Duplicating an Object

1. Click the object.
2. Press **Ctrl+C**.
3. Press **Ctrl+V** to paste a duplicate copy.

OR
1. Click the object.
2. Hold down **Ctrl** and drag to place the duplicate in the desired location.

Aligning and Distributing Objects
1. Click the objects you want to align and distribute.
√ *Hold down Ctrl to select multiple objects.*
2. Click the **Drawing Tools Format** tab.
   Arrange Group
3. Click the **Align** button ⊫ ▾.
4. From the menu, click the desired option.

Using Office Help
1. Click the File tab.
2. Click the **Help** button **?** in the upper-right corner.
3. At the Support-Office.com page, click in the search box, type the topic for which you need help, and press Enter.
OR
1. In an open Office application, click in the *Tell me what you want to do* box to the right of the Ribbon tabs.
2. Type a topic or query.
OR
1. Press F1 to open the Help Viewer.
2. Enter the topic for which you need help in the search box, or use the Top categories list to search for a topic.

Viewing File Properties
1. Click **File**.
2. On the Info tab, review the file properties listed on the right.

Using Access Keys
- Press Alt to activate access keys.
- Press the keyboard character to execute the desired command.

Using the Mini Toolbar
1. Select text you want to format.
2. On the Mini toolbar, click the desired formatting options.

Using a Shortcut Menu
1. Right-click an object or selected text.
2. From the shortcut menu, select the desired option.

Using Dialog Box Options
- Use a list box to display a list of items from which a selection can be made.
- Use a palette to select an option, such as a color or shape.
- Use a drop-down list box to either type a selection in the text box or select from a drop-down list.
- Click a check box to select an option. A check mark indicates the option is selected.
- Click a command button to execute a command. An ellipsis on a command button means that clicking it will open another dialog box.
- Click a tab to view additional pages of options.
- In the Preview area, you can preview the results of your selections.
- Use increment boxes to type a value, or use increment arrows to increase or decrease the value.
- Use a text box to type variable information.
- Use an option button to make one selection from a group.

Displaying Task Panes
- Click a dialog box launcher ⌐₃ on a tab to open a task pane.

Formatting Text

Formatting Selected Text
1. Click the **Home** tab.
   Font Group
2. Click the desired formatting options.

Formatting New Text
1. Click the **Home** tab.
   Font Group
2. Click the desired formatting options.
3. Enter the text.

Changing the View

Word, Excel, and PowerPoint
- Click the View shortcut buttons on the status bar.
OR
- Click the **View** tab and select options as desired.

Access
- Use the Views button to switch between an object's views.

Using Multiple Program Windows
- Click a button on the Taskbar to display the desired window.
- Click a group button on the Taskbar and select the desired window to display.
- Tile windows to see all of them at the same time. Right-click on a blank area of the Taskbar. From the shortcut menu, click the desired tiling option.

Arranging Multiple Files within Word, Excel, and PowerPoint
1. Click the **View** tab.
   Window Group
2. Click the desired window arrangement option.

Showing or Hiding Nonprinting Characters

1. Click the **Home** tab.
   Paragraph Group
2. Click the **Show/Hide ¶** button ¶.
3. Click the **Show/Hide ¶** button ¶ again to toggle off.

Showing or Hiding the Ruler

1. Click the **View** tab.
   Show Group
2. Click the **Ruler** check box.
   √ *A check in the check box indicates the ruler is displayed.*

Changing the View

1. Click the **View** tab.
   View Group
2. Click the desired View button:
   - **Read Mode** 📖
   - **Print Layout** 📄
   - **Web Layout** 🌐
   - **Outline** ▣
   - **Draft** ▤

OR

   - Click a **View** button on the status bar:
   - **Read Mode** 📖
   - **Print Layout** 📄
   - **Web Layout** 🔖

Switching between Open Documents

- Click in the document window you want to make active.

OR

- Click the program's taskbar button and click the document you want to make active.

OR

1. Click the **View** tab.
   Window Group
2. Click the **Switch Windows** button 🗗.
3. Click the document you want to make active.

Arranging Multiple Documents

1. Open all documents.
2. Click the **View** tab.
   Window Group
3. Click the **Arrange All** button ▤.

Closing a Document

- Click the **Close** button ✕.

OR

1. Click **File**.
2. Click **Close**.

Entering Text and Data

Typing in a Document

- Press **Enter** to start a new paragraph.
- Press **Backspace** to delete one character to the left of the insertion point.
- Press **Delete** to delete one character to the right of the insertion point.
- Press **Escape** to cancel a command or close a dialog box.

Using Overtype Mode

1. Right-click the status bar.
2. Click **Overtype** on the shortcut menu.
   √ *A check mark next to the command on the shortcut menu indicates it is selected.*
3. Click **Insert** on the status bar to change to overtype mode.

Finding and Replacing

Using Find

1. Click the **Home** tab.
   Editing Group
2. Click the **Find** button 🔍.
3. In the text box at the top of the Navigation pane, enter the text you want to find. Word displays a list of occurrences in the Navigation pane.

Using Advanced Find

1. Click the **Home** tab.
   Editing Group
2. Click the **Find** button drop-down arrow 🔍.
3. Click **Advanced Find**.
4. In the Find and Replace dialog box, enter the text to find in the Find what text box.
5. Click **Find Next**. A message box appears when all occurrences have been found.

Using Find and Replace

1. Click the **Home** tab.
   Editing Group
2. Click the **Replace** button ᵃᵇ/ₐᵪ.
3. In the Find and Replace dialog box, enter the text to find in the Find what text box.
4. Enter the replacement text in the Replace with text box.
5. Click the **Replace** button to replace each separate occurrence; click **Replace All** to replace all occurrences.

Changing Case

1. Select the text whose case you want to change.
2. Click the **Home** tab.
   Font Group
3. Click the **Change Case** button Aa ▾.
4. On the menu, click the desired case option.

Applying Text Effects

1. Select the text.
2. Click the **Home** tab.

   Font Group

3. Click the **Text Effects** button Ⓐ ▾.
4. Click the desired effect from the gallery.

Using the Format Painter to Copy Formats

1. Select the text whose format you want to copy.
2. Click the **Home** tab.

   Clipboard Group

3. Click the **Format Painter** button ❖.
4. Select the text to which you want to apply the copied format.

Copying Formatting to Multiple Selections

1. Select the text whose format you want to copy.
2. Click the **Home** tab.

   Clipboard Group

3. Double-click the **Format Painter** button ❖.
4. Select the text to which you want to apply the copied format, and repeat for additional blocks of text.

Highlighting Text

1. Select the text you want to highlight.
2. Click the **Home** tab.

   Font Group

3. Click the **Text Highlight Color** drop-down arrow ☀ ▾.
4. Click the desired highlight color.
OR
1. Click the **Home** tab.

   Font Group

2. Click the **Text Highlight Color** drop-down arrow ☀ ▾.
3. Click the desired highlight color.
✓ The mouse pointer changes to the Highlight Text pointer ▨.

4. Drag across the text you want to highlight.
5. Click the **Text Highlight Color** button ☀ ▾ again to turn off the feature.

Clearing Formatting

1. Click the **Home** tab.

   Font Group

2. Click the **Clear All Formatting** button ❖.

Revealing Formatting

1. Click the formatted text.
2. Click the **Home** tab.

   Styles Group

3. Click the **Styles** group dialog box launcher ⌐.
4. In the Styles task pane, click the Style Inspector button.
5. In the Style Inspector task pane, click the Reveal Formatting button.

Setting Alignment

Aligning Text Horizontally

1. Click the **Home** tab.

   Paragraph Group

2. Click the desired alignment button:
   - **Align Left** ≡
   - **Center** ≡
   - **Align Right** ≡
   - **Justify** ≡

Aligning a Document Vertically

1. Click the **Layout tab**.
2. Click the **Page Setup** group dialog box launcher ⌐.
3. Click the **Layout** tab.
4. Click the **Vertical alignment** drop-down arrow.
5. Select the desired alignment from the menu.
6. Click **OK**.

Printing a File

1. Click **File**.
2. Click **Print**.
3. Click the **Print** button 🖶.

Previewing and Printing a File

1. Click the **File** tab.
2. Click **Print**.
✓ In Backstage view, print settings display on the left, and a preview of the file displays on the right.

2. Use the **Next Page** and **Previous Page** arrows under the preview to view other pages
3. Use the **Zoom** controls under the preview to adjust the preview magnification.
4. Click the **Print** button 🖶.

Changing Print Options

1. Click the **File** tab.
2. Click **Print**.
✓ In Backstage view, print settings display on the left, and a preview of the file displays on the right.

3. In the **Copies** box, enter the number of copies.
4. Under Printer, select the printer to use.
✓ Click Printer Properties to set options for the selected printer.
5. Under Settings, select options:
   - What to print
   - Pages to print
   - One sided or two sided printing
   - Collated or Uncollated
   - Landscape or Portrait orientation
   - Page Size
   - Margin width
   - Pages per sheet
✓ Click Page Setup to open the program's Page Setup dialog box for additional options.

6. Click the **Print** button 🖶.

Setting Document Spacing

Setting Paragraph Spacing
- Click the **Layout tab**.

Paragraph Group

- Use the **Spacing Before** box increment arrows to set the spacing before the paragraph.
- Using the **Spacing After** box increment arrows to set the spacing after the paragraph.

OR

1. Click the **Layout tab**.
2. Click the **Paragraph** group dialog box launcher ⌐.
3. Click the **Indents and Spacing** tab.
4. Under Spacing, enter the desired spacing in the **Before** and **After** boxes.
5. Click **OK**.

OR

1. Click the **Home** tab.
2. Click the **Line and Paragraph Spacing** button ⌸ ▾.
3. Click the **Remove Space Before Paragraph** or **Remove Space After Paragraph** option from the menu.

Setting Line Spacing
1. Click the **Home** tab.

Paragraph Group

2. Click the **Line and Paragraph Spacing** button ⌸ ▾.
3. Click the desired line spacing option from the menu.

OR

1. Click the **Home** tab.
2. Click the **Paragraph** group dialog box launcher ⌐.
3. Click the **Indents and Spacing** tab.
4. Click the **Line spacing** drop-down arrow.
5. Select the desired spacing option from the menu.
6. Click **OK**.

Formatting Pages

Selecting a Preset Margin
1. Click the **Layout tab**.

Page Setup Group

2. Click the **Margins** button ⊞.
3. On the menu, click the desired margin setting.

Setting Custom Margins
1. Click the **Page Layout** tab.

Page Setup Group

2. Click the **Margins** button ⊞.
3. On the menu, click **Custom Margins**.
4. In the Page Setup dialog box, under Margins, set the margins as desired.
5. Click **OK**.

Selecting a Paper Size
1. Click the **Layout tab**.

Page Setup Group

2. Click the **Size** button ◻.
3. Click the desired page size.

Setting Page Orientation
1. Click the **Layout tab**.

Page Setup Group

2. Click the **Orientation** button ⌧.
3. On the menu, click the desired orientation.

Applying a Page Border
1. Click the **Design** tab.

Page Background Group

2. Click the **Page Borders** button ◻.
3. In the Borders and Shading dialog box, click the **Page Border** tab.
4. Select the Setting, Style, Color, and Width as desired.
5. Click **OK**.

Setting Indents

Adjusting the Left Indent by 0.5"
1. Click the **Home** tab.

Paragraph Group

2. Click the indent option as follows to adjust the indent by 0.5":
   - **Decrease Indent** button ⮌
   - **Increase Indent** button ⮎

Setting a Left or Right Indent Precisely
- Click the **Layout tab**.

Paragraph Group

- Use the **Indent Left** box increment arrows to set the left indent.
- Use the **Indent Right** box increment arrows to set the right indent.

Setting Indents Using the Paragraph Dialog Box
1. Click the **Layout tab**.
2. Click the **Paragraph** group dialog box launcher ⌐.
3. Click the **Indents and Spacing** tab.
4. Under Indentation, use the **Left** and **Right** increment arrows to set the left and right margins, respectively.
5. If desired, click the **Special** drop-down arrow to set the indent on the first line.
6. Click the **By** increment arrows to adjust the indent on the first line, if desired.

Setting a Hanging Indent
1. Click the **Layout tab**.
2. Click the **Paragraph** group dialog box launcher ⌐.
3. Click the **Indents and Spacing** tab.
4. Click the **Special** drop-down arrow and click **Hanging**.
5. Click the **By** increment arrows to adjust the indent on the hanging indent, if desired.

Setting Tabs

Setting Tabs Using the Horizontal Ruler

1. To select a tab type, click the Tab selector box at the left end of the horizontal ruler until the tab you want to use displays, as follows:
   - **Left** ⌐
   - **Right** ⌐
   - **Center** ⊥
   - **Decimal** ⊥
   - **Bar** ⊥
2. Click at the position on the horizontal ruler where you want to set the tab.

Setting Tabs in the Tabs Dialog Box

1. Click the **Home** tab.
2. Click the **Paragraph** group dialog box launcher ⌐.
3. Click the **Tabs** button.
4. Type the tab stop position in the **Tab stop position** text box.
5. From the Alignment option, select the desired tab type.
6. Click **Set**.
7. Click **OK**.

Using the Horizontal Ruler to Adjust and Clear Tab Stops

- Position the insertion point in the line of text for which the tab has been set.
- To clear a tab stop, drag the tab stop off the horizontal ruler.
- To adjust a tab stop, drag it to the desired position on the horizontal ruler.

Selecting a Tab Leader

1. Click the **Home** tab.
2. Click the **Paragraph** group dialog box launcher ⌐.
3. Click the **Tabs** button.
4. In the Leader area, click the desired leader style.
5. Click **OK**.
6. In the document, press **Tab** to advance to the tab stop and insert the selected leader.

Working with Breaks

Inserting a Hard Page Break

1. Position the insertion point where you want to insert the page break.
2. Click the **Insert** tab.

   #### Pages Group

3. Click the **Page Break** button ⌐.

OR

2. Click the **Layout tab**.

   #### Page Setup Group

3. Click the **Breaks** button ⌐.
4. From the Breaks gallery, click **Page**.

Deleting a Hard Page Break

1. Position the insertion point on the page break.
2. Press **Delete**.

Inserting a Section Break

1. Position the insertion point where you want to insert the break.
2. Click the **Layout tab**.

   #### Page Setup Group

3. Click the **Breaks** button ⌐.
4. From the Breaks gallery, click the desired break type.

Deleting a Section Break

1. Position the insertion point on the section break.
2. Press **Delete**.

Inserting Symbols

1. Position the insertion point where you want to insert the symbol.
2. Click the **Insert** tab.

   #### Symbols Group

3. Click the **Symbol** button Ω.

√ *If the symbol you want displays in the Symbols gallery, click it to insert it in the document.*

4. Click **More Symbols**.
5. In the Symbol dialog box, select a font if necessary, and then click the desired symbol.
6. Click **Insert**.

Inserting Special Characters

1. Position the insertion point where you want to insert the character.
2. Click the **Insert** tab.

   #### Symbols Group

3. Click the **Symbol** button Ω.
4. Click **More Symbols**.
5. In the Symbol dialog box, click the **Special Characters** tab.
6. Click the desired character.
7. Click **Insert**.

Creating Lists

Creating a Bulleted List

1. Click the **Home** tab.

   #### Paragraph Group

2. Click the **Bullets** button drop-down arrow ⌐.
3. Click the desired bullet style from the Bullet Library.

OR

1. Click the **Home** tab.

   #### Paragraph Group

2. Click the **Bullets** button drop-down arrow ⌐.
3. Click **Define New Bullet** on the menu.
4. In the Define New Bullet dialog box, click the **Symbol** button, **Picture** button, and/or **Font** button to define a new bullet.

Creating a Numbered List

1. Click the **Home** tab.

   #### Paragraph Group

2. Click the **Numbering** button drop-down arrow ⌐.
3. Click the desired numbering style from the Numbering Library.

Changing an Item Level in a Numbered List

1. Click the **Home** tab.

   #### Paragraph Group

2. Click the **Decrease Indent** button ⌐ to promote the item one level, or click the **Increase Indent** button ⌐ to demote the item one level.

Creating a Multilevel List
1. Click the **Home** tab.
   #### Paragraph Group
2. Click the **Multilevel List** button ⌄.
3. Click the desired numbering style from the List Library.

Changing the Bullet or Number Formatting
1. Right-click the bullet or number.
2. On the shortcut menu, click **Font** or **Paragraph** to open the corresponding dialog box and change formats as desired.

Inserting Page Numbers
1. Click the **Insert** tab.
   #### Header & Footer Group
2. Click the **Page Number** button ▣.
3. On the menu, click the desired location for the page number.
4. From the gallery, click the desired format for the page number.

Changing the Page Number Format
1. Double-click in the header or footer containing the page number.
2. On the Header & Footer Tools Design tab, click the **Page Number** button ▣.
3. On the menu, click **Format Page Numbers**.
4. In the Page Number Format dialog box, set the formatting as desired.

Working with Headers and Footers

Typing in the Header or Footer
1. Double-click in the header or footer area to make it active.
2. Type the header or footer information.
3. Double-click in the main document area to make it active.
   OR
1. After typing the header or footer information, click the **Header & Footer Tools Design** tab.

   #### Close Group
2. Click the **Close Header & Footer** button ⊠.

Inserting a Header or Footer
1. Click the **Insert** tab.
   #### Header & Footer Group
2. Click the **Header** button ▢.
   OR
   - Click the **Footer** button ▢.
3. Click the desired style.
4. Type and format the header or footer information.
5. Click the **Header & Footer Tools Design** tab.
   #### Close Group
6. Click the **Close Header and Footer** button ⊠.

Modifying a Header or Footer
1. Click the **Insert** tab.
   #### Header & Footer Group
2. Click the **Header** button ▢ or click the **Footer** button ▢.
3. Click **Edit Header** or click **Edit Footer**.
4. Modify the header or footer information.
5. Click the **Header & Footer Tools Design** tab.
   #### Close Group
6. Click the **Close Header and Footer** button ⊠.

Working with Styles

Applying a Built-In Style
1. Click within the line of text.
2. Click the **Home** tab.
   #### Styles Group
3. Click the desired style from the Styles gallery.

Creating a Custom Style
1. Format text.
2. Select the formatted text.
3. On the Mini toolbar, click **Styles**.
4. Click **Create a Style**.
5. Type a style name.
6. Click **OK**.

Modifying a Style
1. Click the **Home** tab.
   #### Styles Group
2. Click the desired style from the Styles gallery.
3. Select the text and modify the formats as desired.
4. With the text still selected, right-click the style in the Styles gallery and click **Update [style name] to Match Selection**.

Changing the Style Set
1. Click the **Design** tab.
   #### Document Formatting Group
2. Click the desired style set from the Style Set gallery.

Using Desktop Publishing Features

Creating Newsletter Columns
1. Select the text or click in the section of text that you want to format in columns.
2. Click the **Layout tab**.
   #### Page Setup Group
3. Click the **Columns** button ▦.
4. From the gallery, select the desired number of columns.

Setting Column Width
1. Click the **Layout tab**.
   #### Page Setup Group
2. Click the **Columns** button ▦.
3. Click **More Columns**.
4. In the Columns dialog box, set the column width and spacing as desired.
5. Click **OK**.

Inserting a Column Break
1. Position the insertion point where you want to insert the break.
2. Click the **Layout tab**.
   #### Page Setup Group
3. Click the **Breaks** button ⊢.
4. From the Breaks gallery, click **Column**.

Balancing Columns

1. Position the insertion point at the end of the text in the last column on the page.
2. Click the **Layout tab**.

Page Setup Group

3. Click the **Breaks** button ⊬.
4. From the Breaks gallery, click **Continuous**.

Applying a Page Background

1. Click the **Design** tab.

Page Background Group

2. Click the **Page Color** button 🖳.
3. Click the desired color from the color palette.

OR

3. Click **Fill Effects** on the menu.
4. In the Fill Effects dialog box, select the gradient, texture, pattern, and picture formats as desired.
5. Click **OK**.

Inserting Dropped Capitals

1. Click in the paragraph where you want to insert the dropped capital.
2. Click the **Insert** tab.

Text Group

3. Click the **Drop Cap** button 𝐀≡.
4. From the menu, click the desired format.

Customizing a Dropped Capital

1. Click in the paragraph where you want to insert the dropped capital.
2. Click the **Insert** tab.

Text Group

3. Click the **Drop Cap** button 𝐀≡.
4. From the menu, click **Drop Cap Options**.
5. In the Drop Cap dialog box, click the desired position for the drop cap.
6. Under Options, set the desired font, lines to drop, and distance from text.
7. Click **OK**.

Enhancing a Paragraph with Borders

1. Position the insertion point in the paragraph to which you want to add a border.
2. Click the **Design** tab.

Page Background Group

3. Click the **Page Borders** button 🗋.
4. In the Borders and Shading dialog box, click the **Borders** tab.
5. In the Style list box, click the desired line style for the border.
6. Click the **Color** drop-down arrow and click the desired color for the border.
7. Click the **Width** drop-down arrow and click the desired line width for the border.
8. In the Setting list, click the desired effect for the border.
9. Click **OK**.

Enhancing a Paragraph with Shading

1. Position the insertion point in the paragraph to which you want to add shading.
2. Click the **Design** tab.

Page Background Group

3. Click the **Page Borders** button 🗋.
4. In the Borders and Shading dialog box, click the **Shading** tab.
5. Click the **Fill** drop-down arrow and click the desired color for the shading.
6. Under Patterns, click the **Style** drop-down arrow and click the desired pattern for the shading.
7. Under Patterns, click the **Color** drop-down arrow and click the desired color for the pattern.
8. Click **OK**.

Inserting the Date and Time

1. Click the **Insert** tab.

Text Group

2. Click the **Date & Time** button 🕮.
3. In the list of Available formats, select the desired format.
   √ *Click the Update automatically check box if you want the date and time to update automatically every time you save or print the document.*
4. Click **OK**.

Sorting Paragraphs

1. Click the **Home** tab.

Paragraph Group

2. Click the **Sort** button ⬆↓.
3. In the Sort Text dialog box, click the **Ascending** button or the **Descending** button.
4. Click **OK**.

Creating Tables

Inserting a Table

1. Click the **Insert** tab.

Tables Group

2. Click the **Table** button ⊞.
3. Click **Quick Tables**.
4. From the gallery, select the desired Quick Table.

OR

3. Position the mouse pointer on a cell to highlight the desired number of rows and columns.
4. Click to insert the table.

OR

3. Click **Insert Table**.
4. In the Insert Table dialog box, set the number of rows and columns and the AutoFit options as desired.
5. Click **OK**.

Entering Text in a Table

- Click in a cell and type the entry.

OR

- Press **Tab** or an arrow key to move to a cell and type an entry.

Converting Text to a Table

1. Select the text to convert.
2. Click the **Insert** tab.

Tables Group

2. Click the **Table** button ⊞.
3. On the menu, click **Convert Text to Table**.
4. In the Convert Text to Table dialog box, click **OK**.

Drawing a Table

1. Click the **Insert** tab.

Tables Group

2. Click the **Table** button ⊞.
3. Click **Draw Table**.
   √ *The mouse pointer changes to* ✏.
4. Drag to create table cells as desired.

Changing Table Structure

Viewing Gridlines

1. Click in the table to select it.
2. Click the **Table Tools Layout** tab.

Table Group

3. Click the **View Gridlines** button ⊞.

Selecting in a Table

1. Click in the table.
2. Click the **Table Tools Layout** tab.

Table Group

3. Click the **Select** button ⌖.
4. Click the desired selection on the menu.

Selecting a Table

- To select the table, click the **Table Selector** button ⊞, that appears outside the upper left corner of the table.

Selecting a Row

1. To select a row, position the mouse pointer outside the table, to the left of the row.
2. When the mouse pointer changes to ⬈, click to select the row.

Selecting a Column

1. To select a column, position the mouse pointer outside the table, just above the column.
2. When the mouse pointer changes to ⬇, click to select the column.

Selecting a Cell

1. To select a cell, position the mouse pointer outside the cell, at the bottom left corner.
2. When the mouse pointer changes to ⬈, click to select the cell.

Selecting Multiple Components in a Table

- To select contiguous cells, drag across them.

OR

- Select the first cell and press and hold **Shift** to select additional cells.
- To select noncontiguous cells, select the first cell and press and hold **Ctrl** to select additional cells.

Inserting Rows and Columns

1. Click where desired in the table.
2. Click the **Table Tools Layout** tab.

Rows & Columns Group

3. Click the options, as follows:
   - **Insert Above** ⊞
   - **Insert Below** ⊞
   - **Insert Left** ⊞
   - **Insert Right** ⊞

Deleting in a Table

1. Click in the cell, row, or column to be deleted.
2. Click the **Table Tools Layout** tab.

Rows & Columns Group

3. Click the **Delete** button ⊟.
4. Click the desired option to delete on the menu.

Deleting a Table

1. Click in any cell of the table.
2. Click the **Table Tools Layout** tab.

Rows & Columns Group

3. Click the **Delete** button ⊟.
4. Click **Delete Table** on the menu.

Merging Cells

1. Select the cells to merge.
2. Click the **Table Tools Layout** tab.

Merge Group

3. Click the **Merge Cells** button ⊞.

OR

1. Click the **Table Tools Layout** tab.

Draw Group

2. Click the **Eraser** button ⌦.
   √ *The mouse pointer changes to* ⌫.
3. Click on a cell divider to merge the cells.

Splitting Cells

1. Select the cell to split.
2. Click the **Table Tools Layout** tab.

Merge Group

3. Click the **Split Cells** button ⊟.
4. In the Split Cells dialog box, set the number of columns and rows for the split cell.
5. Click **OK**.

Formatting a Table

Applying a Table Style

1. Click in the table to select it.
2. Click the **Table Tools Design** tab.

Table Styles Group

3. Click the **Table Styles More** button ⊽.
4. Click the desired style.

Applying Formats to Cell Contents

1. Select the text to be formatted.
2. Click the **Home** tab.
3. Apply formats from the Font and Paragraph groups as desired.

Applying Cell Borders

1. Select the cell(s).
2. Click the **Table Tools Design** tab.

Borders Group

3. Click the **Line Style** button
   ⎯ .
4. From the Line Style gallery, click the desired line style.

5. Click the **Line Weight** button ☐.
6. From the Line Weight gallery, click the desired line weight.
7. Click the **Pen Color** button drop-down arrow ✐.
8. From the palette, click the desired color.
9. Click the **Borders** button drop-down arrow ⊞.
10. From the Borders gallery, click the desired border style.

Applying Cell Shading
1. Select the cell(s).
2. Click the **Table Tools Design** tab.
   ### Table Styles Group
3. Click the **Shading** button drop-down arrow ⬚.
4. From the color palette, click the desired shade.

Setting Column Width and Row Height
1. Click a cell in the column or row you want to adjust.
2. Click the **Table Tools Layout** tab.
   ### Cell Size Group
3. Click the **AutoFit** button ☐.
4. Click the desired option from the menu.
OR
1. Rest the pointer on the column divider or row divider.
2. Drag to the desired width or height.
OR
1. Click a cell in the column or row you want to adjust.
2. Click the **Table Tools Layout** tab.
   ### Cell Size Group
3. Click the **Table Row Height** ↕ increment arrows or the **Table Column Width** ↔ increment arrows to adjust the size as desired.

OR
1. Click the **Table Selector** button ⊞ to select the table.
2. Click the **Table Tools Layout** tab.
   ### Cell Size Group
3. Click the **Distribute Rows** button ⊞ to distribute the rows evenly, or the **Distribute Columns** button ⊞ to distribute the columns evenly.

Setting Alignment in a Table Cell
1. Click in the cell(s) in which you want to set the alignment.
2. Click the **Table Tools Layout** tab.
   ### Alignment Group
3. Click from the alignment options, as follows:
   - **Align Top Left** ▤
   - **Align Top Center** ▤
   - **Align Top Right** ▤
   - **Align Center Left** ▤
   - **Align Center** ▤
   - **Align Center Right** ▤
   - **Align Bottom Left** ▤
   - **Align Bottom Center** ▤
   - **Align Bottom Right** ▤

Using Mail Merge
1. Click the **Mailings** tab.
   ### Start Mail Merge Group
2. Click the **Start Mail Merge** button ☐.
3. Click **Step by Step Mail Merge Wizard**.
4. In the Mail Merge task pane, click **Next: Starting document**.
5. Click **Next: Select recipients**.
6. Under Use an existing list in the task pane, click **Browse**, and then navigate to and open the file.
7. In the Mail Merge Recipients dialog box, click **OK**.
8. Click **Next: Write your letter** at the bottom of the task pane.
9. Click to place the insertion point in the letter where you want to insert the address block field.
10. In the task pane, click **Address block**. Click **OK**.

11. Insert other merge fields as desired.
12. Click the **Mailings** tab.
    ### Preview Results Group
13. Click the **Preview Results** button ☐ to preview a copy of the merged letter.

Merging to a New Document
1. Click the **Mailings** tab.
   ### Finish Group
2. Click the **Finish & Merge** button ☐.
3. On the menu, click **Edit Individual Documents**.
4. In the Merge to New Document dialog box, click **OK**.

Creating a New Address List
1. Click the **Mailings** tab.
   ### Start Mail Merge Group
2. Click the **Select recipients** button ☐.
3. Click **Type a New List**.
4. In the New Address List dialog box, type the address of the first recipient.
5. Click **New Entry** to complete the entry and move to a new row to enter another recipient, if desired.
6. When you have entered all the recipients, click **OK**.
7. In the Save Address List dialog box, enter a name for the list and select the location where you want to save the file.
8. Click **OK**.

Using an Existing Data Source
1. Click the **Mailings** tab.
   ### Start Mail Merge Group
2. Click the **Select Recipients** button ☐.
3. On the menu, click the desired type of data source.

Adding Records to the Data Source

1. Click the **Mailings** tab.

   Start Mail Merge Group

2. Click the **Edit Recipient List** button .
3. In the Data Source box, click the data source you want to edit.
4. Click **Edit**.
5. In the Edit Data Source dialog box, click **New Entry**.
6. Enter new recipients as desired.
7. Click **OK**.

Using an Excel File as a Data Source

1. Click the **Mailings** tab.

   Start Mail Merge Group

2. Click the **Select Recipients** button .
3. On the menu, click **Use an Existing List**.
4. Navigate to and open the desired Excel file.
5. In the Select Table dialog box, click the sheet to be used as the data source.
6. Click **OK**.

Matching Fields to a Data Source

1. Click the **Mailings** tab.

   Write & Insert Fields Group

2. Click the **Match Fields** button .
3. In the Match Fields dialog box, match the fields in the data source as desired.
4. Click **OK**.

Creating an Envelope

1. Click the **Mailings** tab.

   Create Group

2. Click the **Envelopes** button .
3. In the Delivery address box, type the name and address to which the envelope will be sent.

   √ *Click the Omit check box if there is a return address printed on your envelopes already, or if you plan to use return address labels.*

4. Click in the Return address box and type the return address.

5. Click **Print**.
6. Click **No** to continue without making the return address the default.

Starting a Labels Mail Merge

1. Click the **Mailings** tab.

   Start Mail Merge Group

2. Click the **Start Mail Merge** button .
3. Click **Labels**.
4. In the Label Options dialog box, click the **Label vendors** drop-down arrow and click the desired label type.
5. In the Product number list, click the desired label size.
6. Click **OK**.

Arranging the Labels

1. Click the **Mailings** tab.

   Write & Insert Fields Group

2. Click the **Address Block** button .
3. In the Insert Address Block dialog box, verify that the Insert recipient's name is in the desired format. Verify that the **Insert postal address** check box is selected and that the **Only include the country/region if different than** option button is selected. Verify that the **Format address according to the destination country/region** check box is selected.
4. Click **OK**. The <<AddressBlock>> merge block is inserted in the first cell.
5. Click the **Mailings** tab.

   Write & Insert Fields Group

6. Click the **Update Labels** button to copy the layout from the first cell to the remaining cells.

Previewing and Printing the Labels

1. Click the **Mailings** tab.

   Preview Results Group

2. Click the **Preview Results** button to preview the labels.

3. If necessary, make adjustments to the label arrangement and formatting.
4. Click the **Mailings** tab.

   Finish Group

5. Click the **Finish & Merge** button .
6. Click **Print Documents**.
7. In the Merge to Printer dialog box, click **OK**.

Using Language Tools

Correcting Spelling as You Type

1. Right-click the misspelled word.

   ✓ A red wavy line under a word indicates a possible spelling error. A blue wavy underline indicates a possible word choice or grammatical error.

2. Click the desired option on the shortcut menu.

Correcting Grammar as You Type

1. Right-click the text marked with the blue, wavy underline.
2. Click the desired option on the shortcut menu.

Checking Spelling and Grammar

1. Click the **Review** tab.

   Proofing Group

2. Click the **Spelling & Grammar** button .
3. Click options to correct or ignore errors identified in the Spelling or Grammar task pane.

Using the Thesaurus

1. Right-click the word for which you want to find a synonym.
2. On the shortcut menu, click **Synonyms**.
3. On the submenu, click the desired synonym.

OR

1. Click the word for which you want to find a synonym or antonym.
2. Click the **Review** tab.

   Proofing Group

3. Click the **Thesaurus** button .
4. In the Thesaurus task pane, select the desired synonym or antonym.

Using Content Controls

1. Click a content control to select it.
2. Type replacement text as desired.

Removing a Content Control

1. Right-click the content control.
2. On the shortcut menu, click **Remove Content Control**.

Managing Document Properties

1. Click **File**.
2. On the Info tab, in the Preview pane under Properties, review the document's properties or click available content controls as desired.
3. If desired, click **Show All Properties** to display all properties.

Viewing a Properties Dialog Box

1. Click **File**.
2. On the Info tab, in the Preview pane, click **Properties**.
3. Click **Advanced Properties** to display the document's Properties dialog box.
4. Add or modify properties as desired.
5. Click **OK** to close the dialog box.

Printing Document Properties

1. Click **File**.
2. Click **Print**.
3. Under Settings, click the top button.
4. On the menu, click **Document Info**.
5. Click the **Print** button 🖶 .

Managing Sources and Citations

Inserting Citations

1. Position the insertion point where you want to insert the citation.
2. Click the **References** tab.

   Citations & Bibliography Group

3. Click the **Style** button drop-down arrow 🔖 .
4. On the menu of available citation styles, click the desired style.
5. Click the **Insert Citation** button ⤵ .
6. From the menu, click **Add New Source**.
7. In the Create Source dialog box, select the type of source and enter the source information.
8. Click **OK**.

Creating a Reference Page

1. Position the insertion point at the end of the document and insert a hard page break.
2. Click the **References** tab.

   Citations & Bibliography Group

3. Click the **Bibliography** button 📑 .
4. From the gallery, click the desired format.

Tracking Revisions

Turning Tracking On or Off

1. Click the **Review** tab.

   Tracking Group

2. Click the **Track Changes** button 📝 .

Accepting or Rejecting Changes

1. Click the **Review** tab.

   Changes Group

2. Click the **Next** button ⤵ to move to the next tracked change in the document.

OR

   Click the **Previous** button ⤴ to move to the previous tracked change.

3. Click the **Accept** button ☑ to accept the change.

OR

   Click the **Reject** button ☒ to reject the change.

Accepting All Changes

1. Click the **Review** tab.

   Changes Group

2. Click the **Accept** button drop-down arrow ☑ .
3. Click **Accept All Changes**.

OR

   Click **Accept All Changes and Stop Tracking**.

Rejecting All Changes

1. Click the **Review** tab.

   Changes Group

2. Click the **Reject** button drop-down arrow ☒ .
3. Click **Reject All Changes**.

OR

   Click **Reject All Changes and Stop Tracking**.

Working with Comments

Inserting a Comment

1. Select the text on which you want to comment.
2. Click the **Review** tab.

   Comments Group

3. Click the **New Comment** button 💬 .
4. Type the comment in the comment balloon.

Displaying or Hiding the Reviewing Pane

1. Click the **Review** tab.

   Tracking Group

2. Click the **Reviewing Pane** button 🗔 .

Editing a Comment

1. Position the insertion point within the comment text.
2. Edit text.

Moving through Comments

1. Click the **Review** tab.

   Comments Group

2. Click the **Next** button 💬 .

OR

   Click the **Previous** button 💬 .

Deleting a Comment
1. Click the comment to delete.
2. Click the **Review** tab.
   #### Comments Group
3. Click the **Delete** button ⌧.

Deleting All Comments
1. Click the **Review** tab.
   #### Comments Group
2. Click the **Delete** button ⌧ drop-down arrow.
3. Click **Delete All Comments in Document**.

Protecting a Document

Encrypting with Password
1. Click the **File** tab.
2. On the Info tab, click the **Protect Document** button 🔏.
3. Click **Encrypt with Password**.
4. In the Encrypt Document dialog box, enter the desired password.
5. Click **OK**.
6. In the Reenter password box, type the password again.
7. Click **OK**.

Open an Encrypted and Password-Protected Document
1. Open the protected document.
2. In the Password dialog box, type the password.
3. Click **OK**.

Stop Protection
1. Click the **Review** tab.
   #### Protect Group
2. Click the **Restrict Editing** button 🔒.
3. In the Restrict Editing task pane, click **Stop Protection**.

Saving a Word Document as a PDF
1. Click **File**.
2. Click **Save As**.
3. In the Save As dialog box, enter the file name and select the location where you want to save the file.
4. Click the **Save as type** button.
5. Click **PDF**.
6. Click **Save**.

Saving a Word Document as a Web Page
1. Click **File**.
2. Click **Save As**.
3. Navigate to the location where you store files.
4. Click the **Save as type** button.
5. Click **Single File Web Page**.
6. Change the page title as desired.
7. Enter a file name for the page.
8. Click **Save**.

Changing a Web Page Title
1. Click **File**.
2. Click **Save As**.
3. Navigate to the location of your file.
4. Click the **Change Title** button.
5. In the Enter Text dialog box, type the title text.
6. Click **OK**.
7. Click **Save**.

Sending a Word Document as an E-mail Attachment
1. Click **File**.
2. Click **Share**.
3. Click **Email** 📧 and then click **Send as Attachment**.
4. Enter the e-mail information as necessary.
5. Click **Send**.

Working with Hyperlinks

Inserting a Hyperlink
1. Select the text or object to hyperlink.
2. Click the **Insert** tab.
   #### Links Group
3. Click the **Hyperlink** button 🌐.
4. In the Insert Hyperlink dialog box, locate and select the hyperlink destination.
5. Click **OK**.

Creating a Hyperlink to a Web Site
1. Click the **Insert** tab.
   #### Links Group
2. Click the **Hyperlink** button 🌐.
3. In the Insert Hyperlink dialog box, type the Web site address in the Address text box.
4. Click **OK**.

Testing a Hyperlink
- Hold down the **Ctrl** key and click the hyperlink.

Editing a Hyperlink
1. Right-click the link.
2. On the shortcut menu, click **Edit Hyperlink**.
3. Edit the link as desired.
4. Click **OK**.

Removing a Hyperlink
1. Right-click the link.
2. On the shortcut menu, click **Remove Hyperlink**.

Creating a Blog

Starting a Blog Post
1. Click **File**.
2. Click **New**.
3. Click **Blog Post**.
4. Click **Create**.
5. Register your blog service if desired.
6. Type the blog text.

Registering a Blog Server
√ *You must have a blog account in order to register a blog server.*
1. In your blog file, click the **Blog Post** tab.
   #### Blog Group
2. Click the **Manage Accounts** button 👤.
3. In the Blog Accounts dialog box, click **New**.
4. In the New Blog Account dialog box, click the **Blog** drop-down arrow and click your provider.
5. Click **Next**.
6. Enter your user name and password, and click **OK**.
7. Click **Yes** to confirm.
8. At the message that the registration was successful, click **OK**.
9. Click **Close**.

Selecting Objects

1. Click the **Home** tab.

   Editing Group

2. Click **Select** ⌖ and then click **Selection Pane**.
3. Click the desired object in the Selection Pane.

Modifying a Text Box

Changing the Font

1. Click the text box to select it.
2. Click the **Home** tab.

   Font Group

3. Click options to apply the desired font formatting.

Inserting a Caption

1. Click to select the object to which you want to add a caption.
2. Click the **References** tab.

   Captions Group

3. Click the **Insert Caption** button.
4. In the Insert Caption dialog box, select options as desired.
5. Click OK.

Saving Compatible File Types

1. Click **File**.
2. Click **Save As**.
3. In the Save As dialog box, click the **Save as type** button to display a list of compatible file types.
4. Select the desired file type.
5. Enter the file name and select the location where the file will be saved.
6. Click **Save**.
7. Click **OK** in the File Conversion dialog box.

Creating a Document Based on a Template

1. Click **File**.
2. Click **New**.
3. Click the desired template.
4. Click the **Create** button.

Inserting a File in a Document

1. Click the **Insert** tab.

   Text Group

2. Click the **Object** button drop-down arrow ▭.
3. On the menu, click **Text from File**.
4. In the Insert File dialog box, navigate to the file you want to insert and select it.
5. Click **Insert**.

Checking the Word Count

1. If the word count is not automatically displayed on the status bar, right-click the status bar.
2. On the shortcut menu, click **Word Count** to display the number of words in the status bar.
   - ✓ Selecting text will display the word count for the selection as well as the entire document.

Creating a Table of Contents

1. Click the **References** tab.

   Table of Contents Group

2. Click the **Table of Contents** button ▭.
3. From the gallery, click the desired style.

Updating a Table of Contents

1. Make changes to the document's headings as desired.
2. Click anywhere within the table of contents.
3. Click the **References** tab.

   Table of Contents Group

4. Click the **Update Table** button ▭.
5. In the Update Table of Contents dialog box, click to select the desired update option.
6. Click **OK**.

Inserting an Online Video

1. Click the **Insert** tab.

   Media Group

2. Click the **Online Video** button ▭.

3. In the Insert Video dialog box, search for or select a video.
4. Click **Insert**.

Formatting a Video

1. Select the video file to format.
2. Click the **Picture Tools Format** tab.

   Arrange Group

3. Apply formatting options as desired.

Copying Data from a Web Page to a Word Document

Copying Text

1. Display the Web page in a browser.
2. Select the text you want to copy.
3. Press **Ctrl+C**.
4. Click in the Word document where you want to paste the copied text.
5. Press **Ctrl+V**.

Copying Graphics

1. Display the Web page.
2. Right-click the graphic you want to copy.
3. On the shortcut menu, click **Copy**.
4. Click in the Word document where you want to paste the graphic.
5. Press **Ctrl+V**.

Saving a Document to the OneDrive

1. Click **File**.
2. Click **Save As**.
3. Click **OneDrive** ☁ in the Save As list.
4. Click the desired OneDrive folder in the right pane.
5. In the Save As dialog box, enter the file name as desired.
6. Click **Save**.

View and Edit a Document on the OneDrive

1. Sign in to your OneDrive account.
2. Open the document you want to view or edit.
3. Click **Edit Document**.
4. Click either **Edit in Word** or **Edit in Browser** (to edit in Word Online).

Navigating a Worksheet

- Press **Ctrl + Home** to return to cell A1.
- Click the up or down scroll arrows on the vertical scroll bar to scroll one row up or one row down.
- Click the right or left scroll arrows on the horizontal scroll bar to scroll one column right or one column left.
- Click above or below the scroll box on the vertical scroll arrow to scroll one screen up or one screen down.
- Click to the left or right of the scroll box on the horizontal scroll arrow to scroll one screen left or one screen right.
- Drag the scroll box on either scroll bar to bring the desired portion of the worksheet into view.
- Use the mouse wheel to scroll up or down in the worksheet.

Changing the Worksheet View

Showing and Hiding Worksheet Elements
1. Click the **View** tab.
   Show Group
2. Click to mark the check box for **Ruler**, **Gridlines**, **Formula Bar**, and **Headings**.
   √ *A check in the check box indicates the element is displayed.*

Hiding the Ribbon
1. Double-click the selected tab to hide the Ribbon.
2. Double-click the tab to redisplay the Ribbon.

Changing the View
1. Click the **View** tab.
   Workbook Views Group
2. Click the desired View button:
   - **Normal**
   - **Page Break Preview**
   - **Page Layout**
   - **Custom Views**

OR

- Click a View icon on the status bar:
- **Normal**
- **Page Layout**
- **Page Break Preview**

Changing the Active Worksheet

- Click the sheet tab of the sheet you want to display.

Splitting a Worksheet into Panes
1. Click the cell to the right and below where you want the split to occur.
2. Click the **View** tab.
   Window Group
3. Click the **Split** button .

Removing a Split
1. Click the **View** tab.
   Window Group
2. Click the **Split** button .

Switching between Open Workbooks
1. Click the **View** tab.
   Window Group
2. Click the **Switch Windows** button .
3. Click the desired workbook.

OR

Hover the mouse pointer over the Excel button on the taskbar, and click one of the other open workbooks.

Arranging Multiple Workbooks
1. Click the **View** tab.
   Window Group
2. Click the **Arrange All** button .
3. In the Arrange Windows dialog box, click the desired arrangement.
4. Click **OK**.

Closing a Workbook
1. Click **File**.
2. Click **Close**.

Entering and Editing Data

Entering Data
- Click in the cell and type the label.
- Press **Enter** to complete the entry and move to the cell below.
- Press **Tab** to complete the entry and move to the cell to the right.
- Press an arrow key to complete the entry and move to the cell in the desired direction.

Editing Data
- Click in the cell and type new text to replace the existing entry.
- Double-click in the cell and move the insertion point as necessary to edit the text.
- Select the cell, click in the formula bar, and move the insertion point as necessary to edit the text.

Clearing Cell Contents

1. Click the desired cell(s).
2. Click the **Home** tab.
   ### Editing Group
3. Click the **Clear** button 🖉 Clear ▾ .
4. On the menu, select the desired clear option.

Inserting and Deleting Columns and Rows

Inserting a Column

1. Click the heading of the column that will be to the right of the new column.
2. Click the **Home** tab.
   ### Cells Group
3. Click the **Insert** button drop-down arrow 🔢 .
4. Click **Insert Sheet Columns**.

Inserting a Row

1. Click the heading of the row that will be below the new row.
2. Click the **Home** tab.
   ### Cells Group
3. Click the **Insert** button drop-down arrow 🔢 .
4. Click **Insert Sheet Rows**.

Deleting a Column or Row

1. Click the heading of the column or row that you want to delete.
2. Click the **Home** tab.
   ### Cells Group
3. Click the **Delete** button 🗙 .

Using Find and Replace

1. Click the **Home** tab.
   ### Editing Group
2. Click the **Find & Select** button 🔍 .
3. On the menu, click **Replace**.
4. In the Find and Replace dialog box, enter the text or values you want to find in the Find what box.
5. Enter the replacement text or values in the Replace with box.
6. Click the **Options** button to further specify the search.

7. Click **Find Next** to find each occurrence and then **Replace** to replace each occurrence. Click **Replace All** to replace all occurrences.
8. Click **Close**.

Checking the Spelling in a Worksheet

1. Click the **Review** tab.
   ### Proofing Group
2. Click the **Spelling** button ✓ .
3. Misspelled words are displayed in the Spelling dialog box, where you can choose to ignore or change them.

Applying Number Formats

1. Click the **Home** tab.
   ### Number Group
2. Click the **Number Format** drop-down arrow [General ▾] .
3. From the gallery, select the desired format.

Aligning Data in a Cell

Setting Horizontal and Vertical Alignment

1. Click the **Home** tab.
   ### Alignment Group
2. Click the alignment option as follows:
   - **Top Align** ≡
   - **Middle Align** ≡
   - **Bottom Align** ≡
   - **Align Left** ≡
   - **Center** ≡
   - **Align Right** ≡

Wrapping Text in Cells

1. Click the **Home** tab.
   ### Alignment Group
2. Click the **Wrap Text** button 📑 .

Formatting Cells

Applying Cell Styles

1. Click the **Home** tab.
   ### Styles Group
2. Click the **Cell Styles** button 📝 .
3. From the gallery, click the desired style.

Applying Borders

1. Right-click the selection to format.
2. Click **Format Cells**.
3. Click the **Border** tab.
4. Under Style, click the border line style.
5. Click the **Color** drop-down arrow and click the border color.
6. Click a **Presets** button.
OR
   - Click one or more **Border** buttons.
7. Click **OK**.

Applying Fills

1. Right-click the selection to format.
2. Click **Format Cells**.
3. Click the **Fill** tab.
4. Under Background Color, click the fill color.
5. Click **OK**.

Entering Dates

   - Press **Ctrl+;** to insert the current date in the mm/dd/yyyy format.
OR
1. Click the **Home** tab.
   ### Number Group
2. Click the **Number Format** drop-down arrow [General ▾] .
3. From the gallery, select **Short Date** or **Long Date**.

Merging Cells

Merging and Centering Across Cells

1. Select the cells that you want to merge and center.
2. Click the **Home** tab.
   ### Alignment Group
3. Click the **Merge & Center** button ▦ .

Merging Across Cells

1. Select the cells that you want to merge.
2. Click the **Home** tab.
   ### Alignment Group
3. Click the **Merge & Center** drop-down arrow ▦ .
4. Click **Merge Across**.

Merging Cells

1. Select the cells that you want to merge.
2. Click the **Home** tab.
   Alignment Group
3. Click the **Merge & Center** drop-down arrow ▤.
4. Click **Merge Cells**.

Removing a Merge

1. Select the cells that you want to unmerge.
2. Click the **Home** tab.
   Alignment Group
3. Click the **Merge & Center** drop-down arrow ▤.
4. Click **Unmerge Cells**.

Copying Formats

1. Click the cell whose formats you want to copy.
2. Click the **Home** tab.
   Clipboard Group
3. Click the **Format Painter** button ✋.
4. Click the cell to which you want to copy the formats.

OR

1. Double-click the **Format Painter** button ✋.
2. Click each cell to which you want to copy the formats.
3. Press **Esc**.

Inserting Comments

1. Click the cell where you want to insert the comment.
2. Click the **Review** tab.
   Comments Group
3. Click the **New Comment** button 🗨.
4. Type the comment text.

Deleting a Comment

1. Click the cell containing the comment.
2. Click the **Review** tab.
   Comments Group
3. Click the **Delete** button 🗨.

Changing Column Width and Row Height

Changing Column Width

1. Position the mouse pointer on the right border of a column header.
2. When the pointer changes to ⊹, drag to the desired width as indicated in the ScreenTip.

OR

1. Click the **Home** tab.
   Cells Group
2. Click the **Format** button ▦.
3. Click **Column Width** on the menu.
4. In the Column Width dialog box, enter the desired width.
5. Click **OK**.

Changing Row Height

1. Position the mouse pointer on the bottom border of a row header.
2. When the pointer changes to ⊹, drag to the desired height as indicated in the ScreenTip.

OR

1. Click the **Home** tab.
   Cells Group
2. Click the **Format** button ▦.
3. Click **Row Height** on the menu.
4. In the Row Height dialog box, enter the desired width.
5. Click **OK**.

Resolving a #### Error Message

- Double-click the right border of the column header to resize the column to the longest entry.

OR

1. Click the **Home** tab.
   Cells Group
2. Click the **Format** button ▦.
3. Click **AutoFit Column Width** on the menu.

Working with Ranges

Selecting a Contiguous Range

1. Click the cell in the top-left corner of the range.
2. Drag to select the remaining cells to be included in the range.

OR

Press and hold **Shift** and use the arrow keys to extend the selection as desired.

OR

Press **Shift** and click the cell that's at the lower-right corner of the range.

Selecting a Noncontiguous Range

1. Select the first portion of the range using one of the methods previously described.
2. Press and hold **Ctrl** to select additional portions.

Filling Range Cells with the Same Entry

1. Select the range.
2. Type the entry.
3. Press **Ctrl + Enter**.

Filling a Range with a Series

1. Select the cells with the series starting value(s).
2. Click the **Home** tab.
   Editing Group
3. Click the **Fill** button ⬇.
4. Click **Series** on the menu.
5. In the Series dialog box, specify if the series will fill a row or column, the type of series, and the step and stop values.
6. Click **OK**.

Making a Range Entry Using a Collapse Dialog Box Button

1. In the dialog box, click the **Collapse Dialog** button ▦, which normally appears at the end of the text box in which you are to enter the range address.
2. In the worksheet, select the range.
3. Click the **Collapse Dialog** button ▦ to redisplay the dialog box.

Defining a Range Name

1. Select the range you want to name.
2. Click in the **Name Box**.
3. Type the desired range name and press **Enter**.

OR

1. Select the range you want to name.

2. Right-click the selected range.
3. Click **Define Name** on the shortcut menu.
4. In the New Name dialog box, type the desired range name in the Name text box.
5. Click **OK**.

OR

1. Select the range you want to name.
2. Click the **Formulas** tab.

   Defined Names Group

3. Click the **Define Name** button ⊡.
4. In the New Name dialog box, type the desired range name in the Name text box.
5. Click **OK**.

Using AutoFill

Using AutoFill to Complete a Series

1. Select the range that will begin the series.
2. Click the **AutoFill** handle ▄ and drag to the desired cell to complete the series.

Using AutoFill to Create a Trend

1. Select the range that will begin the series.
2. Right-click the **AutoFill** handle ▄ and drag to the desired cell to complete the series.
3. When you release the mouse button, click the desired trend on the shortcut menu.

Using the Fill Button to Create a Linear Trend

1. Select the range that will begin the series.
2. Click the **Home** tab.

   Editing Group

3. Click the **Fill** button ⬇.
4. Click **Series**.
5. In the Series dialog box, click **Rows** or **Columns** for the direction to fill.
6. Click the **Linear** type of series
✓ Enter a step and stop value if desired.
7. Click **OK**.

Using Formulas

Entering a Formula

1. Click the cell.
2. Type =.
3. Type the formula.
4. Press **Enter**, **Tab**, or an arrow key to complete the entry.

OR

   Click the **Enter** button ✓ on the formula bar.

Using Parentheses in a Formula

- Excel calculates the part of the formula enclosed in parentheses first.
- When there are multiple nested pairs of parentheses in a formula, Excel calculates from the innermost pair to the outermost.

Editing a Formula

- Click in the cell and type a new formula to replace the existing formula.
- Double-click in the cell and move the insertion point as necessary to edit the formula.
- Select the cell, click in the formula bar, and move the insertion point as necessary to edit the formula.
- Select the cell, press **F2**, and move the insertion point as necessary to edit the formula.

Entering a Cell Reference in a Formula

1. Click the cell to contain the formula.
2. Type =.
3. Begin entering the formula.
4. At the location where you want to enter a cell reference, type the cell or range reference.

OR

- Click the cell or select the range to reference.

✓ You may click a cell or select a range on any worksheet.

5. Continue entering the formula until it is complete.
6. Press **Enter**, **Tab**, or an arrow key to complete the entry.

OR

   Click the **Enter** button ✓ on the formula bar.

Entering an Absolute Cell Reference

- Type a dollar sign (**$**) before the column letter and again before the row number of the cell you want to make an absolute reference.

OR

- Press **F4** to insert the dollar signs.

Copying a Formula Using the Fill Handle

1. Click the cell.
2. Drag the fill handle ▄ to copy the formula to the desired cells.

Creating a 3-D Reference in a Formula

1. Click the cell where you want to enter the formula.
2. To enter a cell reference or range from another worksheet, click the sheet tab, select the cell or range of cells, and press **Enter**.

OR

   Type the sheet name and cell reference or range address directly in the formula using the following guidelines:

- Use an exclamation point (!) to separate the sheet name(s) from the cell reference(s).
- Use a colon (:) between sheet names to indicate a range of worksheets.
- Use single quotation marks to surround a sheet name that contains a space.

Displaying and Hiding Formulas

1. Click the **Formulas** tab.

   Formula Auditing Group

2. Click the **Show Formulas** button ▓.
3. Click the **Show Formulas** button ▓ again to hide formulas.

OR

- Press **Ctrl+`** to toggle formulas on and off.

Printing Formulas
1. Click the **Formulas** tab.
   #### Formula Auditing Group
2. Click the **Show Formulas** button.
3. Click **File**.
4. Click **Print**.
5. In the Backstage view, click the **Print** button.

Working with Functions

Entering a Function
1. Click the cell in which you want to enter the function.
2. Type **=**, the function name, and then an opening parenthesis.
3. Type the range address or drag over the range on which you want to perform the function.
4. Type a closing parenthesis.
5. Press **Enter**.

Using AutoSum Functions (SUM, AVERAGE, MAX, MIN, and COUNT)
1. Click the cell in which you want to enter the function.
2. Click the **Home** tab.
   #### Editing Group
3. Click the **AutoSum** drop-down arrow.
4. Click the desired function from the menu.
5. Verify the range.
6. Press **Enter**.

Inserting Other Functions
1. Click the cell in which you want to enter the function.
2. Click the **Formulas** tab.
   #### Function Library Group
3. Click one of the function category buttons and click the desired function from the menu.
OR
   Click the **More Functions** button, point to a category, and click the desired function.

Previewing and Printing a Worksheet

Previewing and Printing a File
1. Click **File**.
2. Click **Print**.

3. Check the preview in the Backstage view.
4. Click the **Print** button.

Changing Print Options
1. Click **File**.
2. Click **Print**.
3. In the Copies box, type the number of copies to print.
OR
   Click the increment arrows to set the number of copies to print.
4. Under Settings, specify the page setup options as desired.

Printing a Selection
1. Select the range you want to print.
2. Click **File**.
3. Click **Print**.
4. In the Backstage view, under Settings, click the first drop-down arrow.
5. Click **Print Selection**.
6. Click the **Print** button.

Formatting Worksheets

Selecting a Preset Margin
1. Click the **Layout tab**.
   #### Page Setup Group
2. Click the **Margins** button.
3. Click the desired margin setting.

Setting Custom Margins
1. Click the **Layout tab**.
   #### Page Setup Group
2. Click the **Margins** button.
3. Click **Custom Margins**.
4. Under Margins, set the margins as desired.
5. Click **OK**.

Selecting a Paper Size
1. Click the **Layout tab**.
   #### Page Setup Group
2. Click the **Size** button.
3. Click the desired page size.

Setting Page Orientation
1. Click the **Layout tab**.
   #### Page Setup Group
2. Click the **Orientation** button.
3. Click **Portrait** or **Landscape**.

Scaling to Fit
1. Click the **Layout tab**.
   #### Scale to Fit Group
2. Click the **Scale to Fit** dialog box launcher.
3. In the Page Setup dialog box, on the Page tab, click the **Fit to** button.
4. Adjust the Fit to settings as desired.
5. Click **OK**.

Inserting a Built-In Header or Footer

Using the Insert Tab
1. Click the **Insert** tab.
   #### Text Group
2. Click the **Header & Footer** button.
3. Click in the placeholders and type the desired header or footer text.
OR
   From the menu of built-in headers or footers, select the desired format.
OR
1. Click the **Header & Footer Tools Design** tab.
   #### Header & Footer Elements Group
2. Click an element to insert it as desired.

Using Page Layout View
1. Switch to Page Layout view, if necessary.
2. Click a placeholder in either the header or footer area.
3. Click the **Header & Footer Tools Design** tab.
   #### Header & Footer Group
4. Click the **Header** button or the **Footer** button.
5. Click the desired built-in option from the menu.

Using the Page Setup Dialog Box
1. Click the **Layout tab**.
2. Click the **Page Setup** dialog box launcher.
3. In the Page Setup dialog box, click the **Header/Footer** tab.

4. Click the **Header** drop-down arrow or the **Footer** drop-down arrow.
5. Click the desired header or footer.
6. Click **OK**.

Inserting a Custom Header and Footer

Using Page Layout View
1. Switch to Page Layout view, if necessary.
2. Click the desired placeholder in either the header or footer area.
3. Type the desired text in the placeholder.

OR

3. Click the **Header & Footer Tools Design** tab.

Header & Footer Elements Group
4. Click a button to insert the desired element.

Using the Page Setup Dialog Box
1. Click the **Layout tab**.
2. Click the **Page Setup** dialog box launcher ⌐.
3. In the Page Setup dialog box, click the **Header/Footer** tab.
4. Click the **Custom Header** button or the **Custom Footer** button.
5. In the Header dialog box or the Footer dialog box, type the desired text or use the buttons to enter information in the Left section, Center section, and Right section boxes as desired.
6. Click **OK**.

Changing the Font of a Header or Footer
1. Switch to Page Layout view.
2. Select the text in the header or footer section whose font you want to change.
3. Click the **Home** tab.

Font Group
4. Use buttons in the Font group to change the font and other formatting as desired.

Working with Excel Tables

Creating a Table
1. Click in the range of data that will make up the table.
2. Click the **Insert** tab.

Tables Group
3. Click the **Table** button ▦.
4. In the Create Table dialog box, verify the range containing the table data.
5. Click **OK**.

Applying a Table Style
1. Click any cell in the table.
2. Click the **Home** tab.

Styles Group
3. Click the **Format as Table** button ▧.

OR

2. Click the **Table Tools Design** tab.

Table Styles Group
3. Click the Table Styles **More** button ▾.
4. Click the desired table style.

Inserting a Total Row
1. Click any cell in the table.
2. Click the **Table Tools Design** tab.

Table Style Options Group
3. Click the **Total Row** check box.

Converting a Table to a Range
1. Click any cell in the table.
2. Click the **Table Tools Design** tab.

Tools Group
3. Click the **Convert to Range** button ▦.
4. Click **Yes** in the dialog box to confirm the conversion.

Sorting and Filtering Data

Sorting Rows
1. Click a cell in the column by which you want to sort.
2. Click the **Data** tab.

Sort & Filter Group
3. Click the **Sort A to Z** button ↕ to sort in ascending order, or the **Sort Z to A** button ↕ to sort in descending order.

Filtering Rows
1. Click anywhere in the range you want to filter.
2. Click the **Data** tab.

Sort & Filter Group
3. Click the **Filter** button ▼.
4. Click the arrow next to the heading of the column you want to filter.
5. From the menu, click the filter you want to apply.

Sorting a Table
1. Click the down arrow on the desired table column header.
2. From the menu, click the desired sort option.

OR

1. Click the **Data** tab.

Sort & Filter Group
2. Click the **Sort** button ▦.
3. In the Sort dialog box, set the sort options as desired.
4. Click **OK**.

Filtering a Table
1. Click the down arrow on the desired table column header.
2. From the menu, click to mark the desired column entries you want included in the filter.

Sorting in a Table by Formatting
1. Click the arrow next to the heading of the column by which you want to sort.
2. From the menu, click **Sort by Color**.
3. Select the desired cell or font color.

Creating a Custom Sort
1. Click a cell in the column by which you want to sort.
2. Click the **Data** tab.

Sort & Filter Group
3. Click the **Sort** button ▦.
4. In the Sort dialog box, in the **Sort by** box, select the first column by which you want to sort.

5. Click the **Sort On** arrow to specify the type of sort.
6. Click the **Add Level** button to add sort levels.
7. Specify the type of sort for each column.
8. Click **OK**.

Removing a Sort
- After applying a sort, click the **Undo** button ↶ on the Quick Access Toolbar to remove the sort.

Removing a Filter
1. Click any cell in the list.
2. Click the **Data** tab.
   #### Sort & Filter Group
3. Click the **Filter** button ▼.

Working with Charts

Creating a Chart
1. Select the range of data you want to chart.
2. Click the **Insert** tab.
   #### Charts Group
3. Click the desired chart category button.
4. In the gallery, click the chart style.

Deleting a Chart
1. Click the chart to select it.
2. Press **Delete**.

Resizing a Chart
1. Click the chart to select it.
2. Position the pointer on a corner handle.
3. When the pointer changes to ⤢, drag to the desired size.

Applying a Chart Layout
1. Click the chart to select it.
2. Click the **Chart Tools Design** tab.
   #### Chart Layouts Group
3. Click the **Quick Layout** button 🖿.
4. Click the desired layout from the gallery.

Applying a Chart Style
1. Click the chart to select it.
2. Click the **Chart Tools Design** tab.
   #### Chart Styles Group
3. Click the Chart Styles **More** button ▼.
4. Click the desired style from the gallery.

Resizing a Chart Element
1. Click the chart to select it.
2. Click the chart element you want to resize.
3. Drag a corner sizing handle to resize the element as desired.

Moving a Chart Element
1. Click the chart to select it.
2. Click the chart element you want to move.
3. Position the mouse pointer on the border of the element.
4. When the pointer changes to ⬚, drag the element to the desired location.

Deleting a Chart Element
1. Click the chart to select it.
2. Click the chart element you want to delete.
3. Press **Delete**.

Changing Chart Text
1. Click the placeholder for the chart text you want to change, or click within a placeholder and select the text.
2. Edit the text as desired.
OR
1. Click the chart to select it.
2. Click the **Chart Elements** shortcut button ➕.
3. Click **Data Labels**, **Axis Titles**, or **Chart Title** from the Chart Elements list.
4. Click the arrow and select the desired option.

Changing Data Series Orientation
1. Click the chart to select it.
2. Click the **Chart Tools Design** tab.
   #### Data Group
3. Click the **Switch Row/Column** button 🖽.

Copying Formulas Containing a Relative Reference
1. Click the cell containing the formula you want to copy.
2. Click the **Home** tab.
   #### Clipboard Group
3. Click the **Copy** button 🖹.
OR
   Press **Ctrl+C**.
4. Click the cell where you want to paste the copied formula.
5. Click the **Home** tab.
   #### Clipboard Group
6. Click the **Paste** button 📋.
OR
   Press **Ctrl+V**.

Copying a Formula Using an Absolute Reference
1. Click the cell containing the formula you want to copy.
2. Enter a dollar sign (**$**) before both the column letter and row number of the cell you want to make an absolute reference.
OR
   Press **F4** to insert the dollar signs.
3. Copy the formula using the procedures discussed above.

Inserting and Deleting Cells

Inserting Cells
1. Click the cell that will be below the inserted cell.
2. Click the **Home** tab.
   #### Cells Group
3. Click the **Insert** button 🖽.

Deleting Cells

1. Right-click the cell you want to delete.
2. Click **Delete**.
3. In the Delete dialog box, specify the direction in which you want cells to shift.
4. Click **OK**.

Cutting and Pasting Data

1. Select the cells you want to cut.
2. Press **Ctrl+X**.

OR

- Click the **Home** tab.

   Clipboard Group

- Click the **Cut** button ✂.
3. Click the cell where you want to paste the cut data.
4. Press **Ctrl+V**.

OR

- Click the **Home** tab.

   Clipboard Group

- Click the **Paste** button 📋.

Applying Conditional Formatting

1. Select the range to which you want to apply the conditional formatting.
2. Click the **Home** tab.

   Styles Group.

3. Click the **Conditional Formatting** button.
4. Point to the desired type of conditional format.
5. From the format's gallery, click the desired style.

Modifying a Rule

1. Click the **Home** tab.

   Styles Group.

2. Click the **Conditional Formatting** button.
3. Click **Manage Rules**.
4. In the Conditional Formatting Rules Manager dialog box, click the **Edit Rule** button.
5. Modify the rule as desired.
6. Click **OK**.
5. Click **OK**.

Saving Excel Data in CSV File Format

1. Click **File**.
2. Click **Save As**.
3. Browse to the location where you want to save the file.
4. In the File name box, enter the name for the file.
5. From the Save as type drop-down list, select **CSV (Comma delimited)**.
6. Click **Save**.
7. In the message box, click **Yes**.

Saving a Workbook as a PDF or XPS File

1. Click **File**.
2. Click **Export**.
3. Click **Create PDF/XPS Document**.
4. Click **Create PDF/XPS**.
5. Browse to the location where you want to save the file.
6. In the File name box, enter the name for the file.
7. From the Save as type drop-down list, select either **PDF** or **XPS Document**.
8. Click **Publish**.

Inserting Pictures

1. Click the cell where you want to insert the picture.
2. Click the **Insert** tab.

   Illustrations Group

3. Click the **Pictures** button 🖼.
4. In the Insert Picture dialog box, navigate to the location where the picture is stored.
5. Select the picture and click **Insert**.

Inserting an Online Picture

1. Click the cell where you want to insert the picture.
2. Click the **Insert** tab.

   Illustrations Group

3. Click the **Online Pictures** button 🖼.
4. In the Insert Pictures search box, type the keyword(s) for the clip art you want to insert.
5. Press **Enter**.
6. Select the desired image and click **Insert**.

Creating a New Workbook from a Template

1. Click **File**.
2. Click **New**.
3. In the Suggested searches list, click the desired category.
4. Click the desired template.
5. Click **Create**.
6. Personalize the information as desired and then save the workbook file.

Starting Access and Creating a New Database

1. Click the Windows button on the Taskbar ■.
2. Begin typing *Access*.
3. Click **Access 2016** in the Search list.
3. In the Access Welcome screen, click **Blank database**.
4. In the File Name box, type the name of the new database.
5. Click the **Browse** button 🖿 and navigate to the location where you want to save the file.
6. Click **Create**.

Creating a Database

Creating a New, Blank Database

1. Click **File**.
2. Click **New**.
3. Click **Blank database**.
4. In the File Name box, type the name of the new database.
5. Click the **Browse** button 🖿 and navigate to the location where you want to save the file.
6. Click **Create**.

Changing the View

Collapsing and Expanding the Navigation Pane

1. In the database window, click the **Shutter Bar Close** button « to collapse the Navigation pane.
2. Click the **Shutter Bar Open** button » to expand the Navigation pane.

Changing the View of the Navigation Pane

1. If necessary, click the **Shutter Bar Open** button » to expand the Navigation pane.
2. Click the **down arrow** button ⊙ at the top of the Navigation pane.
3. On the menu, click the desired view option.

Opening and Closing the Field List

1. Open a form or report in Layout view or Design view.

2. Click the **Form Design Tools Design** tab.

   Tools Group

3. Click the **Add Existing Fields** button 🗐.
4. Click the **Close** button × to close the Field List task pane.

Saving a Database

Saving Changes to a Database

- Click the **Save** button 🖫 on the Quick Access Toolbar.

OR
1. Click **File**.
2. Click **Save**.

Saving a Copy of a Database

1. Click **File**.
2. Click **Save As**.
3. Click **Save Database As**.
4. In the Save As dialog box, navigate to the location where you want to save the file.
5. In the File name box, type the database file name.
6. Click **Save**.

Opening a Database

Opening a Recently Used Database

1. Click **File**.
2. Click **Recent**.
3. Click the desired database to open it.

OR
1. From the Access Welcome screen, click **Open Other Files**.
2. On the Open menu, click **Recent**, if necessary.
3. From the Recent list, click the desired file.

Opening a Saved Database

1. Click **File**.
2. Click **Open**.
3. In the Open dialog box, navigate to the file you want to open and select it.
4. Click **Open**.

Opening a Database Exclusively

1. Click **File**.
2. Click **Open**.

3. Navigate to and select the file to open.
4. Click the **Open** button drop-down arrow.
5. Click **Open Exclusive**.

Closing a Database

1. Click **File**.
2. Click **Close**.

Managing Tables

Saving and Closing a Table

1. Right-click the table tab.
2. On the shortcut menu, click **Close**.

OR
   Click the **Close** button × in the upper right corner of the datasheet.
3. In the message box, click **Yes** to save the table.
4. In the Save As box, type the table name.
5. Click **OK**.

Opening a Table

- In the Navigation pane, double-click the table.

Renaming a Table

1. In the Navigation pane, right-click the table you want to rename.
2. On the shortcut menu, click **Rename**.
3. Type the new table name and press **Enter**.

Creating Additional Tables

1. Click the **Create** tab.

   Tables Group

2. Click the **Table** button 🞐.

Creating a Field in a Datasheet

1. In the open table, click **Click to Add**.
2. Click the desired field type on the menu.
3. Type the field name and press **Enter**.

Adding Records to a Table

1. Click in the first field.
2. Type the field entry.
3. Press **Tab** to move to the next field.

Editing Field Data

- Double-click the field entry and type the replacement entry.
- Click the field entry, position the insertion point where desired, and type the edits or press **Backspace** or **Delete** to delete characters as desired.Position the mouse pointer in the upper-left corner of the field entry. When it changes to ⊕, click to select the entire field. Press **Backspace** or **Delete** to delete the entry, or type the replacement entry.

Selecting Records

- Click the record selector to select the desired record.
- To select multiple records, click the record selector of the first record, hold **Shift**, and click the record selector of adjacent records.
- Press **Ctrl+A** to select all records.

Deleting Records

1. Click the record selector of the record you want to delete.
2. Press **Delete**.
3. In the message box, click **Yes** to confirm the deletion.

Managing Fields in Datasheet View

Changing the Data Type

1. In Datasheet view, click in the desired field.
2. Click the **Table Tools Fields** tab.

Formatting Group

3. Click the **Data Type** drop-down arrow.

4. On the menu, click the desired field type.

Making a Field Required

1. In Datasheet view, click in the desired field.
2. Click the **Table Tools Fields** tab.

Field Validation Group

3. Click the **Required** check box.

Making a Field Unique

1. In Datasheet view, click in the desired field.
2. Click the **Table Tools Fields** tab.

Field Validation Group

3. Click the **Unique** check box.

Adding a Field by Right-Clicking

1. Right-click the field header that will be to the right of the new field.
2. On the shortcut menu, click **Insert Field**.

Adding a Field from the Ribbon

1. Click in the field that will be to the left of the new field.
2. Click the **Table Tools Fields** tab.

Add & Delete Group

3. Click the button for the desired field type.

Renaming a Field

1. Double-click the field column heading.
2. Type the new name for the field and press **Enter**.

OR

1. Right-click the field column heading.
2. On the shortcut menu, click **Rename Field**.
3. Type the new name for the field and press **Enter**.

Moving a Field

1. Click the column heading of the field you want to move.
2. Click and hold the mouse button down and drag the field to the desired location.

Deleting a Field

1. Click the column heading of the field you want to delete.
2. Click the **Table Tools Fields** tab.

Add & Delete Group

3. Click the **Delete** button ✖.
4. In the message box, click **Yes** to confirm the deletion.

Hiding and Unhiding Fields

1. Right-click the column heading of the field you want to hide.
2. On the shortcut menu, click **Hide Fields**.
3. To unhide a column, right-click the column heading of any field.
4. On the shortcut menu, click **Unhide Fields**.
5. In the Unhide Columns dialog box, click to select the field you want to unhide.
6. Click **Close**.

Changing Table Field Widths

1. Position the mouse pointer on the right border of the column heading.
2. When the pointer changes to ⊞, drag the column to the desired width.

OR

1. Double-click the right border of the column heading.

OR

1. Right-click the column heading.
2. On the shortcut menu, click **Field Width**.
3. In the Column Width dialog box, enter the desired width.
4. Click **OK**.

Freezing Fields

1. Select the fields you want to freeze.
2. Right-click the selected fields.
3. On the shortcut menu, click **Freeze Fields**.
4. To unfreeze the fields, right-click the column heading of a field.
5. On the shortcut menu, click **Unfreeze All Fields**.

Working With Tables in Design View

Opening a Table in Design View
1. Right-click the table name in the Navigation pane.
2. On the shortcut menu, click **Design View**.

OR

1. With the table open in Datasheet view, right-click the table tab.
2. On the shortcut menu, click **Design View**.

Creating a Table in Design View
1. In the open database, click the **Create** tab.

   Tables Group
2. Click the **Table Design** button.
3. Set the field names, data types, and field properties as desired.

Setting a Primary Key
1. Open the table in Design view.
2. Click the field you want to set as the primary key.
3. Click the **Table Tools Design** tab.

   Tools Group
4. Click the **Primary Key** button.

Inserting a Field
1. In Design view, click the field selector of the field that will follow the new field.
2. Click the **Table Tools Design** tab.

   Tools Group
3. Click the **Insert Rows** button.

Moving a Field
1. In Design view, click the field selector to the left of the desired field.
2. Holding the mouse button down, drag the field selector to the desired location in the field list.

Deleting a Field
1. In Design view, click the field selector of the field you want to delete.

2. Click the **Table Tools Design** tab.

   Tools Group
3. Click the **Delete Rows** button.

Changing a Field's Data Type
1. In Design view, click the **Data Type** drop-down arrow of the desired field.
2. On the menu, click the desired data type.

Modifying a Field's Properties
1. In Design view, click the field selector of the field whose properties you want to modify.
2. In the Field Properties pane, modify the properties as desired.

Previewing a Datasheet
1. Click **File**.
2. Click **Print**.
3. Click **Print Preview**.

Printing a Datasheet
1. Click **File**.
2. Click **Print**.
3. Click **Print**.
4. In the Print dialog box, select options as desired.
5. Click **OK**.

Modifying Database Properties
1. Click **File**.
2. On the Info tab, click **View and edit database properties**.
3. In the Properties dialog box, modify properties as desired.
4. Click **OK**.

Protecting a Database

Setting a Database Password
1. Open the database exclusively (see preceding procedure).
2. Click **File**.
3. On the Info tab, click **Encrypt with Password**.
4. In the Set Database Password dialog box, type the password in the Password box.
5. Type the password again in the Verify box.

6. Click **OK**.

Opening a Password-Protected Database
1. Open the database exclusively (see procedure above).
2. In the Enter database password dialog box, type the password.
3. Click **OK**.

Removing the Password from a Database
1. Open the database exclusively.
2. Click **File**.
3. On the Info tab, click **Decrypt Database**.
4. In the Unset Database Password dialog box, type the password.
5. Click **OK**.

Creating a Simple Query
1. In the open database, click the **Create** tab.

   Queries Group
2. Click the **Query Wizard** button.
3. In the New Query dialog box, click **Simple Query Wizard**.
4. Click **OK**.
5. In the Simple Query Wizard dialog box, click the **Tables/Queries** drop-down arrow.
6. Click the table or query on which the new query will be based.
7. Select fields from the Available Fields list box to move to the Selected Fields list box.
8. Click **Next**.
9. Enter the title for the query.
10. Click **Finish**.

Creating a Quick Form
1. In the Navigation pane, click the table on which you want to base the form.
2. Click the **Create** tab.

   Forms Group
3. Click the **Form** button.

Sorting

Sorting Records in a Table
1. With the table open in Datasheet view, click in the field by which you want to sort the records.

2. Click the **Home** tab.

Sort & Filter Group

3. Click the **Ascending** button ↓ to sort in ascending order or the **Descending** button ↓ to sort in descending order.

Removing a Sort

1. Click the **Home** tab.

Sort & Filter Group

2. Click the **Remove Sort** button ↓.

Sorting Using Multiple Fields

1. With the table open in Datasheet view, arrange the fields in the order you want to sort them so they are adjacent to each other.
2. Select the fields by which you want to sort.
3. Click the **Home** tab.

Sort & Filter Group

4. Click the **Ascending** button ↓ to sort in ascending order or the **Descending** button ↓ to sort in descending order.

Filtering

Filtering by Selection

1. With the table open in Datasheet view, select the field value for which you want to filter.
2. Click the **Home** tab.

Sort & Filter Group

3. Click the **Selection** button ▼.
4. On the menu, click the desired filter option.

Removing a Filter

1. Click the **Home** tab.

Sort & Filter Group

2. Click the **Toggle Filter** button ▼.

Working with Queries

Creating a Query in Design View

1. In the database window, click the **Create** tab.

Queries Group

2. Click the **Query Design** button.

---

3. In the Show Table dialog box, click the table or query on which the new query will be based.
4. Click **Add**.
5. In Query Design view, drag fields from the table window to the grid as desired.

OR

Click in the Field row in the query grid, click the drop-down arrow, and click the field to add.

OR

Double-click a field in the table field list to add it to the grid.

Removing Fields from the Query

1. In the query grid, click anywhere in the field's column that you want to remove.

OR

In the query grid, click on the thin gray bar above the desired field to select the column.

2. Click the **Query Tools Design** tab.

Query Setup Group

3. Click the **Delete Columns** button ✖.

Running a Query

1. In Query Design view, click the **Query Tools Design** tab.

Results Group

2. Click the **Run** button **!**.

Saving a Query

1. In Query Design view, click the **Save** button 🖫 on the Quick Access Toolbar.
2. In the Save As dialog box, type the query name.
3. Click **OK**.

Printing a Query

1. With the query open in Datasheet view, click **File**.
2. Click **Print**.
3. Click the **Print** button 🖶.
4. In the Print dialog box, set the print options as desired.
5. Click **OK**.

Creating a Multi-Table Query

1. In the database window, click the **Create** tab.

Queries Group

2. Click the **Query Design** button.
3. In the Show Table dialog box, double-click the tables on which the new query will be based.
4. Drag fields from the table windows to the grid as desired.

Sorting Query Results

1. Open the query in Design view.
2. In the query grid, click in the **Sort** row for the field on which you want to sort.
3. Click the drop-down arrow and click **Ascending** or **Descending**.

Reordering Fields in a Query

1. Open the query in Design view.
2. In the query grid, click the gray bar above the field you want to move.
3. Drag the field to the desired location.

Using All Fields of a Table

1. In the database window, click the **Create** tab.

Queries Group

2. Click the **Query Design** button.
3. In the Show Table dialog box, double-click the table on which the new query will be based.
4. In the table window, double-click the asterisk (*) at the top of the table field list.

Changing a Column Name

1. Open the query in Design view.
2. In the query grid, click in the **Field** row of the column you want to rename.
3. Position the insertion point to the left of the current field name.
4. Type the new name followed by a colon.

Specifying Criteria in a Query

1. Open the query in Design view.
2. In the query grid, click in the **Criteria** row for the desired field.
3. Type the criteria as desired.

Filtering by an Undisplayed Field

1. Open the query in Design view.
2. In the query grid, click in the **Criteria** row for the desired field.
3. Type the criteria as desired.
4. Click the field's **Show** box to deselect it.

Filtering for Null Values

1. Open the query in Design view.
2. In the query grid, click in the **Criteria** row for the desired field.
3. Type **Is Null**.

Using Wildcards and Operators in a Query

Using Wildcards

1. Open the query in Design view.
2. In the query grid, click in the **Criteria** row for the desired field.
3. Type the criteria, using the asterisk (*) wildcard character to specify any number of characters, or the question mark (?) wildcard character to specify a single character.

Using the Like Operator

1. Open the query in Design view.
2. In the query grid, click in the **Criteria** row for the desired field.
3. Type **Like**, followed by the criteria as desired.

Using the Between...And Operator

1. Open the query in Design view.
2. In the query grid, click in the **Criteria** row for the desired field.
3. Type the criteria in the format, **Between *criteria* and *criteria***.

Using the In Operator

1. Open the query in Design view.
2. In the query grid, click in the **Criteria** row for the desired field.
3. Type the criteria in the format, **In (criteria)**.

Using the Or Operator

1. Open the query in Design view.
2. In the query grid, click in the **Criteria** row for the desired field.
3. Type the criteria in the format, ***criteria* Or *criteria***.

Using a Comparison Operator in a Query

1. Open the query in Design view.
2. In the query grid, click in the **Criteria** row for the desired field.
3. Type the criteria with comparison operator as desired.

Using Calculated Fields in a Query

1. Open the query in Design view.
2. In the query grid, click in a blank column and type the field name followed by a colon (:).
3. Click the **Query Tools Design** tab.

Query Setup Group

4. Click the **Builder** button.
5. In the Expression Builder, select from the Expression Elements, Expression Categories, and Expression Values as desired.
6. If necessary, delete the Expr text.
7. Click **OK**.

Creating a Form

Creating a Form in Layout View

1. In the Navigation pane, click the table on which you want to base the form.
2. Click the **Create** tab.

Forms Group

3. Click the **Blank Form** button ⬚.
4. Drag the fields from the field list to the form layout as desired.

Creating a Form in Design View

1. Click the **Create** tab.

Forms Group

2. Click the **Form Design** button.
3. Click the **Form Design Tools Design** tab.

Tools Group

4. Click the **Add Existing Fields** button.
5. In the Field List pane, click **Show all tables**.
6. Expand the fields of the table that you want to add to the form.

7. Double-click the desired fields to add them to the form.

Managing Records in a Form

Adding a Record

1. In Form view, click the **New (blank) record** button at the bottom of the form.
2. Type the record data in the fields.

Navigating Records in a Form

- Click the navigation buttons as follows:
  - **First record** ⏮
  - **Previous record** ◀
  - **Next record** ▶
  - **Last record** ⏭

Deleting a Record from a Form

1. In Form view, click in the record you want to delete.
2. Click the **Home** tab.

Records Group

3. Click the **Delete** button.
4. On the menu, click **Delete Record**.
5. In the message box, click **Yes** to confirm the deletion.

Creating and Viewing a Tabular Report

1. In the Navigation pane, click the table on which you want to base the report.
2. Click the **Create** tab.

Reports Group

3. Click the **Report** button.
4. Click the **Report Design Tools Design** tab.

Views Group

5. Click the **View** button drop-down arrow.
6. Click **Report View**.

Creating a Report in Layout View

1. Click the **Create** tab.

Reports Group

2. Click the **Blank Report** button ⬚.
3. Click the **Report Layout Tools Design** tab.

Tools Group

4. If necessary, click the **Add Existing Fields** button ▦.
5. In the Field List pane, click **Show all tables**.
6. Expand the fields of the table that you want to add to the report.
7. Double-click the desired fields to add them to the report.

Deleting Fields from a Report Layout

1. In Layout view, click the field you want to delete.
2. Click the **Report Layout Tools Arrange** tab.

Rows & Columns Group

3. Click the **Select Column** button ▦.
4. Press **Delete**.

Changing Field Widths in a Report

1. In Layout view, click the field whose width you want to change.
2. Position the mouse pointer on the right edge of the selected field.
3. When the pointer changes to ↔, drag to the desired width.

Creating a Report Using the Report Wizard

1. Click the **Create** tab.

Reports Group

2. Click the **Report Wizard** button ▦.
3. In the Report Wizard dialog box, select the table on which you want to base the report.
4. Select fields in the Available Fields list box and move them to the Selected Fields list box.
5. Click **Next**.
6. Select a grouping field if desired.
7. Click **Next**.
8. In the next dialog box, set a sort order if desired.
9. Click **Next**.
10. In the next dialog box, click the desired layout and orientation for the report.
11. Click **Next**.
12. In the next dialog box, enter the title for the report.
13. Click **Finish**.

Previewing and Printing a Report

1. With the report open, right-click its tab.
2. On the shortcut menu, click **Print Preview**.
3. Click the **Print Preview** tab.

Print Group

4. Click the **Print** button 🖶.
OR
1. With the report open, click **File**.
2. Click **Print**.
3. Click **Print**.
4. In the Print dialog box, set print options as desired.
5. Click **OK**.
OR
1. With the report open, click **File**.
2. Click **Print**.
3. Click **Quick Print**.

Working with Report Sections

Selecting Sections of a Report

1. Open the report in Design view.
2. Click the bar of the section you want to select.

Resizing a Section

1. Click the bar of the section you want to resize.
2. Position the pointer on the top border of the bar.
3. When the pointer changes to ╪, drag to the desired size.

Moving a Control Between Sections

1. Open the report in Design view.
2. Click the control you want to move.
3. Press **Ctrl+X**.
4. Click where you want to move the control.
5. Press **Ctrl+V**.

Modifying a Report

Adding Page Number Codes

1. Open the report in Design view.
2. Click the **Report Design Tools Design** tab.

Header/Footer Group

3. Click the **Page Numbers** button ▯.
4. In the Page Numbers dialog box, set the form, position, and alignment of the page numbers as desired.
5. Click **OK**.

Sorting Report Data

1. Open the report in Layout view.
2. Click the **Report Layout Tools Design** tab.

Grouping & Totals Group

3. Click the **Group & Sort** button ▦.
4. In the Group, Sort, and Total pane, click Add a sort.
5. On the pop-up menu, select the field you want to sort by.
6. Click to select the sort order (with A on top or with Z on top).

Grouping Report Data

1. Open the report in Layout view.
2. Click the **Report Layout Tools Design** tab.

Grouping & Totals Group

3. Click the **Group & Sort** button ▦.
4. In the Group, Sort, and Total pane, click Add a group.
5. On the field list that opens, click the desired field on which you want to group records.

Working with Print Preview and Report View

Opening Print Preview

1. Click the **Home** tab.

Views Group

2. Click the **View** button drop-down arrow.
3. Click **Print Preview**.

Opening Report View

1. Click the **Home** tab.

Views Group

2. Click the **View** button drop-down arrow.
3. Click **Report View**.

Changing the View

1. Click the **View** tab.

   ### Presentation Views Group

2. Click the desired View button:
   - **Normal** 🔲.
   - **Outline View** 🔲.
   - **Slide Sorter** 🔲.
   - **Notes Page** 🔲.
   - **Reading View** 📖.

OR
- Click a View icon on the status bar:
   - **Normal** 🔲.
   - **Slide Sorter** 🔲.
   - **Reading View** 📖.
   - **Slide Show** 🖳.

Showing and Hiding On Screen Elements

1. Click the **View** tab.

   ### Show Group

2. Click to mark the **Ruler** check box, the **Gridlines** check box, and the **Guides** check box.

Adjusting Grid and Guide Settings

1. Click the **View** tab.

   ### Show Group

2. Click the Show dialog box launcher 🔲.
3. In the Grid and Guides dialog box, adjust the settings as desired.
4. Click **OK**.

Displaying the Outline

1. Click the **View** tab.

   ### Presentation Views Group

2. Click the **Outline View** button 🔲.

Navigating in the PowerPoint Window

Navigating in Slides View

- In the Thumbnail pane, click the desired slide to display it.

OR
- Click the **Previous Slide** button ▲ or click the **Next Slide** button ▼.

OR
- Click the vertical scroll bar to bring slides into view.

Navigating in Reading View

1. On the status bar, click the **Reading View** button 📖.
2. To scroll through the presentation, click the **Next** button ⊙ and **Previous** button ⊙.

OR
   a. Click the **Menu** button 🔲.
   b. From the menu, click the desired option.

Switching between Open Presentations

- Click in the presentation window you want to make active.

OR
- Click the program's taskbar button and click the presentation you want to make active.

OR
1. Click the **View** tab.

   ### Window Group

2. Click the **Switch Windows** button 🔲.
3. Click the presentation you want to make active.

Arranging Multiple Presentations

1. Click the **View** tab.

   ### Window Group

3. Click the **Arrange All** button 🗗.

Entering and Editing Text

General Typing

- Press **Enter** to start a new paragraph.
- Press **Backspace** to delete one character to the left of the insertion point.
- Press **Delete** to delete one character to the right of the insertion point.

Typing in a Placeholder

1. Click in the desired placeholder.
2. Type the text.

Typing in an Outline

1. Display the outline.
2. Click the slide where you want to enter text.
3. Type to enter a title.
4. Press **Ctrl + Enter** to start a new bullet line.

OR
- Press **Enter** to insert a new slide.

Typing Notes

1. In the Thumbnail pane, click the slide to which you want to add speaker notes.
2. Click the **View** tab.

   ### Presentation Views

3. Click the **Notes Page** button 🔲.
4. Click in the Notes placeholder and type the desired notes text.

OR
1. In Normal view, click the **Notes** button 🔲 on the status bar.
2. Click in the Notes pane of the desired slide and enter the note.

Inserting a New Slide

Inserting a New Slide Using the Previously Used Layout

1. Click the **Home** tab.

   ### Slides Group

2. Click the **New Slide** button 🔲.

Inserting a New Slide with a Different Layout

1. Click the **Home** tab.

   Slides Group
2. Click the **New Slide** button down arrow ⬛.
3. From the gallery, click the desired layout.

Selecting in a Presentation

Selecting Text
- Click and drag across the text you want to select.

Selecting Placeholders
- Click the placeholder you want to select.

Selecting Objects
- Click the object you want to select.

Selecting a Slide
- In the Slides pane, click the slide you want to select.

Checking Spelling in a Presentation

1. Click the **Review** tab.

   Proofing Group
2. Click the **Spelling** button ✓.
3. In the Spelling task pane, click to **Change** or **Ignore** the suggestions.
4. Click **Close**.

OR

1. Right-click a word that has been identified as misspelled.
2. On the shortcut menu, click the desired spelling.

Finding and Replacing Text

Finding Text
1. Click the **Home** tab.

   Editing Group
2. Click the **Find** button 🔍.
3. In the Find dialog box, type the text you want to find.
4. Click **Find Next**.

Replacing Text

1. Click the **Home** tab.

   Editing Group
2. Click the **Replace** button 🔤.
3. In the Replace dialog box, enter the text to find in the Find what text box.
4. Enter the replacement text in the Replace with text box.
5. Click the **Replace** button to replace each separate occurrence; click **Replace All** to replace all occurrences.

Copying Text Formatting

1. Select the text or placeholder whose formatting you want to copy.
2. Click the **Home** tab.

   Clipboard Group
3. Click the **Format Painter** button 🖌.
4. Select the text or placeholder to which you want to copy the formatting.

Clearing Formatting

1. In the Thumbnail pane, click the slide from which you want to clear the formatting.
2. Click the **Home** tab.

   Font Group
3. Click the **Clear All Formatting** button ❖.
4. Click the **Home** tab.

   Slides Group
5. Click the **Reset** button 🖼 to reset the position, size, and formatting of the slide placeholders to their default settings.

Aligning Text

1. Select the text or placeholder.
2. Click the **Home** tab.

   Paragraph Group

3. Click the desired alignment button:
   - **Align Left** ≡
   - **Center** ≡
   - **Align Right** ≡
   - **Justify** ≡

Adjusting Paragraph Spacing

1. Select the text.
2. Click the **Home** tab.

   Paragraph Group
3. Click the **Paragraph Group** dialog box launcher ⌐.
4. In the Paragraph dialog box, in the Spacing section, set the Before and After spacing as desired.
5. Click **OK**.

Adjusting Line Spacing

1. Select the text.
2. Click the **Home** tab.

   Paragraph Group
3. Click the **Line Spacing** button ↕≡▾.
4. From the menu, click the desired spacing option.

OR

1. Select the text.
2. Click the **Home** tab.

   Paragraph Group
3. Click the **Paragraph Group** dialog box launcher ⌐.
4. In the Paragraph dialog box, click the **Line Spacing** drop-down arrow, and click the desired line spacing.
5. Click **OK**.

Using AutoFit Options

1. Select the placeholder.
2. Click the **AutoFit Options** button ⬍.
3. From the menu, click the desired option.

Adjusting and Formatting Placeholders

Adjusting Placeholders
1. Click the placeholder.
2. Click and drag a sizing handle to resize the placeholder.

Formatting Placeholders
1. Click the placeholder.
2. Click the **Home** tab.
   Drawing Group
3. Click the **Quick Styles** button ⬧.
4. From the gallery, click the desired style.

Working with Lists

Changing a List Level
1. In the Thumbnail pane, click in the line of text whose level you want to change.
2. Click the **Home** tab.
   Paragraph Group
3. Click the **Decrease List Level** button ⬅ or the **Increase List Level** button ➡.

Applying Bullets
1. Select the item or list to which you want to apply bullets.
2. Click the **Home** tab.
   Paragraph Group
3. Click the **Bullets** button ⬝ ⌄.

Removing a Bullet
1. Select the item or list from which you want to remove bullets.
2. Click the **Home** tab.
   Paragraph Group
3. Click the **Bullets** button ⬝ ⌄.

Modifying the Bulleted List Style
1. Drag across the entire bulleted list to select it.
OR
   Click in the bulleted list and press **Ctrl+A**.
2. Click the **Home** tab.
   Paragraph Group
3. Click the **Bullets** drop-down arrow ⬝ ⌄.

4. From the gallery, click the desired style or click **Bullets and Numbering**.
5. In the Bullets and Numbering dialog box, customize the list style as desired.
6. Click **OK**.
OR
5. In the Bullets and Numbering dialog box, click **Customize**.
6. In the Symbol dialog box, select the desired bullet character.
7. Click **OK** twice.

Formatting the Slide Background

Changing a Slide Background Style
1. Click the **Design** tab.
   Document Formatting Group
2. Click the **Variants More** button ⬇.
3. Click **Background Styles**.
4. From the gallery, click the desired style.

Applying a Background Fill Color
1. Click the **Design** tab.
   Customize Group
2. Click the **Format Background** button ⬙.
3. In the Format Background task pane, click the **Fill** icon ◇.
4. Select the fill options as desired.

Formatting a Slide Background with a Picture
1. Click the **Design** tab.
   Customize Group
2. Click the **Format Background** button ⬙.
3. In the Format Background task pane, click the **Fill** icon ◇.
4. Under Fill, click **Picture or texture fill**.
5. Under Insert picture from, click the desired location from which you will insert the picture.
6. Navigate to the location where the picture file is stored.
7. In the Insert Picture dialog box, click the picture and click **Insert**.

Resetting the Slide Background
1. Click the **Design** tab.
   Customize Group
2. Click the **Format Background** button ⬙.
3. At the bottom of the Format Background task pane, click **Reset Background**.

Changing a Slide Layout
1. In the Slides pane, select the slide to change.
2. Click the **Home** tab.
   Slides Group
3. Click the **Slide Layout** button ▦.
4. From the gallery, click the desired layout.

Printing a Presentation
1. Click **File**.
2. Click **Print**.
3. In the Backstage view, set the print options as desired.
4. Click the **Print** button 🖶.

Previewing and Printing All Slides
1. Click the **File** tab.
2. Click **Print**.
✓ In Backstage view, print settings display on the left, and a preview of the current slide displays on the right.
3. Use the **Next Page** and **Previous Page** arrows under the preview to view other pages.
4. Use the **Zoom** controls under the preview to adjust the preview magnification.
5. Click the **Print** button 🖶.

Changing Print Options
1. Click the **File** tab.
2. Click **Print**.
3. In the **Copies** box, enter the number of copies.
4. Under Printer, select the printer to use.
✓ Click **Printer Properties** to set options for the selected printer.

5. Under Settings, select options:
   - Which slides to print.
   - What to print (Slides, Notes, Outline, or Handouts).
   - One sided or two sided printing.
   - Collated or Uncollated.
   - Landscape or Portrait Orientation (not available when printing full page slides).
   - Color, Grayscale, or Pure Black and White
   ✓ Click **Edit Header & Footer** to open the Header and Footer dialog box for additional options.
6. Click the **Print** button 🖨.

Managing Slides

Copying Slides
1. In the Thumbnail pane, click the slide you want to copy.
2. Click the **Home** tab.
   Clipboard Group
3. Click the **Copy** button 📋.
4. Click between the slides where you want to copy the slide.
5. Click the **Home** tab.
   Clipboard Group
6. Click the **Paste** button 📋.

Duplicating Slides
1. In the Thumbnail pane, click the slide you want to duplicate.
2. Click the **Home** tab.
   Clipboard Group
3. Click the **Copy** drop-down arrow 📋.
4. On the menu, click **Duplicate**.

Deleting Slides
1. In the Thumbnail pane, click the slide you want to delete.
2. Press **Delete**.
OR
2. Click the **Home** tab.
   Clipboard Group
3. Click the **Cut** button ✂.

Rearranging Slides

In Slide Sorter View
1. In the status bar, click the **Slide Sorter** button 🔠.
2. In Slide Sorter view, click the slide you want to move.
3. Drag the selected slide to between the slides where you want to reposition it.

In the Slides Pane
1. In the Slides pane, click the slide you want to move.
2. Drag the selected slide to the new location.

Adding Slide Transitions
1. Click the slide to which you want to add the transition.
2. Click the **TRANSITIONS** tab.
   Transition to This Slide Group
3. Click the **Transition to This Slide More** button 🔽.
4. From the gallery, click the desired transition.

Adding Transition Effects
1. Click the slide with the transition.
2. Click the **TRANSITIONS** tab.
   Transition to This Slide Group
3. Click the **Effect Options** button.
4. From the menu, click the desired effect.

Controlling Slide Advance
1. Display the presentation in Slide Sorter view.
2. Click the **TRANSITIONS** tab.
   Timing Group
3. From the Advance Slide options, click **On Mouse Click**, or click the **After** box and set the timing as desired.

Applying Animations

Applying Effects Using the Animation Gallery
1. Select a placeholder or object to which you want to apply the animation.
2. Click the **Animations** tab.
   Animation Group
3. Click the **Animation More** button 🔽.
4. From the gallery, click the desired animation.

Setting Effect Options
1. Select the placeholder or object to which you have applied the animation.
2. Click the **Animations** tab.
   Animation Group
3. Click the **Effect Options** button ↑.
   √ *The graphic on your Effect Options button will depend on the animation already applied to the object or placeholder.*
4. From the menu, click the desired effect.

Using the Animation Painter
1. Select the placeholder or object with the animation you want to copy.
   Advanced Animation Group
2. Click the **Animation Painter** button ⭐.
3. Click the placeholder or object to which you want to apply the animation.

Applying Animation to Objects, Charts, and Diagrams
1. Select the graphic or object to which you want to apply the animation.
2. Click the **Animations** tab.
   Animation Group
3. Click the **Animation More** button 🔽.
4. From the gallery, click the desired animation.

Previewing a Slide Show
- Click the **Slide Show** button 🖥 near the right side of the status bar.

Working with Notes Pages

Typing Notes Pages
1. In the Thumbnail pane, click the slide to which you want to add speaker notes.
2. Click the **View** tab.
   #### Presentation Views
3. Click the **Notes Page** button ▣.
4. Click in the Notes placeholder and type the desired notes text.

Printing Notes Pages
1. Click the **File** tab.
2. Click **Print**.
3. Under Settings, click the second option button (what to print).
4. Under Print Layout, click **Notes Pages**.
5. Select additional options as necessary.
6. Click the Print button 🖶.

Printing Handouts
1. Click the **File** tab.
2. Click **Print**.
3. Under Settings, click the second option button (what to print).
4. Under Handouts, click the handout layout you want to print.
5. Select additional options as necessary.
6. Click the Print button 🖶.

Inserting Headers and Footers
1. Click the **Insert** tab.
   #### Text Group
2. Click the **Header & Footer** button 🗋.
3. In the Header and Footer dialog box, click the desired options on the Slide tab.
4. Click **Apply to All**.

Inserting Graphics

Inserting a Picture from a File
1. On the Thumbnail pane, click the slide on which you want to insert the picture.
2. In the slide content placeholder, click the **Pictures** icon 🖾.

OR
  a. Click the **Insert** tab.
   #### Images Group
  b. Click the **Pictures** button 🖾.
3. In the Insert Picture dialog box, navigate to the location where the picture file is stored.
4. Click the picture and then click **Insert**.

Inserting Online Pictures
1. In the Thumbnail pane, click the slide on which you want to insert an online picture.
2. In the empty content placeholder, click the **Online Pictures** icon 🖾.
3. In the Insert Pictures dialog box, click in the search box and enter a search string for the type of picture for which you are searching.
4. Press **Enter**.
5. Click the desired image and click **Insert**.

Working with Text Boxes

Inserting a Text Box
1. Click the slide where you want to insert the text box.
2. Click the **Insert** tab.
   #### Text Group
3. Click the **Text Box** button 🄰.
4. On the slide, drag to draw the box the desired size.
5. Type the text as desired.

Creating a Multiple Column Text Box
1. Click the outer border of the text box to select it.
2. Click the **Home** tab.
   #### Paragraph Group
3. Click the **Add or Remove Columns** button ☰ ▾.
4. On the menu, click the desired column setting.

Working with Video

Inserting a Video from a File
1. In the slide's content placeholder, click the **Insert Video** icon 🖵.

OR
  a. Click the **Insert** tab.
   #### Media Group
  b. Click the **Insert Video** button 🎞.
2. In the Insert Video dialog box, navigate to the location where the video file is stored.
3. Click the file and then click **Insert**.

Inserting an Online Video
1. Click the slide on which you want to insert the video.
2. Click the **Insert** tab.
   #### Media Group
3. Click the **Video** button 🎞 drop-down arrow.
4. Click **Online Video**.
5. In the Insert Video dialog box, type keyword(s) in the **Search YouTube** box and press **Enter**.
6. Click the desired clip and click **Insert** to insert it on the slide.

OR
Paste the embed code for the video you want to insert in the **Paste embed code here** box and press **Enter**.

Previewing a Movie in Normal View
1. Click the video to select it.
2. Click the **Video Tools Playback** tab.
   #### Preview Group
3. Click the **Play** button ▶.

OR
Click the **Play/Pause** button ▶ on the video itself.

Viewing a Video in a Slide Show
1. In the status bar, click the **Slide Show** button 🖵.
2. Hover the mouse over the video.
3. Click the **Play** button ▶.

Working with Sound

Inserting Sounds or Music from a File

1. Click the slide on which you want to insert the music.
2. Click the **Insert** tab.
   ### Media Group
3. Click the **Audio** button 🔊.
4. On the menu, click the type of audio you want to insert.
5. In the Insert Audio dialog box, navigate to the desired audio file.
6. Click the file and then click **Insert**.

Hiding the Audio Icon

1. Click the audio icon on the slide.
2. Click the **AUDIO TOOLS PLAYBACK** tab.
   ### Audio Options Group
3. Click to select the **Hide During Show** check box.

Setting Audio to Play Continuously

1. Click the audio icon on the slide.
2. Click the **AUDIO TOOLS PLAYBACK** tab.
   ### Audio Options Group
3. Click to select the **Loop until Stopped** check box.

Setting Audio to Rewind

1. Click the audio icon on the slide.
2. Click the **Audio Tools Playback** tab.
   ### Audio Options Group
3. Click to select the **Rewind after Playing** check box.

Setting the Playback Volume

1. Click the audio icon on the slide.
2. Click the **Audio Tools Playback** tab.
   ### Audio Options Group
3. Click the **Volume** button 🔊.
4. Click the volume level.

Trimming an Audio Clip

1. Click the audio icon to select it.
2. Click the **Audio Tools Playback** tab.

Editing Group
3. Click the **Trim Audio** button 🎬.
4. Drag the green handle on the left to trim the beginning of the audio.
5. Drag the red handle on the right to trim the end of the audio.
6. Click **OK**.

Working with WordArt

Applying WordArt Styles to Existing Text

1. Select the text you want to format as WordArt.
2. Click the **Drawing Tools Format** tab.
   ### WordArt Styles Group
3. Click the **WordArt Styles More** button ⊡.
4. From the gallery, click the desired style.

Inserting WordArt

1. Click the **Insert** tab.
   ### Text Group
2. Click the **WordArt** button 𝐴.
3. From the gallery, click the desired style.
4. Select the placeholder text and type your text.

Formatting WordArt

1. Click the WordArt object.
2. Click the **Drawing Tools Format** tab.
   ### WordArt Styles Group
3. Click the desired format buttons as follows:
   - **Text Fill** 🅰
   - **Text Outline** 🅰
   - **Text Effects** Ⓐ
4. From the menu, click the desired option.

Working with SmartArt

Converting a Bulleted List to SmartArt

1. Select the entire list.
2. Right-click the selected list.
3. On the shortcut menu, click **Convert to SmartArt**.

4. From the gallery, click the desired SmartArt.

Inserting a New SmartArt Object

1. On a blank slide, click the **Insert SmartArt Graphic** icon 🖼 in the content placeholder.
2. In the Choose a SmartArt Graphic dialog box, click the category from the left pane.
3. In the middle pane, choose the SmartArt style.
4. Click **OK**.

Removing a Shape from a SmartArt Object

1. Click the shape you want to remove.
2. Press **Delete**.

Adding a Shape to a SmartArt Object

1. Click a shape in the SmartArt object.
2. Click the **SmartArt Tools Design** tab.
   ### Create Graphic Group
3. Click the **Add Shape** button 🗀.

Resizing a Shape

1. Click the shape you want to resize.
2. Click and drag a sizing handle to resize as desired.

Reordering Diagram Content

1. Click the shape within the diagram that you want to move.
2. Click the **SmartArt Tools Design** tab.
   ### Create Graphic Group
3. Click the reorder options as follows:
   - **Promote** ← to increase the level of the shape
   - **Demote** → to decrease the level of the shape
   - **Right to Left** ⇄ to switch the layout
   - **Move Up** ↑ to move the current selection forward in the sequence
   - **Move Down** ↓ to move the current selection backward in the sequence

Changing the SmartArt Style
1. Click the SmartArt to select it.
2. Click the **SmartArt Tools Design** tab.
   SmartArt Styles Group
3. Click the SmartArt Styles **More** button ⏷.
4. From the gallery, click the desired style.

Changing the SmartArt Colors
1. Click the SmartArt to select it.
2. Click the **SmartArt Tools Design** tab.
   SmartArt Styles Group
3. Click the **Change Colors** button ⸭.
4. From the gallery, click the desired color.

Working with Photo Albums

Creating a Photo Album
1. Click the **Insert** tab.
   Images Group
2. Click the **Photo Album** button 🖼.
3. In the Photo Album dialog box, click the **File/Disk** button.
4. In the Insert New Pictures dialog box, navigate to the picture files.
5. Click the files you want to insert, holding down the **Ctrl** key to select multiple files.
6. Click **Insert**.
7. In the Photo Album dialog box, edit the pictures as desired.
8. Click **Create**.

Editing a Photo Album
1. Click the **Insert** tab.
   Images Group
2. Click the **Photo Album** drop-down arrow 🖼.
3. On the menu, click **Edit Photo Album**.
4. In the Edit Photo Album dialog box, click the photo you want to edit.
5. Edit the photo as desired.
6. Click **Update**.

Applying a Theme to a Photo Album
1. Click the **Insert** tab.
   Images Group
2. Click the **Photo Album** drop-down arrow 🖼.
3. On the menu, click **Edit Photo Album**.
4. In the Edit Photo Album dialog box, click the **Browse** button next to Theme.
5. In the Choose Theme dialog box, click the desired theme.
6. Click **Select**.
7. Click **Update**.

Working with Tables

Inserting a Table
1. Click the slide on which you want to insert the table.
2. In the content placeholder, click the **Insert Table** icon ▦.
3. In the Insert Table dialog box, specify the number of columns and rows.
4. Click **OK**.
OR
1. Click the **Insert** tab.
   Tables Group
2. Click the **Table** button ▦.
3. On the menu, drag the pointer over the grid to specify the desired number of columns and rows.

Applying Table Formats
1. Click the table to select it.
2. Click the **Table Tools Design** tab.
   Table Styles Group
3. Click the **Table Styles More** button ⏷.
4. From the gallery, click a style.

Applying Shading Formats
1. Click the table to select it.
2. Click the **Table Tools Design** tab.
   Table Styles Group
3. Click the **Shading** drop-down arrow 🎨.
4. From the palette, click the desired color.

Applying Border Formats
1. Click the table to select it.
2. Click the **Table Tools Design** tab.
   Table Styles Group
3. Click the **Borders** drop-down arrow ⊞.
4. From the menu, click the desired border.

Applying Effects
1. Click the table to select it.
2. Click the **Table Tools Design** tab.
   Table Styles Group
3. Click the **Effects** drop-down arrow 🌀.
4. From the menu, point to the desired effects category.
5. From the submenu, click the desired effect.

Inserting a Row
1. Click the **Table Tools Layout** tab.
   Rows & Columns Group
2. Click the **Insert Above** button ▦ to insert the row above the selected table cell.
OR
   Click the **Insert Below** button ▦ to insert the row below the selected table cell.

Inserting a Column
1. Click the **Table Tools Layout** tab.
   Rows & Columns Group
2. Click the **Insert Left** button ▦ to insert the column to the left of the selected table cell.
OR
   Click the **Insert Right** button ▦ to insert the column to the right of the selected table cell.

Deleting Part of the Table
1. Click the **Table Tools Layout** tab.
   Rows & Columns Group
2. Click the **Delete** button ▦.
3. On the menu, click the desired part of the table you want to delete.

Merging Table Cells

1. Select the cells you want to merge.
2. Click the **Table Tools Layout** tab.

   Merge Group

3. Click the **Merge Cells** button ⊞.

Distributing Rows and Columns Evenly

1. Click the **Table Tools Layout** tab.

   Cell Size Group

2. Click the **Distribute Rows** button ⊞ to distribute rows evenly.

OR

   Click the **Distribute Columns** button ⊞ to distribute columns evenly.

Working with Charts

Inserting a Chart

1. Click the slide on which you want to insert the chart.
2. In the content placeholder, click the **Insert Chart** icon ▮▮ .

OR

   a.   Click the **Insert** tab.

   Illustrations Group

   b.   Click the **Chart** button ▮▮ .

3. In the Insert Chart dialog box, click the type of chart in the left pane.
4. In the right pane, click the style of chart.
5. Click **OK**.
6. Enter data in the worksheet as desired.

Changing the Chart Type

1. Click the chart to select it.
2. Click the **Chart Tools Design** tab.

   Type Group

3. Click the **Change Chart Type** button ▮▮ .
4. In the Change Chart Type dialog box, click the type of chart in the left pane.

---

5. In the right pane, click the style of chart.
6. Click **OK**.

Applying a Chart Style

1. Click the chart to select it.
2. Click the **Chart Tools Design** tab.

   Chart Styles c

3. Click the **Chart Styles More** button ▾ .
4. From the gallery, click the desired style.

Editing the Chart Data

1. Click the chart to select it.
2. Click the **Chart Tools Design** tab.

   Data Group

3. Click the **Edit Data** button ▦ .
4. Select the option to edit the data in the Microsoft PowerPoint chart or to edit in Excel, and then edit the data as desired.

Switching Rows and Columns

1. Click the chart slide
2. Click the **Chart Tools Design** tab.

   Data Group

3. Click the **Switch Row/Column** button ▦ .

Selecting Data to Chart

1. Click the chart to select it.
2. Click the **Chart Tools Design** tab.

   Data Group

3. Click the **Select Data** button ▦ .
4. In the Select Data Source dialog box, update the data range as necessary.
5. Click **OK**.

Changing Chart Layout

1. Click the chart to select it.
2. Click the **Chart Elements** button ✚ .
3. On the pop-out list of chart elements, click the elements as desired to modify the layout.

Animating a Chart

1. Click the chart to select it.
2. Click the **Animations** tab.
3. Click the Animation **More** button ▾ .
4. From the gallery, click the desired animation.

Creating Links in a Presentation

Inserting Hyperlinks on Slides

1. Click the slide on which you want to insert the link.
2. Click the placeholder or object for the link.
3. Click the **Insert** tab.

   Links Group

4. Click the **Hyperlink** button ⊕ .
5. In the Insert Hyperlink dialog box, click the desired option in the Link to pane.
6. Fill in the linking information as necessary and click **OK**.

Inserting an Action Button

1. Click the slide on which you want to insert the button.
2. Click the **Home** tab.

   Drawing Group

3. Click the **Shapes More** button ▾ .
4. Under Action Buttons, click the desired button.
5. On the slide, drag to place the button as desired.
6. In the Action Settings dialog box, specify the desired settings on the button.
7. Click **OK**.

Sending a Presentation for Review

1. Click **File**.
2. Click **Share**.
3. Click **Email**.
4. Click the desired option for sharing the presentation via e-mail.

Using Comments

Displaying Comments
1. Click the **Review** tab
   #### Comments Group
2. Click the **Show Comments** button ▭.
3. Review the comment and if desired, click in the Reply box and enter a reply.

Inserting a Comment
1. Click the slide on which you want to insert the comment.
2. Click the **Review** tab
   #### Comments Group
3. Click the **New Comment** button ▭ and enter the comment in the comment box.

OR

2. Click the **Review** tab.
   #### Comments Group
3. Click the **New Comment** button ▭.
4. In the Comments task pane, enter the comment in the comment box.

Viewing Comments
1. Click the **Review** tab.
   #### Comments Group
2. Click the **Next** button ▭ or the **Previous** button ▭ to move from comment to comment.

Deleting a Comment
1. Click the comment to select it.
2. Click the **Review** tab.
   #### Comments Group
3. Click the **Delete** button ▭.

Controlling Slides During a Presentation

1. Click the **Slide Show** tab.
   #### Start Slide Show Group
2. Click the **From Beginning** button ▭.
3. Right-click the screen and from the shortcut menu, click the desired option for controlling the slide show.

OR

Press the following keys to advance through the slide show:
- **N**
- **Down arrow**
- **Right arrow**
- **Enter**
- **PgDn**
- **Spacebar**

Press the following keys to move backward through the slide show:
- **P**
- **Up arrow**
- **Left arrow**
- **PgUp**
- **Backspace**

Preparing a Presentation for Delivery

Rehearsing Timings
1. Click the **Slide Show** tab.
   #### Set Up Group
2. Click the **Rehearse Timings** button ▭.
3. Advance from slide to slide at the desired pace.
4. At the end of the show, click **Yes** to keep the slide timings, or **No** to discard them.

Setting Slide Show Options
1. Click the **Slide Show** tab.
   #### Set Up Group
2. Click the **Set Up Slide Show** button ▭.
3. In the Set Up Show dialog box, click the options as desired.
4. Click **OK**.

Creating a Looping Presentation that Runs Automatically
1. Click the **Slide Show** tab.
   #### Set Up Group
2. Click the **Set Up Slide Show** button ▭.
3. In the Set Up Show dialog box, under Show type, click **Browsed at a kiosk**.
4. Under Show Options, click **Loop continuously until 'Esc'**.
5. Click **OK**.

Check a Presentation for Issues

1. Click **File**.
2. Click **Info**.
3. Click the **Check for Issues** button ▭.
4. On the menu, click **Inspect Document**.
5. In the Document Inspector, click to mark options as desired.
6. Click **Inspect**.
7. Review the inspection results and then click **Close**.

Saving a Presentation as a Show

1. Click **File**.
2. Click **Save As**.
3. Navigate to the location where you want to store the show.
4. Type the name for the presentation.
5. Click the **Save as type** drop-down arrow and click **PowerPoint Show**.
6. Click **Save**.

Saving a Presentation as a Video

1. Click **File**.
2. Click **Export**.
3. Click **Create a Video**.
4. In the Create a Video pane, click the **Presentation Quality** button and select the desired quality.
5. Select if you want to record timings and narrations.
6. If desired, change the number of seconds for each slide.
7. Click **Create Video**.
8. In the Save As dialog box, navigate to the location where you want to store the video.
9. Type the name for the video.
10. Click **Save**.

Saving a Presentation to OneDrive

1. Click **File**.
2. Click **Save As**.
3. Click your **OneDrive** ☁ account.
4. Click the **Documents** folder in the right pane.
5. In the Save As dialog box, enter the file name.
6. Click **Save**.

Presenting a Slide Show Online

1. Click the **Slide Show** tab.

Start Slide Show Group

2. Click the **Present Online** button ☁.

OR

a. Click **File**.
b. Click **Share**.
c. Click the **Present Online** button ☁.

3. Read the information in the Present Online dialog box, and click **Connect**.
4. In the next Present Online dialog box, specify how you want to send the notification to attendees.
5. When you and your attendees are ready to begin the presentation, click **Start Presentation**.
6. Click **End Online Presentation** when the slide show ends.

Resizing and Positioning Online Pictures

Sizing Pictures

1. Click the picture.
2. Drag a sizing handle to resize it as desired.

OR

1. Right-click the picture.
2. On the shortcut menu, click **Format Picture**.
3. In the Format Picture task pane, click the **Size & Properties** button.
4. Click **Size**.
5. Set the height and width.

OR

1. Click the **Picture Tools Format** tab.

Size Group

2. Click the **Shape Height** ↕ and **Shape Width** ↔ increment arrows to set the size as desired.

Positioning Pictures

1. Click the picture.
2. Position the pointer on the border.
3. When the pointer changes to ⬚, drag the picture to the desired position.

OR

1. Right-click the picture.
2. On the shortcut menu, click **Format Picture**.
3. In the Format Picture task pane, click the **Size & Properties** button.
4. Click **Position**.
5. Set the horizontal and vertical positions as desired.

Formatting a Clip Art Illustration

1. Click the clip art you want to format.
2. Click the **Picture Tools Format** tab.

Adjust Group

3. Click the **Color** button 🖼.
4. From the menu, set color options as desired.

Formatting a Text Box

1. Click the outer border of the text box to select it.
2. Click the **Drawing Tools Format** tab.

Shape Styles Group

3. Click options as desired to format the text box.

Changing the Text Box Shape

1. Click the outer border of the text box to select it.
2. Click the **Drawing Tools Format** tab.

Insert Shapes Group

3. Click the **Edit Shape** button ⬚.

---

4. On the menu, click **Change Shape**.
5. From the gallery, click the desired shape.

Adding Effects to the Text Box

1. Click the outer border of the text box to select it.
2. Click the **Drawing Tools Format** tab.

Shape Styles Group

3. Click the **Shape Effects** button ☁.
4. In the gallery, point to the desired effect category and then click the desired effect.

OR

1. Right-click the text box to select it.
2. On the shortcut menu, click **Format Shape**.
3. In the Format Shape task pane, click the **Effects** icon ☁.
4. From the task pane, click the desired effect.

Drawing Shapes

1. Click the **Insert** tab.

Illustrations Group

2. Click the **Shapes** button ⬡.
3. From the gallery, click the desired shape.
4. Drag on the slide to draw the shape.

Moving and Sizing Shapes

Moving Shapes

1. Click the shape.
2. Position the pointer on the shape's border.
3. When the pointer changes to ⬚, drag the shape to the desired position.

OR

1. Right-click the shape.
2. On the shortcut menu, click **Format Shape**.
3. In the Format Shape task pane, click the **Size & Properties** icon 🖼.
4. Click **Position**.
5. Set the horizontal and vertical positions as desired.

Sizing Shapes

1. Click the shape.
2. Drag a sizing handle until the shape is the desired size.

OR

1. Click the shape.
2. Click the **Drawing Tools Format** tab.

   Size Group
3. Click the **Shape Height** ⬍ and **Shape Width** ⬌ increment arrows to set the size as desired.

Applying Fills and Outlines

Applying Fills

1. Click the shape.
2. Click the **Drawing Tools Format** tab.

   Shape Styles Group
3. Click the **Shape Fill** drop-down arrow ⬥.
4. From the palette, click the desired color.

Applying Outlines

1. Click the shape.
2. Click the **Drawing Tools Format** tab.

   Shape Styles Group
3. Click the **Shape Outline** drop-down arrow ⬔.
4. From the palette, click the desired outline.

OR

1. Right-click the shape.
2. On the shortcut menu, click **Format Shape**.
3. In the Format Shape task pane, click the **Fill** & **Line** icon ⬥.
4. Click **Fill** or **Line** in the task pane.
5. Under each heading, click the desired format options.

Applying Shape Effects

1. Click the shape.
2. Click the **Drawing Tools Format** tab.

   Shape Styles Group
3. Click the **Shape Effects** button ⬡.

4. In the gallery, point to the desired effect category and then click the desired effect.

OR

1. Right-click the shape to select it.
2. On the shortcut menu, click **Format Shape**.
3. In the Format Shape task pane, click the **Effects** icon ⬠.
4. From the task pane, click the desired effect.

Applying Shape Styles

1. Click the shape.
2. Click the **Drawing Tools Format** tab.

   Shape Styles Group
3. Click the Shape Styles **More** button ⬛.
4. From the gallery, click the desired style.

Adding Text to a Shape

1. Click the shape.
2. Type the text you want to add.

Rotating Text in a Shape

1. Right-click the shape.
2. On the shortcut menu, click **Format Shape**.
3. In the Format Shape task pane, click **Text Options**.
4. Click the **Textbox** icon ⬛.
5. Click the **Text direction** drop-down arrow.
6. Click the desired rotation.

Stacking Objects

1. Click the object whose stacking order you want to change.
2. Click the **Drawing Tools Format** tab.

   Arrange Group
   - Click the **Bring Forward** button ⬛ to move the object forward one layer at a time; click the **Bring Forward** drop-down arrow and click **Bring to Front** to move the object all the way to the top of the stack.

   - Click the **Send Backward** button ⬛ to move the object back one layer at a time; click the **Send Backward** drop-down arrow and click **Send to Back** to move the object all the way to the bottom of the stack.

Hiding an Object

1. Click the **Drawing Tools Format** tab.

   Arrange Group
2. Click the **Selection Pane** button ⬛.
3. Click the eye symbol � to remove an object. Click it again to redisplay the object.

Grouping Objects

1. Drag around all the objects to lasso them in a group.
2. Click the **Drawing Tools Format** tab.

   Arrange Group
3. Click the **Group** button ⬛.
4. On the menu, click **Group**.

Combining Shapes to Create a New Shape

1. Select the shapes you want to combine.
2. Click the **Drawing Tools Format** tab.

   Insert Shapes Group
3. Click the **Merge Shapes** button ⬡.
4. From the menu, select the desired merge style.

Rotating and Flipping Objects

Rotating an Object

1. Click the graphic you want to rotate.
2. Drag the rotation handle as desired.

OR

2. Click the **Drawing Tools Format** tab.

Arrange Group

3. Click the **Rotate** button
   ⬛▾ .
4. From the menu, click the desired rotation and flipping option.

Compressing Pictures

1. Click the picture you want to compress.
2. Click the **Picture Tools Format** tab.

Adjust Group

3. Click the **Compress Pictures** button ⬛ .
4. In the Compress Pictures dialog box, click the desired compression and target output options.
5. Click **OK**.

Modifying Video Appearance and Length

Cropping a Video

1. Click the video to select it.
2. Click the **VIDEO TOOLS Format** tab.

Size Group

3. Click the **Crop** button ⬛ .
4. Drag the cropping handles as desired.
5. Click the **Crop** button ⬛ again to complete the edit.

Applying Video Styles

1. Click the video to select it.
2. Click the **VIDEO TOOLS Format** tab.

Video Styles Group

3. Click the **Video Styles More** button ⬛ .
4. From the gallery, click the desired style.

Trimming a Video

1. Click the video to select it.
2. Click the **VIDEO TOOLS PLAYBACK** tab.

Editing Group

3. Click the **Trim Video** button ⬛ .
4. Drag the end point arrow to the desired end time.
5. Click **OK**.

Creating a New Theme

1. Click the **View** tab.

Master Views Group

2. Click the **Slide Master** button ⬛ .

Creating Custom Theme Colors

1. In the Background group, click the **Colors** button ⬛ .
2. From the menu, click the desired color scheme or click **Customize Colors**.
3. In the Create New Theme Colors dialog box, select the new theme colors as desired.
4. Enter a name for the new theme colors.
5. Click **Save**.

Creating Custom Theme Fonts

1. Click the **SLIDE MASTER** tab.

Background Group

2. Click the **Fonts** button ⬛ .
3. From the menu, click the desired font, or click **Customize Fonts**.
4. In the Create New Theme Fonts dialog box, select the fonts as desired.
5. Enter a name for the new theme fonts.
6. Click **Save**.

Saving a Theme

1. Click the **Design** tab.

Themes Group

2. Click the **Themes More** button ⬛ .
3. From the gallery, click **Save Current Theme**.
4. In the Save Current Theme dialog box, enter the name for the theme in the File name box.
5. Click **Save**.

Applying a Custom Theme to an Existing Presentation

1. Open a blank presentation.
2. Click the **Design** tab.

Themes Group

3. Click the **Themes More** button ⬛ .
4. From the Custom section of the gallery, click the desired theme.

Creating a New Mail Message

1. Click **Mail** in the Navigation Bar at the bottom of the Outlook window.
2. Click the **Home** tab.

New Group

3. Click the **New Email** button ✉.

OR

1. Click the **New Items** drop-down arrow.
2. On the menu, click **E-mail Message**.

Creating and Sending a Mail Message

1. In the e-mail message window, click in the **To** box and type the recipient's e-mail address.
2. If desired, click in the **Cc** box and type the e-mail address of the copied recipient.
3. Click in the **Subject** box and type the subject of the message.
4. Click in the message window and type the message text.
5. Click the **Send** button ✉.

Receiving Messages

1. Click the **Send/Receive** tab.

Send & Receive Group

2. Click the **Send/Receive All Folders** button.

OR

- Click **Send/Receive All Folders** in the Quick Access Toolbar.

Reading Mail

1. In the Folder Pane, click **Inbox**.
2. In the message list, click the message you want to read to display it in the Reading Pane.

OR

- In the message list, double-click the message you want to read to display it in a message window.

Formatting Message Text

1. In the e-mail message window, select the message text you want to format.
2. Click the **Format Text** tab.
3. Click the button or its drop-down arrow to apply the desired format. Some common formats are:

Font Group

- **Font** Calibri (Body)
- **Font Size** 11
- **Bold** B
- **Italic** I
- **Underline** U
- **Text Highlight Color**
- **Font Color** A

Paragraph Group

- **Align Left**
- **Center**
- **Align Right**
- **Justify**
- **Bullets**
- **Numbering**

Checking Spelling in a Message

1. Click the **Review** tab.

Proofing Group

2. Click the **Spelling & Grammar** button ✓.
3. In the Spelling and Grammar dialog box, click the desired option to change or ignore the word.
4. When the spelling check is complete, click **OK** in the message box.

Creating a Folder for Storing Mail

1. Click the **Folder** tab.

New Group

2. Click the **New Folder** button.
3. In the Create New Folder dialog box, type the name of the new folder.

4. Select where you want to place the folder.
5. Click **OK**.

Printing an E-mail Message

1. Select the message you want to print.
2. Click **File**.
3. Click **Print**.
4. In Backstage view, set the print options as desired.
5. Click the **Print** button 🖨.

Replying to Mail

1. Select the message to which you want to reply.
2. Click the **Home** tab.

Respond Group

3. Click the **Reply** button.

OR

- Click the **Reply All** button.

4. Type your reply.
5. Click the **Send** button ✉.

Forwarding a Message

1. Select the message you want to forward.
2. Click the **Home** tab.

Respond Group

3. Click the **Forward** button.
4. In the message window, enter the e-mail address in the To and Cc boxes of the recipient to which you want to forward the message.
5. Type a message if desired.
6. Click the **Send** button ✉.

Working with Attachments

Attaching a File to a Message

1. Compose the e-mail message.
2. Click the **Message** tab.

OR

Click the **Insert** tab.

Include Group

3. Click the **Attach File** button 📎.
4. In the Insert File dialog box, navigate to the location where the file is stored.

5. Click the file and then click **Insert**.

Opening an E-mail Attachment

1. Display the message in the Reading Pane.
2. Double-click the attached file in the message header to open the file in its native program.

Previewing an Attachment

1. Display the message in the Reading Pane.
2. Click the attached file in the message header to display its contents in the Reading Pane.

Saving an Attachment

1. Display the message in the Reading pane.
2. Click the attached file in the message header that you want to save.

   Actions Group

3. Click the **Save All Attachments** button 🖫.
4. In the Save All Attachments dialog box, verify the file to save.
5. Click **OK**.
6. In the Save Attachment dialog box, navigate to the location where you want to save the file.
7. Enter a file name and set the file type, if desired.
8. Click **Save**.

Managing Messages

Deleting a Message

1. Right-click the message you want to delete.
2. Click **Delete**.

OR

1. Click the **Home** tab.

   Delete Group

2. Click the **Delete** button ✕.

Moving a Message

1. In the message list of the mail window, select the message you want to move.
2. Drag the message to the desired folder in the Folder Pane.

OR

1. Click the **Home** tab.

   Move Group

2. Click the **Move** button 🖿.
3. From the menu, click the desired folder.

Copying a Message

1. In the message list of the mail window, select the message you want to copy.
2. Hold down **Ctrl** and drag the message to the desired folder in the Folder Pane.

OR

1. Click the **Home** tab.

   Move Group

2. Click the **Move** button 🖿.
3. From the menu, click **Copy to Folder**.
4. In the Copy Items dialog box, click the folder to which you want to copy the message.
5. Click **OK**.

Flagging a Message for Follow-up

1. Select the message to flag.
2. Click the **Home** tab.

   Tags Group

3. Click the **Follow Up** button ⚑.
4. From the menu, click the desired follow-up deadline.

Adding an Entry to the Address Book

1. Click the **Home** tab.

   New Group

2. Click the **New Items** drop-down arrow 🖃.
3. On the menu, click **Contact**.
4. Complete the contact form as desired.
5. Click the **Save & Close** button 🗗.

OR

1. Click the **Home** tab.

   Find Group

2. Click the **Address Book** button 🖳.
3. In the Address Book dialog box, click **File**.
4. Click **New Entry**.

5. In the New Entry dialog box, click **New Contact**.
6. Click **OK**.
7. Complete the contact form.
8. Click the **Save & Close** button 🗗.

Entering an E-mail Address Using the Address Book

1. Create a new e-mail message.
2. Click the **To** button ⌨.
3. In the Select Names dialog box, click the recipient's address.
4. Click **To**.
5. Click **OK**.

Searching Mail

1. In the Folder Pane, click the folder you want to search.
2. In the Search text box at the top of the message list, type the text for which you want to search.
3. Press **Enter**.

Creating a Distribution List

1. Click the **Home** tab.

   Find Group

2. Click the **Address Book** button 🖳.
3. In the Address Book dialog box, click **File**.
4. Click **New Entry**.
5. In the New Entry dialog box, click **New Contact Group**.
6. Click **OK**.
7. In the Contact Group window, click in the **Name** box and type the name for the contact group.
8. Click the **Contact Group** tab.

   Members Group

9. Click the **Add Members** button 🖳.
10. Click the resource from which you will add members.
11. In the Select Members dialog box, double-click member names.
12. When you have selected all the members, click **OK**.
13. Click the **Save & Close** button 🗗.

Viewing a Web Page in a Browser

1. Click the Windows button on the taskbar ▦.
2. Click the **Microsoft Edge** tile.
3. Click in the **Search or enter Web address** box and type the Web page address.
4. Press **Enter**.

OR

1. Click the Windows button on the taskbar ▦.
2. Type the Web page address in the Search the web or Windows box.
3. Press **Enter** or click the page name in the results list.

Going to a Different Web Page

1. Click in the Edge Address bar.
2. Type the Web page address.
3. Press **Enter**.

Navigating Web Pages

- Click the **Back** button ← to return to the previously viewed page.
- Click the **Forward** button → to go to the page you were on when you clicked the Back button.

Using a Web Site's Navigation Bar

1. Locate the navigation bar, typically located at the top of the Web page or along the left side.
2. Click a link within the navigation bar to go to that Web page.
3. Click the **Home** link within the navigation bar to return to the Web site's home page.

Finding Specific Information on a Web Site

- Use the Web site's navigation bar to go to pages with more specific information.
- Click in the site's Search box and type the keyword(s) for which you are searching.
- Press **Ctrl+F**, type the text you want to find, and then press **Enter**.

Refreshing a Web Page

- Click the **Refresh** button ↻.

OR

1. Right-click the page's tab.
2. On the shortcut menu, click **Refresh all tabs**.

Opening a New Tab

1. Click the **New tab** button +.
2. Click in the **Address bar** and type the address of the Web page you want to open.

Closing a Tab

- Click the **Close** button × on the tab of the page you want to close.

Copying Data from a Web Page

Copying Text
1. Display the Web page.
2. Select the text you want to copy.
3. Press **Ctrl+C**.
4. Click in the file where you want to paste the copied text.
5. Press **Ctrl+V**.

Copying Graphics
1. Display the Web page.
2. Right-click the graphic you want to copy.
3. On the shortcut menu, click **Copy**.
4. Click in the file where you want to paste the graphic.
5. Press **Ctrl+V**.

Printing a Web Page

1. Display the Web page.
2. Press **Ctrl+P**.
3. In the Print dialog box, select the printing options as desired.
4. Click **Print**.

Showing History of Recently Visited Web Sites

1. In Edge, click the **Hub** button ≡ on the toolbar.
2. In the Hub task pane, click the **History** button ⟳ to display the History pane.

Navigating to a Recently Visited Site
1. Click the desired time frame in the History pane to list the sites visited during that time.
2. Click a site to list the Web pages visited at that site.
3. Click a page to display it.

Deleting an Item on the History List
1. Right-click the item you want to delete.
2. On the shortcut menu, click **Delete**.

Clearing the History List
1. In the History pane, click **Clear all history**.
2. Select the checkbox next to the items you want to clear.
3. Click **Clear**.

Using a Search Engine

1. In the Address bar, type the address for the desired search engine and press **Enter**.
2. In the Search box, type the subject for which you are searching and press **Enter**.
3. In the list of Web sites that meet the search criteria, click the site you want to visit.

Working with Search Tools

Using Keywords

- In the Search box, type as specific a keyword as possible to help focus the search.

Using Quotation Marks

- In the Search box, type the search string enclosed in quotation marks to return only those pages with an exact match.

Using Boolean Operators

- Use the AND operator to find pages that include more than one search term; for example, type **dogs AND terriers** to find pages that contain both "dogs" and "terriers."
- Use the OR operator to find pages that include one search term or another; for example, type dogs OR terriers to find pages that contain either of the terms.
- Use the NOT operator to find pages that contain one search term but exclude other terms; for example, type **Harvard NOT University** to find pages that contain the word "Harvard," but not the word "University."

Using Wildcard Characters

- Use the asterisk (*) wildcard character to substitute for any number of characters.
- Use the question mark (?) wildcard character to substitute for a single character.

Using Natural Language

- In the search box, type a question or phrase describing what you are searching for; for example, type **conducting effective Internet searches** to return pages that contain information on the topic.

Using Subject Directories

- In the Address bar, type the address of the subject directory you want to search. If you do not know the Web address, use a search engine to find a subject directory.

Adding a Site to Favorites in Microsoft Edge

1. Display the desired Web page in Edge.
2. Click the **Add to favorites or reading list** button ☆.
3. Click the **Favorites** button ☆, if necessary.
4. In the Name box, enter a name for the favorite.
5. If desired, click the **Save in** drop-down arrow and select a folder in which to store the site address.
6. Click **Add**.

Using Favorites

1. In Edge, click the **Hub** button ≡ on the toolbar.
2. In the Hub task pane, click the **Favorites** button ☆ to display the Favorites pane.

Downloading a File from the Internet

1. Display the Web page from which you want to download the file.
2. Click the file to download and then click the page's **Download** button
   - ✓ You may see a message box asking you to accept a service agreement concerning the download.
3. Proceed through the installation steps.

Viewing Downloaded Files

1. In Edge, click the **Hub** button ☰ on the toolbar.
2. In the Hub task pane, click the **Downloads** button ↓ to display the Downloads pane.

Display Microsoft Edge Settings

1. In Edge, click the **More** button ⋯ at the right end of the toolbar.
2. Click **Settings**.
3. Edit the settings as desired.

Controlling Pop-ups

Turning Off Pop-up Blocker

1. In Edge, click the **More** button ⋯ at the right end of the toolbar.
2. Click **Settings**.
3. Click **View advanced settings**.
4. Click the left side of the Block pop-ups toggle.

Turning On Pop-up Blocker

1. In Edge, click the **More** button ⋯ at the right end of the toolbar.
2. Click **Settings**.
3. Click **View advanced settings**.
4. Click the right side of the Block pop-ups toggle.

Resolving Page Not Found Errors

- Refresh the page.
- Check for errors in the URL and/or retype the URL in the Address bar.
- If applicable, move up one directory level at a time in the URL until you connect to a page.
- If available, click a link that redirects you to the site's Home page and use the site's Search feature to find the desired page.

Keyboarding Essentials

appendix B

LEARNING TO KEY CORRECTLY

The human body is not designed for long sessions of repetitive movement. You might even know someone who has strained their hands and fingers by playing video games. Keyboarding can present similar dangers. When you key, you repeat many small movements with your hands and fingers. You might be keying for a long time. If you position yourself correctly, however, and use ergonomic tools and techniques, you can avoid strain and fatigue.

Even if you do not practice healthy, ergonomic keying techniques, you might not experience any problems while you are young and flexible. However, over the years, if you don't begin to key correctly, you will repeat thousands of stressful movements. You risk painful long-lasting injury that can reduce the quality of your life and your ability to work. It pays to develop healthy, ergonomic keying habits now.

ADJUSTING YOUR WORKSTATION

In a classroom you do not usually have much choice in the equipment you must use. However, flexible equipment and a little imagination can help you adjust your workstation.

Adjusting Your Keyboard and Mouse You want your fingers to gently curve over the keys while your wrist is in a flat, neutral position.

- If wrist rests are available, place one in front of the keyboard as a guide. Never rest your arms, hands, or wrists while you are keying.
- Place your mouse or trackball at the same height as your keyboard, in easy reach of your preferred hand.

Adjusting the Slope of Your Keyboard If your keyboard slants toward you, you need to adjust it so it is flat or slopes down away from you.

- Flatten the kickstand at the back of the keyboard.
- Alternatively, raise the front of the keyboard about ¾" by using door wedges, a wood strip, or a box.

Adjusting the Lighting It is important to arrange lighting so you can clearly see the images on your monitor without any glare.

- Position your monitor at an angle to windows and bright lights, so reflections do not wash out the monitor image.
- Keep task lighting focused on your desk to illuminate reading and writing material, but use indirect light to illuminate your monitor.
- Adjust the monitor brightness based on the available light.

Figure B-1 At the beginning of each class, adjust your workstation.

TECHNIQUE TIP

Never rest your arms, hands, or wrists on anything while you are keying.

CORRECT KEYING POSTURE

After you have adjusted your workstation, you need to maintain the correct keying posture. Following are some guidelines for keying correctly:

- Center your body on the J key, about a hand's length from the keyboard and directly in front of the monitor.
- Hold your head straight over your shoulders, without straining forward or backward.
- Position the monitor at eye level, about arm's length away, so you look down about 10 degrees.
- Elongate and relax your neck.
- Keep your shoulders down.
- Tilt your keyboard slightly down toward the monitor. This helps you keep your wrists neutral and your fingers relaxed and curled.
- Adjust your chair and keyboard so your elbows bend at right angles.
- Keep your arms close to your sides, but free to move slightly.
- Keep your wrists relaxed and straight in a "neutral" position.
- Keep your back upright or tilted slightly forward from the hips. Keep the slight natural curve of your lower back. Use a cushion or adjust the chair to support your lower back.
- Keep your knees slightly lower than your hips.
- Adjust your chair so your feet are well supported. Use a footrest, if needed.

AVOIDING STRESS WHEN KEYING

There are two ways to avoid stress when keying. First, you need to maintain the correct keying posture as you key. Second, you need to take a short break every 20 to 30 minutes and perform stretching exercises designed to help you avoid strain, fatigue, and injury.

Maintaining a Correct Keying Position It's easy to start keying by using the correct keying position. As we key, however, many of us lose our focus, and bad habits begin to creep in. It's important to check your keying position to make sure you are still keying correctly. The following figures show some guidelines for maintaining correct keying positions.

Figure B-2 (Left) Maintain a correct upright posture. (Right) Avoid slouching, extending your elbows, or bending your wrists.

Figure B-3 (Left) Maintain a neutral position with your hands. (Right) Avoid twisting your hands inward or outward.

Figure B-4 (Left) Maintain a neutral wrist position with gently curled fingers. (Right) Avoid bending your wrists or using an upward-sloping keyboard.

Stretching and Resting   When you key for a long time, your muscles stiffen. You become fatigued and risk injury. You build tension in many parts of your body, including your neck, arms, and wrists. To relieve the tension and reduce the threat of injury, you should stretch before you start keying. You should also take short breaks from keying every 20 to 30 minutes and stretch.

Stretch 1: Neck Stretch

Sitting tall, bring your chin toward your chest, stretching the back of your neck. Slowly repeat two times. See Figure B-5.

Figure B-5 Neck stretch.

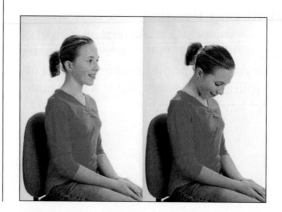

Stretch 2: Head Turn

Begin with your head in a neutral position. Look all the way to the right without moving your chest or upper back. Then, look to the left. Slowly repeat two times. See Figure B-6.

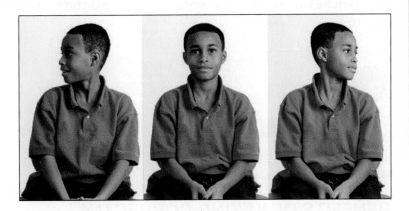

Figure B-6 Head turn.

Stretch 3: Head Tilt

Begin with your head in a neutral position. Bring your ear toward your shoulder without turning your head or lifting your shoulder. Hold for a count of five. Reverse directions. See Figure B-7.

Figure B-7 Head tilt.

Stretch 4: Downward Wrist Stretch

With your left fingers pointing down and your palm in, place your right hand over your left knuckles. Extend your arms straight out. Gently press back with your right hand to a count of ten. Reverse hands. Repeat the stretches using a fist. See Figure B-8.

Figure B-8 Downward wrist stretch.

Stretch 5: Upward Wrist Stretch

With your left fingers pointing up, place your right hand over your left palm. Extend your arms straight out. Gently press back with your right hand to a count of ten. Reverse hands. Repeat the stretches with fingers pointing down and the palm out. See Figure B-9.

Figure B-9 Upward wrist stretch.

BENEFITS OF KEYING CORRECTLY

Training takes effort and time. If you already use a keyboard, you might have to re-teach your body to use correct techniques. You might ask yourself "Why make the effort? I'm already keying fast enough."

Just imagine you will probably be using a computer for the rest of your life. If you don't learn now, you will probably need to learn later. There's really no escaping it. Besides, if you learn to key correctly, you will:

- Increase your speed.
- Increase your efficiency, making fewer errors.
- Increase your effectiveness because you can see your work and screen while your hands are free to work.
- Stay healthy, avoid injury, and remain productive over your lifetime.

BREAKING BAD HABITS

Many of you might have been keying for years. However, without any formal training, you could easily have developed bad habits.

The best way to correct bad habits is to use natural breaks as checkpoints. For instance, look at your own habits at the end of each exercise, paragraph, or page you type. Consider your posture, sitting position, hand position, keying technique, and work habits.

To help you break your bad habits, consult the following "Bad Habits Checklist." Check it when you start keying and when you take a break. If you know you have a particular bad habit, try to focus on the correction at the beginning of every keying session. Eventually the bad habit will be replaced by the good habit. It takes work, but it's worth it.

Bad Habit	Correction
Slouching	Sit up straight with your feet flat and well supported.
Reaching too far for the keyboard or the mouse	Sit one hand's length from the keyboard. Keep elbows at right angles.
Leaning your hand on the keyboard or the wrist support	Hover your hands over the keyboard; curl your fingers slightly.
Bending your wrists forward, back, left, or right	Keep your forearms and wrists straight and in the neutral position.
Pounding the keys	Strike keys lightly.
Looking at the keyboard	Position the workstand close to the monitor at eye level. Keep your eyes on your work.
Raising your elbows	Keep your arms close to your body.
Raising your shoulders	Keep your shoulders relaxed, with your chest open and wide.
Keying with the wrong fingers	Practice with correct fingers until you establish the right habit. Your speed will then improve.

Figure B-10 Many of us have developed bad habits that we need to break.

Learn the Home Keys

LEARN AND PRACTICE

Begin keying by placing your fingers on the eight keys—called the *home keys*— 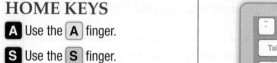 and semicolon as shown below.

HOME KEYS

A Use the **A** finger.

S Use the **S** finger.

D Use the **D** finger.

F Use the **F** finger.

J Use the **J** finger.

K Use the **K** finger.

L Use the **L** finger.

Use the finger.

The semicolon (;) is typically used between two independent clauses in a sentence. In a sentence, key one space after a semicolon.

KEYBOARDING TIP

On only the semicolon is colored. This is because the key is used for two different characters. In this lesson, you learn how to key the semicolon. In a later lesson you will learn how to key a colon.

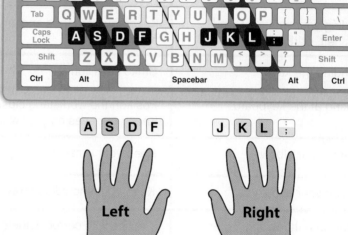

The index finger of your left hand should rest on **F**, your second and third fingers rest on **D** and **S**, and the little finger of your left hand rests on **A**. For your right hand, your index finger should rest on **J**, your second and third fingers rest on **K** and **L**, and your little finger rests on .

From now on, the finger you use to press a key will be named for its home-key letter. For example, your left little finger is the **A** finger Your right index finger is the **J** finger.

From the home keys, you can reach all the other keys on the keyboard. The keyboard diagram shows which homekey finger is used for each key. For example, you use the **D** finger to key all the keys in the band of green on the left. You use the **L** finger to key all the keys in the band of red on the right, and so on. When any finger is not actually pressing a key, you should keep it resting lightly on its home key.

The row of keys containing the home keys is called the *home row*. The row below the home row is the *first row*. The row above the home row is the *third row*.

Use the thumb of your writing hand.

Enter Use the ⟨;⟩ finger.

Learn and Practice the Spacebar   Notice that on the keyboard diagram, the keys you have learned are darker and tinted with their background color. Now locate the Spacebar on the diagram. You use the Spacebar to insert spaces between letters and words. You press it by using the thumb of your writing hand (that is, the hand you use for writing). You do not use the thumb of your other hand.

Key the home-key letters, inserting a space after each letter by pressing the Spacebar quickly and lightly. (Drill lines are numbered. Do not key the green numbers.)

```
1 a s d f j k l ;
```

Learn and Practice Enter   You do not have to wait for a text line to be "full" before starting a new line. Pressing the Enter key starts a new line of text whenever you need one. You press Enter by using the ⟨;⟩ finger. Try to keep the ⟨J⟩ finger on its home key when you press Enter.

Now press Enter (↵) to start a new line. Key each of the lines below twice. Press Enter (↵) after each line.

```
2 asdf jkl; asdf jkl; asdf jkl;↵
3 ;lkj fdsa ;lkj fdsa ;lkj fdsa↵
4 fd jk sa l; fds jkl dsa kl;↵
5 dfsa l;kj ddss kkll ffaa ;;jj fjdk ls;a↵
```

Learn and Practice Double-Space   You can add a blank line between lines of text by pressing Enter twice. This is how you *double-space* text. (Two consecutive Enters are sometimes referred to as a double line-space.)

Key a line of text, press Enter, and then key it again. After you key a line the second time, press Enter twice before keying a new line. Using this method, key each line twice, and double-space after each pair of lines.

```
6 adfs jlk; aj sk dl f; aaa jjj sd kl ldsk↵
7 fjjf dkkd slsl da l; ks fj ;f sss lll dl↵
8 kkd dlk ds ddd ;f ff ;; fdl; sl f; ds kl↵
9 a as dad sad fads lads lass falls flasks↵
```

TECHNIQUE TIP

Begin with your fingers curled and lightly touching the home keys.

TECHNIQUE TIP

Make sure your back is straight or tilted slightly forward from the hips.

Review the Home Keys

REVIEW

The keyboard shows the keys you have learned so far. This lesson focuses on the keys highlighted in dark blue.

WARM UP

Key each line twice. Double-space after each pair of lines (remember, that means pressing Enter after you key the line the first time and pressing Enter twice after you key the line the second time).

```
1 asdf jkl; asdf jkl; asdf jk l; as df jkl↵
2 ;lkj fdsa ;lkj fdsa a;sl dkfj fdjk sa l;↵
3 fk dk sl a; fds jkl asd ;lkj k fd asf lj↵
4 sdl fdk kls ad; jfd salk klas dsf; flks;↵
```

TECHNIQUE TIP

Concentrate on pressing the correct keys. Read silently letter-by-letter as you key. In this Warm Up do not focus on your speed.

BREAKING BAD HABITS

Do not hammer your fingers on the keyboard. Strike keys with a light tap.

PRACTICE

Key each line twice. Double-space after each pair of lines.

Left-Hand Focus

```
5 fdsa asdf ff dd ss aa fd sa ds af asf fd↵
6 asdf df df sd sd as as fa af das fad saa↵
7 fads df as dfaa ddfs fada dada fafa sasa↵
```

Right-Hand Focus

```
8 jkl; ;lkj jj kk ll ;; jk l; kl j; jk; jk↵
9 jkl; l; l; kl kl jk jk ;j j; ;lk ;lk kjj↵
10 jlkj l; jk jll lkjj kkjl klk jkkl; kllj;↵
```

Home Keys

```
11 asdf jkl; fjdk l;sa fjk jfd dkl kds; all↵
12 jk df dk jf sl a; fjd kds; akl kdsl dkll↵
13 adkl dajk kads lfds; ljds jfds lks; jdlk↵
14 as a dad; all lads; all fads; as a lass;↵
15 lads; dads; as sad; lass; as all; a fad;↵
```

Learn **E** and **H**

WARM UP

Key each line twice. Double-space after each pair of lines. Do not look at the keyboard when you are keying.

```
1  a dd aaa as asd sdf j jj jjj jk jkl jkl; ⏎
2  as ads ask; lass dada jask fads dads sad⏎
3  lads dada daff; jajs ja salad dads; saks⏎
4  jakk jall; jadd dajs ladd saddl aja had; ⏎
```

LEARN

Reach your **D** finger up and slightly left when you key **E**. Keep your **A** and **S** fingers anchored on their home keys. Reach your **J** finger directly left to key **H**. Keep the other right-hand fingers anchored on their home keys.

PRACTICE

Key each line twice. Double-space after each pair of lines.

Practice e
```
5  d e d ddd eee de ede eed lee eel del eel
6  eee ddd lll eel led eee dell lee led lee
7  eee ddd elk elf sell eee ddd see lee fee
```

Practice h
```
8  j h jjj hhh jh hj jhj hjh jjj hhh jj hhh
9  aaa hhh ash sss ash hh ss aa has sa sash
10 ha had aha has heel she hee half hah has
```

Practice e and h
```
11 he he eh eh hhh eee she he eh she eh hee
12 hhh eee easel feed seed heed lead she he
13 jade desks head sake head lead seal jade
14 has heed; lad had; heel hale; seek sale;
```

NEW KEYS

E Use the **D** finger.

H Use the **J** finger.

KEYBOARDING TIP

Press Enter at the end of every line unless you are told specifically to use word-wrap. From this point on, the Enter symbol (⏎) is not shown.

Learn R and I

WARM UP

Key each line twice. Double-space after each pair of lines. Concentrate on pressing the correct key each time.

```
1  ff fff ddd fd df jj jkj lkj fjk fdjk hhj
2  fed fej fek dek dell jade dale fake keel
3  lease lash lake ladle leak led leek feel
4  flea fled sea seal sell sleek shake heel
```

NEW KEYS

R Use the **F** finger.

I Use the **K** finger.

LEARN

Reach your **F** finger up and slightly left when you key **R**. Keep the other left-hand fingers anchored on their home keys. Reach your **K** finger up and slightly left to key **I**. Keep the other right-hand fingers anchored on their home keys.

PRACTICE

Key each line twice. Double-space after each pair of lines.

Practice r

```
5  fff frf frf fff rfr rffr fff rrr fff rrr
6  ra are far raf dare reef fear free freed
7  red jar lard reel dark darker hares rare
```

Practice i

```
8  k kk iii kik kkk ikki iki kk ii kkk kiki
9  ii ll jj kij sill jik ilk fill dill kids
10 if is silk kid hid kill ilk kiss hi hide
```

Practice r and i

```
11 ri ire ride sir rife fire dire sire rise
12 if ride hire hare hers rides fries dries
13 lair fair hair raid rid dill drill frill
14 riff sheared shire sear fire liars fried
```

TECHNIQUE TIP

Adjust your chair and keyboard so your elbows bend at right angles.

Review E H R and I

REVIEW

The keyboard shows the keys you have learned so far. This lesson focuses on the keys highlighted in dark blue.

WARM UP

Key each line twice. Double-space after each pair of lines.

```
1  all ale ad else sled sell sale lass less
2  sheer shear share ail air rile lair fair
3  hash flea his head lead lease deals dash
4  here hares hire hair jars jeer rear dear
```

PRACTICE

Key each line twice. Double-space after each pair of lines.

Practice e and h

```
5  ddd dde ded dde eed ed deeds sea eel see
6  hhh hjh jhj jjj jjh hh ja had he has she
7  had shed he she jade lake head ease heed
8  deed heed seed heal seal fed easel lease
```

Practice r and i

```
9  rrr ffr frf rfr re are red her fair here
10 iii iki kik kki if ire dire kid lie like
11 rise iris frail rail err dear dire fires
12 sire fire liar lair rail hail jail riser
```

Practice e h r and i

```
13 heir hare hair heard hire here rare rear
14 lairs said share shire red her idea dare
15 jeers; sir fir hear; fare hare hair lair
16 sear shared; liars rails hired fired ire
17 hailed fresher fished rides herds shades
```

Learn **T** and **O**

WARM UP

Key each line twice. Double-space after each pair of lines. Keep your fingers anchored on the home keys.

```
1  f ff fff fir fire fir fire fff ff fff ff
2  l ll lll lad lade lad lade lll ll lll ll
3  fall fell fill earl leaf field fife life
4  hall hall lire dire rare rash dash flash
```

NEW KEYS

T Use the **F** finger.

O Use the **L** finger.

LEARN

Reach your **F** finger up and right to key **T**. Keep your **A**, **S**, and **D** fingers anchored on their home keys. Reach your **L** finger up and slightly left to key **O**. Keep the other fingers of your right hand anchored on their home keys.

BREAKING BAD HABITS

Do not rest your hands or arms on any support. Keep your hands over the keyboard as you key.

PRACTICE

Key each line twice. Double-space after each pair of lines.

Practice t

```
5  f ff ttt ftf tft fftt the that this tree
6  this tall tree; tear it; lift the tires;
7  at all; third three first; at tea three;
```

Practice o

```
8   o ll o oo lol olo old lot soak sold told
9   ode doe rot dot lot lost slot joke joker
10  oars are solid; oats look food; a lot of
```

Practice o and t

```
11  ff tt trt ll oo lo ol ooo of to too toto
12  foot fool tools loot took jots lots soot
13  hoot; odes to; store; lots of lost tools
14  hold those; if told; he dotes; too short
```

Learn G and N

WARM UP

Key each line twice. Double-space after each pair of lines. Keep your wrists and fingers relaxed.

```
1 f ff fff fit file fail fir fr ftr ftt tf
2 j jj jjj jar jail has hill jhj jj hhj jj
3 feel foil life half heal this that those
4 joke hers rake fast haste hoist lash lid
```

LEARN

Reach your **F** finger directly right to key **G**. Keep the other fingers of your left hand anchored on their home keys. Reach your **J** finger down and left to key **N**. Keep the other fingers of your right hand anchored on their home keys.

PRACTICE

Key each line twice. Double-space after each pair of lines.

Practice g

```
5 g gg ggg fgf fgtg tgf go gal got get lag
6 sag sage stag stage gas rag egg edge leg
7 dog ledge keg grog get tiger grade grail
```

Practice n

```
8 n nn nnn jnj jnhn hnjn no on in kin none
9 rind seen lane train lane lean nine lion
10 tan ten ton tin tones none nasal tinnier
```

Practice n and g

```
11 ff gg gg jj nn nn gn ng ing ing nag ring
12 nag anger gnarl range longer green grind
13 ring grand glean grin gone gentle ginger
14 tangle dangle strange slings and strings
```

NEW KEYS
G Use the **F** finger.
N Use the **J** finger.

TECHNIQUE TIP
When keying, hold your head straight, without tilting it forward or backward.

Learn Left **Shift** and **.**

WARM UP

Key each line twice. Double-space after each pair of lines. Keep your fingers curved.

```
1  a aa aaa j jj jjj; a aa aaa j kk lll jkl
2  l ll lll lag lags land doll dill toil in
3  all lie like kite kin of ode or ore idea
4  lashes slides knell soil sails rill roil
```

NEW KEYS

 Use the **A** finger.

Use Left Shift for right-hand capital letters (and for all other shifted right-hand characters).

. Use the **L** finger.

A period is used in abbreviations and to mark the end of a sentence. Typically, one space follows a period.

LEARN

Reach your **A** finger down and left to press the Left **Shift** key. With Left **Shift** pressed, you can strike any right-hand key. Then, release Left **Shift**. Reach your **L** finger down and slightly right to key **.** . Keep your **J** finger on its home key.

BREAKING BAD HABITS

Do not slouch. Sit up straight with your feet flat and supported.

PRACTICE

Key each line twice. Double-space after each pair of lines.

Practice Left Shift

```
5  jJ Jj Jd kK Kk Kf lL Ll Ls JdJ fKKf sLLs
6  hH Hj Ha aHHa; Jill Hill Lee; Hall Iris;
7  Hi there Hello; Here he is; Leo the lion
```

Practice Period

```
8  a. l. s. k. d. j. f. e. r. t. i. o. n. a
9  adj. alt. art. e.g. gal. i.e. inf. sing.
10 in. ft. kil. gr. lit. orig. transl. del.
```

Practice Left Shift and Period

```
11 Kan. La. OH OK HI N.H. N.J. Jos. I. Kant
12 Long. Lat. N.H.L. Joe and Jed; King Lear
13 I see. I said. I sit. I sat. I do. I do.
14 Ode to Leo. Oh. His is. No. One. Listen.
```

Review Left [Shift] [T] [O] [G] [N] and [.>]

REVIEW

The keyboard shows the keys you have learned so far. This lesson focuses on the keys highlighted in dark blue.

WARM UP

Key each line twice. Double-space after each pair of lines. Concentrate on pressing the correct key each time.

```
1  t to to tot toe not note got gotten tote
2  jJ kK lL hH iI oO. Joke; Kids like Jake.
3  Joanne is terse. Nora nods. Kane is kin.
4  Kirk tends to the garden. Lana looks on.
```

PRACTICE

Key each line once. Double-space after each group of lines.

Practice t and o
```
5  ttt ooo fff lll to too toot tot toe tote
6  to tone toner foot oat lot jot rote goat
7  toast knots trots lost stones toes ghost
```

Practice g and n
```
8  ggg nnn ggg nnn no go; gone; genes; sign
9  long longer longest longing song singing
10 no nod node; note done; gig agog; gotten
```

Practice Left Shift and Period
```
11 JKL; IO. KNOLL. Jr. Kg. Lg. Kg. Jds. Hd.
12 Kin are kind. Logan Hotel. Otis loiters.
13 L. L. H. H. K. K. J. J. I. I. I. Hi. No.
```

Practice t o g n Left Shift and Period
```
14 to go to. Nine tons. No one going. Ogden
15 green gnarl great gross gnats grain gilt
16 N.J.L. L.J.K. J.I.N.; Old Ohio. Old Hat.
```

TECHNIQUE TIP

Center your body on [J], about a hand's length from the keyboard, directly in front of your monitor.

Learn **C** and **U**

WARM UP

Key each line twice. Double-space after each pair of lines. Strike the keys with a light tap.

```
1 d dd ddd sad sat dot dog done dotes adds
2 j jj jjj Jill Join hill her his hat hits
3 Lili held on. Jade is green. Jess holds.
4 does he dial one or three; drifted east;
```

NEW KEYS

C Use the **D** finger.
U Use the **J** finger.

LEARN

Reach down and slightly right with your **D** finger to key **C**. Keep the **A** and **S** fingers anchored on their home keys. Reach up and slightly left with your **J** finger to key **U**. Keep the **K**, **L**, and **;** fingers anchored on their home keys.

PRACTICE

TECHNIQUE TIP

Hold your head up and relax your neck.

Key each line twice. Double-space after each pair of lines.

Practice c

```
5 d dd c cc dc dc dcd cad cat cater decade
6 lacks class clicks coins; Nick can cook.
7 lace cask flock shock Jack likes cheese.
```

Practice u

```
8 j jj u uu ju ju juj ujuj us use sue uses
9 due hue hurt huge urge; He is Uncle Kurt.
10 Used lutes and flutes; noun run nuts hut
```

Practice c and u

```
11 cur cue cut cud curt cute cuff cure curd
12 cull could cough couch accuse occur ouch
13 curls cushion curious cluck scour ruckus
14 such clubs culture course cruel function
```

Learn W and Right Shift

WARM UP

Key each line twice. Double-space after each pair of lines. Keep your arms close to your sides but free to move.

1 s ss sss sash ski skits sour sell sister
2 so; does; sun; stars; sass; losses; dust
3 Hugh shares his fish. He leads us south.
4 sack; cast; usage; soccer; lesson; sense

LEARN

Reach up and slightly left with your S finger to key W. Keep your F and D fingers anchored on their home keys. Reach your ; finger down and right to press the Right 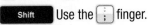 key. (Keep your J and K fingers anchored on their home keys.) With Right Shift pressed, you can strike any left-hand key. Then, release Right Shift.

PRACTICE

Key each line twice. Double-space after each pair of lines.

Practice w
5 s w ss ww sss ws sws wsw sss www sws wsw
6 saw awe dew draw jaw law wall well wills
7 sag wad owe we wan wall week wear wealth

Practice Right Shift
8 S; St; SA; W.A.G. F Fa Go Ta Da Ed We Fr
9 Fast Far Face Dad Dash Deal Sad Sash Add
10 AHA; Cold Drinks; Fine Sand; Grills Fish

Practice w and Right Shift
11 The Fresh Air Fund; The Far East; C.O.D.
12 WAAF Go slowly. Walt thinks; Tess walks;
13 Glow Aware Flaw Waist Rower Ewe Chew Few
14 Raw Flow Worn Waif Grown Stew Stow Worth

NEW KEYS

W Use the S finger.

Shift Use the ; finger.

Use Right Shift for left-hand capital letters (and for all other shifted left-hand characters).

TECHNIQUE TIP

Remember to use the Right Shift key for left-hand capital letters and the Left Shift key for right-hand capital letters.

Learn ⊠ and ⊠

WARM UP

Key each line twice. Double-space after each pair of lines. Keep your wrists relaxed.

```
1  s ss sss w ww www sw wsw sw saw sew swat
2  j jj u uu jiujitsu Julio jingle just jaw
3  Chris Wes Wendi sacks socks clock roasts
4  as is was SST Sid idle snack snake straw
```

NEW KEYS

⊠ Use the ⓈＳ finger.

⊠ Use the Ⓙ finger.

LEARN

Reach down and slightly right with your Ⓢ finger to key ⊠. As you make the reach, keep your Ⓕ finger anchored on its home key. Reach down and slightly right with your Ⓙ finger to key ⊠. Keep your Ⓚ, Ⓛ, and ⨟ fingers anchored on their home keys.

TECHNIQUE TIP

Keep your shoulders down.

PRACTICE

Key each line twice. Double-space after each pair of lines.

Practice x

```
5  s ss x xx sx xsx xs xss S X XSX six axis
6  ax axe axel ox oxen fox flex sax sox FAX
7  Rex hoax nix next index annex Saxons XXI
```

Practice m

```
8  j jj jm mj jmmj mmjm mm mmm JM MJ me mom
9  Milk makes more might. gamma mailman mum
10 mammoth makes mole mire magma Mark merge
```

Practice x and m

```
11 wax tax lax gum gem exam remix minx coax
12 mold mile mere more magic marred maximum
13 Tom Mix; Max; Mr. Maxwell; Ms. M. Maxine
14 maxim mixture axiom Manx matrix exclaims
```

Review C U W X M and Right Shift

REVIEW

The keyboard shows the keys you have learned so far. This lesson focuses on the keys highlighted in dark blue.

WARM UP

Key each line twice. Double-space after each pair of lines.

```
1  Dd Ss Cc Jj Uu Ww Xx Mm cue cruel tuxedo
2  sugar smudge mail male malls urges under
3  Ursa Essex Tom mow met metric metal axle
4  Caitlin wash wish wells waxes masc. fem.
```

PRACTICE

Key each line twice. Double-space after each pair of lines.

Practice c and u

```
5  muck duck duct tuck luck lucid cull cuss
6  cute could crush crust touch truck scull
7  deuce stuck stack sticks success custard
```

Practice w and Right Shift

```
8   William Washi Wen Winslow Woodrow Wilson
9   Wolfgang Winona Wade Wheeler Wilma Wendi
10  Willow Wallace Wanda Ward Wes Walt Willa
```

Practice x and m

```
11  mix Mexican maximum maximal Maddox moxie
12  mixer Alex examined axmen taxman Maxwell
13  mass exits extremes exhumes sixth summer
```

Practice c u w Right Shift x and m

```
14  Cellist Cancels a Concert. Felix meowed.
15  Dexter Wexler Chuck chum chew chow exits
16  Sammie worries that few hear much music.
```

TECHNIQUE TIP

Key by using the correct reach; other fingers should remain in their home positions.

Learn B and Y

WARM UP

Key each line twice. Double-space after each pair of lines. Do not look at the keyboard.

```
1  if elf fast fill fun effort effect faded
2  end hen den jail Julie hale hinge jogger
3  gas sash fish half fresh joshes freshman
4  Edward jest heft cleft gash grass jagged
```

NEW KEYS

B Use the F finger.

Y Use the J finger.

LEARN

Reach your F finger down and right to key B. Keep your A finger anchored on its home key. Reach your J finger up and left to key Y. Keep the other right-hand fingers anchored on their home keys.

PRACTICE

BREAKING BAD HABITS

Do not reach far for the keyboard. Keep elbows at right angles, but free to move slightly.

Key each line twice. Double-space after each pair of lines.

Practice b

```
5  fff fbf bfb bbb fbf bbb fb bf baa be fib
6  bee bib bat bar rub dub cub club tub but
7  been bias bunt tuba stub beef bark about
8  cable rabbit cabbie ribbon rubber bubble
```

Practice y

```
9   jjj jyj yyj jjy jyj yyy jy yj yd jay hay
10  you yet yes say sty dry day aye fly away
11  joy jay jury ray rely yolk yen nosy body
12  Young York Yak yam yummy tiny teeny tidy
```

Practice b and y

```
13  Bryce buys a bulb to brighten the lobby.
14  Buddy the bulldog labors to bury a bone.
15  Brody yearns for a yacht; bye bye money.
```

Learn V and P

WARM UP

Key each line twice. Double-space after each pair of lines. Key by using the correct reach.

```
1  ff gg bb fbf fans feels Biff baffles bye
2  j; Jill; lo; hi; his; hers; their; lake;
3  good friend; forge ahead; lost messages;
4  ironclad; tea for two; title match; I.D.
```

LEARN

Reach your **F** finger down and slightly right to key **V**. Keep your **A** and **S** fingers anchored on their home keys. Reach your **;** finger up and slightly left to key **P**. Keep the other right-hand fingers anchored on their home keys.

PRACTICE

Key each line twice. Double-space after each pair of lines.

Practice v
```
5  fff fv fv vf fvv vfv vgf fvf fvv vet eve
6  vow van vat vex vote vast vase vest vary
7  ivy ever even envy eave avid alive above
```

Practice p
```
8  ;; ;p; pp; ;pp p; pp; ;p ppp pat pad ape
9  pep papa pass pond pane pick paste price
10 sap clap tape press supper paddle puddle
```

Practice v and p
```
11 pave peeve prove privy vamp VIP provider
12 vapors viper verve pivot private prevail
13 evil powers oval pools develop viewpoint
14 vampire approve overlap overpaid popover
```

NEW KEYS

V Use the **F** finger.

P Use the **;** finger.

TECHNIQUE TIP

When using your **;** finger to reach for **P**, keep your right elbow close to your side.

Learn Q and ,

WARM UP

Key each line twice. Double-space after each pair of lines. Strike each key with the correct finger.

1 as aim aide avid aster ashes adapt adept
2 key kid king kit kiss kiln milks kippers
3 okay lanes lake like lamb Luke live long
4 all alarm call rail raffle river Alabama

NEW KEYS

Q Use the **A** finger.

, Use the **K** finger.

The comma is used to separate words and phrases for clearness.

LEARN

Reach your **A** finger up and slightly left to key **Q**. Keep your **D** and **F** fingers anchored on their home keys. Reach your **K** finger down and slightly right to key the comma **,**. Keep your **L** and **;** fingers anchored to their home keys.

PRACTICE

BREAKING BAD HABITS

Do not bend your wrists forward, back, left, or right. Keep them relaxed and straight.

Key each line twice. Double-space after each pair of lines.

Practice q

5 aa aq aqqa qqaa aqa qqa qa qua aqua quad
6 quit quay quite quick quill quilt quaint
7 equip equal squid squad quest quack Que.

Practice ,

8 k, kk, ki, jk, A, B, C, D, E, F, G, H, I
9 one, two, three, four; red, white, blue,
10 Joaquin owned a cat, a dog, and a mouse.

Practice q and ,

11 quiet, quota, quote, squat, squaw, squib
12 Raquel, quail, squirrel, sequel, conquer
13 equate, equator, Quincy, squares, squirt
14 Queen, quake, quasi, qualm, quirk, quash

Review B Y V P Q and ,

REVIEW

The keyboard shows the keys you have learned so far. This lesson focuses on the keys highlighted in dark blue.

WARM UP

Key each line twice. Double-space after each pair of lines.

```
1  fad frail Frank Alfred bug bud bush vast
2  hen Hanna vary very your young yell yelp
3  bevy; pamper; prove; pixie; posh; gladly
4  year, ache, acre, squish, piquant, quint
```

PRACTICE

Key each line twice. Double-space after each pair of lines.

Practice b and y
```
5  byte ruby abyss shabby tabby bygone days
6  bay birthday yellow belly bully boundary
7  gabby cubby abbey bubbly burly hobby buy
```

Practice v and p
```
8  vapor vapid pensive pave preview prevent
9  Vice President V.I.P. overpaid passivity
10 Pablo plays the vibraphone very happily.
```

Practice q and ,
```
11 Quite, squab, quickens, quibble, quantum
12 Queens, quits, toque, quarrels, quantity
13 Quinn squashed it quickly and then quit.
```

Practice b y v p q and ,
```
14 pay pry bypass bumpy pebbly pygmy opaque
15 brave, vinyl, brevity, behave very badly
16 Bowery Boys, Marquis, Beverly, Quasimodo
```

TECHNIQUE TIP
Make sure your back is straight or tilted slightly forward from the hips.

Learn **Z** and

WARM UP

Key each line twice. Double-space after each pair of lines. Keep your wrists relaxed and straight.

```
1  debut past perk park chances dares tries
2  flurry hurry scurry enjoy delays happens
3  salve settles vessel vassal caste create
4  Frasier will pursue a career in finance.
```

NEW KEYS

Z Use the **A** finger.

: Use Left [Shift] and the **:** finger.

The colon (:) is used in numerical expressions and to direct attention to information that follows (as in "For example:").

LEARN

Reach your **A** finger down and slightly right when you key **Z**. Keep the left-hand fingers anchored on their home keys. Keying the colon is like keying a capital letter. Hold down the Left [Shift] key and strike **:**. Then, release Left [Shift].

SPACING TIP

In a sentence, you use one space after a colon.

PRACTICE

Key each line twice. Double-space after each pair of lines.

Practice z

```
5  a az aza zza zaz aqza za azq zza zap zoo
6  zoom zest zeal Zen zinc zone cozy zipper
7  Zuni fizz fuzz zigzag zebra zero pizzazz
8  zip quiz lazy mezzo muzzle zenith frozen
```

Practice :

```
9  ; ;: :: ;: :; ::: Sirs: Ext: As follows:
10 Memo To: From: Date: Subj: RE: CC: ATTN:
11 To Whom It May Concern: Dear Madam: Ref:
```

Practice z and :

```
12 Dear Elizabeth: To: Mrs. Dezanne Ziegler
13 Puzzle answer: ZIP Code: Zone: Size: NZ:
14 Zoe: Zora: Oz: Ziggy: Ezra: Zelda: Buzz:
```

Learn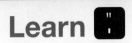

WARM UP

Key each line twice. Double-space after each pair of lines. Keep your eyes on the page and not on the keyboard.

```
1 fizz fuzz dizzy gaze buzzer prized gizmo
2 Abbot alley fast has lasts dash flag lab
3 play; pram; pads; my pals; swamps; pique
4 Name: Address: FAX: cars, planes, trains
```

LEARN

Reach your ⬚ finger right to key an apostrophe ⬚. Keep the J, K, and L fingers anchored on their home keys. To key a quotation mark, hold down Left **Shift**, reach your ⬚ finger right, and strike ⬚.

PRACTICE

Key each line twice. Double-space after each pair of lines.

Practice '
```
5 ;' ;';' ';'; 's s' it's I'm isn't aren't
6 Jill's Dave's Omar's didn't don't aren't
7 isn't hadn't should've would've could've
```

Practice "
```
8 ;" ";"; "x" "y" "A" "B" "My Way" "Okay."
9 "Not me." "Maybe soon." "See you later."
10 "Just enough," she said. "Oh, we agree."
```

Practice ' and "
```
11 "It's Magic" "Let's Dance" "That's Life"
12 "Don't hang up." "I'll call." "I'm Sue."
13 "Malcolm's moved the boxes," Rubin said.
14 It's the book "Emma" for Mr. Hu's class.
15 "Lillie won't travel on New Year's Eve."
```

NEW KEYS

⬚ Use the ⬚ finger.

The apostrophe (') has many purposes. Use it to form contractions (don't) and possessives (John's).

⬚ Use Left **Shift** and the ⬚ finger.

Use quotation marks (" ") to enclose direct quotations, to emphasize words, and to display certain titles.

BREAKING BAD HABITS

Do not key with the wrong fingers. Practice with correct fingers until you establish the right habit.

Learn  and

WARM UP

Key each line twice. Double-space after each pair of lines. Hold your head straight, without leaning it forward or backward.

```
1  "Let's go pick apples," Sophie proposed.
2  Paul's parrot piped up, "I'm not Polly."
3  Shipped to: Paul Lopez; PS: Please RSVP.
4  Piper liked papaya; Piper's aunt didn't.
```

NEW KEYS

 Use the <key>;</key> finger.

A hyphen (-) is used for compound words. It is also used to divide words between lines, although most word-processing programs do this automatically.

 Use the <key>;</key> finger.

A diagonal (/), often called a forward slash, is used in abbreviations, in fractions, and to express alternatives or relationships.

LEARN

To key a hyphen, reach your <key>;</key> finger up and slightly right and strike . Keep the <key>J</key> finger anchored on its home keys. To key a diagonal, reach your <key>;</key> finger down and slightly right and strike . Keep the other right-hand fingers anchored on their home keys.

SPACING TIP

In normal use, do not space before or after the diagonal.

PRACTICE

Key each line twice. Double-space after each pair of lines.

Practice -

```
5  ;p; ;p-p; ;-; ;-; -er one-on-one T-shirt
6  side-by-side, after-effects, part-timers
7  toll-free, good-humored, close-captioned
```

Practice /

```
8  ;/; ;//; ;//;/ a/b I/we he/she East/West
9  true/false, owner/manager, and/or, AM/FM
10 his/her, on/off, either/or, input/output
```

Practice - and /

```
11 best-case/worst-case, high-rise/low-rise
12 left-hand/right-hand, mid-week/mid-month
13 paper-thin/see-through, ice-cold/red-hot
14 tax-exempt/tax-sheltered one-way/two-way
```

Review Z ; " - and ?/

REVIEW

The keyboard shows the keys you have learned so far. This lesson focuses on the keys highlighted in dark blue.

WARM UP

Key each line twice. Double-space after each pair of lines. Begin with your fingers curled and lightly touching the home keys.

```
 1  brazen shilly-shally sizzle crazy quartz
 2  Don's fez, Via: tilt-a-whirl willy-nilly
 3  mightn't hadn't "Don't say such things."
 4  http://www.si.edu "wall-to-wall" mi./hr.
```

PRACTICE

Key each line twice. Double-space after each pair of lines.

Practice z and :

```
 5  Price per dozen: Prize: Size: Zookeeper:
 6  Zone: Bronze medal: Tarzan: Waltz: Czar:
```

Practice ' and "

```
 7  "Neither a borrower nor a lender be." S.
 8  "Don't just say 'Don't' like that's it."
```

Practice - and /

```
 9  street-smart/quick-witted/sharp-sighted;
10  He/she must give a blow-by-blow account.
11  She provides on-site support for E-mail.
```

Practice z : ' " - and /

```
12  "door-to-door" 'self-employed' in-house:
13  log-jam low-flying "Long-Range" two-term
14  Zig Lenz: Writer/Producer; life-or-death
15  A day of dappled sea-born clouds. -Joyce
```

SPACING TIPS

Remember: Do not key a space before or after a hyphen in a hyphenated word. Do not key a space before or after a diagonal.

Lesson 22

Learn  and

WARM UP

Key each line twice. Double-space after each pair of lines. Focus on your technique, not on speed.

```
1  AR append alternate Aswan Dallas daisies
2  Q.E.D. client-server peer-to-peer hi-res
3  Pass/Fail E/G/B/D/F play-by-play on-site
4  La Paz quizzical A-OK on-again/off-again
```

NEW KEYS

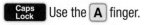 Use the **A** finger.

Use Caps Lock to key capital letters without pressing Right Shift or Left Shift.

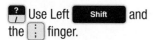 Use Left **Shift** and the finger.

Use a question mark (?) at the end of a sentence that asks a question.

LEARN

Reach your **A** finger left to press **Caps Lock**. Keep all other fingers on their home keys. (Once you press **Caps Lock**, it stays on until you press it again.) The question mark is a shifted diagonal. Press Left **Shift**, reach your finger down and slightly right and strike.

TECHNIQUE TIP

The Caps Lock key works only on letter keys. You still have to press Left Shift to key punctuation such as a question mark, a colon, or a quotation mark.

PRACTICE

Key each line twice. Double-space after each pair of lines.

Practice Caps Lock

```
5  NBA, NFL, AND NCAA ANNOUNCE RULE CHANGES
6  ASPCA FINDS LOST DOG; ROVER RETURNS HOME
7  IMAGINE: MEN WALK ON MOON; READ ABOUT IT
```

Practice ?

```
8  ;/; ;?; :?? ?:? ?;? ?/?/? Who? How? Why?
9  Me? When? Soon? What day? Are you going?
10 Can you? Would you? Could you? Call me?
```

Practice Caps Lock and ?

```
11 VISITOR FROM SPACE? AN ECONOMIC SETBACK?
12 PRESIDENT'S TRIP ON HOLD? TWO TEE TIMES?
13 VIKINGS IN THE NEW WORLD? KENNEWICK MAN?
14 MASSIVE CALCULATION ERRORS TO BLAME? US?
```

Learn

WARM UP

Key each line twice. Double-space after each pair of lines.

```
1  adamant ACADEMIA adzuki AARDVARK amalgam
2  Alabama Havana Agra Qatar Panama Jamaica
3  La Salle, La Mancha, La Plata, La Spezia
4  aquatic AQUARIUS aqueous AQUILA aqueduct
```

LEARN

Reach up and left with your A finger to key Tab . Keep the F finger on its home key. Keep your elbows close to your sides.

NEW KEYS

Tab Use the A finger.

Press Tab to align items into columns or to indent text for paragraphs. Tabs are automatically set every half-inch.

PRACTICE

Key each line twice. Press Tab where you see an arrow. Double-space after each pair of lines.

Practice Letters and Tab

```
5  aba→ bcc→ cdd→ dee→ efe→ ghh→ hii→ ijj
6  jkk→ llm→ mnn→ opo→ qrr→ stt→ uvw→ xyz
7  DMA→ UPS→ CPU→ CRT→ LCD→ IRQ→ KBD→ I/O
```

Practice Short Words and Tab

```
8  all→ ad→ cat→ cot→ dot→ lot→ rot→ not
9  be→ bit→ bat→ do→ to→ tot→ in→ the
10 if→ so→ then→ who→ call→ to→ tell→ me
11 TO→ BE→ OR→ NOT→ TO→ BE→ THAT→ IS
```

Practice Indenting with Tab

Key the following text as a paragraph. Use word wrap. To indent the paragraph, press Tab where you see the arrow.

```
12 →Qatar is an independent Arab state
13 in the Middle East, bordering the
14 Persian Gulf. It is a major exporter of
15 oil and natural gas.
```

SPACING TIP

Do not key a space before or after pressing Tab.

Review   and Tab

REVIEW

The keyboard shows the keys you have learned so far. This lesson focuses on the keys highlighted in dark blue.

WARM UP

Key each line twice. Double-space after each pair of lines.

1 A diller a dollar, a ten o'clock scholar
2 Everyone's seen a movie, no? We did not.
3 a/b/c/d/e/f/g/h/i/j/k/l/m/n/o/p/q/r/s/t/
4 Del thinks he's all that. Al thinks not.

PRACTICE

BREAKING BAD HABITS

Do not raise your elbows. Keep your arms close to your body.

Key each line twice. Double-space after each pair of lines. Where you see an arrow, press Tab.

Practice Caps Lock

5 PHASE One; PHASE Two; PHASE Three; RESET
6 MONDAYS, WEDNESDAYS, and FRIDAYS AT NINE
7 Jamal: WISHING YOU A VERY HAPPY BIRTHDAY

Practice ?

8 Who said that? Why? Where is Paul going?
9 Well, which is it? What? You don't know?
10 How are you? Yes? No? Do you? Won't you?

Practice Tab

11 eucalyptus→ hemlock→ sycamore→ larch
12 hickory→ dogwood→ chestnut→ willow

Practice Caps Lock ? and Tab

13 TO:→ FR:→ RE:→ CC:→ FAX:→ EXT:→ FL:→ DEPT:
14 VOL→ HIGH→ LOW→ DATE→ OPEN→ CHG→ YTD→ INT
15 ADRIANA, did ALEJANDRO call the station?
16 Narrator: WHO KNOWS WHICH WAY THEY FLED?

Learn the Ten Key

LEARN

If you are doing something—like a science fair project—that requires you to enter lots of numbers, you will benefit from using the ten key pad or "ten key." This is the number pad to the right of the letters on your keyboard or the ten keys on calculators and adding machines. (Most laptop computers do not have a ten key pad. Numbers are on the top row of the keyboard.) Good ten key skills may help you get your work done faster and more accurately.

Your home row is now a home key 5 in the middle of the 4 5 6 row. This key usually has a small raised line to guide you, so you don't have to look when placing your right hand lightly on the keys. Even lefties must use the right hand for the ten key, unless they have a specially designed keyboard with the number pad on the left.

You will use your index finger for 4, your middle finger for 5, and your ring finger for 6. The same arrangement goes for the 1 2 3 row below, and the 7 8 9 row above. You use your thumb for the 0 Ins on the bottom and your pinkie for the / * - and + and Enter keys.

PRACTICE

Rest your right hand lightly on 4 5 6 and + keys, with your index finger on 4, your middle finger on 5 (the home key), your ring finger on 6, and your pinkie on +.

Double-space after each line, using your pinkie on the Enter key to return:

```
1   4,5,6 and +
2   0456++65400
3   6645+455650
4   400+566+450
5   5+566465++4
```

Keyboarding Activities

DIRECTIONS: *You will build your keyboarding skill. Each group of five strokes is considered a "word" (spaces and Enter count as strokes). Your speed is measured by how many five-stroke words you can type in a minute. For example, if you type ten five-stroke "words" in a minute, your "words per minute" (abbreviated WPM) is 10. Each of the following exercises is a one-minute drill with the focus on the alphabet keys. It is important that you do these drills in sequential order since they build on one another; do not skip around.*

1. Start a word-processing program. Save the new, blank word-processing document as **KB-1_Drills_xx**. Replace *xx* with your own initials or name, as directed by your teacher, and type your name and today's date in the header.

2. Key the text in each of the following speed drills for one minute. Press Enter after each line. If you reach the end of a drill before time is up, press Enter and start over immediately from the beginning of the drill.

3. Take these speed drills for home keys:

   Drill 1 (Goal: 8 WPM)
   ```
   lads fall; as a fad
   lass adds; sad lads
   ```
   Drill 2 (Goal: 8 WPM)
   ```
   as a lass; all dads
   alas as a lad falls
   ```
   Drill 3 (Goal: 10 WPM)
   ```
   as a sad lass; add a lad
   lads fall; fads; add all
   ```

4. Take this speed drill for keys E and H (Goal: 10 WPM).
   ```
   he has a sled; she asked
   she has a sash; he sells
   ```

5. Take this speed drill for keys R and I (Goal: 11 WPM).
   ```
   she shares a fare; he is fair
   her red dress has real frills
   ```

6. Take this speed drill for keys E, H, R, and I (Goal: 12 WPM).
   ```
   he fries fish; she feels fair
   free idea; he likes fresh air
   ```

7. Take this speed drill for keys T and O (Goal: 13 WPM).
   ```
   those tools are foolish; these too
   jets dot the air; lift off so fast
   ```

8. Take this speed drill for keys G and N (Goal: 14 WPM).
   ```
   sitting in this light; long nights
   golden raisins and grains are good
   ```

9. Take this speed drill for Left Shift and Period (Goal: 14 WPM).
   ```
   Ken likes Jen. He said John is in.
   Hold on. OK. I see. No one has it.
   ```

10. Take this speed drill for keys T, O, G, N, Left Shift, and Period (Goal: 15 WPM).
    ```
    Nikki greets Lara. I told Ossie a joke.
    He kids Les. Nan is Irish. Lea led Nat.
    ```

11. Take this speed drill for keys C and U (Goal: 16 WPM).
    ```
    Julia hugs her cousin Lucie once again.
    Urge Louis to accrue one hundred coins.
    ```

12. Take this speed drill for keys W and Right Shift (Goal: 16 WPM).
    ```
    Shawn wanted to write. Rowan went west.
    Dan is a D.A. in D.C. He was a witness.
    ```

13. Take this speed drill for keys X and M (Goal: 17 WPM).

```
Mr. Marx meets Xena in March.
Tim fixes machines in Mexico.
Matt Solomon mined metal ore.
```

14. Take this speed drill for keys C, U, W, X, M, and Right Shift (Goal: 18 WPM).

```
Michi locates the crux of it.
Dr. Dux makes music on a sax.
Her hat is crushed in a rush.
```

15. Take this speed drill for keys B and Y (Goal: 18 WPM).

```
Moby brings Ben a toy rabbit.
Becky enjoyed yoga yesterday.
Rob blabbed about your story.
```

16. Take this speed drill for keys V and P (Goal: 19 WPM).

```
Vince has one pct peeve. Liv appeared very peppy.
View Venus and the moon. Buy very purple violets.
```

17. Take this speed drill for keys Q and Comma (Goal: 19 WPM).

```
Quentin quips about age. Buy quarts, not gallons.
She asks for equal time. Do not quibble with him.
```

18. Take this speed drill for keys B, Y, V, P, Q, and Comma (Goal: 20 WPM).

```
Jane bought a new Viper.
I provided yellow paper.
Pave your patio, please.
Quit playing that piano.
```

19. Take this speed drill for key Z (Goal: 21 WPM).

```
A piazza is an Italian public square.
Zika saw lots of zebras at the zoo.
Zanesville is located in Ohio.
```

---

20. Save the document. With your teacher's permission, print it, and then close it.

21. Exit your word-processing program.

22. Evaluate your speed and accuracy. Assess your posture and keyboarding technique. Did you remember to maintain your correct keyboarding posture and to keep your eyes on the copy?

Keyboarding Activities

DIRECTIONS: *You will increase your keyboarding speed. Each group of five strokes is considered a "word"(spaces and Enter count as strokes). Your speed is measured by how many five-stroke words you can type in a minute. For example, if you type ten five-stroke "words" in a minute, your "words per minute" (abbreviated WPM) is 10. Always use the correct techniques when you type. It is important that you do these drills in sequential order since they build on one another; do not skip around.*

1. Start a word-processing program, and create a blank document. Save the word-processing document as **KB-2_Drills_xx**. Type your name and today's date in the header.

2. The first three of the following drills are in pairs. For the first drill in each pair, press Enter at the end of each line. For the second drill in each pair, start with a tab and use word wrap. If you reach the end of a drill before time is up, press Enter and start over immediately from the beginning of the drill.

3. Take these speed drills using keys 4, 5, 6, and 7:
   One-Minute Drill (Goal: 12 WPM)
   ```
   You can get 4 of the 5 items.
   Wait, 5 and 6 do not match.
   ```
   One-Minute Drill (Goal: 26 WPM)
   ```
       The Moai statues on Easter Island average over fourteen feet tall.
   The builders of these stone statues thought they were sacred.
   ```

4. Take these speed drills using keys 8, 9, and 0:
   One-Minute Drill (Goal: 13 WPM)
   ```
   I let 9 kids make 8 tents at camp.
   Jo hit 80 of 90 balls in the game.
   ```
   One-Minute Drill (Goal: 27 WPM)
   ```
       The blue pike once swam the cool waters of Lake Erie. With
   overfishing, changes in habitat, and pollution, the fish has become
   extinct.
   ```

5. Take these speed drills using keys 1, 2, and 3:
   One-Minute Drill (Goal: 14 WPM)
   ```
   There are 21 men and 3 women here.
   I found 32 rocks on my trip today.
   ```
   One-Minute Drill (Goal: 27 WPM)
   ```
       Most students do not look forward to exams. It feels great when an
   exam is over, but the best feeling of all is when you ace an exam.
   ```

6. Review the number keys. One at a time, key each sentence of the following drill as many times as you can in 30 seconds (Goal: 14 WPM for each line).
   ```
   He has 2 birds, 4 dogs, and 1 cat.
   Of the 63 hours, 20 were overtime.
   All 8 students had 50 or 75 cents.
   It is 85 or 90 degrees in the sun.
   ```

7. Key the following paragraph for 2 minutes. Start with a tab, and use word wrap. If you reach the end before time is up, start again from the beginning (Goal: 27 WPM).
   ```
       Of all the people in the public eye, think of someone who you feel
   is a good role model for you and your friends. It might be someone in
   the arts, in sports, or even in your town. It might be someone you
   know. List things about this person that makes him or her special.
   ```

8. Save the document. With your teacher's permission, print it, and then close it.

9. Exit your word-processing program.

10. Evaluate your speed and accuracy. Assess your posture and keyboarding technique. Did you maintain your correct keyboarding posture and to keep your eyes on the copy?

DIRECTIONS: *You will improve your keyboarding skill. Each group of five strokes is considered a "word"(spaces and Enter count as strokes). Your speed is measured by how many five-stroke words you can type in a minute. For example, if you type ten five-stroke "words" in a minute, your "words per minute" (abbreviated WPM) is 10. Always use the correct techniques when you type. This activity consists of 30-second, 60-second, and 2-minute drills.*

1. Start a word-processing program, and create a blank document. Save the word-processing document as **KB-3_Drills_*xx***. Type your name and today's date in the header.

2. For each of the following drills, key each paragraph for the specified amount of time. Start each paragraph with a tab and use word wrap. If you reach the end of a drill before time is up, press Enter and start over immediately from the beginning of the drill.

3. Take these 30-second drills (Goal: 35 WPM for each sentence):

A river is a natural stream of water that empties into an ocean, lake, or other river. A delta is a landmass that forms at the mouth of a river by layers of sand and gravel.

4. Take these 60-second drills (Goal: 35 WPM for each paragraph):

A reef is a ridge of sand, coral, or rock lying at or near the surface of the water. Coral reefs are found in tropical climates. They are made of the remains of sea animals.

Sally had to change a flat tire. She had never done it before, but had seen other people do it. She found the spare tire and the tools, and made the switch in twenty minutes.

5. Take this 2-minute drill (Goal: 35 WPM):

Jerry always wanted to write a mystery novel. He had all the details in his head before he even sat down to start writing. He knew the names of all the people in the story. He had the plot worked out. He knew how it would start and end. When he began writing on his laptop, the words flowed like water. Before long, he was ready to write the sequel.

6. Save the document. With your teacher's permission, print it, and then close it.

7. Exit your word-processing program.

8. Evaluate your speed and accuracy. Assess your posture and keyboarding technique. Did you remember to maintain your correct keyboarding posture and to keep your eyes on the copy?

Web Page Development and Computer Programming

Web Design and Programming Logic Have Value

Even if you don't plan to pursue a career in Web development or computer programming, understanding the logic and processes that go into designing effective Web sites and building functioning programs can help you succeed. These skills rely on problem solving, attention to detail, and analysis, all of which are useful in any career you choose. In this appendix, you will explore the requirements for using HTML to create a Web page with both a text editor and a graphical user interface (GUI) editor. You will also learn some of the basic processes for designing a computer program.

Chapter Outline

 Lesson C–1

Web Page Development

 Lesson C–2

Computer Programming

Web Page Development

Objectives

- Compare and contrast HTML text editors with GUI editors.
- Demonstrate the ability to design, create, and revise a Web site.

As You Read

Organize Information   Use a main idea/detail chart to help you identify details about Web Page Development as you read.

🔑 Key Terms

- attributes
- Cascading Style Sheets (CSS)
- end tag
- Graphical User Interface (GUI)
- singletons
- start tag
- style sheet
- syntax

Designing and Developing for the Web

An effective Web site not only looks good, but also conveys a message and is easy to use. A successful Web developer uses the principles of design, color theory, and organization to communicate useful information quickly and efficiently. Knowing how to use the available Web development tools will help you plan, design, create, publish, and maintain a successful Web site.

Hypertext Markup Language

Recall that Hypertext Markup Language (HTML) is the most common language used to define how a Web page should look. A markup language requires marks, called tags, to provide the instructions for formatting the page and the page content. You can type them manually using an HTML text editor such as Notepad, or you can use an authoring tool which writes the HTML code automatically. Other common markup languages include Extensible Hypertext Markup Language (XHTML), which is HTML in XML syntax, and Dynamic Hypertext Markup Language (DHTML), which is a combination of HTML and other technologies used to add interactivity and animation to Web pages.

Tags

Tags are words or abbreviations enclosed in angle brackets (< >). There are strict rules, called **syntax,** that control how you enter tags. If you follow the rules, your page will look the way you want. You use most tags in pairs to surround the content you want to format. The **start tag,** or open tag, is placed at the beginning, and the **end tag,** or close tag, is placed at the end. The end tag must have a slash (/) between the tag name and the left bracket. HTML5 requires tags to be entered in all lowercase, so, the HTML5 start tag for applying bold formatting is <bold>, and the end tag is </bold>.

Singletons Some tags are called **singletons** because they do not work in pairs, generally because they do not surround anything. For example, tags used to insert something like an image, video, or horizontal line only require one tag. For singletons, the syntax has a slash between the tag name and the right angle bracket. So, the tag for inserting a horizontal line is <hr/>.

Attributes Some tags have **attributes,** which you combine with values to provide additional information about how you want the page to look. For example, you might want to use a width or height attribute with the tag for inserting an image to control the size of the image, or a color attribute to set the font color. The syntax for an attribute is the attribute name, followed by an equals sign (=), followed by the value enclosed in quotation marks. So, the start tag for changing the font color to red is <font color="red">.

Required Tags There are a few required tags for all HTML documents. These include the following:
- <!doctype html> This singleton is the document type declaration for HTML5, and must be the first tag entered. It tells the browsers that the document is an HTML5 file.
- <html> The HTML tag surrounds everything else in the document.
- <head> The head tag surrounds the tags that describe the characteristics of the page, such as the character set used and the title.
- <body> The body tag surrounds the rest of the Web page content.

Figure C.1.1 HTML tags organize and define Web page content.

Start Tag	EndTag	Result
<title>	</title>	Identifies a title
<h1>	</h1>	Identifies a top level heading
<h2>	</h2>	Identifies a second level heading
<p>	</p>	Identifies a paragraph
<b>	</b>	Applies bold
<i>	</i>	Applies italic
<ol>	</ol>	Identifies a numbered list
<ul>	</ul>	Identifies a bulleted list
<li>	</li>	Places a number or bullet at the start of a line in a list
<img src="name">		Inserts the image file identified by the src attribute "name" value (src stands for source)
<a href="name">	</a>	Inserts a hyperlink to the location identified by the href attribute "name" value (href stands for hyperlink reference)
<table>	</table>	Identifies a table
<table border="n">		Sets the width of a border around table cells to the value "n"
<table width="n">		Sets the width of a table, in pixels, to the value "n"

Cascading Style Sheets

Originally, HTML was developed to define the organization of content on a Web page, not format it. In HTML 3.2, formatting tags such as <font> </font> were added. Although formatting tags made it possible to add color and other formatting to a Web page, it also made writing HTML more time-consuming. In HTML 4 and 5, **Cascading Style Sheets (CSS)** are used for all HTML formatting. A **style sheet** is a separate document that describes the styles, or rules, that define how the elements look on the page. CSS are called *cascading* because they describe a hierarchy of style rules. Rules with a higher priority will be applied over rules with a lower priority. This insures that the formatting will be consistent. Because the CSS is stored in a separate file, you can attach it to more than one page. You can also change it and have the change affect all pages attached to it.

The syntax for a CSS rule is a little more complex than an HTML tag. It includes a selector, which identifies the HTML element you are going to format, and a declaration block enclosed in curly braces, which specifies the formatting. The declaration block can include one or more declarations, separated with semicolons. Each declaration includes a property name, such as color, a colon, and a value, such as red. It is a good idea to put each declaration in a block on a separate line just to make it easier to read. The CSS rule for formatting a heading with bold and blue is:

```
h1 {
    color: blue;
        font-weight: bold;
            }
```

Using a GUI Authoring Tool

Although you can type HTML tags, it is much easier to use a **Graphical User Interface (GUI)** authoring tool or editor. Adobe Dreamweaver is a popular HTML GUI authoring tool. There are also many that are available free for downloading or for use on Web hosting sites. Also called a "What You See is What You Get" (WYSIWYG) authoring tool or editor, these programs let you enter text and content as if you are working in a word-processing document. The program automatically writes the HTML code to create the Web page. Most GUI editors today include both a text editor for entering the text and tags, if you want, and a WYSIWG, or visual, editor, which lets you drag-and-drop objects to build the site.

GUI authoring tools include features to make it easy for you to create and publish a Web page, or even a Web site. Most come with built-in templates that include page and text formatting as well as placeholders for graphics and other elements. Some templates even include navigational elements. You can use a template to quickly create a professional-looking Web page, and you can edit the template to suit your own needs. Most GUI authoring tools also let you create your own Web page template and save it to use to create consistent pages.

Other features include spell check, automatic line numbering, Web page preview so you can see how your page would look in a browser, support for CSS, and automatic publishing so you can upload your Web page files to your Web server. They may integrate an FTP client so you can upload the files using FTP.

Navigation

A single Web page might look nice, but the purpose of the Web is to enable browsing from one page to another. To accomplish this, you use hyperlinks that let a visitor navigate to a different location on the same page, to a different page within the site, and to a page at an external site. A Web site's navigation scheme should be logical, simple, and consistent so visitors can find what they need quickly and easily.

Two of the most effective navigation schemes are simply highlighting text and graphic hyperlinks so they are easily identified, and using a navigation bar, which presents a series of links across the top or along the side of the page. For both, using descriptive text or images to identify links is important, so visitors know where the link will take them. With HTML you use the anchor tag, <a> </a>, to surround the text or insert image tag you want to use as the link. You add the href attribute to the anchor start tag to identify the destination that will display when the visitor clicks the link. (href stands for hyperlink reference.) So, this code will result in the word HOME that links to a site's home page: <a href=http://www.sitehomepage.com>HOME</a>.

Computer Programming

Objectives

- Explain basic programming logic structures.
- Demonstrate the ability to use a high-level programming language.

As You Read

Organize Information   Use an outline to help you organize details about computer programming as you read.

Introduction to Computer Programming

A computer program is the software instructions, or **source code,** that tells a computer what to do. Some programs stand on their own, like a calculator or contact list. Others are part of a larger system, such as one that imports records into a database, or plays a video in a Web browser.

Computer programming means writing **algorithms,** which are the specific steps the computer must follow in order to solve a problem or complete a specific task. The steps must be exact, so the computer can follow them over and over and always get the desired result. They must also take into consideration all possibilities that might occur, and still allow the computer to get the desired result.

The algorithms must be written in a language the computer can understand, and that means following the rules, or syntax, required by that language. There are many, many computer programming languages available. Most programming languages used today are **high-level programming languages,** which means they are not dependent on a particular type of computer. They often use natural language, or English elements, that are more intuitive and easier to understand and use.

Compiled vs. Interpreted Languages

A compiled language uses source code that cannot be executed by a computer until it has been translated by a compiler program into **binary** form. Binary code uses only two possible values: 0 and 1. The result, called **object code,** can be read and acted on by a computer. C++ is a compiled language.

 **Key Terms**

- algorithms
- binary
- bytecode
- decision
- high-level programming languages
- iteration
- loop
- object code
- pseudocode
- sequence
- source code
- variable

An interpreted language does not need a compiler program to translate the code. Instead, it uses a program called an interpreter to translate the source code directly into actions. Perl, Python, and HTML are interpreted languages.

Some languages, such as Java, are compiled into bytecode. **Bytecode** is an object code that can be processed by a virtual machine program instead of by a computer's processor, enabling it to be used on any computer platform. That is why Java programs can be transmitted across a network and run on any computer that has the Java Virtual Machine program installed.

Programming Variables

In computer programming, a **variable** is a symbol or name that stands for a value. They are important because programmers can write code using variables, which are replaced by real data when the program is executed. This lets the same program be executed multiple times, using different data.

Variables have a name and a data type. Some common data types include string, which is a sequence of characters that does not contain numbers used for calculations; numeric, which is numbers or amounts that are used in calculations; character, which is text; integers, which represent whole numbers; and date, which is the method of coding dates.

Basic Logic Structures

The three basic logic structures in computer programming are **sequence, decision,** and **loop.** The sequence is the order of operations. The decision, which may also be called the selection or branch, is the choice made at the end of each step. The loop is a repeated action that occurs until the desired result is achieved.

Each occurrence of a loop is called an **iteration.** In computer programming, iteration statements are used to repeat code using different variables. The code uses a variable to set a condition, and then instructs the computer to start a sequence, check for a certain condition, and, based on the condition, either start another iteration or exit the loop. Some common iteration statements include:

- for   The for loop is a control statement that is usually used when there is a finite, or limited, number of iterations you want. For example, a for loop might be used in a customer database to total outstanding payments. The program would instruct the computer to start with the outstanding payment for customer record 1, add the outstanding payment for customer record 2, and so on. After the last customer record, the program exits the loop.

- while   A while loop causes the program to repeat the code if a particular condition is true. If the condition is false, the program exits the loop. If the condition is false at the beginning of the loop, the loop is never executed.

- do-while   A do-while loop is similar to a while loop except that the condition is not checked until the end of the first iteration, so the sequence is always executed at least once.

The Software Development Process

Every computer program solves a problem, usually by turning input into output. There are seven basic steps in the software development process:

1. Identify the problem.

2. Identify the solution. This includes identifying the criteria for achieving a successful solution as well as any constraints or limitations.

3. Design and document an algorithm showing all of the steps required to solve the problem.

4. Code the program.

5. Test the program.

6. Debug the program.

7. Repeat steps 1 through 6 until the problem is solved.

Career Corner

Software Engineer/Programmer/Coder Although some people use these terms interchangeably, software engineer, programmer, and coder are very different occupations. A software engineer is often a manager who also writes code. He or she has in-depth knowledge of the product, and has the skills to work with customers and users, write documentation, and provide training and support. A programmer's primary responsibility is to design and write code. He or she is also very familiar with the product, can develop test data for testing and debugging the program, and can discuss and explain the code to others. A coder is simply anyone who can write code that compiles and runs.

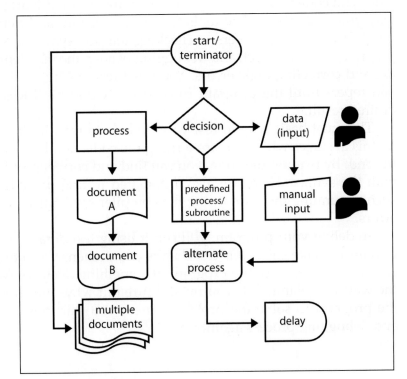

Figure C.2.1 A flowchart is one way to document a program algorithm.

If you are working for someone else, documenting the output, input, and logic for a program will help you define and understand the scope of the project. In addition, your employers will be able to review the information and approve it.

Think About It!

Which of the following are reasons why an employer might want to review the output, input, and logic for a program?

➤ so she can write the code herself

➤ so she knows exactly what you are going to do

➤ so she can check to make sure the program is what she wants

Program Design

In order to design a computer program, you need to know and document the following:

- What will the output of the program be? This involves analyzing the problem to determine everything that the user will see while using the program, such as screens, fields, buttons, and even printed reports. You will create lists of these items and even draw or create samples.

- What data is needed to produce that output? This also involves analyzing the problem to determine everything that the user will enter while using the program, such as information typed in a field. Again, you will create lists and samples.

- How will the computer process the input in order to produce the output? This is the logic you will use to write your code to produce the desired result, and you can document it using algorithms in the form of flowcharts or **pseudocode.** Pseudocode lets you write logic using specific words instead of flowcharts. It relies on structural conventions used when coding software, but since it doesn't have to be executed by a computer, it omits details such as variable declarations. It simply spells out how the program is going to work in a language that is easier to understand than code or a flowchart. You may also use a storyboard to model the program flow and functionality.

Testing and Debugging

After you code your program, you must make sure it works the way you designed it. The tools for this are testing and debugging. Testing usually refers to checking that the syntax in your program code is correct, and debugging usually means identifying and correcting logic errors. You must test, debug, evaluate, and repeat until the program runs correctly and produces the desired result.

The most basic way to test your code is to read it. You can do this at stages while you are writing the code, or all at once at the end. By reading the code, you can find and correct problems with the syntax. There are also automated testing procedures, such as running the code through a compiler to identify syntax errors.

To debug your program, you run it using test data. It is important to make sure your test data is comprehensive so that it will test every part of the program. If something does not work the way you planned it, you must figure out why, and modify the program to solve the problem. Then, you start the testing and debugging process again.

⬤ Think Critically

Directions: *Answer the following questions.*

1. Compare and contrast HTML text editors with GUI editors.

2. Describe iterative programming structures, such as for, do, and do-while, and explain how they are used in programming.

3. Explain the types and uses of variables in programming.

4. Compare and contrast programming languages that are compiled with programming languages that are interpreted. Explain why Java does not fit in either category.

⬤ Extend Your Knowledge

Directions: *Choose and complete one of the following projects.*

A. Use an HTML text editor to create a Web page using basic HTML tags. Include the required tags as well as tags for elements such as lists and tables. Use formatting tags to apply character styles and text alignment. Insert at least one image and a link to an external Web site. Test your Web page, and make corrections as necessary so that it looks the way you want in a browser. Share your page with a partner or the class, and discuss the process of writing HTML.

B. Use a GUI authoring tool to create a Web site based on a template. Modify the template as necessary to achieve an effective look and feel for your site. Use the principles of design and color theory to make the Web pages attractive, engaging, and efficient. Create a well-organized navigation scheme so visitors will be able to find the information they need. Create hyperlinks using text and images. Publish the site using FTP. Present your site to a partner or to the class, explaining why you chose the colors, design, and navigation structure.

C. Design and create an effective Web page template that demonstrates an understanding of color theory and the color wheel, and allows for the integration of audio, animation, and video on the page. Use the template in a GUI editor to create a Web site with attractive, engaging, and efficient Web pages that include audio, video, and animation. Use Dynamic HTML (DHTML) to enhance the interactivity of at least one Web page in the site. Publish the Web site. Present your site to a partner or the class.

Extend Your Knowledge

D. Plan, design, and create a program using a high-level programming language. Start by identifying the problem your program will solve and the steps you will take to achieve the solution. As part of the design process, use pseudocode that uses structured programming to document the program flow you are going to use to solve the problem. Check the logic in your pseudocode, and correct it as necessary. When you are ready, convert the pseudocode into the programming language. Analyze and test the code to identify and troubleshoot errors, and then use debugging procedures to make the changes necessary to insure the program will run correctly and produce the desired result. Demonstrate your program to a partner or to the class.

E. Use a high-level programming language to create an interactive program such as a video game or interactive video based on telling a story. Plan to create and integrate animated objects in the program. Start by identifying the problem your program will solve. Use the design process to determine the steps you will take to solve the problem, as well as the criteria and constraints you will face. Create storyboards to model the program flow and functionality. When you are ready, write the appropriate code. Test and evaluate the program, and modify it as needed to insure the program will run correctly and produce the desired result. Demonstrate your program to a partner or to the class.

Glossary

Numerals

@ in an e-mail address, a symbol used to separate the user name from the name of the computer on which the user's mailbox is stored (for example, frodo@bagend.org); pronounced "at"

10 baseT an Ethernet local area network capable of transmitting 10 megabits of data per second through twisted-pair cabling

3-D graphics adapter a video adapter that can display images that provide the illusion of depth as well as height and width

3-D reference a reference to a cell or range on a specific worksheet in a 3-D spreadsheet

3-D rendering transforming graphic images by adding shading and light sources so that they appear to be three-dimensional

3-D Secure a security protocol for online transactions

3-D spreadsheet a spreadsheet that uses multiple worksheets in the same file

3-D video accelerator a computer card that helps display graphics quickly

40-bit encryption a minimal level of encryption supplied with most Web browsers

A

absolute reference the method of copying or moving a formula that keeps its cell references exactly as they are

acceptable use policy (AUP) a policy—published by a school district, business, or other organization—that identifies rules of behavior that must be followed by anyone using that organization's telecommunications equipment, computers, network, or Internet connection

access time the amount of time required for a disk drive's read/write head to locate data on the surface of a disk

activate authorize legal use of a software program

active cell the current, or selected, cell in use in a spreadsheet application

add-on code designed specifically to add a feature to a Web browser, modify a Web page, or integrate your browser with other services

algorithm a sequence of instructions that result in a predictable outcome, or solve a specific problem

alert box a dialog box that warns users that an action cannot be completed or will result in an error

alias an informal name by which an e-mail user is known

Align the tool in a draw program that determines how images will be placed in relation to one another

alignment the placement of text and objects so they line up within a space

All-in-One printer a printer that combines printing, scanning, copying, and faxing capabilities

alt newsgroup a newsgroup formed to discuss very specific topics

American Standard Code for Information Interchange (ASCII) a system that uses eight-bit codes to represent 256 characters

analog a type of system that sends electrical signals that match the human voice and other sounds

animation the process of showing many images in rapid sequence to make them appear as if they are in motion

anonymity the state of being unknown, or out of the public spotlight

antimalware program a program that protects computers from malware

antivirus program a program that protects computers from viruses

applet a small application with limited features and functions

application software a program or group of programs designed to perform specific tasks, such as create documents, store information, or edit videos

application workspace the large area of a program's window that displays the content currently in use

apps third-party software programs developed specifically for smart phones, tablet computers and some PCs

archival storage a storage device for information that is not frequently used

argument the data that a function will use

ascending order the sorting of data by increasing value

aspect ratio the relative proportion of an image's height and width

asynchronous training Web-based training without a live instructor

attachment a file sent with an e-mail message

attributes properties or characteristics that can be set to different values

augmented reality an emerging technology in which cameras and mobile devices are used to layer virtual information on to real information

authentication the process of confirming a valid user

authentication cookie a piece of data stored by a Web site on your computer to allow you to log in to a secure Web site using a secure account

authoring tool a program that includes tools for creating multimedia programs

AutoContent wizard in some applications, a series of dialog boxes that helps the user create a new presentation

Autocorrect a feature that fixes common spelling mistakes as they are typed

AutoFill a spreadsheet command that automatically enters related, sequential data (such as the days of the week) into a connected set of cells

Autosave the feature in an application program that saves the current file after a specified amount of time has elapsed

AutoShapes a list of ready-to-use shapes in the Draw tool

avatar graphic icon that represents a user in the virtual reality world

B

Back button a tool that lets users reload the previously viewed page in a browser

backbone high-speed lines that carry data through a network

back up to copy or archive files for safekeeping

backup a copy or archive of a file

backup utility a program that automatically copies data from the hard drive to a backup storage location

balance the way objects are arranged in an image or on a page; symmetrically arranged objects are evenly balanced; asymmetrically arranged objects are unevenly balanced

bandwidth the amount of data that can travel through a network connection

bar-code reader a device used to scan product labels

Basic Input/Output System (BIOS) a set of programs, built into a PC's ROM chips, that controls the function of the computer's keyboard, disk drives, monitor, and several other components; the programs also help the computer start itself when the power is turned on

batch processing a way of changing a database that delays updates until a group of data is ready to process

beta version a working copy of a program from early in the development, used for testing prior to release

binary a numbering scheme in which there are only two possible values for each digit: 0 and 1

binary large object (BLOB) a database feature that allows the user to specify a data type to handle large objects

bit the smallest unit of information with values of either 0 or 1; a number that is a building block for computer languages; short for *binary digit*

bitmapped graphic an image formed by a pattern of dots; also called raster graphic

bits per second (bps) the amount of data that can be sent in one second

blended learning a method of learning by combining traditional classroom and Web-based training

blog short for "Web log," a Web page that a writer updates regularly with news or opinions

Bluetooth wireless technology that uses radio signals to allow devices to connect over short distances

Boolean algebra a form of algebra that only has two values: true and false

Boolean search a type of search that uses an operator to link keywords

boot to start a computer

bounce message a notice that e-mail could not be delivered

brand an image or identity assigned to a person or product based on how they are perceived by others

breadcrumbs links displayed in a browser window that help you keep track of what page you are viewing in a Web site or on a server by displaying the path you followed to get there

broadband the general term for all high-speed digital connections of at least 1.5 megabits per second

browse to find information in a database by looking at records one at a time; also, to move from one Web page to another while using a Web browser

browser a program that enables users to navigate the World Wide Web and locate and display Web documents

buddy list a list of people with whom a person with an instant messaging program interacts

bus topology a network design that connects the network to a single line

business-to-business (B2B) a transaction between companies

byte a group of bits combined into groups of eight or more

bytecode an object code that can be processed by a virtual machine program instead of by a computer's processor

C

cable modem a device that allows a computer to access the Internet through a cable television connection

cache memory hardware that stores program commands and data that are accessed often to save processing time

call center a central place where an organization's inbound and outbound calls are received and made

cascading style sheet a style sheet used for HTML that describe a hierarchy of style rules

cathode ray tube (CRT) a type of monitor that produces images by making phosphors glow

Cave Automatic Virtual Environment (CAVE) a virtual reality environment where images of the virtual world are projected on the walls of a real room

CD-ROM drive a read-only optical storage device

cell the box in a table or worksheet where a column and row meet; also, a geographic area to which a signal can be transmitted

cell address a unique name by which each cell on a worksheet is identified

cell reference the shorthand command that tells a spreadsheet program to use the information inside a certain cell

cell site the location of the radio tower that sends and receives radio signals for a particular cellular phone

cellular phone a mobile phone that uses radio waves to communicate

censor to ban or block

central processing unit (CPU) a piece of the computer's hardware that processes and compares data, and completes arithmetic and logical operations

certificate authority (CA) a third-party organization that validates digital signatures

channel a chat group

character set a system for coding letters and numbers

chart a graphical image, such as a pie or a set of columns, used to visually display numerical data, making it easy to understand and analyze

chat room an informal, public, real-time teleconference

circuit in electronics, a path between two or more points along which an electrical current can be carried; in telecommunications a specific path between two or more points along which signals can be carried

circuit board an insulated board on which microchips and other components are mounted or etched

circuit-switching a technology that provides an unbroken connection between two computers, enabling them to exchange data quickly; also used in telephone networks to open a dedicated line (a circuit) for a phone call and leave the circuit open for the duration of the call

citation a reference to a source that gives credit to the source and provides the tools a reader needs to locate the source on his or her own

click-and-mortar store a business that offers products online

client a workstation computer attached to a network, which is controlled by a server

client/server network a network system that uses a central server computer

clip art a graphic that has already been created for use by others

Clipboard a tool that temporarily stores cut or copied data

close tag code the code that indicates the end of a Hypertext Markup Language (HTML) instruction

cloud apps applications that are stored on cloud servers instead of on local computers

cloud computing using the Internet and central remote servers to host, or store, data and/or applications

cloud storage areas on Internet servers where data and applications can be stored and accessed

CMOS a battery-operated chip on the motherboard that stores information and settings about computer components

collaborative software application software designed to be used by a group of people working together

collision a problem in networking that occurs when two computers try to transmit data across a network at the same time, causing data packets to collide and both transmissions to fail

color an element of design that describes the way eyes see light

color depth the number of colors that can be displayed on a monitor at one time

color palette a display of options that allows the user to choose a color

command an instruction that tells a software program what action to perform

command button an icon on a toolbar or Ribbon that tells the computer to perform an action when the icon is clicked

command prompt a symbol displayed in a command line, or text-based, computer interface that indicates where to enter a command

commercial software copyrighted software that must be purchased before it can be used

compatibility the ability to share files between two different application programs or operating systems

compiler a program used to translate the source code of a computer program into binary form using only 0s and 1s

compress to reduce the size of a file

computer a machine that changes information from one form into another by performing input, processing, output, and storage

computer crime any act that violates state or federal laws involving use of a computer

computer system several different parts of a computer that perform the four basic functions of computing: input, processing, output, and storage

computer-assisted design/computer-assisted manufacturing (CAD/CAM) a method of creating a 3-D model that links 3-D design to the manufacture of that object

computer telephony integration technology that links computers to telephone systems

congestion delay caused by too much traffic on a network

contention the condition that occurs when two computers try to access a network at the same time

contrast the difference between the colors of the pixels in an image

cookie a file left on a hard drive by a Web site that the user visits

Copy to place a duplicate of a selection on the Clipboard

copy protection a physical device or software tool that keeps users from making unauthorized copies of the software

copyright the right to control use of creative, literary, or artistic work

corrupted describes a computer file that has been damaged

cracker a cybercriminal who tries to access and damage secure networks

crash to suddenly stop working

crop to trim the edges from a graphic to make it fit a space or to remove an unwanted part of the image

cross-platform a type of software or hardware capable of running the same way on more than one platform

cross-platform compatibility ability to share files across operating systems

current the flow of electricity through a wire

Cut to remove a selection from a document and place it on the Clipboard

cyberbullying to use electronic communications to threaten or harass someone

cybercrime the use of the Internet or private networks to violate state or federal laws

cylinder the same track location on the platters of a hard drive

D

data raw, or unprocessed, information

data decay the loss of information due to the gradual wearing down of a storage medium

data glove a glove equipped with sensors to measure movements of the hand and fingers

data integrity describes the availability and usability of data stored on a computer

data loss occurs when information on a storage device is damaged or made unusable

data maintenance the upkeep of a database that includes regular updates, modifications, and deletions

data mining to find valuable information by examining trends in large amounts of data

data projector a device that shows a computer's video output on a screen

data series a set of data that changes by a constant value

data source a file containing variable data used for customizing a mail merge document

data structure the way a database is organized

data transfer rate the number of bits per second at which data is transferred

data type settings applied to a database field, which allow the field to store only information of a specific type and/or format

data warehouse a large collection of data

database an organized collection of information that may or may not be stored in a computer

database management system (DBMS) a software program used to manage the storage, organization, processing, and retrieval of data in a database

decision a choice; in programming, one of the three basic logic structures, which is the choice made at the end of each step; also called the selection or branch

dead link a connection to a Web document that no longer works

decrement the number by which each value in a series decreases

default the preset options in a program

demodulation the process that changes the analog signal received by a modem to the digital signal used by a computer

denial of service attack a method used by hackers which prevents legitimate users from accessing an online service

descending order the sorting of data by decreasing value

desktop the workspace on a computer screen

desktop computer an individual's personal computer that resides on a desk or table

desktop publishing a program with expanded design options to create documents for publication

destination file the file in which you place shared or pasted data; also the file that displays when a link is clicked

device a hardware component installed for use with a computer system

device driver the software utility that allows the operating system to communicate with a device

dialog box on-screen message box for users to supply information or convey requests

digital connection a method of using computer codes to transmit voice, data, and video

digital audio tape (DAT) a storage medium that uses high-capacity magnetic tape enclosed in a cartridge

digital camera a camera that records and stores photos in a digital form that the computer can work with

digital projector a projector that displays digital information on a projection screen

digital signature a method to verify the source and content of an e-mail message or application file

digital video camera a camera that records moving images in digital form

digitize to change information of any kind into digital format

directory a hierarchical filing system

disk cache software that uses space on the hard drive to store data that is used most frequently

disk management utility a software program such as a disk scanner, disk defragmenter, or disk cleaner that helps you maintain and repair storage devices

disk operating system (DOS) an operating system that uses a keyboard to type specific commands into the computer

disk scanner a utility that checks magnetic disks for errors

Distribute the tool in a draw program that determines the distance between two objects

distribution list a list of e-mail contacts saved with a single group name so they can easily be sent the same message; also called a contact group

document camera a device that captures images and transmits them to a projector, monitor, or computer

document map an outline of a word-processing document that can be seen in a separate pane

documentation instructions on how to install a program, use the application, and troubleshoot any problems

Domain Name Server a server used to match a domain name to the correct Internet protocol (IP) address

Domain Name System (DNS) a naming system using letters as well as numbers to identify one or more computers on the Internet

domain name the phrase used to identify one or more Internet protocol (IP) addresses

download to transfer copies of files from a remote computer to a local computer by means of a modem or network

downtime a temporary stop to all work on a network

drag handle one of the eight small rectangles or circles that appears at a graphic's four corners and four edges that is used to resize the image

draw program a program used to create and edit vector images

driver utility software that contains information needed by application programs to properly operate input and output devices

duplex communication in which both sides can send and receive messages at the same time, like on a telephone call

Dynamic Hypertext Markup Language (DHTML) a programming language that adds interactivity to a Web page

E

e-commerce the use of telecommunications networks or the Internet to conduct business

electronic data interchange (EDI) a business-to-business wide area network

e-mail an electronic communication method in which messages are sent and received over the Internet

e-mail client a program, on a user's computer, that enables the user to create, send, receive, and manage e-mail messages

e-mail folder a folder used to store and organize related messages from your Inbox

e-mail server a program, on an Internet service provider's server computer, that sends, receives, and delivers e-mail messages to client computers

e-mail virus a program sent in an e-mail message to deliberately cause computer problems for the recipient

embed to copy an object into a document; both the object and the document remain independent when changes are made to either one

emerging technology new, innovative technology developed to meet a need

emphasis in graphic design, creating a visual focal point

emulator software program that allows two incompatible computers to work with each other

encoder a software program that converts a file

encryption the process of encoding data so that it cannot be used without first being decoded

end tag the code that indicates the end of a Hypertext Markup Language (HTML) instruction

End User License Agreement (EULA) a legal contract that states the terms of use for a software program

enterprise storage system technology that allows networked computers to access one or many different types of storage devices

ergonomic designed to provide comfortable use and avoid stress or injury

e-tailer a retailer that primarily uses the Web to sell goods or services

Ethernet a networking technology used for local area networks

ethics moral principles

evolving technology existing technology that is changed to be more efficient or meet a different need

exclusion operator a minus sign or the word NOT used to search for Web pages that do not contain certain words

executable file a file that carries out instructions as part of a program

expenses money you owe

expert system a complex program that uses artificial intelligence techniques to manipulate a large, detailed database

export to format data so it can be used in another program

Extensible Markup Language (XML) the code that describes the format for constructing Web queries and processing database queries

extension an additional set of up to four letters that is separated from the file name by a period and that generally identifies the type of data in the file

external a component located outside the computer case

extranet a wide area network designed to look and work like the Internet that allows for limited public access

Eyedropper a tool that picks up and works with a specific color from an image

F

fair use the use of copyrighted material in a review, in research, in schoolwork, or in a professional publication, which does not necessarily require permission from the material's owner

fax machine a device that makes a digital copy (a "facsimile") of a document, then transmits the data to another device, such as a computer modem or other fax machine

fiber-optic cable strands of pure glass that transmit digital data by pulses of light

field the part of a database that holds an individual piece of data

field name identifier for a database field

field width maximum number of characters a field can contain

file a unit or grouping of information that has been given a unique name

file compression a way of reducing file size so that large files can travel more quickly over a network or consume less disk space

file compression utility a software program that reduces the size of a file for storage or transmission purposes

file extension two or three letters following a period that indicate the application a file was created in

file format standards used to write data to a disk

file fragmentation the allocation of a file to noncontiguous sectors on a floppy disk or hard drive

file name a series of characters that gives each document in a folder a unique name

file server the main computer in a client/server system

file sharing making files available to more than one user on a network

filter to select or display items based on whether they meet or match specific criteria; also, a feature in some e-mail programs that can delete certain messages or file messages in folders

find and replace a feature that locates a word or word combination and then changes it to a different word or combination

firewall hardware or software that prevents access to a network

firmware permanent instructions stored in read-only memory (ROM) that control computer components

flame to insult online in a text message, e-mail, or other communication

flash drive a small storage device that uses flash memory and connects to the computer through a USB port; also called a pen drive, jump drive, or thumb drive

flash memory storage medium that has no moving parts and stores data in electronic cells

flat-file database a database that can work with only one file at a time

form an on-screen window for users to view, enter, and edit data

format prepare a storage medium to be used by a specific type of computer

formula a mathematical expression used to link and perform calculations on numbers in worksheet cells

Forward button a tool that lets users move ahead to previously viewed pages in a browser

frame an empty section in a document that will eventually hold text or graphics; or a section of a Web page window; also, an individual still image in an animated sequence

frame rate the number of still images displayed every second in a full-motion video or animation

frame relay a communications technology used by most permanent virtual circuits that allows voice, data, and video to travel on the same line at the same time

freeware copyrighted software given away free

full back-up to duplicate all files on a hard drive

function a commonly used formula that is built into a spreadsheet program

function key a shortcut key at the top of a keyboard that is labeled with the letter F and a number

G

garbage in, garbage out (GIGO) a phrase that stresses the importance of inputting accurate data in a database

gateway a node on a network that enables communication with other networks

global unique identifier (GUID) a unique identification number generated by hardware or by a program

grammar checker a word-processing tool that identifies problems with verb tense, sentence structure, pronouns, punctuation, and capitalization

graphic anything that can be seen on a computer's screen

graphical browser a Web navigation program that shows pictures and text

graphical user interface (GUI) a visual display that allows the user to interact with the computer by using graphical objects on the screen

graphics tablet a hardware device used for drawing

Grid an advanced graphics tool that displays a grid on-screen to assist with alignment

gridline a line extended from chart axis to body so data will be clearer; also, non-printing lines displayed on-screen to help align and format objects on a page

group to combine separate vector images into one image; also part of a Microsoft Ribbon tab that displays related tasks

groupware software that supports multiple users working on related tasks

H

hacker a computer hobbyist who tampers with systems to find mistakes and weaknesses

half-duplex communication in which both sides can send and receive messages but not at the same time, like using a walkie-talkie

handheld computer a small palm-size computer mainly used for personal assistance

handwriting-recognition software software that converts handwritten text to digital format

haptic interface a method of communicating with a computer through a device that senses body movement through touch

hard drive the most commonly used type of secondary storage device, which stores bits of data as aligned particles on the surface of a magnetic disk

hardware the physical parts of a computer

harmony a principle of design created when elements of a graphic or design come together as a complete idea

hashtag (#) a symbol (#) added to the beginning of search terms or key words in a tweet to identify related tweets, making it easier for users to follow a specific topic

head-mounted display (HMD) a helmet that wraps around the head; used for virtual reality experiences

hexadecimal value a six-digit code that uses the hexadecimal system to represent color; the first two digits represent the intensity of red, the second two represent the intensity of green, and the last two represent the intensity of blue

hibernate mode a power state in which data from RAM is saved to the hard disk and then power is shut down

hierarchy the categories in which Usenet newsgroups are organized

hierarchical multilevel

high definition television (HDTV) a type of television that produces a sharper image than regular television

high-level programming languages programming languages that are not dependent on a particular type of computer

holographic data storage system (HDSS) a future storage technology in which data is stored in images called holograms on optical cubes

home page the front page of a Web site

horizontal application a type of application software that is designed to meet the needs of many different users

hub a connection point for computers, printers, and other equipment on a network

hue the actual color as shown in the spectrum or range of colors

hyperlink a link from one document to another

hypermedia system a system of connecting resources online (via the Internet, for example) that lets users click links to access resources in different types of media, such as text, audio, or video

hypertext a type of document that is published on the World Wide Web

Hypertext Markup Language (HTML) the code that describes the format, layout, and structure of a document for publication on the World Wide Web

hypertext transfer protocol (HTTP) the protocol that governs how Web pages are transmitted across the Internet

I

icon an on-screen picture that represents an object, resource, or command

identity theft the taking of another person's identity for the purpose of committing illegal acts

if-statement a statement in an algorithm that defines conditions that must be met to move to the next step

image editor an advanced paint program that edits bitmapped images

impact printer a printer that uses keys or pins to strike an ink ribbon to create an image on paper

import to bring information into a program from another program

inclusion operator a plus sign or the word AND; used to search pages to find a match for specified words

income money you earn

increment the number by which each value in a series increases

incremental backup to copy only the data that has changed since the last full backup

information kiosk an automated system that provides information or training; usually has a touch screen to allow input

information overload the result of a computer user being overwhelmed by the amount of information generated by his or her computer

infrared light waves that cannot be seen by the human eye

infringe undermine or interfere with; also, to break the terms of a law or agreement

input raw information, or data, that is entered into a computer; also, to enter data into a computer

insertion point a mark that indicates where entered text will appear in a document

install prepare a computer to run a specific program or use a specific device, usually by copying the necessary instructions to the computer's hard drive

instant messaging (IM) the system on the Internet that allows people who are online to communicate by typing messages

integrated software a program that combines the basic features of several applications into one package

intellectual property someone's creative, literary, or artistic work

interactive multimedia a program that uses different types of media (such as text, sound, animation, and others) to convey its message, and which allows the user to choose the content that will be displayed next or direct the flow of the content

interface a means for users to control or operate the computer

internal located inside the computer case

Internet a vast network that links millions of computers around the world

Internet 2 (I2) high performance network to test new technologies

Internet client the computer and related software that requests a service on the Internet

Internet protocol (IP) address a four-part number separated by periods that identifies each computer connected to the Internet

Internet Relay Chat (IRC) an Internet service that enables the user to join chat groups

Internet service provider (ISP) a company that provides the actual link between a computer and the Internet

Internet telephony the use of the Internet to complete real-time voice communication

interpreter a program used to translate source code directly into actions

intranet a private network that uses the same protocol as the Internet

iteration repetition; in programming, each occurrence of a loop

K

key field an element that links tables in a relational database

keyboard shortcut a combination of keys that carries out a specific action

keyword in a spreadsheet function's syntax, the name of the function; also, text or a phrase used in a search

knowledge base a database of information usually related to a specific subject

L

label text or a combination of numbers and text typically used for titles or explanation in a worksheet

land a flat, reflective area on the surface of an optical disc

laptop a personal computer that is small enough to be carried around

laser sensor a laser-operated tool in an optical drive that reads information

Lasso the tool in an image editor program that selects complex or freehand shapes

launch to start an application program

layer to stack parts of a bitmapped image on top of another level

layout an on-page arrangement of text, graphics, backgrounds, images, and other design elements

Learning Management System (LMS) an application designed for education that can manage records, report grades, and deliver subject matter content

leased line a permanent connection between the mobile telephone switching office (MTSO) and the long-distance providers that will complete the call

libel false statements that might hurt someone's reputation

line an element of design used to create form and perspective and to draw shapes

link to create a connection between an object's source application (the program in which an object was created) and a destination application (a program into which the object is copied), allowing the object to be edited in either program

liquid crystal display (LCD) monitor panel that produces color by using an electric field to combine crystals of different colors

list server a program that handles e-mail messages automatically

local area network (LAN) a network in which all workstations and equipment are near each other

local loop the network that connects to the phone company's central office

lossless compression a method of reducing the size of a file so that it can be returned to its original state without losing any data

lossy compression a method of reducing the size of a file so that some data may be lost when the file is decompressed;

M

macro a set of mouse actions, keystrokes, or commands recorded for repeated use

macro virus a series of commands that is hidden in a document

Magic Wand the tool in an image editor program that selects all the touching pixels of a similar color

mailbox name a part of an e-mail address before the "at" sign

mail merge a process that inserts variable information into a standardized document to produce a personalized or customized document

mainframe a type of computer used by many people at the same time to allow access to the same secure data

maintenance release a minor revision to correct errors or add minor features to a software program

malware any type of software designed to damage or disable your computer system or data

Marquee a tool in an image editor program that highlights a simple shape

master page the pattern that sets the basic features of a document's look for all the other pages to follow

master slide a default template that is applied to all slides of a certain type

master view a view in a presentation program used to make universal style changes

maximize to make an application window as large as possible

memory specialized chips, connected to the computer's motherboard, which store data and programs as they are being used by the processor

memory shave to steal some of a computer's memory chips

menu a list of commands

menu bar the bar generally located below an application's title bar where a set of commands is listed

merge combine into one

mesh topology a network design in which all components are connected directly to other components

message header information located at the top of an e-mail that identifies the sender, other recipients, the date, and the subject

meta data information stored with a file to help identify the file

metropolitan area network (MAN) a network that covers a large area such as a university campus or a city

microwave a high-frequency radio wave

minimize to make an application window as small as possible

minimum system requirements the system components you need to run software

mobile device any portable computer, particularly smart phones, handhelds, and wearable devices.

modem a device that allows a computer to transmit data to other computers through telephone lines

modulation the process that changes the digital signal from a computer to the analog signal of a telephone

motherboard the primary circuit board to which all devices are connected and through which all data passes

multicore processors single integrated circuits with two or more CPUs

multimedia using different types of media (such as text, graphics, video, animation, or sound) at the same time

multitask to work with more than one computer application at a time

Musical Instrument Digital Interface (MIDI) an interface that connects a computer to electronic musical instruments, to control the instruments and record their output

N

navigate to move through a network or program to find resources or files

navigation button a tool that lets users perform routine operations with a browser

nest include an item such as a function or a table, within another, similar item

netiquette an informal set of rules for how to behave online

network two or more computers connected to each other to share resources

network architecture the science of designing a network

network interface card (NIC) a hardware device that physically connects a computer to a network

network layer a subset of protocols that govern how data is handled and transmitted over a network

network operating system (NOS) a set of programs that manages and secures a network

network traffic the electronic pulses of information that carry data through a network to its destination

newsgroup a discussion group in which users communicate by posting messages about a particular topic

node anything connected to a network, such as a computer, printer, or fax machine

nonimpact printer a printer that uses spray or powder to create an image on paper

normal view the view used most often

Notes Page view a view in a presentation program that you use to view and edit notes

O

object a piece of data such as an image, chart, video or sound clip, or a section of text

object code readable instructions created by compilers translating the source code into binary form

object-oriented database a database that stores objects, such as sound, video, text, and graphics

object-oriented programming a method of programming that provides rules for creating and managing objects

offsite a location remote or separate from a company's main location

Ohm's law a rule that describes how electricity will behave as it travels through circuits

online analytical processing processing used for storing current data

online banking using a Web browser to pay bills and access accounts online

online service a business that provides access to the Internet as well as to custom content, discussion groups, news, shopping services, and other information that is available only to its paying subscribers

online support Internet-based service that provides answers or other help

online transactional processing (OLTP) a way to immediately approve Internet credit-card purchases

on-screen presentation a display of slides on a computer screen

open protocol a standard that anyone can use

open source software software for which the source code is made available to the public

operating system (OS) a system that allows hardware devices to communicate with one another, run efficiently, and support software programs

operator a character, symbol, or string that represents a specific action

optical character recognition (OCR) software used by most scanners that turns text into a digital file

optical storage device a storage device that uses laser beams to read the information stored on the reflective surface of a disc

Order a tool that changes the position in which objects are stacked or layered

order of evaluation the rule that tells a spreadsheet program which operation to do first in a multiple-operation formula

organic light emitting diode (OLED) a technology used for monitors and screens that is made from sheets of organic material that glows when an electrical field is applied; OLED monitors do not require backlighting or diffusers

output the result of a computer's processing, displayed on-screen, printed on paper, or heard through a speaker

output device any piece of hardware that shows the result of computer processing

P

packet tiny segment of information transmitted over a network

packet sniffer a program that examines data streams on networks to find information such as passwords and credit-card numbers

packet-switching a method of transmitting data across a network by breaking it into tiny segments called packets

page formatting the arrangement of text on a page

pagination the automatic division of a document into pages

paint program a basic program for working with a raster or bitmapped image

pane a section of a document after the window has been split

paragraph any amount of text up to a forced new line

parse a spreadsheet feature that breaks down data into parts that will fit into the spreadsheet cells

password a word, or a string of letters and/or numbers, that is used to gain access to a computer system or network and that is usually known only to the user and an administrator

Paste to insert an item copied or cut to the Clipboard

patent the exclusive right to make, use, or sell a device or process

path the route through the filing system that leads to the specified file or folder

peer-to-peer network (P2PN) a small network that usually includes from two to ten computers but no server

pen-based graphics tablet a touchpad that uses a stylus to create images

peripheral separate input, output, and storage hardware

permanent virtual circuit (PVC) a circuit that allows multiple users' data to travel at the same time on the same line

personal digital assistant (PDA) a small, highly portable handheld computer that is used for taking notes or keeping track of appointments

personal information manager (PIM) program a program responsible for storing phone numbers and addresses and creating schedules

personal productivity program a horizontal application used to help people work more effectively

phishing a method by which cybercriminals lure users into revealing account codes and passwords by pretending to be a legitimate Web site

physical media the wires, cables, or wireless transmitters and receivers used to connect the computers in a network

pit an indented area on the reflective surface of an optical disc that scatters light from a laser

pixel a single point in a bitmapped graphic

placeholder an area within a slide layout designed to hold data, such as text or pictures

plagiarism illegal copying of creative material owned by another person

platform a kind of computer that uses a certain type of processor and operating system

platter one of a stack of metal disks that store information in the hard drive

player software a program that plays audio or video files

Plug and Play (PnP) capability of Windows-based PC operating systems to detect new, compatible devices

plug-in a program that adds new features to an application on the computer

podcast an audio or video file that is created for downloading to an iPod or an MP3 player

point of presence (POP) a local connection to a wide area network

pointer a cursor that shows your location on a computer screen

pointing device a device such as a mouse used to point to elements on a monitor

point-of-sale (POS) a type of system used at retail checkout counters (the point of sale), which scans product codes for items being purchased, verifies the items' prices, and usually updates inventory and customer information through a connection to the seller's network

Point-to-Point Protocol (PPP) a method of connecting to the Internet in which Transmission Control Protocol/Internet Protocol (TCP/IP) packets are sent from a computer to a server that puts them on the Internet

pop-up menu a list of shortcut commands that appears when an area of the screen is right-clicked or the mouse button is held down

port software that creates a connection between two computers or network devices through which data is shared; also a socket for connecting peripherals

portal an Internet service that provides an organized subject guide to Internet content, news, weather, sports, e-mail, etc.

power surge a sharp increase in power coming into the computer system

power-on self test (POST) series of tests a computer performs while booting

preference a choice for the way a program will operate

premium apps apps that cost money

presentation software a specialized software that is used to create and display visual information

primary storage memory chips that are built into a computer, such as random access memory (RAM)

print area a portion of a worksheet intended to be printed

Print Layout view the view of a word-processing document that shows how the document will appear when printed

Print Preview the feature in a program that shows how a document will look when printed

procedural programming a method of programming that uses step-by-step instructions

processing a task a computer carries out with data in response to a command

productivity suite a program that combines several programs and all of their features

product key a string of characters that certifies that a user is authorized to install a program

program the coded instructions that tell a computer what to do; also to write the code for a program

programmer an expert who writes the instructions for software

programming language a coded language used to write instructions for a computer

property a piece of data attached to or associated with a file, folder, program, or device; also called metadata

proportion the size and location of one object in relation to other objects

proprietary protocol a standard that only certain people can use

proprietary software copyrighted software that you must buy before using it; also called commercial software

protect to block accidental changes in a file or on a device

protocol standard format and rules for handling data

protocol stack a set of small protocols used to set standards for the Internet

protocol suite a collection of individual protocols that determines how a network operates

proximity in graphic design, using the closeness between objects to indicate a relationship

proximity operator a Web query that searches for words that appear close together

pseudocode a method of writing programming logic using specific words instead of flowcharts

public data network a network that allows different companies to set up their own networks

public domain software a program distributed for free without a copyright

pull-down menu a list of options

Q

quarantine disable and isolate a file thought to be infected with a virus

query a request to search a database

query language a set of characters, terms, symbols, and rules used in the construction of database queries

query-by-example (QBE) to request information from a database by providing an example

R

random access memory (RAM) special chips that store data and instructions while the computer is working

random access storage device a storage device that lets the computer go directly to the needed information

range in a spreadsheet, a group of cells that are next to each other

raster graphic an image formed by a pattern of dots; also called bitmapped graphic

reading view a view in some applications that makes it easier to read on-screen content

read/write device a storage device that allows users to access information and save it to the device

read/write head in a disk drive, the component that writes data to and reads data from the surface of a disk

read-only device a storage device that allows users to access information but not save or change it

read-only memory (ROM) chips on the motherboard that contain the instructions that start the computer and control some input and output devices

reboot restart the computer

recommended system requirements the system components you need to run the software at its best

record a part of a database that holds data about a particular individual or item

Redo a command that puts a change back in effect after it was cancelled with Undo

rehearsed presentation a slide show timing method that changes from one slide to the next according to the will of the creator so that the presentation moves at the exact desired speed

reinstall install a program or device again

relational database a database in which shared key fields link data among tables

relative reference the method of copying or moving a formula that changes the values in the formula depending on its new location

remote resource information and components available via a network

repetition when color, shape, or pattern is repeated throughout a graphic

repetitive strain injury (RSI) nerve damage in the hand caused by continued use of a keyboard or mouse

replicate to copy

report an ordered list of selected database records and fields in an easy-to-read format

report template a pattern that controls how data will be displayed in a database report

resistance a condition caused by anything that obstructs or inhibits current

resolution for a raster image, the number of pixels in a certain section of the image; for a monitor, the number of pixels that are displayed on the screen at any given time, used as a measure of sharpness of picture quality

restore replace or recreate data using back-up files

Ribbon a toolbar area in Microsoft Office applications since 2007

ring topology a network design that connects all devices into a circle

rip to copy music from any source, such as an audio compact disc, to a hard drive

root directory the main storage location in a hierarchical filing system

router a network device or program that determines which path a packet will follow to reach its destination

S

safe mode a method of starting a computer with a limited set of files and drivers so you can identify and fix problems

sans serif font a font that has no serifs, or lines, projecting from its ends

scale the range of values against which data is measured; also, to change the size of an object, proportionately

scanner a device that converts printed images into a digital form

scanning a type of cybercrime that uses programs to try different passwords until one works

screen saver a utility program that changes the screen display after a preset period

screen-magnifier software software that makes images larger and changes colors to make text easier to see on a monitor

scroll to move from one part of a document to another on the screen

search engine software that finds a list of Web sites that meet a specified search

secondary storage computer disk drives such as the hard drive and CD-ROM drive used to store large amounts of data

section a part of a document that contains specific format settings

sector a section of a track on a computer disk

Secure Electronic Transactions (SET) a standard that uses digital signatures to protect buyers and sellers online

select a feature that allows the user to highlight, or select, data such as text or objects on-screen

selection tool a tool that can select a portion of an image to be moved, enlarged, or edited

self-running presentation a slide show timing method that changes from one slide to the next at a given increment of time

sequence in programming, one of the three basic logic structures, which is the order of operations

sequential storage device a storage device that requires a computer to scan from the beginning to the end of stored information

serif font a font that has serifs, or lines, projecting from its ends

server a computer that manages data and programs used in a network

server address a part of an e-mail address after the "at" sign

shape an element of design that defines the outline or form of an object

shareware copyrighted software that can be sampled before it is purchased

simulations a virtual reality program that mimics a specific place, job, or function

single-seat license a license to install and use software on only one computer

singletons HTML tags that are used alone instead of in pairs

single-user license a license to use one copy of a commercial software program

site license a license that allows a group to install software on a specific number of computers for internal use only

slander false statements that might hurt someone's reputation

sleep mode a power state in which power is shut off to non-essential components but some power is used and data remains in RAM

slide a separate page in a presentation program on which information is organized smart phone

Slide Show view a view in a presentation program used to display the slide show presentation

Slide sorter view a view in a presentation program used to display thumbnail-sized versions of all slides at once

smart phone a device that includes telephone, text, and data capabilities

social networking virtual online communities that facilitate communication between users

software programs that tell a computer what to do and how to do it

Software as a Service (SAAS) programs stored on a server, which customers pay for by subscription and access via the Internet

software license the document that contains permission for a buyer to install and use a program

software piracy the illegal copying of computer programs

solid state disk (SSD) a high-capacity storage device that contains high-speed random access memory

sort to arrange data in a specific order

sound card a circuit board chip that converts sounds in analog form into digital form and vice versa

source code the instructions that programmers write

source file the location from which data was collected

space an element of design that defines the distance between objects in a graphic or on a page

spam unrequested e-mail messages and advertisements

speech synthesis software a type of software that lets a computer read text files aloud

speech-recognition software software used for inputting text or commands by speaking into a microphone

spelling checker a tool that checks each word in the text against a dictionary built into the program to identify potential errors

spoof to use a false IP or e-mail address

spreadsheet a software program used for processing numbers that are stored in tables, such as budgets or financial statements

standalone program application software that specializes in one task

standby mode a power state in which power is shut off to non-essential components but some power is used and data remains in RAM

star bus topology a network design that connects multiple star networks in a local area network

star topology a network design that connects each network device to a hub

start tag the code that indicates the beginning of a Hypertext Markup Language (HTML) instruction

status bar the area below the application workspace that shows information about the program or document

storage the action by which a computer saves information so the information is available for use and reuse

storage area network (SAN) a network of storage devices that can be accessed by multiple computers

storage device a computer component that retains data after the power is turned off

storage media the material that retains the stored information in a computer storage device

storyboard a map of a project such as a Web site or video that helps you plan the project's structure, content, and organization

stream to transmit data over a network or Internet connection without interruption

Structured Query Language (SQL) a standard database query language

style a set of formats for similar elements in a document

style checker a tool that suggests ways to improve the writing style in a document

style sheet in word-processing, a collection of predefined formats that can be applied to a document; in Web page design, a document that describes rules used to define how the elements of the pages in a Web site will look

stylus a pointing device used for drawing on a graphics tablet

subdirectories folders stored within the root or other folders

subnotebook computer a small portable computer, such as a netbook

subroutine in programming, a sequence described in a single line of code

supercomputer a large and powerful scientific computer that can process large amounts of data quickly

superzapper a program that accesses data by avoiding security measures

synchronous training a Web-based classroom to which students log on at a preset time to watch a recorded lecture

synergy the combined effect group effort can create

syntax in a spreadsheet, the rules for entering a function; in programming and Web page design, the rules that control how you enter code

synthesize to create sounds imitative of actual musical instruments using a computer

system administrator person responsible for maintaining a computer system

system requirement the minimum equipment a computer needs to run an application

system software programs that help the computer work properly

T

T1 line copper or fiber-optic lines that allow data to be sent at more than 1.5 million bits per second

tab a part of the Ribbon in Microsoft Office applications since 2007 that contains related groups of commands

table data organized into rows and columns

tablet computer a computer that combines the features of a graphics tablet with the functions of a personal computer

tag a code used in HTML for formatting Web pages

telecommunications the process of sending information over a telephone network

telecommute to work from home by communicating with a workplace through a network

teleconference a live meeting using computers and telecommunications equipment that allows two or more people in different locations to participate

template a preformatted version of a certain type of document

temporary files data temporarily stored by the computer during processing

terabyte a unit of measure equal to 1024 gigabytes

terminal a keyboard and monitor attached to a shared, central computer

texture an element of design that defines the quality of the surface of shapes

thermal transfer printer a printer that uses heat to transfer color dyes or inks onto paper

thumbnail a small, representative version of a graphic

time bomb a computer virus programmed to perform a task (often a destructive one) at a specific date and time

time-limited trial a type of software that stops working after a certain number of uses or days

title bar the top row of an application window where the program name and often the name of the document is shown

token a unit of data used in ring topology to prevent collisions; or a handheld electronic device that generates a log-on code

toolbar a row of icons that represent the program's most commonly used commands

top level domain the suffix of an Internet domain that identifies the type of organization that registered the name

topology the layout of the physical structure of a network

Track Changes a feature that marks each editing change made by one or more members of a group working on the same document

track one of a set of uniform circles made on a disk

tracking when a Web site gathers information about your Web browsing activity

trademark a symbol that indicates that a brand or brand name is legally protected and cannot be used by other businesses

transactional processing a way of changing a database that keeps its records up to date at all times

transformer a device that transfers electricity from one circuit to another

transistor a switch contained in a circuit

transition effect in a presentation program, a special effect that adds visual interest when the current slide disappears and the next slide appears on the screen

Transmission Control Protocol/Internet Protocol (TCP/IP) the set of rules for formatting and transmitting data over the Internet, used by every computer that is connected to the Internet

trap door a type of virus that enables an unauthorized user (such as a hacker) to secretly gain access to a computer

troll someone who posts rude, mean comments intended to upset people; also, to post rude, mean comments on the Internet

Trojan horse a program disguised as useful but that is destructive to the data on a hard drive

troubleshoot to correct a problem with a piece of hardware or a software program

tween the ability of a graphics program to determine in-between frames

twisted pair a pair of copper wires that are twisted together and commonly used as a networking medium

U

UEFI (Unified Extensible Firmware Interface) a standard firmware interface for PCs, designed to replace the BIOS (basic input/output system)

Undo a command that reverses the previous action

ungroup to separate combined vector images into individual images

Unicode a system using 16 bits to encode characters, creating more codes for foreign languages

uniform resource locator (URL) the unique address given to a document on the Internet

uninstall to remove a program from a computer

uninterruptible power supply (UPS) a device that aims to prevent interruption of power to a computer

unity in graphic design, when a third object is used to establish a connection between two other objects

universal product code (UPC) a pattern of bars printed on packages or labels to indicate price

universal serial bus (USB) a standard that allows communication between devices, such as between a flash drive and a computer

update to install a fix or repair for an operating system or program; also, the software used to update

upgrade to install a new and improved version of an operating system or program

upload to send data from a client computer to a server computer through a network or Internet connection

USB flash drive a small storage device that uses flash memory and connects to the computer through a USB port; also called a pen drive, jump drive, or thumb drive

Usenet a discussion system computer users can access through the Internet

user account a collection of information used to identify a person and grant him or her access to a computer system or network

username the online identity of a person who is accessing a system or network

user rights settings assigned to a user account to limit or allow access to a computer system

utility software programs that are used to maintain and repair the computer

V

value a number, such as a whole number, a fraction, or decimal; also, a numerical representation of a color in a graphics program

variable in programming, a symbol or name that stands for a value

variety in graphic design, the use of different colors and shapes to create visual interest

vector graphic an image that is created using paths or lines

version a release of a software program, usually identified by a unique number to distinguish it from previous releases

versioning saving previous or incremental versions of programs or files

vertical application a type of application software that is designed for a very limited purpose in a field or business

video adapter circuit board that creates the images seen on a monitor

video capture card a circuit board chip that converts analog video images into a digital file

video editor a program that combines and edits video and audio files

video memory (VRAM) video adapter's memory used to store video images

videoconference a meeting that provides audio and visual contact for participants in different locations

viewable area a portion of the screen where an image can be shown

virtualization physical storage pooled from multiple network storage devices into what seems to be one single storage device managed from a central console

virtual memory space set aside on the hard drive for the operating system to temporarily store data

virtual private network (VPN) a private network set up through a public network

virtual reality (VR) a computer-generated, realistic, three-dimensional world a user can "enter" and explore

virus a program whose purpose is to damage or destroy computer data, cause a computer to behave in unexpected ways, or interfere with the operation of a network, all while concealing and replicating itself

visual aid a graphic that helps convey information to an audience

Voice over Internet Protocol (VoIP) technology that sends digital voice data over the Internet to enable Internet-based telephone calls

voltage electric pressure

volume license a license that allows a group to install software on a specific number of computers for internal use only

W

wearable computer mobile device designed to be worn on the body, leaving the hands free for other tasks

Web apps applications that are stored on cloud servers; sometimes called cloud apps

Web browser a program used to view Web pages

Web cache a temporary location for storing Web pages during browsing to make reloading the pages faster

Webcam a digital camera used to capture and transmit video over the Internet or other network

Webcast a live broadcast of audio and video over the Internet

Web feed a service that automatically downloads Web page content that a user has signed up for

Web host a company that leases Web space for Web sites

Web Layout view the view in a word-processing program that shows how a document will appear when published on the World Wide Web

Webmaster the person responsible for the creation and maintenance of a Web site

Web page a single document on the Web

Web server a computer that maintains Web sites

Web site a collection of related pages on the Web

Web-based training educational courses available via the Internet

whiteboard an electronic equivalent of a chalkboard

WHOIS database the central database of domain names

wide area network (WAN) a network that connects computers and other resources over great distances

widgets interactive elements on a Web site used to perform a function or access a service

Wi-Fi wireless networks that use radio signals to connect computers

wiki a Web site that contains information created and updated by anyone who has access to the site

wildcard a symbol that stands for one or more characters; used to search pages with variations of a word in the search

window a rectangular, on-screen frame used to view a program or document

wizard a series of dialog boxes that gives a step-by-step guide through a procedure

word wrap the automatic starting of a new line of text when the previous line is full

word-processing program a program used to create documents through typing, editing, formatting, and printing functions

worksheet a grid made of vertical columns and horizontal rows in a spreadsheet program

worksheet tab a tag that identifies each worksheet in a spreadsheet program

workspace the blank area where a graphic will display in a paint or draw program

workstation a computer connected to a computer network

World Wide Web (Web) part of the Internet comprised of linked documents

worm a computer virus that spreads over a network without user execution

write the process of storing information on a storage device

write-protect switch a sliding bar on a USB flash drive that can be set to prevent changes to the data stored on the drive

WYSIWYG behind-the-scenes programming that stands for "What You See Is What You Get"

Z

zoom to focus on a part of a document

Index

computer telephony integration (CTI), 345, 345f
computer-based training (CBT), 444
computer-controlled robots, 6, 79
computers, defined, 4
conditional functions, 196
confidentiality agreement, 479
configuration options, 90–91
conflicts in operating systems, 78
congestion, 359
connections, Internet, 39-9–10
connectors, 9, 9f
content blocking, 39-18
content creation programs, 38-3
content management system (CMS), 417–418
content validity, of Web information, 423, 423f
contrast, 246
conversions, 198
cookies, 406, 420, 467, 467f, 37-11
cooperation, 497–498
COPRA (Children's Online Privacy Protection Act), 392
Copy command, 131, 140, 140f, 141, 38-4
copy editors, 138
copy protection, 123
copyright, 44, 479, 39-17
Corel WordPerfect Office, 110
Corning, Inc., 332
corrupted files, 95
cost estimator, 197
cover letters, 512
CPU (central processing unit), 7, 37-11
crashed programs, 78
creative commons license, 113, 39-17
Creative Suite Design Premium, 110
critical thinking, 496
cropping, 148, 38-8
cross-platform compatibility, 95, 391–392, 391f
CRT (cathode ray tube), 36
CSMA/CD (Carrier Sensing Multiple Access/Collision Detection), 371
CSS (Cascading Style Sheets), 403, C-4–5
CTI (computer telephony integration), 345
currency data, 224
current, electrical, 19
custom software, 12
customer service, 516
customer-support technicians, 129

customization
desktop, 37-6
operating system (OS), 37-6–7
Cut command, 131, 140, 140f, 38-4
cyberbullying, 481, 498
cybercrime, 481
cost of, 470
defined, 470
fighting, 470
password theft and, 471
personal data protection, 472
social networking and, 473, 473f
techniques, 468–469
types of, 469
cylinders, in hard drive, 64, 64f

D

DARPA (Defense Advanced Research Projects Agency), 379
data
backing up, 54, 67, 69, 483–484, 483f
bits of, 4
Bluetooth used to transfer, 9
compression of, 44, 83
decay of, 71, 71f
digital vs. analog, 4
formats for, 189
input of, 4–5, 32
integrity of, 72, 215
loss of, 67
maintenance of, 225
protecting from loss, 67, 67f
protection of, 67, 37-19
redundancy in, 215
removing, 484
restoring, 484
security of, 215
sharing among programs, 181–182, 182f, 183f
sorting, 176, 213
storage of, 7–8
transfer rate, 69
translating, 11
data entry, automatic, 193, 193f
data glove, 316, 316f
data projector, 46
data series, 193
data source, 141
data structure, 222
data types, 21, 210, 224
database
adding data to, 226, 227f

Index

P

W

Index

Credits